1- 19

The late ROBERT S. WOODWORTH was Professor of Psychology at Columbia University. He exercised an immeasurable influence on the development of psychological thought in many parts of the world, and was the first recipient of the gold medal award of the American Psychological Foundation.

MARY R. SHEEHAN, Ph.D. Columbia University, is Professor of Psychology at Hunter College of The City University of New York. She did her doctoral research under the direction of Dr. Woodworth.

ROBERT S. WOODWORTH

CONTEMPORARY SCHOOLS OF PSYCHOLOGY

By

ROBERT S. WOODWORTH
Late of Columbia University

In collaboration with

MARY R. SHEEHAN
*Hunter College of the
City University of New York*

Third Edition

THE RONALD PRESS COMPANY • NEW YORK

Preface

In the Spring of 1958, New York newspapers carried an account
of Robert S. Woodworth's second retirement from Columbia where
since 1945, the year of his first and official retirement, he had continued to lecture to large classes on dynamic psychology or the
contemporary schools. At almost the same time his *Dynamics of
Behavior* representing the rich synthesis of more than forty years of
his characteristic thinking on the relation of motivation to the complexities of "dealing with the environment" was published. One
would expect that at the age of eighty-eight, under these circumstances, a man might well decide to clear his desk and with a serene
sense of mission accomplished settle back to relax in an easy chair.
But for this man there was a job waiting to be done and he turned
to it next with deep satisfaction.

The Second Edition of *Contemporary Schools of Psychology* was
at that time ten years old, and much had been happening during
those ten years. Woodworth was soon at work, staking out contemplated changes with marginal notes in a copy of the old text; building up his card file with selected new references, many of them with
lengthy stenotyped summaries of the topics to be featured. The
Third Edition, he told newspapermen at the time of his retirement,
would include an account of the recent work of Soviet psychologists;
but he proposed to give greater representation as well to developments in psychology in all parts of the world, and to expand the
book accordingly.

He continued to work on the book during 1959 and 1960 and had
made substantial progress on topics which are now included within
the first eight chapters before failing health forced him into the role
of advising partner. When he committed to me the completion
of the task he had begun we recalled with amusement that at the
conclusion of an earlier collaboration "Woodworth and Sheehan"

had agreed it would be hard for either to identify in the final joint product the specific ideas or sentences each had originally contributed. From this we took hope that some common trend of thought or style might in this instance, too, assure a degree of unity for the Third Edition, or at least help to make the seams less conspicuous.

In the Third Edition the old sequence of topics has for the most part been retained. However, some changes will be quickly apparent. The number of chapters has necessarily increased and their length is generally greater. The new title for Chapter 11 will appear to be a radical departure from the policy of identifying the chapters with the names of the several schools, but it seemed to admit of more extended coverage than the "Hormic and Holistic" title used in the 1948 Edition. Although these two designations have been reduced to subtitles within the chapter, the corresponding schools have been in no sense "demoted."

The student may on occasion be surprised to come upon a "visiting professor" in a part of the book where one would not have expected to find him. Such displacements are generally understandable on the basis of the flexible boundaries of the schools; but I have on a few occasions departed from orthodoxy to point up a contrast or an unexpected similarity, or the better to focus attention on a whole issue rather than presenting one part at a time.

An effort has been made to preserve the readability that has won for Woodworth's books the approval even of the students who use them. Some consideration has been given, however, to the fact that greater exposure to well-documented information about scientific psychology through television and other media is producing a generation of students prepared to cope with some less elementary content. We would say that the goal has been to keep the book, as it has been, at a level within the competence of the young student, but by no means beneath the notice of more mature readers.

There remains to be mentioned the paradox of a book on contemporary schools of psychology which despite its long chapter on functionalism contains no solid account of the contributions of the man who throughout his long and distinguished career was an outstanding representative of that position. As a result, the reader who meets Robert S. Woodworth casually for the first time in this Third Edition may be left with only the impression of him conveyed by scattered references throughout the book, and a text which must inevitably reflect some of the opinions of the second author notwithstanding the latter's close and willing discipleship. An alternative—which would have been most distasteful to Woodworth himself—

might have been to incorporate a section explicitly dealing with the details of his career, his theories, his writings. But just such a record has already been prepared by Professor Albert T. Poffenberger, whose close professional association and long friendship with Woodworth especially qualified him to provide a three-dimensional picture of the man who had come to be known as "the dean of American psychologists." Even a brief glance at the Woodworth bibliography (pages 391–403) will give the reader some measure of his scholarship and the scope of his interests.

I resist the temptation to add some observations based on my personal acquaintance with Professor Woodworth as his student and later as his collaborator. There is no need for further evidence of his intellectual stature, and an anecdote or two could scarcely do justice to the traits which distinguished him as a person. Along with the integrity that was a cardinal feature of his personality I think of his kindness, his modesty, and his delightful humor as the qualities most characteristic of him. It is not surprising that they should be, for are these not the qualities—if a psychologist may be allowed the indiscretion of speaking off the record—which constitute true greatness?

I wish to express my sincere thanks to Mrs. Enrica Tunnell, Professor Poffenberger, Professor Karl M. Dallenbach of the *American Journal of Psychology*, and Columbia University Press for permission to reproduce the complete Woodworth bibliography. I am also deeply indebted to Mrs. Tunnell, long in charge of the Graduate Psychology Library at Columbia University and for many years Professor Woodworth's capable secretary, for her thoughtful engineering of the transfer of the writing task from the senior to the second author and for her continued warm interest in its progress. I am grateful to Dr. Neal E. Miller of Yale University for checking my interpretation of his proposal of an alternative to the drive reduction hypothesis. Dr. Albert E. Goss of the University of Massachusetts has offered some valuable suggestions which have been incorporated into the text. I have drawn upon the time, patience, and judgment of many of my good friends and colleagues at Hunter, including Professors Dorothy M. Barrett, William J. Bryar, Jewell H. Bushey, Ruth C. Conkey, Dorothy Doob, Olive Huber, Catherine F. Reid, and Eleanor E. Reilly. My thanks go also to the ever helpful Miss Lucille E. Bailey, Miss Dorathea R. Wesel, and Mr. Arthur Goldzweig who in their respective librarian roles quickly resolved some problems of bibliography. This by no means exhausts the list of those whose wisdom, concern, and encouragement have given me reason to be deeply grateful. I would thank especially my brother,

Charles V. Sheehan, whose wit and wisdom have done much to reduce the "crises" of the past three years to their proper proportions.

I gratefully acknowledge the courtesy of the many publishers,
organizations, and individuals who have permitted the use of numerous quotations appearing in this book. Specific acknowledg-
ment is given in the References and Author Index section.

MARY R. SHEEHAN

New York, N. Y.
March, 1964

Contents

CONTEMPORARY SCHOOLS
OF PSYCHOLOGY

1

The Schools of Psychology and Their Background

It is safe to say that psychology is as old as the inquiring, self-conscious mind of man. From the beginning, man's dependence upon his environment would not have allowed him to be indifferent to the effects of its objects upon himself; and one aspect in particular, the living objects—human and animal—that shared his world and figured in his daily activities, must surely have aroused his special interest. The first great chapters about man's speculations on his mental functions and behavior, and on how in these respects he resembled or was distinguished from other living beings, come to us from the history of philosophical thought. The history of philosophy has traditionally been a history of controversy, so it is not surprising that when psychology, in the last quarter of the nineteenth century, followed the lead of physics, chemistry, and biology in taking on the discipline of science, it lost none of its dispute-provoking character. New issues shortly arose as to what exactly could be considered the proper content of the new science and what methods were to be used in its study.

For one group of psychologists the proper content seemed reasonably to be man's conscious experience, which they held could be investigated through *introspection*. This is a method of self-observation which, as we shall see later, may take a variety of forms, ranging from the simple reporting of one's immediate sensory impression of a stimulus to long-extended probing, during analytical therapy, of one's emotional experiences. Unlike as these "introspections" may seem, they have in common a private quality which

3

appears to distinguish them from the methods of physics or chemistry or biology. In these sciences any number of observers can report on what is visible in the test tube or under the microscope, whereas the psychological "experience" can be reported by only one observer.

How real this distinction is remains a perplexing epistemological problem. Does each observer see in the test tube or under the microscope a bit of the real external world, or does each merely report on his subjective experience resulting from some emanations of the real world? If the latter is the case a sharp line cannot be drawn between the data of the "objective" sciences and the subjective data of psychology. In all cases the observing subject would be reporting the private content of his own "consciousness."

Before the end of the second decade of the twentieth century, however, a number of psychologists, mostly Americans, had come to repudiate the idea of a subjective science of psychology built up by use of the subjective method of introspection. There appeared some valid grounds for complaint, one of them being the irreconcilable differences in the introspective reports issuing from different laboratories investigating the same questions. For example, do we have mental pictures—imagery—as we solve a problem? Some introspectors were convinced they did; others could find no evidence of it, although they might describe in elaborate detail sensations of muscle tension or eye movement or organic changes which would never be noticed by an ordinary, untrained "thinker." The intangible events of consciousness reported with such dubious accuracy did not seem to the insurgents the right sort of building blocks out of which to construct the new science. Let the psychologist concern himself, rather, with behavior-study exclusively, and commit himself to demonstrating the validity of his theories by pointing to facts of behavior which can be checked by many observers.

This movement toward "behaviorism," soon to become a dominating trend in American psychology, was further strengthened in the 1920's and 1930's by developments in the philosophy of science. With some variations, the movements known as logical positivism, operationism, and physicalism (Stevens, 1939)[1] set out to purify the language of science and to rid science itself of the "pseudo-problems" which arise in the attempt to translate into the language of physical reality that which is itself unobservable or metaphysical or physically undemonstrable. In describing the effect of these

[1] Citations in parentheses can be used to locate complete titles in the References and Author Index, beginning on p. 405.

developments on his own thinking at that time, Edwin G. Boring, one of our distinguished American psychologists (born 1886, now Edgar Pierce Professor Emeritus, Harvard University), provides in his illustration of operationism a revealing clue as to how radically it was bound to affect the new science of psychology:

> Physicalism, in its most modern phase which is often called *operationism*, is the view that consciousness, as an object of observation by science, reduces to the operations by which consciousness becomes known to scientists. A sensation, for instance, is not an immaterial something such as redness or pain or bitterness, but the observed data, a man reporting in words the difference between two hues, the rat reporting in action that he knows dark from light. Since the man's words are discriminative behavior, and the rat's behavior is similarly discriminative, and behavior is a physical phenomenon, we can manage in this way to avoid dualism and bring all science, psychology and physics, into relation (1961, page 52).

For the behaviorists, then, introspective study of consciousness or "immediate experience" was ruled out in favor of the study of behavior. Sometimes the behavior studied is verbal, but in the most orthodox form of behaviorism a subject's *verbal report* of his private experience is treated just as any other motor response he might make to the stimulus presented. The subject has *said* the word "blue," or "brighter," or "louder." It is this *response* to the stimulus (S–R), rather than the subject's reconstruction of what went on in his "consciousness," that becomes the primary datum for the experimentalist.

Although they quarreled over method, introspectionist and behaviorist alike generally assumed in the early years of scientific psychology that the reasonable way to understand what is complex is to reduce it to its elements. Physics has used this method; logically, it should work also for psychology. But this logic was disputed by a relatively small group of psychologists, most of them German, who before the 1920's had built up a formidable array of evidence suggesting that a psychological event must be understood as a whole, and that breaking it down into elements, whether elements of consciousness or elements of behavior, at best leaves it unexplained, and at worst destroys its meaning. "The whole is more than the sum of its parts" came to epitomize the new *Gestalt* psychology that took its place in the scientific arena along with the earlier schools. The name "Gestalt" focused attention upon the importance of the inherent organization of the pattern or configuration. Put down three dots, about a half-inch apart but not in a straight line. What do you see? A triangle—not just three dots. Now add one more dot close to the three. The triangle gives way to a quadrilateral. With effort you may get back the triangle and see the added dot as a separate thing, but the quadrilateral seems more real, unless you have put one of the dots at a considerable distance from the others. It seems that some internal relationship within the figure has more to do with what you see than any effort you may make to group or associate the "elements" that "compose" it.

"Association," the principle relied upon by the earlier schools to account for the complex wholes they reduced to elements, seemed to the gestaltists nothing more than a device invented to put Humpty-Dumpty together again. They characterized element-centered theories as "brick-and-mortar psychology"—but without the mortar. On the other hand, the Gestalt school found no fault with introspection as a method, provided it was not used in such a way as to destroy the meaningfulness of the data by analysis. The free, natural reporting of conscious experience—that is, of *phenomena,* or the way things appear to the subject—has always been regarded by this group as a valid and valuable method. They describe it as *phenomenological observation.*

There remains to be added one more angle to complete this sketchy and tentative framework of the schools as they were developing in the early years of the twentieth century. Psychoanalysis may seem very remote from the theories and controversies we have been talking about, yet both as a theory and as a clinical method it is deeply concerned with the problem of consciousness. Evidence of a pathological breach in "consciousness" appears again and again in one form or another in the consulting room of a psychiatrist: a temporary loss of sight unaccounted for by any organic damage; the unexplainable loss of a whole system of memories while other memories remain undisturbed; the development of disabling, irrational fears; or the commission of compulsive acts of violence of which the doer later retains no recollection. These and other less dramatic symptoms which the psychiatrist must treat throw doubt on the adequacy of a definition of psychology which limits its scope to the study of "consciousness."

On the other hand, as we have already pointed out, the psychoanalytic *method,* in which the patient tracks down the elusive fragment of experience by long, continued free association, is a form of introspection although it is used with very different effect from that sought in the psychology laboratory. It might appear that psychoanalysts and the introspective psychologists might early have found some common ground of interest, but the fact is that there was little interchange between the theorists of the laboratory and the theorists of the consulting room. The distrust was mutual, for the average psychiatrist was likely to be as skeptical of the practical value of the artificial laboratory approach as the average experimentalist was scornful of what he considered undisciplined theorizing by the practicing analyst. Only in recent years have there been promising signs of greater tolerance on both sides, but there still remains a great gap even though a beginning has been made toward reconciling some of the concepts of these two widely different approaches to the problems of psychology.

So the issues and the schools began to multiply at about the turn of the century or within a few years after. In the following list, some names will be well known, while others will be less familiar to the general reader and have, in fact, not been very prominent in psychology itself:

> *Functional psychology:* very old, wide in scope and not sharply defined, named in America in 1898
>
> *Structural psychology:* German in origin, with 1879 as an outstanding date; named and sharpened in America in 1898
>
> *Associationism:* an old British school, taking stimulus-response form in America in 1898, in Russia in 1903
>
> *Psychoanalysis:* originating in Austria about 1900
>
> *Personalistic and organismic psychologies:* originating in both Germany and America about 1900
>
> *Purposivism or hormic psychology:* originating in Britain in 1908
>
> *Behaviorism:* originating in America in 1912
>
> *Gestalt psychology:* originating in Germany in 1912

For each of these schools there has been a major focus of interest. Roughly speaking, for structural psychology it has been sensation, for Gestalt psychology it has been patterned perception, for associationism it has been learning and memory. Behaviorism has concentrated on conditions determining motor activity, while psychoanalysis and hormic psychology have been more concerned with the emotional forces determining behavior. Personalism and organismic psychology are interested in the individual as a whole. Functionalism has been tacitly accepted by so many psychologists of varied persuasions that perhaps it should not be counted among the schools, but the reason for including it will be shown in the next chapter.

The dates assigned for the origin or rejuvenation of the schools are also worthy of notice, and it is quite in order to ask how much of their original identity they have retained in the intervening years. The term *schools* suggests orthodoxy, followership, uniformity. It tends to conjure up images of disputants taking sides in a perennial debate, more interested in keeping the argument alive and defending their own positions than in reaching a point of mutual agreement from which both sides might work together toward a more satisfactory solution. In an age and a society which stress the values of thoughtful individuality more than conformity there would be reason to doubt the healthy status of a young science which could show over a period of more than half a century little or no evidence of the restructuring that is a mark of maturity. The chapters which follow will provide much evidence on which the reader may base his own judgment, but tentatively we may say that a charge of inflexibility or rigidity can hardly be sustained against psychology considered as a whole. It is true that most of the schools continue to exist, some less active than in the past, others appreciably changed but still essentially identifiable. Yet signs of *rapprochement* have begun to appear in spots. Perhaps the lines of cleavage were never as sharp as the chapter headings of a book make them appear to be. Indications that this was in fact true of the early period of the schools will shortly be cited. But in more recent years, particularly since the midpoint of the century, there have been the more hopeful signs of a conscious reaching out toward better understanding and closer communication among those who have undertaken sincerely the demanding obligations of psychological research. Sometimes this has appeared in the form of a significant variation on a major theme of one or another school, which has had the effect of pointing the way or at least offering hope for future reconciliation of theoretical differences.

Combating the threat of blind spots and provincialism in a different way have been the special symposia which have made it possible for psychologists known for their widely different viewpoints to thrash out their differences with colleagues who do not share their opinion on some important problem such as motivation (the annual Nebraska Symposium on Motivation). Other meetings have been international in scope, some of them including among their participants distinguished scientists of other disciplines closely related to psychology: biologists, physiologists, mathematicians. And not least important, from the point of view of inviting an overall comparison of the contributions of the several schools, has been "Project A," inspired by the Policy and Planning Board of the American Psychological Association, and taking shape under the critical editing of Sigmund Koch (1959, 1962). This presents in a series of volumes comprehensive statements of outstanding theories representative of the schools, prepared by well informed contributors according to a common outline. It is, in a sense, a progress report on the science of psychology as it entered the last quarter of its first century of existence. We shall have reason to refer to it again.

Returning to the matter of dates, we might ask why the dawn of the present century should have been so remarkably prolific in new schools of psychology. To gain perspective [2] we must glance briefly at the state of the science in 1900. Each school began as a revolt against the established order and cannot be fully understood without taking account of its historical background. An interesting fact about the established order of 1900 which provoked revolt was that it was young and had itself been revolutionary not long before. In fact, there was an old tradition in psychology to rebel against tradition. At the beginning of the modern scientific movement in the seventeenth century, we find such philosophers as Descartes and Hobbes rebelling against the psychology that had come down from the Greeks and Scholastics, thus making a start toward modern psychology. Without attempting to divorce psychology from philosophy they endeavored to bring their psychology into line with the new developments in physical science. Early in the seventeenth century Galileo and others revolutionized physics and astronomy by showing that many and perhaps all physical processes could be described in terms of motion and inertia; and Harvey, by discovering the circulation of the blood, made a start toward explaining physiological processes in physical terms. Without delay, Descartes applied the new physics to human and animal behavior. Behavior he based on what we now call reflex action; and a reflex he conceived as the motion of a fluid along the nerves from the sense organs to the brain and out again to the muscles. The soul he located in the brain, and he supposed it to intervene in certain processes between the incoming and outgoing motions in the nerves. Animals, however, Descartes believed, had no soul; their behavior consisted purely of physical motion. The human soul, with its faculty of thinking, he held to be non-physical.

Hobbes went even further by reducing all mental processes to physical motion. External motion striking the sense organs was communicated to the nerves, brain, and heart, and this internal motion, once started, persisted by inertia in the form of memories and ideas. Hobbes's revolt against the traditional psychology was certainly radical, but it was sketchy in detail; the task remained for the English philosophers of the following century to develop this line of thought, as they did in the associationist psychology. They tried to reduce all mental processes to the single process of association, as we shall see in Chapter 3. With many variations in their theory as to the physical nature of associations, with many applications to morals, economics, and the social sciences in general, and in spite

---

[2] For a fuller perspective, reference may be made to the excellent histories by Murphy (1949); Boring (1950); Roback (1952); Peters-Brett (1953). Full titles are given in the References and Author Index, beginning on p. 405.

of numerous objections raised by their contemporaries, the associationists grew in influence and dominated the field in the early nineteenth century.

THE NEW PSYCHOLOGY OF THE NINETEENTH CENTURY

Just as the physics of Galileo's time exerted an immediate influence on psychology, so, early in the nineteenth century, two newly developed sciences made themselves felt. The wonderful achievements of chemistry led the philosophers of the time to project an analytical psychology which sought to discover the elements of conscious experience and their laws of combination. This was an attractive program and proved to be feasible to a certain extent. More influential, however, was the example of physiology, which began early in the nineteenth century to be an experimental science. Soon it had remarkable achievements to its credit, and some of them bordered closely on the proper domain of psychology. The workings of the sense organs, nerves, and brain were intensively studied by physiologists during the nineteenth century. Their findings gained a place in the current books on psychology, and their methods were taken up by the new group of experimental psychologists. Out of the physiological laboratory grew the psychological laboratory, though it was not until 1879 that the first recognized psychological laboratory was set up by Wundt at Leipzig. Soon there were many laboratories, especially in Germany and the United States, and the "new psychology," as it was described in 1900, was experimental psychology.

This new psychology rebelled against the older tradition in respect to methods and scientific standards rather than in respect to theory. Where the earlier psychologist had been satisfied with evidence from his memory and ordinary experiences, the experimentalist insisted on definite recorded data. Experiments on the senses and muscular movements were followed by cleverly designed experiments on learning and memory, and hope was strong that all psychological problems could in time be attacked by the new method.

We have not yet displayed the full scope of psychology in 1900, and our sketch of the nineteenth century developments would be incomplete if we failed to mention the influence of still two other sciences. General biology, and especially the theory of evolution, from 1860 on brought into view a whole mass of problems that were quite foreign to the older psychology and also to physiology, chemistry, and physics. Mental development in the race and in the individual as influenced by heredity and environment, child psychology, animal psychology, differences between individuals and between races, and similar topics began to appear in psychological writings toward the end of the nineteenth century, largely through the influence of Darwin and Galton. Tests for measuring individuals were first invented for use in such studies and were added to the laboratory type of experiments as part of the psychologist's stock of methods.

The remaining influence came from psychiatry, and the history of psychiatry throughout the nineteenth century would well repay an extended review. In summary, the treatment of the mentally ill advanced from an utterly unscientific to a highly promising state. All through the century psychiatrists were divided into two main schools, the psychic and the somatic, the one seeking causes in the mental sphere and the other looking for some brain disturbance behind every abnormality of behavior. Brain disturbance was actually found in some kinds of mental illness but could not be demonstrated in other kinds. Where it could not be demonstrated the somatists assumed it to exist in some elusive form. On the whole the somatic school dominated psychiatry and had the greater influence upon the psychology of the time.

All these new problems and methods tended to break the traditional connection of psychology with philosophy, and one by one the American universities, at least, created separate departments of psychology. The decade of the 1890's was a period of great psychological activity. Laboratories were springing up, journals were started, the American Psychological Association was founded, international congresses were held. Great books were published, fruitful new methods were designed. The psychologists of 1900 were an active and aggressive group, small in size but rapidly recruiting itself from the younger generation, hopeful of its newly acquired technique of tests and experiments, finding new fields to explore year by year, beginning to study the child, the animal, the mentally ill as well as the normal adult, maintaining contact with the workers in several other sciences, and ready to break loose from philosophy and set up an establishment of its own. In theory the psychologists of 1900 subscribed to the orthodox definition of psychology as the science of consciousness; but in practice they were studying man's performances rather than his states of consciousness. In theory they stood for an analytical psychology patterned after chemistry, with elementary sensations, images, and feelings, and with complex thoughts and emotions composed of these elements; but in practice they often disregarded this scheme. In theory they were mostly associationists, but not dogmatically so; the high noon of associationism was already past.

These discrepancies between theory and practice, between orthodox definition and actual research work, were an open challenge to
the younger psychologists of the period. Was consciousness the
proper subject matter for the psychology of the future, with introspection as the only direct method of investigation? The younger
psychologists, during the first decade of the twentieth century, even
before the outburst of behaviorism, were more and more inclined to
emphasize behavior rather than consciousness and objective rather
than introspective methods; and from a totally different angle of
approach the psychoanalysts urged that the deeper field for investigation lay not in consciousness but in the unconscious. Was the old
slogan, "association of ideas," a true guide to a theory of learning?
The connection of stimulus and response might be a much better
guide. Was behavior a collection of simple and complex reflexes?
Desire and purpose, and the unity of the organism as well, seemed
to be left out of this picture. Was consciousness itself made up of
sensory elements in varied combinations? Here the unity of the
person and the consciousness of being oneself were missing, and
there was no room even for the unity of a perceived object and the
meaning of any experience to the individual.

Apart from these flaws in its general theory, the psychology of
1900 was necessarily open to the criticism of immaturity and meager
accomplishment. Such minor defects could gradually be corrected
by intensive work on specific problems, and to this sort of work the
great body of psychologists has devoted itself for more than half a
century. Hypotheses have been set up and tested. Findings have
sometimes been disputed, and opinions have sometimes clashed.
Such controversies can be settled by the weight of evidence, but the
merits of the different schools cannot be appraised in so direct and
scientific a manner. The major tenets of a school can scarcely be
proved or even disproved. The test of a school is its long-run fruit-
fulness or sterility. Each school points the way for psychology to
follow; psychology is attempting to advance in all directions; and
the questions are which path will yield the great discoveries of the
future, and whether synthesis of the different lines of advance will
not sometime prove to be possible.

2

Functional and
Structural Psychology

A very genuine psychological interest is apt to awaken in anyone who has the opportunity of watching the development of a young child. How many different things even an infant can do! He sleeps, awakes, sucks and swallows, breathes, coughs and sneezes at times, cries and vocalizes in various ways, lies placid or throws his arms and legs around. After a while he begins to "take notice," to look and listen, to recognize persons, to reach for things and handle them with increasing skill. Months later he begins to understand words that are spoken to him and a little later still to speak a few words and then more and more words. Dozens of items could be added, as any young parent finds who undertakes to keep a "baby diary."

Such a record, psychologically considered, consists of answers to the question, "What did the child do?" This question "What?" is one of the three types of questions that are asked by any inquiring person—by a scientist, for example. The others are "How?" and "Why?" These questions, too, are likely to occur to the observer of a child. How does he creep? Why does he cry? They are harder questions to answer. The "How" question inquires into the process by which a result is reached, and the "Why" question seeks for the cause behind an action. The process may be too complex and rapid to follow with the eyes, besides being partly concealed inside the body and even in the brain. The cause of an action—often we can call it the motive—is very likely to be invisible.

THE BEGINNINGS OF FUNCTIONAL PSYCHOLOGY

If such a diary were continued through childhood and youth and on into adult life, the number of things recorded would be so enormous that some kind of classification would be found necessary; and since the interest presumably would be in the *person* rather than in the numerous objects involved in his activities, the variety of objects could be disregarded and the "things done" brought under a relatively few heads according to the results accomplished. All the different words and sentences spoken could be brought under the head of "talking," all the games played under the head of "playing," all the lessons learned under the head of "learning," all the various facts remembered under the head of "remembering." So the final answer to the "What" question would be a more or less systematic list of kinds of results accomplished. Meanwhile the answers to the "How" and "Why" questions would be lagging behind because of their difficulty.

Something like this, as far as we can make out from the available sources, was the early history of psychology. In the time of the ancient Greek philosophers such classes were recognized as: perceiving objects by the senses, remembering, imagining things never seen, choosing between alternative possible actions, and carrying out one's chosen plan. Knowing and willing seemed to be the most inclusive classes possible above the physiological level of digesting, sensing, and moving. This classification was obviously an answer to the "What" question. Aristotle made an important start toward answering the question how we remember (see page 60), and other philosophers gave some very naive answers to the question how we perceive objects. The "Why" question received a very general answer from the hedonists, who asserted that all human activity is dominated by a desire for pleasure. On the whole the psychology that came down from the Greeks consisted in a set of broad classes of results accomplished by the human mind.

Aristotle employed verbal nouns equivalent to our *remembering, willing*, etc., as names for his classes. When his works were translated into Latin, a slight change of form was required to fit the Latin idiom. The translation became "faculty of remembering," "faculty of willing," etc. The word *faculty* was not intended to add any new meaning, though it does of course imply that a man *can* remember, the evidence being that he does remember. So the list of faculties was nothing more or less than a list of classes of "things done," an answer still to the question "What?" No doubt the great thinkers who spoke of the faculties of the mind were perfectly clear on this matter, but many lesser men, even down into the nineteenth century, were betrayed by the form of expression into supposing that the faculties were processes, an answer to the question "How?" But a student who is told that we remember by virtue of the faculty of memory is not much wiser about the process or operation by which remembering is made possible.

A list of faculties is a respectable answer to the question "What" but only a list of problems for the psychologist who is beginning to take the "How" question seriously. It is not even safe to assume that to each faculty there corresponds one distinct mental operation. To remember a face so as to recognize it may require an operation different from that of remembering a poem so as to recite it. In terms of operation there may be many memories rather than a single one. Or, on the contrary, there may be fewer fundamental operations than there are faculties. This last view was that of the associationists, who tried to show that all mental operations were essentially the one operation of association (see the following chapter).

A psychology that attempts to give an accurate and systematic answer to the question,"What do men do?" and then goes on to the questions, "How do they do it?" and "Why do they do it?" is called a *functional psychology*. Men not only know and will, but also feel, and their emotions as well as their intellectual and executive functions are included in the scope of functional psychology. Just as the physiologist, starting with the digestion of food as a result accomplished, seeks to discover the operations that produce this result, so the functional psychologist starts with the fact that objects are perceived and asks how they are perceived, or starts with the fact that problems are solved and asks how they are solved; or he starts with the fact that men get angry and asks how they get angry. He asks "Why?" as well.

In the United States, where psychology of the armchair variety was a very active academic subject as early as 1830, long before the advent of experimental psychology, a favorite expression was the "workings of the mind" to indicate the subject matter. It was evidently a functional psychology that these "mental philosophers" were attempting to develop. They used whatever results they could glean from the contemporary physiologists and psychiatrists but were after all rather abstract. The ideal which they had before their eyes was well expressed by the chemist Edward L. Youmans in his introduction to an American edition of Alexander Bain (1868; see pages 65–66 in the next chapter):

In the whole circle of human interests there is no need so vital and urgent as for a better understanding of the laws of mind and character. . . . The acquirement of true ideas concerning human nature, the springs of its action, the modes of its working, and the conditions and limits of its improvement, is indispensable for all. . . . The extension of the subject of Mental Philosophy so as to include the physiological elements and conditions . . . is therefore an important step in the direction of our greatest needs. . . . In place of the abstraction *mind*, is substituted the living being, compounded of mind and body, to be contemplated, like any other object of science, as actually presented to our observation and in our experience.

EXPERIMENTAL FUNCTIONAL PSYCHOLOGY

It is all very well to ask the question "How?" but the difficulty is to find adequate methods for tracing the hidden process that leads to an observed result. Three approaches were commonly used during the nineteenth century, two of which—the *physiological method* and the *method of varied conditions*—would still be acceptable in a strictly behavioristic science. The third, the controversial *introspective method*, now has dubious status, as we have seen; yet in one form or another the psychologist must have recourse to it whenever his inquiries lead him to the private or subjective aspects of his problem. The three methods are by no means to be thought of as mutually exclusive; they are often combined, and the method of varied conditions may, in fact, be thought of as a logical device for insuring against premature conclusions reached through the use of other methods. Let us consider the separate merits and deficiencies of these three, which still seem to cover adequately for our present purposes the current approaches used in experimental psychology.

THE PHYSIOLOGICAL METHOD. If the question is how we see, the anatomy and physiology of the eye will supply part of the answer. The eye muscles that make it possible to see things in focus, the iris that regulates the amount of light admitted, the retina with its rods and cones and photochemical substances that contribute to clear night-and-day vision, the conduction of impulses by the optic nerve —all tell part, but only part, of the story of how we see.

The same limitation holds for the physiological approach to other psychological phenomena. The study of "brain waves" has revealed some interesting facts about brain functioning during mental activity. Stages of dreaming, for instance, can be differentiated from dreamless sleep by the character of the waves in the frontal and occipital lobes of the cortex (Dement and Kleitman, 1957), and these distinctive patterns seem to alternate several times during the night. Yet we still cannot tell the content of the dream without awakening the dreamer. The electrical phenomena tell us about as much as we would learn about the operations of a factory by listening to the noise coming out of the window. Although recent research has vastly increased our knowledge of the physiology of the nervous system, the physiological method still cannot provide us with all the answers we want to know about the processes of perceiving, learning, thinking, choosing, etc. The psychologist must supplement this source of knowledge. We shall have reason to discuss this subject again (pages 177–78).

THE METHOD OF VARIED CONDITIONS. This is simply the general method of experimental science applied to the performances of an individual. He is given a task to perform, and we wish to discover how he performs it. If he can do it under certain conditions but not under others, or does it better under some conditions than others, we have some indication of his mode of operation. We may have to try out many hypotheses by appropriate control of the conditions before we obtain anything like a complete picture of the process. For example, he perceives the distance of objects in the third dimension. What are his cues or indicators of distance? Several cues are suggested and tested by comparing his success when a cue is present and when it is absent. Does he get any help from using both eyes? Compare his success with one eye open and with both. For a simple test, let him take a pencil in each hand and hold them pointing toward each other about a foot in front of his face. Let him close one eye and bring the pencil points toward each other till they almost touch—and then let him open the closed eye and see if he can improve the setting. Following this lead the physicist Charles Wheatstone in 1838 invented the stereoscope and proved that the somewhat different views obtained by the two eyes were an important cue of distance when the object is within a few feet of the eyes.

In the area of vision Zener and Gaffron (1962) have more recently applied the method of varied conditions in a revealing study of the effects produced by inversion of a picture. It would seem that an assemblage of "objects" represented on a two-dimensional surface would appear much the same whether seen as they are arranged on the original plate or negative, or as they are arranged in the mirror-image print. A careful phenomenological study of the different effects of plate and print of Dürer's *Melancolia* and of Rembrandt's *Death of St. Mary* brings to light subtle differences in the organization of the patterns which not only alter the appearance of the objects but also the viewer's feelings of relationship to them and consequently his mood or "affective" reaction.

Ebbinghaus's pioneer experiment on memory (1885), from which came the well-known "curve of forgetting," is a good example of the method of varied conditions. Is forgetting a gradual process? The condition varied was the elapsed time since the learning of a fixed quantity of unfamiliar material (nonsense syllables), and the results showed that when the material had been just barely learned, it was forgotten rapidly in the first few hours after learning, and then more and more slowly. Another variation of conditions was to have the material "overlearned" (more than barely learned) and the result was that it was forgotten more slowly. Another, much more recent experiment was to have the subject go to sleep immediately after learning, and the result showed that forgetting was slower than under the waking condition. The experiment has been varied in many different ways during the past eighty years, for the purpose of getting as complete a picture as possible of the process of forgetting.

Other examples could be added indefinitely. In short, the great body of experimental work in psychology, in both the nineteenth and the twentieth centuries, has used some form of this method of varied conditions. In order to keep our historical perspective clear we should take careful note of the fact that this objective method has been dominant throughout the scientific period of psychology.

THE INTROSPECTIVE METHOD. You are with a friend who is driving to the suburb of a medium-sized city. A few miles from the city he comes to a stop at the entrance to a side road and silently deliberates for a while, then takes the side road. You ask him how he reached his decision, and he replies, "This side road seems to run in the general direction we want and I figured we might lose less time this way than in the city traffic." Your friend has given you an introspective account of his thought process and probably a correct account as far as it goes. At the beginning of the present century, when the schools were taking shape, much doubt was expressed regarding the validity of the introspective method. (A brief account of the early behaviorist reaction against it has already been given on page 4). At the time mentioned, too, a common accusation against the older psychology was that it had been merely introspective; but this was a false accusation in two respects. Many objective experiments had already been carried out, as we have seen; and even the old "mental philosophers" had not depended much on introspection in an exact sense. They had sometimes appealed to the introspection of their audience in support of a statement, as in the famous American controversy over free will. Jonathan Edwards (1754) had offered a strong logical argument against free will: "Nothing ever comes to pass without a cause. . . . The will is always determined by the strongest motive." Several of his successors, as Henry P. Tappan (1841), sought to rescue free will: "We appeal directly to consciousness; and as a result, we find that . . . there is nothing intervening between the will and its act of choice."

What we miss here is a report of certain occasions when the subject said, "I was conscious of choosing A rather than B as a perfectly un-caused, unmotivated act." The modern introspectionist would re-quire definite data, not general appeals; and he would feel that such introspections as Tappan called for were too difficult to be reliable.

Strange as it may seem, psychology learned the accurate use of introspection not from philosophy but from physics and physiology. Physics used it in studying light and sound, and physiology in study-ing the sense organs. Light and sound, we must remember, are not absolutely objective facts, for light is not simply radiation, but visi-ble radiation, and sound is not simply vibration, but audible vibra-tion. There is much vibration that is not audible and much radiation that is not visible. The most convenient way to determine the limits of the visible spectrum is to apply different wave lengths of light to the eyes of an observer and ask him to report when he sees the light and when not. Since Newton's time physicists have been interested in these subjective phenomena of light and sound. With the rapid development of physiology in the early nineteenth century, some of the physiologists began to experiment on the operation of the sense organs. An obvious approach was to apply a suitable stimulus to a sense organ and ask for a report on the sensation produced. This way of securing introspective (or at least subjective) data may be called *the method of impression*. Apply a stimulus and ask your observer what impression he gets. In the hands of the sense physi-ologists and later of the experimental psychologists the method of impression has yielded much accepted information.

One general problem in each sense is the search for the elements. The skin sense, for example, gives us any number of impressions: the size, shape, weight, and texture of objects; warmth, cold, moisture, and dryness; roughness and smoothness; hardness and softness; and still others. But many of these impressions might be complex, while the elementary sensations were much fewer. Experiments finally showed that there were certainly four elementary skin sensations—warmth, cold, pain, and pressure—and that probably all the others were blends of these four. This analysis was accomplished by ex-ploring the skin with different stimuli and finding little spots sensi-tive to warmth, other spots sensitive to cold, and so on. In some-what the same way the surface of the tongue was explored and four elementary taste sensations were demonstrated: sweet, sour, bitter, and salty. The numerous "tastes" that we ordinarily speak of are blends of these elements with odor sensations and also with pressure and temperature sensations from the mouth. The taste of cold lem-onade is a blend of cold, sour, sweet, and lemon odor. By calling it a blend we mean that in spite of the complex of elements the total impression is unitary.

The sense of smell is more difficult to analyze. The great variety of odors has been reduced to some kind of order, but we are still not sure of the elements. In the senses of sight and hearing the method of impression has yielded many significant results.

The method of impression has been used in many different ways. It got its name in experiments on feelings, likes and dislikes, and esthetic judgments. You show a person a color and ask whether he likes it, whether it makes a pleasant or unpleasant impression. You show him two colors and ask which makes the pleasanter impression. You show him two pictures and ask which seems to him the more beautiful, or you ask the same question regarding two faces. You cannot call his judgments on such matters either correct or incorrect, though you may be able to trace the effects of prejudice. But you do assume that he reports his actual feelings or impressions. To that extent the method of impression calls for a simple form of introspection.

But is this form of introspection really any different from our ordinary objective observation of external facts? Those psychologists who insist always on objective methods dislike the method of impression as if it were tainted with subjectivism. But it seems perfectly objective to the person who receives the impression and gives the verbal report. You show him a color and he reports, "It is green," rather than that it gives him a green impression or sensation. Even when you ask whether he likes it, he is apt to say, "It is beautiful," rather than that it gives him a pleasant impression or feeling. His attitude is that of the ordinary objective observer.

If the method of impression is unsound, all scientific observation must be unsound, since it makes the same demands on the observer. In testing a technician for a job, a chemist will set out test specimens for the applicant to analyze. Having prepared the specimens he knows their nature; but he does not know the skill of the applicant. After using the known specimens to find out what he wants to know about the applicant, he will use the known technician to find out what he wants to know about unknown specimens. Both in the test situation and the job situation the technician has merely reported his experience as an objective observer. The data were alike, but were used first for a psychological purpose and later for a chemical purpose.

The human organism is a delicate registering instrument capable of registering the environment. It happens also to be capable of making a verbal report which may be used as an indicator of the registering process. Words may offer a greater hazard of misinterpretation than an unambiguous pointer-reading, but this hazard can be reduced in certain types of study by limiting the subject's responses to a choice of words about which there can be no misunderstanding: in a *psychophysical* experiment, for instance, the answer "yes" or "no" will indicate whether or not the subject perceives a certain light stimulus, the purpose of the experiment being to measure capacity for sensory discrimination.

But sometimes the psychologist is interested in obtaining a descriptive report from his subjects. In this case he must allow them a broader choice of words, and the problem arises as to the scientific treatment of such "raw data." C. H. Graham describes this as one of the "major problems of psychology." He points out that:

> In particular, the problem of analysis and classification of responses does not involve accepting them as understandable conversation, but is one of formulating their uniformities and rules in a system where they are taken *as* behavior. This sort of analysis provides the anomaly that conversation is not viewed as such, but is considered in terms of other words or symbols—that is, scientific description that formulates the rules of the subject's conversation (1958, page 66).

We have here again an illustration of the objective discipline of operationism to which an earlier reference was made (pages 4–5). In the hands of a psychologist who rules out introspection in favor of purely objective methods, verbal report becomes an objective method. The experimenter now becomes the scientific observer, and the object of his study is the behavior of the subject toward the stimuli the experimenter has prepared for him. Bergmann and Spence (1944) present the matter in this way:

> Scientific empiricism holds to the position that all sciences, including psychology, deal with the same events, namely, the experiences or perceptions of the scientist himself. . . . In the schema outlined by the scientific empiricist the experiences of the observing scientist do indeed have a privileged, even unique position. . . . the empiricist scientist should realize that his behavior, symbolic or otherwise, does not lie on the same methodological level as the responses of his subjects. . . . all his terms should be behavioristically defined. . . . In studying his subjects, including their symbolic responses (object language), the behavior scientist himself uses a different language (pragmatic metalanguage). . . . Assume that a scientist calls a behavior fragment of a subject aggressive if 8 out of 10 judges apply this word to the behavior in question. In doing so our scientist has made use of what might be termed the *human yardstick* in the introduction of *his* term "aggressive." The latter lies in the scientist's metalanguage and must, therefore, be carefully distinguished from the judges' term which belongs to the object language. . . . If [concepts introduced without the use of the human yardstick] are called *strict behavioristic terms*, one would have to say that the scientist of our illustration

describes, in strict behavioristic terms, not the behavior of his subjects, but rather the behavior of the group composed of his subjects *and* of his judges. . . . The clinician who applies mentalistic, not strictly introduced, terms to his patients is indeed the limiting case of the schematic situation; in this instance the single judge coincides with the observing scientist. There is, of course, no objection against calling all these procedures behavioristic, but then the word refers to nothing more precise than what is usually called the experimental attitude.

Laudable as this scrupulous precision on the use of terms is, applied too rigorously it could exclude from psychological consideration many of the most significant problems which do not lend themselves to a formalized approach of the type described. Imposing too many methodological rules and conventions during the early development of a science can have the effect of shutting the door against the emergence of new and better techniques which might otherwise have been discovered; or it may result in driving young scientists away from real problems to search for something insignificant or irrelevant "where the light is better."

The heritage of psychology would be less rich without such studies as Francis Galton's questionnaire on mental imagery which established the fact of wide individual differences (1880), or Sigmund Freud's self-analysis as it is recorded in *The Interpretation of Dreams* (1900). McKellar (1962) cites, along with these and other important contributions based on the introspective approach, specific areas of psychology which can profit from the use of the introspective method even when it is not the only or the main method used. Referring to his own experience with mescaline, he describes the difficulty of communicating verbally the character of the imagery the drug produced. His method of solving the problem, and the ingenious devices used by others similarly frustrated in their effort to describe in words the character of their inner experience, raise a reasonable doubt about the adequacy of verbal reports exacted from each subject in a standard form, or translated into a code found most convenient for statistical processing.

FURTHER DEVELOPMENT OF THE INTROSPECTIVE METHOD. The purpose of introspection in functional psychology is to obtain from the person who has performed a task some inside information on how he did it. To be accurate enough for scientific use, an introspective report should be made right after the task is completed and it should not attempt to cover too much ground, since it depends on the person's memory of what has just "passed through his mind." The method of impression is ideal in these respects. Processes that are more complicated and take more time can nevertheless be observed

WILHELM WUNDT

EDWARD BRADFORD TITCHENER

WILLIAM JAMES

JOHN DEWEY

JAMES ROWLAND ANGELL

and reported to some extent. There is an old standard experiment in which the subject compares two weights that are almost equal by lifting first one and then the other. Usually all he is asked to report is his impression as to which is heavier. But how can he compare the weight he is now lifting with the one he has already put down? The sensation of lifting the first weight is past and gone. The older theory was that a memory image of the pull of the first weight remained and was compared with the actual pull of the second. But why not have him describe the experience of comparing the weights, as a test of the theory? When the subject did so, the theory was not confirmed. His report was that he did not remember, nor try to remember, the pull of the first weight, but simply felt all ready for the second. When he lifted the second weight, it felt light or heavy and he accordingly called it lighter or heavier than the first —and was usually right. The experimenter by watching the subject's hand could clearly see in some cases that a weight which seemed light to the subject had come up quickly when lifted, while one which seemed heavy had come up slowly. Now if the subject adopted a standard force of lifting, adjusted always to the first weight, the second weight would come up easily if it were lighter than the first, but slowly if heavier. The process of comparison accordingly made use of a muscular adjustment instead of a memory image. This theory, which was confirmed by variations of the experiment, was based on a combination of introspective data from the subject with objective observations by the experimenter. From such experiments came the important concept of a preparatory set or state of readiness, a concept that has a wide range of application.

The type of introspective report first obtained in this experiment stands to the credit mostly of G. E. Müller (1850–1934), one of a small number of German psychologists who, without being pupils of Wundt—being rivals, rather—had started laboratories not long after Wundt. (The experiment cited dates from 1889.) Müller went on to use his new introspective method in his long-continued studies of memory (1911, 1913, 1917). The excellent pioneer work of Ebbinghaus (already noted on pages 17–18) had used objective data exclusively. It had seemed to indicate that a list of nonsense syllables was memorized by a mechanical, though very intense, process of linking syllable to syllable, quite in line with the old associationist theory. Müller, entertaining some doubt of this interpretation, required his subjects to report their experiences in memorizing the material. The subjects found a good deal to report. They seemed to be very active while memorizing, by no means receiving the material passively and letting it link itself together by some automatic process. They grouped the items, such as numbers or nonsense syllables, put the series into rhythmical form, noted similarities and contrasts, lugged in meanings where possible, and in general actively organized the material. Müller found the combination of objective and introspective methods an excellent approach to the question of how we learn.

About 1900 another great psychologist, Alfred Binet of Paris (1857–1911), began to use introspection in an experimental study of the process of thinking. In his early days Binet had written a book on the psychology of reasoning, quite in the old style, without bothering to obtain any firsthand data, but trusting to logic and the theory of association to furnish a scheme of the reasoning process. In that book he assumed that reasoning must be a process of calling up and manipulating memory images. In a later work (1903) he based his conclusions on actual thinking processes reported by his two young daughters, who were of secondary school age. He gave them problems to solve and had them notice and report how they solved them. He would quiz them: "Just how did you think of that object? Did you see it? Or say its name to yourself?" Sometimes his subjects reported images, but in many instances they denied the presence of any images, and Binet was thus forced to abandon the theory that thinking consisted essentially in the manipulation of images. Thinking seemed to go on largely in just "thoughts," "*pensées*"—he could find no better word. These thoughts—"imageless thoughts" they were often called—could be described as "thinking of" a certain object or "thinking that" so and so was the case; but this sort of description was not accepted as expert introspection by all psychologists. Even so, the introspective method had scored two successes: it had disproved an old theory; and it had shown that the general course of a thought process could be reported, even if the details were not adequately described.

A school of *Denkpsychologie* ("thought psychology") arose in Germany under the leadership of Oswald Külpe (1862–1915), a pupil of Wundt who broke away in certain respects from his master's teaching. This school, comprising many distinguished psychologists, flourished in Germany up to the time of the First World War and has been continued independently in Belgium by Albert Michotte, professor at Louvain, and his students.[1] The Külpe group made systematic use of the combined introspective and objective methods, with more emphasis on the introspective reports, which tended to be very elaborate. They fully confirmed Binet's imageless thoughts and added many other facts on the process of thinking;

[1] We shall hear more of Michotte's work later (pp. 49–50).

and they found Müller's "preparatory set" important in both simple and complicated thought processes.

There can be no reasonable doubt, in spite of the behaviorists, that introspection affords some very good glimpses of the processes of learning, problem solving, and reaching a decision. As was said before, however, the objective method of varied conditions has been the favorite of functional psychologists. Many of them think of introspection as belonging to another school with which they are not in sympathy. We may well be curious to know what other school there could be in view of the broad scope of functional psychology. What other goal could psychology set before itself except that of discovering what the organism does and how and why?

THE STRUCTURAL PSYCHOLOGY OF CONSCIOUS EXPERIENCE

William James (1842–1910), a truly great psychologist, in offering a *Briefer Course* in psychology for the college student in 1892, started off with a definition which was regarded as standard at the time: "The definition of psychology may be best given . . . as the description and explanation of states of consciousness as such." A much-used English textbook of the period was *Outlines of Psychology*, 1884, by James Sully, who said: "I abide by the old perception that psychology is distinctly marked off from the physical or natural sciences as . . . having to do with the phenomena of the inner world, and employing its own method or instrument, namely, introspection." Wilhelm Wundt (1832–1920), certainly a leader in psychology, said in 1892: "Psychology has to investigate that which we call internal experience—i.e., our own sensation and feeling, our thought and volition—in contradistinction to the objects of external experience, which form the subject matter of natural science." In 1896, however, he replaced the words "internal experience," by the improved formula "immediate experience," so as to include what obviously was a part of psychology's subject matter, our experience of external objects. We are conscious of objects outside us as well as of thoughts and feelings inside us, and a science of conscious experience must cover both. Undoubtedly it is the inner experience that first awakens the interest of students who approach psychology from this angle. James said in a well-known passage of his larger work, *Principles of Psychology* (1890, Vol. I, page 550):

> The manner in which trains of imagery and consideration follow each other through our thinking, the restless flight of one idea before the next, the transitions our minds make between things wide as the poles asunder . . . all this magical, imponderable streaming has from time immemorial excited the admiration of all whose attention happened to be caught by its omnipresent

mystery. And it has furthermore challenged the race of philosophers to banish something of the mystery by formulating the process in simpler terms.

If conscious experience was set apart as the field for a science of psychology to explore and reduce to order, the project was similar to that of chemistry. Discover the elements of conscious experience and their modes of combination. So it seemed to Wundt anyway, though in James's view, on the contrary, the main requirement was to bring out clearly the fluid, streaming, personal nature of consciousness. It was Wundt, not James, who mapped out the field of *structural psychology*, which, however, he called simply "psychology." All our experiences—perceptions of external objects, memories, emotions, purposes—are complex and call for scientific analysis.

The elements of conscious experience, in Wundt's analysis, were of two main classes: the sensations which seem to come to us from outside, and the feelings which seem to belong to ourselves. The elementary sensations were teased out by the sense physiologists— the colors, the tones, the elementary tastes, the elementary skin sensations. For the functional psychologist these sensory elements helped to explain how we see, hear, etc., but for the structural psychologist they were significant as being the simplest possible kinds of experience, except, perhaps, the feelings. Of the elementary feelings, the pleasant and unpleasant were universally agreed on, and Wundt proposed two additional pairs: the excited and the quiet; the tense and the relaxed. These elements could combine into many blends and patterns of feeling. Emotion was explained as a complex experience composed of feelings and bodily sensations, and the experience of willing as a certain time-pattern of emotion, characterized by an abrupt change of feeling at the moment of decision. Throughout, Wundt aimed to describe not what man does but what his experience is—not his acts but the contents of his consciousness.

Of Wundt's laws of combination the most interesting was his "law of psychic resultants" or "principle of creative synthesis." Combination creates new properties. "Every psychic compound has characteristics which are by no means the mere sum of the characteristics of the elements" (1896, page 375). Something very much like this law is to be found in the teachings of the associationists before Wundt and of the Gestalt psychologists after Wundt.

As the revered head of the Leipzig laboratory, where many of the young leaders were trained at about the turn of the century, Wundt exerted great influence on the psychology of that period. Few of his numerous American pupils seem to have carried away a hearty acceptance of the structural point of view; they remained functionalists at heart. But Wundt had at least one vigorous representative in the United States from 1892 on for over three decades.

Edward Bradford Titchener (1867–1927), an English student of Wundt, would have preferred on obtaining his doctor's degree in 1892 to be the pioneer in Britain of the new experimental psychology, but the time was not ripe, the British being skeptical of the new approach to one of their favorite philosophical subjects. Titchener accepted a position at Cornell University and remained there the rest of his life, directing a very active laboratory and training a loyal band of structural psychologists. He promptly took up the cudgels in support of the Wundtian structural psychology as against the functional psychology which he found dominant in the United States. It was Titchener at this time who coined the terms *functional* and *structural psychology* (1898, 1899). We can speak of the structure of a machine and of its function or use. We can speak of the structure of the eye and of the function or operation and use of each part of the structure. In biology we have structural sciences and functional sciences, human anatomy being structural, while physiology is functional. The structure of an organ is what it is; the function is what it does, what it is for. Both kinds of science are important, but the structural would seem to have priority, since the function of an organ could not very well be investigated until the organ itself was known.

Psychology was the science of consciousness, according to general agreement at that time. Titchener held that this science, like biology, would include a study of structure and a study of function. The structure of consciousness would be what consciousness is "as such," and the function of consciousness would be what it does, what use it is in the life of the individual and of the social group. Structural study should have priority over functional, for until we know thoroughly what conscious processes are we are not ready to investigate what they do for the organism. Functional psychology must continue to be speculative until structural psychology has provided a scientific foundation.

How, according to this view, would the structure of consciousness or of any conscious process or experience be described? Every experience, as Wundt said, is complex and calls for scientific analysis; and when analysis has gone as far as possible and reached the elements of conscious experience, description must advance to synthesis in order to show how the elements fit together to produce the conscious experience. Recognizing a person in the street as an old acquaintance is a complex experience, some elements of which are supplied by the sense of sight, some by memory. But structural psychologists would go beyond this to examine whether the memory is an image of some past experience or merely a sense of familiarity. Observational analysis of such everyday experiences may be very difficult except for the introspectionists trained to report only what is factually present in the experience, not the logical meaning or the practical value of the elements. A coin, for example, cannot be described as a "shilling." The introspective observer must strip off meanings and values. Although these are indeed present in the experience, they are not elements; they are elusive compounds which must be analyzed if possible. One who reports objects inferred from elements commits the *stimulus error*. Titchener's emphasis on the unelaborated mental content as the proper datum of introspection led to the labeling of his special form of structuralism as "existentialism." (This use of the term is not to be identified in any way with the philosophy of Kierkegaard, Heidegger, Jaspers, Sartre, etc., or with the more recent adaptation of existentialist philosophy to personality theory.)

With conscious experience as the subject matter of psychology, the questions "What?" and "How?" take on a new aspect. "What?" becomes "What are the elements?" and "How?" becomes "How are they combined?" The "Why?" question calls for explanation and for fitting conscious experiences into the organism and the world at large (Titchener, 1909–1910, page 41). The question "What for?" has no place in existential psychology, being the appropriate question for a functional psychology, and corresponding to the "What?" question of the genuine functional psychology. That is, the genuine functional psychology starts not from consciousness, but from man's doings, and uses introspection to give some indications of how he does and what he does. If consciousness is the only proper starting point for any psychology, as was generally assumed in 1900, man's doings can be regarded as what consciousness is for, i.e., as the value, use, or function of consciousness.

The word *function* has two related but rather confusing meanings. It means "use or value"; and it means "operation or process." If you look under the hood of an automobile and discover a certain structure there called a carburetor, you ask, "What is the function of this thing? What is it for? What does it do? What is its use in the running of the automobile?" But if you start with the automobile as a whole, a functional whole, you ask what operations must go on in it, what internal functions (not external uses) it must have; and you see that it has the function of supplying its own energy by burning gasoline. Then you ask how this function is carried out and discover that gasoline and air are mixed in the carburetor. In the same way you could start with a bodily organ such as the stomach and ask what its function is, or you could start with the function of digestion and ask how it operates. At the psychological level you could, as a structuralist, start with memory images and then, turning functionalist, ask what use they have for the organism; or, being a functionalist from the start, you would note that the organism has the function of remembering past events and then, asking how this function is performed, find that memory images play a part. Either approach is legitimate, but the thoroughgoing functional approach seems more promising if what you want in the end is a functional psychology. And the actual work in functional psychology, of which a few samples were cited earlier in this chapter, has approached its problems not from the side of conscious experience but from the side of results accomplished. (There is still a third meaning of *function*, taken over from mathematics, and probably more common than either of the others in present-day psychology. *Y* is a function of *X*, i.e., depends on *X*, varies systematically with *X*. Appetite is a function of the time since eating; forgetting is a function of the time since learning; intelligence is a function of age. The numerous "curves" which psychological investigators put out to show their results are functions in this sense, or represent functions. Surely they also, for the most part, belong under the head of functional psychology.)

Though Titchener won quite a number of adherents, especially among his students, his crusade for a structural psychology did not carry the day with American psychologists in general. Instead, great and increasing doubt was voiced as to whether psychology was properly the science of consciousness as such or was not better called the science of behavior. Titchener granted that there could be a science of behavior but denied that it was psychology. Instead it would necessarily be a part of biology. According to Titchener (1929) the biological and psychological viewpoints are radically different, since biology views the organism in relation to the environment while psychology views conscious experience in relation to the organism. Conscious experience has direct relations, not with the environment, but only with processes occurring within the organism, especially in the nervous system. But behavior is directly related to the environment and so belongs in the province of biology.

In spite of this attempt to draw a sharp line between genuine psychology and the science of behavior, Titchener still regarded the two sciences as closely related. In his general textbooks (1909–1910, 1915) he introduced functional as well as structural material. He projected a comprehensive, advanced treatise on structural psychology; but this project bogged down for some reason, perhaps because of the difficulty of fitting into his scheme the newer developments in introspective psychology. He evidently had considerable sympathy with the *Denkpsychologie* (see page 24) but could not accept "imageless thought" as adding anything to the conscious elements of sensation, image, and feeling (1909). He may well have had a similar sympathy for the emerging "phenomenological psychology" (pages 36–37) and even for Gestalt psychology (page 219); but to fit these into his system would have been almost impossible. At any rate, his comprehensive treatise was never completed, and only the introductory groundwork was published (1929). His *magnum opus,* a great contribution to the advancement of our science, was his four-volume *Experimental Psychology* (1901, 1905). Here, too, functional as well as structural experiments were included. In fact anyone would find it very difficult to draw the line. The quantitative study of sensation ("psychophysics") can evidently be regarded as belonging to structural psychology, but at the same time it is a study of the *functions* of discrimination and estimation. The same can be said of the valuable work on the "dimensions" of a sensation, such as tonal pitch, loudness, volume, and density (Boring and Stevens, 1936). Titchener's pupils can certainly not be accused of any narrow outlook (Pillsbury, 1911; Washburn, 1916, 1930; Boring, 1930, 1942, 1950; Bentley, 1926, 1930).

THE CHICAGO SCHOOL OF FUNCTIONAL PSYCHOLOGY

Titchener's challenge to the functionalists was promptly accepted by a vigorous group at the University of Chicago under the leadership of John Dewey (1859–1952) and James Rowland Angell (1869–1949), two of the most distinguished men in our whole list—Dewey the great philosopher, Angell later influential as President of Yale. In their stand for a functional psychology they were influenced by William James's conviction that consciousness was not a mere frill or epiphenomenon but rather a genuine causal factor in life and biological survival. Every sensation or feeling, besides its mere existence, has a function as referring to some kind of an object, knowing it and also choosing or rejecting it. Moreover, "every possible feeling produces a movement," or sometimes an inhibition of movement. Conscious processes are thus tied in with the environment on both sensory and motor sides (1890, Vol. I, pages 271, 478; Vol. II, page 372).

Like James, the early Chicago functionalists accepted the definition of psychology as the science of consciousness and held that conscious processes should be studied not only as existential facts but also as playing their parts in the development of the individual and his adaptation to the environment. A few citations from Angell's *Psychology, An Introductory Study of the Structure and Function of Human Consciousness* (1904) will bring out the point of view.

> Psychologists have hitherto devoted the larger part of their energy to investigating the *structure* of the mind. Of late, however, there has been manifest a disposition to deal more fully with its functional and genetic phases. To determine how consciousness develops and how it operates is felt to be quite as important as the discovery of its constituent elements. . . . The fundamental psychological method is introspection . . . the direct examination of one's own mental processes. . . . We are able to supplement introspection by immediate objective observation of other individuals. . . . Animal psychology is engaged with the study of consciousness, wherever . . . its presence can be detected. . . . We shall adopt the biological point of view . . . we shall regard all the operations of consciousness—all our sensations, all our emotions, and all our acts of will—as so many expressions of organic adaptations to our environment, an environment which we must remember is social as well as physical. . . . If the reflexes and the automatic acts were wholly competent to steer the organism throughout its course, there is no reason to suppose that consciousness would ever put in an appearance.[2]

Here we see an outspoken functionalism making its debut in psychology, but it was not identical with the broad, implicit functionalism of the experimental work mentioned earlier in the chapter. It did not start with results accomplished by the individual and ask how they were accomplished, but it started with conscious processes and asked what their use might be in organic and social life. It sought to discover what needs of the organism were met by sense perception, by memory images, by emotion. Taking the evolutionary point of view, it sought to divine at what stage in the development of the race the need for each mental process must have led to the emergence of that particular ability. The simpler forms of consciousness probably emerged when reflexes were unable to meet the organism's needs, and the higher mental processes emerged when a wider and more flexible control of the environment became necessary. Thus functional psychology aimed to give psychology a place in the general field of biological science. It aimed also to be of practical use, especially in the field of education. Dewey, besides his eminence as the philosopher of pragmatism, was a pioneer in progressive education, which, he said, should be based on an understanding of the child's needs as he develops.

Believing so strongly in developmental psychology, the Chicago functionalists soon possessed an active animal laboratory. Consciousness could be assumed, according to Angell's view, whenever an animal adjusted to a novel environment or solved a problem.

---

[2] Angell (1904), pp. iii, 4, 6, 7, 50. See also Angell (1907, 1936); Hunter (1949).

Without regard to this particular assumption the laboratory became and long remained very productive of experimental work on animal learning. Under the direct leadership of Angell's junior colleague and later successor, Harvey Carr (1873–1954), the Chicago group lost most of that great emphasis on introspection and most of those speculative and philosophical interests (Carr, 1930, 1936), and it trained and sent out to all parts of the country many productive research psychologists. The Chicago school has been a very important psychological center, though Angell never aspired to establish a "school" in our sense. In the course of time the Chicago brand merged with the "implicit" brand, which has remained a tendency strong in American psychology (Hilgard, 1956, pages 328–67), but by no means confined to this country.

CARRYING ON THE CHICAGO TRADITION

Following Angell and Carr in the functionalist tradition at Chicago were Edward S. Robinson and John A. McGeoch. Among these four men there was considerable community of interest in theoretical and practical problems of learning. Later, at Yale, Robinson's concern for the practical use of psychology in the interests of society was expressed in his volume *Law and the Lawyers* (1935). In this he pleaded for a realistic revision of legalistic concepts such as "insanity," "intent," "the reasonable man," and fossilized ideas of motives and responsibility that have no better argument in their favor than that they have existed for centuries and so give society a sense of security. Yet he recognized that disagreements among the "schools," the preoccupation of experimental psychologists with refinements of techniques, and the statistical generalizations of science were unlikely to bring much enlightenment to jurists on the handling of the individual case. The only solution seemed to be for the man of law to be aware of the psychological aspects of the problems he must handle and to participate in the search for answers:

A jurisprudence dominated by the interrogatory attitude of psychology will do far more than throw light upon the law. It will turn up inquiries that are new to the psychologist himself and it will bring to the solution of psychologically important problems a type of factual material which has thus far played but little part in the determination of our thinking about human nature. The psychologist has . . . avoided law except to suggest that he might some day render it technical service. Yet, in the existing legal materials there is a mine of data for psychological investigation. . . . when the legal scholar himself begins to pursue psychological investigations we may expect him to show that the average law library has within it more psychological stuff than is contained in the reports of all the laboratories (1935, page 120).

Carr and Robinson were both identified with a search for quantitative laws of associative learning, and Robinson produced a list of nine (1932), including the apparently reasonable factors of *contiguity, frequency, intensity,* and *individual differences.* He did not claim his list was exhaustive, and he admitted that the separate laws might be further broken down, which is in fact the case. They have not played an important part in the history of learning theory.

Robinson's name is more familiarly identified with his studies of the work curve and the factors which account for work decrement. In *Work of the Integrated Organism* (1934) he provided an analysis and summation of the principles which emerged from studies then available on physical and mental fatigue, boredom, etc., including a number of his own and his students' experiments. One well-known study with Arthur G. Bills (born 1895; now professor at the University of Cincinnati) compared the work decrement in three tasks varying in degree of homogeneity. Subjects were required to read cards on which 100 quarter-inch letters had been pasted. On one of the cards eight different letters were repeated in random order, on another four, and on the third only two. Speed of reading the eight-letter combination was markedly slower than that for the other two cards, but there appeared less evidence of work decrement in this task. Robinson attributed the greater decrement on the two-letter card to the greater homogeneity of the task.

Bills carried on the investigation of factors involved in work efficiency including the phenomenon of mental "blocking," which is also increased by homogeneity. When a subject is required to add in his mind a succession of numbers cumulatively, the smooth flow is repeatedly interrupted by instants of "blankness"—the inability to come up with any response. Bills has suggested that these "refractory phases" make possible the apparent relative unfatiguability of our mental equipment (1931, 1935). He has demonstrated the increase of blocking also when the oxygen content of the blood is reduced (1937). His *Psychology of Efficiency* (1943) reports a number of studies of his own and of other investigators which have practical personal or industrial application.

John A. McGeoch (1897–1942) has been perhaps best known for his careful analysis of the phenomenon of retroactive inhibition. Along with proactive inhibition this factor is generally acknowledged to be one of the imps that confound us in our efforts to remember. But exactly how it operates to have that effect is not yet clearly understood. We do know that when the learning of task A is followed by the learning of task B the latter is likely to interfere with the recall of A through items from B that intrude or threaten to intrude into the A content. Thought of in a slightly different way, retroactive inhibition might be described as *negative transfer* of training, inasmuch as the new material learned interferes with the recall or the relearning of the earlier task. McGeoch and McDonald (1931) investigated the relationship between the degree of similarity of the interpolated material and the original learning, using for the former synonyms that had been carefully evaluated for their degree of similarity to the adjectives used in the original list. They found that the greatest interference came from the most similar words.

But a puzzling contradiction suggests that there is more to the story than these experiments tell. What happens when the second task is almost identical with the first rather than just "very similar"? When we repeat what we have learned on an earlier occasion we do not expect the repetition to *weaken* our grip on the associations that have been formed. A number of solutions have been suggested, the relative merits of which we cannot consider here. (The interested reader is referred to Hilgard, 1956, Osgood, 1953, and Woodworth and Schlosberg, 1954, for a fuller discussion of the problem.)

The question has been raised as to the effect of the timing of the interpolated material in retroactive inhibition. The theory of Müller and Pilzecker (1900) who first reported the phenomenon was that it could be explained as the result of too early interference with some perseverative process which followed the formation of any association and which allowed it to "soak in" or become consolidated. If this is the case, and some good evidence can be found to support the idea, the second task would be most damaging to the first learning if it followed promptly rather than after some delay. McGeoch, however, favored the idea that interference was the result of competition between the earlier and the later learned items at the time the earlier had to be recalled. In this case the interference effect would be greater if the new material were introduced immediately before the recall of the old. Experimental findings on this question are still conflicting, and some suggest that the effect would be marked at both the beginning and end of the interval between first learning and recall (Postman and Alper, 1946). The theory has also been advanced (Melton and Irwin, 1940) that part of the retroactive inhibition effect is the result of "unlearning" the original material in the course of trying to learn the new material. If the learner suppresses the first association each time it comes to his mind in favor of a new, correct one, the former will gradually be weakened; but in addition, as Underwood has pointed out (1945), the old association under such conditions will have less chance of competing with other associations when the time comes later for it to be put back into use. The theory of unlearning, then, is quite compatible with the theory of competition, and McGeoch and Underwood (1943) have produced evidence to support the idea that they work together.

Obviously in all such studies much will depend upon the nature of the content used and the degree to which the new and the old material have been learned. Assuming that the intruding errors will be less well learned than the content the subject is trying to recall, McGeoch predicted that spaced practice should be more effective than massed practice in reducing the effect of retroactive inhibition, since after a brief lapse of time the unwanted errors will have been forgotten more than the wanted associations (McGeoch, 1942; McGeoch and Irion, 1952). Experimental results have not supported McGeoch on this theory of *differential forgetting*, however.

Eleanor J. Gibson has also proposed a theory of differential forgetting (1940) based on the principle of generalization of response as it has been described by Pavlov. (See pages 76–77, this book.) In the early stages of learning or of perceiving objects fine discrimination does not occur. Only after a particular spot on the skin has been frequently associated with a shock or with feeding does the animal gradually begin to differentiate it from spots nearby which have not been so treated. The animal—or human—subject must learn to inhibit the tendency to respond to the irrelevant spots, and the progress of learning is marked by more certain and, up to a degree, finer discrimination as measured by appropriate response to the positive spot and inhibition of that response to the negative spots.

Think now of the learning of nonsense syllables in the same way. At first one syllable will be much like all the others; but with some consistent differentiating effect, one can be made to stand out from the others for the learner so that eventually that one becomes the "right" one and the others which had at first competed with it are repressed. But as with the spots touched in the first illustration, so with the nonsense syllables. The closer the spots, the more difficult the discrimination; the more similar the nonsense syllables, the more difficult the discrimination. If this reasoning based on a theory of a *gradient of generalization* is correct, then spaced practice might prove less effective than massed practice, because it would allow a chance for these difficult-to-make and tenuous distinctions between the positive and the negative stimuli to disappear in the rest intervals. Experimental results in general seem to support Mrs. Gibson's predictions more than McGeoch's, but many complicating factors make the results inconclusive.

Benton J. Underwood (born 1915; now professor at Northwestern University), with his collaborators, has done a series of studies on distributed practice over a period of years, systematically varying such factors as stage of learning, speed of presentation of items, length of rest interval, inter-list and intra-list similarity, nature of the learned material—whether nonsense or meaningful, individual items or serial, etc. (1961). Once again, the evidence does not support any simple formulation of a rule. There seems some reason to believe that any immediate advantage of distributed practice gives way after a period of rest to advantage for massed practice, and increasing the time *per item* for a list to be learned may do more good than allowing a rest interval between lists (Underwood and Viterna, 1951). It appears also that high similarity among the items that compose a list may work two ways: first, to complicate the learning of the items because of the chance of confusing them; and second, supporting Gibson's generalization theory, to assure a greater immunity from *inter-list* interference because of the distinctive character of the high-similarity list. Whatever early advantage a low-similarity list may have is gradually lost as learning progresses. Underwood's results have led him to emphasize the effect of *proactive inhibition* even more than *retroactive inhibition*. Lists learned before a "test list" have been found to transfer negatively to the latter, the degree of interference being directly related to the number of prior lists (1957). Problems in the interrelated areas of retroactive and proactive inhibition and transfer of training continue to offer a challenge to a great number of investigators. (For other studies and a more complete account of the experimental work on this aspect of learning the reader is referred to Cofer, 1961; Underwood and Schulz, 1960; Keppel and Underwood, 1962; Postman, 1962; Postman and Stark, 1962.)

EUROPEAN FUNCTIONALISTS

Of the older German psychologists, we have already counted G. E. Müller as an important contributor to the experimental methods of functional psychology; and it will be fair to count in at least two of Müller's pupils.

David Katz (1884–1953; long Müller's assistant at Göttingen, then professor at Rostock in Germany and later at Stockholm in Sweden) is well known for his varied studies in animal, child, and applied psychology, but especially for his "phenomenological" studies of color (1911, 1930) and of touch (1925). By *phenomena* we mean "appearances." By touch phenomena, then, we mean the impressions the ordinary observer gets from touching and handling objects and different materials. We do not tell our observer about the "elements": warmth, cold, pain, and pressure. We leave him psychologically unsophisticated and simply ask him to report how these things feel. He reports that one thing is rough and hard, another thing soft and bulky, and uses quite a variety of such descriptive words. The structuralist may object that such impressions are contaminated with meanings acquired in past experience, and so are not pure sensory data. The phenomenological point of view is that these naive, "holistic" impressions are important for a comprehensive psychology, fully as important as the "atomistic" elements of the structuralist. Katz certainly used this method very effectively and made notable contributions to the functional psychology of the cutaneous senses. His study of object colors and "color constancy" —the tendency for colors to appear relatively unchanged in different lights—was equally significant.

Katz's holistic approach and phenomenological method were quite acceptable to the Gestalt psychologists who appeared on the scene right after his first major work. There might be some doubt whether he should be classed as a functionalist or as a gestaltist—especially as he later published a book on *Gestalt Psychology* (1950). Yet in this as well as in his *Autobiography* (1952) he draws a distinction between his psychology and that of the major Gestalt group. "In spite of the fact that my views are close to those of the Gestalt psychologists in many, perhaps even in most respects, . . . I do not believe that all psychological facts are in accord with the Gestalt viewpoint" (1950, Preface). There is much more of value in the older work than the Gestalt group admits. For one thing, the gestaltists have mostly neglected the study of motor skill and of mental work, to which Katz applied his holistic concepts with considerable success (1950).

Edgar Rubin (1886–1951; professor at Copenhagen) was another exponent of phenomenology. His great contribution was a study of "figure and ground" (1915, 1921). The "figure" is whatever stands out from a background. The figure is a compact part of the total visual field; at least it has some apparent form, while the ground appears like formless space. Unless the visual field is perfectly uniform, some portion of it will certainly appear as the figure. The figure usually catches the observer's attention, but he can easily attend to the ground; so that the figure-ground distinction is not merely the difference between the focus and margin of attention. Figure and ground are not limited to the visual field. A rhythmical drumbeat or the chugging of a motorboat stands out from the formless background of vague noise; something moving along the skin stands out from the vague mass of touch sensation. The facts are obvious enough but were disregarded by psychological theorists until their significance was pointed out by Rubin who held that the figure-ground organization must be as natural and fundamental as the seeing of colors or the hearing of tones and noises. Figure and ground were soon adopted by the Gestalt school (page 220) and made part of their system. Rubin's personal attitude was much like that of Claparède: "Psychological schools are a nuisance. As a rule the association of the members with each other serves as a help toward the continued belief in some unproved favorite notions which characterize the school. As a rule the founders of a school are not so bad as the pupils" (1930).

Egon Brunswik (1903–1955) spent the first ten years of his career at the University of Vienna and the last eighteen years at the University of California in Berkeley. He was perhaps best known to American psychologists, even before he took up permanent residence in this country, for his important contributions to method and theory in the study of perceptual constancy, but these represented only one aspect of his broader interest in the problem of "achievement," by which he meant the relative success with which the organism arrives at an approximately correct impression of an object in spite of the complex and misleading cues which make up "the causal texture of the environment." For example, when a "distal" visual stimulus from an object one hundred yards away produces a "proximal" effect upon the retina, why do we usually interpret it correctly as a large object at a distance rather than a small object near at hand? There are, of course, numerous cues that enter into our judgment of its relative distance and size; but Brunswik pointed out the uncertainty and ambiguity of such information: the circumstances of the moment will determine how many and which of these cues will be present and it would be futile to attempt to explain size constancy or the estimation of distance in terms of their individual separate effects. He therefore proposed a probabilistic (statistical) approach in which, instead of specific cues, alternating groups of cues in representative situations would be the object of study.

Brunswik also applied his "probabilistic functionalism" to learning, thinking, and social perception. In advocating the statistical approach to such problems he anticipated by about fifteen years the current behaviorist trend toward mathematical learning theory (pages 209–10, this book). In an experiment he designed specifically to test the effect of different frequencies of reward received for a right turn and for a left turn in a T-maze, the rats eventually chose the arm which had been rewarded 75 per cent of the time in approximately three-quarters of their runs, as against one quarter for the other arm. (For other results, see Brunswik, 1939.) This was the first of a number of experiments in which psychologists have sought the answer to the question of whether the subject's ultimate (asymptotic) performance will be wholly in the direction of the more frequently "rewarded" alternative, or will show a tendency for the subject to learn to match his responses to the ratio of "successes" to "failures." Brunswik considered that this sort of experiment presented a more realistic situation than one in which one or the other response is invariably rewarded. In actual life the subject does not find the pathways through the "mazes" he must traverse so conveniently distinguished. They often remain ambiguous, and he must make his choice on the basis of a "higher or lesser degree of probability" (1939, page 175).

In his synthesis of perception and motor behavior from this functionalist point of view (1952, 1956) Brunswik's position in many respects approached that of his University of California colleague, E. C. Tolman, whose "cognitive behaviorism" will be discussed in Chapter 6. After Brunswik's death, Tolman wrote an appreciative review of his contribution (1956), and with Leo Postman prepared a summary of probabilistic functionalism (Postman and Tolman, 1959).

Edouard Claparède (1873–1940) was the most outspoken European functionalist, and there are many parallels between his work at Geneva in Switzerland and the practically simultaneous work of the Chicago group. Early in his career he adopted a point of view which he first called biological and later functional. The functional conception, he said, "considers psychical phenomena primarily from the point of view of their function in life. . . . This comes to the same thing as asking one's self: What is their use?" (1930, page 79). Their function is to meet a person's needs and interests. He set up an animal laboratory in his department of the university. Because of his dissatisfaction with the traditional methods of elementary teaching and his belief that "the teacher should learn from the child," he founded at Geneva the now world-famous J. J. Rousseau Institute for the study of the child and for the development of progressive methods of teaching. He found John Dewey's ideas on education very much to his liking. Believing in introspection, he would not by any means restrict it as Titchener did to the observation of meaningless existential content. For the study of thought processes he adopted a method which he called *réflexion parlée* or "thinking aloud" (1933). Claparède had no desire to found a "school" of psychology. A peace-loving man of wide acquaintance among psychologists, for many years the secretary of the International Congresses of Psychology, he regarded the controversies between schools as wasted energy which might better be turned into productive channels. "What is the use of wantonly limiting the scope of psychology, prescribing beforehand the concepts which will be of value to it? I believe one should be eclectic and adopt provisionally all those points of view which would appear to be of practical value, even if they be contradictory" (1930, page 96). There should not be many "psychologies," but a single, all-inclusive psychology.

Jean Piaget, professor at the University of Geneva, has been well known to English-speaking psychologists through his early writings, particularly *The Language and Thought of the Child* (1923), *Judgment and Reasoning in the Child* (1924), and *The Child's Conception of Physical Causality* (1927). His conclusions have provoked much research on these topics in America and elsewhere (McCarthy, 1954; Mussen, 1960; Hunt, 1961; Kessen and Kuhlman, 1962); but probably in the final appraisal of Piaget's contributions to psychology these early studies will be recognized as the promising products of a warming-up period in a long program and a distinguished career dedicated to study of the origin and development of human knowledge. From his autobiography we learn some of the reasons why his interests took this direction.

Born in Neuchâtel in 1894, he was trained by a scholarly father to make precise observations, and to write them down systematically. His first publication, an article on biology in a local natural history journal, won him an informal apprenticeship to the director of the natural history museum where he soon became a "specialist" in classifying mollusks. In his years at Neuchâtel, philosophy also had a great claim on his interests, and he read avidly for himself, among others, the writings of Bergson, Kant, Durkheim, James, and Janet, continuing his scrupulous note-taking and commentaries. He was fascinated by the problem of universals and reality, and the relationship of parts to the whole: "If I had known at that time (1913–1915) the work of Wertheimer and of Köhler, I would have become a Gestaltist . . ." (1952, page 242).

After receiving his doctorate, Piaget moved to Zurich where he had his first contact with psychoanalytic theory in Bleuler's clinic. Here he heard Jung lecture, and he read Freud. But some months later he went to Paris where, at Simon's invitation, he undertook to standardize for Parisian children Burt's tests of reasoning, using Binet's unoccupied laboratory as his workshop. It was at this time that he began to use the probing questions which have since been a distinctive feature of his method of studying the thought of children.

In 1925 his work attracted Claparède's attention, and he was offered the post of "director of studies" at the Jean Jacques Rousseau Institute. There, for the next few years, he carried on the research which provided the content of his first five books (1923; 1924; 1926; 1927; 1932) and which activated a flurry of counter-research and criticism of conclusions which Piaget himself has conceded may have been premature.

During a busy period (1925–1933) in which his activities were divided between duties at Neuchâtel and Geneva, Piaget undertook a study of his own three children. What he learned provided him with the foundation he regarded as essential to the building of a sound theory of mental development. We cannot do justice here to the assortment of ingeniously contrived "little experiments" and the penetrating analysis of the children's reactions. Piaget's own detailed accounts are now available in English translations (1936; 1937) and an excellent summary of these studies has been provided by Hunt (1961).

His years at Geneva since 1940 as Claparède's successor in the Institute of Educational Sciences and Director of the Psychology Laboratory, have been crowded with activities including a program in which he has associated with himself a number of collaborators whose names have become well known to those acquainted with the rich output of "the Geneva group." With Inhelder, Lambercier, Szeminska, and others, he has continued to trace the development of perception and thought through childhood and adolescence. These later studies use relatively large groups of subjects and introduce problems solvable only by manipulation, so meeting, to some extent, the criticisms that his earlier conclusions were based on too few cases and depended too heavily upon children's verbal responses, which could not be assessed with any degree of certainty. However, Piaget's "clinical" technique of pressing the child to account for each action or any hypothesis continues to be an important feature of his method. (This verbal approach has not been universally accepted; see Braine, 1959; Kessen, 1960.)

The intensive observations of his own children and these laboratory studies have led Piaget to his conclusions on the nature of the changing "structures" which characterize the perception and thought of the child as he passes through four distinguishable stages from infancy through adolescence. But before we attempt any differentiation of these stages it will be helpful to consider two principles which Piaget regards as essential to all developmental change.

It is not surprising that the thought of Piaget the psychologist should be strongly influenced by the knowledge of Piaget the biologist. If the physical growth and adaptation of the organism depend on the quality and quantity of its "aliment" why should not the same apply to mental development? He uses the term *assimilation* to describe the incorporation of external reality (aliment) into the existing mental organization at any level of development. In early infancy this would result in the transformation of the native reflexes into more effective *schemata* which as the child advances in age gradually become more complexly coordinated, making it possible for him to cope with his constantly broadening environment. Such adaptation has a circular effect, because as the child acquires through assimilation greater sensory and motor competence—as he focuses more accurately, judges distance more adequately, grasps objects with more assurance and intent, moves about more freely—he is daily confronted with new experiences which require *accommodation*. Assimilation and accommodation operate together throughout life. Needless to say, at any stage the new experiences must be within relatively easy reach of the existing schemata if accommodation is to take place; but on the other hand each new mental structure assimilated initiates a need and search for new experience. The *equilibrium* which is established at each of these moments of coping successfully with the environment is a temporary, "unstable" sort of equilibrium. If the environment does not soon present some new problem, the child will find one for himself!

THE FOUR STAGES OF DEVELOPMENT. All development then, according to Piaget, is a matter of successive integration at higher levels of the schemata which have developed at earlier levels. An illustration of the effect of such coordination in the first or *sensorimotor stage* would be the infant's progression from closing his fingers reflexly over one's finger to his achievement several months later when, seeing an object within arm's reach in front of him, he stretches out his arm and successfully picks it up. Although it might seem to the casual observer that the same motor reaction—grasping —has occurred in both situations, many schemata involving several separate senses must have developed and must have become coordinated as inter-sensory schemata to make the second response possible. In the grasping which appears at the very beginning of a baby's life, and which, in fact, occurs before birth, the object grasped is not recognized as an "object." It does not exist for the infant outside of his own subjective experience. Before he can begin to see it as an object his visual experiences must provide him with schemata that will help him to recognize the size, distance, and color of objects he sees at different distances, and in different lights, at different angles, etc. Without such schemata the same object would never have any constancy in its appearance. Mother's full face is quite different from her profile or any of the views in between. Once he has got Mother "figured out" she may upset his equilibrium by appearing in a glamorous new hat which his present schemata cannot handle, and he reacts with a loud expression of surprised disapproval. So with the smaller objects within his universe: he must learn to see them in a variety of forms before he can identify them with assurance. With that much visual sophistication he will have gradually learned also to judge whether or not they are within his reach. But, as the reader can probably guess, before he can reach for them in the right direction and at the right distance he must also have the necessary motor schemata. Even when the motor and visual schemata have formed the integrated schemata needed for reaching, there still remains the problem of grasping. One might expect that the original reflex could still serve that purpose; but this, too, has been undergoing transformation as the baby's hands have clutched at a variety of objects around him in the first months of his life. These experiences have built up an assortment of schemata controlling hand and finger movements which can now be coordinated with those assimilated through any other channel of experience.

Piaget offers an interesting explanation of why one of his children was slower than the other two in developing this "looking-at grasping" response, as he calls it. Laurent did it shortly after reaching three months; Lucienne was midway between her fourth and fifth month before she did it. But Jacqueline, who had spent the early winter months of her life bundled up securely in her crib on an outdoor balcony, did not show the response until she was six months old. Her brother and sister who had enjoyed greater freedom of movement had profited by the additional "aliment" and so were provided earlier with the mental structures required for this adjustment to their environment.

His children's behavior during the first two years provided Piaget with a rich assortment of evidence that only during the last quarter of the first year do children begin to treat objects as though they continue to exist when they are out of sight. At first an object which disappears is promptly replaced by a new interest. Later, a missing object may be sought, but with a misdirection of search that suggests the baby believes that his own actions have something to do with the disappearance and reappearance of the object. For example, a toy which the baby had just succeeded in finding under one pillow was then hidden as he watched, under a different pillow. Where did he look for it? Under the first pillow! Another example: Piaget was greeted joyfully by the baby who was being held in her mother's arms. Mother asked, "Where's Daddy?" Quickly the baby turned toward the window where she had become accustomed to see her father regularly at work. Piaget links this early unconscious egocentricity and delusion of omnipotence to the fact that there is at that time no objective organization of space or permanence of objects.

YEARS TWO TO SEVEN. By the end of the second year, which would also mark the end of the sensorimotor stage of development, much of the doubt about the constancy of familiar objects has been taken care of through accommodation and assimilation; but the child now enters a more complicated world in which people, language, and a more extended past and future make new demands on the schemata he has at his disposal. By this time he has some understanding of his position as one object among many. He seems to recognize, at least partly, that he has little to do with how these other objects behave, for he spends much time imitating them, and he appeals to his more effective elders to reproduce results he has seen them produce before. He even begins to represent in anticipation through bodily gestures some of the effects he hopes to see reappear, as when his mouth opens slightly while he watches an adult prepare to open a match-box.

His egocentricity has not yet been completely routed, however. Piaget says, ". . . for a long time (he) remains enclosed in his own point of view before placing it among other points of view." This shows itself in several ways. When he explains the behavior of other objects, he is likely to refer that behavior to himself or to his now somewhat extended social circle. The sun is something to keep him warm, the snow is something for him and his playmates to have fun in, etc. Many of the definitions of four- or five-year-olds will show this conception of a universe organized about their needs. Children also project their original delusion of omnipotence into other objects, so that, asked to explain what makes things act as they do, they offer animistic explanations: the cloud driven by the wind is credited with the power to move by itself; a pebble dropped into a glass of water "weighs" on the bottom of the water and "forces" it to rise in the glass (Piaget, 1954, page 378). At this period, Piaget concludes, all actions, whether of people or objects, imply to the child that there is some purpose and some goal.

The reactions of one five-year-old in justifying his rather confused ideas about what determined whether objects of various sizes and weight would float or sink (Inhelder and Piaget, 1958) reveal in an amusing way how this egocentricity veiled his view of reality. Confronted with a plank of wood and asked what would happen to it when it was placed in the water, he assured the experimenter it would sink. The plank chose to float; whereupon the child pressed it down, chiding, "You want to stay down, silly!" When he was later asked whether the same plank might sink to the bottom another time he answered "yes." We can imagine an adult doing much the same sort of thing in a petulant manner when something does not behave as he wants it to; but he would do it with no expectation that his action could produce any permanent change in the situation. Nor would he expect the behavior of the plank to be so whimsical as to float one day and sink the next. If such a thing did happen he would look for causes outside the plank, rather than explain them animistically.

Communication is one of the areas where the child's egocentricity is clearly manifested during the early years of language development. Piaget's early studies at *La Maison des Petites* brought him to the conclusion that much of the young child's language is not socially directed at all, such as the babbling and iteration of sounds during the imitative phase of development, or the senseless repetition of new words that have come into his experience, with ingenious variations. Just producing the sounds seems to provide its own satisfaction. [Such a view would be quite consistent with the idea that new schemata actively seek out ways to exercise themselves, or with White's theory of *competence* (page 294, this book) or any capacity-primacy theory of motivation. Acts that relate the child to his world seem to delight him (Woodworth, 1958, page 127).]

It has been Piaget's appraisal of the degree of egocentricity in what on the surface appear to be social uses of language during early childhood that has probably been least understood and least accepted by American investigators. Children of four or five are prone to carry on long discourses with no clear direction to any particular audience nor any consistent sequence of ideas. Piaget has called such exercises *dual, or collective, monologues.* These seem to show something of the same veiled contact with reality that we recognized before in the child's speculations about the way the plank of wood could be expected to behave in the water. In these cases the child's behavior can be thought of as social to the extent that he involves at least one other person in his chatter, but Piaget notes that he "does not attempt to place himself at the point of view of the hearer" (Piaget, 1926). It appears that this is true even of his more socialized efforts at communication. When, at five or six years of age, he is given the task of retelling a story which has been told to him, and the details of which he has understood, as his answers to the experimenter have demonstrated, he will usually present a sketchy, muddled, disordered assortment of the facts instead of a reasonable account of what he has heard.

Both the collective monologues and the garbled stories would seem to be explained, at least in part, by Piaget's hypothesis that the child supposes everybody sees things just as he sees them: why then is there any need to clarify further? The thought may occur to the reader that such an attitude is not limited to five- and six-year-olds. College professors find the same failure to take into consideration their point of view on the examination papers written by their students, and students "reverse the charges" when they criticize some of their professors' lectures. Husbands and wives often exchange similar recriminations.

Piaget's finding that 38 per cent of the speech of two six-year-olds observed at play was egocentric has not been generally confirmed in American studies. Part of the reason may be in the differences between one nation and another, one generation and another, or one family and another in their child-raising practices. By Piaget's own reasoning a child brought up under circumstances which encourage him to communicate will probably sooner reach a high standard of social speech than one left much to his own resources. McCarthy (1954) has provided a summary of the research on this issue, concluding that "differences in definition and interpretation of terms" play an important part in accounting for the wide range of percentages reported. The greater accessibility of Piaget's whole program of research, made possible by the more recent translations and discussions of his theories (Kessen and Kuhlman, 1962) should at least have the effect of correcting one unfortunate misinterpretation of his concept of *egocentrism* in some of these critical studies. The egocentrism of the child in Piaget's sense of the term cannot be measured operationally by counting the number of times first-person pronouns appear in his speech. Piaget describes it as a broad, undiscerning identification of others with himself. The personal pronoun count would measure an interest in self which would exclude others.

THE OLDER CHILD AND THE ADOLESCENT. Piaget's developmental studies beyond the age of early childhood have led him to more intensive analysis of the thinking of the preadolescent and adolescent in contrast with that of the child under seven. Inhelder and Piaget (1958) have provided a detailed account of how young subjects between the ages of four and sixteen deal with such problems as how to position a ball-projecting plunger so that the ball will hit a target from an angle, or how to balance scales by adding or removing weights or placing the weights at different distances from the fulcrum. As they grappled with each problem the subjects were questioned about their "reasons" for what they were doing; and in their answers as well as their methods of proceeding Piaget found confirmation for his own belief that the "algebra of logic can . . . help the psychologist, by giving him a precise method of specifying the structures which emerge in the analysis of the operational mechanisms of thought" (1953, page xviii).

Only a brief summary of Piaget's development of this theme can be presented here, but the reader acquainted with abstract algebra may supplement it with the exhaustive account of the Geneva group's study (Inhelder and Piaget, 1958), a briefer treatment of his theory by Piaget (1953), or Hunt's account (1961) which places Piaget's contribution against the background of other important contemporary theory and research.

Piaget describes the thinking of the child during the years up to age seven, following the sensorimotor period, as *pre-operational*. An "operation" is an "internalizable" and, to some degree, integrated action. But the problem-solving efforts of young children are impulsively overt and uncomplicated. They plunge directly into the job of solving the problem without stopping to think about how it might be solved or why their efforts fail. Piaget emphasizes also the "static" quality of their observations at this age. When a plasticene ball is pressed into a flat form, a child may insist that in its new shape there is less plasticene than in its original shape, even though he has watched the transformation take place. He may judge that water poured from a low beaker into a tall, slender one has increased in quantity, even though, again, he has observed the transfer. Reasoning about reality implies some intuitive understanding that objects have certain constant properties even though there are circumstances under which these may appear changed. The child must also realize that these properties and the environment have a constant interrelationship over which he has only indirect control. The five-year-old who expected the plank to sink when he pushed it down had not yet developed the schemata necessary for this complete understanding of the facts, yet he was showing rudimentary signs, in this "intuitive regulation," of the future mental structures which would make a more satisfactory solution possible.

The difference appears in the solutions offered by slightly older children in the *concrete operational stage* (7–11 years). In this period, as at the pre-operational level, a child does a good deal of thinking with his hands, but his actions and his explanations show that more goes on behind the scenes (internalized operations) than at the earlier age. Yet he still seems to fall short of finding a conclusive principle for facts he is sometimes very quick to notice. When he is urged to account for his observations, he regularly turns back to the apparatus on which he has been working and demonstrates what he means by several more examples. His proof consists in accumulating more facts, and if these do not always agree with his conclusion because of some complicating factor he has overlooked, he is likely to brush the exception off lightly, or give up. In the problem of balancing the scales, he no longer depends on pressing down on the higher pan; he adds weight. If the added weight is too great, he removes it—the operation of *inversion*—and replaces it with a lighter weight. (His choice of the lighter weight gives evidence of the fact that he has at this stage developed some schemata for ranking objects according to size, weight, etc.) He discovers other ways to balance the scales. Instead of removing the too-heavy weight, he may equalize it with more weight on the other side—the operation of *reciprocity*. At first he does not notice that the effect of a particular weight depends on how far out along the arm of the scale it is hung. During the second half of the concrete operational phase he shows a dawning awareness of a relationship between adding or subtracting weights and pushing them farther away or nearer to the fulcrum: "You have to change the position of the sack, because at the end it makes more weight" (Rol, aged ten years, ten months). But for a while the relationship between these two factors remains a qualitative one for him. It is usually not much before the age of twelve that the young thinkers recognize the mathematical ratios involved: a fifty-gram weight at four unit-lengths from the center will balance a hundred-gram weight on the other side at two unit-lengths from the center: $50:100 = 2:4$. Piaget sees in this recognition evidence of a new and higher coordination of the operations of inversion and reciprocity, schemata which up to this point have operated separately, so preventing the child from recognizing relationships which become clear only when these operations are combined into a single "structured whole."

In describing the developments of the *formal operational period* covering years 12–16 and beyond, Piaget notes that the haphazard, incompletely thought-out procedures and conclusions of the younger child are now replaced by a systematic checking of all the relevant implications of any hypothesis suggested by the facts they observe. Their reasoning has become *hypothetico-deductive*, and although the checking may involve active dealing with the apparatus, the substance of their thinking is now internalized and expressed in the form of propositions. Yet each propositional statement of the thinker reflects a far more complicated and coherent mental structure than the piecemeal operations of the concrete stage. Piaget makes it clear that the essential feature of this new stage is not the verbal form which reasoning takes, but the newly "integrated structure at the interior of his thought, a structure of which he is naturally not aware" (Inhelder and Piaget, 1958, page 321). As long as the limited schemata of the younger child allowed him to cope only with the weights, or only with the effects of the distances—depending on the operations of inversion and reciprocity *separately*—he could not perform the complex mental operations necessary to solve problems in which these variables interacted in complicated ways; and he certainly could not be expected to rise above the concrete details of the situation in front of him to formulate a generalization or "law" that would apply in all situations. Recognition of the quantitative relationship between a transformation by inversion and a transformation by reciprocity signaled the readiness of the new mental structure to function not only with the effect of more *stable* equilibrium as far as the present problem was concerned, but also with more *mobile* equilibrium in adaptability to new problems.

Piaget has dealt only briefly with the personality development of the adolescent. In this period the youth prepares to assume an adult role, but one he would idealistically reform. In this respect he carries over from formal operational thought the tendency to build systems or theories, or he acclaims the theories of others, which emphasize the *possible* rather than the immediately present *real*. A third phase of egocentrism occurring at this stage reinforces this tendency. As in the sensorimotor period, and again in the period of early childhood, the adolescent passes through a phase of failing to discriminate the viewpoints of others from his own; but "decentering" occurs as his views are challenged by the peer groups who share his reforming zeal; and even more effective is his coming to grips with reality in the career he adopts. Adolescence is also the period for the first emergence of genuine social values which become organized in a hierarchy as the youth develops a life plan and adopts an adult role. Personality, as Piaget defines it, is the individual's shaping of a social role in which he makes practical application of the scale of values he has adopted.

Albert Edward Michotte, Baron van den Berck (born 1881; professor at Louvain, Belgium) might be counted as a functionalist or as a gestaltist. Either school would be proud of him. He is distinctively an experimentalist and has succeeded in devising exact methods for the study of complex human performances, both perceptual and motor. In his *Autobiography* (1952) he divides his research career into three main periods. Up to the outbreak of the

First World War, he used Külpe's method of introspection combined with objective timing for the analysis of such processes as logical memory and voluntary choice. Driven from his laboratory by the enemy in 1914, he took time to reconsider his previous methods critically, particularly the validity of introspection.

I became convinced that it was a vain task to try to describe internal events and analyze them into elements, and that the only value of introspection must be an *informative* one. . . . I had, indeed, become convinced that psychology was not a science of mental life but rather a science of behavior and actions. Nonetheless it seemed entirely evident to me that to make an exhaustive study of behavior it is essential to take into account the way in which men or animals understand the situation in which they are placed (1952, pages 220, 222).

When he got back to his laboratory in 1920 he began a long series of experiments on motor patterns, reaching conclusions that were more or less analogous to the visual findings of Gestalt psychology. This motor period lasted till 1939, when he switched to "certain fundamental problems of phenomenology, the problems of causality, of permanence and of apparent reality in outer experience" (*ibid.*, page 227). His thorough study of apparent causation (1946, 1963) is an outstanding piece of experimental work. His ingenious apparatus presents to the observer two small black squares, both stationary at first. One square then moves toward the second and stops when it reaches it; and the second square immediately moves away in the same direction. Every observer reports the clear impression of cause and effect: the first square acts on the second and causes it to move. There is nothing inferential about this impression; it seems perfectly direct and perceptual, as direct as the apparent motion in Wertheimer's famous experiment (see pages 216–17). By variation of the spatial and temporal conditions Michotte was able to predict and control the subject's impression and report.

FUNCTIONALISM AND THE PSYCHOLOGY OF PERCEPTION

In the course of this chapter purportedly describing the views of structuralists and functionalists we have occasionally made excursions into the associationist or the behaviorist "sector." These have been useful, if not actually necessary, for pointing up the interests which link the schools as well as the issues which have divided them. Were our book organized around problems of learning, motivation, and perception we would meet the same psychologists here classified as members of one or another school; yet judged on the basis of their common interest in some significant question, they might lose their "school" identity, and not infrequently we might find it hard to recognize in their work the systematic or methodological issues on which they would split.

The problems of perception might well be used to illustrate the point. The everyday experiences we take so much for granted present conundrums which have defied philosophers for centuries and which remain to challenge psychologists. Some of the conundrums have been suggested in the theories earlier described. How does Piaget's infant progress from his earliest incoherent awareness of the effects of objects upon him to the perception of objective and independent reality? How does it happen that the numerous ambiguous and sometimes conflicting cues on the basis of which, according to Brunswik, our probabilistic judgment of an object is formed can give us an impression of the constancy of things and qualities? How does it happen that our adjustment to the environment these variant cues structure for us—or lead us to structure—is adequate more often than not: we usually find the chair where we see it; we are not even likely to be far off in our visual judgment of the weight of an object, or in our visual judgment of the texture of food taken into the mouth. "Lightness," "crispiness," "chewiness" seem to be visual qualities of the object as well as "muscular" or kinesthetic effects. This immediate perception of qualities is even more strikingly illustrated in aesthetic experience. Where is the *beauty* we find in a work of art, a piece of literature, a symphony? It seems to be as "objective" as the canvas, the printed page, or the orchestra. We meet the same perplexing question in trying to understand the response to Michotte's moving squares: How can we explain the insistent cause-and-effect impression? We might multiply our "How" question to provide endless experimental programs to occupy psychologists. Let us take a brief survey of some recent work and theory in this area.

It would be a mistake to say that the study of perceptual functions went into total eclipse with the downgrading of the introspective method. The objective approach to sensory discrimination was still open through the behavioristic form of verbal report, and physiological studies yielded some important data; but elaborate analyses of complex conscious experiences in the Wundt-Titchener tradition became archaic. Following Titchener's death much of the research on perception in America took a psychophysical form (see page 30). Studies which used the phenomenological approach were largely of European origin or were the work of psychologists in America who were sympathetic to Gestalt principles, or who had remained unconvinced that science could be best served by the rigid exclusion of introspective data interpreted at their face value. Certainly the volume of work on perceptual problems was relatively slight in comparison with that on learning and motivation.

Since midcentury the picture has changed: perception has become a strong competitor of learning and motivation as a source of research projects and a focus of theory. The phenomenologists continue to be well represented, but along with them we find functional psychologists and behaviorists; and it is not always easy to decide in which of the latter two groups a particular investigator should be classified. We have already seen why a distinction might be difficult (page 28). Those who study perception as "a process by which an individual maintains contact with his environment" (Gibson, 1959) are certain to become concerned with "function" in one or another sense of the term.

Although they may agree on the adaptive function of perception, theorists in this field divide on other questions. Of several such issues we might consider one which has received a good deal of attention and inspired some ingenious experimental studies. We could formulate the question in this way: To what extent, if at all, does the perceiver have an active role in the determination of what he perceives? In that double form the question must obviously be followed by another when we have disposed of the "if at all" clause: At what stage of the perceptual act does the perceiver make his contribution? And that question would in turn be followed by a third: How?

The *transactionalist* view proposed by the late Adelbert Ames, Jr. (1880–1955), as its title suggests, takes the position that the individual has an important part in structuring his perception of the environment (Kilpatrick, 1952). Ittelson and Kilpatrick represent the theory as holding that "the world each of us knows is a world created in large measure from our experience in dealing with the environment" (1952, page 175). The raw data out of which the individual creates that world is chaotic and ambiguous; he must therefore integrate it on the basis of "assumptions" that stand for a sort of "weighted average" of his accumulated experience. On the strength of these assumptions he "predicts" or "makes a bet" as to the nature or quality of the reality with which he is confronted. He can never know the true reality, but the veridicality of his bet will in any instance be tested through the *actions* that follow the directive the bet provides. In this way not only the object world, but also the world of people and the world of values are interpreted. The transactionalist theory of perception would therefore have significance in the psychology of aesthetics and personality; and it would have application also in the field of psychotherapy.

We recognize in this position a close kinship with Brunswik's probabilistic functionalism (pages 38–39). In its acceptance of the operation of *unconscious inference*, it resembles also Helmholtz's solution to similar questions.

The evidence for the theory has been provided by experiments which have, justifiably, received much attention from psychologists. How conflicting "assumptions" are resolved has been studied by manipulating the cues upon which such factors as size and distance judgments would be based. These are arranged in a way to obscure the information the perceiver might be expected to depend upon. Ames' distorted room, designed to look normal when viewed monocularly from a certain position, is one of the best known. Actually the floor of the room and the rear wall are sharply slanted in such a way that a small child assumes towering proportions by filling up the whole space between floor and ceiling in one corner, while a full-grown man shrinks into comparative insignificance in another corner which looks the same height as the other but which is really much higher. When the viewer is given practice in touching various parts of the distorted room with a rod, the illusion is gradually replaced by a more correct impression of its shape.

The trapezoidal window, another famous device, consists of an irregularly shaped window, usually with shadows painted on its frame. It is mounted on an axis about which it is rotated. Sometimes an object such as a short rod is attached to the shortest side of the trapezoid. The effect usually reported in this case is that of a rectangle swinging backward and forward, from which, at a certain stage of the swing, the rod separates itself from the rectangle and floats in space until it re-attaches itself as the figure rotates into another phase of its movement.

The transactionalist explanation of these illusions is that the viewer "sees" what is most congruent with the "weighted average" of his experience until new evidence arises which makes his first guess no longer tenable. The weight of our experience with doors opening and closing has made perception of such objects in rectangular form a good "bet," and the movement as swinging rather than rotating. The rod has to be accommodated to such an interpretation: there is no "shortest" side to a rectangle, therefore the rod is left in the air!

For other experiments and fuller details, the reader is referred to Ittelson's account of transactionalism (1960). Descriptions of other functionalist theories of perception may be found in Solley and Murphy (1960).

In contrast to the transactionalist position, James J. Gibson (born

1904; now professor at Cornell University) describes perception as a "function of stimulation." He adds: ". . . and stimulation is a function of the environment; hence perception is a function of the environment" (1959, page 459). As he explains the gradual increase in the veridicality of perception, "differentiation" occurs within the "flowing sea of energy in which the organism is immersed" as practice reduces the amount of stimulus generalization. [We have met this concept earlier in this chapter (page 35) in our discussion of Mrs. Gibson's theory of interference phenomena.] Stimulation is not to be thought of as something which affects single cells; it is rather a complex matter of "pattern and change"—energy affecting groups of cells which are not even always anatomically together. The same perception may result from many different patterns, which seems, indeed, to be what happens when we move our hand over an object or scan it with our eyes. Different skin spots, different retinal points will be involved, yet the same object is perceived. Learning plays a part in making it possible for the individual to discriminate "more variables" or "variables of a higher order." "Higher order variables" would be illustrated by *ratios* of stimulation such as those which function to give us constant impressions even when the circumstances under which we experience the environment are changed. Since change is always taking place in the real world, it is then understandable that the difference between a child's experience and an adult's will be accounted for to some extent by the child's deficiency in detecting the higher order variables. In this way Gibson provides an objective description of what cognitive theorists would account for as the effect of attention or set. Gibson holds that the child lacks the experience necessary for discriminating in the flowing pattern of stimulation such significant features as gradients of light or of texture cues which at a later stage he will immediately perceive as nearness or distance. Such cues are not to be thought of as "enrichment"—something added to or associated with a basic "sensation"; they are "differentiated" high-order variables of stimulation which through conditioning have now come to "specify states of affairs in the external world" (1959, page 486).

Although in this way clearly acknowledging the role of learning in perception the Gibsons favor a nativist rather than an empiricist account of its development. Untangling the influences of nature and nurture is a delicate operation that is never completely successful, and, on the question of their relative contributions to perceptual development, research findings can be offered in support of either position. Rather striking evidence for the nativist viewpoint is provided by the behavior of young animals and babies in the "visual cliff" experiment. On a flat surface designed to give the illusion of an abrupt drop, day-old chicks as well as young rats that had been reared in darkness steered a "safe" path away from the "edge." Four-week-old kittens, also reared in darkness, did not show that same cautiousness immediately, although they seemed to develop it soon after they were exposed to the light even though no reinforcement had been given to such avoidance behavior (Gibson and Walk, 1960; Walk and Gibson, 1961). Babies also seem to respond to the appearance of "depth" in these experiments, but by the time they can be used as subjects, experience has probably come to play some part in shaping their behavior. It is also possible that man's more complex brain requires more environmental "aliment" to enable him to make judgments of depth necessary for adjusting to his complicated world. (For a fuller account of the Gibsons' theory and current issues in the study of perception, see Gibson and Gibson, 1955; J. J. Gibson, 1959, 1960, 1963; and E. J. Gibson, 1963.)

PRESENT STATUS OF STRUCTURAL AND FUNCTIONAL PSYCHOLOGY

Now that the active controversy between these two schools has died down, contemporary investigators very seldom announce themselves as adherents of either school. Structural psychology of the Wundt-Titchener type is relatively quiescent. The elementary sensations were discovered and accepted long ago, except perhaps in the case of color, where competing theories are still active. The attempt to analyze the complex experiences of thinking into sensory and non-sensory elements has been found futile, even as Michotte said, though the "informative" type of introspection is sometimes utilized. Functional psychology is certainly active but is not a closely knit school. We had some doubt whether to classify Michotte and Katz with the functional or the Gestalt school; and in other cases we should hesitate whether to class some psychologist as a functionalist or as a broad-minded behaviorist.

The method used by an investigator is of course more easily identified than the school, if any, to which he adheres. We might expect the *method of impression and verbal report,* which seems so subtly blended with subjectivism, to disappear before the onward march of objective psychology. It has not yet disappeared by any means, even in the United States, the favored home of behaviorism. A count of thirteen major American journals for the year 1958 gave a total of 1,122 research papers, of which 493, or 44 per cent, made some use of impression and verbal report. This is a minority, to be sure, but a significantly large minority. Of the 493 papers mentioned, 184 were studies of some sort of perception, and the remainder belonged mostly in the field of personality study.

What are the "impressions" reported by the human subjects who provide the pointer readings in these numerous investigations? The range is wide. In "psychophysics" the instructions call for a very specific report; for example: "You will hear two tones. Tell me whether the second sounds louder or softer than the first." This procedure would be used by the strict behaviorist as well as by a functional psychologist who does not share the other's antipathy for introspection. But the behaviorist would translate the "object language" of his subjects into the "metalanguage" of his own operational definition of what is to be considered "louder" or "softer" in terms of the percentage of responses one way or the other.

In direct "magnitude scaling" (Stevens, 1956), the subject is told to call the loudness of the first tone "ten" and then to assign a suitable corresponding value, larger or smaller than ten, to the loudness of the second tone. In other words, the subject is asked to estimate the ratio of the two loudness impressions. Intelligent subjects make these estimates with fair consistency and agreement. Loudness depends on the physiological hearing mechanism, and also, of course, on the physical intensity of the sound. To double the loudness the intensity must be increased tenfold. A loudness scale is therefore useful for the engineer who is concerned with the effects of physical sound on the human listener.

When the psychologist moves over from psychophysics to the very different field of personality, methods that are broadly introspective continue to yield important information. Accounts given by subjects of the effects upon them of prolonged sensory deprivation (Heron, 1961), or of the effects of exposure to the devastating social and physical barbarism of concentration camps (Bettelheim, 1943; Frankl, 1955, 1963), are not less useful to psychology for the fact that they do not lend themselves to convenient translation into behavioristic metalanguage.

Clinical data obtained from a patient, or self-reports about personality must frequently be accepted at their face value when the primary object is to come to some conclusion about the individual rather than about the group. When enough data have been accumulated about individuals, generalizations that seem to hold for the group may become apparent. Recent studies of the subjective effects of new psychoactive drugs have proceeded along this line (Wendt, et al., 1956; Gottschalk, 1960).

Questionnaires have long been used by psychologists to obtain information about the individual's personality. Some range widely over the field of personal traits; others concentrate on a single trait, such as proneness to anxiety, which can be measured or estimated by a count of symptomatic responses. A few sample items from current studies will suggest a possible weakness of this method:

I am usually pretty confident of myself.
I lose interest in anything that I cannot finish quickly.
I like to argue with my friends.
It is usually my own fault when I get into trouble.
I like to follow a regular routine almost every day.

It would seem that the subject checking such statements might under some conditions be disposed to check some of them in a way that would show him in the best light; at other times he might be harsher on himself. There is a danger that results with such scales may be unreliable—that is, inconsistent when repeated on the same subjects. However, many of them are not so obvious as they seem. A vast amount of preparatory work goes into the design and improvement of personality scales and inventories which may not be apparent on the surface, but which provides some degree of assurance that they will measure what they aim to measure.

A test that is somewhat harder for the subject to see through has been developed by George A. Kelly for revealing the personal constructs by which an individual interprets his world. The Role Construct Repertory Test (REP) requires the subject to identify from his own acquaintance a separate figure fitting each of twenty-four significant roles: father, mother, most interesting person, most successful person, most liked teacher, most disliked employer, a neighbor who is hard to understand, etc. He is then required to do a job of "sorting" on the people he has fitted into the role titles: confronted with three at a time, he must select the two that he judges most alike and the one that is different, explaining in what respect they are alike or different. Underlying this procedure is Kelly's assumption that we always think in dichotomies, whether we recognize the fact or not. The repeated forced choices of like and unlike items within the triads presented to the subject will throw light, presumably, on the dichotomies that play a significant part in his thinking (Kelly, 1955).

In this test, impressions of other people are made the basis for an appraisal of the individual tested. Sometimes such impressions are used as a measure of the other person. For example, the social behavior of adolescent boys and girls was the theme of an extensive study by Mary Cover Jones (1958). As observers and reporters she used adults who were well acquainted with the children "on playgrounds, in school halls, club meetings, . . . social gatherings, school excursions and the like." These adult observers rated the individual boys and girls for appearance and grooming, for poise, for eagerness, and for their apparent drives toward achievement, management, social recognition, and friendship. The impressions made by the children on their schoolmates in respect to popularity, leadership, friendliness, humor, and daring could also be discovered by an ingenious "Guess-who" technique. These impressional data were correlated with the objective facts of sex, age, physical maturity, intelligence, and frequency of mention in the students' school paper. There was an important relationship between the subjective and the objective estimates.

To track down further the use of subjective methods would quickly take us to the area of clinical theories and techniques which might be classified as "functional psychologies" in the broadest sense, but these we shall deal with under a different category later in this book. On the subject of method we might conclude this chapter with a final note on "introspection." As recently as 1953, in his *History of Introspection*, Boring declared that the word had "dropped out of use," although the method "is still with us, doing business under various aliases, of which *verbal report* is one." The frequency of the appearance of the term in current literature, however, and the articles or incidental comments written in its defense raise some doubt about the finality of its extinction. Perhaps one reason why it will continue to be used is offered in the first paragraph of Hilgard's summary stereotype of the functionalist:

The functionalist is free from self-imposed constraints that have shackled many other systematists. He uses the words from diverse vocabularies, borrowing words freely from other traditions. He is not forbidden the use of older words because today they sound subjective (e.g., "idea," "meaning," "purpose") or because they have occasionally been given systematic connotations that he does not accept ("sensation," "image," "ego"). He does not believe that anything is gained by new terms, unless advance in knowledge justifies the further precision that new words can bring. For example, he believes it premature to call all thinking "implicit verbalization," for the objective terminology is not yet justified by what we know about thinking. Hence he holds to the older word. His definition of the field of psychology is also a tolerant one, and he is ready to accept information obtained by introspection, by objective observation, from case studies, from mental tests. He is tolerant as to method, and he is tolerant as to content. The distinction between pure science and applied science seems to him trivial, so long as either is good science (1956, pages 333–34).

In a later chapter we shall learn more about the "self-imposed constraints" of behaviorism; but first we shall consider some of the influences which have contributed to the development of objective psychologies.

3

Associationism

The topic of learning has a prominent place in present-day psychology, as anyone can see by examining the current textbooks or glancing through the journals that report current research. How we learn—the "we" including animals as well as men—has been for several decades one of the biggest problems for psychological experimenters and theorists. How we learn a poem or a list of nonsense syllables, how we learn to solve a puzzle or to find our way through a maze, how we learn a good or a bad habit, how we learn a face so as to recognize it later, or a scene so as to describe it, or a motor performance so as to execute it with skill and speed—all these and many similar questions have been investigated. Learning is certainly one of the major interests of psychology today.

It is surprising, then, to find no chapter on learning in the older textbooks. Even William James in his great book of 1890, the *Principles of Psychology*, had no such chapter, nor did the term *learning* occur in the index of this two-volume work. The older psychologists had a great deal to say about *remembering* what had previously been learned, but they were slow in coming to grips with the process of learning. They did have a general *theory* of learning: the theory of *association*. They took as their starting point, not the learning process, but the facts of remembering. Remembered ideas they explained as the result of the individual's past experience, and the fact that these ideas occurred in clusters and often in regular sequences they explained as the result of the past linking of sensations that had occurred together or in immediate succession. This was the teaching of the associationists, a predominantly British school.[1]

[1] For the full story of the associationist school, see Warren (1921), and for briefer accounts Heidbreder (1933), Murphy (1949), and Boring (1950).

THE OLDER ASSOCIATIONISM

The germ of associationism can be found even as far back as Aristotle's essay on "Memory." He made the fundamental observation that one thing reminds you of another, and went on to ask this question, in effect: "If A reminds you of B, what is the relation of A and B?" He answered that the relation was sometimes one of *similarity*, sometimes one of *contrast*, sometimes one of *contiguity*. For example, one person reminds you of another because they are so much alike, or because they are markedly different, or because you have seen them together. These three relations were called the "laws of association" by the British associationists, who attempted with some success to reduce them all to the single law of contiguity in experience. If A, a stranger, reminds you of your friend B, the two have obviously never been together in your experience; but if they resemble each other, you must now see something in A which you have previously seen in B, and this something, this common characteristic, furnishes a bridge of contiguity between A and B. Contrast could be plausibly reduced to partial contiguity in somewhat the same way.

While these reductions may be open to question, the concept of association seems too matter-of-fact to arouse controversy or provide the basis for a "school." The British associationists made it the basis of their school by claiming so much for it—by regarding it as the sole mental operation, except for sensation. At once, therefore, they came into conflict with the faculty psychology which assumed a variety of mental operations to account for the various results accomplished. Thomas Hobbes, the first of the British line, already mentioned in our first chapter, had the following to say in his *Leviathan*, 1651:

Concerning the thoughts of man, I will consider them first singly, and afterwards in train, or dependence upon one another. . . . The original of them all is that which we call "sense," for there is no conception in a man's mind which hath not at first, totally or by parts, been begotten upon the organs of sense. . . . As we have no imagination, whereof we have not formerly had sense, in whole or in parts, so we have no transition from one imagination to another, whereof we never had the like before in our senses. . . . All fancies are motions within us, relics of those made in the sense; and those motions that immediately succeeded one another in the sense continue also together after sense. . . .

But the philosophy schools . . . teach another doctrine. . . . Some say the senses receive the species of things, and deliver them to the common sense; and the common sense delivers them over to the fancy, and the fancy to the memory, and the memory to the judgment, like handing of things from one to another, with many words making nothing understood. . . . Those other faculties . . . are acquired and increased by study and industry. . . . For besides sense, and thoughts, and the train of thoughts, the mind of man has no other motion.

In place of the various faculties, then, Hobbes admitted only three (or two) fundamental operations: sensation, recall, and association which governs recall. Hobbes did not use the word *association* which was introduced by later writers, but when he speaks of "fancies," i.e., thoughts and images, as coming in sequences determined by the original succession of sensations, he is speaking of association by contiguity. Hobbes reduces the two or three fundamental operations mentioned to a single one which he calls "motion." An external object affects the senses through what we now call the "stimulus" of light, sound, pressure, or chemical action—some kind of physical motion—and the motion of the stimulus is communicated into the organism through a sense organ. When the stimulus ceases, the internal motion does not cease but continues by inertia though gradually dying away. The original motion is the sensation, and the residual motion is the retained image. A certain sequence of stimuli leaves behind the same sequence of images and so accounts for a later sequence of thoughts. So Hobbes reduced everything to physical terms: motion, the communication of motion, and inertia. But he was forced to recognize one additional factor in the organism. The organism reacts to the stimulus by muscular movement, and the *direction* of this movement is not communicated from outside but originates within the organism. The reaction is either approaching or avoiding, either toward or away from an external object. Desire is an incipient motion of approach, aversion an incipient motion of avoidance. Some desires, such as the appetite for food, are native, and others are acquired from experience of the properties of objects. Hobbes develops this theme extensively, but most interesting to us is his use of desire as a control factor in association. He made the important distinction between what we now call free and controlled association. Because stimuli occur in different sequences at different times, there are many alternative sequences of thoughts available. From A you may pass to B, C, or D, each of which has followed A at one time or another. So thought is free to wander unless there is some active desire present to exercise a selective and directive influence.

This train of thoughts . . . is of two sorts. The first is "unguided," "without design," and inconstant; wherein there is no passionate thought to govern and direct those that follow . . . in which case the thoughts are said to wander, . . . as in a dream. . . . The second is more constant, as being "regulated" by some desire and design. . . . From desire ariseth the thought

of some means. . . . And because the end . . . comes often to mind, in case
our thoughts begin to wander, they are quickly again reduced into the way.
. . . Look often upon what you would have, as the thing that directs all
your thoughts in the way to attain it.

Hobbes was concerned with the sequence of thoughts, the *successive association* of later terminology. John Locke, next in the chronological list of the British school, had more to say of what was later called *simultaneous association*. In his famous *Essay Concerning Human Understanding*, 1690, Locke undertook to prove that all our knowledge is derived from experience. He combated the notion that self-evident or axiomatic knowledge is independent of experience and based upon "innate ideas." Instead, he held that all *simple ideas* are derived from experience, mostly from sensory experience of the outside world but partly from experience of our own mental operations. Given these simple ideas as elements, we are able to put them together into *compound ideas* of endless variety. To test the validity of any idea we have to trace it back to its origin and see whether it is justified by experience. Locke was most interested in this philosophical question of the validity of knowledge, and the philosophical discussion which he started and which continued for a hundred years and more does not concern us here. As to the psychological question of how we combine ideas, he indicates that some are combined because they logically belong together, but others from the mere chance "association of ideas"—this being the first appearance in the literature of that historic expression. He wrote (Book 2, Chapter 33 of the 4th edition of the *Essay*, 1700):

> Some of our ideas have a natural correspondence and connexion one with another: it is the office . . . of our reason to . . . hold them together. . . . There is another connexion of ideas wholly owing to chance or custom: ideas that in themselves are not [at all akin] come to be so united in some men's minds that it is very hard to separate them; . . . the one no sooner at any time comes into the understanding, but its associate appears with it. . . .
>
> *Instances.* The ideas of goblins and sprights have really no more to do with darkness than light: yet let but a foolish maid inculcate these often on the mind of a child, . . . possibly he shall never be able to separate them again so long as he lives; but darkness shall for ever afterward bring with it those frightful ideas. . . . Many children imputing the pain they endured at school to their books . . . so join those ideas together that a book becomes their aversion . . . and thus reading becomes a torment to them, which otherwise possibly they might have made the greatest pleasure of their lives.

It is interesting to find what we now call conditioned fears and antipathies appearing so early in the history of associationism. Many other foretastes of modern scientific results could be culled from the authors who followed Locke in the next century and more, if we had the leisure for such historical research. Just a few salient contributions should be mentioned.

George Berkeley in his *Essay Toward a New Theory of Vision,* 1709, made an important contribution, though he did not use the term *association.* Just as the meanings of words are obviously acquired by associating the words with the objects they stand for, so it is with a great variety of signs and indicators. A certain sound means to the listener "a horse trotting along the road"—evidently because of previous observation of horses making that sort of noise. Since the eye furnishes only a two-dimensional picture, and still reveals the third dimension—the distance of objects—the visual appearance must indicate distance by virtue of association with the bodily movements necessary to reach a seen object. All such sign–meaning associations are successive rather than simultaneous, the sign having the role of a stimulus, in modern terminology, and the meaning the role of a response. Because of constant use, however, and because of predominant interest in the meaning, we are scarcely aware of the sign but seem to ourselves actually to see distance, as we even seem to hear the meanings of words spoken in everyday conversation.

David Hume in his two great books, *Treatise on Human Nature,* 1739, and *Enquiry Concerning Human Understanding,* 1748, carried forward the discussion of the validity of knowledge which had been inaugurated by Locke (and which was later taken up in Germany by Kant and his successors). Hume formulated the problem of the associationist psychology very clearly when he asked whether it was not possible to go behind the "faculties" and discover "the secret springs and principles by which the mind is actuated in its operations." He concluded that such a principle was found in association, a force of attraction between ideas. He recognized the factor of similarity but laid most emphasis on contiguity, especially the immediate succession of one sensation (or "impression") after another. Some sequences of impressions are so frequent and invariable as to become firmly associated, with the result that we cannot see the antecedent occur without expecting the consequent. We then call them cause and effect, and we assume that the effect *must* occur because the cause has occurred. We imagine that we see a "necessary connection" in cases such as the falling of an unsupported body or the putting out of a fire by water thrown upon it—just because we are forced by habitual association to expect the usual consequent after the given antecedent. All our reasoning, except in mathematics, is based on habitual associations. "This is the whole operation of the mind, in all our conclusions concerning matter of fact." [2]

David Hartley, a contemporary of Hume, published in 1749 his *Observations on Man, His Frame, His Duty, and His Expectations,* a book that is less philosophical and more psychological than those of his predecessors. He reduced everything to association by contiguity in experience, either simultaneous or successive. Sensations occurring simultaneously tended to coalesce into a complex sensation, like the taste of lemonade, and left behind a corresponding complex idea; and ideas brought together in the mind tended similarly to coalesce. Muscular movements often occurring in the same sequence became associated into automatic habits. Ideas became associated with movements and so furnished the basis for voluntary action. Emotions were combinations of sensations, including especially pleasure and pain, bound into units by simultaneous association. So Hartley developed associationism into an all-round theory, a theory which, though vigorously opposed in certain quarters, was widely accepted and influential for the hundred years following. Though capable of further development, it remained little changed till the early part of the nineteenth century.

Thomas Brown was professor at Edinburgh—the first professor in our list since Aristotle—and his remarkable, though long-winded, *Lectures on the Philosophy of the Human Mind* were published in 1820. By this time the modern science of chemistry had begun to show its power, and to Brown it furnished a guide or analogy in tackling the problem of simultaneous association. Many sensations, emotions, and ideas are complex and call for analysis; and yet they have characteristics which are not found in their elements, as the taste of lemonade is a blend and not simply a sum of sweet, sour, etc.:

> As in chemistry it often happens that the qualities of the separate ingredients of a compound body are not recognizable by us in the apparently different qualities of the compound itself—so, in this spontaneous *chemistry of the mind,* the compound sentiment that results from the association of former feelings has in many cases . . . little resemblance to these constituents.[3]

This idea of a "mental chemistry" reappeared from time to time in later psychological theories; it was rechristened "creative synthesis" by Wundt and was taken over as a central problem by the Gestalt school.

Brown accepted contiguity in experience as the sole primary law of association but saw that certain secondary laws were needed. Why does A remind me of B at one time, but of C or D at another time, B, C, and D having been contiguous with A at different mo-

[2] *Enquiry,* Section 5.
[3] Lecture 10.

ments of my previous experience? It depends, said Brown, on such factors as the relative *frequency, recency,* and liveliness (later renamed *vividness*) of those previous contiguities.[4] These secondary laws have remained a permanent possession of psychology.

A third major contribution of Thomas Brown may not belong in a strict associationist psychology, since it recognized something besides the combination of ideas or impressions. Objects are not merely associated; they are compared, related to each other:

> There is an original tendency . . . of the mind, by which, on perceiving together different objects, we are instantly . . . sensible of their relation in certain respects . . . coexistence and succession . . . resemblance . . . difference . . . proportion . . . degree . . . the number of relations, indeed, being almost infinite.[5]

He went on to show that knowledge consists very largely in perceived relations. Mathematics and indeed all sciences are concerned wholly with relations.

James Mill's *Analysis of the Phenomena of the Human Mind,* 1829, is regarded as the high point of strict associationism. With his insistence on a rigidly logical and consistent system, Mill discarded mental chemistry and perception of relations, and admitted only simple ideas derived from sensation and mechanically linked by association. When the associations are strong and quick-acting from frequent use, the elements may *seem* to coalesce and the resulting complex idea may seem simple, though it still is composed of all the simple ideas that have entered into it in past experience. The complex idea of a house contains the less complex ideas of walls, windows, doors, floors, roof, and chimney, and these contain the simpler ideas of bricks, boards, and nails, and the still simpler ideas of wood, iron, glass, mortar, etc., combined of course with appropriate ideas of size, shape, position, and strength. Such a complex idea would seem to be unmanageable in any ordinary thinking about a house, without some sort of unifying organization of the total idea. It certainly seemed as if James Mill's logical system amounted to a *reductio ad absurdum* of strict associationism. Accordingly his son, John Stuart Mill, in giving this work a critical revision (1869), reinstated mental chemistry and spoke of the simple ideas as "generating," rather than composing, the complex ones.

Last of the great figures in the British line of associationists was Alexander Bain, whose principal works, *The Senses and the Intellect,* 1855, and *The Emotions and the Will,* 1859, have much of the mod-

[4] Lecture 37.
[5] Lecture 45. Brown probably was indebted to the French psychologist Laromiguière in this matter of perception of relations.

ern atmosphere. But Bain deviated in some respects from the strict associationist doctrine. (1) The first step toward building up knowledge from sensory experience is not association but discrimination, the singling out of an item from the mass. Until it has been separated it is not ready to be combined with other items. (2) Associations are established not by contiguity alone but by perception of likeness and difference, cause and effect, utility and other relations. (3) Being interested in motor behavior as well as in sensations and ideas, he could not say that everything is derived from experience; for the infant possesses some definite reflexes as well as a large stock of "random movements" which furnish the raw material for motor behavior. There are no innate ideas, as Locke rightly insisted, but there are surely innate muscular movements. There is such a thing as instinct, defined as "untaught ability" or as "what can be done prior to experience and education." Associationism had tried to trace everything back to experience, but now the factor of heredity had to be added. The emphasis on heredity was greatly accentuated a little later, when Darwin and evolution began to make an impression on psychology.

British associationism had considerable influence in France but very little in Germany down to the beginning of the nineteenth century. Hume's skeptical theory of knowledge had indeed been a powerful stimulus to German philosophy, but in psychology the faculty theory remained dominant down to the time of Johann Friedrich Herbart and his textbook, *Lehrbuch zur Psychologie*, 1816, and his more extensive treatise, *Psychologie als Wissenschaft* (*Psychology as a Science*), 1824–1825. Herbart is said to have administered a knockout blow to the faculty psychology by arguments already cited in our preceding chapter (page 15).

Herbart's system, by no means the same as associationism, resembles it in being a theory of the interaction of ideas. The difference is that the associationists assumed a single force of attraction between ideas, while Herbart assumed both attraction and repulsion. Ideas that occur simultaneously in consciousness come together and combine so far as they are congruous with each other, but repel or inhibit each other so far as they are incongruous. These forces are due to the unity and limited span of consciousness, or better, of attention. One cannot attend to two ideas at once except so far as they will unite into a single complex idea. When one idea holds the center of the stage, incongruous ideas are forced into the background or off the stage altogether into unconsciousness. They still remain alive, however, and "strive" to get back to the center of the stage, being kept out most of the time by other ideas but being drawn in (recalled) when the dominant idea of the moment is congruous. When two or more ideas have combined, the complex idea behaves as a unit thereafter, being forced out and drawn back as a whole. A combination of many related ideas forms a powerful "apperception mass" which welcomes relevant material but excludes the irrelevant. At this point the theory had an important application to teaching. Before introducing new material, prepare the way for it by building up an apperception mass of familiar and interesting ideas. The Herbartians had much influence on both general and educational psychology for a period of fifty years or more. The concept of inhibition reappears much later, both in the conditioned reflex theory of Pavlov and in Freud's "repression." And inhibition or interference in one form or another comes to light again and again in modern experimental studies of learning and remembering.

The associationists, spread over a period of two centuries, were obviously not a compact school like the Gestaltists or psychoanalysts. There was apparently no personal contact between any of the men mentioned except between John Stuart Mill and his father on one hand and Alexander Bain on the other. More recent psychologists generally accept association as an important fact in psychology without agreeing with the extreme associationists who regarded it as the sole basis for all mental operations.

THE NEWER ASSOCIATIONISM

A new era dawned in 1885 when Ebbinghaus (1850–1909) published his work on memory (already cited, pages 17–18) which was new not only in being experimental but also in studying the formation of associations, the learning process. The older associationists started with associations as they operate in recall and tried to reason back to the process by which these associations were probably established. The new associationists start with the process of forming associations and then test the strength of the associations by later recall. That is, the older associationists started with effects and tried to infer the causes, while the newer ones start with known causes or conditions and observe the effects. The newer procedure is obviously more complete and trustworthy.

Ebbinghaus wished to follow the formation of associations from scratch and therefore needed items not previously associated. He invented nonsense syllables such as *cag, wom, kel,* which nobody has ever associated together. A single pair of these could be learned in one reading and there would be no observable process to follow objectively. With close attention a series of four or five syllables could be learned in one reading, but a long list could be mastered only gradually, by repeated readings. By this and similar methods Ebbinghaus and his successors reduced the law of frequency to quantitative form and worked out the now familiar "learning curves." The law of recency was given quantitative form in the "curve of forgetting." Contiguity itself was found to be a matter of more or less, since associations were formed not only between the adjacent syllables in a series, but also, though less strongly, between syllables lying farther apart in the series. This start toward an exact knowledge of the process of forming associations was quickly followed up by many experimenters.

From Ebbinghaus down, the study of learning has used objective methods in the main, and quite a number of ingenious methods have been devised. But introspection also has proved of value in giving inside information on *how* the learner manages to combine disconnected material such as nonsense syllables. G. E. Müller was especially successful in combining introspection with objective measurement, as we saw in the previous chapter (page 23). Association by contiguity, his results show, is not the whole story. Contiguity is an opportunity rather than a force, and the learner establishes connections largely by perceiving relations.

ASSOCIATION IN ANIMAL BEHAVIOR. The psychological study of animals arose partly from the interest of biologists and physiologists in the sense organs and motor activities of various kinds of animals. There was much experimental work along those lines in the latter half of the nineteenth century. Another very important influence came from Darwin and the theory of evolution. For if all animals are blood relatives in respect to bodily structure, must they not be akin in respect to behavior and mentality? And if the human body has evolved from an ancestral line of animals, must not the human mind have developed from a more primitive animal mind? Such a suggestion was bound to awaken heated opposition not only from the theological side but even from the self-conceit of the common man who regarded himself as radically different from the "brutes," not merely superior to them. The animal was said to be guided by "instinct," not by "reason," which was peculiar to man. To combat this argument the early evolutionists industriously collected instances of animal behavior which seemed to depend on reasoning. There were numerous anecdotes of this sort: A dog, without ever being trained to do it, was observed to open a gate by raising the latch with his muzzle—evidently, so the dog's master felt, because he had figured out the mechanism of the latch or because he had seen it opened by men and reasoned that he could do the same in his own way.

The trouble with such interpretations was that they saw only the alternatives, instinct and reason, instead of the broader choice between instinct and learning. Certainly the dog does not open a gate by instinct, and therefore he must have *learned* to open it. But *how* did he learn the trick? The only way to tell would be to take a dog that has never opened a gate, confront him with the problem of opening one, and watch carefully how he attacks the problem. Give him repeated trials and follow his progress till he is complete master of the trick. Such an experimental study of animal learning was projected in the early 1890's by two eminent psychologists of the day, in Germany by Wundt in the second edition of his *Lectures on Human and Animal Psychology*, 1892 (English translation, 1894), and in Britain by Lloyd Morgan in his *Introduction to Comparative Psychology*, 1894. Both of these men, but especially Lloyd Morgan, had already made some informal homemade experiments and had concluded that dogs learned by forming simple associations (Wundt) or by trial and error (Morgan), and not by reasoning. At least the facts could be explained without the assumption of higher mental processes. And both of these men recommended that animal psychology should observe the *law of parsimony*, "the approved maxim of the exact natural sciences that we should always have recourse to the *simplest* explanation possible" (Wundt)—or in other words that "in no case may we interpret an action as the outcome . . . of a higher psychical faculty, if it can be interpreted as the outcome . . . of one which stands lower in the psychological scale" (Lloyd Morgan's Canon, as it has been called).

These two books no doubt had much influence in turning the attention of the young experimentalists of the time toward the study of animals. Especially in the budding laboratories of the United States animal work soon became established, and of course it tended to change the atmosphere of the department of psychology, which became less philosophical and more biological. Experimental studies of animal learning came out from the Harvard, Columbia, and Clark laboratories before 1900 and from Chicago and several other universities shortly thereafter. This early work can be truly called epoch-making both because of the extensive and fruitful investigations that have followed down to the present day and because of the two theoretical schools that arose from it, Thorndike's connectionism and Watson's behaviorism.

A New Law of Association Revealed in Animal Learning. Now we come to a striking instance of that independent but (almost) simultaneous discovery of the same fact or law which has occurred so often in the history of science (evolution, the conservation of energy, photography, the telephone, and many other examples). Thorndike's law of "effect" was discovered about 1898, Pavlov's law of "reinforcement" about 1902. It was many years before the relationship of these two laws was clarified. The two discoveries were as independent as possible. Thorndike, a young American graduate student of psychology, was following up the evolutionary interest in animal intelligence. Pavlov, an already distinguished Russian physiologist, came upon the "conditioned reflex" in the course of his investigations of digestion and fastened on it as a possible lead toward the understanding of brain physiology. In spite of this great difference in background and aim the two men were alike in scientific spirit, keen alertness, and great energy and persistence.

THORNDIKE'S THEORY OF LEARNING

Edward Lee Thorndike (1874–1949; professor at Teachers College, Columbia University) was a pupil both of James at Harvard and of Cattell at Columbia, but his selection of animal psychology as a fruitful field for experiment was not due to either of them but probably to study of the books of Wundt and Lloyd Morgan already mentioned. He shared with his contemporaries, Linus W. Kline and Willard S. Small, who worked at Clark University, the distinction of introducing the animal into the psychological laboratory. Mazes and problem boxes (or puzzle boxes) were the tasks which they gave the animals to learn. The animal was confronted with the problem by being placed in the maze or puzzle box while hungry, with food present as a reward for the solution of the problem. The animal was left to his own devices, his behavior was watched, and the time required for the first success was noted. He was given trial after trial and the changes in his behavior and the decrease in time of performance were recorded. From these data the animal's progress in mastery of the problem could be plotted in a "learning curve," and some evidence could be obtained as to how the animal learned.

Beginning in 1896 and continuing for several years until his energies were absorbed in educational psychology, Thorndike used these methods with fishes, chicks, cats, dogs, and finally monkeys. His extensive experiments with cats are best known, and his description of the cat's behavior has been so often quoted as to be classic. The cat, usually a young and lively one, was placed while hungry in a slatted cage or box, with food outside as a reward for getting out. The door could be opened in one box by pulling a string, in another by turning a door button, etc.

When put into the box the cat would show evident signs of discomfort and of an impulse to escape from confinement. It tries to squeeze through any opening; it claws and bites at the bars or wire; it thrusts its paws out through any opening and claws at everything it reaches; it continues its efforts when it strikes anything loose and shaky. . . . The cat that is clawing all over the box . . . will probably claw the string or loop or button so as to open the door. And gradually [i.e., in the course of a number of trials] all the other non-successful impulses will be stamped out and the particular impulse leading to the successful act will be stamped in by the resulting pleasure, until, after many trials, the cat will, when put in the box, immediately claw the button or loop in a definite way [1898, page 11].

This "stamping in" or "stamping out" of a response tendency by its favorable or unfavorable results constituted Thorndike's "law of effect," which he formulated a little later (1905, page 203) as follows:

Any act which in a given situation produces satisfaction becomes associated with that situation, so that when the situation recurs the act is more likely than before to recur also. Conversely, any act which in a given situation produces discomfort becomes disassociated from that situation, so that when the situation recurs the act is less likely than before to recur.

A companion law was the law of exercise, or of use and disuse, which stated that any response made to a given situation was thereby associated with the situation, that the more it was used as a response to the same situation the more strongly it was associated with it, whereas prolonged disuse weakened the association. This law of exercise was evidently the old law of association applied to connections, not between ideas, but between situation and response. It was the old law of association with its sublaws of frequency and recency.

The study of animal learning showed clearly that the law of exercise did not cover the ground. In a novel situation such as a maze or puzzle box the animal (or man for that matter) is apt to make a number of different responses before hitting on the successful one. Every one of these responses, according to the law of exercise, becomes associated with the situation. Consider the first response made: as soon as it is made it has a recency and frequency advantage over any alternative response which has not been made, and therefore this first response should be immediately repeated and so gain still more advantage. According to the law of recency alone, the animal would never get away from this first unsuccessful response. There must be some factor at work causing him to desist from this first response and try something else. The law of recency must be counteracted by some other factor or the animal would never reach success. By the time he does succeed he is likely to have repeated certain unsuccessful responses several times during this first trial, but the successful response is made only once because it terminates the trial. At the start of the second trial, then, the successful response is at a disadvantage in respect to frequency, and according to the law of frequency alone it would remain at a disadvantage trial after trial and no improvement could occur. As a matter of fact, however, the unsuccessful responses gradually lose out in spite of their advantage in recency and frequency, and the successful response prevails.

The law of effect, announced by Thorndike, encountered much criticism, stimulated a vast amount of experimental investigation, and led to persistent efforts to work out a complete and satisfactory theory of learning. It is not necessary for our present purposes to follow this discussion. We need consider only the importance of this law in the newer associationism.

The law of effect is a law of association and nothing more. It lays down a certain factor in the strengthening and weakening of associations. When a response is made to a situation, the favorable or unfavorable result of the response is a factor in strengthening or weakening the association of that response to that situation.

The early criticisms of the law of effect failed to notice the precise bearing of the law. It was said, for example, that the law pretended that the outcome of an act worked backward to strengthen or weaken the act just performed, which would, of course, be impossible. What the law actually asserted was that the outcome of an act strengthened or weakened the continuing association—something inviting a neurological explanation, no doubt, but not involving any absurdity.

Again, it was objected that the law assumed blind trial and error in hitting on the successful response. Thorndike seemed to make this assumption, but it has nothing to do with the law of effect, which does not attempt to say how the response is initiated but only that, when initiated and performed, it has results which strengthen or weaken the tendency to make the same response in the future. Perhaps, if an act were done with crystal-clear insight, it would need no further confirmation from successful results; but in the ordinary human cases of partial insight, success certainly has an effect.

It was said, too, that the law had the reprehensible character of being "atomistic"—the cardinal sin to certain schools—but there is nothing atomistic about Thorndike's "situation" and "response," nor about "effect." The total act of a whole organism can have a global effect which strengthens or weakens the tendency to repeat the same total act.

The behaviorists of course took fright at the words *pleasure, dis-*

comfort, satisfaction, and *annoyance* used by Thorndike to indicate the effects of an act and asked what right he had to assume such conscious states in animals or to assume even in man that they could have any effect on the brain so as to strengthen the nerve connections involved in making a certain response to a situation. Thorndike offered possible neural explanations, admitting that they were speculative. Really it is not necessary to work out a neural explanation before accepting a behavioral law such as the law of effect, if only it conforms to the facts of behavior. And it is not necessary to speculate on the animal's conscious states. All we need assume is that success has an effect on the organism, that failure has a different effect, and that these different intra-organic effects can modify the organism's associations or response tendencies. This is the "empirical law of effect," accepted by many psychologists who differ in their theoretical interpretations.

About thirty years after the original animal experiments which led to the law of effect, Thorndike re-examined the matter by extensive experiments on human learning (1932, 1933). The learner's task in these varied experiments was quite different from that of a puzzle box, except that alternative responses were always possible and that one response was successful or correct and was "rewarded" by the experimenter's saying "Right," while other responses were "punished" by being called "Wrong." The results demonstrated a strong positive effect of reward but no comparable negative effect of punishment. Thorndike accordingly revised his law of effect by assigning much greater weight to reward than to punishment. The effect of punishment, he decided, was not exactly to "dissociate a response from the situation" but rather to cause the learner to try something else until a response was found that was rewarded and so positively associated with the situation. Establishment of the correct response would incidentally and automatically eliminate the incorrect ones.

With the law of effect thus simplified, Thorndike was able to offer a physiologically conceivable explanation. The organism, being "set" for reaching a certain goal, makes tentative exploratory movements aimed at the goal; when one of these movements is actually reaching the goal, the whole organism instantly confirms and intensifies it, so giving it an advantage which remains behind as an association of the successful response with the situation and goal. Or, in Thorndike's words (1933, pages 66–67):

> Suppose that in animals possessed of a certain degree of cerebral organization, the acceptability or satisfyingness of a status arouses what we may call the "confirmatory" reaction. . . . Suppose that the nature of this confirmatory

reaction is such that it strengthens whatever connections it acts upon. . . . The confirmatory reaction probably is set up and controlled by large fractions of the "higher" levels of the cortex, often by what corresponds to the general "set" and purpose of the animal at the time. . . . The confirmatory reaction will . . . make the animal more likely to repeat the connection when the situation recurs.

Or again (1943, page 33 ff.):

The strengthening by satisfying consequences may have a biological causation. . . . Perhaps all that is required is that the over-all control of a person or animal (what we used to call the "higher" centers) should be able to react to a certain stimulus by a reinforcement of whatever connection has most recently been active, and that the stimulus that sets off this "confirming reaction" should be satisfying to the over-all control. . . . The confirming reaction is not held in reserve for great affairs. . . . You do not have a dozen a week, but more nearly a dozen a minute. To each phrase that I speak you respond by a certain meaning. If this meaning satisfies you by making sense, the connection is confirmed. . . . But if difficulty or confusion arises, the confirming reaction is withheld.

It is not necessary for our purposes to examine Thorndike's numerous and important contributions to such problems as the nature and measurement of intelligence, the influences of heredity and environment, and many others. In all these studies he was a thoroughgoing associationist, or "connectionist," as he preferred to call himself. He did not believe that mere contiguity of two impressions or ideas in a momentary experience would establish an association between them. For a bond to be formed some response must be evoked as well. He accounted for man's superior mentality on the grounds that human genes enable men to establish more connections and larger systems of connections than are possible for animals. "A good simple definition or description of a man's mind is that it is his connection system, adapting the responses of thought, feeling, and action that he makes to the situations that he meets" (1943, page 22). A critical review of Thorndike's work on learning can be found in Hilgard (1956).

PAVLOV'S PHYSIOLOGICAL THEORY OF LEARNING

THE PAVLOVIAN CONDITIONED RESPONSE. From 1890 until his death Ivan Petrovitch Pavlov (1849–1936) was director of the physiological laboratory at the Institute for Experimental Medicine in St. Petersburg (now Leningrad). In the course of studying the digestive glands, their nerves and reflexes, he devised apparatus which enabled him to collect and measure the saliva secreted by his dog subjects in response to the stimulus of food placed in the mouth. He noticed incidentally that the dogs used in these experiments would begin to salivate before the food actually reached the mouth —just at the sight of the food dish, or at the approach of the attendant who customarily brought the food, even at the sound of his footsteps. This observation, made in 1902 or earlier, was to have a tremendous influence on the later development of psychological theory and the direction of its scientific research. Pavlov recognized that the sight of the dish or the sound of the footsteps—obviously not natural stimuli for the salivary reflex—had come through experience to be a signal to the dog that food was coming. He realized too that such signals must play an important role in the adaptation of an animal to any particular environment. This seemed to offer a promising lead toward research in brain physiology. Physiologists had been trying to study the brain by operations which could not but disturb the normal function; but here was a method which left the brain intact. At first Pavlov called the salivary response to a signal a "psychic secretion," but later he coined the term *conditioned reflex* (CR), to avoid any implications about the dog's mental life. The signal was called the *conditioned stimulus* (CS).

The CR was obviously a learned response, but Pavlov's interest fastened particularly on the fact that it was a cortical event, not just subcortical as a true reflex would be. This was a compact, convenient specimen of "higher nervous activity," readily available for experiment and measurement. He quickly found the way to establish a conditioned salivary response to any stimulus that would attract the dog's attention without arousing fright or anger. A hungry dog was placed in the familiar apparatus and left quiet for a while. Then a metronome began to tick; the dog pricked up his ears. When the metronome had ticked for half a minute, meat powder was put into the dog's mouth, producing the normal reflex flow of saliva. This exact procedure was repeated at intervals of perhaps fifteen minutes, and after a number of such repetitions saliva began to flow during the half-minute interval before the meat powder was given. This was the conditioned response. The quantity was small at first but trial by trial it increased to a moderate amount. The metronome in this experiment was the CS; the meat powder was the unconditioned stimulus (US), also called the *reinforcement* because it produced a much greater flow of saliva than the metronome did even after conditioning.

To establish the conditioned response so thoroughly that it would hold over from day to day might require several days of conditioning, but once established it was retained over a long period of disuse. It could be temporarily *inhibited* by any distracting stimulus that disturbed the dog or made him investigate. Even the experimenter had to be kept out of the dog's sight. Pavlov drew plans for a special CR laboratory in the country with elaborate provisions for excluding extraneous sights, sounds, gusts of air, etc.; and despite the fact that he was a rather outspoken critic of the government when these projected improvements were sought, the Soviet recognized his scientific importance and built him his laboratory early in the 1920's.

But distraction was not the only circumstance producing inhibition. One of Pavlov's important discoveries was extinction of the CR. Even a well-established CR, it appeared, could be extinguished by the same procedure used to establish it, with one important difference: no *reinforcement*. When a hungry dog that had already been conditioned to salivate at the sound of the metronome was exposed to the ticking, trial after trial, without receiving meat powder at the appointed time, the flow of saliva grew less with each repetition until it disappeared altogether. If the metronome had in the first instance become a signal that food was coming, it had now become a signal that no food was coming. Instead of waking the dog's brain to readiness for action, it now seemed to depress brain activity, for the dog became visibly drowsy under these conditions. However, such "extinction" could not be regarded as a permanent loss or forgetting, because after an interval of a few hours of rest the dog would again begin to salivate at the sound of the metronome.

Pavlov concluded that he had found out how to produce two opposite brain states, the state of excitation and the state of inhibition. By use of these two recognized physiological concepts he could formulate hypotheses and put them to the test of experiment. He could predict, for example, that if he kept the metronome ticking and the dog waiting for two minutes instead of half a minute before the food was given, making this the regular procedure for a long series of trials, the conditioned response would become a two-phase affair, inhibition followed by excitation. When the metronome began ticking it would be a signal of "no food coming *for a while*" and so would induce drowsiness without salivation; but after the ticking had continued for a minute or more it would become a signal of "food coming soon" and so would arouse the dog to alertness with salivation. The prediction was verified, and this two-phase response was named the *delayed conditioned reflex*.

Another prediction had to do with *stimulus generalization* and *differentiation*. Pavlov had found that when a salivary response had been conditioned to a slowly ticking metronome, the same response (but less strong) would be made to a faster-ticking metronome. In the same way, a CR to a high-pitched tone would to some degree transfer to one of lower pitch; or a CR to pressure on the dog's shoulder would to a lesser degree be evoked by the same kind of pressure applied to his flank. The effective conditioned stimulus, then, seemed to *generalize*, within limits, to similar stimuli. Pavlov explained this as the result of *irradiation of excitation* about the central cortical point affected by the CS. The question of how to train the dog to differentiate these more or less similar stimuli from the regular CS might be solved, therefore, by applying the procedure used in extinguishing a response. Prediction: if the regular CS is invariably reinforced each time it is presented while the more or less similar stimuli are never reinforced, the generalized response to the latter should be inhibited as the effect of extinction. This prediction was verified, although it often took many trials to eliminate the non-reinforced responses completely. Pavlov found that dogs vary considerably in this respect. Some, apparently disposed toward excitability, condition readily, and their CR's are relatively hard to extinguish; others, more inhibitable, are hard to condition, and their CR's are easily extinguished. Such individual differences are no doubt physiological, and they suggested to Pavlov a lead toward a truly physiological and scientific psychiatry (Pavlov, 1941).

The technique of differentiation produced other significant effects. It provided a method of testing the fineness of the dog's power of sensory discrimination. If over a long series of trials the negative, unreinforced stimulus was made more and more like the positive, reinforced stimulus the dog could be brought to differentiate very small differences in pitch, shape, tactile proximity, or other stimulus qualities. But there would eventually be a limit at which the dog's capacity to discriminate would break down. Some of the animals became emotionally disturbed at this stage and showed frenzied, uncontrolled behavior which would reappear whenever they were returned to the familiar apparatus. They were no longer usable as experimental animals. Pavlov called this disturbed state *experimental neurosis*, and he interpreted it as the effect of the clash of cerebral excitation and inhibition aroused by the ambiguous stimulus.

Many other experiments were done by Pavlov and his students, aimed entirely at an understanding of brain processes. He made no claim to being a psychologist; in fact that is about the last thing he would have claimed. Time and again in his lectures he made a remark of this nature:

In conclusion we must count it an uncontested fact that the physiology of the highest part of the nervous system of higher animals cannot be successfully studied, unless we utterly renounce the untenable pretensions of psychology.

When, at the beginning of all this work in 1902–1903, he asked his psychological colleagues what concepts they would use in explaining his results, they suggested desire, expectation, disappointment, and the like; but he did not find it possible to make effective use of such concepts for devising new experiments or predicting results. When he used his physiological concepts of reinforcement, excitation, and inhibition, he made progress. So he concluded that the key to the understanding of behavior lies wholly in physiology. It is true, however, that on becoming acquainted a few years later with Thorndike's animal experiments he welcomed them as akin to his own and recognized Thorndike's priority (Pavlov, 1927, page 6; 1928, page 39). But Pavlov was never very well pleased with the use made by psychologists of his results (Pavlov, 1932).

In view of his general discontent with psychology, it is interesting that Pavlov's conditioned reflexes at first received more attention from psychologists than from physiologists. One of his best friends among the physiologists wrote to him expressing the hope that he would soon drop this fad and get back into genuine physiology! When psychologists began to learn about the conditioned response they thought of it as a useful technique for measuring the sensory discrimination of animals, and it is still used for that purpose. Then, in the 1920's, it began to serve, particularly in America, as the basis of theories of learning, and has since given rise to a vast amount of experimenting, theorizing, and controversy.

It is interesting to speculate on how much of the controversy may be related to Pavlov's original preoccupation with the salivary response and his choice of the term *conditioned reflex* as a label for the learning process he undertook to study so thoroughly. His real interest, we must remember, was not in learning but in brain conditions of excitation and inhibition; but he had uncritically proposed that when two stimuli are presented simultaneously, one of them being the natural stimulus for a reflex response, this reflex after sufficient repetition of the combination will become attached to the other stimulus (the CS). Closely examined, this will be recognized as a very inaccurate description of Pavlov's actual procedure and results.

It is inaccurate in several respects. (1) It suggests that the two stimuli are presented simultaneously, whereas at least a fraction of a second must separate them. Pavlov himself found this spacing important, and many investigators have confirmed the fact that a stable and substantial CR can be "elaborated" only if there is some interval between the CS and the US. A recent Russian study on this point has even established the interesting fact that a well-learned defensive reflex to electric shock can be *extinguished* by repeatedly presenting the CS and the US exactly at the same time or within an interval of one-tenth of a second of each other (Pakovich, 1958; see Asratyan, 1961a, pages 105, 111, for English reference).

(2) The "substitute stimulus" theory suggests, incorrectly, that the CS—when conditioning has taken place—produces the actual reflex naturally connected with the US. Much attention has lately been focused upon the variety of responses the CS may produce, but even before refinements of technique made it possible to study closely the details of the orienting reflex (see pages 102–5) aroused by the CS, it was clear that the true reflex occurs only when the natural stimulus is presented.

(3) Closely related to this point is the error in thinking that the CR is the same as the natural reflex. Sometimes the two may be completely different. As far as the salivary response is concerned the two may outwardly differ only in quantity, the natural reflex being quicker and more abundant. But the natural reflex to food includes also a chewing movement which, if it appears at all in the CR, is reduced to imperceptible movements of the jaw that can only be recorded by special devices. On the other hand the CR includes some sort of approaching movement. The CR, then, is a *preparatory* response made in advance to the signal of food—a getting ready for the receiving of the food, while the reflex is a *consummatory* response to the food itself. So too with defensive and other kinds of reflex behavior.

Liddell and his co-workers at Cornell (1934) found that when a sheep received an electric shock through an electrode bound to one foreleg, the CS being the tick of a metronome set in action a few seconds before the shock, the animal, as he became conditioned, responded to the sound by lifting the leg slightly and crouching as if to prepare himself for the shock. When the shock came, the reflex response was a full raising of the leg, followed by relaxation of the tenseness of the body. Culler, and others (1935), found that when the shock was administered from a floor grid, the final behavior was different. In this case the animal—a dog—avoided the shock, finally, by lifting his paw coolly and efficiently from the grid with no more accompanying postural adjustment than was necessary to maintain his balance on three legs, although in the early stages of the experiment he had shown the diffuse emotional behavior which was a feature of the sheep's response with the other type of apparatus. The contrast between these two experimental results reveals clearly the new character of the CR and its suitability to the circumstances under which it develops. Many other examples might be cited.

The assorted forms of learning which have been classified under the category of the CR, and the apparently interminable maze of questions uncovered by those who have sought to understand it will make up a substantial part of the content of the next few chapters. A reference to one more recent study will serve to illustrate the complexity of the problems of learning and at the same time to introduce us to a form of conditioning which has received much attention from American investigators.

A CASE OF INSTRUMENTAL LEARNING. R. L. Solomon, who with others has done a great deal of research and theorizing on the effect of anxiety in animal avoidance learning, has described a study on dogs that had been trained to expect an electric shock after a ten-second interval of darkness. They could, however, prevent the shock by pressing a panel of their enclosure within the ten-second period of grace, and this they learned to do. (This is an example of the kind of CR which has been called "instrumental behavior," since the animal's *own* response produces the reinforcement. In the "classical" form of CR studied by Pavlov the reinforcement is given or withheld by the experimenter according to his own design and has no logical relation to the animal's behavior. (See pages 83–85, this book.)

After a dog had learned the instrumental response of pressing the panel, he was given curare, a drug which has the effect of temporarily paralyzing the skeletal muscles. While he was in this incapacitated state he was subjected repeatedly to two new stimuli —tones of different pitch, one of which was always followed by shock, the other never. The dog showed clear evidence of distinguishing the two signals by cardiac acceleration to the shock signal but not to the other tone. This CR to the shock-tone would fit into the "classical CR" category; in this phase of the experiment there was no possibility of an instrumental CR because of the effect of the curare. After he had completely recovered from the paralysis, he was tested on all three signals. As might be expected, he reacted to the darkness signal by pressing the panel. He had never made this response to the warning *tone;* to this his response had been limited to a "classical" physiological reaction—heart acceleration. But the study records that the dogs "typically" transferred the instrumental panel-pressing response to the tone signal which had been followed by shock, whereas they "typically" showed investigatory behavior when the non-shock tone was presented (Solomon and Turner, 1962). The authors emphasize the fact that the transfer occurred appropriately to the new aversive cue even though the

curare had made it impossible for these animals to make the appropriate responses during the period in which it was followed by shock.
In other words, there could be no vestige of the panel-pressing response associated with the warning tone to mediate the appropriate
response later transferred to it.

Our speculations about the results of this experiment bring us
back to two of our basic questions. *What* has the dog learned?
How has he learned it? Is he automatically attaching an old response to a new stimulus, perhaps on the basis of some imperceptible
internal cues—such as might occur in fear—that have been common
to the visual and the auditory signal? Or has he learned the environment and selected the appropriate response to escape from it
or to change it? Is his learning a matter of *knowing* or of *doing?*
These alternatives by no means exhaust the possibilities, but they
are different enough to suggest the kind of thinking a learning theorist must do.

How has the learning occurred? Since mediating motor responses
seem to have been ruled out, what could be the nature of the process
by which signal discrimination and selection of the right response
were made possible? Did the excitation within the visual area "ir-
radiate" to the auditory centers? And if it did, why did the response
transfer to the shock-tone more often than to the unreinforced neutral tone? Or was the motor response center "sensitized" or predisposed by its earlier assocation with the darkness signal, and so more
easily involved when, soon after, a different sensory signal was associated with the shock? Along quite a different line would be an
explanation in terms of complex neural patterns in the cerebrum
widespread enough to allow for the possibility of some overlapping
to account for a common response to the two different stimuli.

Our speculations have gone beyond the purpose of the Solomon
and Turner study, and we leave them without any conclusion. They
have served their purpose if they have made it clear to the reader
that the CR represents the starting point for questions about the
nature of the learning process rather than the final answer to the
question of how we learn. A great deal of research all over the
world is being directed to finding answers to such questions. Russia
and the United States have made the greatest number of contributions in this particular area, although, as we shall see, there have
been differences in the problems studied and the techniques developed in the two countries. A number of international conferences
within the past decade, however, has introduced a new means of
communication and a spur to the development of common research
interests and techniques.

SOME DEVELOPMENTS OF THE CLASSICAL CONDITIONING TECHNIQUE. We have learned much about the great structure that has been and is still being erected upon the solidly laid cornerstone of Pavlov's work. The simple ticking metronome may now be replaced by a compound CS made up of a group of different kinds of stimuli presented all together, or in a sequence, separated by equal or unequal intervals. Beritov, *et al.* (1929) and later Voronin, *et al.* (1959) have used such combinations in varying degrees of complexity as a measure of the relative position in the evolutionary scale of different animal species—a problem which holds a prominent place in Soviet science. Pavlov had studied the effects of combining stimuli and had been able to build up serial responses in an animal to sequences alternated in a stereotyped order: a positive signal—"food coming" —followed by a negative signal—"no food this time." When the order of stimuli in such a *dynamic stereotypy* was altered the trained animal might be thrown into the same sort of experimental neurosis which occurred in tests overstraining the capacity for discrimination (page 77). In actual life situations we are always responding to a complex of stimuli rather than to a single isolated stimulus; and the issue of whether such patterns act upon us as primitive, ready-made figures (*Gestalten*), or must be integrated gradually through learning or some secondary synthesizing function has been one of the basic matters of controversy separating the schools. We shall have more to say on this question in later chapters, but we may mention here that the Russian position on the matter has been that the patterns are built up as a result of association. Certainly their experiments have demonstrated that some patterned CS's become effective in this way. Whether or not they have explained away the possibility of any ready-made patterns can be better judged after we have considered the case for Gestalt psychology in Chapter 8.

Great interest has lately been centered in Soviet research on *interoceptive conditioning* in which either the CS or the US, or both, is applied directly to an internal organ. Here again the origin of this variation on the traditional *exteroceptive* CR model:

$$bell + food \rightarrow salivation,$$

can be traced back to some of the early work of Pavlov and his pupils on digestive responses. In 1905 Boldereff introduced a rubber balloon into a dog's stomach as a means of recording the contractions on a kymograph. The rubber balloon technique is still being used, but may now serve to produce pressure stimulation when it is inflated, or to cause internal temperature changes when it is filled with warm or cold water. Direct stimulation of the internal mucosa of an organ through a surgically produced fistula is another method of interoceptive conditioning. Sometimes such stimulation may be used as the signaling CS for an external US, as when the cooling of the stomach wall regularly precedes the administration of an electric shock to some external part of the body. Sometimes an external stimulus, such as a flash of light, may be used to signal the advent of internal pressure, or the warming or cooling of the stomach wall. One interesting study (Pshonik, 1952) described by Razran (1961a) found that unpleasant physiological consequences—headache, vomiting, and sensory distortions, as well as irregular vascular reactions —resulted from upsetting the dynamic stereotype (see above, page 82) when the subjects had become accustomed to the established sequence of light flashes and the signaled internal stimuli. In his summary remarks on the significance of interoceptive conditioning, Razran says (page 97):

> Interoceptive conditioning, whether involving conditioned or unconditioned interoceptive stimuli, is readily obtainable and is by its very nature largely unconscious in character. . . . the interoceptive kinds of stimulations are . . . by their very nature . . . recurrent, periodic, and organism-bound, making interoceptive conditioning an almost built-in function that is constantly generated and regenerated in the very process of living and acting.

According to the same commentator, as an experimental method interoceptive conditioning has made the unconscious "observable."

THE INSTRUMENTAL CONDITIONED RESPONSE. We have not yet reported the whole story of recent Soviet research on the CR, but we may with some advantage interrupt our account at this point and return to it after we have described in more detail a domestic variant of the CR which we briefly mentioned earlier (page 80). The important question is: What relationship does the *instrumental CR* bear to the *classical CR*, on the one hand, and to Thorndike's trial-and-error learning on the other?

In Pavlov's experiment the dog's conditioned response had nothing to do with his securing the food, for the food was provided at the regular time whatever the dog did. The regular sequence of signal and food, controlled by the experimenter, was the essential feature of the procedure. The conditioned salivary response was preparatory for receiving the food in the mouth, but it did nothing toward securing the food. Pavlov observed a motor aspect of the CR—a turning toward the awaited food—but this response in Pavlov's setup was not necessary for obtaining the food. In a different setup, where the dog is left free to move, and the food pan is placed at a little distance from him, he learns to respond to the metronome signal not only by salivating, but also by approaching the food pan

(Zener, 1937). In this case the approach movement is "instrumental" in securing the food. Sometimes a special device, or gadget, must be manipulated before the food or desired result can be obtained. Thorndike's cats had to operate a crude latch device to get out of the cage; young children must learn to use spoons and cups and other conventional devices to feed themselves. Such behavior is "instrumental," but is also referred to as *operant* when the operation of such a device is involved.

An instrumental—or operant—CR secures the reinforcement and is necessary, under the experimental conditions, for the reinforcement to occur. Instrumental behavior acts on the environment by locomotion or manipulation and so secures rewards and avoids punishments. It is as common as prose. The successful act in a puzzle box is an instrumental response—but can it be called a conditioned response with any propriety? Thorndike's trial-and-error learning and Pavlov's conditioning appeared for decades to be radically different and irreducible. The gap between them was bridged by B. F. Skinner (see our pages 162–69) when he devised a simplified form of puzzle box, now widely known and used under the name of the Skinner box (Skinner, 1932, 1938).

As employed in experiments on that favorite laboratory animal, the white rat, a Skinner box is small and bare, with little opportunity for the varied reactions elicited by a typical puzzle box. It has a little tin pan in one corner, and outside is a machine which can deliver pellets of food through a chute into the pan, each pellet making a *"bing"* as it falls into the tin pan. When a new subject is introduced into the box and has nosed around and become adjusted, the experimenter lets a pellet of food drop into the pan. The rat responds to the *bing* by approaching the food pan, and then responds to the pellet by eating it. Pellets are dropped into the pan at intervals, and the rat soon learns to approach the pan promptly at the sound.

Now let us compare just the *sequence* of events here with that in the Pavlov experiment. In Pavlov's case we have:

metronome—salivate—food—eat

And in Skinner's case:

bing—approach—food—eat

The two sequences are exactly alike except that the salivary CR is not instrumental in securing the food, while the rat's approach to the food pan is instrumental. Let us then agree that this approach movement is a CR, and that the *bing* is a CS.

In preparation for the second phase, the box is equipped with a horizontal bar extending along one wall and hooked up to the pellet-delivering machine so that downward pressure on the bar will release a pellet into the food pan. The subject is let in and left to his own devices. Sooner or later he is sure to get his forepaws on the bar and exert enough pressure to release a pellet with the customary *bing*, to which he responds as before by approaching the food pan. As soon as he goes back and presses the bar again—which some rats do at once and others after some wandering around—a second pellet is delivered. The conditioning is soon complete and the rat, left in the box, continues to press the bar and secure pellets as long as he remains hungry. The operant bar-pressing response can be extinguished, though not very quickly, by stopping the supply of pellets.

The learned sequence in this last experiment is:

bar—press—bing—approach—pellet—eat

The visual or olfactory stimulus from the bar that guides the rat to it is a CS, the bar-pressing a CR, this S–R unit being preparatory to the previously established *bing*–approach unit, and this in turn preparatory to the consummatory unit, pellet–eat. Both the bar-pressing and the approach to the pan are instrumental in obtaining the reinforcement of food. A longer series of such S–R units can be built up by suitable conditioning, but the principle is the same as in the simpler instrumental conditioning or in Pavlovian conditioning.

How does the rat's mastery of the Skinner box differ from the cat's mastery of the Thorndike puzzle box? The Skinner box offers a minimum of false leads, while the puzzle box offers a number of promising leads that have to be tried and eliminated. The two differ in respect to elimination, which is of course an important matter in many problems, but as far as concerns the positive learning of the successful response there is probably no essential difference. The positive learned sequence in a puzzle box is, for instance:

door button—claw it—door opens—go out—food—eat

which is exactly parallel to the sequence learned in the Skinner box. An extinction series was not part of Thorndike's procedure; credit for this important innovation goes wholly to Pavlov. But extinction would certainly occur if, once the animal has learned to press the door button, the setup were altered so that he could no longer release himself by clawing it, but had to manipulate something else in order to obtain the reward. Miller (1948a) has demonstrated such extinction in maze learning.

An early and apparently "reasonable" assumption about the effectiveness of consistent reinforcement was exploded soon after the jamming of a food magazine led Skinner to study systematically the effects of intermittent reinforcement (1938, 1956). He found that the rat's rate of bar-pressing remained high even when the pellet materialized only after a scheduled number of presses or at irregular intervals (pages 164–66, this book). In 1940, L. G. Humphreys demonstrated that extinction of the conditioned human eyelid response and psychogalvanic response (PGR) was considerably slower when these had been built up by a program of *partial reinforcement* than when the reinforcement had been given on every trial. If for a moment we lay aside our rigid objective attitude toward such data it is not difficult to think of a reason why such results should follow. If in the training period the subject, animal or human, comes to recognize the CS as a consistent signal of a coming event, the very first time that event fails to follow is a much more striking reason to reappraise the whole situation than a single omission, or even two or three, when the event has in the past been "unreliable." In the latter case, what we might call the "Oh,-this-has-happened-before attitude," with a consequent delay in the arousal responses of the organism (see pages 102–5), slows up the subject's reinterpretation of the CS as a sign that the event is not going to happen *at all*. Similar explanations of the "Humphreys paradox" have been offered by Hull (1943), by Elam, Tyler, and Bitterman (1954), and by Freides (1957).

WHAT IS ASSOCIATION? As long ago as 1898 Thorndike demonstrated a training procedure which in some respects anticipated the instrumental conditioning which is now the focus of much theory and research. When he rewarded a cat with a morsel of food each time she licked herself the animal eventually became a fastidious self-groomer. Kupalov has more recently reported (1961) that a dog fed whenever he shook himself gradually developed what seemed to be a completely voluntary response of that character.

> The general alimentary excitation, irradiating to the centers of the shaking-off reflex, will elevate their excitability; and weak skin stimulations (irritations) that are always present and do not normally elicit the shaking-off reflex become supraliminal and adequate to elicit the reflex. Eventually the dog begins to shake itself actively, so effortlessly, so accurately, and so often that this essentially involuntary act cannot be distinguished from voluntary movements (page 1051).

Verplanck (1955) has reported engineering in much the same way a gradual increase in the occurrence of an involuntary gesture made by a human subject simply by selecting it arbitrarily for reinforcement each time that particular behavior—touching the ear, for instance—occurred. The subject would be told that he had just scored a point, but he was not told for what. Other investigators (Greenspoon, 1962) have, with variable results, attempted to influence the character and frequency of verbal responses made by subjects in an interview situation, the reinforcement in such cases being a nod or a smile or an "mmm-hmmm" response from the interviewer each time a certain class of verbal behavior appeared: plural nouns, verbs, emotionally toned words or phrases, neurotic responses, etc. Although the general results of these studies give us no immediate reason to believe that our freedom of speech is threatened by such techniques, Verplanck has reported positive results on twenty-three subjects in increasing the rate of expressing "opinions" during a ten-minute period when the experimenter reinforced such statements by agreeing with them or rewording them. In another ten-minute phase of the conversation, when the reinforcement was withheld, the extinction effect to be expected appeared in twenty-one of the cases (1955). [But see also pages 203–4, this book, for additional findings in the work of Spielberger and Levin (1962), Dulaney (1961).]

The building up of connections between irrelevant stimuli and "passive" movements—for example, the imposed, mechanical flexion of a dog's leg—has also been the subject of study. If each time a tone sounds the leg is passively moved, there will eventually appear at the sound of the tone some evidence of innervation of the leg muscles even without the imposed movement. Actual movement may not be visible, but the record of the electrical potentials of the leg muscles will show that some connection has been established. Such "conditioned responses" have been found to be unstable, weak, and easily extinguished (Asratyan, 1961a, page 96).

Can we draw any conclusions from this limited sampling of studies which can trace their origin back to the techniques and theories of Thorndike and Pavlov, and of Skinner, representing a later generation? No; but we can make some guarded observations, and ask some important questions for which the chapters to follow may suggest answers. One observation is that Pavlov's *reinforcement* and Thorndike's *reward* appear to have to some extent a common function. Both contribute positively to establishing an association. Psychologists have come in the course of the years to use the term "reinforcement" rather than "reward," one reason being that many effects which serve to reinforce—an electric shock to a leg, or electrical stimulation of some center deep within the brain (see page 154) —do not fit our usual idea of what a reward should be. This raises the question of whether we are justified in assuming that *reinforce-*

ment is really a single process, physiological or psychological in nature, or whether it is merely a convenient term to describe a number of processes that occur in different kinds of learning.

We might ask, too, what is it that is reinforced? One simple answer has been that the S–R bond is strengthened: the association between the metronome and the salivary response; between the door button and the clawing; between the bar and the pressing. But another answer that has been suggested is that the reinforcement contributes more to giving the subject some important information about his environment; in other words, that it builds up S_1–S_2 associations, or S_1–R–S_2 associations which ultimately lead him to make the most effective response to the situation in which he finds himself. Only under extraordinary circumstances could an isolated S–R connection occur by itself. "Feedback" has come to be recognized as an ever present feature of all normal, neural activity. It would be most strange and disconcerting to talk without having reflected to us the sound of our own speech, or at least, as in the case of the deaf speaker, the sensations of movements made in speaking. The normal adjustment of posture and the movements of walking, reaching, grasping, etc., also depend, for their precision, on the instant-to-instant sensory record we normally receive as we react to any situation. Even before the relatively recent focusing of interest on "cybernetics" through the work of Norbert Wiener (1948), the principle of the "retroflex" formulated by Troland (1928) recognized the fact that the real unit of behavior does not end with the response to a stimulus, but includes adjustment of that response on the basis of further information about the situation. Even the exotic cheese fancier may hold his breath as the first odorous hint comes to him that he is passing a shop which purveys such delicacies; but a tantalizing whiff of a lady's perfumed handkerchief may dispose him to inhale more deeply to prolong the pleasant effect.

There was a time when strict associationism did not recognize any cognitive factor such as the perception of relations. Ideas were merely "connected." The eminent British psychologist, Charles Edward Spearman (1863–1945) based his whole system of intellectual psychology mostly on the perception or "eduction" of relations and correlates (1923). But he did not regard his theory as a form of associationism. Quite to the contrary, he complained that the associationists were "astonishingly crude" in their failure to take into consideration what he called "noegenesis," that is, the discovery of new knowledge and the solution of new problems which emerge in the process of learning. As we shall presently see, the Gestalt psychologists have made a similar criticism, and they have made an important contribution in calling attention to the gap and stimulating research and theory directed toward closing it.

Like other maps of our generation, the boundaries of psychological systems do not long remain fixed. In an earlier edition of this book we have said that not all behaviorists could be counted as associationists; today we might say that not all behaviorists can be counted as behaviorists! We can add that not all associationists are behaviorists, although some are. The full meaning of these cryptic statements will be clearer after we have examined the major branches of behavioristic thought, and beyond that, their more recent offshoots. First, however, let us take the opportunity to follow up the development of psychology in Russia, and see how its course has been influenced by the early studies and thought of Pavlov.

4

Soviet Psychology as a "School"

There were psychologists in Russia before the Bolshevik Revolution of 1917. Some of them had learned experimental psychology in Germany, and a few of these could be said to belong to the Wundtian "structural" school. There were pioneering laboratories in the psychiatric clinics of Korsakov and Rossolimo. These contributors to the general advance of psychology certainly did not constitute a distinctive Russian school.

A school of psychophysiology, however, dates back to Sechenov's *Reflexes of the Brain* (1863) and other important works of this physiologist, and comes forward through Bekhterev and especially through Pavlov to the present. The idea that mental functions are fundamentally physiological readily suggests itself to anyone with some knowledge of the brain. Many physiologists have offered this suggestion; it was worked out most persistently by Sechenov (Razran, 1957b).

Soon after the Revolution it became clear to the psychologists that their theory would have to take account of the official Marxian philosophy, the so-called dialectical materialism of Marx and Engels, dating from 1847. The "idealism" that was opposed by materialism was concerned not with ideals, but with ideas regarded as the fundamental reality of the world. Materialism, then, held that matter, or better, matter in motion, was the only basic reality. There could be a one-way materialism, or a two-way materialism. The one-way, "mechanistic" materialism, which was often proposed, held that brain processes were real, but that mental processes were mere epiphenomena, playing certainly no dynamic role in the life of the organism or in the processes of nature. Marx's "dialectical" materialism was two-way, holding that mental processes were actual brain processes, and just as real whether considered as mental or as physiological. The organization of matter could be at a primitive level or at more advanced levels. At the level of the organism, matter in motion constituted life; at the cerebral level it constituted mental life.

Cerebral activity from this point of view has the remarkable property of "reflecting" the environment, the external material reality. This "reflection" is not merely passive and sensory. The environment can be changed by motor activity, and the brain reflects this active participation. At the human level of planned action on the environment, the reflection includes the changes that are planned, the individual's own goals and purposes. Evidently there were philosophical pitfalls in the way of the psychologist who wished to continue experimental work.

Dialectical methodology, with its sequence of "thesis, antithesis, synthesis," seems to have been adopted wholeheartedly by the group of post-revolutionary psychologists. It calls for vigorous criticism of any theory or thesis that anyone offers, in the hope of supplanting it by an opposing theory and if possible reaching a higher synthesis. What happened after 1917 was a series of hopeful programs, each one soon subjected to destructive criticism and abandoned or drastically revised. This method is a better guide toward criticism than toward any positive line of research. It has had no particular effect on mathematics and the physical sciences, which have prospered under the Soviets, but at times it has almost paralyzed the progress of psychology. We must admire the courage and determination of the Russian psychophysiologists who have kept up the fight during their long time of trouble.

There was an Institute of Psychology in the Moscow Academy of Sciences. At the time of the Revolution, this institute was headed by G. I. Chelpanov, who had installed there a psychological laboratory after inspecting the German and American laboratories. Chelpanov tried to save psychology by arguing that Wundt's views were not inconsistent with materialism; but his argument was beaten down. Wundtian psychology was condemned as "idealistic."

Yet some of Wundt's favorite topics, sensation and perception, continued to be investigated in the Moscow Institute. Kravkov's studies of sensory interaction have been continued from the 1920's right up to the present (Kravkov, 1934; London, 1954). Such studies, like those in mathematics and physics, have no obvious relation to the Marxian dogmas. They are acceptable so long as they promise to be of practical value.

REFLEXOLOGY

In the early 1920's Watson's behaviorism was put forward in Russia as a suitable materialistic psychology. Its denial of any importance to consciousness freed it from any taint of "idealism." Watson apparently made no personal effort to promote his views in Russia. Bekhterev, antedating Watson with his "Objective Psychology" (1907), later renamed "Reflexology" (expounded by Schniermann, 1930), was right on the ground and had many zealous adherents in the Neurological Institute at Leningrad. He insisted that any form of "psychology" was necessarily idealistic and should be thrown out of the universities to make room for reflexology. This argument had some success and a beginning was made in the displacement of psychologists by members of Bekhterev's group. Soon, however, i.e., by 1930–1931, it was decided that reflexology and behaviorism represented only a "one-way," mechanistic materialism which simply shunted mental processes aside and allowed them no positive role in human life (London, 1949).

Pavlov took no active part in this controversy, preferring to enlist continued governmental support for his "strictly physiological" investigation of the "higher nervous activity." He succeeded so well that his institute continued and expanded its work on the conditioned reflex, undisturbed by the metaphysical problems that have plagued the psychologists. These physiologists have kept up their experiments on conditioning in relation to the internal organs, diseases, drug effects; also on verbal conditioning and on animal training.

KORNILOV'S "REACTOLOGY"

The chief protagonist of the psychologists in the controversies of the 1920's was K. N. Kornilov (1879–1957). He made it clear that psychology had its own problems, requiring its own methods, and could not be reduced to physiology. He ruled out Wundtian psychology on one side and reflexology on the other and offered his reactology as a Marxian synthesis. He was the main personal bridge from pre-Soviet to Soviet psychology. At the Moscow Institute of Psychology, he was the chief assistant from 1915 to 1921, being then advanced to Professor and in 1924 to Director. He had devised a method of studying "reactions" of any degree of complexity. His instruments showed the speed, force, and form of the reacting movement, and he also obtained introspections on the meaning or social background of the reaction. So the experiment had a true dialectical form and could not be accused of either "idealism" or mechanistic materialism. The method lent itself, so he believed, to the developmental study of the child in relation to socio-economic background. (See Kornilov, 1930.) Kornilov's books, *Reactology, the Study of Human Reactions*, and the textbook on *Psychology from the Standpoint of Dialectic Materialism*, went through successive editions and represented the standard Soviet psychology during the latter part of the 1920's. He was subjected to mounting criticism, however, from Communist party members among the junior staff of the Institute of Psychology. In Lenin's posthumous *Philosophical Notebooks* (1929–1930) these critics found what they needed to force Kornilov to admit his errors and withdraw his reactology. Lenin emphasized man's activity and initiative; man was active, not merely reactive (London, 1949; Razran, 1958a, b). Kornilov stepped down from his position of leadership as Director of the Institute of Psychology; he was not "purged," however, but remained an active participant in the further development of Soviet psychology.

The Communist party of course expected more of its psychologists than doctrinal Marx-Lenin orthodoxy. It expected them to make practical contributions to the work of the party in establishing socialism and changing the mentality of the people to meet the Soviet requirements. "Soviet psychology must especially concern itself concretely with the special psychological problems of the new Soviet man, and must depict his nature so that the superiority of the socialist order can be made evident to all" (Wortis, 1950, page 24). This was a large order; what the psychologists undertook to do (about 1930) was to help in the selection of workers for different technical jobs and in the training of workers and the education of school children. Much of the experimental work of the Institute of Psychology (now attached to the Academy of Pedagogical Sciences) was directed, and is still directed, to finding methods of educating the young child, discovering his difficulties, and helping him systematically.

Standardized tests and related methods of selection were adopted about 1930 and pushed with great energy. Many of the testers were not well prepared, apparently, and had little background for the interpretation of test results. The claims of the testers as to the educability of individual children were often resented by teachers and parents. The intelligence tests sometimes assigned a low rating to children from the working class and even to the children of party members! Opposition to the tests mounted and in 1936 the party issued a "Decree against Pedology," outlawing the use of standardized tests in the schools and also in industry. The role of the psychologists in the schools was to be made definitely subordinate to the role of the teacher. The psychologist was to devote himself to the task of developing the character of the "new Soviet man."

The decree against pedology threw Soviet psychologists into confusion and panic. . . . Departments of psychology were closed, and teachers of psychology wondered what to teach. Some leading psychologists disappeared from the scene. Kornilov and a group of colleagues began shortly to publish a series of articles setting forth the "correct" position for various topics . . . with specific page references to . . . the classics of Marxism-Leninism (Bauer, 1952, page 128).

The pedologists, like other developmental psychologists, had adhered to a "two-factor theory": the child's development depended on the combined influences of heredity and environment. Soviet theory adds a third factor, "training," and even a fourth, "self-training." Training is really an environmental factor, but it is intentionally applied and adjusted to the child's needs by the trainer. If a child is backward in school, the teacher must accept the responsibility; he cannot lay the blame on the home environment.

Some experimentation on training in school continued, but on the whole, "Soviet psychology was in continuous decline after 1936; it had no periodical of its own and produced little new research and thought" (Razran, 1957b, page 1101). This judgment is perhaps unduly pessimistic, since the War intervened, and the psychologists contributed to military training and to rehabilitation of brain-injured soldiers (Ananiev, 1948). Their own claims were not exactly modest. The leading systematist of this period was S. L. Rubinstein (sometimes Rubinshtein), whose *Foundations of General Psychology*, 1940, remained standard for nearly a decade. The fundamental principles, according to the analysis by London (1949, pp. 267–72), focus on the Marx-Lenin concept of consciousness, which is certainly rather difficult to grasp. Consciousness is an advanced form of material motion (brain action) which "reflects" external reality. But apparently it is not believed to occur in animals, but only in socialized human beings. It has evolved historically in dependence on man's labor and social organization, being therefore something new in the "new Soviet man." Rubinstein's system came in for violent criticism in 1947, as being too dependent on Western psychology—dealing with man in the abstract instead of with Soviet man in his concrete education and labor; as lacking Bolshevik party spirit and impetus, and as being too highbrow in style for the masses (London, 1952; see also Wesley's review of German edition, 1961).

PAVLOVIANIZATION, 1950

Since the 1920's the Soviet psychologists had regarded Pavlov's work as belonging exclusively in physiology and not in the least as a basis for psychology. In 1950, fourteen years after his death, he was politically canonized, we might say, and placed alongside Marx and Lenin as one of the great classics of Soviet psychology, as well as of Soviet physiology and psychiatry. These sciences, it was ordered, must be reconstructed according to Pavlov's teachings. The authority behind this order was ultimately Stalin, who was bent on Russification of Soviet science. Russian predecessors were always to be given credit in preference to non-Russians.

No direct decree came from Stalin to the psychologists. What took place in the summer of 1950 was a week-long joint session of the Soviet Academies of Sciences and Medical Sciences, "dedicated to the physiological teachings of Pavlov," and attended by many hundreds of Soviet physiologists, biologists, physicians, and philosophers. First on the agenda were lengthy expositions of Pavlov's concepts by two of his most active and orthodox followers, Professors Bykov and Ivanov-Smolensky. Then followed criticism of some of Pavlov's old co-workers who had sought to go beyond Pavlov in some respect, being influenced apparently by the physiology of Western Europe. After being severely criticized, these physiologists had an opportunity to defend themselves, but their pleas were not accepted, and some of them lost their positions (Gantt, 1952, pages 18–24; Razran, 1957b). The session set up a continuing committee to carry on its work of criticism and Pavlovianization.

Recovering somewhat from their first bewilderment at this abrupt shift of prescribed theory, the Soviet psychologists began in a year or two to pay their respects to Pavlov in almost every published book and article. Razran (1957a) has counted the references to Pavlov in Russian textbooks of psychology published shortly before and shortly after the edict of 1950: there were very few references, almost none, before 1950, but a great many afterward. The psychologists needed a few years to study Pavlov's works, including the suggestions of the free-ranging "Wednesday Seminars" he had conducted late in life (Pavlov, 1957, pages 551–623). Some of these were fruitful of experimental research. What he called the "second-signal system"—language—opened the door for Soviet scientific studies of thinking and concept formation.

There is no doubt that since about 1953 Soviet psychology has been proliferating. Presumably, a psychology with Pavlov in it, even if it has to have also Marx, Engels, and Lenin, is better off than one with Marx, Engels, and Lenin alone. Or we might say that Soviet psychology had at last found an officially sanctioned . . . framework within which it can operate with a wide margin of safety (Razran, 1957a, page 100).

Pavlovian theory was safe because it fitted the approved two-way materialistic pattern prescribed in dialectical materialism. There-fore a psychologist who speaks of "conditioning" with occasional reference to Pavlov insures himself against the suspicions of dualism or idealism which a psychology of "behavior" or of "learning" might arouse.

Pavlov insisted that his experiments were purely physiological studies of brain processes, especially cerebral processes. Actually his conditioning method did not afford any direct observation of what was going on in the cortex. He observed stimulus and response and offered what seemed to him a reasonable theory of the inter-vening brain processes. This, for example, was one of his inferences (Pavlov, translated by Anrep, 1927, pages 36–37):

All this brings us to the important question of the intimate mechanism by which new nervous connections are established in the hemispheres. It is easy to suggest an explanation on the basis of the actual facts. . . . Any unconditioned . . . stimulus undoubtedly evokes a state of nervous activity in some definite part of the brain. . . . During the period of excitation of such centers all other external stimuli which happen to affect the animal are conducted to these centers, and the paths by which they are conducted through the hemispheres become thereby specially marked out. This is the only pos-sible interpretation of the facts.

In this cerebral theory, the unconditioned stimulus (usually food in Pavlov's studies) is thought of as occurring *first*, and as arousing activity in a certain part of the cerebrum (the alimentary center); this active center would then attract the CS to itself, a new cerebral pathway would be opened up, and the CS would become a substitute stimulus arousing the alimentary center. In his experiments, how-ever, Pavlov found it necessary, as we have seen, to have the CS start *before* the US. The time sequence was very important. Ac-cordingly, when he described the connection in terms of a signaling theory, he was staying closer to his behavioral data. But he regarded the data of conditioning as consistent with his cerebral theory.

He could not be accused of "one-way" materialism for he did not regard the conditioned reflex as a purely mechanical process. Along with the analytic operation of the sensory apparatus (the "an-alyzers"), the conditioned reflex provided the rudiments of knowl-edge. "I am fully convinced that thinking is association. . . . As-sociation is knowledge, it is thinking, and when you make use of it, it is insight" (1957, page 582). So also in Thorndike's puzzle-box experiment: "A connection is formed between . . . the latch or bolt and the opening of the door. This is an association . . . it is knowledge which the cat will use next time; this is comprehension of the relations between objects in the external world" (*ibid.*, page 583). Pavlov had no patience with Gestalt psychology which had belittled his conditioned reflexes and all associations, and had even disputed the fundamental role of scientific analysis. A "Gestalt," he insisted, is a secondary product built up by previous associations. But all these mental processes of conditioning, association, knowledge, and insight are physiological processes in the material brain.

SOVIET PSYCHOLOGY SINCE 1950

The present period has been one of relative calm and increasing productivity. Once more the Russian psychologists have a journal of their own—*Voprosy Psikhologii* (*Problems of Psychology*)—and they are holding annual or biennial meetings comparable to those in Britain and America. Several international conferences, one at Montreal in 1954, one at Moscow in 1958, another at Montevideo in 1959, and still another at New York in 1960, have made possible a profitable interchange of information on current research in America, Russia, and other parts of the world. The discussion of the papers presented, and the published reports of these meetings (Delafresnaye, *et al.*, 1961; Kline, 1961), have been a rich source of enlightenment not only to the participants, but to all interested readers for whom the language barrier had previously made the scientific achievements on the other side of the world appear vague and distorted. Fortunately for many of us who do not read Russian, a good view of the recent Soviet output has been provided by Mintz (1958, 1959) and by Brožek (1962) who have abstracted the outstanding papers and books, and summarized significant current research interests and theories; by Simon (1957) and his associates who have translated over twenty papers selected by the Russians themselves to show the present trend of their psychology; by Kline (1960) who has reported on the closely related field of psychiatric care and research; and by Razran (1957a, 1961a) who has filled in the background of present Soviet theories and methods of studying consciousness and the unconscious, appraising the results in comparison with American learning theory.

THE PSYCHOLOGY OF EDUCATION

The education of young children is still, as it has long been, a major field for Soviet psychology. The Russians distinguish between "education" (*vospitani*) and "training" (*obuchenie*), the former being largely concerned with the development of personality, with great emphasis on moral character traits such as social responsibility, respect for public property, earnest application to study, and recognition of the social significance of learning. A paper by L. S. Slavina considers how "to create habits of punctual, neat, and accurate homework in children in the first grade of school." If the children are kept after school to correct their homework, it makes a great difference whether this overtime is made to appear as a punishment or as a golden opportunity to improve—no improvement in the former case but much in the latter!

Brožek points out that psychologists identified with educational institutions such as the Moscow Academy of Pedagogical Sciences contribute not only to general theory and research, but can claim also a rich output on the application of psychology to teaching special subjects (1962, page 542). Among the findings of this kind of investigation was that in such subjects as arithmetic, geometry, or mechanics the study of abstract rules was ineffective unless combined with concrete examples. Other school experiments have dealt with the learning of speech and reading, concept learning, and problem solving. Mintz (1958, 1959) also reports a variety of laboratory investigations: on rote learning, habit hierarchies, reaction time, perception and illusions, sensory feedback, sensory interaction, individual differences in working efficiency, and group decisions in a "collective." (Strangely enough, however, the Russians take a very dim view of social psychology! In the Soviet delegation's report of the Montreal Congress in their journal *Voprosy Psikhologii* this phase of psychology was dismissed as having "no scientific significance whatever.")

Intelligence and other forms of standardized tests are also still under a cloud. Biographical assessments of intelligence are regularly made of distinguished people, and appraisals of their pupils' approach and enterprise in solving problems are made by teachers without the pupils' knowledge. Pavlov's theory of types has been the point of departure for a number of studies in a two-volume work edited by B. M. Teplov (1956, 1959). In regard to the nervous organization of humans or animals, Pavlov made the strength or weakness of inhibition and excitation, their balance or imbalance, and their mobility or inertness the bases of his type distinctions (compare page 77). The *lively* type combined strength, balance, and mobility; the *sedate* type, strength, balance, and inertness; the *impulsive* type, strength, but overbalanced on the side of excitation; and, finally, the *weak*, inert type. For man he used the relative proportion of dependence on the two signal systems (page 99) as the basis for a different, three-category typology. The *thinking* type represented high development of the second signal system (verbal behavior); the *artistic* type was characterized by dominance of the first signal system; and the *average* type balanced the two (Brožek, page 549).

Practical application, student initiative, and creativity are stressed as educational objectives. The study of the thought process has taken a prominent place both in general research and in educational research. In the latter case the emphasis has been on aspects of the thought process—analysis and synthesis, for example—which, properly used in teaching, will add a dynamic quality to the content taught, encouraging the pupil to think further and to apply his knowledge. A more theoretical approach to thought is represented in a volume of experimental studies edited by S. L. Rubinstein (1960) which he considers a supplement to his own earlier *Thinking and Methods of its Study* (1958). Brožek notes (page 548) that both Rubinstein and Ponomarev, who has also studied the creative thought process experimentally, feature the essential role of continuing interaction between the subject and the environment in the period of working toward the solution of the problem: "The study of the 'movement' of thought was facilitated by the introduction of auxiliary tasks which contained certain links essential to the solution of the principal problem."

THE SECOND SIGNAL SYSTEM; SEMANTIC CONDITIONING

Language, the "second signal system" to which Pavlov made late references in his Wednesday Seminars, has become the subject of much Soviet research since 1950, its significance growing out of the fact that in his capacity to use it man is set off as qualitatively different from animals. The latter, of course, can learn to respond to words, but a command spoken to a trained dog is not essentially different as a CS from the sound of a bell or a buzzer. It is the use of words as surrogates for complexly organized stimuli or responses that constitutes the real function of language. Razran characterizes it as

. . . not a signal of one signal, a simple second-order CR, but a signal of *many* signals, a second-order CR to a compound CS—a system that . . . does not merely link and analyze but synthesizes (abstracts or generalizes) its acquired information. The formulation presumably pertains to the complex R and not the simple S aspect of words: that is, to the emergence of the production and use of language and not to its basic character as a stimulus (1961a, page 126).

Razran proposes that it be promoted to the position of "third signal system" to make room for non-verbal forms of compound and configural conditioning which obviously involve a higher organization of nervous activity than simple conditioning. Compound conditioning may take the form of grouped stimuli which evoke simultaneously a response different from that made to any element of the group alone; or sequences of stimuli the response to which will depend upon the particular temporal pattern—or some other discriminable relationship—of the separate elements (see pages 82–83). It is only in conditioning to these patterned stimuli that higher species are differentiated from the lower evolutionary orders. The latter may even have an advantage over the higher animals and man in simple CR learning.

Razran, who in 1939 introduced semantic conditioning to this country, has now given us an account of typical research in that area more recently carried on in Russia. Razran's original approach was to present visually to his subjects the words *style, urn, freeze,* and *surf,* with food reinforcement. When a stable salivary response to these words had been established, he tested the subjects with the homonyms *stile, earn, frieze,* and *serf,* and with the unlike-sounding synonyms *fashion, vase, chill,* and *wave.* The latter showed more transfer effect (generalization) than the former group. At another time (1949) he studied the transfer effect from a short conditioned sentence to other short sentences having more or less related meaning to the first. Still later he measured the transfer from the conditioned sentence as a whole to the several structural elements that composed it (1952). Such early leads have been elaborated and proliferated in Soviet investigations. For example, conditioned vasoconstriction to the Russian word *dom* (house) transferred to a greater extent to the English *house* than to the phonetically similar Russian *dym* (smoke)—the subjects in this experiment having a knowledge of both languages. However, thirty minutes after the subjects had received a dose of chloral hydrate the transfer to *house* disappeared, and there was a noticeable return of the transfer to *dym* which had been of brief duration in the first place. The results with other words were consistent with these (Razran, 1961a, page 103).

In this experiment and the next which we shall consider, mild shock was used as the unconditioned stimulus (US) and a pattern of vasomotor reaction was used as an index of a conditioned response. Dilatation or constriction of blood vessels will determine the volume of blood in a part of the body; changes in the size of a part, registered by a plethysmograph, therefore provide a measure of vasodilatation or vasoconstriction in that area. Soviet investigators set great store by this measure as a means of differentiating what is merely a state of alerted attention (the orienting reflex) from a defensive reaction. In the former case the pattern seems to be *dilatation* of the blood vessels of the forehead and *constriction* of the blood vessels of the fingers—a combination sometimes referred to as the *disparate* vascular response. When the reaction is defensive, vasomotor constriction occurs in both forehead and fingers—the *conjoint* vascular response.

After seven subjects were conditioned to the sound of the word *skripka* (violin) a plethysmographic record of forehead and finger changes was kept as they listened to other words, some more or less resembling the sound of *skripka,* some more or less like it in meaning, some entirely unrelated. Those which had some degree of meaningful relationship at first drew the conjoint, defensive pattern of response, but this gradually changed to the disparate, orienting response with repetition, and eventually was extinguished altogether. *Skrepka* (paper clip) from the beginning drew only the orienting reaction until this too died out. In the same study it appeared that the reaction to ambiguous words varied depending upon the nature of the words they followed—evidence of the effect of the kind of set which operates when we read words in context.

In another study a differential response was first established to the words *khorosho* (good) and *plokho* (bad) by food reinforcement only to the former. Then over a period of several weeks during which the key words were presented periodically with the same differential reinforcement, the salivary reaction to some propositions which might be expected to elicit a value judgment of good or bad (*khorosho* or *plokho*), along with one proposition of a mixed nature, was measured. At no time were the propositions themselves ever directly associated with the conditioned words, yet the variation in salivary response seemed clearly to be related to the degree of approbation of the information conveyed in each proposition. On successive presentations of *khorosho* the salivary response of the thirteen-year-old boy who was the subject ranged from 9 to 18 drops in a 30-second interval; the unreinforced *plokho* produced no more than 2 drops in the same interval. "The pupil studies excellently" produced 14 drops. "The pupil failed to take the examination" produced 2 drops. "The pupil passed the examination with a mediocre grade" produced an intermediate 10 drops, understandable when we consider the probable conflict of attitudes toward "passing" and toward being "mediocre." What is not so obviously accounted for is that "The Soviet Army was victorious," "The enemy army was defeated and annihilated," "The pioneer helps his comrade," produced 23, 24, and 23 drops respectively, all outstripping the maximum response to *khorosho* itself. It would, of course, be dangerous to speculate on the data from a single case, but if it can be demonstrated that such results are typical and reliable in semantic conditioning it must be recognized that they reflect a much more complicated mechanism of transfer or generalization of response than that represented in transferring a CR attached to a tone of a certain pitch to a tone of a slightly different pitch. In the present case, it would almost appear as if the conditioning of the word *good* carried with it implicitly a potential for an even stronger reaction to the superlative, and that this expressed itself in the greater response to the chauvinistically approved propositions. Pavlov implied some complexity when he referred to the second signal system as a "signal of signals."

THE ORIENTING REFLEX

Pavlov's interest in the primary effect of the conditioned stimulus was almost wholly eclipsed by his major concern with the circumstances under which it would come to evoke or fail to evoke the response originally produced by the unconditioned stimulus. He did, however, observe that the dog's ears would be raised at the sound of the bell, and that other adjustive or investigatory behavior was evident during the early stages of the conditioning process, and that when such responses were very prominent or very feeble, conditioning did not progress well. He called these responses the *orienting reflex*. Since 1950, this one-time stepchild of CR research has come into the limelight and now shares at least equal attention with the highly focused problems of visceral and semantic conditioning. One reason for this newly gained status has been the great increase in research on the limbic and reticular areas of the brain. Evidence of the important effect of these older parts of the brain upon cortical functioning would make them significant to any theory of learning, motivation, or cognition; but for dialectical materialism, with its stress on the identification of mental processes with brain processes, investigation of the functions of the newly discovered "core" brain became imperative.

It was first established that the reticular system, stretching between the lower medulla and the thalamus, had among other properties, the function of general arousal (Moruzzi and Magoun, 1949). The neighboring limbic area has been found to play an important role in emotional behavior. These areas must therefore be involved in the primary response to a novel or unexpected stimulus—a response which Razran describes as "versive," having the effect of alerting the organism to the stimulus and preparing it for the consummatory approach or avoidance behavior which may, or may not, follow.

The Russians have gone far in the development of ingenious methods of recording simultaneously a variety of responses evoked by the unconditioned stimulus (US) or the conditioned stimulus (CS). Such records have shown that the orienting reflex (OR) is by no means a simple response, but a highly complex one varying from species to species in the pattern of elements that compose it, in the speed of its arousal, and in its duration. Typical of the responses that make up the OR are: desynchronization of the alpha rhythm, which means that the slow, high-amplitude waves usually held to be characteristic of relaxation are replaced by rapid, low-amplitude waves usually indicative of arousal and awakening; pupillary dilatation when the stimulus is non-visual, pupillary contraction when it is visual, the latter reaction contributing to the clearness of the image; oculomotor and general postural adjustments in the direction of the stimulus—responses of the sort Razran has called versive and preparatory; the previously described pattern of forehead vasodilatation and digital vasoconstriction (page 101); respiratory reactions; and the neuromuscular and visceral changes which are represented in the electrocardiogram and the psychogalvanic response (PGR) respectively.

Like the CR, the OR undergoes extinction or change, but the several components of the response are not affected at the same rate. The breathing reaction, for example, has been found to be more resistant to habituation than the PGR; and the intensity of the stimulus will be a factor in determining how fast the OR will be transformed into a different kind of response such as defensive, withdrawal, or approach behavior. Stimuli which have ecological significance to an animal will continue to evoke the OR longer than less meaningful stimuli: Razran cites as examples the sound of splintering wood to the beaver, a rustling sound to a hare, the splashing of waves to a fish (1961a, pages 114–15); and these special dispositions have been found in animals so young that it is doubtful previous experience could entirely account for them.

When the OR shows signs of extinguishing, it may be restored to full strength in several ways. Any novelty introduced into the repeated situation will of course revive it. A dog trained to go to one dish for meat at the sound of a tone, and to another dish for bread at the flash of a light will show exactly the "surprise" we might expect when he finds bread in his meat dish. Not only his overt behavior but also his electroencephalogram and other OR measures will register the effect of the change. The OR may also be directly reinforced. Fox cubs that heard the squeak of mice in the laboratory soon began to ignore the sound; but after they were allowed to catch some of the mice they were instantly alerted by further squeaks. In the case of human subjects, requiring that they perform a task or make an observation each time the stimulus is introduced maintains the OR at high level (Razran, 1961a, page 118).

It has been demonstrated that the OR may be present without consciousness of the stimulus, as in the case of subliminal effects, or in pain stimulation under certain types of anesthesia; it is also true that consciousness may be present without the OR, as in the case of habituation to a stimulus. Yet along with semantic conditioning the OR is considered to offer one of the main avenues of approach to experience of a cognitive nature. As we have seen, to the Russians semantic conditioning reflects the highest mental functioning which is uniquely human. In the OR, perception, attention, expectancy—states commonly shared by man and animals—appear at times to be implicit. For any psychology limited to an objective approach these lines of study provide access to what Razran calls the "inferable conscious" (1961a, pages 120–22).

But to understand the difference between the ways these approaches would be developed by the Soviet psychophysiologist and by the American psychologist we must recall the Marxist prescription that consciousness is identified with brain action (matter in motion), and that "idealism"—trafficking in ideas divorced from matter —is beyond the pale of science. This cramping ideological control is probably responsible for what has been described as the "unsophisticated" state of Soviet psychophysiological theorizing (Razran, 1961a, page 138). It obviously also accounts for Soviet preoccupation with physiological detail. In the Pavlovian tradition, conceptualization must take its departure from this rather than from identifiable patterns of behavior or from introspective reports of conscious experience. Although the prevailing trend in American psychological theorizing is to focus first on the psychological events and to turn later to physiological and anatomical data for confirmation or correction of hypotheses, the significance of the contributions made by approaching the problems of psychology "from below" rather than "from above" should not be underestimated.

A neuronal theory proposed by E. N. Sokolov (1960) to account for the OR is in some respects like a proposal of the Canadian psychologist Hebb which we are later to consider at some length (see page 185). According to Sokolov's conception, when a stimulus occurs which does not quite match an already existing "cell assembly" in the cortex that embodies all the features of earlier similar experiences, nerve impulses generated in the cortex discharge into the reticular system. The orienting response is the effect of this discharge. On the other hand, when the stimulus corresponds with the existing cell assembly, inhibiting impulses arising in the cortex have the effect of preventing sensory impulses from arousing the reticular system. In this situation the organism responds automatically to the stimulus in the habitual way with little or no evidence of the alerting, investigatory behavior which the novel stimulus would evoke.

At the Montevideo Symposium on Brain Mechanisms and Learning in 1959, P. K. Anokhin, a member of the Academy of Medical Sciences of the U.S.S.R., presented another matching theory in his conception of the physiological architecture of the CR. Enough has already been said of the various kinds and vicissitudes of the CR to make it clear that a simple S–R formula falls far short of telling the whole story of its neural structure. Nothing could be farther from the truth than that—as the CR *naturally* develops—a simple bond linking two centers in the brain can account for a salivary response or withdrawal of a paw at the sound of a bell. Even in the simplest forms of CR the response may vary in latency, in quantity, in whether or not it appears at all, depending upon the circumstances under which the CS is received. In semantic conditioning, as we have seen, there is even greater evidence of the probable complexity of the neural mechanism involved. The CR is never the result of an isolated CS, but rather of a focal "dynamic pattern"—the term is Pavlov's—combining all the attendant circumstances. The same CS which in the morning has produced a salivary response can, in the afternoon, produce paw withdrawal. A distraction of which the experimenter himself may be unaware may result in the inhibition of a well-learned CR and the appearance of the alerted complex of behavior we have been considering in this section—the OR.

In the course of conditioning, Anokhin asks, of the infinite possible combinations of excitations occurring in the central nervous system, what determines which will become integrated? Of all the possible adaptive responses, what determines which will be the end result in the conditioning process? How does the organism know when the right response has been made? These are questions which take the physiologist beyond the bounds of his own science and well into the speculative area of neuropsychology. Anokhin has been one of the Soviet investigators of brain functioning, however, who has been relatively well-disposed toward hypotheses relating physiology to psychology. In his hypothetical proposal in this case he suggests neuronal correlates of such psychological phenomena as "set," "anticipation," and to some extent even of the satisfaction, surprise, or disappointment which may be the effect of set or antici-

pation. A quotation from his own presentation of his theory at the
Montevideo meeting will help to make his position clear (Anokhin,
1961a, page 204):

> . . . many investigators do not as yet adequately understand that in a psy-
> chological sense the emergence of an "intention" to perform some action *is an
> absolutely indispensable* stage which antedates the action itself and that, con-
> sequently, we, physiologists of the nervous system and higher nervous activ-
> ity, must strive to analyse the physiological correlates of this "intention."

The first stage in the development of the CR, Anokhin believes,
is that of *afferent synthesis*. During this phase all the afferent impulses aroused by the situational conditions, along with the trigger-
ing bell, shock, word, or other CS, and with the related afferent
impulses of the reticular system become integrated. He stresses the
great importance of the reticular contribution and the orienting reflex in assuring sharp discrimination at this stage. As soon as afferent synthesis has been achieved, the second phase begins. This consists in the formation of the apparatus of the *acceptor of action* which
Anokhin describes as "an afferent reflection of the results of future
action." More simply and psychologically, it may be said to be a
representation or "emergence of the 'idea,' 'intention,' or 'aim' to
perform the given action," and so defined it seems to bear some relationship to the "idea" or image of an act which William James believed to be the basis for voluntary or "ideomotor" behavior (James,
1890). The acceptor of action is an organization within cortical and
subcortical centers of seemingly appropriate bonds selected from
those formed by previous experience and now aroused to activity
as a result of the current afferent synthesis. This excitation really
acts as a set which determines the choice of a response. When the
response has been made, the *return afferentation*—what would more
commonly be called "feedback"—provides information about the results of the behavior. If there is a discrepancy between anticipation
and result, as when a dog finds bread—or nothing—in the dish where
he had expected to find meat, there is a pronounced change in the
character of his response. The investigatory OR replaces the originally intended response, and a new phase of afferent synthesis begins
another cycle that will lead to the shaping of a different CR.

Anokhin recognizes that behavior is always a complex affair, combining many CR units, and that this sequence of determining neural
events must be represented by "an uninterrupted chain of afferent
excitations" to take care of the entire response from start to finish.
He recognizes also that his theory requires further physiological research to support it. Yet it holds special interest for features it

shares with a number of other theories which have grown up in quite different contexts (Hebb, 1949; G. Miller, *et al.*, 1960; and Neal Miller, 1963), but which also stress the dynamic effect of "discrepancy," or "dissonance," or "incongruity" in accounting for behavioral development.

Through the use of microelectrodes implanted so as to make possible the recording of the electric activity of single cells or groups of cells in circumscribed areas of the cortex or reticular formation, Anokhin has also made important contributions to knowledge of the *specific* activating functions of the reticular formation. He has reported, for example (1961b), that a tranquilizer, chlorpromazine, completely eliminated the desynchronization and stress rhythms typical of a defensive reaction to shock, and restored a shocked rabbit's interest in food which he had a moment before tensely refused. The chlorpromazine was obviously not blocking the animal's feeding behavior or general wakefulness, but apparently was blocking his defensive responses—a fact which Anokhin interprets as an argument that these functions must have a separate and distinct organization within the reticular tract. Other investigators have reported results not wholly in agreement with Anokhin's on details of the localization of centers for approach or avoidance reactions, but the specific functioning of the reticular formation is now generally accepted as well as its early-recognized, non-specific, arousal function. However, within this area of fast-moving research and discovery, premature overassurance and conclusiveness are out of order.

OTHER ASPECTS OF CR THEORY

At the Montevideo Symposium, E. A. Asratyan presented new data on an old problem: the issue of whether the bond between two stimuli separated by an interval develops only in the forward direction, or in both directions. A great deal of evidence has been accumulated supporting the view that "backward conditioning," when it appears at all, is really not true conditioning. If an animal has been shocked first and a few seconds later hears a buzzer, any response he may show thereafter to the buzzer could be the effect of *sensitization* to the whole experimental setup. An animal that has never been exposed to the shock and buzzer together has been shown to give the same response. According to Asratyan, however, under certain conditions the reverse response can be elicited, although it is usually a weak one and scarcely observable when it does occur. When two unconditioned stimuli such as shock and food are combined, circumstances which make one of the stimuli stronger than the other can lead to a backward response. Describing a 1958 experiment of Lyan-Chi-an, Asratyan explains (1961a, page 101):

> For example, in an experiment in which stimuli are applied in the sequences "electrical shock—food," the presentation of food evokes a conditioned reflex lifting of the animal's leg more frequently and more distinctly if the leg was previously stimulated by a stronger shock than usual, or if, prior to the experiment, the dog was deliberately fed to satiety.

On the other hand, after subjection to the shock—food sequence a very hungry animal will not show the reverse shock reaction when food is presented, nor will the backward CR occur if the initial shock has been a very weak one. These data seem to warrant another review of the problem of the effect of the sequence of stimuli on the strength of the connection.

At the 1960 meeting in New York, Asratyan directed himself to the problem of the specific site of the neural process of *inhibition*. Inhibition is the theoretical function by which Pavlov accounted for such phenomena as the extinction of the CR, the delayed reflex, and the gradual learning to discriminate between closely similar stimuli. He conceived of it as originating in cortical cells at the site of the CS. Anokhin assigns it to the site of the US. Kupalov has thought of it as arising simultaneously at both these centers. Asratyan has offered still another alternative: that inhibition occurs in the conditioned connection between the centers affected by the CS and the US. He bases his argument on the evidence which comes from "trans-switching" experiments—a very complicated form of conditioning in which the same CS comes to evoke a *salivary* response in the morning and a *defensive* response in the afternoon; or "double trans-switching," in which two different stimuli—bell and light—alternately evoke now salivation, now defensive withdrawal, each response under the appropriate conditions. Such results would be impossible, according to Asratyan, if inhibition were active at the site of either the CS, the US, or at both sites (1961b).

P. S. Kupalov, who was also a participant in the New York conference on higher nervous activity, and who, of those present, could claim the earliest association with Pavlov, dating back more than fifty years, introduced in his report a reference to a pathological reaction which has sometimes been found to occur as a sequel to the internal inhibition presumably required in a delayed conditioned response (1961). At first limited to the brief period during which salivation is withheld after the CS has been presented, the inhibition in these cases seems to extend its effect, so that salivation does not begin even when the animal is given his food. At a more advanced stage the animal may refuse to eat at all—suggesting that the inhibition has irradiated to the motor centers as well. (As we have noted above, Kupalov has maintained that inhibition may arise and spread from more than one center of the cortex.)

We have presented in the last few pages some illustrations of the theories that outstanding Russian investigators have offered to integrate and lend meaningfulness to the assemblage of physiological data which their ingeniously devised techniques have made available. Even from this limited sampling it is clear that the conceptualizations proposed tend to waiver between the realms of physiology and psychology—a flexibility which is scientifically dangerous since a term used in one of these disciplines does not necessarily mean the same thing when it is used in the other. "Inhibition" is a good example. It would certainly be risky to conclude that the pathological inhibition Kupalov has described is identifiable either with Hull's "reactive inhibition" or with the inhibition psychoanalysts invoke to account for certain neurotic symptoms. But even more easily overlooked is the possible equivocal use of "inhibition," or any other single term to describe what may in fact be two (or more) quite different neurological phenomena. A good example, noted earlier in our discussion of semantic conditioning (pages 101–2), is the Pavlovian concept of "irradiation," which has been used to explain generalization or transfer of response from one situation to another. It is unlikely that *failure to distinguish* between two rather similar stimuli and the *deliberate transfer* of a response found suitable in one situation to another situation recognized as essentially similar can both be the result of irradiation or spread of neural activity about a central point. Razran has developed this criticism further in his discussion of papers presented at the New York Academy of Sciences Conference on Higher Nervous Activity (1961b, pages 1070–71).

There is no doubt that what most distinguishes the Soviet contribution to "psychological" research and theory from the work of most of the traditional "schools" is the extent to which the former consists in the amassing of physiological facts, in contrast to the moderate distrust expressed by many learning theorists about reducing psychological problems to physiological terms. An equally prominent feature of the Soviet system is the relatively inflexible control exercised over research programs designed to achieve the objectives set out in an officially determined five- or ten- or fifteen-year plan. Kline (1960) has provided some instructive examples of such assignments undertaken by various research institutes under the Academy of Medical Sciences (pages 208–17). Along with strictly medical problems we find references to problems of the development of higher nervous activity in children, the need for clarification of the "general and specific laws of operation of the second signal system," study of the evolutionary development of higher nervous activity in vertebrates, study of the effects of hormonal and pharmacological substances on stimulation and inhibition, etc.

Although Razran does not believe that the psychophysiologists who have been devoting their energies to these problems which lie in the middle ground between psychology and physiology have been seriously limited by the Pavlovianization Resolution of 1950, the record shows that some outstanding scholars including Kupalov and Anokhin were pilloried for heresy against Pavlovian orthodoxy. That they have returned to the fold seems significant. Since any arbitrary constraint, whether it be state-imposed, "school"-imposed, or self-imposed, is not likely to be conducive to optimal production, we are inclined to credit the notable advances of Soviet science under disciplinary "facilitation," yet to wonder what might have been their scholars' achievement under a less rigid policy of motivation.

5

Early Behaviorism

In the half-century of its existence behaviorism has passed through several stages and taken on somewhat diverse meanings. It grew out of the study of animal behavior, but to define it simply as the science of behavior would be to miss the force of the "ism." In fact, some of the leading workers in animal psychology—Edward Thorndike and Harvey Carr of whom we have already spoken, Henri Pieron of France, Robert Yerkes—refused to join the ranks of the behaviorists. Behaviorism was expressly developed as a "school" in opposition to the apparently dominant school of structuralism and to the functionalism of William James and of the Chicago group. As the old controversies have died down, behaviorism has become less negativistic and more a component part of the general stream of progressive psychology. Our aim will be to show what behaviorism was at the start, to follow its development, and finally to see what it has now become.

WATSONIAN BEHAVIORISM

Although John Broadus Watson (1878–1958), the founder of American behaviorism, began graduate study in philosophy at the University of Chicago, he changed over to psychology and neurology, and, after receiving his doctor's degree, joined the teaching staff and set up one of the early animal laboratories. In 1908 he became full professor at the Johns Hopkins University. By 1912 he was well known for his many studies of animal behavior.

As a teacher of psychology he became more and more disgusted with "intangibles and unapproachables," and determined to teach a psychology dealing with concrete facts. Another cause of his irritation was the ambiguous status of animal psychology, his field of

111

research. According to the orthodox definition at the time, psychology was the science of conscious experience. Now, since the days
of Descartes it had been recognized that consciousness in animals
can neither be directly observed nor logically proved to exist. At
best, animal behavior could only be a psychological sideshow.
Meanwhile the animal psychologists were obtaining excellent results on learning and problem solving—certainly psychological problems—and were inclined to resent the disparaging attitude of the
structuralists. Watson decided to take the offensive with the force-
ful claim that the animal psychologists were doing the truly scientific research and leading the way for all psychologists to follow—the
non-introspective, non-mentalistic way.

Watson's behavioristic manifesto, as we may call it, was promul-
gated in some lectures and a journal article (1913) and in his book,
Behavior, in 1914. A few extracts from this notable document will
show what behaviorism meant to its founder (1914, pages 1, 7, 8, 9,
11, 13):

Psychology as the behaviorist views it is a purely objective experimental
branch of natural science. Its theoretical goal is the prediction and control
of behavior. Introspection forms no essential part of its methods, nor is the
scientific value of its data dependent upon . . . interpretation in terms of
consciousness. . . . The time seems to have come when psychology must discard all reference to consciousness; when it need no longer delude itself into
thinking that it is making mental states the object of observation. . . . Our
psychological quarrel is not with the . . . structural psychologist alone. The
last fifteen years have seen the growth of what is called functional psychology. . . . The difference between functional psychology and structural psychology, as the functionalists have so far stated the case, is unintelligible.
The terms sensation, perception, affection, emotion, volition are used as much
by the functionalist as by the structuralist. . . . We advance the view that
behaviorism is the only consistent and logical functionalism.

It is possible to write a psychology, to define it . . . as the "science of
behavior," and never go back on the definition: never to use the terms consciousness, mental states, mind, content, will, imagery, and the like. . . . It
can be done in terms of stimulus and response, in terms of habit formation,
habit integration, and the like. . . . The reason for this is to learn general
and particular methods by which behavior may be controlled. . . . Those
who have occasion to apply psychological principles practically would find no
need to complain as they do at the present time. . . . If this is done, work
. . . on the human being will be directly comparable with the work on animals.

This stirring appeal got an immediate response from the American Psychological Association which by a plurality vote elected
Watson to be its President for the year 1915. Many of the younger
psychologists felt he had succeeded in clearing away old mysteries
and complexities, a heritage from philosophy which the older generation had not been able to shake off. In their enthusiasm they exag-

gerated the extent of the revolution. In order to keep the historical record straight, we must analyze this manifesto and see how much of it was new, original, and progressive. The following points were made clear:

1. *Definition:* Psychology is to be the science, not of consciousness, but of behavior.

2. *Scope:* It is to cover both human and animal behavior, the simpler animal behavior being indeed more fundamental than the more complex behavior of men.

3. *Method:* It is to rely wholly on objective data, introspection being discarded.

4. *Concepts:* It is to avoid "mentalistic" concepts such as sensation, perception, and emotion, and employ only behavior concepts such as stimulus and response, learning and habit. Presumably, mentalistic concepts are suggested by human conscious experience and introspection, while behavior concepts are suggested only by objective observation of animals and human beings. Since behaviorism is to be "the only consistent and logical functionalism," the admissible concepts would apparently be concepts of functions.

5. *Application:* A scientific basis is to be provided for the practical control of behavior, and for dealing with "behavior problems" as they appear in a guidance or psychiatric clinic.

6. *Metaphysics:* The old mind–body problem and the rival theories of interaction and parallelism disappear, as shown in unquoted passages, with the disappearance of mind. There is no mystery in the relation of body and behavior. Psychologists have introduced unnecessary mystery by replacing the mind or soul by the inaccessible brain. Behaviorism must not make a fetish of the brain but must keep its eyes fixed on the peripheral organs, the sense organs, muscles, and glands. Only objectively observable facts are admissible.

This list consists largely of "thou shalt nots": drop the mind, say no more about consciousness, cease introspecting, eliminate mentalistic concepts, stop speculating on what goes on in the brain. It was this negative emphasis that was novel. Objective methods had been in use for a long time, as we saw in an earlier chapter (page 18), and functional concepts had predominated from the first. Animal learning had thrown light on human learning. Objective tests had been devised to aid in the prediction and control of behavior. Watson recognized some of this work and complained only that the conclusions were often tainted with superfluous references to "consciousness"—as was true to a certain extent.

With regard to the proper definition of psychology, the ground had been well prepared for Watson. It is true that around 1900 most psychologists, even when working on functions or performances, gave formal assent to the orthodox definition of psychology as the science of consciousness. These active laboratory workers scarcely attempted to define their science in terms of their work. The first to do so was probably James McKeen Cattell (1860–1944), a pupil of Wundt at Leipzig, a co-worker with Galton in London, the founder of the psychological laboratories at Pennsylvania and Columbia, a pioneer in the development of mental tests, and in some ways the most influential American psychologist of his time, though not much given to theoretical writing. In 1904, however, in connection with the World's Fair at St. Louis, he was designated to make an address on the scope and method of psychology, and expressed himself as follows:

> The task has been assigned to me of considering the scope, conceptions and methods of psychology, and it is my business to define the field of psychology or to acknowledge my inability to do so. I must choose the latter alternative. I can only say that psychology is what the psychologist is interested in *qua* psychologist. . . . I am not convinced that psychology should be limited to the study of consciousness as such. . . . I admire . . . the ever-increasing acuteness of introspective analysis . . . but the positive scientific results are small in quantity when compared with the objective experimental work accomplished in the past fifty years. There is no conflict between introspective analysis and objective experiment—on the contrary, they should and do continually cooperate. But the rather widespread notion that there is no psychology apart from introspection is refuted by the brute argument of accomplished fact. It seems to me that most of the research work that has been done by me or in my laboratory is nearly as independent of introspection as work in physics or in zoology. . . . I see no reason why the application of systematized knowledge to the control of human nature may not in the course of the present century accomplish results commensurate with the nineteenth century applications of physical science to the material world.

Watson, if he noticed Cattell's pronouncement, regarded it as too tame for his own purposes, which were not simply to promote objective psychology, but to get rid of everything else. For the same reason he was not satisfied with certain other proposals of the same period.

The first man to define psychology as the science of behavior was apparently the young English experimentalist, William McDougall, whom we shall meet again in a later chapter (page 336). In his little book on *Physiological Psychology*, published in 1905, he had this to say on the matter of definition:

> Psychology may be best and most comprehensively defined as the positive science of the conduct of living creatures. . . . Psychology is more commonly

defined as the science of mind, or as the science of mental or psychical processes, or of consciousness, or of individual experience. Such definitions . . . express the aims of a psychologist who relies solely upon introspection, the observation and analysis of his own experience, and who unduly neglects the manifestations of mental life afforded by the conduct of his fellow-creatures.

Here he used the word *conduct*, but in 1908, in his *Introduction to Social Psychology*, a book which immediately gained a wide audience, he added the word *behavior* to his definition:

Psychologists must cease to be content with the sterile and narrow conception of their science as the science of consciousness, and must boldly assert its claim to be the positive science . . . of conduct or behavior. . . . Happily this more generous conception of psychology is beginning to prevail.

Many psychologists were strongly inclined toward this new and broader definition of psychology. An influential representative of this tendency was Walter Bowers Pillsbury (1872–1957), one of Titchener's early pupils who devoted himself more to functional than structural investigations. Pillsbury published in 1911 his *Essentials of Psychology*, a standard college textbook, and his definition was acceptable to a large share of his contemporaries:

Psychology may be most satisfactorily defined as the science of human behavior. Man may be treated as objectively as any physical phenomenon. . . . Viewed in this way the end of our science is to understand human action. The practical end is . . . to discover means of increasing man's efficiency. . . . Even if we regard the understanding of human behavior as the ultimate end of psychology, consciousness must still play a very important part in our science. By consciousness we mean a man's awareness of his own acts and their antecedents. . . . Behavior is to be studied through the consciousness of the individual and by external observation.

Pillsbury was saying, in effect, that conscious experience was valuable to psychology for the light it threw on behavior, while the structuralists said that behavior was valuable for the light it threw on conscious experience. But Watson complained that Pillsbury was "going back on his definition" by allowing some value to introspection and using terms like *consciousness* and *imagery*. For Watson, behavior and consciousness were mutually exclusive, and to define psychology as the science of behavior was to make a radical departure and rule out all introspection, all reference to conscious experience, and so practically all of the psychological work down to 1912.

Why was Watson so set against introspection? Primarily, no doubt, because it was put forward by the structuralists as the essential method of psychology, while it was obviously unavailable to the animal psychologist, who was thus left out in the cold. He had other reasons as well. He was suspicious of the accuracy of introspection. Titchener had admitted or rather insisted that only well-trained introspective observers could be trusted. But Watson pointed an accusing finger at the imageless thought controversy (our pages 22–25) and other recent examples of divergent results obtained in different laboratories by presumably well-trained introspectionists. If even your best observers cannot agree on matters of fact, he said, how can you ever make psychology a science instead of a debating society? Here Watson was overplaying his hand, for there were many matters of fact on which introspective observers did agree, the examples of disagreement being such as made extra-heavy demands on keen observation—and in the matter of imagery individuals differ anyway and quite properly report different observations. Watson admitted a little later (1919, page 39) that a person can observe his own behavior to some extent so as to report, for example, "that I am writing, that my face is flushed, etc." And in his autobiography (1936) he includes many personal introspections of this type: "I enjoyed . . . ," "I hated to leave," "The thought presented itself," "I honestly think . . . ," "I still believe . . . ." Watson's argument on the score of reliability did not succeed in disproving a conservative statement such as that introspection can be trusted if too much is not demanded of it.

But Watson had a more radical objection to introspection, an objection that began by being very practical and ended by being altogether metaphysical. He wanted to deal with tangibles, visibles, audibles—things or happenings that he could point out to a fellow-observer as the chemist points at the contents of a test tube. He did not want to have anything going on in his laboratory that was not objectively observable. Introspection pretended to report something going on in an organism that was not objectively observable. Now of course there is much going on inside the organism's skin that is practically unobservable—movements of the viscera, secretions of the various glands, minimal contractions of the various muscles, nerve impulses running to and from the brain. All such internal motions and secretions belong under the head of behavior. They are not overt behavior, to be sure, but they are "implicit behavior."

In introducing this famous concept of implicit behavior Watson was relaxing his original requirement that everything in psychology should be actually observable, and retreating to the philosophical demand that everything must be potentially observable. All that goes on in the organism is organic behavior, and even implicit behavior is potentially observable as a physical process. Some introspectionists have claimed to observe processes of an entirely different order, not conceivably observable by any refinement of physical instrumentation; but this claim cannot be allowed by the behaviorist. The parallelists have assumed two entirely different processes keeping step in the brain, one being purely physical, the other purely psychical (and sometimes conscious); but the metaphysical behaviorist, discarding the psychical process from his theory, has only behavior to consider, all of it being of the same order as the actually observable movements of the organism.

This *metaphysical behaviorism,* however fascinating to a philosopher, is wholly irrelevant in scientific psychology. It has no bearing on the methodological question as to whether introspective data are ever reliable and useful.

Methodological behaviorism—the insistence on objective methods exclusively—loomed very large at first but proved to be of minor importance. Watson himself came to make some use of introspection, but in the form of verbal report. On the positive side the behaviorists had nothing revolutionary to contribute, for the excellent reason that objective methods had been a major concern of psychology ever since it began to be an experimental science.

Conceptual behaviorism had more to contribute to the progress of psychology. It helped in the clarification and sharpening of the functional concepts, particularly the "What" concepts (our page 14).

What does the organism do? Watson's emphasis on muscular and glandular action laid him open to the charge that his behavior psychology was only a little piece of physiology. Against this charge he had a strong defense (1919, pages 19–20):

> It has been claimed by some that behavior psychology is really physiology. That this is not the case appears from even a casual examination. . . . Physiology teaches us concerning the functions of the special organs. . . . Certain combined processes are studied, such as metabolism . . . but nowhere in physiology do we get the organism, as it were, put back together again and tested in relation to its environment as a whole. . . . The physiologist *qua* physiologist knows nothing of the total situations in the daily life of an individual that shape his action and conduct.

Psychology, then, should concern itself with the doings of the whole organism in relation to its environment. The actual experiments of many psychologists had placed the individual in known situations and noted his responses, but a comprehensive formula for this kind of experiment had perhaps not been given. "Behavior of the organism in relation to its environment" was a good framework for the "What" question.

Watson's proposal to shift the general headquarters of psychology from the human to the animal field seemed like mere adolescent bravado at first, but in the course of time it exerted no little influence on the conceptual framework of psychology. Let us assume for the moment that the fundamental relations of the organism to the environment must be common to men and animals, and that probably certain fundamental ways of dealing with the environment can be more easily seen in animals than in man's more complicated behavior. From this point of view it would seem desirable to work out a basic system of concepts free from "anthropomorphism" and strictly applicable to animal behavior. Into this basic framework could then be fitted the secondary concepts demanded by human behavior. This strategy has been used in the investigation of learning, problem solving, and motivation. It has not worked well, or rather has not been tried, in research on perception of the environment.

The word *perception* was regarded by Watson as old-fashioned and mentalistic. Human observers can report what they see or hear —the apparent size, distance, and other properties of objects in the environment. The lead in this field has therefore been taken by non-behavioristic human psychology, and the behavioristic influence for two or three decades was negative. Military skills required in World War II were found to be perceptual–motor rather than merely motor, which is one reason that perception has been coming back into the psychological picture in recent theories.

The behavioristic manifesto of 1912–1914 had considerable success with younger American psychologists of the time. Many of them were quite willing to forswear introspection and all attempts to describe consciousness, and instead to devote themselves to research on animal behavior. There was much opposition, however, from well established psychologists. Not wishing merely to establish a separate "school"—hoping, rather, to convert the main body of psychologists to his point of view—Watson felt compelled to work out a comprehensive *Psychology from the Standpoint of a Behaviorist,* which was published in 1919. Although his academic career ended in 1920, he continued to promote the cause of behaviorism by popular lecture courses which were later published in his book, *Behaviorism* (1925, 1930), and by other books which were widely read during that period.

STIMULUS AND RESPONSE.   Just as Wundt had said that conscious experiences are complex and call for analysis into simple sensations and feelings, so Watson said that behavior is complex and capable of analysis into simple stimulus–response units. He called these units "reflexes," defined as including not only the typical physiological reflexes such as the knee jerk but also the miscellaneous movements which he observed in his intensive studies of newborn babies.

IVAN PETROVITCH PAVLOV

JOHN BROADUS WATSON

"Instinct and habit are undoubtedly composed of the same elementary reflexes. . . . In instinct the pattern and order are inherited, in
habit both are acquired during the lifetime of the individual" (1919,
pages 272–73). Such statements made it easy for the *Gestalt* and
organismic schools, later, to accuse Watson of "atomism." Neither
his experimental work nor his theorizing, however, ran much to
atomism. His examples of a *stimulus* start with light entering the
eyes, sound entering the ears, etc., and proceed to objects in the
environment and to total situations. His examples of *response* start
with the knee jerk but advance to acts such as taking food, unlocking
a door, writing a letter, and even building a house. Watson's major
interest is not in the analysis of behavior into elementary muscular
(and glandular) responses to elementary stimuli, but, quite to the
contrary, in what the individual will do in a given situation. For
example, the "stimulus" is a stick of candy dangled in front of a baby
and the "response" (at a certain age) is a reaching out, grasping the
candy, and putting it into the mouth. Or, the "stimulus" is a baseball thrown by the pitcher, and the response is a fly to the outfield.
In strictness we should speak in such cases not of stimulus and response but of objective situation and objective results produced by
the individual's response. It is in that sense that Watson should be
understood when he says that the goal of behavior psychology is
the "ascertaining of such data and laws that, given the stimulus,
psychology can predict what the response will be; or, on the other
hand, given the response, it can specify the nature of the effective
stimulus" (1919, page 10).

Responses can be classified as learned or unlearned, and also as
explicit and implicit. It was important for behavior psychology to
distinguish between what was instinctive and what was learned, and
to discover the laws of learning or habit formation. Still another
way of classifying responses is according to the sense organ receiving the stimulus. So an "auditory response" is any sort of physical
response aroused by a stimulus to the ears, whether it be a startle
response to a pistol shot or a verbal report that a tone is high or low.
An "olfactory response" may be a sniffing movement or a verbal report of smelling something like violets or like tar. But how can a
speech movement be called olfactory or auditory? It seems a strange
use of terms. To see why the behaviorists felt compelled to speak
in this way we need to examine their attitude toward sensation.

SENSATION AND PERCEPTION. Since we cannot assume consciousness in animals, we have no right to say that they see, hear, or smell.
However, since they demonstrably make motor responses to visual,
auditory, and olfactory stimuli, there is no objection to saying that

they make "visual responses," etc., with the meaning just explained. Our objective data in the case of an animal are the stimulus and the motor response. With a human subject before us we wish to be equally objective. His conscious experience, if he has any, is invisible to us. We wish to find out what his "visual response" will be to light of a certain wave length, and to make things simple for him we use the everyday expression, "Tell me what you see." He replies that he sees blue. This verbal response is a perfectly objective phenomenon. We need not assume that he has any conscious sensation but only accept the fact that he makes the verbal response. If we make the blue stimulus fainter till he says that he no longer sees blue, we learn as much about his color sense by simply accepting his verbal response as by assuming any conscious sensations in him which we cannot observe. But for the behaviorists to deny that the human subject, at least, is actually seeing or hearing when he so reports, seems pedantic to say the least. The behaviorist certainly admits that he himself can see and hear; in fact he presents what *he* can see and hear as scientific data.

The method of impression (page 19) was an old stand-by of the introspectionists, but Watson believed he could transform it into an acceptable objective method by rechristening it the method of *verbal report*. He did not like this method very well and even proposed to substitute for it, as far as possible, the conditioned reflex method which Pavlov had found useful in testing the animal's powers of sensory discrimination. Watson proposed (1916, 1919) to use the motor conditioned response which V. M. Bekhterev (1857–1927), a Russian contemporary and rival of Pavlov whose work has already been mentioned in Chapter 4, had introduced with human subjects. Bekhterev had written an *Objective Psychology* in 1907 which became known to our psychologists through the German and French translations of 1913. Watson did not care much for Bekhterev's general treatment of the subject, but he did like the motor conditioned response, because it was so purely behavioral and free from any suspicion of introspection. But Watson could not afford to throw overboard all the results obtained in the study of the senses by the method of impression. For example, he did not want to discard the visual after-image as a mere introspective delusion and relic of the old religious psychology. Thus he says (1919, page 91):

One of the most interesting sets of phenomena to be met with in the whole of sensory physiology appears in the after-effects of monochromatic light stimulation. After the eye has been stimulated for a time by a monochromatic light which is then removed, one of two things may be reported by the subject: The subject may react as though he were stimulated anew by the original light, the so-called "positive after-image"; or, as though he were stimulated by light the wave length of which is complementary to the original light, the "negative after-image." We can illustrate this by data obtained by the verbal report method. If we stimulate with . . . blue and the subject then looks at a gray screen, he will say, "I see yellow." . . . Stating these phenomena in physiological terms, we may say . . . .

From these phenomena, he continues, something can be learned regarding the physiological processes that occur in the eye.

We must be on our guard here, for Watson may be claiming too much and widening the scope of his behaviorism by appropriating data which do not properly belong in his system. So long as he says "verbal response" he remains a behaviorist, for he himself heard the subject say, "I see yellow," and is fully entitled to record that objective fact. But now Watson shifts to saying "verbal report," and we must ask, "Who makes this report, and what does he report?" And we find that the *subject* makes the report and that he reports *"seeing."* If Watson accepts this report, he admits "seeing" into his system, while pretending to have a system which excludes all such subjective contraband. And he cannot pretend that after all he means nothing more than "verbal response," for the mere speech movements of his subject give no indication of the physiological processes in the eye, except so far as they are a report of seeing. The "phenomena" which Watson finds so interesting and valuable in the after-image experiment are the after-images themselves, not the subject's speech movements. We must conclude that verbal report is not a behavioristic method and that Watson's use of it is practically a confession of defeat for methodological behaviorism. From the history of American psychology following Watson it seems, in fact, that behaviorism exerted a deadening rather than a stimulating influence on research into human sensation and perception.

MEMORY IMAGES. Behavior in Watson's view is an activity of the whole organism in which the brain serves to connect the sensory with the motor nerves and so link the sense organs with the muscles. Nerve impulses coming into the brain by the sensory nerves are instantly transmitted to the motor nerves, he believed, and all behavior is sensorimotor. If any process can go on entirely within the brain, it is too inaccessible to be included under behavior. Now memory images—visual, auditory, or tactile, sometimes olfactory—are reported by almost every person who is asked to call to mind a friend's face, or a bit of music, or the feel of velvet, or the odor of peppermint. These images resemble sensations, though they are not produced by any present stimulus to the eyes or ears or skin or nose. They seem to be "centrally aroused sensations," purely cerebral affairs accessible to introspection but not to the behavioral methods of observation. Watson attempted to show (1914, pages 16–21) that the so-called images were really sensorimotor affairs. The visual image could consist partly in after-images from the eye, partly in kinesthetic impulses from the eye muscles, and partly in implicit speech movements.

FEELING AND EMOTION. Like the image, the feelings of pleasantness and unpleasantness seemed to many psychologists to be purely central affairs, without any sense organ to arouse them and without any distinct motor expression. Efforts had been made to discover definite expressive changes in the heartbeat, blood pressure, and breathing, but these efforts had led to no clear result. Watson suggested (1914, pages 21–26) that pleasantness was a true sensorimotor affair, the sensory impulses coming in from tumescent sex organs (or other erogenous zones), and the motor impulses going out to muscles and arousing incipient movements of approach—with the reverse conditions in unpleasantness.

From our point of view as students of the schools, it is not important to decide whether Watson made a good guess or a wild one in his attempt to explain feeling or memory images. It is important for us to notice two things: (1) he evidently did not regard feelings or images as mere unreal ghosts, for then he would not have attempted to explain them; (2) if they were sensorimotor processes, they were behavior and quite acceptable to him, even though both the stimulus and the response were implicit and hypothetical. Nothing must go on in the organism except sensorimotor processes—that was the behaviorist's demand or postulate.

Emotion was universally admitted to be more complex than pleasant or unpleasant feeling, and psychologists had long noticed the rapid heartbeat and breathing and the tense muscles of strong emotion. The old view was that the stirred-up bodily state was aroused by the conscious emotion, while the famous James–Lange theory, dating from 1884–1885, held that the perception of danger, for example, directly caused the bodily changes, and that the mass of resulting bodily sensations was the emotion as we experience it. To convert this theory into Watson's, say simply that the presence of danger causes bodily changes. Watson, of course, would not admit any conscious "perception" of danger, or any conscious "mass of sensations" from the bodily organs. What he said was that emotion consists in "profound changes of the bodily mechanism as a whole, but particularly of the visceral and glandular systems," each separate emotion being a particular pattern of such changes (1919, page 195). "Notwithstanding the fact that in all emotional responses there are overt factors such as movement of the eyes and the arms and the legs and the trunk, visceral and glandular factors predominate" (1925, page 130).

Watson felt that his simplified theory opened the door for a developmental study of emotions in children. He made some challenging contributions along this line. In very young infants he found three well-marked patterns of emotional behavior, distinguished, however, in terms of external situation and overt response rather than in terms of implicit visceral behavior. These three primal emotions he called fear, rage, and love. As he could distinguish no others in infants, he regarded these three as the only native emotions, all others being built up by processes of learning. The natural or original stimuli of fear were loud sounds and loss of support (slipping or falling); for rage, interference with the infant's freedom of movement; for love, patting and stroking. Other stimuli could be made effective by the conditioned response technique. He was able to develop a conditioned fear in a child of eleven months by "punishing" with a loud, harsh noise each of the child's efforts to reach a white rat, an animal that up to that time had always got a positive response from the child. The loud noise made the child start and sometimes whimper and give other signs of fear or discomfort; and by repeating the punishment every time the child reached for the rat, the experimenter soon established a conditioned avoiding response to the animal. Moreover, this conditioned fear persisted. Such fears are in fact difficult to extinguish. These early results of Watson's are historically important, even though they do not exhaust the subject of native and acquired emotions (1925, page 120).

His data and conclusions on the patterns of infants' emotions were soon challenged by Sherman's study (1927) of the interpretations made by observers (1) when they knew the circumstances causing the babies' emotions; (2) when they were allowed to see only the behavior; (3) when a switch was made in the movie on which the judgments were based so as to mislead the observers about the circumstances. In the first situation the judges generally agreed: a baby that had been disturbed by a sudden jolt was "frightened"; one that was pinched was "angry," etc. But the observers who saw only the response did not agree about what the emotion was; and those who were tricked by the switch were likely to judge the emotion to be one reasonably related to the false circumstances. In other words, it seems as if the judges in this experiment—and probably Watson too, in his—were drawing on their own recollections of how they would feel and act if they were hungry, or startled, or hurt, rather than basing their interpretations solely on the objective data before them.

This raises some doubt about the validity of the purely behavioristic approach to the study of emotions. If our purpose is to understand better the psychological part they play in the life of the organism we must apparently identify in some way with the behaving subject. Sherman's study shows this to be the case, but it is even more realistically demonstrated in our everyday social relationships. Sometimes we are aware of an emotional reaction in a person to whom we are talking, even though we would be unable to report any change in his behavior that could be reasonably called "emotional." Sometimes we tactfully avoid discussing a subject we feel might be painful to our listener. Heider (1958) has made a distinction between two forms of inter-personal perception. In one the perceiver is simply aware of objects and persons in the environment; in the other, the perceiver recognizes the other person as also perceiving. To the extent that the observer can maintain the former attitude—which is doubtful—the description of emotion will be reduced to a few overt responses which become so conventionalized according to the culture pattern that they shed little light on the real nature of emotion. There are, of course, also physiological reactions which can be recorded: the psychogalvanic response, breathing and circulatory changes, etc.; but do these add up to that experience known *psychologically* as an "emotion"? In the introduction to her two-volume treatise on *Emotions and Personality* (1960), Magda Arnold presents the phenomenologist's position in these terms (page 12):

> Throughout this discussion I am going to talk about emotion as a human experience, a human activity, and shall not apologize for taking as fact what you, the reader, and I, the writer, experience first hand and can identify without scientific terminology. . . . If I experience joy, no measurement of muscular tension or patterns of autonomic excitation can give a more valid account of this particular experience. If a theorist should insist that this pattern *is* the experience of joy, we cannot follow him: we are not aware of a pattern of excitation but of a quality of experience that is *sui generis,* whatever may be the sensations and other excitations included in it.

Apparently this "experience" is what the observer "intuits" in perceiving the emotional behavior of another person. We must grant that there are individual differences in the shrewdness of the intuition, but to the degree that it can occur at all, it presents a difficult problem to the psychologist. He has invented terms to describe the fact: empathy, projection, identification, etc. But the terms must themselves be explained. What makes it possible for any individual to know anything about the conscious experience of another? Pointing to the immediacy of this communication, Asch (1952) says: "Often there is virtually no lag between the psychological event in one person and its grasp in the other. We may even anticipate the thought and feelings of those we know, and it would appear that we are as directly connected with others as with our own psychological processes" (page 142).

THEORY OF LEARNING.   As you will recall from Chapter 3, Thorndike had modified the older association theory by adding to the law of contiguity, which he renamed the law of exercise, a new law, the law of effect. Successful responses to a situation, by giving satisfaction to the learner, were gradually stamped in, while the unsuccessful ones were stamped out by the discomfort of failure. Although satisfaction and discomfort could be regarded as physiological states, and although Watson himself suggested a behavioral theory for them (see above, page 122), the law of effect seemed to assume conscious feelings in the animal subject and even to allow them a causal influence on behavior. Therefore Watson attempted to eliminate the law of effect by reducing it in some way to the law of exercise. He at first pinned his faith to the long-accepted laws of frequency and recency, those sublaws under the law of exercise. He pointed out that an animal learning to run a maze is bound to take the correct path at least once on every trial before reaching the food box, whereas any particular blind alley may be skipped in some trials. Thus the successful response would gradually acquire a balance of frequency over the unsuccessful. Thorndike, in reply, pointed out that the same blind alley was often entered several times in the same trial, so that the advantage in frequency would favor that alley, trial after trial, and the blind alley never could be eliminated on the basis of frequency. Thorndike had the best of the argument (pages 71–72).

Later, Watson came to rely mostly on the conditioned response. He had at first adopted the Pavlov and Bekhterev techniques only as convenient objective methods in certain problems. In 1919 he utilized the conditioned response concept for explaining acquired fears, and we have seen how he developed a conditioned fear in a child. By 1924 he had come to suspect that the conditioned response might afford the key to all habit formation—a suggestion first made, apparently, by Smith and Guthrie in a book with decided behavioristic leanings (1921). But neither these writers nor Watson himself recognized the basic importance of Pavlov's law of reinforcement, which seems (pages 83–85) to be somehow related to the law of effect. Watson's theory of learning, therefore, belongs with the older

associationism and has few adherents among present-day behaviorists. (See Hilgard, 1956.)

THEORY OF THINKING. Among psychologists at least, Watson's
reduction of thinking to implicit motor behavior is the most famous
and distinctive of all his theories. He started from his regular postulate that all "mental activity" must be sensorimotor behavior of some
sort and decided that implicit speech movements were the most
likely behavior for thinking. People, especially children, often think
aloud. The young child says what he is doing, naming the objects
he is playing with and the results he is producing. He gives up talking aloud for whispering to himself, gives up whispering for inaudi-
ble lip movement, and reaches the stage of talking to himself without any visible movement. He learns to talk to himself not only
about what he is now doing but also about what he has done or intends to do, and so reaches the adult form of thinking. Watson
suggested, then, that the implicit behavior of silent thought consisted mostly of minute speech movements (1924). He readily conceded that implicit gestures also might play a part in thinking. In
the case of deaf people who talk with their hands he held that they
must think by implicit hand movements. He had no objection to
including other implicit movements, insisting indeed that we think
with our whole body, but he always came back to his original emphasis on subvocal talking (1914, page 19; 1919, pages 322–28; 1920;
1924; 1925, pages 191–99).

Watson's theory of thinking strikes many people as reasonable
because they are aware of talking to themselves, more or less, while
thinking. The theory was not novel but had been proposed time
and again without any reference to behaviorism. What behaviorism
demanded was that silent speech should consist of actual implicit
movements. To some persons silent speech seems to be felt in the
mouth and throat and chest as if actual movements were occurring
there; but to others it seems to be auditory rather than motor. Introspection cannot tell whether the theoretical implicit movements are
actually occurring. Watson proposed to apply sensitive recording
apparatus to the speech organs in the hope of securing objective
evidence for his theory. The larynx seemed to him at first the most
likely "organ of thought" and the best organ to approach with external recording instruments. When his attention was called to individuals whose larynx had been surgically removed but who were
still able to think, he shifted his emphasis to the mouth and tongue.

For a hypothesis of purely theoretical interest, without any possible bearing on the practical question of how to promote better
thinking, Watson's suggestion was surprisingly stimulating to the ex-

perimentalists. It was a challenge to their technical abilities. Could they demonstrate the supposed implicit speech movements during silent thought or show conclusively that such movements did not occur? Mechanical recorders used by the first experimenters failed to yield any clear result. Electrical registration with amplification of the little "muscle currents" that occur when a muscle is even minimally active was more dependable. By this test the tongue muscle proves to be active sometimes but not all the time during silent speech (Jacobson, 1932). More accessible are the forearm muscles employed by a deaf person in talking with his hands; by the electrical test these muscles often show some activity when he is engaged in difficult thinking, but not when his thinking is easy and smooth (Max, 1937). Even today there is no conclusive evidence either for or against the theory.

Behaviorism does not stand or fall with the fortunes of this particular theory. Even if speech movements were always detected during silent thought, the question would remain whether the brain activity responsible for the muscular action were not the essential thing. On the other hand, if speech movements were found to be certainly non-existent in some thinking, other possible muscular activity might be supplying the sensorimotor process demanded by behaviorism.

Watson's Environmentalism. In the 1920's Watson became widely known for his strong emphasis on environment as against heredity. What appeared to the public to be most characteristically behavioristic was his rejection of instincts and of hereditary mental traits. "Has the boomerang an instinct to return to the hand of the thrower? . . . Well, why does it return? Because it is made in such a way that it must return. . . . Man is made up of certain kinds of material—put together in certain ways." Man's unlearned behavior is "no more mysterious than that of the boomerang." "Let us, then, forever lay the ghosts of inheritance of aptitudes, of 'mental' characteristics, of special abilities." His strongest claim for environment was that he could "guarantee," given a free hand in controlling a child's environment and training, to take any normal infant "and train him to become any type of specialist I might select—doctor, lawyer, artist, merchant-chief and, yes, even beggar-man and thief, regardless of his talents, penchants, tendencies, abilities, vocations and race of his ancestors." He admitted that he was going beyond the known facts and was hoping to enlist support for the extensive program of research needed to check his claims (1925, pages 82–85).

Extreme environmentalism is not logically a corollary of behaviorism. It has nothing to do with rejection of introspection and insist-

ence on objective methods. Some behaviorists reject it and some
non-behaviorists accept it. It is not an issue separating one psychological school from another. It is a question of fact and evidence,
and the evidence is still coming in from those who work, not for or
against behaviorism, but simply as scientific investigators of the
problem. On the one hand is the great building of knowledge about
heredity through research on the DNA molecule; on the other is the
accumulation of evidence that the period of prenatal development
and the early postnatal years play a very important part in determining the ultimate achievement of the individual. In drawing conclusions from a rich assortment of relevant data on this subject, Hunt
(1961) rejects the "belief that the wherewithal to solve problems
comes automatically with the maturation of somatic tissues, especially with the neural tissues of the cerebrum" (page 6), but finds
rather that:

> It is fairly clear from the evidence surveyed in these chapters that impov-
> erishments of experience during the early months can slow up the develop-
> ment of intelligence. In terms of the traditional measurement of intelligence,
> this means reducing the IQ. Various bits of the evidence have strongly sug-
> gested that such slowed development is permanent, that it may result not
> only in a permanently reduced IQ but in a failure of the basic criterion ca-
> pacities of individuals to develop to the degree that they might have devel-
> oped under other, more varied programs of encounters with the environment
> which were appropriately matched to the intellectual structures developing
> within the child. But much remains to be learned about the degree of per-
> manence in such failures to develop and about the conditions under which
> these failures to develop become permanent (page 346).

Although Watson's immoderate claims for the effect of environment
are by no means supported by such a statement, it moves us to reappraise the significance of an IQ, particularly as a basis for comparison of individuals or groups whose "encounters with the environment" have not been comparable. It also suggests that there may
be much greater flexibility in this measure especially during the
early years of life than has sometimes been attributed to it.

Watson's strong popular appeal during the 1920's depended a
great deal on his environmentalism and on his enthusiastic confidence that a well-developed science of behavior could make over
the human and social world. Behaviorism in this sense seemed to
hold out a fresh hope to many young, disillusioned idealists of that
generation. For the psychologists of the time, it was not so much
Watson's actual scientific achievements, which were considerable,
nor even his system of concepts and methods, that made him a stand-
ard-bearer in the forward march of the science. It was, rather, his
boldness, tough-mindedness, scorn of tradition and mystery, along

with his optimistic faith in the capacity of science to take charge of human affairs.

SOME OTHER EARLY BEHAVIORISTS

Though Watson was undoubtedly the outstanding pioneer in the behavioristic movement and its most prominent representative for a couple of decades, there were a few other eminent psychologists who almost simultaneously reached the same point of view.

Edwin Bissell Holt (1873–1946; at Harvard, 1901–1918; at Princeton, 1926–1936) was a very influential protagonist of this general point of view, according to the testimony of such men as Carmichael (1946) and Elliott (1952) who studied with him in those days. Holt speaks of Watson's 1914 book as being "valiant and clearheaded," but as lacking an adequate definition of behavior. A few sentences from Holt's book of 1915 will show his approach.

> We are prone, even the "behaviorists" among us, to think of behavior as somehow consisting of reflex activities. Quite true, so far as it goes. . . . But our account has overlooked the most essential thing of all—the *organization* of these processes. . . . Behavior is not a function of the immediate stimulus. . . . This fact . . . is the interesting point about the integration of reflexes. . . . The organism "behaves" with regard only to the distant object. . . . This fact offers no opening for the introduction here of "subjective" categories: the investigator continues to ask, merely, What is the organism doing? The answer will be in strictly objective terms. . . . Every living thing is at every waking moment doing something or other to some feature or other of its environment. . . . One could not describe what the animal as a whole is doing in terms of the immediate stimuli; but . . . only in terms of the environing objects toward which the animal's response is directed (pages 160–68, 58, 76).

In his later and more elaborate book (1931) Holt makes a determined effort to trace the development of the individual's behavior from the fertilized egg up to the adult state—and to do so in purely physiological terms. The diffuse sensorimotor discharge of "random movement" seen in the newborn animal or child becomes canalized into definite habits by the processes of the circular reflex, the conditioned reflex, and the chaining of reflexes. When a habitual response encounters an obstacle, the organism reverts to random movements which vary until some one of them succeeds in circumventing the obstacle; so emerges trial-and-error behavior, which plays a part in all the higher forms of learning. If the obstacle is not too obstructive, it will "hold the attention," as shown by exploratory movements of the hand or eyes. So behavior becomes related to objects and integrated in relation to the environment. When two incompatible responses are simultaneously aroused, there are conflicting muscular tensions which do not at once give rise to overt behavior but which constitute "thought" and "ideational" trial and error. The "higher mental processes" occur as advanced stages of sensorimotor physiological activity.

In the picture which I have endeavored to present of the living and responding organism, I believe that every statement rests on plain biological foundations . . . and that I have nowhere surreptitiously introduced any "psychic" principle. . . . From the point where we now stand it is but one short step to a definition of awareness and consciousness in terms of physiological process (Holt, 1931, pages 256, 263).

Evidently Holt did not share Watson's horror of consciousness and mental processes; he pinned his faith to an adequate physiological description of integrated behavior.

Max Meyer (born 1873; long professor at the University of Missouri), writing in 1911 on *The Fundamental Laws of Behavior*, anticipated the views of behaviorism and has since been regarded as a behaviorist. He was a pupil of the famous German psychologist, Carl Stumpf (1848–1936) of the University of Berlin and was influenced by Stumpf's great interest in the psychology of hearing and of music to study the mechanism of the ear and the brain. Although this specialty might seem to invite the use of introspection, Meyer came to believe that a true science of psychology should confine itself to the study of "the nervous laws of behavior." Much like Pillsbury, he decided that the "scientific value of introspective psychology consists merely in the fact that it aids us in discovering the laws of nervous function." Beyond that the proper scope of a scientific psychology is the study of "the other one." Meyer incorporated this objective concept into the title of a textbook which he published in 1921.

Albert Paul Weiss (1879–1931), a pupil of Max Meyer, was certainly a behaviorist. In his book, *A Theoretical Basis of Human Behavior* (1925, 1929), he was concerned over psychology's dubious status among the natural sciences. He urged psychologists to give up certain pretentions which he thought were alienating them from other scientists. Psychologists should not pretend to have access through introspection to any realities which are immaterial and therefore inaccessible to a natural scientist. Psychology must freely admit that there are no ultimate entities besides those recognized in physics—which at that time were the electron and the proton. All biological and psychological processes must accordingly consist ultimately in the motion of electrons and protons—until physics has something better to offer! Psychology should not assume any mental forces separate from the physiological forces, which are themselves reducible to physical forces.

In ordinary common-sense talk we imply that the feelings are causes of behavior, causing us to do what is pleasant and avoid what is unpleasant. Psychologists should not speak in this way unless they are prepared to regard the feelings as physical processes in the nervous system (Weiss, 1928).

However, Weiss did not wish to restrict psychology to physiological concepts. In a social group one individual's behavior is a stimulus arousing responses from others, and each person's behavior and development are largely controlled by the social situation. Recognizing this social nature of human behavior, we must not forget that it is always biological as well. In becoming socialized the child does not become any less biological. In order to do justice to both aspects of human behavior, Weiss coined the descriptive term, *biosocial*. Psychology is the biosocial science, and its main task is to trace the development of the human infant into the socialized adult. In this task such mentalistic concepts as sensation, perception, feeling, thinking, or striving cannot help. Rather, Weiss argued, they will hamper research. The development of conscious experience cannot be followed from infancy, since the infant's feelings, for example, are not directly observable. Behavioral indicators have to be used from the start, and only in behavioral terms can a complete developmental history be worked out. Weiss inaugurated a comprehensive program at The Ohio State University for following the development of behavior in the young child. Unfortunately he did not live to see the program through.

Walter S. Hunter (1889–1954) was well started on his psychological career before the date of Watson's manifesto, but it was not until later that he made a definite shift to behaviorism. He reported in his *Autobiography* (1952, pages 172, 186):

By 1922 I had come to the belief that behaviorism represented essentially the only adequate scientific point of view in psychology and that some of Watson's pronouncements represented less the necessary details of behaviorism than his own prodigious effort to fill in the experimental gaps with hypotheses pending further work. . . . I am happy to be counted among the many workers who have brought about the change from a psychology of experience to a psychology of behavior. . . . Behaviorism is the point of view in psychology which holds that an adequate account can be given of psychological problems without reference to the terms consciousness and introspection.

With regard to the older schools Hunter admitted that in the days of Wundt and Titchener there was good reason to expect that an introspective experimental psychology might be fruitful; but he was convinced that it had proved to be relatively sterile. An analysis of conscious experience does not yield much in the way of real discoveries because the main facts are known to everyone. "The discovery of seeing, feeling and thinking . . . was made by common-sense observation at some unrecorded time in the past" (1932, page 5). The great variety of detailed "conscious content" does not appear to the ordinary man as mental at all but appears to belong to the environment.

> The . . . Wundtians abstract qualities, intensities, durations . . . from the environment and call the material selected experience. The users of meaning take concrete objects from the environment and call these experience (1926, page 88).

Or, in other words:

> If we ask any contemporary psychologist [not behaviorist] what he means by the term consciousness, or experience, he will reply by enumerating such things as sweet, red, and kinesthetic strain . . . or he will reply by enumerating such things as roses, books, configurations, and melodies. . . . I wish to point out that consciousness or experience for the psychologist is merely a name which he applies to what other people call the environment (1930, pages 282–83).

A good stiff argument could be directed against Hunter on this last point, for the environment is not the same thing as the individual's perception of the environment. To perceive the size, shape, color, and distance of an object is really a remarkable achievement, and it is a task for functional psychology (in the broad sense; see page 31) to discover how this result is accomplished. Hunter, however, is engaged here in combating the structural, not the functional, psychologist.

Along with his active life of administration at Texas, Kansas, Clark, and Brown Universities, his work for the National Research Council and his organization and direction of *Psychological Abstracts* were important contributions. In the area of behaviorist methodology he can be credited with the development of the temporal maze and the delayed reaction experiment.

6

The Later Behaviorists

The somewhat arbitrary division into early and later behaviorists is justified by the fact that behaviorism had something like a new birth about 1930, with new names coming into view and new forms of behaviorism emerging. The movement branched out into sub-schools which have been quite controversial in respect particularly to their theories of learning. A critical but impartial survey of these theories is provided by Hilgard (1956). Continued animal experimentation and theoretical discussion have come from the four behavioristic subschools headed by Tolman, Hull, Guthrie, and Skinner.

Edward Chace Tolman (1886–1961) was one of the early converts to behaviorism. In his very informative *Autobiography* (1952) he tells how he got to know Watson's 1914 *Behavior* in 1914–1915, his final year as a graduate student at Harvard where he was also being indoctrinated in the Wundt-Titchener introspective psychology. He had become somewhat skeptical of the value of introspection, so that his "introduction . . . to Watson's behaviorism came as a tremendous stimulus and relief." Yet it was several years before he definitely became a behaviorist—at Berkeley where he had begun to teach comparative psychology and conduct laboratory experiments on animal learning with rats as subjects.

In his early years as a working behaviorist he got himself "into a sort of in-between position. On the one hand I sided with Watson in not liking the Law of Effect. But, on the other hand, I also did not like Watson's over-simplified notions of stimulus and of response. . . . That is, I was already becoming influenced by Gestalt psychology and conceived that a rat in running a maze must be learning a lay-out or pattern." (Tolman had spent the summer of 1912 with

Koffka in Germany and in 1923 he went back for a couple of months to learn more of Gestalt psychology.)

As early as 1920 and 1922 Tolman was announcing himself as a behaviorist or sometimes as a "purposive behaviorist." There was some doubt in the minds of most psychologists whether his *purposive behaviorism* could properly be called behaviorism. As the experimental work in Tolman's active animal laboratory proceeded, the methods were seen to be behavioral methods, beyond doubt, and the behavioral basis of his system of concepts was rather convincingly set forth in his 1932 book on *Purposive Behavior in Animals and Men.* From that time to the present, purposive behaviorism has been generally recognized as truly a form of behaviorism, though differing from the original Watsonian variety.

Tolman's espousal of behaviorism was from the beginning coupled with rather severe criticisms of Watson's views. Watson had waved "purpose" aside as an introspective superstition of no interest to a behaviorist. Tolman, less impatient and more subtle, believed he could discern an objective purposiveness in behavior itself.

Watson had been far from clear and consistent in his definition of behavior. He had insisted that behavior was something that could be seen, objectively observed; yet he had postulated implicit behavior which could not actually be observed. He had emphasized the role of muscles, glands, and the viscera; and yet, to distinguish behavior study from physiology, he had said (1919, page 195): "It is perfectly possible for a student of behavior entirely ignorant . . . of the glands and smooth muscles . . . to write a thoroughly comprehensive and accurate study of the emotions." He had distinguished fear, rage, and love as the emotions observable in infants without making any attempt to get at the visceral processes in the infants so as to discover whether there actually were three distinct patterns of visceral behavior. Instead, he had observed three types of overt behavior aroused by three types of external situation. He had observed, for instance, that the infant screamed and made slashing or striking movements of the arms and legs when his movements were hampered by the experimenter. The angry behavior was a fighting against interference. The stimulus varied and the response also varied and still the behavior was clearly angry. A critical review of this work led Tolman (1923) to draw a significant conclusion: "It is not a response, *as such*, nor a stimulus situation, *as such*, that constitutes the behavior definition of an emotion, but rather the response as affecting . . . the stimulus situation." Behavioristically, an emotion is a "tendency toward a particular type of behavior-result." What Watson actually described was the infant's behavior in the true sense; what he said he ought to describe amounted to visceral and other physiological processes (Tolman, 1922).

As Tolman put the matter later (1932, pages 6–7):

> In short, our conclusion must be that Watson has in reality dallied with two different notions of behavior, though he himself has not clearly seen how different they are. On the one hand, he has defined behavior in terms of its strict underlying physical and physiological details. . . . We shall designate this as the *molecular* definition of behavior. And, on the other hand, he has come to recognize . . . that behavior, as such, is more than and different from the sum of its physiological parts. Behavior, as such, is an "emergent" phenomenon that has descriptive and defining properties of its own. And we shall designate this latter as the *molar* definition of behavior.

Physiological analysis of a behavior act, perfectly legitimate and desirable in its place, does not bring out the behavioral character of the act. Clutching at your hat when the wind threatens to blow it off is a behavior act, a relatively small one and yet big enough to involve a host of physiological details. As a bit of behavior it has a start and a finish: it starts from a certain situation and terminates in a certain change effected in the situation. A strictly "molecular" or a physiological description could not mention such "molar" items as the hat, the threatening wind, and your attempt to rescue the hat —all part of the total response.

The rat's trial-and-error behavior in mastering a maze—once food has been found in the food box—is visibly goal-seeking. If the food is not reached by one route, other routes are tried until the goal is reached. Not any single trial but a *series of trials* demonstrates the goal-seeking. The elimination of blind alleys and the final adoption of the shortest available route show that the animal is learning the route to a goal, the means to an end. This *learning* is the decisive evidence of goal-seeking—or of "purpose" as Tolman called it. It is also evidence of "cognition," i.e., of getting acquainted with the maze. Purpose and cognition may seem rather scholarly terms to apply to a rat, but Tolman insisted that they are appropriate at a rudimentary level (1932, pages 10–21).

As can be readily imagined, Tolman had to entrench himself against serious attacks from behaviorists and introspectionists alike, both contending that knowing and purposing could not be attributed to animals except on the assumption that the animals were conscious. Tolman insisted that he neither knew nor cared what knowing and purposing *felt like* to the animals. If a rat has any conscious foresight of the goal or any conscious preference for the shortest route, it is his private affair and we have nothing to do with his private feelings. Even in the case of human beings, Tolman went on to say, the "raw feel" of their sensations and emotions is their private possession and incommunicable. If I try to describe to you my sensation of the color red, I find it cannot be done. I can point to a red object, I can say that red is somewhat like orange or purple, and very different from green and blue, rather a stimulating color, very good for a tie but a little too gay for a professor's overcoat—I can put red in many such relations but I cannot describe the sensation itself. I should have the same difficulty in trying to describe my feelings of pleasantness. Now what is essentially private cannot be made the subject matter of science, for science is social. The data of science must be public or capable of publication. The "mentalists" have tried to create a science of private experience, while the behaviorists of all varieties reject any such possibility. Only to the extent that private experience can be *reported*, made public, can it have any place in science.

This apparently clear distinction between behaviorism and mentalism, however, does not stand up very well under analysis. The structuralists, who seem to be the typical mentalists, do insist on verbal report of all introspective observations. Their data are made public and on this basis should be acceptable to the behaviorists. If so, the behaviorists have no real quarrel with the structuralists, except so far as the structuralists attempt (or once did attempt) to rule behavioral data out of psychology. Similarly, the structuralists have no real quarrel with the behaviorists except so far as the latter attempt to rule the former out of scientific psychology. From the broad functionalist point of view (page 15) both kinds of data can throw some light on the difficult "How" question, and accordingly both structuralists and behaviorists are accepted for their positive contributions, while both are rejected for their negativistic tendencies. Tolman, it must be said, was less negativistic than most other behaviorists. He was open-minded toward all the schools and found concepts that he could utilize even in the theories of such anti-behavioristic schools as Gestalt psychology and psychoanalysis (1932, 1942, 1948b, 1949a, b). Indeed Tolman seemed to claim for "behaviorism" any psychological work using objective methods or objective concepts, concepts that can be expressed in behavioral or even in hypothetical physiological terms (1935).

To Tolman apparently goes the credit of first clearly formulating the concept of *intervening variables* (1935, 1938). The primary task of any psychological experimenter is to observe what a given individual does in response to a given situation. The experimenter knows in advance the situation and such facts about the individual as his heredity, age, and past experience (this ideal being more attainable in animal than in human experiments). In a series of experiments the situation is varied or individuals of varying heredity, age, or experience are compared. Whichever factor is varied is the *experimental variable,* also called the *independent variable,* while the resulting behavior shows the *dependent* or *behavior variable.* The experimenter's task is to observe the behavior under the different experimental conditions—to discover the relation of the behavior variable to the experimental variable—to work out the "function" (in the mathematical sense, page 29), represented schematically by the equation,

$$B = f(S, A)$$

where B stands for behavior variables, S for situation variables, and A for antecedent variables such as heredity, age, and previous experience.

So far, what the experimenter has is an elaborate answer to our question "What?" But he would like also to attack the question "How?" He tries to imagine the internal process leading from the given situation to the observed response. In terms of another familiar formula, S—O—R, he tries to imagine what goes on in O between S and R. The intervening process must vary with the experimental variables, and so give rise to the behavior variables. The intervening variables, which he imagines, have no scientific value unless they can be tied in with the experimental variables on the one hand and with the behavior variables on the other. The best example is hunger, conceived as a demand for food or an active tendency to seek food. The animal's demand for food is not directly observable, but it can be tied to a certain experimental variable: the time since last feeding. And it can be tied to a certain response variable: speed of eating when food is obtained. Tolman found at least two kinds of intervening variables useful in explaining animal behavior: *demand* variables and *cognitive* variables. In the class of demands are sex, hunger, demand for a safe spot in face of danger, and demand for a good bed after prolonged activity. The cognitive or "know-how" variables include perception of objects, recognition of previously explored places, motor skill, etc. The cognitive variables might be called abilities, and answers to the question "How?"; the demands would be motives, and answers to the question "Why?"

In a reorganization of his thinking on intervening variables, Tolman, in 1951, added a new category to the demand variables and the "know-how" variables. These were now grouped as *need systems* and *behavior spaces,* the latter covering the inner *cognitive* aspects of learning what to do about what. Objects in the learner's behavior space take on positive or negative valences on the basis of his expectations, and he moves toward or away from them accordingly. But in the psychological reckoning of his behavior the *belief-value matrix* is also significant. Goal objects in the environment are not all equally desirable or appropriate for meeting a need. They fall into an order of preference which may be determined by past individual experience or which may be the product of cultural pressures. More must be known about the relative values of the various types of goal object "arrayed along a given generalized dimension" (1951, page 334) to understand or predict the behavior or course of learning at a given moment. If the hypothetical intervening variables can be successfully tied in with the experimental and behavioral variables, they make up an acceptable theory of behavior; but the task is a towering one.

TOLMAN'S THEORY OF LEARNING

Neither Tolman nor other behaviorists engaged in lasting polemics against the Wundt-Titchener structural psychology. They simply brushed it aside as useless for a science aiming at the prediction and control of behavior. Controversy arose, however, among the behaviorists themselves. They argued about *What* was learned and *How* it was learned. Thorndike, though not himself a behaviorist, had put forward a learning theory from which many behaviorists took their start. There developed theories which diverged from Thorndike's and from one another. *What* was learned, according to Thorndike, consisted of S–R bonds—connections linking a situation with a motor response: given such a situation and the well-established connection, the response would follow. To account for *How* the connection was established, Thorndike relied principally on his Law of Effect: a reward or satisfaction immediately following a response strengthened the S–R connection. This was only the core of Thorndike's whole theory, but it was from this core that the controversial behavioristic learning theories took their start.

Thorndike's theory, then, was that learning occurred in the course of a situation–response–reward sequence, the reward serving as a dynamic factor strengthening the S–R connection. The reward itself was not said to be learned. We may say "reinforcement" instead of "reward," and represent reinforcement by the symbol "Rf," and so we have the sequence S–R–Rf, with Rf the dynamic factor establishing the connection S–R, but with only S–R learned. But why should not Rf also be learned? *Because the theory calls only for the learning of motor responses to stimuli.*

Tolman rejected this restriction; he said that the whole sequence was learned. And he rejected "effect" or "reinforcement" as the prime factor in learning.

My objection to Thorndike's Law of Effect was not to the importance of motivation as a factor in learning, but rather to his wholly mechanical notion as to its operation by way of effect. According to Thorndike, an animal learned, not because it achieved a wanted goal by a certain series of responses, but merely because a quite irrelevant "pleasantness" or "unpleasantness" was, so to speak, shot at it, as from a squirt gun, after it had reached the given goal-box or gone into the given *cul de sac*. And it is this same quite mechanical and irrelevant notion as to the operation of the modern successor of Effect—"Reinforcement"—which underlies, I believe, my main objection to *it* (1952, pages 329–30).

In place of the Law of Effect, Tolman proposed a *cognitive* theory of learning. The animal gets to *know* a bit of the environment. In a simple sequence, S_1–R–S_2, S_1 is the initial situation, R is a motor response, and S_2 is the resulting situation. For example, S_1 is the entrance to a maze, R is the rat's entering and turning left, and S_2 is the dead end of that alley. Or, R is going to the right, and S_2 is the food box at the end of that alley. The rat gets to know both the blind alley and the "good" alley, but more particularly the "good" alley because the food box is more significant and impressive than the dead end. What is established is not primarily the motor response of turning to the right, but an "expectancy" of finding food in that direction. If the food is found there, the expectancy is confirmed and strengthened. This confirmation takes the place in the cognitive theory of reinforcement in the S–R theory.

From such elementary bits of learning, Tolman held (1948b), a rat builds up a comprehensive acquaintance with a whole maze or with any familiar environment. "We believe that something like a field map of the environment gets established in the rat's brain." So the animal can go from one spot to another without being limited to any fixed series of bodily movements.

This same 1948 paper gives an outline of thirty years of experimental work in Tolman's laboratory, bearing on the question of cognitive learning. One line of experiments dealt with "latent learning." Rats were given plenty of time to explore an empty maze (no food being present); then food was placed in the food box, and the question was whether, after once finding the food, the rats would avoid most of the blind alleys. If so, they must have become pretty well acquainted with this maze without any food reward or other obvious reinforcement. This sort of experiment has been tried many times in different laboratories, with several variations, intended to exclude minor reinforcements. On the whole the results have been positive, though puzzling problems of interpretation remain. In a very serious and thorough scrutiny of Tolman's theory, MacCorquodale and Meehl (1954) reach the conclusion that "it seems safe to say that the current state of the evidence is at least encouraging to the theorist oriented to some form of expectancy theory" (page 213). These authors, not belonging to Tolman's group nor predisposed to his theory, have attempted to work out a more precise formulation based on Tolman's relatively loose and programmatic statements; and Tolman (1955) welcomed some of their suggestions.

One objection sometimes made to Tolman's theory is that he does not show how *knowing* the environment generates actual motor behavior. Tolman met this objection in 1955 and 1959a by the concept of *performance vectors*. A vector has both direction and strength. A performance vector is directed toward a reward or away from a punishment. It is a tendency to approach food when one is hungry, with some expectancy of reaching the food; and the strength of this vector depends on the degree of hunger drive, the amount and palatability of the food incentive, and the strength of the expectancy. The expectancy (in a maze, for example, with food out of sight from the entrance) has been acquired in previous learning, but would not, according to the theory, generate motor behavior in the absence of present need (or drive) and the current incentive. Thus the performance vector toward entering and running a maze is made up of three positive factors:

> Drive
> Incentive
> Expectancy (probability) of finding food in the goal box

and of three corresponding negative factors:

> Disinclination to work, a negative *drive*
> Amount of work to be done, a negative *incentive*
> Expectancy (*probability*) of having to do this work

The former three factors combine multiplicatively, and the latter three combine multiplicatively. If any one of the positive factors is zero, the performance vector is zero, and no behavior will appear. Any one or all of the negative factors would reduce the effect of the positive factors and their product is subtracted from that of the positive factors. Despite this amendment to his theory Tolman's critics still argue that he has failed to solve the problem of the transition to behavior.

Tolman's positive and negative factors are really much like those previously adopted by Hull (1943, 1950) who, of all the behaviorists, probably developed the most elaborately conceived and thought-fully formulated theoretical system. Let us consider some of its features and then compare in more specific detail these two histori-cally important theories.

HULL'S THEORY OF LEARNING

The youthful interests of Clark Leonard Hull (1884–1952) might have led him to be a mathematician, a logician—they did, in fact, turn him first toward a career in mining engineering; but eventually they found their fulfillment in the young, developing science of psy-chology. He remained at the University of Wisconsin as a member of its faculty for a decade after receiving his doctoral degree; then, in 1929 he became a research professor at Yale where he remained until his death. He will be remembered always as one of America's most distinguished determiners of the course of learning theory and research.

Hull early made the acquaintance of both behaviorism and Gestalt psychology. He gave them a fair hearing but was not fully satisfied with either. "Personally, while inclined to be sympathetic with Watson's views concerning the futility of introspection and the gen-eral virtues of objectivity, I felt very uncertain about many of his dogmatic claims" (1952a, page 153). And of Koffka's presentation of Gestalt theory on a visit to the University of Wisconsin Hull wrote:

. . . his expository approach was strikingly negative. At least half of his time was spent in attacking Watson. . . . I came to the conclusion not that the Gestalt view was sound but rather that Watson had not made out as clear a case for behaviorism as the facts warranted. Instead of converting me to Gestalttheorie, the result was a belated conversion to a kind of neo-behaviorism —a behaviorism mainly concerned with the determination of the quantitative laws of behavior and their deductive systematization (1952a, page 154).

When the English language edition of Pavlov's Conditioned Reflexes appeared (1927), Hull found it very rich in suggestions for his own work.

Hull's early research included an important experiment on the learning of concepts, a purely objective study (1920). Without dis-paraging the introspective experiments of his predecessors in this field—which had yielded some interesting qualitative results—he pointed out that the "functional and quantitative" development of the subject still awaited the invention of suitable objective methods; and he showed how the Ebbinghaus memory methods could be adapted to the purpose. That Hull did not at the time consider his work behavioristic is shown by his incidental use of mentalistic

terms like *mental activity, focus of consciousness, memory images,*
and *unpleasantness.* But the emphasis was strongly on objective
methods and functional laws.

Hull's early work was directed also to the projection of an elaborate system of aptitude tests (1928) and to the development of practical statistical methods, including the invention of a machine for
computing correlations (1925). Also notable was his experimental
work on hypnosis and suggestibility (1933). Brother psychologists
were surprised to see him desert these early interests and devote his
energies to the working out of a theory of behavior based on Pavlov's
laws of conditioning.

Always the inventor, Hull was evidently fascinated by the problem of designing a theoretical system from which definite laws of
behavior could be logically deduced for submission to the test of
experiment. The conflicting schools meant to him that psychology
had not yet advanced to a truly scientific stage of development.
Various broad theories were being offered, but only in very sketchy
outline, none of the theorists having the patience to work out the
implications of a theory far enough to make sure whether it could
predict phenomena not yet observed. Good work was being done
by the experimentalists in the testing of particular hypotheses, but
what was lacking was a comprehensive system of concepts, a "hypothetico-deductive" system. Such a system, much like geometry,
starts with certain postulates and definitions which can be combined
to yield logical deductions. The deduced propositions must be as
logical as those of geometry, once the premises are granted. Of
course in an empirical science like psychology the deduced propositions must be put to test in the realm of observable facts. When the
predicted results are not verified the postulates and definitions must
be re-examined in the hope that some minor revisions will save the
system as a whole. The enterprise may run on for many years, paying its way as it goes by the mass of scientific knowledge gathered
by the experimenters who test the hypotheses derived from the system (1935).

Besides his objective of constructing a "system," Hull had another
goal in view. He wished to show that learning, motivation, and the
higher "mental processes" were truly biological in nature. He did
not doubt the reality of Tolman's "purpose" and "cognition," but he
tried to show that they were derived from simple conditioning
(1930). In one of his major books (1943, page 25) he wrote: "An
ideally adequate theory even of so-called purposive behavior ought
. . . to begin with colorless movement and mere receptive impulses
as such, and from these to build up step by step both adaptive and

maladaptive behavior," with the biological needs as the primary motivating factors.

Hull was especially intent upon deriving expectant or anticipatory behavior from Pavlov's conditioned reflex. He adopted the substitute-stimulus theory of conditioning which we have criticized on pages 78–79. One of his postulates (1943, page 178) was that any stimulus occurring "in close temporal contiguity" with a reinforced response becomes connected with that response so as to evoke it later (after enough repetitions of the combination). This statement says nothing about the *sequence* of the two stimuli. Actually, in Pavlov's experiments it appeared that the conditioned stimulus (CS) had to precede the unconditioned stimulus (US), or at least had to begin first for conditioning to succeed. Hull's statement also implies that the conditioned response (CR) is the same as the unconditioned response (UR), except that it is now attached to a new stimulus. We have seen that this is not the case (see page 79 in this book). The CR has the features of a preparatory response, not a *premature* response as Hull's statement would make it. If we grant the preparatory nature of the CR, we are coming closer to the concept of expectancy.

Genuinely premature responses are often observed in the rat's behavior as he learns the maze. If the last turn before reaching the food box is a turn to the left, a rat is prone to make a left turn prematurely wherever such a turn is possible. This is an error, not a preparatory reaction. The rat has made an *anticipatory goal reaction,* according to Hull. When, instead, the rat makes a *fractional anticipatory goal reaction* (r_G)—that is, if he turns his head slightly to the left or begins to move toward the left as he runs down the alley—his response suggests to the non-behavioristic observer that he is oriented toward the goal. Hull, however, did not interpret the r_G in Tolman's *cognitive* sense of "expectancy." He regarded these "antedating" reactions merely as fractions of the final response which have become conditioned to features of the situation in the course of learning. The r_G itself gives rise to other stimuli—*goal stimuli* (s_G)—which help to keep the rat on the right track as the runs are repeated. Hull referred to some *fractional antedating (anticipatory) goal reactions* as "pure stimulus acts," since they seemed only to serve the function of guiding and in a sense motivating the sequence of behavior, even the behavior we call "thought." After all, Hull was framing a theory to account for all behavior, not just that of an experimental animal in a learning situation. Pure stimulus acts, therefore, offered a convenient mechanism to account for internal directives: "Slow down"; "Buy birthday card"; "Divide by six"; "higher up"; "on the other hand"; "every other one"; etc., which would provide a behavioristic "set" determining the course of thought as well as of overt behavior. This will become more evident as we consider the behaviorist's $r_G \sim s_G$ combination further.

Stimuli resulting from the fractional antedating goal reaction also provide *secondary reinforcement*. Primary reinforcement results from the reduction of a drive: a response which has the effect of supplying food to a hungry animal is consequently reinforced. But other stimuli related to environmental and somatic experiences produced by the response may become signs that the goal object is near or on its way. These goal stimuli become secondary reinforcers which tend to confirm the response made at each stage of a performance. Such reinforcing stimuli will have something to do with determining the relative strength of possible alternative responses in a learning situation. Any behavior which brings the goal object to the learner quickly, or the learner quickly to the goal object, will tend to take precedence over behavior which produces slower results. In this case the learner will choose his alternatives in a preferred order, resorting to the less favored only when the more favored are blocked for some reason. Hull described such a system of related responses as a *habit-family hierarchy*. The habit-family hierarchy concept is an especially promising contribution in the sense that it invites study of the possible relationship between laboratory phenomena and problems of the psychological clinic such as regressive behavior or patterns of substitute response in the neurotic. The resemblance between Hull's habit-family hierarchy and Tolman's *belief-value matrix* (page 138 in this book) is apparent.

Hull's variables and his conception of their interaction changed from time to time in the evolution of his thinking, but within the space allowed here there is room for only a sketchy account of salient features and some of the problems of his theory that are relevant to other theories which we shall consider later.

DRIVE AND DRIVE STIMULI. Hull's drive concept, for example, holds considerable interest not only because of some paradoxical features but also because it has been closely related to the thinking that Spence, Miller, Mowrer, and other learning theorists have done on the subject. He conceived of drive, first, as an energizing or activating force growing out of a biological need. It has been established that a hungry rat will expend more energy running in an activity cage than one that is well-fed. Furthermore, if thirst is added to hunger, the total drive will be increased even in the absence of any incentive.

For Hull, reinforcement depended upon drive reduction. But

biologically hunger is not reduced, and appetite certainly not satiated, when food is taken into the mouth. Digestion is a lengthy process, and there would therefore be no reason to expect that a food pellet delivered into a tray could on its own account produce any reduction in the hunger drive level. If reduction occurs it must be accounted for in some other way. Hull gradually supplemented *drive* (D) with *drive stimuli* (S_D), and finally gave a major role to S_D as the reinforcing factor: it was food in the mouth, slaking of thirst in the throat, the immediate allaying of pain or discomfort that increased the tendency for the effective stimulus–response connection to be repeated.

But, according to Hull, through association with neutral stimuli, the rapid reduction in drive stimuli could produce two quite different secondary effects. Such associated stimulus traces could, on the one hand, develop the characteristics of a secondary drive, so contributing to the energizing effects of the primary drive. The same stimulus traces could, on the other hand, serve to provide secondary reinforcement by bringing about reduction of S_D. At first glance these two developments seem to be utterly irreconcilable; but let us see if they really are.

Suppose a hurt animal fleeing from tormentors finds safe refuge in a tree where his fright soon subsides. It is reasonable to assume that after one or more such experiences the immediate vicinity of the tree would have acquired some of the positive reinforcing character of the tree itself. On the other hand, the tree has been associated with the animal's pain, and with the fear that was the induced reaction to pain. It would be understandable, then, if the animal looked over his shoulder and hastened his steps when he came in sight of the tree and objects in its neighborhood. The paradox can be rather easily explained in cognitive terms: we might say that he has ambivalent feelings about the site of his harrowing experience; he has "memory images," he "knows," he has "expectancies" that on the one hand increase his agitation, on the other give him a sense of security. But the Hullian behaviorist is committed to explaining the observable state of affairs in terms of intervening variables that will interact with quantitative accuracy within the framework of CR theory. In a sense Hull's system of postulates and corollaries undertook to predict in such terms *what* response would occur in certain circumstances, to account for *why* it would occur, and to show *how* it would occur.

LEARNING VERSUS PERFORMANCE. If we return for a moment to the treed animal that has learned to respond to the tree both as an object of fear and an object of safety, the reasonable question occurs as to what will determine the selection of competing potential responses under any particular circumstances. Habit strength will clearly be one important consideration. But the fact that a certain response has been reinforced frequently by no means insures that it will occur in a given instance. The beleaguered cat may make a bee-line to his tree when the chase is hot, but on other occasions he may have other objectives. All the factors contributing to D may be operating to energize his behavior, but if the drive stimuli of hunger are especially prominent after several hours of fasting, his response will more likely be one related to food-foraging, and, of the various alternate paths to food, he may be expected to choose that which promises the best results (*incentive motivation* or K in Hull's terminology), and, other things being equal, that which will get him to the food with the least delay (J).

As a systematic study of behavior, therefore, Hull's theory, and others which have followed it, focus more on *performance* than on *learning*. E becomes an important intervening variable representing *reaction potential* (sometimes called also *excitatory potential*). H (or $_sH_R$, if we use the complete symbol) stands for an acquired *ability* to make the response R to the stimulus S; but E ($_sE_R$) is an active *readiness* to exercise that ability when the conditions are favorable. We have already seen what some of those conditions will be: habit strength, drive, and incentive. These along with stimulus intensity (V) Hull conceived to combine multiplicatively in the calculation of $_sE_R$:

$$_sE_R = D \times V \times K \times _sH_R$$

A possible response may be subject to inhibition, of which there are several kinds. Besides that which occurs in experimental extinction there is *reactive inhibition*, illustrated by readiness to stop doing what one has been doing for some time. I_R, which builds up gradually as an activity continues, is what we know as fatigue or boredom. *Conditioned inhibition* ($_sI_R$), or conditioned non-activity would be illustrated by the lingering disposition to avoid working in the presence of stimuli regularly associated with the stopping of work. The comfortable lounge chair or the pleasant, awninged terrace which has regularly served as a refuge after a period of fatigue or stress becomes a conditioned stimulus for the habit of resting. But perhaps it would be better to use an example from the animal laboratory: a rat that has built up a considerable amount of I_R in the course of running a maze will tend to develop the habit of *not* running as the reduction of the I_R effected by stopping reinforces his inactivity disposition. $_sI_R$ has proved itself a very useful construct in Hull's system for various reasons, one being that its *habit* character made it more adequate in accounting for relatively permanent, as against merely temporary, extinction of a CR. Reactive inhibition and conditioned inhibition may combine to make for total inhibition, or—in Hull's terminology—*aggregate inhibitory potential* (I_R). Obviously, the chance of the occurrence of a possible response will depend heavily upon these variables.

As we pointed out earlier (page 140), there is a close parallel between Tolman's and Hull's intervening variables. Both recognized the importance of Drive (Hull's D), Incentive (Hull's K), and the inhibitory factor of work (Hull's I_R). Although quite differently conceived, Tolman's Expectancy may be thought of as the counterpart of Hull's Habit strength in the sense that both are built up through reinforcement. Tolman's Performance Vector, as a resultant of the several positive and negative factors described on page 140, corresponds closely to Hull's Reaction Potential (E). In the absence of drive (D) or incentive (K), or with too much inhibition (I_R) even a well-established habit may not show up in performance.

At best, Hull could not expect his "conceptual machine" to operate with perfect precision. He had to allow for unpredictable variations in conditions. *Stimulus generalization* or *response generalization* would occur as the stimulus varied from time to time, or as the response had to be adapted to obstacles. The S–R bond, though still there, would be less dependable. Often two simultaneous stimuli would interfere with each other's operation. He had also to allow for oscillation of readiness (O) from moment to moment, and for individual differences in the operation of all the factors. So, though Hull could and did work out a diagram showing the interaction of all his factors, he did not make the diagram or formula strictly quantitative. According to Koch's logical analysis, Hull could not possibly have constructed a complete, well-knit, quantitative system. Such a system still lies far beyond the scope of psychological knowledge. "Hull's theoretical efforts as a whole [are] the most intensive and persistent attempt of any learning theorist to achieve rigor" (Koch, 1954, page 82); but he left many loose joints in the theoretical structure.

Besides many papers on special problems, Hull offered a brief "miniature" view of his system in 1937, a rigidly "mathematico-deductive" presentation in 1940, and a more complete and more generally intelligible treatment in 1943. The 1943 *Principles of Behavior* was accepted by psychologists as a definitive statement of Hull's psychology; but Hull sought to apply the abstract principles further to various forms of individual and social behavior. Of the two volumes projected, he was able, unfortunately, because of failing health, to finish the manuscript of only the first—*A Behavior System*—published in 1952.

As he progressed with this writing, however, he became increasingly determined to improve the abstract system itself. He felt it his duty to perfect its postulates and their quantitative relations. "I became convinced of the necessity for making these quantifications before proceeding any further. This turned out to be a very laborious process requiring several years of meticulous labor" (1952a, page 160). Much new experimentation was needed but could not be undertaken for lack of time. Instead he made use of such near-relevant experiments as could be found in the literature. The result was not wholly satisfactory, though some postulates were certainly improved. The revised postulates and corollaries were published in 1950 and 1951 as well as in the 1952 book.

Hull did not often call himself a behaviorist, believing perhaps that that name belonged to the adherents of Watson's very different system. Hull called his own concepts "objective" or "naturalistic," and endeavored to prune them of all traces of introspection and anthropomorphism. For Thorndike's "satisfaction," which seemed to imply a conscious state, Hull substituted "reduction of a need," or, in his later formulation, reduction of drive stimuli (our pages 142–43; 144–45). All admissible concepts, even though referring directly to "molar behavior," must refer ultimately to bodily processes. What we ordinarily call mental processes are doubtless composed of physicochemical processes.

> What, then, shall we say about consciousness? Is its existence denied? By no means. But to recognize the existence of a phenomenon is not the same thing as insisting upon its basic, i.e., logical priority. Instead of furnishing a means for the solution of problems, consciousness appears to be itself a problem needing solution (1937, page 30).

He challenged anyone to start with well-defined conscious processes and work out a logical system that would predict actual behavior in animals or men.

Whatever may be the merits of his system, Hull soon gathered around him at Yale a productive group of young investigators, a distinctive school of behaviorism. And this school ramified widely throughout the United States and elsewhere. Many graduate students found Hull's ideas a feasible lead to concrete experiments with tangible results. There were lots of theorems to test and lots of parameters to work out quantitatively. Hull's theory certainly generated a vast amount of experimental work. "It may well be said to have been the most influential of the theories between 1930 and 1950, judging from the experimental and theoretical studies engendered by it, whether in its defense, its amendment, or its refutation" (Hilgard, 1956, page 182). During the decade 1941–1950, a very large share of American experimental papers on learning and motivation made some reference to Hull, according to Spence's count (1952a). And as recently as 1957–1958, a review of current studies indicated "that if there is one influence that dominates most, but certainly not all, of the past year's work in the psychology of learning, it is the formulation of Clark Hull. But the strong influence Hull exerts on contemporary learning psychology results more from his failures than from his successes" (Kendler, 1959).

HULL'S SUCCESSORS

Following Hull's example, his numerous loyal students and "grand-students" have remained active and progressive, contributing to and working over some of Hull's postulates and theorems.

Neal Elgar Miller (born 1909; now professor at Yale) has investigated intensively the broad field of motivation, often in collaboration with John Dollard, a Yale colleague whose special province is social psychology and psychotherapy. (See their two books: Miller and Dollard, 1941; Dollard and Miller, 1950.)

In their study of imitative behavior Miller and Dollard come to the conclusion that this form of social behavior can be explained as the product of learning. Against the common belief that it is instinctive they offer evidence that neither rats nor children show any pronounced disposition to follow a leader unless they are rewarded for doing so; and when the response of *not* following the leader is rewarded, there develops a disposition to be non-imitative. As a behavior model of their concept of *matched-dependent behavior* they use the example of a small boy who, apparently without intending to imitate an older brother, happened to be running after him when the brother was on the way to greet their father. Both children received a candy. On the safe assumption that both of them had a desire (a *drive*) for candy their *response* was reinforced by the drive-reducing *reward*. The only difference was in the fourth fundamental element of the learning situation: the *cue* to which each was responding. For the older boy it was the sound of his father's footsteps; for the younger it was the sight of his brother running. Through consistent rewarding of such "matching" responses a secondary drive to imitate may develop, and the question has been raised as to what extent dependency and conformity traits of personality may be traced to the effects of such early experiences too often repeated. Life soon does force on the young learner, however, the need for some discrimination in the matter of when to match and when not to match, as a small boy learns when he discovers that he does not share his father's appreciation of a good cigar!

Miller and Dollard distinguish matched-dependent behavior from *copying*, the term by which they describe behavior gradually built up in imitation of a model, the cues for which are first provided by the model but later developed by the learner as mediating, self-directive stimuli associated with reinforced responses. The authors use voice training as an illustration. Skill in a sport, in the precise use of a new language—in contrast to tourist jargon which would belong more in the matched-dependent category—or in style of writing, painting, etc., may also be the result of copying. The process involved in such learning would be described as "acquired distinctiveness."

To the learner of a new language the nod of a listener's head or his air of comprehension may be the primary reinforcement which converts inner response-produced motor or auditory cues, or even feelings of satisfaction, into secondary reinforcing agents. But in the early stages there will be more responses that draw perplexed looks or smiles from the listener, and these come to provide internal cues which will discourage or inhibit repetition of the errors. Further cues, provided by the amount and direction of the discrepancy between the rewarded and the unrewarded behavior, will gradually help the learner to make a finer selection from among alternate responses. *Drive-induction* results from failure; *drive-reduction* results from success. Relative failure or success depends upon the learner's recognition, through information fed back from his own responses, of how nearly his pronunciation has approximated his internalized standard of the required sound. Miller describes such learning as "cybernetically guided," and points out the familial resemblance between his theory and that of O. H. Mowrer (pages 194–98). Although originally conceived to explain the learning that takes place through copying, the same principles have been used by Miller to acount for other behavior changes leading to adjustment (1959, pages 248–52).

One other form of "imitation," differentiated by Miller and Dollard as *same behavior,* is really not imitative at all when it represents a common response made independently by two or more people to the same situation. The crowds of people who converge upon the public transit system of a large city when it is time to go to work or to go home are not imitating one another. However, there are times when it is difficult to tease out these three elements which may be present in various degrees in certain kinds of mass or conformity behavior. We may ask ourselves the question: What draws the crowds to a sell-out theatrical performance? The authors recognize that the three principles they have defined do not necessarily work separately.

Miller begins his comprehensive survey of *Learnable Drives and Rewards* (1951) with the statement, "People are not born with a tendency to strive for money, for the discovery of scientific truths, or for the symbols of social status and security. Such symbols are learned during socialization." Animals, he goes on to show experimentally, acquire a fear of a place where they have received painful electric shocks. The shocks can be discontinued after a few such experiences, and still the animals will struggle to get out and avoid the (non-existent) shocks, and will, if possible, learn some means of getting out. Their fear or anxiety is diminished when they do get out, and thus the learned avoidance behavior is reinforced.

Dollard and Miller (1950), accepting both Hull's learning theory and a large share of Freud's psychoanalysis, have endeavored to bring the two together. They have tried to give a behavioristic account of the development (learning) of a neurosis and of its cure (unlearning—learning something better) in psychotherapy. Freud's "pleasure" from release of inner tension can be identified with Hull's "reinforcement" from drive reduction. The psychoanalyst's "ego strength" consists largely in the free and adequate use of language. The neurotic patient cannot talk freely about his conflicts which are largely unverbalized and unconscious. The psychotherapist permissively induces the patient to talk about relevant matters and accepts what the patient says, so reinforcing the patient's attempts. Inhibiting anxieties give way to rational talk and thought. Much more of interest could be cited from this book. (See also Miller, 1948a, 1948b.)

In an experiment often cited as reducing to behavioristic terms Freud's mechanism of *displacement* (page 267, this book), Miller placed a small rubber doll in a cage with rats conditioned to spar with each other to avoid an electric shock. After the response had been well established, one rat was removed, leaving the other alone with the rubber doll. In the group of rats so trained there was a pronounced tendency for the lone rat to strike at the doll after his original partner had been withdrawn, even though he had ignored the doll before that time (1948b). It seemed in effect that the doll was made a "scapegoat," although another explanation would be that the apparently aggressive behavior was merely a generalized response resorted to as a means of stopping the shock (Arnold, 1960, Vol. I, page 262).

Although Miller has not committed himself, as Hull and Spence have, to quantification in the working out of assumptions about the interaction of intervening variables, he has not hesitated to deal with problems which at a more sophisticated level of theory development would require mathematical validation. One such project carried on with his colleagues and students over a period of years has been a study of the relation of approach to avoidance behavior in conflict situations. What principles of drive interaction or central mechanisms can account for the vacillation of a rat—or a human—drawn on the one hand toward a goal, but halted midway, apparently by some counterforce?

According to Hull's and Spence's concept of a *gradient of reinforcement* the closer a positive goal is the stronger the drive to reach it becomes. By much the same reasoning it may be argued that the more imminent an unpleasant or *aversive* experience is the stronger will be the disposition to draw away from it. Miller describes these two tendencies respectively as the *Gradient of Approach* and the *Gradient of Avoidance*. By adding the assumption that the gradient of avoidance is steeper than the gradient of approach he offers a plausible account of why an animal that has been given an electric shock while receiving food in the goal-box will thereafter at some point in his progress toward the food "get cold feet." The gradient of avoidance has at that spot, presumably, caught up with and cut across the gradient of approach, so causing the rat to stop in his tracks or turn back.

Miller recognizes the complications that limit generalization of conclusions based on animal experiments to problems of human behavior; but conceding these limitations he still considers that the work done on his "miniature system" has yielded some deductions that can prove useful "first approximations" in the area of clinical psychology. From a series of such deductions he ventures some predictions about the probable nature of the displacements which may be expected under various degrees of conflict or in its absence. He suggests, as an example, that a girl whose sweetheart dies might be expected, when she has recovered from her grief, to prefer the suitor who most resembles him. Not so where there has been conflict: if the broken match results from a lovers' quarrel the girl will likely pick a substitute who is different, but only moderately different. But if the inhibiting avoidance response is very strong, the new choice will probably be a totally dissimilar sort of person.

Reasonable as such an application to human behavior would seem to be, the difficulties which stand in the way of validating it are obvious. (For a fuller account of approach-avoidance behavior in conflict situations, and the applications of the theory, see Miller, 1959, particularly pages 203–30.)

Miller made an important contribution to Hull's theory of reinforcement. Hull, striving to be perfectly objective, had identified reward or reinforcement with the reduction of a need. When a hungry animal takes the correct route to the food box and has a bite to eat, his need for food is reduced to some extent and thus his relevant $_sH_R$, his tendency to respond to the local stimuli by following the correct route, is strengthened. Unfortunately for this theory, food reinforcement has to follow the correct behavior within less than a minute in order to produce learning in the rat, whereas any genuine physiological reduction of need for food has to wait till the food is digested and absorbed into the blood stream. Some much quicker process of reinforcement is demanded by the combination of physiological and behavioral facts. Now, need for food generates stomach movements and stimuli (well known as hunger pangs), and there are also thirst stimuli, fatigue stimuli, pain stimuli from electricity, etc. Miller and Dollard (1941) suggested that stimuli generated by the different needs were the actual drives to action. "A drive is a strong stimulus which impels action. Any stimulus can become a drive if it is made strong enough" (1941, page 18). Reinforcement would accordingly be the reduction of a drive *stimulus.* Hull adopted these revised conceptions of drive and reinforcement, speaking of Primary Reinforcement as "the diminution in the receptor discharge characteristic of a need" (Hull, 1950, page 173).

When Miller speaks of drive-reduction as a reinforcement, then, he means reduction in intensity of the drive stimulus. Certainly *some* reinforcements are drive-reducing, but do *all* reinforcements belong in this category? Can we say that drive-reduction is the only mechanism of reward and reinforcement? Miller has become somewhat skeptical of this doctrine and inclined to subject it to rigorous and varied tests (1957). One experiment made use of saccharin, the sweet but unnutritious substance already known to serve as an effective reward for rats when taken by mouth. But when injected directly into the stomach it had no such effect. It reduced the sweet-hunger when taken by mouth but not when the mouth was by-passed. The effectiveness of oral reward was evidence against need-reduction, but not against drive-reduction.

Other experiments have been made, both in Miller's laboratory and elsewhere, by the use of minute electrodes permanently implanted in definite regions of a rat's or cat's brain (Bower and Miller, 1958; Olds, 1958; Miller, 1961b). The electrical stimulation at certain points of the interbrain is rewarding, since an animal will learn to press a bar that turns on the current. At some of these points a paradoxical dual result is obtained, since the animal learns to turn on the current by pressing one bar and then quickly turn it off by pressing another bar—as if the brain system stimulated "responded with pleasant sensations at first, which continue to increase until they become unbearable . . . contrary to the drive-reduction hypothesis" (Miller, 1957, page 1277). Without adopting this interpretation, Miller leaves the possibility open.

Such a revision of Hull's system, however serious it may seem, would not necessarily destroy the system as a whole. Like an automobile, Hull's system is an assembly of several subsystems, each of them designed to play a necessary part in the total performance. Hull labeled the subsystems H, D, K, I, etc., and labored valiantly to design each of them so that it would do what was required of it. If some subsystem—the carburetor, for example, or the learning system H—has to be redesigned, the whole assembly may need only minor readjustments.

Miller maintains with his students a heavy schedule of research on a wide assortment of topics of old and recent vintage. A study of the effects of sodium amytol and chlorpromazine, tranquilizing drugs, is reported along with another on the problem of whether or not fear experience becomes consolidated unless the subject is quickly re-exposed to the fear-inducing situation minus the traumatic event. On these questions and that of the possibility of increasing resistance to stress by gradual habituation, his findings are somewhat surprising but still tentative (1961a). They will need, and will undoubtedly be given, further study.

In his Presidential address to the 1961 Convention of the American Psychological Association he reviewed a series of ingenious new studies in which hunger and thirst were stimulated in a number of ways including direct electrical methods of stimulating brain centers, intravenous saline injections, brain stimulation by hormones and drugs applied through cannulae devised for direct "feeding" of a brain area, etc. The inconsistencies in the animal's behavior in response to the hunger or thirst induced through these several methods led Miller to the conclusion that:

We no longer view the brain as merely an enormously complicated telephone switchboard which is passive unless excited from without. The brain is an active organ which exerts considerable control over its own sensory input. The brain is a device for sorting, processing and analyzing information. The brain contains sense organs which respond to states of the internal environment, such as osmotic pressure, temperature and many others. The brain is a gland which secretes chemical messengers, and it also responds to such messengers, as well as to various types of feedback, both central and peripheral (1961b, page 753).

Incompatible results on rats' behavior as a consequence of injections of the appetite-reducing drug dexedrine—less interest in eating, but more interest in bar-pressing which produced hunger-satisfying self-stimulation of brain centers—leave him still in doubt about the drive-reduction hypothesis.

At the 1963 Nebraska Symposium on Motivation Miller surveyed current learning theory and the problems which specific theories present or at best leave unsolved. Although not yet quite ready to abandon the drive-reduction hypothesis, he has proposed a tentative alternative which he believes incorporates salvageable elements of other theories without their defects. The product is a theory in which reinforcement of the classical conditioning variety, rather than drive-reduction, becomes the primary factor in establishing S–R connections. He arrives at this change in position by reinterpreting the increased vigor of response a shocked animal will show once he discovers the device that turns off the shock. This vigor could be, Miller reasons, the effect of an energizing "go mechanism" within the nervous system, automatically brought into action by the sudden relief from pain. As the result of its activity not only present cues and responses but also traces of immediately preceding events will be intensified.

In other words, Miller now conceives of reinforcement as occurring whenever appropriate centers are energized either by an unconditioned stimulus, as in classical conditioning, or by the "go mechanism" which serves a similar function for instrumental responses. The exact nature of the "go mechanism" he leaves undefined, other than to suggest in passing that it might have some connection with the reticular formation, or have something of the character of an electrical brain potential, or be somehow related to those brain areas which have been found upon electrical stimulation to have a "rewarding" effect. The stimuli which might evoke the "go mechanism" are presumably as numerous as those which would be included under the empirical law of effect (page 73, this book): besides pain reduction Miller lists specifically as examples the immediate and delayed effects of eating, the unblocking of inhibitions in conflict situations, and "removal of a discrepancy between an intention and an achievement" (1963, page 95). However, since the "go mechanism" operates in the same manner as an unconditioned response, it becomes itself conditioned to the cues and responses which are present when it is evoked. By the same reasoning, responses such as turns into blind alleys, which provide no occasion for release of the energizing effect, will be gradually extinguished by repeated absence of the intensified trace, which would be, in effect, the unconditioned stimulus.

Miller notes the close resemblance of his "go mechanism" to Thorndike's central "confirming reaction" (pages 73–74, this book), but points out that intensification of current activities, rather than strengthening of a connection, is the primary role of the "go mechanism." He presents also an instructive brief comparison of his theory with others bearing some significant similarity as well as significant differences. Although parts of his account will take on fuller meaning when the reader has completed several other sections in the pages which follow, the value of Miller's summary justifies introducing some excerpts at this point:

The present hypothesis has obvious resemblances to Mowrer [1960a, 1960b] except for the crucial fact that, like the original analysis of copying [Miller and Dollard, 1941], it does *not* rule out connections between cues and motor responses, and therefore does have a way of eliciting immediate responses. . . .

The present formulation also resembles . . . some of the recent emphasis by Spence [1956] on the incentive value of the anticipatory goal response, except that it does *not* limit itself to incentives based on the conditioning of peripheral consummatory responses, and does specifically include an incentive based on the termination of noxious stimulation. While Spence, who has primarily used the empirical law of effect, prudently has not clearly made up his mind, the present formulation differs from what seems to be Spence's present position in that it clearly and definitely does not assume different processes for appetitive and aversive learning, or for the acquisition of habit strength and incentive strength.

While the present formulation does use association by contiguity, it differs from Guthrie [1952] in using the booster or "go mechanism" to explain the obvious selectivity of learning, instead of relying on stimulus change to protect certain elements . . . from being unlearned. . . .

The present formulation is similar . . . to Tolman's and different from most other CR formulations in that it does not place all of its emphasis on peripheral mediating responses, but allows for the possibility of central perceptual, imaged or other processes utilizing the myriad potential interconnections in the brain. It is different from Tolman in that it conceives of these central processes as obeying the same fundamental laws as overt responses, and hence refers to them as cue-producing "responses."

The central responses, which have been a part of my thinking for a long time, obviously resemble Hebb's [1949] cell assemblies and phase sequences, but in the "go mechanism" and experimental extinction, the present formulation has selective factors which are essential to prevent Hebb's cell assemblies and phase sequences from continuing to grow from association by contiguity until they elicit one grand convulsion (1963, pages 97–98).

Kenneth W. Spence (born 1907; now professor at the State University of Iowa) is another loyal but independent pupil of Clark Hull. He studied with Hull at Yale and later corresponded actively with him from Iowa. He has developed a very productive laboratory and has steered many of his students into research on problems related to Hull's system. He sets forth his own theory in an important book, *Behavior Theory and Conditioning* (1956), in which he says,

> The approach to be taken in the present work is basically similar to that of Hull. . . . However there were a number of matters on which Hull and I never did agree. . . . Hull was not in the least afraid of being wrong, and he held to the point of view that one should proceed with the best hypothesis available at the moment. Experimentation, he believed, would provide the necessary corrective for any mistakes. In contrast I have always been inclined to keep my theorizing much more closely tied to the available empirical data" (pages 54, 56).

Hull was prone to embellish his abstract intervening variables with some rather speculative neurophysiology; so he got himself involved, as Spence pointed out, in wholly irrelevant controversies. Hull's need-reduction theory of reinforcement was a bit of superfluous physiology from which Spence did not succeed wholly in prying him loose.

On the whole the two theorists made an effective team. The fundamental strategy on which they agreed was to start with conditioning, both Pavlovian and instrumental (see our pages 83–85), to work out a theory for these single-response forms of learned behavior, and then to extend this conditioning theory, if possible, to cover discrimination and choice responses. Having discovered in conditioning experiments how to control the factors H, D, K, etc., for each *separate* response, one can figure out which alternative has the stronger response tendency and will therefore be chosen. If all the other factors are held constant, the H factor will determine the choice; the alternative receiving the more numerous reinforcements will gain the advantage.

A striking application of this method in Spence's early research on discrimination learning (1936, 1937) dealt a critical blow at what had seemed a strong Gestalt argument against behavioristic learning theory. Consider what might happen if an animal that has regularly found food behind a door marked with a 3-inch square B, and never behind another marked with a 2-inch square A, is confronted with a new combination in which the old, positive B remains, but in which the alternate door is now marked with a 4-inch square C. Where will he now look for his food? According to the

view that he has been conditioned to the absolute stimulus properties of B, that door should be his choice; but if he is responding to
the pattern as a whole and has a direct perception of relationship, as
the gestaltists believe, we could expect him to choose the larger
square C. That this seems to be what does frequently happen has
been used by the gestaltists against S–R theory (pages 233–34, this
book.) Spence, however, demonstrated another way to account for
how the choice would fall in any particular experiment. He assumed there would be a gradient of excitation on either side of the
reinforced B-trace, and a gradient of inhibition on either side of the
unreinforced A-trace. Spence showed that the probability of the
selection of the smaller or the larger stimulus could be calculated on
the basis of the overlapping of these two curves. In other words,
whether the larger or the smaller square in our example will be
chosen would depend on the relative strength of the interacting excitation and inhibition effects upon each stimulus *separately*.

Some experimental results have supported Spence's ingenious
proposal; some have not. Apparently a number of factors, including the age of the learner, the stage of language development, the
distinctiveness of the stimuli, and the amount of discrimination
training on the initial pair, have something to do with whether or not
transposition will occur when the new combination is presented.
Spence has agreed that the circumstances may determine whether,
in a given instance, discrimination will be made on the basis of
absolute or relational cues (1952b).

The S–R theory of anticipation—the theory of a "fractional anticipatory goal reaction" which we mentioned on page 143—was proposed by Hull as early as 1931, but was later put to a new use by
Spence (1956, pages 126, 134). Spence uses r_G and s_G to explain
the development of the incentive motivation, K. The food or other
incentive in the goal box is invisible at the maze entrance; but after
it has been found once or twice, the animal's behavior at the entrance indicates anticipation in some form. An anticipatory *image*
would be unbehavioristic, but an anticipatory muscular, glandular,
or emotional activity is quite acceptable. Such secondary reinforcers would operate not only at the goal site but also, with reduced effect, at distances removed from the goal. The scent of food
at a distance can produce excitement; the loss of the scent, frustration. Spence's K would include, then, along with the primary
reinforcing goal object, an indefinite number of secondary reinforcing effects covered under the symbol $r_G \sim s_G$. So conceived, K contributes substantially to the energizing of behavior, a role which
Hull had originally assigned primarily to D.

Spence played a part, along with some non-Hullian investigators, in leading Hull to attribute the level of performance more largely to current motivation and less largely to habit strength—more largely, that is, to factors such as D and K and less largely to H. Hull's final revised formula for habit strength made it depend entirely on the *number* of previous reinforcements and not on their amount or delay, i.e., not on the factors K and J. These motivating factors are held to affect performance (E) but not learning (H). Hull's final formula for E (page 146, this book) shows D, K, and H among the variables that are combined multiplicatively in the calculation of reaction potential, but Spence has been testing a modified formula in which D and K are added:

$$E = H \times (D + K)$$

Hilgard presents a clear demonstration of how, in a specific problem, this change in the theory may give weight to K rather than D as the determinant of reaction potential (1956, pages 418–19).

Spence has also deviated from Hull's position on reinforcement. He seems to accept it, somewhat dubiously, as a factor in classical aversive conditioning, as when the eye-blink becomes conditioned to a buzzer which has been regularly followed by a puff of air directed against the eyeball. But the habit strength of appetitive instrumental behavior such as food-seeking he considers a function of the number of times the response occurs in the specific situation. (For a good illustration of the bearings of this departure from Hull's thinking see Spence, 1958, pages 89–90.) He admits that this "two-factor" theory of motivation is tentative and subject to change if his continuing research turns up data that suggest a better hypothesis. This qualification applies to all of Spence's thinking. He has never shared Hull's dedication to the drive-reduction hypothesis, and has expressed indifference to the "Why?" of reinforcement, just continuing to plan his studies on the basis of the empirical law of effect. In one of his often quoted Silliman Lectures (1956) he clarifies his position on instrumental learning by conceding that reinforcement may play a part in strengthening reaction potential rather than the learning of an association.

Spence has taken great interest in Hull's concept of *general drive* and has designed many ingenious experiments for putting this concept to the test. According to Hull, any specific drive, such as hunger, thirst, or fear, feeds into the general drive, and this general drive can activate any learned performance which the occasion demands. Pavlov had noticed a temperamental difference among his dogs, some being excitable and others quiet and inhibitable. People differ similarly, and the Janet Taylor Manifest Anxiety Scale, developed in the Iowa laboratory (1953), was used to pick out from a college population those students presumably high or low in general drive. High subjects should be more easily startled and more quickly conditioned to such responses as the eye-wink from a threatened puff of air or the hand-withdrawal from a threatened electric shock. These predictions were readily verified. Suppose, however, that two competing responses are about equally associated with the same stimulus, as two nouns may be about equally pre-associated with the same adjective in paired-associates learning—presumably the high-drive individuals would be more hampered by conflict. Predictions were made for a variety of conditions with fair but not complete success. Spence's conclusion is: "I suspect that, as yet, we have hardly begun to uncover all of the complexities that underlie even such simple learning behavior as is involved in these situations. I also believe that progress . . . will be greatly facilitated if psychologists will but learn to make more effective use of theories" (1956, pages 233–34).

Edwin Ray Guthrie (1886–1960) was entirely independent of both the Hull and the Tolman subschools of behaviorism. He was independent of Watson as well. "My prejudice in favor of a behavioristic attack," he reports, "dates from . . . 1910 [when] I heard Professor E. A. Singer deliver an address . . . on 'Mind as an Observable Object.' That address remains the most stirring event of my academic life. Singer's contention that a relatively objective method could be applied to the scientific treatment of mind revived an interest in psychology" (1952, page vii). Guthrie was influenced also by his colleague Stevenson Smith with whom he collaborated in writing a behavioristic textbook (our page 125). He may be called the most radical of all associationists. He rejects Thorndike's Law of Effect, and he even rejects the old Law of Frequency. If a stimulus once elicits a response, this S–R association is established —like the closing of an electric switch. If the same stimulus—or stimulus pattern—recurs, it will again elicit the same response.

How then does Guthrie circumvent frequency? Many repetitions are certainly required to establish some associations firmly. The trouble is that the same combination of stimuli does not recur. Even when the external situation is the same, the internal stimuli from the viscera and the proprioceptive stimuli feeding back into the brain from the postural and other active muscles are likely to be different. When we are introduced to a person and say his name while looking at him, the name is attached to the whole combination of stimuli received at that moment. So many of these stimuli are changed when we next see this person that it is no wonder we do not recall the name. The first time a few elementary associations were formed, the next time a few more, and so on until the total linkage from person to name is comprehensive enough to function in all circumstances. (Of course there are ways of cutting this process short.)

How does Guthrie circumvent effect or reinforcement? The "empirical law of effect" seems practically certain, though the theories differ on its dynamics, Thorndike appealing to "satisfaction," Hull to "need-reduction" or reduction of the "drive stimulus." Guthrie does not credit the reward or reinforcement with any power to strengthen an association, for in his view an association is already established in full strength by the mere making of a certain R to a certain S. All the reward can do is to terminate the trial-and-error process, so leaving the successful (and therefore final) response established and undisturbed. As long as the cat is in the cage trying to get out to the bit of fish, she makes a series of varied responses, each association being fully formed but quickly broken by the making of another response to the same situation; but the successful response lets the cat out of the cage and so remains the established response to the cage situation.

Guthrie's rule for predicting and controlling behavior is basically simple. Since a person is most likely to do what he last did in the same circumstances, you should reproduce the circumstances if you wish to secure the same response and build up the habit; but if you wish to break the habit you should change the circumstances in some significant respect. A little girl went through a regular routine every schoolday at noontime. She threw her coat on the vestibule floor, rushed into the dining room and at her mother's command went back to the vestibule and hung up her coat. She was keeping this chain of associations firm and unbroken. What to do? At the psychologist's advice, the mother required the girl to put on her coat again, go out to the street, come back in, and hang up her coat *before* entering the dining room.

Guthrie's interest in psychotherapy is shown by his book on *The Psychology of Human Conflict* (1938). Often, even typically, the individual is assailed by more than one pattern of stimuli at the same time, the different patterns calling for incompatible responses. The most normal result is for one pattern to dominate and totally inhibit the other. "Conflict is a failure of inhibition" (page 27), and gives rise to emotional tension and ineffective behavior. While giving much credit to "the brilliant and original mind of Sigmund Freud," Guthrie found more substantial instruction in the work of Pierre Janet. Janet had in fact welcomed behaviorism and had developed a practical and clinical objective psychology which he called the psychology of conduct (Janet, 1930).

Burrhus Frederic Skinner (born 1904; now professor at Harvard), although much younger than Hull or Tolman, was their active contemporary in the new birth of behaviorism which occurred in the early 1930's. He invented the "Skinner box" for the study of "operant conditioning," as already described on pages 83–85.

In his *Case History in Scientific Method* (1956) Skinner has told how he came to be the kind of behaviorist he is. Entering graduate school as a biologist, he read Watson and Pavlov very seriously. He went to work in an exploratory way, "looking for lawful processes in the behavior of the intact organism. . . . I had the clue from Pavlov: control your conditions and you will see order." He sampled several bits of rat behavior, designing several pieces of ingenious apparatus for controlling the conditions. He saw how to exclude extraneous stimuli and how to eliminate superfluous portions of his animal's performance, how to standardize reinforcements, how to get results with only intermittent reinforcements, and how to have his animal's responses recorded automatically in a cumulative curve. In all this work, culminating in his *Behavior of Organisms*, 1938, he found no use for treatises on scientific method.

> I never faced a Problem which was more than the eternal problem of finding order. I never attacked a problem by constructing a Hypothesis. I never deduced Theorems or submitted them to Experimental Check. So far as I can see, I had no preconceived Model of behavior—certainly not a physiological or mentalistic one and, I believe, not a conceptual one (1956, page 227).

There were some "principles," however, which Skinner found useful in his search for order: "When you run onto something interesting, drop everything else and study it"; "Some ways of doing research are easier than others"; make use of your good and even your bad luck; the best thing you find may not be what you were looking for. The most exciting thing Skinner found "by accident" was the orderly process of operant extinction (page 225); it was pure behavior, uncomplicated by the physiology of eating, and he was led to the discovery the first time the food magazine of his contrived apparatus jammed.

A little later in his career he experimented with large groups of rats, using averages and tests of significance on the data he obtained, but he found this approach unsatisfactory because of its lack of flexibility. Averages often eliminate troublesome variability; but adequate control of conditions will do the same and yield a smooth curve even for the single case. Control of the individual animal is essential to the trainer who is preparing for exhibition or for some wartime application. Skinner found himself "face to face with the engineering problem of the animal trainer. . . . Manipulation of environmental conditions alone made possible a wholly unexpected practical control. Behavior could be shaped up according to specifications and maintained indefinitely almost at will" (1956, page 228; see also Breland and Breland, 1951).

Skinner now calls his particular brand of behaviorism by a name which he and his pupils have incorporated in the title of their new *Journal of the Experimental Analysis of Behavior* (1958). It is intended to foster adequate experimental handling of the individual case—adequate behavior technology both in animal training and in human education. Besides the practical results to be expected:

> A second consequence of an improved technology is the effect upon behavior theory. As I have pointed out elsewhere, it is the function of learning theory to create an imaginary world of law and order and thus to console us for the disorder we observe in behavior itself. . . . When we have achieved a practical control over the organism, theories of behavior lose their point. . . . When behavior shows order and consistency, we are much less likely to be concerned with physiological or mentalistic causes (1938, page 230).

Now there are theories and theories. What we may call "mature theories" would be acceptable to Skinner, except that behavior science is not yet mature enough to supply the numerous empirical laws which a mature theory would integrate into a system. "Juvenile theories" offer hasty explanations of striking peculiarities of behavior, such as the extinction of a well-learned act when the customary reward is discontinued. "It is due to loss of interest," says one who favors mentalistic explanations. "It is due to brain fatigue," says one who prefers physiology. Both of these theories try to escape from the realm of observed behavior and to take refuge in a world of "events taking place somewhere else, at some other level of observation, described in different terms" (Skinner, 1950, page 193). Such theories do not help the experimenter who is trying to *control* behavior.

Intervening variables are small-scale theories of the "juvenile" type. Although he tolerated them as convenient in his pioneering 1938 book, Skinner argued strongly against them in his more comprehensive *Science and Human Behavior* (1953a):

> . . . the variables which are immediately available for scientific analysis . . . lie outside the organism, in its immediate environment and in its environmental history. . . . We have a causal chain consisting of three links: (1) an operation performed upon the organism from without—for example, water deprivation; (2) an inner condition—for example, physiological . . . thirst; and (3) a kind of behavior—for example, drinking. . . . The second link is

useless in the control of behavior unless we can manipulate it. . . . We usually set up the second link through the first . . . we must always go back beyond the second link for prediction and control (pages 31–35).

In short, the behavioral engineer cannot manipulate the inner processes directly but has to go back to the environmental variables which he can control; so he has a chance to control behavior and discover the laws of behavioral dependence on the environment.

In the further development of his animal work Skinner has made much use of a different organism. The pigeon is a hard-working organism that performs at a rapid rate and does not have to take time out to chew its food rewards. An enormous body of data, largely in the form of performance curves, is presented in the book by Ferster and Skinner (1957), and some of the main findings were reported by Skinner (1953b). The pigeon is maintained considerably under weight so that it is always ready to eat. His preliminary learning process goes through three stages: (1) he becomes conditioned (emotionally adjusted) to the work cage; (2) he learns to find his food in a tray just behind a hole in one wall of the cage; (3) he learns to peck at a disk higher up on the wall. The disk is an electric-circuit key; it operates a machine which brings the food tray within reach and supplies reinforcement. The food tray remains in reach for four seconds at a time, so that several bits of food constitute a single reinforcement. At first each single peck gets a reinforcement; later various "schedules" of reinforcement may be introduced. A *fixed interval* schedule presents the food tray at the first peck after the lapse of a certain time, for example, five minutes following the last reinforcement. This would give the bird four seconds every five minutes to gorge himself. A *fixed ratio* schedule presents the tray after a certain number of pecks on the disk, say once for every fifty pecks. Besides the fixed interval or fixed ratio scales, *variable interval* or *variable ratio* schedules may be used; or schedules may be alternated.

The timing of reinforcement has always been recognized as a factor of considerable importance in conditioning. Apart from any neural process which may play a part in facilitating or inhibiting learning, there is the quite practical consideration which Skinner points out: while a rat is trying to find the food at the end of the maze, or while the seal has to wait for his fish after he has bounced the ball off his nose, some new activity may get under way which diverts the effect of the reinforcement to itself. Skinner has taken the precaution, therefore, of providing an immediate conditioned reinforcement to the pigeon's pecking at the disk: at that very instant, even before he can pull his head away, a sound announces that the tray is coming. Even a slight departure from this timing produces changes in the curve.

There was good reason, then, to investigate the effects of the complex interval and ratio scales. In *Schedules of Reinforcement* (1957), Ferster and Skinner describe as their primary purpose ". . . to evaluate the extent to which the organism's own behavior enters into the determination of its subsequent behavior" (page 3). They found, for example, that when a pigeon has become accustomed to receiving food at five-minute intervals, he will pause after each reinforcement and more or less gradually resume a moderate pecking rate. His eating activity produces stimuli which apparently become a cue that food is not coming soon. The introduction of the variable interval schedule at this stage can make the slowdown disappear and keep the pecking rate steady for long periods of time. "Both the circuit and the behavior, then, contribute to the reinforcing contingencies. It follows that the effect of any circuit depends upon the behavior the organism brings to it. Some complex schedules can be studied only by taking the organism through a series of simpler schedules into the final performance" (1958a, page 96).

This procedure corresponds to the "shaping" or *approximation conditioning* by which Skinner gradually secures from his subject the response he wishes him to learn. At first it may be necessary to reinforce behavior that has little resemblance to the desired response: the rat may be rewarded when he turns toward the lever, then when he advances in its direction, etc. Eventually, he goes to work on the lever itself, and with less delay than if he had been allowed to discover its function purely by chance. But neither in the process of shaping behavior nor in that of controlling the animal's rate of behavior through scheduling can the experimenter expect results without careful grading of the succession of performances or of conditions.

In the usual study of problem solving, for example, the experimenter constructs a complex set of contingencies and simply waits for it to take hold. This is no test of whether the organism can adjust to these contingencies with a performance which would be called a solution. . . . It is dangerous to assert that an organism of a given species or age *cannot* solve a given problem. As the result of careful scheduling, pigeons, rats, and monkeys have done things during the past five years which members of their species have never done before. It is not that their forebears were incapable of such behavior; nature had simply never arranged effective sequences of schedules (1958a, page 96).

To the pigeon it apparently becomes a matter of importance how long and how hard he must work before he collects his reward: when he is repeatedly subjected to mixed and alternating schedules, he may peck faster on the same variable interval schedule to get to one alternate than to get to another. Industrial production curves early reflected the effect of piece-rate pay plans as motivating devices. In fact, Skinner and others who have become interested in this new technology of studying the "lawful processes" of behavior have not only discovered interesting parallels between the effects of schedules and schedule combinations on animals and on man, but have also found promising areas of application of the method.

What conditions will alter the expected appearance of the cumulative curve? A beginning has already been made in investigations of the effects of tranquilizers, of cerebral lesions, of psychoses (Skinner, 1957a). Obviously the field of education offers a rich opportunity for engineering human behavior through effective reinforcement schedules. The policy of "Wait until your father hears about this"; or the test paper returned at the end of the semester cannot be expected to contribute much to the learning process. Even the constant watchfulness of the teacher is not sufficient to prevent the contamination of well-meant reinforcement by irrelevant stimuli present with or immediately following the right response. Such reasoning turned Skinner's attention toward the possibility of developing mechanical teaching devices which could incorporate the principles of behavior-engineering brought to light in his research program. He has described the rationale and construction of his teaching machines (1954, 1958b); and those concerned with education or personnel training are watching with interest the reports of their effectiveness.

Finally, but not least of all, we must recognize the patriotic contribution of "pigeons in a Pelican" through whose systematic responses missiles could be guided to a target. The account of "Project Pelican" is a most persuasive argument for Skinner's thesis that adequate behavior technology will result in lawful behavior (1960).

A notable extension of Skinner's work into the human field is his *Verbal Behavior*, published in 1957 after more than twenty years of preparation. Its aim is to bring speaking and writing of all kinds and levels into the realm of the conditioned operant, where they can be subjected to experimental analysis and brought under engineering control. The book is not packed with experiments, however, since "the basic facts to be analyzed are well known to every educated person" (page 11). The data are found in the nursery, in everyday conversation, in lectures and speeches and in many varieties of literature, from poetry to mathematics.

Primary verbal behavior requires the interaction of two persons, a speaker and a listener. The speaker emits some form of verbal response to a stimulus, and the listener supplies reinforcement, non-reinforcement, or even punishment for what the speaker has said. So the listener increases or decreases the probability that the speaker will later emit that same response to the same or a similar stimulus. The listener's behavior may not be verbal at all; it is only the speaker's operants that are to be considered.

There are two basic kinds of verbal response, the *mand* and the *tact*. The mand is typically the speaker's response to an internal or aversive stimulus such as hunger or pain, and it calls on the listener for attention or help. The listener can supply reinforcement by paying attention or giving help. A tact is the speaker's response to an external stimulus—typically to "a particular object or event or property of an object or event" (page 81). By differential reinforcement from the listener, or more broadly from the "verbal community" in which the language behavior occurs, the child learns to say the names of persons, objects, colors, games, etc., and so is able to talk about the environment. If his pronunciation is at first inaccurate or incomplete, the listener, acting as teacher, can have the child say a word or phrase after her, "echoically," with gradual insistence on closer approximation before supplying reinforcement in the shape of an "OK." Similar devices are used in teaching a child to read.

With the growth of a speaking or reading vocabulary, secondary factors come into play that affect the choice of words. One word suggests another if they have been associated in familiar phrases, jingles, pairs of synonyms or antonyms. So a good deal of *intraverbal behavior* is generated. Again, given the words needed to make a report, the speaker has to put them together in grammatical forms approved by the community, and he may have to qualify his statement by inserting "perhaps" or "certainly," "yesterday" or "tomorrow," "always" or "never," "if," "although," or other relational words. All these, as well as punctuation, come under the head of what Skinner calls *autoclitic* behavior (verbal behavior dependent on other, more fundamental verbal behavior; pages 315, 355).

Having thus worked out fundamental methods by which the verbal community controls the verbal behavior of the individual, Skinner goes on to show how various higher-level "uses of language" are brought into his system. He analyzes literary composition and editing, the communication of information, scientific research and reporting, and thinking. As to thinking, no doubt it often goes on as subvocal verbal behavior, but there is no point in stressing the "subvocal," for one often thinks aloud when alone. And though it is tempting to identify thought entirely with verbal behavior, there is also much non-verbal thinking, and the only comprehensive statement is that "thought is simply *behavior*—verbal or nonverbal, covert or overt" (page 449).

Skinner seems inclined to relax somewhat the traditional behavioristic taboo against introspection. So he says:

> In a sense verbal behavior which cannot be observed by others is not properly part of our field. It is tempting to avoid the problems it raises by confining ourselves to observable events, letting anyone extend the analysis to his own covert behavior who wishes to do so. But there would then be certain embarrassing gaps in our account. . . . When someone solves a problem in "mental arithmetic," the initial statement of the problem and the final overt answer can often be related only by inferring covert events (page 434).

Covert speech cannot only be "inferred"; it can often be reported by the silent thinker and accepted as genuine by the investigator. The prospective speaker serves as his own preliminary audience and edits his speech in advance. He casts about for the right words, and tries out on himself alternative ways of beginning his speech. Many other examples of "self-editing" are given (pages 369–417).

Skinner's *Verbal Behavior* was, however, intended as a contribution, not to methodological behaviorism, but to metaphysical behaviorism (see our pages 115–17). As he reports on page 456, it took its start back in 1934 when he tried to convert the philosopher, Alfred North Whitehead, to behaviorism and was challenged to show how human speech could be fitted into the behaviorist's deterministic scheme of things. Skinner took the challenge very seriously and believes he has made a good case for concluding that verbal behavior, like all other operant behavior, is determined by stimuli and reinforcements.

> Whenever some feature of the environment—past or present—is shown to have an effect upon human conduct, the fancied contribution of the individual himself is reduced. The program of a radical behaviorism left no originating control inside the skin. . . . No scientific advance has ever actually damaged man's position in the world. It has merely characterized it in a different way. . . . If we eventually give a plausible account of human behavior as part of a lawfully determined system, man's power will increase even more rapidly. Men will never become originating centers of control, because their behavior will itself be controlled, but their role as mediators may be extended without limit (pages 459–60).

In short, the way will be opened for the "human engineer" in education and other human affairs. Of course, the engineer cannot claim to be more than a "mediator," but he may solace himself with the thought that nowhere in nature, inside the skin or outside, can we discover any "originating center of control."

Like other behaviorists, Skinner unnecessarily limits the scope of his psychology by refusing to consider perceptual factors. The child hears a great deal of talk before he begins to talk himself. Someone opens the outside door and calls "Kitty, Kitty," and the cat comes running in; so the sequence is set up for him to associate the name with the object. The proof that many words, phrases, and simple grammatical forms are first learned by listening comes out when he begins to speak: new words appear, sometimes a dozen a day, without any direct prompting; they have been picked up over the preceding days and weeks in the course of listening to people talk. His listening vocabulary always remains greater than his speaking vocabulary, even as, later, his reading vocabulary will far exceed the number of words he will spontaneously use in writing.

7

Behaviorism: The Nature of the Mediating Process

A history of psychology could be written on the theme of the small dash that connects stimulus with response in the "S-R" symbol. So far no one has thought seriously of replacing the dash with a question mark, but that device might well be used as a shorthand description of the puzzle which some of those engaged in research on perception, motivation, and learning have been trying to solve. Instead of a question mark an O has often been inserted between the S and the R as a reminder that the stimulus and the response must be related to the functioning of a living *organism*. Tolman's "intervening variables" gave some features to the blank "O," and Hull's symbolic monograms—$_sH_R$, $_sE_R$, $_sI_R$, etc.—spelled out the nature of each hypothetical construct implied. Much has been written about the different types of intervening functions implied in various theories (Hilgard, 1956; MacCorquodale and Meehl, 1948). Hull described his own variables as "molar" in the sense that they did not reduce the causal explanation of the association to physiological processes. Drive, habit strength, inhibition, oscillation, etc., are all treated as psychological phenomena, even though it would be possible to reduce these concepts one step further to a "molecular" physiological explanation—a temptation which, according to Spence, Hull sometimes found hard to resist.

In the present chapter we shall carry on the story of current behaviorism by describing characteristic theories representing quite different views as to what is the most promising approach to the problems of perception, motivation, and learning. We shall begin with the contributions of a psychologist who has been eminently identified with the physiological approach: Karl Lashley.

PHYSIOLOGICAL EXPLANATIONS OF BEHAVIOR

KARL S. LASHLEY. Physiological hypotheses are not uncommonly offered to bridge the gap between stimulus and response. A common assumption in the past has been that cortical sensory and motor areas are linked through the "switchboard" of the cortical association areas. There was some speculation also about the respective roles of the various intricately related subcortical nuclei, and through methods of tracing tracts, surgical extirpation, and pathological data, probable functions were gradually assigned to some of these. But without precision techniques and adequate controls, findings based on these methods were not infrequently upset by later research. Efforts to find the neural correlates of language behavior, of memory, of motor habits, and of emotion met with repeated failure. The brilliant studies of Karl S. Lashley (1898–1958) could be described in a sense as frustrating if only positive gains in knowledge about the nervous system are to be counted. But his contribution has been inestimable in the fact that he uprooted the oversimplified chain-reflex assumption of the functioning of the higher centers.

Lashley, who was a pupil of John B. Watson, declared himself a behaviorist in an early theoretical paper (1923), but he could better be classified as a neuropsychologist because of the nature of his research and the independence of his thinking. He was opposed to subjectivism or the use of introspection to study "a universe of nonmaterial things" such as sensations and images; but he believed that trustworthy introspective data could be expressed in objective terms and so have a place in behavioristic psychology.

Lashley devoted many years to an untiring investigation of the brain in relation to learning and other psychological functions. Localization of functions in the cerebral cortex had been a major enterprise of the physiologists in the latter part of the nineteenth century, and they had shown that each of the senses is connected to a definite cortical area. Besides these sensory areas, a motor area was identified. But all these areas, sensory and motor combined, made up but a small proportion of the cortex in man. Plenty of cortex remained for the higher functions. If these were to be localized, it was time for psychologists to unite their forces with the physiologists.

Credit for initiating this neuropsychological line of investigation belongs to Shepard Ivory Franz (1874–1933), a pupil of Cattell and a fellow-student of Thorndike. Franz devised a combination of Thorndike's methods of studying animal learning and the physiologists' methods of studying localization. For example, to discover whether the cat's frontal lobes were involved in learning to escape from a puzzle box, he had the animal learn the trick and then removed its frontal lobes. After a period to allow for general recovery he then tested the animal for retention of the trick. If there was no retention he gave the animal a chance to learn the trick again. Unless it had been very thoroughly learned the ability to do the trick disappeared with the loss of the frontal lobes, but the animal's capacity to relearn it did not; and the *well-learned* trick survived the operation. This was only one of Franz's important and mystifying discoveries (1902, 1907, and other papers).

Lashley collaborated with Franz in this type of study, and in 1917 they applied the method to that favorite laboratory animal, the white rat. This is a convenient animal for such studies, but its brain is, of course, much less complicated than man's. As Lashley continued his investigations he reached the baffling conclusion that although the loss of any considerable amount of the cortex slows a rat's maze-learning, it seems to make little difference to the rat what particular part of the cortex is removed and what part is left for him to learn with. He apparently learns the maze as well with one part as with another. The greater the amount of cortex removed, the more is he hampered in his learning. Easy tricks are learned rather quickly with only half of the cortex left, but difficult tricks require a larger mass of cortex. Lashley summarized his findings under two principles (1929):

1. *The principle of equipotentiality:* One part of the cortex is potentially the same as another in the capacity to learn a maze or other performance. There are some exceptions: visual perception of a shape or pattern can be accomplished only with the occipital (rear) area, though within that area the parts are largely equipotential.

2. *The principle of mass action:* The more cortex left, the better the learning.

Lashley himself was surprised by these results and checked them over very carefully. He began this work with the expectation of finding definite sensorimotor connections, definite paths through the cortex, laid down by heredity for instinctive reactions, established by conditioning for learned reactions. But the whole tendency of his results was against accepting the simple reflex arc as the basic unit in brain function. Superimposing the conditioned reflex on the native reflex did not provide the key to learned behavior. It became obvious that the brain must function in some other way not yet clearly discerned.

Regarding the change in his own views Lashley had this to say (1931, page 14):

> I began life as an ardent advocate of muscle-twitch psychology. I became glib in formulating all problems of psychology in terms of stimulus-response and in explaining all things as conditioned reflexes. . . . I embarked enthusiastically upon a program of experiments to prove the adequacy of the motor-chain theory of integration. And the result is as though I had maliciously planned an atttack upon the whole system. . . . The conditioned reflex turned out not to be a reflex, not the simple basic key to the learning problem. . . . In order that the concept of stimulus–response should have any scientific value it must convey a notion of how a particular stimulus elicits a particular response and no other. . . . When viewed in relation to the problems of neurology, the nature of the stimulus and of the response is intrinsically such as to preclude the theory of simple point-to-point connection in reflexes.

The last sentence refers to such facts as these: (1) in looking repeatedly at the same object, you change your fixation point and so bring into play different rods and cones and different nerve fibers leading to the brain, and yet the object appears the same and gets the same response; (2) the motor response, too, varies in the exact muscles used and still produces the same result. The cat that has learned to turn the door button of a puzzle box gets somewhat different stimuli and makes somewhat different responses, neurologically, from one trial to the next, and still her behavior remains essentially the same. The brain, therefore, must do something more than merely switch incoming nerve currents over into outgoing nerves. Watson in his desire not to make a fetish of the brain had allowed it only this switching function, and the early conception of the conditioned response had envisaged specific sensorimotor connections established in the brain. Lashley's own experiments and his critical survey of other results led him to view the brain as having a more active role. "This evidence seems to favor the older doctrine of imagery and to throw us back upon the concept of activity maintained within the central nervous system for an understanding of serial habits and the mechanisms of thinking" (1934, pages 482–83). Nor could Watson's extremely negative view of instinct and heredity be maintained (1947).

No doubt Lashley's views and findings came as a shock to many behaviorists, who liked the reflex and the conditioned reflex as furnishing a simple scheme of behavior and banishing "mystery." Yet it must be said that behaviorism is not bound to any single hypothesis or explanation so as to be seriously shaken when that hypothesis is displaced by one that is more adequate. Concepts must be allowed to change provided they remain true to the spirit and attitude of behaviorism. Lashley's concepts were dictated in part by the requirements of neurophysiology.

In one of his papers Lashley described the behavior of rats after removal of some of their cerebral cortex, in comparison with the behavior of normal rats, in the "latch box" (1935, pages 31–35).

The behavior of animals with cerebral lesions in the latch box situation suggests two more general defects which may have contributed to their poor records . . . a general reduction in sensitivity . . . and . . . exploratory activity . . . [and] a lack of aggressiveness. . . . In addition to these differences between normal and cerebral operated cases a third may be significant. The normal rat rather quickly modifies his reactions to the latch so that, whereas his original movement in springing it may have been a random stumbling, his subsequent movements are directly adapted to operating it with a minimum of effort. . . . Such behavior suggests that the normal rat . . . comes to identify the movable latch as a distinct object connected with the opening of the door. . . . Whatever the explanation of behavior of this character, animals with extensive cerebral lesions show a limitation in acquiring it. Their behavior is more stereotyped in that they tend to repeat the movements which were first successful. . . . The observations may be summarized by the statement that the rats with extensive cerebral lesions are less observing, have less initiative, and show less insight into the relations of latch and door than do normal animals.

In previous discussions of the effects of cerebral lesions I have striven to avoid such psychological interpretations of behavior. They do not give us any understanding of the cerebral mechanisms involved and tend to obscure the issues by presenting a pseudoscientific explanation in terms of empathy. . . . I therefore present the above psychological interpretations, not because they have any explanatory value, but in order to make the dynamic concepts of cerebral function sound less strange by identifying them with terms which, though scientifically meaningless, are familiar.

In observing animal behavior we tend by "empathy" to put ourselves in the animal's place, even while avoiding anthropomorphism as far as possible, and we say that the animal seems to perceive objects and relations. But we cannot apply such concepts directly to brain processes. The concept of "connections" can readily be applied to the brain, which shows in its microscopic structure innumerable nerve fibers connecting one part of the cortex with another. But Lashley's work indicates that connections do not tell the whole story. In reviewing his whole long series of brain studies, he was able to conclude:

It is not possible to demonstrate the isolated localization of a memory trace anywhere within the nervous system. . . . The so-called associative areas are not storehouses for specific memories. They seem to be concerned with modes of organization and with general facilitation or maintenance of the level of vigilance (1950, page 478).

How far Lashley had moved away by that time from the position of his early mentor, Watson, is nowhere more evident than in his article one year later on "The Problem of Serial Order in Behavior." The hierarchical organization of language seemed to him to present "in a most striking form the integrative functions that are character-istic of the cerebral cortex" (1951, page 113). The chain-reflex the-ory could not adequately explain the different well-functioning chains that are composed of the same motor elements. The words "right" and "tire" afford a simple example. The sequence of words in a sentence, or of sentences in a paragraph would be illustrations at a higher level of organization. A skilled translator will directly convey the meaning of a passage in one language through another, using the idiom and sentence structure of the second, with a speed that belies the hypothesis that he is chaining together isolated re-flexes as he speaks. So in other "fluent" sequences of behavior: the *prestissimo* performance of a virtuoso executing a brilliant cadenza could never take place if each separate finger movement depended upon the one directly preceding it. Even with the minimal reaction time physiologically possible, nothing resembling such speed of ac-tion could occur. Anokhin's theory described on page 106 gives evi-dence of his recognition of this problem of the "engineering" of complex, goal-directed behavior sequences. We shall find it again a focus of consideration in a thought-provoking volume by Miller, Galanter, and Pribram (1960) soon to be discussed (pages 206–8).

THE CENTRAL NERVOUS SYSTEM AND THE CONCEPTUAL NERVOUS SYSTEM. Wilder Penfield and his associates, in the mapping of brain areas which is preliminary to brain surgery, have received reports of startlingly vivid "flashbacks" from their conscious patients who seem generally to agree, however, that these experiences aroused by the surgical "stimulator" do not have the quality of a normal mem-ory experience, but seem rather a brief reliving of an isolated instant of the past. Sometimes the stimulator evokes merely a false sense of familiarity similar to the normal experience known as *déjà vu;* or the patient may report, on the contrary, that everything seems strange or absurd, or very far away. Both these "experimental" and "interpretive" phenomena have occurred in the exploration of the temporal lobe in particular, and a very small area of the adjoining parietal lobe. In commenting on these data Penfield points out that it would be a mistake to conclude that the memory is recorded or stored at the exact point in the gray matter to which the electrode is applied. The local effect of the electric current at that immediate spot would, in fact, probably interfere with the production of the memory were that spot its fixed and permanent repository. "But a stream of neuronal impulses might well leave the area of electrical application and be conducted along nerve fibers to *some more distant area* where the ganglionic record could thus be activated in a normal physiological manner" (Penfield and Roberts, 1959, page 49; italics added).

Uncertainty about the functioning of the nervous system has lent force to the argument of those who, like Skinner (1938), have protested against "explaining" behavior in terms of a "conceptual nervous system" (CNS):

> The use of terms with neural references when the observations upon which they are based are behavioral is misleading. An entirely erroneous conception of the actual state of knowledge is set up. An outstanding example is the systematic arrangement of data given by Pavlov. The subtitle of his *Conditioned Reflexes* is "An Investigation of the Physiological Activity of the Cerebral Cortex," but no direct observations of the cortex are reported. The data given are quite obviously concerned with the behavior of reasonably intact dogs, and the only nervous system of which he speaks is the conceptual one. . . . This is a legitimate procedure so long as the laws established are not turned to "explain" the very observations upon which they are based . . . (page 427).

Since Skinner wrote this passage, knowledge about the functioning of the nervous system has advanced with unprecedented speed. Much of the impetus for the research that is being done has come from the pioneer study of Moruzzi and Magoun (1949) which demonstrated that electrical stimulation of the reticular formation, an intricate network of neurons in the brain stem, has the power of activating the cortex. The EEG promptly reflects its effect. If an animal is registering the slow-wave pattern characteristic of light sleep reticular stimulation transforms it into the fast waves typical of alertness and activity. The same effect could be produced by stimulation through the usual sensory channels. The inference, which has at least been partly confirmed by later studies, is that a function of the reticular formation is to act as an arousal system working along with the traditional spinothalamic tracts which carry sensory impulses to the several projection areas of the cortex. With the development of more refined techniques this original finding has been amended, and research has been extended to investigation of the function of the limbic system comprising a number of nuclei in the midline area separating the cerebral hemispheres. These structures, including the hippocampus, the septal and amygdaloid areas, mamillary bodies, fornix, etc., are connected not only with one another, but with the sensory and motor areas of the cortex as well; and since they have been generally found to be related to affective experience, they may be thought of as playing a significant part in the motivation of behavior (Arnold, 1960; Brady, 1962). Support for this view is offered in the startling results reported in 1954 by Olds and Milner that rats trained to press a lever which sets up a current in electrodes chronically implanted in the limbic area would continue to stimulate themselves in this way without any other reinforcement.

Much of the progress that has been made toward a better understanding of the functioning of the nervous system has been due to the development of ingenious techniques which make possible precise stimulation of finely localized points in the brain tissue and continuous exact recording of the simultaneous electrical, glandular, and muscular reactions which occur. Microelectrodes, insulated except at the very tip, may be permanently implanted in an otherwise intact animal brain; or micropipettes may be used for introducing into an exactly defined area chemical solutions—psychoactive or tranquilizing drugs, hormones, alcohol, etc. By such procedures the differential effects of the stimulation on other brain centers or on peripheral responses can be established. A number of other devices and techniques might be cited.

Although much credit for developing new methods and initiating research in neuropsychology goes to American investigators, the movement has been international. The importance of the contribution of Russian physiologists can be estimated from the sampling of studies earlier described (Chapter 4). The seven-hundred-page report of the Montevideo symposium on *Brain Mechanisms and Learning* (Delafresnaye, 1961) provides not only a valuable fund of information about ongoing research, but also gratifying evidence of communication among scientists of various disciplines and various national backgrounds on problems that have great significance to all of us.

Yet even with more adequate knowledge of the nervous system a long-standing issue will remain as to the extent to which psychology should draw upon physiology for its explanations. No one would deny the close relationship between the two disciplines, nor the satisfaction of establishing reliable "mind–body" correlates. A great many psychologists, including some of the most distinguished ones referred to in this book, have had intensive training in physiology, but many of them take the firm position that *psychological* facts must be explained at the *psychological* level. In quite another connection, paradoxically, the Soviet physiologist, Anokhin, provides what might be called the seed of an argument for this viewpoint. He points out (1961b, pages 901–2) that the same cortical cell may connect with a muscle that will take part in operations as diverse as pulling a trigger, writing a love letter, or turning on a motor. Knowing all about the nerve–muscle connections, or the fine details of sense-functioning and feedback, as well as the intricate central adjustments that make any one of these responses physically possible, would still not give us a psychological understanding of the act itself. There are two points involved here: one is the question of whether we have really accounted for behavior at the molar level when we reduce it to the molecular level; the other is whether we have fulfilled our obligation as psychologists by moving into the realm of physiology in search of an explanation. In discussing the question elsewhere (Woodworth, 1958), the author has presented at greater length his reasons for approaching the study of behavior at the molar level. A rather similar view has been expressed by W. C. H. Prentice (1961) in urging a reconsideration of all the relevant facts of motivation. He says:

> I have no objection to physiology. In fact, I look forward to the day when we will have a physiological account of every behavioral fact or relationship, but the behavioral facts and relationships must come first. And we must not delay longer in finding out what kinds of psychological situation produce what kinds of behavior, writing first approximations to laws about the structure of such situations, and then beginning to seek the biological substrate (page 511).

DONALD O. HEBB.   The Canadian psychologist, Donald O. Hebb (born 1904; now professor at McGill University) does not fit neatly into any one of the traditional schools, as we can see from his appraisal of the behaviorist "revolution" in psychology:

> My own introduction to the subject was a deep immersion in Freud, Pavlov, and Köhler . . . before taking on my present protective coloring of pseudo-behaviorism. It was no accident of birth or involuntary exposure to the ideas of the American Revolution in psychology that leads me to the conclusion that it was a tremendous achievement. . . . In the psychological revolution, the second phase is just now getting under way. The first banished thought, imagery, volition, attention, and other such seditious notions. . . . it is the task of the second phase to bring them back, brainwashed as necessary. In other words: my thesis . . . is that an outstanding contribution to psychology was made in the establishment of a thoroughgoing behavioristic mode of thinking. But this has been achieved, too frequently, only by excluding the chief problem of human behavior. The second contribution must be to establish an equally thoroughgoing behavioristics of the thought process (1960, pages 735, 736).

Tolman, Hull, Lashley, and other behaviorists have in their different ways, as we have seen, faced the "central" problems that a rigid S–R model of behavior, in its avoidance of "mentalism," does have difficulty in handling. The uncompromising theorist, who in

his zeal for scientific purity, attempts to cleanse psychology of phenomenological "blemishes" such as set, attitude, expectancy, purpose, attention—all "unobservables," yet tremendously important in
determining what the organism will respond to and which of many
possible responses it will select—does indeed throw the baby out
with the bath water!

In *The Organization of Behavior* (1949) Hebb has brought back
into focus and suggested a hypothetical central structure for such
neglected features of behavior within the framework of a rather daring theory of neural functioning. Lashley's data on equipotentiality
(page 172, this book) had apparently destroyed the hope of explaining learning in terms of fixed and invariable neural connections.
Köhler, the gestaltist, as we shall see (page 220), had rejected any
form of neural "switchboard theory," proposing instead an explanation of perceptual and learning phenomena in terms of changing
field effects in the cortex, created by electrical currents arising from
nerve impulses (Köhler, 1951, 1958a). Hebb's own research in
neurophysiology had shown that substantial masses of an adult's
cortex could be removed without appreciably lowering the IQ. One
such patient, after removal of a pre-frontal lobe, had an IQ of 160,
was later graduated with honors from college, and continued to do
credit to himself in medical school (1949, pages 289–91). On the
other hand a small area of damage to an infant's brain might be followed by serious mental retardation in later years. Any hypothesis
which offered even a tentatively consistent explanation of such facts
as well as of the operation of set, expectancy, attention, insight, motivation, and emotion, would not be likely to be overlooked, and
Hebb's volume certainly was not.

Although in the years since its publication advances in knowledge
about the reticular formation and related systems have made it necessary to amend features of his theory (1955, 1959, 1963), it continues
to play a significant part in our thinking on many neuropsychological problems; and, as we shall see, it has opened new ways of thinking about old problems such as maturation and learning, and even
psychopathological behavior (1949). Hebb himself has been quick
to concede that the new brain physiology has raised serious questions
about the validity of some of his speculations, but he has recently
reaffirmed his faith in the idea that it will be some theory of the same
class that will ultimately provide the answers needed to understand
perception and thought. He has also offered a rebuttal of criticisms
of his view that perceptions are to some extent dependent upon
learning, and that primary learning is slower in organisms with relatively large association areas than in those with more primitive

brains (1963). Let us consider his early arguments on these issues.

ARE PERCEPTIONS READY-MADE? THE ROLE OF LEARNING. The surprising tenacity of old learning even in the face of disease or massive damage to the cortex was Hebb's point of departure in theorizing about neural organization. As we have seen, the facts ruled out the traditional explanation in terms of fixed neural chains, linked by lowered synaptic resistance, along which impulses passed from sensory to motor centers through the association areas. Yet Hebb was unwilling to accept Köhler's alternate proposal of electrical fields.

He took issue, too, with the Gestalt view that form perception is an instantaneous process. Were this true, the image of a square formation of unrelated letters should be just as easily "read" backward as forward, which is not the case (Woodworth, 1938, page 42). But more dramatic evidence against the idea had been provided by von Senden's studies of congenitally blind patients for whom vision became possible with the removal of cataracts in their mature years (1932). These took weeks to build up the ability to make immediate visual identifications of objects or faces already familiar and recognizable through the sense of touch. Riesen (1947) and others offered evidence on the relatively slow development of effective vision in animals reared in darkness, when they are at last introduced to a normal environment. All this suggested to Hebb that some organization of the association areas through contact with the environment is necessary before perceptual forms become available for ready use. Once developed, such patterns can be used, as the gestaltists conceived them to operate, in closure, pregnance, and insightful solutions to problems (pages 221–22; 232–33).

His speculations on this "primary" learning led Hebb to another interesting observation and a corollary hypothesis. The dark-reared rat may acquire the ability for visual discrimination in a fifteen-minute period; the chimpanzee takes several days to make the adjustment even under strong motivation; man needs weeks to develop the effective use of his new sensory capacity. Once the primary learning has been achieved, of course, man far surpasses the animals in the levels of learning he can reach; but how can his early disadvantage be explained? Hebb does not believe that rate of maturation is the answer—at least, not the whole of it. He suggests that part of the explanation lies in the relative extent of the association areas of the cortex in proportion to the sensory areas: the A/S ratio.

The sensory projection areas are directly under environmental control; and if they are large, with respect to the association areas, and so project a large number of fibers into the association cortex, their control should be quickly established. If the sensory projection is small, association cortex large, the control will take longer; the period of "primary learning," that is, will be long (1949, page 124).

We might stop here to consider the complications involved in "establishing a first environmental control over the association areas." The symbol S in the formula S–R is deceiving in that it suggests that we are responding repeatedly to the same stimulus; but a moment's thought will show that it is actually a kaleidoscopic assortment of experiences. His mother's face, the bottle she brings in to him, the family dog—all of the common objects he will eventually come to identify—will be seen first by the infant in a variety of perspectives and illuminations which make quite understandable his slow progress in object recognition. Just the same will be true of the once-blind man who receives the gift of sight. These fragments of object-vision must somehow all come to stand for the same object before it can be identified without hesitation.

Hebb grants that primitive figure-ground differentiation is unlearned, but he holds that any specific figure will be seen (or perceived through other senses) only as a result of cumulative learning which builds up a *non-sensory* organization of responses made to parts of the figure. The problem, then, is to translate such learning into neurological form. How can a succession of experiences result in some lasting neural organization which will be flexible enough at the same time to allow an organism to identify an object and even distinguish it from a similar object when it is only partly present to the senses, or when part of the neural pattern has been destroyed by disease or surgery?

THE CELL ASSEMBLY AND PHASE SEQUENCE. Hebb's answer was a theory which at first glance seems to have some kinship with the old theory of neurons linked by lowered synaptic resistance. But the *cell assembly* as he conceived it was a build-up of a multiloop system of neurons which over a period of time, through proximity to one another and occasional simultaneous excitation, become linked in a complex and widespread pattern. The advantage of this intricate design over the traditional chain is that it would make possible greater "reverberation" of the nerve impulse once it is aroused by a stimulus. In fact, even after stimulation has ended the impulse may move from one loop to another, providing a greater chance for some immediate learning through association of the loops involved; and with repeated stimulation of this kind structural changes at the synapses would assure more permanent learning. Hebb suggested the structural change might be in the nature of the growth of synaptic knobs of which many are found in the unmyelinized areas of the axons lying close to the cell bodies and dendrites of other neurons.

A second effect of the complex, intercommunicating loop system would be that excitation of any one loop might be the result of an outside stimulus, or it might be the result of arousal through the activity of another loop in the system. The external stimulation would occur in the presence of an object or some partial cue or symbol representing the object; but the activity so initiated could lead to associated ideas or images quite unrelated to the present stimulus, as when, for example, a stranger's eyes or smile bring to mind a friend's face.

A cell assembly would be built up slowly, and a different one would be developed for each part of an object that is newly perceived. Hebb calls a series of cell assemblies which have gradually become associated through experiencing the whole object a *phase sequence*. He describes the "primary learning" of a triangle to illustrate this process. As the retina is being stimulated by one line or angle, the muscles tend to move the eyes on toward the next, at which point another cell assembly gets under way. While this is happening reverberation continues through the first neural loops, so increasing the chances for association of these two experiences with each other as well as with the accompanying eye movements. In the same way the third line or angle becomes part of the organization, so that eventually the sight of angle a or of angles a, b tends to facilitate the seeing of the whole figure, t. In the course of the process neurons will be added and neurons will be dropped out of the organization, but because of the complexity of the system the effect of these specific alterations may be negligible. Once a fairly stable core pattern has been established, activation of part of the circuit can reinstate the whole; and if the core pattern remains intact, damage to less essential cells in the complex loop system may not make any obvious difference in perception or the related response.

The full implications of Hebb's 1949 theory cannot be included here with full justice to its broad coverage. Attention, expectancy, conceptual learning, and quick, mature, "insightful" learning were among the many phenomena which came within the purview of his hypothesis. We shall have more to say later about Hebb's development of the theme in the direction of motivation theory, emotions, and sensory deprivation; but first let us consider the status of the cell assembly concept as its creator viewed it fourteen years after its introduction to psychology.

Phase sequences represent an integration of cell assemblies. But are there conditions under which the integration may break down and reveal the elements of its composition? We might suppose that circuits linked by many synaptic knobs would be insured against such fragmentation; but structural growth of the neural connections alone does not insure the endurance or the priority of any sequence of neural action. Without regular environmental renewal through sensory stimulation—"aliment," to borrow Piaget's term—an assembly or a phase sequence will undergo disorganization. Most of us have made the interesting discovery that staring at a common word like "is," or repeating it aloud again and again, will drain from it all its meaning and familiarity. The results of this kind of intensive, unvarying stimulation have been studied systematically by the use of contact lenses to which geometrical forms have been affixed so that, except for possible slippage, they will constantly stimulate the same retinal points even when the wearer turns his eyes (Pritchard, 1961).

Hebb has studied the nature of the disappearance and reappearance of parts of several types of figure under these conditions, and has come to this conclusion:

> The data . . . strongly indicate that something like the postulated cell as-sembly exists and plays a major role in perception. The data also allow us to make some reasonable inferences concerning locus, separating for example field effects in the visual cortex from the activity of the closed systems that also function. At the same time the data contradict the theory as it stands, showing clearly that it needs modification or extension if it is to comprehend the facts (1963, page 22).

Line figures, such as triangles and squares, accommodatingly broke up into fragments that suggested support for the cell assembly hypothesis; but the changes that took place in solid-color forms, parallel lines, and meaningless irregular designs seemed to indicate that field forces, closure, or the tendency to replace a missing part with a "better" figure—all Gestalt principles—were operating alone, or along with some other principle.

LEARNING, MOTIVATION, AND EMOTIONS. Hebb applied his concept of interacting central neural organizations to phenomena of learning and motivation as well as to perception. Mature learning occurs once complex, enduring patterns have been established. In contrast to early learning it may take place very quickly, involving as it does some interaction of the already organized systems. System A, for instance, may share loops with system C even though these two may never have functioned together in their entirety. This overlap makes it possible for A to arouse or "facilitate" C, or vice versa (1949, page 132). Some interaction of this sort could provide the neural basis for concept formation, which amounts to the identification of some common factor distinguishing a group of otherwise different objects. Or it suggests an explanation for striking metaphors that seem to catch subtle similarities between two events. Hebb notes that the effect of inter-system facilitation need not be consciously apparent or articulately definable by the one who experiences it. It may be quite "unconscious," or the subject may find himself at a loss for words to account for what has happened to make him suddenly change his approach to a problem that had a moment before defied solution. In other terms, inter-system facilitation could account for the sharp drop in learning curves which has been described as, or ascribed to, "insight."

Motivation is also related to these constantly active and interactive phase sequences, and at any instant the character of the motivation depends on what patterns are dominant.

It then follows that the experimenter who wants an animal to learn some particular thing must achieve some control of the phase sequence. . . . Putting an animal into a particular situation does not determine what particular conceptual activity will result. Therefore, it cannot determine that a facilitation will be established between the conceptual activities the experimenter is interested in. When the experimenter takes further steps to limit the variety of conceptual activity that will occur in an animal, he sets up a *motivation*. The term motivation then refers (1) to the existence of an organized phase sequence, (2) to its direction or content, and (3) to its persistence in a given direction, or stability of content (Hebb, 1949, page 181).

Hebb's theory predicates that the "timing" or "firing" of any cell in an assembly must be consistent with that of the other cells. Conditions which change the timing would result in the elimination of cells from the assembly and its disorganization if enough cells drop out. Metabolic changes related to fatigue and hunger, for instance, could produce such a disruptive effect. Hebb uses hunger as one of his illustrations of how the mechanism of learning is involved in the development of the "motivating" effects of a "biological need." In infancy, before any significant learning has taken place, hunger stimuli simply have the effect of disrupting ongoing brain activity and producing restlessness and irritability. After the child has accumulated enough experience through feeding to have developed interacting sequences that relate the sight, smell, taste of food, and eating responses with hunger pangs, "hunger" is no longer limited to a biological need. The problem of salted nuts is a case in point. It is wise to place the salted nuts beyond easy arm's reach of the guest who is trying to reduce, for one ill-advised sampling can be disastrous to the diet! "Hunger has increased: but how?" Hebb asks. His answer is that hunger is not a precise biological state nor specific sensations from the stomach, but rather "an organized neural activity that can be aroused in several ways." Savory odors, attractively served food, the initial taste of food itself can all contribute to "appetite"—and appetite to Hebb is hunger. Once aroused, it may have a disorganizing effect even upon the adult if food is lacking or the means of getting to it unknown.

By 1955 the advances in neurophysiology had convinced Hebb that the general arousal function of the reticular formation must be recognized as an important factor in the organization of cortical activity. Cues are provided by impulses from the direct sensory pathways to the appropriate cortical areas, so making learning possible. Moderate activation through the reticular formation will allow the organism to use such information adaptively, but more intense arousal will produce emotional disturbance. The effect of the general arousal or drive can therefore be described by an inverted U-curve: too little activation, or too much, will work against effective learning. On the other hand a moderate fear or frustration will have a positive incentive value (1955).

Hebb explains the psychological experiences of indifference, interest, pleasure, and emotional disorganization as effects of the congruence or relative degree of discrepancy between a new phase sequence and an expected, familiar sequence. When the excitations set in motion by a present event match the expectations associated with a customary phase sequence, the present event is accepted as a matter-of-fact affair. With constant repetition of that experience there will be a breakdown rather than a reinforcement of that sequence, and boredom or inattention will result. Some variety in the component cell assemblies is necessary for maintaining alertness and interest. Some novelties or small surprises are interesting, even pleasant. Hebb defines pleasure as "fundamentally a directed *growth* or *development in cerebral organization*" (1949, page 232). Those things are pleasant which contribute to this development or to the elimination of a condition which prevents development. We can think of many illustrations of this principle. One long-recognized in music theory is the gradual acceptance of musical intervals or sequences once considered dissonant, and their later rejection as commonplace after long repetition. Wit also depends for its success on some divergence from the obvious and the expected. Even in the problems of daily life, sparkle is added by a new feature—not too different, but different enough to be challenging.

Apparently this characteristic is not limited to man. Studies by Hebb and Mahut (1955) and Berlyne (1955) have shown what effect novelty has upon animals. In the Hebb and Mahut experiment hungry rats preferred to take the *longer* path of a maze to the food box as long as it continued to offer novel features. Berlyne's animals showed renewed interest when some novel, inedible object was introduced into a place they had given up exploring.

But too great a discrepancy between the expected and the new stimulus will have a different effect. When there is no relationship at all, the unfamiliar may be treated as irrelevant and ignored. But when the familiar is presented with some radical change it may create excitement and even panic. Hebb has reported that models of human or ape heads terrified chimpanzees. Adult animals were even more distressed than the youngsters, presumably because the young ones had not yet developed assemblies and sequences with which these bizarre experiences would conflict. In terms of Hebb's reticular hypothesis such experiences would be expected to touch off the arousal function of that system, and the degree of arousal would determine how effectively the disrupted phase sequences could be reorganized into adaptive patterns (new learning). If the inverted U-curve describes the relationship between motivation and learning, moderate arousal should produce optimal results.

STUDIES OF EFFECTS OF ENVIRONMENTAL IMPOVERISHMENT. Much important research has been stimulated by Hebb's emphasis on the threat that sensory deficit or a restricted environment presents to normal development. The dogs which he and his colleagues raised under such conditions took prizes, but not for intelligence or social responsiveness (1958; Hebb and Thompson, 1954). Harlow's studies of the immediate and long-range effects of sensory and emotional deprivation on young monkeys have added further details to the picture of abnormal social development (1962). We shall describe his results later (pages 192–94). But Hebb considers that animal studies provide only collateral data on the really important issue of what the intellectual and social consequences of environmental deprivation may be on man's development. Some evidence on this question comes from the psychoanalytically oriented studies of Ribble (1943), R. A. Spitz (1946, 1955), and Bowlby (1951, 1960). They report that children deprived of "normal" mothering care because of institutional placement or other unfavorable circumstances in early stages of their development frequently show the consequences in immediate physical and emotional symptoms—the "psychotoxic diseases" and anaclitic depression of infancy—or in the delayed and cumulative effects of intellectual deficiency and social maladjustment.

But can an experimental approach be devised to determine the effects of a measurable reduction in man's normal quota of sensory stimulation? In an era of space-travel which demands that men adjust themselves to weightlessness and other environmental shocks, the question becomes one of more than theoretical interest. It is pertinent also to the effectiveness of the methods used by some governments to extort information from war prisoners or, by reducing them to "unreasonable" facsimiles of themselves by extended and abnormal solitude, to induce them to subscribe to propositions wholly contradictory to their traditional principles and to the truth. It is not surprising that under the provocative influence of Hebb's theory and research an extensive program to investigate the effects of sensory deprivation should have developed at McGill University under his aegis, but executed by Bexton, Heron, and Scott (1954) and Heron, Doane, and Scott (1956; see also Solomon, et al., 1961). The subjects were college students who were paid to indulge in what has been the cherished dream of many college students: just to lie on a comfortable couch for twenty-four hours a day, for four days—if they could take it! Eighteen of the twenty-nine experimental subjects reneged before the end of the second day. What were the conditions which could make such a comfortable and lucrative contribution to science intolerable?

The bed was in a small, almost sound-masked cubicle. This had a small window, but since the subjects wore translucent goggles they could see only diffused light without form. Sensory stimulation of their arms and fingers was reduced by gloves and long, inflexible cuffs which extended from below their finger tips to their elbows. An "intercom" device made it possible for them to carry on conversation with the experimenter when conversation was necessary and in order. Such occasions arose during the intervals in which periodic, brief tests were administered. These consisted of problems selected from various intelligence tests, and the performance of the subject at the several stages at which they were given was used as a measure of the deterioration of his alertness and mental effectiveness. The only other interruptions to his isolation and the reduced "sensory input," except for meals and time-out for toilet activities, came in the form of a series of records purporting to prove the scientific validity of psychic phenomena. The first of these was introduced after the subject had been in isolation for eighteen hours, and he was invited to listen to the others when he chose and as often as he chose. A comparison of the experimental subjects with a control group that took all the tests, including the test of attitudes toward spiritualistic phenomena, showed results generally in accord with what we might expect. The experimental subjects were more affected by the "propaganda," became progressively less efficient in solving the mental problems, and complained of difficulty in concentrating on any task, and sometimes of difficulty in thinking of something to think about. Hallucinations were common. In the early stages these were simple and almost negligible, but they became progressively more insistent and in some cases caused the subject to withdraw from the experiment. When opaque glasses replaced the translucent lenses, the hallucinations seemed to diminish or disappear after a couple of hours, and the suggestion has been made on the basis of this and studies showing similar results that unpatterned stimulation is more likely than total elimination of stimuli to foster hallucinatory visions. These are not uncommon in patients with eye cataracts.

Individual differences in the reactions to sensory deprivation and isolation cannot be ignored. In a collection of related studies reported at a symposium at the Harvard Medical School (Solomon, et al., 1961) these differences manifested themselves in various ways:

The length of time a subject could tolerate the rigid limitations;
The degree of spatial and temporal disorientation and the methods used by subjects to reduce these anxiety-producing effects;
Physiological effects, including EEG's, EKG's, etc.;
Dependency, or resistance to dependency, upon the experimenter in the course of the isolation period and even in the months following it, when some subjects showed a disposition to avoid contacts with him;
Amount and character of verbalization during the experiment.

These are just a sampling of the kind of data provided by studies of sensory deficit.

That such studies have proliferated so richly during the past decade may be credited in part to the effect of Hebb's theorizing, in part to the renewed interest in physiological psychology because of its recent revelations and improved methods, and in some unmeasurable degree to what Professor Edwin G. Boring has referred to as the Zeitgeist (1961), a force growing out of social interaction which fosters, and at the same time controls, original thinking. Whatever may be the final verdict about the validity of Hebb's original speculations they will always be recognized for their influence in focusing the spotlight on some neglected central factors in behavior and awakening psychologists to the necessity of giving them closer scientific scrutiny.

LEARNING SET THEORY

HARRY F. HARLOW. Sets, concepts, the effects of early learning, species differences in learning, and motivation have been matters of concern also to Harry F. Harlow (born 1905), although the results of his experimental program at the University of Wisconsin have not always led him to share Hebb's views on the same subjects. Among his other research interests he is identified with "learning set" (LS) theory. Studies of learning set differ from the usual discrimination learning experiments in presenting the subject with a succession of paired objects or groups of which only one, but that one consistently, will be associated with the reward. After four or six presentations of one such group, it is replaced by another entirely different, except for the fact that, again, one object will carry the reward throughout the appearance of the new series. That series will be followed by a third, having nothing in common with the others except the reliability of the identification of one particular object with the reward. So what the subject must learn is not a pattern of distinguishing physical characteristics such as size, shape, color, or pitch, but a *principle*. Once he has caught on to the rule the experimenter has adopted he can quickly solve all the later problems put before him. If the problems contain just two objects, his first guess may be wrong, but his second will surely be right and he must stay with it until the next set of objects is presented. In the "oddity" problem, the experimenter will present three or more objects, all of which are alike except one, that being the one consistently associated with the reward. This principle, too, will eventually be grasped, even by animals of the higher species.

On the subject of interspecies differences, however, all the evidence points to the greater difficulty of acquiring learning sets than making simple discriminations of the traditional sort. Although there are great gaps in the data, the information available indicates that the docile laboratory rat does not distinguish himself in LS problems. Cats are better, but still less capable than primates; and of the latter the young do not show much aptitude for LS before the second or third year, although they may be able to learn simple discriminations in the second or third month. Man's performance is conspicuously at the top of the list, and in this generalization Harlow includes the performance of nursery school children despite some claims to the contrary (1959, pages 504–8). He therefore takes issue with Hebb on the subject of relative rates of first learning, at least as far as LS learning is concerned. This capacity he finds directly correlated with the structural complexity of the cortex, offering in support of this view data from the Wisconsin laboratory and from Riopelle's studies (1958) of a number of primate subspecies. Man's association areas should therefore not be considered an early handicap.

A comparison of LS learning curves at early, middle, and late stages of an experiment is instructive. Although, as Harlow points out, there is no single "ideal" curve, it is obvious that a great change will take place in the course of several hundred trials. Much will depend on the kind of problem and on the kind of subject involved; but if a learning set is finally successfully established it will manifest itself in the final phases of the experiment as a sudden change from a wrong or vacillating response to an almost instantaneous solution of one problem series after another. At this stage the learning curve has the characteristics of "insight" learning curves described by the gestaltists (page 232); but Harlow believes that all such curves must be accounted for as the result of learning set, and that without previous learning there can be no such thing as insight.

In fact Harlow advances the hypothesis that "all concepts such as triangularity, middle-sizedness, redness, number, and smoothness evolve only from LS information" (1959, page 510). He describes an experiment (Andrew and Harlow, 1948) in which sixteen monkeys developed a "generalized concept of triangularity" as a result of being trained first to discriminate a triangle from a circle, then in a later series to select the "more triangular" figure in each of fifty pairs. He questions whether this "broad stimulus generalization" could ever have evolved if training had been limited to the single discrimination type of problem. There is a subtle danger, however, in this identification of the term "concept" with "broad stimulus generalization." We have run into this problem before (page 109). This time the question is whether the *concept* of triangularity in its logical or mathematical meaning can ever have a "more" or "less" dimension. Harlow may well be correct in his claim that all the mammalian species he has tested for learning set show some degree of capacity for generalizing perceptual experience, but it is doubtful that his LS results exhaust the full meaning of the term "concept."

ERROR FACTORS AND THEIR RELATION TO LEARNING. Harlow introduces an interesting hypothesis about the effect of errors in slowing up first learning. Errors are frustrating and tempt the learner to stop working on the problem. Once the errors begin to diminish, motivation improves. Then the insights which have been built up at the earlier stages are put to use and

. . . learning within the same area becomes simple and effortless. Both the intellectual and emotional problems associated with learning to read disappear so completely that reading becomes an automatic process for most students. Similar phenomena are associated with such learnings as those involved in arithmetic and foreign languages. It remains as a possibility that the resistance of elderly people to new learning may relate more to associated problems of frustration than to learning limitations (1959, pages 511–12).

Learning set has often been described as "learning to learn." In the course of several hundred trials the subject learns to ignore irrelevant details and to concentrate on cues that will lead to the incentive. From this it would follow that learning consists simply in eliminating the *error factors* (EF's) which interfere with the occurrence of the correct response. Harlow has identified four classes of EF: *stimulus perseveration,* apparently reflecting a prejudice for or against one of the stimuli which causes the subject to repeat the same error again and again; *differential cue errors* resulting from associating the reward with the position of the object in which it is found rather than with the object itself; *response shift* suggesting a capricious change of taste in a subject that has long since shown signs of having discovered the "rule"; and *position-habit errors* probably related to right- or left-side preferences.

Harlow believes that a full understanding of the operation of these error factors would not only account for the course of learning, but also for some of the puzzling facts which have appeared in LS experiments. He predicted, for example, that once a discrimination had been established, it would be very difficult for an animal to make the opposite choice. This turned out not to be the case. EF analysis makes the ease with which *discrimination-reversal* can be accomplished more comprehensible. Only one of the four EF's, stimulus perseveration, would be working against the new object choice; the inhibition of the other three factors, developed during the discrimination learning, would transfer to and so facilitate learning of the discrimination-reversal task (1959, page 520).

In accounting for change in behavior as the effect of inhibition of error factors Harlow finds "no need to postulate formations of new associations" (1959, page 531). As soon as the learner suppresses the tendency to respond to "stimulus objects" rather than to the incentive, the appropriate behavior will occur without the necessity of new associations. When a change occurs and a new problem presents itself the inhibited error factors will reappear, as they must if an appropriate adjustment is to be made in the new situation.

IMPORTANCE OF THE ENVIRONMENT. Mutterings against reinforcement theory as an explanation of learning are becoming louder and more frequent, although it still has loyal adherents. Testimony against it has come from Breland and Breland (1961) who have for years applied the psychology of conditioning professionally in training "career" animals to give public performances (page 163, this book). Despite their experience they find themselves frequently confronted with unexplained aberrations on the part of their stars —chickens, rabbits, raccoons, porpoises, pigs, whales, even reindeer—

that seem suddenly to become unduly engrossed in what Harlow calls the "impedimenta," apparently forgetting all about the meal that is theirs for the earning. But let us give the authors a chance to present a bit of their own evidence:

> . . . a pig was conditioned to pick up large wooden coins and deposit them in a large "piggy bank." The coins were placed several feet from the bank and the pig required to carry them to the bank and deposit them, usually four or five coins for one reinforcement. . . .
>
> Pigs condition very rapidly, they have no trouble taking ratios, they have ravenous appetites (naturally), and in many ways are among the most tractable animals we have worked with. However, this particular problem behavior developed in pig after pig, usually after a period of weeks or months, getting worse every day. At first the pig would eagerly pick up one dollar, carry it to the bank, run back, get another, carry it rapidly and neatly, and so on, until the ratio was complete. Thereafter, over a period of weeks the behavior would become slower and slower. He might run over eagerly for each dollar, but on the way back, instead of carrying the dollar and depositing it simply and cleanly, he would repeatedly drop it, root it, drop it again, root it along the way, pick it up, toss it up in the air, drop it, root it some more, and so on.
>
> We thought this behavior might simply be the dilly-dallying of an animal on a low drive. However, the behavior persisted and gained in strength in spite of a severely increased drive—he finally went through the ratios so slowly that he did not get enough to eat in the course of a day. Finally it would take the pig about 10 minutes to transport four coins a distance of about 6 feet. This problem behavior developed repeatedly in successive pigs (1961, page 683).

The unaccountable change to preoccupation with the stimulus object rather than the incentive would seem to justify classifying this as an illustration of the EF which Harlow describes as *response shift* (page 191). Recognizing that in their performers the unscheduled act represents a regression to primitive species behavior, the Brelands describe it boldly as *instinctive drift* (1961, page 684). Harlow seems to be saying much the same thing when he reports that the "difficulty encountered in training infant monkeys, most chimpanzees, and all human children is their persistent tendency to disregard both appetite and hunger and to respond to the stronger motives afforded them by the impedimenta" (1959, page 530).

Harlow's theory of motivation takes its place among the growing number in contemporary psychology that recognize interest in the environment as a primary force in behavior and not one derived from biological needs such as hunger, thirst, sex, etc. He does not deny the importance of these, but he believes they have been overemphasized in current learning theory to the relative neglect of curiosity, exploration, and manipulation which, in his own studies (1953b, 1954), he has found to play an even more important part in learning. Monkeys well fed before the experiment learned to solve difficult mechanical puzzles even when they were allowed to continue eating during the trials regardless of right or wrong responses (1953a). Other monkeys successfully solved discrimination problems in a small dark box when their only reward for a correct solution was a chance to look out a little window for a moment (1954).

In opposition to Harlow's theory that curiosity, exploration, and manipulation have the status of primary drives, O. H. Mowrer argues that they are more correctly considered as forms of behavior used in the service of primary motives through the secondary reinforcement of fear reduction (1960a, 172f). J. S. Brown (1953) and N. E. Miller (1954) had earlier pointed out that fear reduction might be a factor in the reinforcing effect of the outside "view," under the circumstances of the confined quarters within which the monkeys worked. This interpretation would bring the "rewarding" responses and their effects under the Hullian formula $r_G \sim s_G$ (our pages 143–44). Harlow's rejoinder to the proposition that fear could have been a factor was that there were none of the usual objective evidences of fear. The argument that relief of "boredom" might have been the reinforcing factor suggests the questions: What is boredom, and when or why does it occur—in monkeys?

In his well-known studies of monkeys separated at birth from their natural mothers and assigned to the less tender mercies of wire or stuffed mother-surrogates, Harlow has provided evidence that affectional responses develop through contact comfort and clinging rather than through feeding satisfaction. Even the infants that had been regularly fed by a wire "mother" model would scramble in panic to a padded "protector"; and, allowed the chance to look out of the window of the little dark box described earlier, they spent as much time watching the padded mother as they spent on another baby monkey, while the wire surrogate which had fed them was treated with ungrateful neglect. Still later studies (1962) which have subjected the infant monkeys to stressful experiences as they cling to the surrogate mother have demonstrated how persistent the dependency relationship is. At this early stage of development it is apparently not easy to produce an experimental neurosis. But Harlow has now plenty of evidence of the long-term effects upon the earlier batch of monkeys separated at birth from their real mothers and brought up under unusual conditions. Among these are monkeys that spent the first year of life in separate cages, within sight and earshot of one another, but out of range for any physical contact. These as well as the surrogate-reared animals show a variety of abnormal symptoms: schizoid, manic, self-punitive. They appear to be incapable of normal social or sexual responses. Even the contact comfort provided by the padded mother-models did not equip these children for later normal adjustments to real monkeys.

O. Hobart Mowrer (born 1907; now Research Professor at the University of Illinois) has for many years been identified with research and theory in both the areas of learning and clinical psychology. His wide acquaintance with the current issues in these two fields and with the studies that have raised or tried to resolve them has led him to formulate a model of his own which he believes can synthesize the facts already established at the level of animal learning and those still left unexplained at the higher levels of behavior involving symbolic processes. This is indeed an ambitious project! But Mowrer has not been fazed by the failure of earlier attempts to do the same thing. His plan, he says, has been to use the theories of the past that have been found wanting, "as the very cornerstones and building blocks for our present edifice, but with the privilege of reshaping and reinterpreting them, so as to make them fit more smoothly into a new, overall system which, hopefully, will have both greater scope and power than any of the earlier conceptual schemes, taken separately" (1960a, page x). Though a theory of learning in name, Mowrer's "edifice" is planned to house all the facts of personality development. Among the "building blocks" we find in it are those characteristic of the architecture of most behaviorist theories: drive-reduction, homeostasis, primary and secondary reinforcement, contiguity learning (CR), and feedback. But scattered among these are some which look strangely foreign in such a structure—*image, hope, disappointment,* etc.—although we are becoming accustomed to comparable incongruities in the liberalized S–R models built to accommodate the cognitive "in-laws" of behavior.

Mowrer's earlier "two-factor learning theory" assigned a separate role to contiguity as it seems to operate in Pavlov's classical CR, and a different role to reinforcement or the law of effect as it was thought to operate in Thorndike's trial-and-error learning. Contiguity, Mowrer suggested, accounted for *sign* learning, which would involve only the conditioning of emotional responses through the autonomic system. Reinforcement accounted for *solution* learning in which the central nervous system and the skeletal muscles combine to produce an instrumental response (1953). In this way he sought to reconcile features of the contributions to learning made by Pavlov, Thorndike, Hull, Tolman, and Guthrie. It will be noticed too that Mowrer has cast contiguity and reinforcement in learning roles just the reverse of those assigned to them in Spence's later proposal (page 159, this book).

But flaws in this theory have now led Mowrer to a revision which uses as its base Thorndike's original idea of reward and punishment. These now become, respectively, *decremental reinforcement* and *incremental reinforcement*—unfortunately confusing designations unless regularly reinforced with the reminder that a decremental reinforcement *reduces* a drive or need whereas an incremental reinforcement *induces* a drive or need which the organism seeks to satisfy. But rarely, according to Mowrer, would such reduction or induction occur directly or only as the effect of the reward or the punishment. It occurs rather when an emotion that the reward or punishment has elicited becomes conditioned to the various external and internal stimuli acting upon the subject at the same time. To illustrate: a hungry rat touches a lever and receives an electric shock. The shock causes some pain, but, more than that, arouses fear. The fear attaches itself not only to the sight of the lever but to other surrounding objects, to the muscular sensations connected with his approach and reaching for the lever, with the tactile sensations as he touches it, etc. It would not require many repetitions of such an experience to make the rat freeze in his tracks rather than go near the lever. But suppose that on the other side of his cage there is a lever which dispenses food pellets when he presses it. The food pellets would in some learning theories be described as reinforcing to the approach and lever-pressing behavior. But to Mowrer even more important than the pellets is the pleasurable emotion they produce in the rat: he calls it *hope.* As with fear in the earlier situation, hope, in this, becomes conditioned to all the stimuli, external and internal, that have been connected with the rat's behavior. As he approaches the treacherous lever the "danger signal" is on; as he approaches the hospitable one the danger signal is off. Sometimes, of course, the supply of pellets may run out—a state of affairs which produces *disappointment* in the hungry, hopeful rat. This, obviously, is the experimental pattern which, if continued, would extinguish the positive response. But Mowrer treats it as another form of punishment which, like fear, will become conditioned to all the response-connected stimuli, and eventually inhibit the lever-pressing. *Relief* would play a corresponding part when there is some sign of the abatement of pain or other form of punishment.

In this version of the theory all learning is the result of conditioning. Fear begins to anticipate the arrival of the shock, hope the arrival of the food, and one or the other emotion becomes conditioned to the pattern of stimuli that existed just before the shock or the food was presented. If we think of the shock and the food as primary reinforcers, the emotions they arouse must be secondary reinforcers, and as Mowrer points out the latter operate in two different ways.

This feature of the theory cannot be evaluated in a few sentences and we can only refer the reader to Mowrer's documentation of his own position against the arguments of the opposition (1960a, Chapters 4, 5, 6). In noting the resemblance of the theory to his own recent thinking on the subject, Miller does, however, challenge the idea that only motivational responses can be learned. If habits are selected in the manner proposed by Mowrer, how, Miller asks, is the speed with which an appropriate response is selected to be explained? (1963, pages 85–86; see also the discussion on pages 155–56, this book.)

Habits, according to Mowrer, are not learned; they do not fit into the classical conditioning pattern as emotions do. They are, rather, forms of behavior—even passive, imposed movements—which rewarding circumstances have endowed with a hope-reinforced, or a relief-reinforced, feedback. In simpler terms we might describe them as "green light" responses which the learner is disposed to repeat. When a need arises these have this advantage over behavior with a neutral or negative feedback, and are therefore more likely to occur. The first response selected may not be appropriate in the new situation. If that happens, *fear* or *disappointment* will give another response the advantage, and this substitution will continue until the right response is found. "Present theory holds that a response which arouses *no* stimuli with secondary reinforcing properties possesses, ergo, *no* 'habit strength'" (1960a, page 233).

Mowrer cites in support of his mediational hypothesis his experience in training some talking birds, including a parrot and a myna bird with which his method was quite successful (1960b). As he supplied them with food and water, and petted them, he spoke the relevant words he wished them to learn. In this way he established a beforehand "built-in" reinforcement for the sounds they heard him produce but had not yet produced by themselves. As their vocalizations progressed these sounds came to be used more often than those which had not been so reinforced, and as the training progressed further the use of the right word at the right moment by a strongly motivated bird provided further reinforcement. Mowrer suggests that a mother and others concerned with the early care of an infant can apply the same principle to good effect in his word-training. In these instances the learner seems to be imitating a model as he gives preference to the reinforced sounds; in habits which appear without the mediation of a model the mediation is being provided by the internal cues of "hope-reinforced" or "relief-reinforced" behavior. In a sense the learner is imitating his own past successful responses. (Compare the theory of Miller and Dollard, page 150.)

Although the parrot or the myna bird will never put his words to better use than to make limited responses to concrete signs, the higher reaches of language behavior available to man set him distinctly apart from even the highest apes, not only in the kind of problem he can solve but even in the kind of problem he can recognize as a problem! Concepts, meaning, symbols have long been substantially ignored in behavioristic thinking, or have been operationally defined in terms that would fit the behaviorist "last." Mowrer acknowledges the necessity of building up this relatively unexplored area, and he attempts to assimilate some of its problems consistently in his own mediational hypothesis. Meaning, for instance, is not adequately accounted for, as Watson thought it could be, by the simple explanation that certain "muscle-twitches," implicit behavior, have become associated with the word *pencil,* and mean *pencil,* because the name of the object has become conditioned to the act of writing with it. Osgood's use of the semantic differential (page 199 in this book) approaches the problem of word-meaning at a more sophisticated level, and Mowrer construes as support for his new emotion-mediation theory of learning Osgood's finding that the "evaluative" factor far outstripped any other in the analysis of the dimensions of the "semantic space." Words obviously do quickly pick up an emotional connotation, a fact which was recognized and exploited long before "Madison Avenue" or the professional political propagandist began to use it systematically to achieve mass conversions.

But informational content as well as feeling must be represented if meaning is to be complete. This aspect of the mediating response Mowrer assigns to the image—not the scorned mental element of the introspective school, but a construct which meets the specifications of S–R theory. An image is a conditioned sensation, learned in the way of all conditioned responses through the principle of contiguity. The image may acquire through generalization the affective quality related to the parent sensation, and so carry across a period of time behavioral effects that would otherwise be difficult to explain. Mowrer speculates on various ways in which this newly adapted mediational agent might contribute to the understanding of the storage and classification of knowledge and the conditions under which it becomes—or fails to become—available when needed for the thoughtful solution of a problem. If his theory is not yet ready to account for all the experimental results and the unsolved questions he has laid out for consideration in his inquiry into symbolic behavior (1960b), he has at least added support to a growing dissatisfaction with the idea that we have only to extrapolate from studies of the white rat or some other animal that adapts well to laboratory life to gain a complete comprehension of man's mind and personality.

THE MEANING OF MEANING

Charles E. Osgood (born 1916; now Director of the Institute of Communications Research, University of Illinois) has for a number of years been occupied with an active group of fellow-workers on a program designed to measure meaning. The meaning of meaning has been a subject of controversy for many centuries, challenging philosophers, who identified it as a fundamental distinctive feature of the human mind, and challenging semanticists, whose interest was primarily in the precision and adequacy of communication. Within the past twenty years the whole topic of verbal behavior has become in psychology an area of accelerated research and theorizing (pages 99–102; 200–4).

Osgood's interest in meaning has been focused on the "mediational process" rather than on how meaning is reflected in conditioned behavior. In fact, in his search for a satisfactory definition, he has rejected the "naive application of Pavlovian principles by early behaviorists like Watson" because it suggests that a word (the sign) will produce as the result of conditioning just the same response the original stimulus (the significate) produced—which is usually not the case (Osgood, et al., 1957, pages 4–5). But Osgood has been equally cautious against admitting into his definition anything which could be construed as a "mentalistic" explanation of meaning. Ideas or images are excluded.

He describes his own theory of meaning as a two-step *representational mediation process*, explaining carefully his choice of each of these descriptive terms: it is representational because the sign-produced behavior is a fractional part of the behavior aroused by the original stimulus; it is mediational because that fractional response serves (as Hull's r_G) to produce self-stimulation (corresponding to Hull's s_G), and so mediates or determines the selection of some appropriate mode of response from the hierarchy of habits the organism has to draw upon. (Refer to pages 143–44 in this book.) Finally, he has chosen the term "process" rather than "reaction" to allow for the possibility that the mediating factor may be neural rather than a pattern of skeletal or glandular behavior. In a later paper he has, in fact, speculated that synesthetic [1] and metaphorical effects which appear in the measurement of meaning could well be the products of the affective reaction system—"the nonspecific projection systems

---

[1] A definition of synesthesia is given on page 248. It is interesting to note the relationship between Osgood's and Asch's work in the area of synesthesia and metaphor.

from the hypothalamic, reticular, or limbic systems and their cortical connections in the frontal lobes . . ." (1962, page 21).

Osgood has taken his lead for measuring the meaning of concepts from factorial studies of traits, abilities, and attitudes (1953, page 712). The complicated derivation of the *semantic differential,* the instrument of measurement, is described in detail in *The Measurement of Meaning* (Osgood, *et al.,* 1957), and only a brief account of its features will be attempted here. Underlying its use is the basic assumption that any concept will have its place in a multidimensional "semantic space," and that therefore it should be possible to plot the position of the concept once the dimensions of that space are reliably identified. The measurement of the meaning of a concept would then be somewhat analogous to the description of a color in terms of its hue, its brightness, and its saturation.

A series of factor analyses of semantic judgments of various sorts involving common adjective-pairs—good-bad, honest-dishonest, nice-awful; strong-weak, hard-soft, heavy-light; fast-slow, tense-relaxed, active-passive, etc.—gave rather consistent evidence that they fell into three clusters. The first three pairs we have used as illustrations, with a number of other pairs closely correlated, seemed to represent an *evaluative* dimension or factor; the middle three pairs, with others, suggested a *potency* factor; the last three and others like them were interpreted as typical of the *activity* factor. Osgood has called attention to the parallel between these three main dimensions of meaning which have emerged through factor analysis, and Wundt's tridimensional theory of feeling which identified pleasantness-unpleasantness, strain-relaxation, and excitement-quiescence as its elementary properties. Wundt's analysis was, of course, the product of careful introspection.

The use of the semantic differential is simpler than the account of its derivation would suggest. Suppose that you were confronted with an assortment of words such as "intelligence," "automobile," "whale," "clock," etc., and you were asked to rate each of these on seven-point scales ranging from *cold* to *hot, tense* to *relaxed, fresh* to *stale* and other such polar adjective scales selected to define the semantic space. You would probably begin by protesting that many of the adjectives had no application to the concepts in question, but if you were prodded to follow the instructions you might be surprised to discover in some cases a sense of relationship you would find hard to explain.

Strangely, such forced choices seem to produce more agreement than could be expected on the basis of logic alone; and from this observation Osgood and his associates have been prompted to investigate systematically to what extent their semantic factor structure holds up when tried out on different kinds of subjects ("generality across people"), and when applied to the measurement of different concepts ("generality across concepts").

The answer to the first question appears to be favorable: the evaluation-potency-activity pattern seems to have been maintained by different subgroups of English-speaking Americans even though the meanings they have assigned to the concepts have varied. Early returns from an extensive international test of the device have also been promising on this point (1962). The same cannot be said for generality across concepts. Here the three-aspect semantic structure seems to break down, particularly in the activity dimension. Osgood offers some possible explanations of why this could happen, and with his associates is busily following up the problem of whether certain classes of concepts may not require more specialized instruments than the general "semantic differential" for the purpose of more adequate measurement. Work is already under way to construct on the same model a *personality differential*. Among the factors which have already been isolated for this test, *morality, volatility*, and *toughness* have appeared most consistently. A second look at these will show that they have more than a passing resemblance to the evaluation-activity-potency triad.

VERBAL MEDIATING RESPONSES

Osgood's representational mediation process would not be limited to, but would obviously include, verbal mediating behavior. This form of intervening variable has in recent years become a subject of renewed attention particularly to a group of behaviorists who find in Hull's and Spence's device, the $r_G \sim s_G$ earlier described on page 143, a solution to many problems including that of the selection or direction of behavior. We have seen the role it plays in determining the habit-family hierarchy, and we have illustrated it in operation in the verbal directives which may accompany the performance of our daily tasks. These intervening response-produced stimuli are not necessarily verbal; they may be the effect of fragmentary behavior which has been positively reinforced or punished, and which has in this way achieved the status of a secondary conditioning agent. So, just as the sight of the dentist's chair or the sound of his drill has become a secondary stimulus for flight, the stimuli related to each forward step we take toward his office may contribute to making us quail the more. And verbal stimuli whether spoken aloud or intervening in some fragmentary or "implicit" way may also compound our fear or aversion when the dreaded visit is due.

We have said that "renewed" attention was given to the idea of verbal mediators because the idea that language has a role in thinking is certainly not new. It was not new when Watson proposed it; it was not even new when the nominalists and idealists of the Middle Ages argued about the nature of concepts. That the connection between thought and language has been a recurrent topic of debate is not strange in view of the fact that man alone has been able to build a scientific and social civilization through the use of words as symbols. That fact, however, was not of primary interest to Watson. What was of interest was the possibility of dealing with language behavior as a surrogate for the conscious phenomena his behavioristic philosophy would not tolerate.

> . . . Since, according to my view, thought processes are really motor habits in the larynx, improvements, short cuts, changes, etc., in these habits are brought about in the same way that such changes are produced in other motor habits. This view carries with it the implication that there are no reflective processes (centrally initiated processes) (1913, page 174).

Watson's views were shared at that time more or less by Max Meyer, A. P. Weiss, J. F. Dashiell, and others caught up in the first, fine, careless rapture of the new behaviorism. Unfortunately for the immediate future of the verbal theory of thinking there were few encouraging experimental findings nor, in fact, were there many experimental studies at all.

Some credit for the recent resurgence of interest in the relation of language to thought is due to the writings of the late Benjamin Lee Whorf whose avocational studies of inter-cultural language differences led him to conclude that the thinking of the people of a given culture is determined and limited by the structure of their language (1956). An illustration Whorf drew from his engineering experience will make clearer how he saw in our own language shaping forces which determine our interpretation of situations and our responses to them:

> . . . around a storage of what are called "gasoline drums" behavior will tend to a certain type, that is, great care will be exercised; while around a storage of what are called "empty gasoline drums," it will tend to be different—careless, with little repression of smoking or of tossing cigarette stubs about. Yet the "empty" drums are perhaps the more dangerous, since they contain explosive vapor. Physically the situation is hazardous, but the linguistic analysis according to regular analogy must employ the word "empty," which inevitably suggests lack of hazard. The word "empty" is used in two linguistic patterns: (1) as a virtual synonym for "null and void, negative, inert," (2) applied in analysis of physical situations without regard to, e.g., vapor, liquid vestiges, or stray rubbish, in the container. The situation is named in one pattern (2) and the name is then "acted out" or "lived up to"

in another (1), this being a general formula for the linguistic conditioning of behavior into hazardous forms (1956, page 135).

Brown and Lenneberg (1954), and Carroll and Casagrande (1958), among others, have undertaken to test Whorf's hypothesis experimentally by comparing the responses of English-speaking and of American Indian subjects on test content which might be expected to reveal the effects of their different language structures. The results obtained have been considered moderately but not overwhelmingly favorable to the Whorfian theory. There appears however to be some agreement among the S–R psychologists that Watson and Whorf exaggerated the role of motor or language effects to the relative neglect of perceptual processes. Charles N. Cofer, who has provided an account of experimental studies of the role of verbal behavior in thinking, suggests that the available data are consonant with "weak forms of these hypotheses, that is, that much thought involves or, if you will, *is* verbal process and that the form and content of a language probably make some kinds of thinking and perceiving easier in one language community and harder in another" (1960, page 94).

Laboratory studies dealing with the effect of verbal mediation in perception, learning, and concept formation have, since the mid-1950's, proliferated at a rate which would make any comprehensive treatment of them in this place impossible. The appearance in 1962 of a new medium for reporting such studies, the *Journal of Verbal Learning and Verbal Behavior* under the editorship of Leo Postman assisted by a distinguished editorial board, is an indication of the lively activity within the field. Albert E. Goss who, with his students, has been a frequent contributor to the literature on the subject has provided historical accounts of the early and more recent experimental developments (1961a, 1961b) including a theoretical analysis of the ways in which different patterns of relationship among the initiating stimuli, mediating responses and stimuli, and terminating responses might produce different results (1961b). Dr. Tracy S. Kendler has provided an excellent brief summary of the literature in her survey of concept formation in the 1961 *Annual Review of Psychology*.

From the numerous studies which have been done, the work of Howard and Tracy Kendler and their associates may serve to illustrate a typical technique and, at the same time, allow us to consider an interesting fact it has uncovered. The experiment requires the subjects to select from a pair of objects the one which the experimenter has arbitrarily designated as "right." Let us suppose the objects to be cubes: some black, some white; some five inches in diameter, some three inches in diameter. There are, therefore, four possible combinations in which the cubes will appear: large-white, small-white, large-black, small-black. The subjects working on the selection task find that they are "rewarded" in some way when they choose the large cubes, regardless of color. Size, in other words, is the relevant dimension, and color is irrelevant. Suppose, now, that after they have learned this trick of discrimination, the experimenter arbitrarily changes his reward system. Half of the subjects are now rewarded whenever they pick a *white* cube, regardless of size. These must change over to the earlier irrelevant dimension and choose on the basis of color rather than of size. The other subgroup is rewarded when they shift to the opposite value in the dimension first used: now it is the small cube which must be picked. The latter change is called *reversal shift;* the former, *non-reversal shift* (1960).

Which should be easier to learn? It appears that for rats, and for young children, up to 5 or 6 years, before dependable language responses are available, the non-reversal shift is easier; for adults the reversal shift is more quickly learned. The difference is understandable on the basis of an inferred mediating verbal response which, in the adult subjects, serves as a common link to either value within a given dimension. For the non-reversal shift, on the other hand, a correct response will depend upon the learning of a new mediating response and correct associated behavior. On the basis of the "single unit" or "one stage" paradigm which presumably accounts for the animal's and the small child's behavior, the prediction could be made that the non-reversal shift would be the more readily learned. Mrs. Kendler calls attention to the possible analogy between this S–R finding and Piaget's observations on the young child's gradual recognition of reversibility (page 48, this book). She finds pertinent also much of the Soviet research on the second signal system (Kendler, 1961).

Much of the current output on thinking and verbal behavior is related to Hull's system and proceeds with behavioristic rigor to make inferences consonant with the system which might account for the observable facts. The assumptions about what goes on between the S and the R must then be justified experimentally. The neobehaviorist thus sets himself a difficult task, and it is not surprising that his data frequently fall short of the required level of statistical significance. Spielberger and Levin have challenged indifference to the data of consciousness in such studies on the grounds that it shuts out the possible fact that awareness itself may be a mediating factor in learning. Dulany had earlier decided (1961) that automatic reinforcement alone was not enough to account for the kind of conditioning described by Verplank (1955) and Greenspoon (1962) in which a gesture or a verbal response of a subject was arbitrarily rewarded by the experimenter, with the effect that such rewarded responses appeared more frequently than those not so treated. (See our pages 86–87.) On a sentence construction task some of the subjects in the Spielberger and Levin experiment showed evidence of similar conditioning when "good" was said in an offhand manner whenever they began a sentence with "I" or "We." However, it appeared from the data obtained in a standardized interview conducted directly after the conditioning session that only those subjects who gave evidence that they had been aware of the "correct response-reinforcement contingencies" during the experiment had learned the responses. The authors conclude that awareness is a mediating factor.

In approaching our next section we may quote from a commentary made by Professor Jerome S. Bruner of Harvard University on computer studies of thinking, a passage which has equal relevance in the present context:

> . . . What is particularly striking about these [computer] studies is the degree to which the step-by-step behavior of the thinker and the problem solver must be described and conceptualized before it can be simulated. The work has freed us from the rather bizarre compulsion to describe all behavior in terms of stimulus–response connections and, at that, to describe only those features of the behavior the psychologist thought well enough of to reward. Perhaps the new science of programming will help free us from our tendency to force nature to imitate the models we have constructed for her (1960, page 23).

MATHEMATICAL LEARNING THEORY AND MODELS

The term "model," long used in other sciences and technology, has recently been added also to psychological jargon. "Analogy" could serve in its place, as Chapanis has pointed out in an illuminating history and critical commentary on its usage:

> A model is an analogy and no one expects an analogy to be completely accurate. . . . Theory, on the other hand, is a conceptual system which attempts to describe the real thing. . . . Whereas a model can tolerate some facts which are clearly not in accord with it, facts which do not agree with theory are fatal to the theory (Chapanis, 1961, pages 118, 119).

High among the advantages of using models is that they can change the direction of our thinking on a subject and so lead us to new insight and a better solution of a problem. On the other side of the ledger is the danger that the model selected may beguile the thinker into forgetting the essential differences between it and the reality for which it substitutes.

Models may vary from precisely scaled-down or scaled-up replicas of the actual object under consideration, through such symbolic analogies as road maps or globes, to the abstract formulas of physics or chemistry, or mathematical equations. Helmholtz based his theory of hearing on an analogy between the fibers of the basilar membrane and the strings of a piano. In our own day von Békèsy has carried out his brilliant study of auditory functioning with the help of a skin model of the cochlea, selected because of a number of common characteristics between the ear and the skin receptors. A dramatic and instructive use of models in recent psychological research has been made possible by the adaptation of the digital computer to the study of thought and the learning process.

A move in chess or the play of a card at a critical stage in a bridge game may entail a long extension of that dash between the S and the R while the player silently works through the possible consequences of conceivable strategies. We know that the human strategist does not always come up with the right answer. A computer adequately programmed with the necessary basic information and the rules for using it might do a better job in a shorter time. But if a man can "teach" a computer to "think" what has he to learn about thinking by studying its "simulated thinking"? Let us review some of the kinds of study that have been done.

Instructions provided by the programmer can take either of two forms. If the problem is a very simple one, the solution might be reached by trying out all the conceivable possibilities or combinations involved. We might quickly illustrate the limitations of this *algorithmic* approach by likening it to the procedure of a forgetful individual who doggedly searches for a temporarily mislaid name by trying each letter of the alphabet until he comes to one that has an aura of familiarity, and accepts that as the initial letter. Then he returns to the beginning of the alphabet to find the second letter. Now obviously many combinations, such as Db, Dd, Dq, etc., will be worthless, and little is to be gained by giving them any consideration at all. Besides, if this unimaginative and compulsive procedure had to be used to aggregate all the letters of a long name, time would run out. It has been estimated that even with the lightning speed of an electronic computer millions of years of continuous operation would be required to deal with all the permutations and combinations involved even in what may appear to be relatively simple problems. In this fact we have one answer to the question of what computers can tell us about the human thought process: No thinker—not even our most deliberate bridge opponent—depends on algorithms! Some short-cut strategies must be used.

The *heuristic* method of programming uses reliable strategies of this sort. The instructions given to the computer will include not only positive rules for proceeding, but also rules for rejecting fruitless or unpromising alternatives. The instructions may even direct the computer to select and "store" for later use solutions that have proved successful in the earlier problems. Newell, Shaw, and Simon (1958) demonstrated in an interesting study how their "Logic Theorist" (LT) made use of its hardware memory in proving some of the theorems of symbolic logic. As a first step they provided the computer with the necessary axioms and techniques, and instructions to store each proof and make use of it in later solutions. LT worked out 38 of the 52 theorems. In the next phase, LT was given the same basic information to work with, but without the memory of the theorems it had proved. This time it was unable to find a proof for a theorem it had solved earlier in ten seconds. In a third phase of the experiment it was given the axioms and one theorem. This time it succeeded in proving the theorem it had failed to prove on the previous test, but it took fifteen minutes to do it.

Miller, Galanter, and Pribram have drawn some inferences from computer operations which could have far-reaching effects on psychological thinking. After reading Kenneth Boulding's book, *The Image*, they became collectively engrossed in the question of what role this neglected cognitive factor in man's life played in his behavior. "Unless you can use your image to do something, you are like a man who collects maps but never makes a trip" (1960, page 2). This led them to tackle again the problem Tolman faced in explaining what drove his rat to act at the choice point where, according to Guthrie, the animal had been "left buried in thought." (See page 140, this book.) The performance of the computer suggested an analogical hypothesis. The computer solves, or fails to solve, its problem on the basis of a set of instructions carefully worked out by the programmer. These reduce the complicated task to a series of subunits each of which must be completed before the machine moves on to the next level. Behavior, therefore, is more accurately described as hierarchical in structure rather than as consisting of a simple chain of reflexes. Whether we think of man dealing with the everyday problems of life, or formulating the instructions for the computer, we can assume that along with the Image which incorporates his knowledge of the world and himself, whether right or wrong, and the values he attaches to those convictions, there must go a *Plan*. The housewife says, "That chair is shabby; tomorrow I'll call the upholsterer, and when I drop Tommy off at the dentist, I'll use the time to shop for fabrics." The businessman-golfer plans:

"If I can reach Smith tomorrow morning by phone, I can get him started working on the deal; then I should be able to get away by noon, drive to the club, have lunch there and be ready to tee off by two-thirty." Implicit in each of these calculations is the planner's appraisal of reality and of his own potentials and limitations. The housewife is not planning to take over Tommy's dental care, nor the upholstering job; but she is realizing her Image of herself as a good mother and a good housekeeper by a Plan which will at the same time ultimately contribute to improving Tommy's teeth and the décor of the living room. In the same way, the businessman has found a Plan by which he can make use of Smith's competence, his own driving ability, and the facilities of his club to enable him to indulge in his favorite sport.

But for both man and computer the best-laid plans may run into difficulties, and so there is need for a master plan, a *Metaplan,* for devising alternate procedures should the first Plan fail. For the man and for the computer the Metaplan may consist of working through a habit hierarchy (page 144, this book) of procedures that have worked in other situations like the present one. The significant fact is that behavior continues directed toward the goal until the goal is achieved or the Image is modified. The college student who plans a career in one of the major professions may have to revise his estimate of himself and of the favored profession if he finds no graduate school willing to accept a second-rate record. The Image and the Plan, then, are essentially *integrated* and *interacting:*

A Plan can be learned and so would be part of the Image.

The names that Plans have must comprise a part of the Image for human beings, since it must be part of the person's Image of himself that he is able to execute such-and-such Plans.

Knowledge must be incorporated into the Plan, since otherwise it could not provide a basis for guiding behavior. Thus, Images can form part of a Plan.

Changes in the Images can be effected only by executing Plans for gathering, storing, or transforming information.

Changes in the Plans can be effected only by information drawn from the Images (Miller, Galanter, and Pribram, 1960, page 18).

The authors recognize that admitting a future goal as an influence on behavior raises again the problem of teleology. How can a future goal "cause" present behavior? But they argue that the principle should be less objectionable to the mechanistically minded theorist as long as something like "purpose" can be demonstrated in the behavior of a man-made machine. As a matter of fact, the "cybernetic hypothesis" introduced by Norbert Wiener (1948) reopened the whole question of "teleological" effects in human behavior by pointing up the resemblance between the operation of a feedback device such as a thermostat, and the continuing adjustments of the organism made on the basis of information constantly supplied by the sensory systems. Until the temperature of the room matches the requirement set by the thermostat, the fuel system continues to work. Normally, until the kinesthetic feedback of the stair-climber matches his Image of how far his foot must be raised to clear the next step, motor impulses to muscles involved in the response will continue to move it. So considered, our responses cannot be adequately described as all-or-none reflexes to separate stimuli, but rather as geared to some internal measure of how closely the present response fits the requirements of the situation. (Compare Anokhin's "acceptor of action," page 106, this book.)

Miller, Galanter, and Pribram have therefore proposed a new hypothetical construct to replace the reflex as the fundamental unit of behavior. They call it *TOTE*, a name made up of the initials of the cybernetic operations: "Test-Operate-Test-Exit." TOTE has the advantage of flexibility. It would cover the most elaborate scheme of Metaplan, Plan, and sub-Plans represented in the life style of an individual; it would cover his program for a single day, or his method of solving a complex problem. But it would equally describe the humble task of hammering a nail into the wall. The hammering of the nail involves more than a chain of violent reflex attacks upon the target; it is rather a series of modulated actions initiated by a Plan, and guided constantly by current information on how closely each operation satisfies the test for that phase of the task. The distance the hammer is lifted in preparation to striking must be tested in terms of the Image of the size of the nail and the probable resistance of the surface it must penetrate; when it has been drawn back far enough, the first blow is struck, with proper regard for the fingers holding the nail in place. This operation is in turn tested, and the next operation of drawing back the hammer will depend on how nearly the new position of the nail meets our requirements; also, in some unfortunate cases, on the fate of the fingers. As soon as a test establishes that the nail is just where we want it, that part of the task is over. Test-Operate-Test-Exit, then, is a formula which can describe man's handling of the complexities of a problem he must solve himself, or his scheme for programming a computer that will do his thinking for him. *Plans and the Structure of Behavior* presents many applications of the concept in the behavior of humans, animals, and computers; and suggests unsolved psychological issues which might well be clarified by the TOTE model.

Carl I. Hovland (1912–1962), late of Yale University, who had in the last ten years of his life identified himself with the study of concept development in human learners (1952, 1953, 1960), was preparing an elaborate computer study of the problem at the time of his death. He has left a thoughtful account and evaluation of the computer approach to psychological questions, citing among its merits the fact that it forces a precise formulation of the specific operations theoretically assumed to take place in any mental process. "It is one thing to say . . . that problem solving involves . . . preparation, incubation, illumination, and verification,[2] and quite another thing for one to specify exactly what is involved in each stage" (1960, page 691). Simulating a thought process by programming a computer is essentially theorizing about what goes on mentally under complex, realistic conditions. If the "theory" holds true for one subject, it may be used as the basis for predicting what others will do; and if it holds generally, it may be used to good advantage in the study of individual differences and the conditions which make for deviations from the normal pattern.

STOCHASTIC MODELS AND STATISTICAL LEARNING THEORY. Disenchanted with the prospect for a fruitful yield from theoretical systems which continued to multiply intervening variables in an effort to describe the learning process, a mathematically minded group of psychologists have decided to approach the problem from another direction. William K. Estes (born 1919; now professor at Stanford University), one of the leaders of the new movement, describes this transition in thinking which began about 1950 in this way:

> The procedure adopted was to take as the primary theoretical dependent variable, not a hypothetical strength, force, or potential, but simply the probability of classes of observable behaviors, and to state psychological assumptions in terms of the ways in which probabilities, or changes in the probabilities, are related to determining conditions (1962, page 109).

This would involve planning experiments with "determining conditions" relevant to the "psychological assumptions," then matching the data obtained against the probabilities mathematically predictable in terms of the theory.

Mathematically, a sequence of events linked by probability is a stochastic process, and Bush and Mosteller, also pioneers in this area, have described their theory as based on a *stochastic* model. Estes has called his *statistical*, although in terms of their mathematical treatment the two approaches are very much alike. (For an account of the mathematical development of the theories see Hilgard, 1956;

---

[2] The steps identified by the eminent mathematician Henri Poincaré in his analysis of the process of creative thought (1913).

Bush and Estes, 1959; Estes, 1959). The major differences between the two theories have been in their basic assumptions about what determines the probabilities or changes in response probabilities. Bush and Mosteller go along with Hull and Skinner in assuming the influence of positive or negative reinforcement. Estes, on the other hand, has moved close to, if not into, the Guthrie camp, stressing contiguity as the determining factor in learning. He believes that stimulus–response bonds are not built up slowly and gradually through "some deterministic growth process," but are established at once, if at all. If learning curves give the appearance of gradualness, it is because averaging group data has obscured what really takes place in the individual on successive trials.

To consider his reasoning in a simplified form, suppose we assume that of the entire set of stimuli operating in an experimental situation, only a sampling—a *subset, S*—will be actually available, for one reason or another, on any one trial. *S'* would represent the elements not operating on that occasion. Each stimulus element of the subset *S* would then become conditioned to the response just by virtue of having been present when R occurred. But between that trial and the next, the subset population will change: conditions can never be identical on two occasions. The probability of the occurrence of R on any subsequent trial, therefore, will depend upon the proportion of elements of the entire set which remain conditioned to that particular R or response class as against those which continue to fluctuate because of the variability of the experimental conditions or the variability of the conditions of the organism. Presumably with repetition of pretty much the same conditions this proportion will increase, and the learning curve will reflect the fact. Estes and his colleagues have provided some challenging data in support of his all-or-none theory of learning (Estes and Burke, 1955; Estes, 1959, 1960, 1962). Needless to say, the challenge has not been ignored!

In the very early stages of statistical learning theory, the problems investigated were of a simple nature, usually limited to two-choice situations such as the T-maze, word associations, or predictions by the subject of whether or not a certain event would follow a signal reinforced according to schedules planned by the experimenter. But with the refinement of mathematical methods (finite Markov chains), and with the accumulated experience from early studies, the "probabilistic behaviorists" have come to handle somewhat more complex projects. For an account of the contributions made by Atkinson, Restle, Suppes, Luce, and others, the reader is referred to Estes' report on current learning theory in the *Annual Review of Psychology* for 1962.

INFORMATION THEORY AND DECISION MAKING. Paralleling the growth of interest in statistical learning theory has been the development of a more practical alliance between the psychologist and the mathematician. The tremendous technological achievements of our day in the service of national defense and the opening of new scientific frontiers in space exploration, medicine, or industry are all man-centered, not only in the sense that they are designed to satisfy his needs, but also in the sense that they depend for their success on his effective participation. The same can be said of non-technical programs involving man. Even where mutual understanding is the goal, whether it be at the international level or among the members of a single family, the willingness and ability of an individual to fit into a prescribed role will be a measure of the probable success of the proposed solution. The probabilistic chain is only as strong as its weakest link! The most sensitive radar system will not be effective if its signals are misinterpreted; the clearest dials and most precise instruments will not insure safe flying if the pilot's reaction time is too slow. These two illustrations represent areas of research in which the mathematician and the psychologist are both heavy stockholders—the problem of the effectiveness of communication systems, and the problem of determination of choice under conditions of uncertainty. Both are now being put to use in human engineering research toward perfecting the "man-machine system" which seems to be demanded in our "hardware age." These excerpts from an account of this development by Franklin V. Taylor tell part of the story (1957, pages 254–55):

> . . . the human in a man-machine system can be considered as an information transmission and processing link between the displays and the controls of the machine. When so viewed, his behavior consists of reading off information, transforming it mentally, and emitting it as action on the controls. . . . The operator of a man-machine system is always consciously trying to perform some task. . . . Perhaps it is . . . to see a visual target imbedded in "noise" and to signal its position. . . . to watch a bank of displays in order to determine malfunction and to take action where necessary. . . . System psychologists also view him as a multipurpose computer. . . . The virtue of these engineering models is that they furnish ready-made a mathematics which has already proved itself of value when applied to the inanimate portions of the man-machine system and which may turn out to be useful for the human element as well. . . . Whereas orthodox psychology still speaks in a construct language consisting of terms such as stimulus, response, sensation, perception, attention, anticipation, and expectancy, the new "hardware" school is rapidly developing a concept argot which, although quite unintelligible to outsiders, is providing considerable inspiration to the initiates. . . . Questions of human behavior are now being asked experimentally which were literally inconceivable a few years ago.

But man's "reprogramming" propensities—his inventiveness—have been a source of trouble to those who hoped to apply the same mathematical models to the animate and inanimate parts of the system; and his tendency to seek additional information, or to use it "in a novel way in decision making," have made it clear that early assumptions were oversimplified, and that a great deal more research is needed on man's intellectual functions and team functions. How is he persuaded? By whom? Under what conditions does he become more susceptible to persuasion? These and many other questions must be further explored if we are adequately to understand man's information processing and decision making (Bray, 1962).

Meanwhile the "concept argot" of information theory has found its way into psychological literature, sometimes expressing the concepts, sometimes merely the argot. *Input* and *output, encoding* and *decoding, channel capacity, noise, bit* are some of the terms used by the communication engineer in predicting to what extent the message received at its destination will correspond with the message despatched from the source, taking into consideration possible channel distortions. The standard unit of measurement is the *bit,* and for an account of its derivation, the reader is referred to Hilgard's brief exposition (1956, page 379) or to the more technical treatments by Frick (1959) and Garner (1962).

Noise is any disturbing condition which affects the channel during the transmission of the message. Enough noise can make the message unintelligible, particularly if the latter has been stripped to the essential minimum. If it has some *redundancy*—repetition, or sequence of symbols—this danger is lessened because enough may remain of the original pattern to allow for reconstruction of the meaning. *Input* would be the information, and *encoding* would be the form appropriate to the channel through which it would be sent. At the other end, the receiver would *decode* the message as he construed it, and act upon the information (output). For the uses and limitations of information theory as a model, the reader is referred to Frick (1959) and to Garner (1962).

On the subject of uses and limitations of mathematical models in general, psychologists are not of one mind. Admittedly mathematics is the language of science, but some doubt is expressed as to whether psychology is old enough to talk in more than halting syllables. Such criticism, oddly enough, has come from psychologists who are themselves distinguished in the application of mathematical procedures (McGill, 1960; McNemar, 1960). One common objection has been that by settling too early upon a method, the psychomathematicians may dwarf the development of psychological research, limiting it too long to those areas or problems that lend themselves to their specialized approach. Another complaint, or perhaps the same one seen from a somewhat different angle, has been that too much emphasis on the elegance of the mathematical tool displaces interest from the problem itself, where the focus of interest should be, to the refinements of techniques which may or may not prove viable.

8

Gestalt Psychology

The year 1912 was a "time of troubles" for the old, standard theory of psychology. Then, or just about then, behaviorism in America was starting its violent assault, while in Germany an equally determined attack was being launched by the new school of Gestalt psychology.

This was no concerted war; neither rebellious party had any knowledge of the other party's plan of attack. The behaviorists knew nothing of the gestaltists, nor the gestaltists of the behaviorists. When they got to know of each other, a few years later, they found they were as hostile to each other as both of them were to the older views of Wundt and Titchener.

The behaviorists proposed to abandon the study of conscious experience, and to analyze behavior into its component reflexes and conditioned reflexes—instead of analyzing experience into elementary sensations and feelings. The gestaltists proposed to continue the study of conscious experience but to abandon the dismemberment of meaningful experiences into meaningless elements. When they became acquainted with behaviorism they objected just as strongly to the dismemberment of meaningful actions into meaningless reflex elements.

Tolman, as we have seen on page 135, combined both of these rebellions; but the typical behaviorists and gestaltists were not disposed to follow him. The gestaltists believed that much could be learned by use of the "phenomenological" form of introspection (page 37). The behaviorists were suspicious of "meaning" and wished to exclude it altogether from the groundwork of their system, as Hull insisted (our page 148).

KURT KOFFKA

MAX WERTHEIMER

WOLFGANG KÖHLER

FOUNDING OF THE GESTALT SCHOOL

In 1912 it happened that three young German psychologists, who had previously been together for some years as research students at the University of Berlin, were located in and near the city of Frankfurt. These three men were Max Wertheimer (1880–1943), Kurt Koffka (1886–1941), and Wolfgang Köhler (born 1887; professor at Berlin and later at Swarthmore and at Dartmouth). Each of them had already produced psychological work of some distinction. Wertheimer had shown how the free association test could be used for the detection of an individual's hidden knowledge, as of a person suspected of a crime. Koffka had done important work on imagery and thought. Köhler had specialized effectively on problems of hearing. These three friends had become profoundly discontented with the dominant psychology represented by Wundt, the "brick-and-mortar psychology" as they called it, the bricks being the sensory elements and the mortar mere association by contiguity. A collection of elements deprived of meaning and plastered together by meaningless associations seemed to them a travesty of human experience. Conscious experiences are not only complex—as Wundt had said—but they are also meaningful, and the type of introspective analysis which pushes the meaning aside in order to get at the bare sensory elements may do good service for the special student of the senses but at the cost of losing the larger values of psychology. These men did not share Watson's disgust with all introspection; quite the contrary, they believed that excellent psychological data could be gained from "direct experience." They admitted that analysis was necessary, but the analysis must not destroy the meaning and value of experience or behavior. Science in spite of its magnificent achievements seemed to many young intellectuals of that day to be depriving human life of all significance by reducing its values to mere illusions; but these young critics believed the trouble to lie in the scientist's infatuation with "elements" and in his effort always to work "from below upward" and never "from above downward," never from the meaningful whole down to parts which are still meaningful because of their role in making up the whole. If a cause and its effect are taken as separate events, Hume was right in asserting that no necessary connection between them can be seen (page 63), but if the entire happening, cause and effect included, is viewed as a whole, cause and effect are meaningful parts of the whole. The Humean and associationist skepticism should not blind the psychologist to the reality of meaningful experience. Wertheimer and his two younger associates were convinced that they had the germ of a new and revolutionary method of attacking all the problems of psychology.

In the Frankfurt laboratory in 1911 and 1912, Wertheimer was conducting experiments on the seeing of motion, and Koffka and Köhler were serving as subjects. The problem was to account for the motion we see in looking at a motion picture. The motion picture camera takes a rapid series of snapshots which are "stills"; nothing moves perceptibly in any one still or the result is a blur and not an appearance of motion. In projection each snapshot stands still on the screen, and the light is cut off while the shift is made from each frame to the next, for if the picture were allowed actually to move on the screen you would see a blur rather than a moving object. Therefore if you saw what is physically presented on the screen, you would see a rapid series of snapshots separated by intervals of darkness. You do not and cannot see what is physically taking place on the screen. You cannot see the dark intervals because the visual sensation outlasts the physical stimulus and holds over till the next exposure, provided the interval is short. (If it is too long, you see some flicker.) Thus retinal lag bridges the time gaps between the successive still views. But what bridges the space gaps and enables you to see an object in the picture moving smoothly along instead of jerking from one place to another as it actually does in the series of views? That is the problem.

Wertheimer was attracted to this problem because the whole experience of seeing an object move in the picture evidently had an important and meaningful property (the motion) which was not to be found in the separate still views. The problem could be attacked by study of the conditions that must be met for motion to appear. He simplified the "picture" to the limit, making it consist simply of a vertical line which could be given an apparent motion in one direction or another. He exposed to view first one line and then a similar line a little to the right or left. A short, blank time interval separated the two exposures. Wertheimer found the length of the blank time interval important. If it were as long as one second, the observer simply saw one still line and then the other still line, in full agreement with the physical facts. If the interval were cut down to one fifth of a second the observer continued to see the two still lines in succession. But when the interval was further diminished the observer began to get a glimpse of something moving across from one position to the other; at one fifteenth of a second the motion was very clear, a single line appearing to move across from one end position to the other. With shorter time intervals the motion became less clear, and at one thirtieth of a second no apparent motion remained but the two presented lines seemed to stand side by side.

All these effects are even clearer if the two lines, A and B, are exposed repeatedly, A-B-A-B-A-B . . . , one at a time in alternation; at the one-fifteenth-second interval the side-to-side swing is very striking and at one-thirtieth of a second the two lines stand steadily side by side.

Wertheimer varied the experiment in several ways. He exposed a vertical followed by a horizontal line; and the observer saw a line swinging around through ninety degrees. By suitable arrangements he could make one line appear to move to the right and another line simultaneously move to the left—just as in a movie two figures are often seen to move in different directions at the same time. This result was important as ruling out the eye-movement explanation of the apparent motion. It had been suggested that the eyes by moving from one position to the other created the impression of motion; but the eyes could not move in two directions at the same time! Another old explanation was that all you really *see* is the series of still views and that you then *infer* the motion; for if a thing is here one moment and there the next moment, it must have moved from here to there in the interval. Against this theory Wertheimer appealed to direct experience: Are you aware of the separate positions first and then of the motion, or do you get a direct sensation of motion? He could also appeal to the peculiar effects of different time intervals. If the interval is too long, you see two separate lines in succession and do not infer any motion; if the interval is too short, you see two separate lines side by side and no motion; but if the interval is just right you get the clear impression of one line in motion. Wertheimer concluded that when the interval was right, the brain response to the first position merged by a continuous process into the response to the second position, so that there was actual motion in the brain.

Wertheimer's experiment on visual movement was certainly interesting and important, but we may query why it was regarded as important enough to inaugurate a new school of psychology. Well, it was a clear case of a whole which was not a mere sum of parts. An object seen in motion is not merely seen in a series of positions; in fact the separate positions are not seen distinctly because they merge into the motion which is clearly seen. A snapshot of a person running or walking often catches him in what looks like a very odd position. You can scarcely believe that he took that position in the course of his movement; and yet the camera did not lie. You saw him in that position, or rather you saw him passing through that position. You saw his movement as a dynamic whole. Seen movement was important to the Gestalt psychologists as a clear example of the dynamic whole, the whole which dominates its parts. Another clear case was the shape of an object. "Shape" in German is *Gestalt*, and to see why this school called themselves the Gestalt psychologists we must go back two decades from 1912 and take notice of an important forerunner of the Gestalt school.

GESTALT QUALITIES, FORM QUALITIES

The fact that we see shapes as well as colors and shades is obvious enough, but the older psychologists made little of this fact. We remember that Thomas Brown early in the nineteenth century had emphasized the seeing of relations (page 65). Relations are akin to shapes; when we see the front of a church as taller than the rear, we are seeing a relation and we are seeing a shape. It was Christian von Ehrenfels (1859–1932), an Austrian philosopher-psychologist, who in 1890 brought the problem of shape out into the open. What he called a Gestalt quality, or form quality, is present in a whole but not present in any of the parts making up the whole. Take the same collection of parts and arrange them in different ways and you get different wholes possessing different qualities. For example, take the notes of the musical scale: arrange them in one order and you have one tune; give them another order and you have a different tune. The tune is not present in the notes taken separately, but only in the whole arrangement. A skeptic might say, "What have you got there besides the notes?—Nothing!" The answer is that the arrangement must be just as real as the notes, since different arrangements give different tunes which have different effects on the listener. If the skeptic is not convinced you can bring forward another fact: the same tune can be made of entirely different notes. That is, the tune can be *transposed* from one key to another and still be the same tune. If it is transposed into a higher key it may sound more brilliant; if into a lower key, more mellow. But it remains the same tune and is recognized as such. When you recognize a tune, it is not the notes you recognize but the tune as a whole. To hear a tune, then, is a real experience, not decomposable into the experiences of hearing the separate notes. The tune has a quality of its own, a form quality.

There are many other examples. Using a dozen red blocks you can build patterns of many shapes, the patterns being as real as the blocks; and you can "transpose" any one pattern from red to blue, if you happen to have a dozen blue blocks available. A dressmaker can make "the same dress" out of various materials, as well as different dresses out of the same material. The point for psychology is that the same pattern can be seen and recognized in spite of differences of material, and that different patterns can be distinguished in spite of sameness of material. To state it more generally, patterns and shapes are psychologically as real as the elementary tones and colors—a fact which from 1890 on the psychological theorists were forced to admit. You hear tunes as truly as you hear tones, and you see squares and circles as truly as you see colors and shades. But by what psychological process do you get the patterns? Do you sense them as you sense tones and colors, or do you construct them by some higher mental process? There soon arose an Austrian Gestalt school which adopted the second alternative (see von Ehrenfels, 1937; Boring, 1950, pages 442–47). In this view tones and colors and other elementary sensations are raw materials provided by the senses, while the patterns are constructed by the observer. The composer constructs a tune by putting notes together in a certain arrangement, and the listener also has to exercise some constructive ability in order to hear a tune rather than a mere jumble of notes.

This theory of the Austrian Gestalt school was rejected by the Berlin Gestalt school, the school founded at Frankfurt in 1912 under the leadership of Wertheimer, Koffka, and Köhler. Both before and after that date they were closely associated with the University of Berlin but they later came to the United States. This is the group which is known today as the Gestalt school, without qualification. Their position has been that a higher mental process of combining and constructing is not required in simple cases of seeing or hearing patterns, because the sensory process itself is a process of organization. The stimuli reaching the sense organs are unorganized, uncombined. But the nerve impulses from the sense organs on reaching the brain immediately interact, attracting and repelling each other and so organizing themselves into patterns. "Organization," a favorite word in Gestalt psychology, is likely to create a false impression. It sounds as if there were an organizer in the form of some higher mental process which imposed organization on unorganized sensations—the view of the Austrian school. But this is just what the Berlin group rejected. What they meant was that the sensory field as a whole is *self-organizing*.

FACTORS IN ORGANIZATION

In a perfectly uniform visual field, such as you can secure approximately by closing the eyes in a light room, there is no observable organization. But as soon as the field is uneven, spots begin to appear, figures against a background, lines, contours, and other signs of organization (Koffka, 1935, pages 110, 124). Organization at a sensory level occurs whenever shapes and patterns are seen or heard, while organization at a higher level, more dependent on past experience, takes place when figures are named and objects recognized.

As we open our eyes we find nothing in sight, let us suppose, except a green blotch on a gray background. We immediately see the blotch as a whole, a vague shape standing out from the background. We could scarcely force ourselves to see part of the green area combined with part of the adjacent gray as a unit, and we should find it even more difficult to see a part of the green area united with a more distant part of the gray. Why is this? Why do we spontaneously see compact, uniform areas as units? The associationists —some of them—had answered that this manner of seeing was the result of past experience, that we *learn* to take compact spots for units because we often find such spots to be objects that we can manipulate or that are of some practical importance. If we had to learn this lesson, we certainly learned it well, for it is almost impossible for us now to see in any other way. On this point our "direct experience" favors the Gestalt theory that the primary brain process in seeing is a dynamic system and not an assembly of little separate activities. The visual area of the brain, in the Gestalt theory, is not like a telephone switchboard, the elements of which remain separate till connected by the operator's cord (corresponding to an association). Instead, the theory holds that the brain is a dynamic system such that the elements active at a given time interact, those that are close together tending to combine, and those that are similar also tending to combine, while those that are unlike and far apart remain separate.

This primitive organization does not consist simply in combination; separation is equally important. The laws of aggregation are at the same time laws of segregation. William James in a famous passage (1890, Vol. I, page 488) had vividly insisted on combination but he had not regarded separation as equally primitive. He said,

The law is that all things fuse that *can* fuse, and nothing separates except what must. . . . The baby, assailed by eyes, ears, nose, skin, and entrails all at once, feels it all as one great blooming, buzzing confusion.

This passage has often been misquoted by omitting the little word "one" in the last line, so giving the impression that James, of all men, was arguing for atomism, which is the very view he combated over and over again. But the Gestalt psychologists are probably right in insisting that things separate as naturally as they combine, according to such factors as distance and dissimilarity. When the baby first opens his eyes upon the world, he certainly does not see a world of objects as he will later, but if there is some compact bright splash in his visual field, due to a face bending over his crib, this probably stands out against the blooming background. If he sees the face as a separate blotch, he is making a start toward seeing it as a face. If he did not naturally take a blotch as a unit separate from the background, his task of coming to know objects by sight would be very difficult (Koffka, 1925, page 145).

Wertheimer (1923) made effective use of dots and lines scattered over the background in demonstrating important factors in aggregation and segregation, also called "field forces" or "principles of organization." Dots are likely to be seen as if falling into groups, and the question is under what conditions a group is easily segregated from the mass. One favorable condition is nearness or proximity of the dots to each other. Another favorable condition is similarity (including equality) of the dots. If the field contains dots of two shapes, or better still of two colors, those which are alike can easily be seen as forming a group. A "continuity" factor shows up when several dots form a row or smooth curve, and a factor of "common motion" when several dots move together in the same direction. The principle of "closure" is very important in the Gestalt theory. If a figure is drawn with small gaps in it, the gaps are apt to be overlooked or disregarded by an observer. Sometimes, indeed, the gaps stand out as the striking thing about a figure, but on the whole the tendency is to close up small gaps. This tendency to close a gap is regarded as revealing a fundamental principle of brain dynamics, a tendency of the brain activity to bridge a gap, like the tendency of an electric current to jump a small gap in the circuit. Tension is built up on both sides of the gap. With the gap present there is a state of unbalanced tensions, but closure brings equilibrium. The sensory brain activity tends toward equilibrium or minimum tension, just as other continuous physical systems do—drops of water, soap bubbles, or electric networks. The physics of this theory has been handled very competently by Köhler (1938, 1940).

The tendency to close a gap is akin to the tendency to overlook irregularities, and in general to see as "good" or "pregnant" a figure as possible under the given conditions. A figure is "good" if it is symmetrical, simple, or in some such respect appealing to the observer. A figure is "pregnant" if the nature of the whole figure is carried out as fully as possible by the parts. If the star figure (Fig. 3) is seen as a gappy figure, the observer will tend to emphasize and exaggerate the gaps and make it as gappy as possible. What is sometimes called "Wertheimer's law" seems to include both pregnance and good figure: "The principle contends that organization of a field

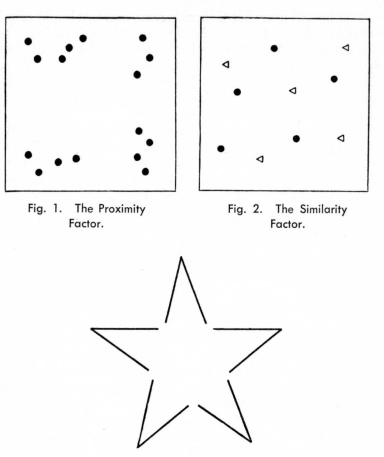

Fig. 1.   The Proximity
Factor.

Fig. 2.   The Similarity
Factor.

Fig. 3.   The Closure Factor.

tends to be as simple and clear as is compatible with the conditions given in each case" (Köhler, 1938, page 251).

Besides these organizing factors which do not depend on higher mental processes or on past experience, Gestalt theory recognizes two other factors which do so depend: the factor of familiarity and the factor of set or attitude. If some of the dots in a collection make up the outline of a face or of any familiar object, such as a letter of the alphabet, it is easy to see that figure. And if the observer is actively looking for a certain figure he is more likely to find it than if he had no such intention. The Gestalt psychologists warn us not to overemphasize these traditional factors of familiarity and set, for we are much too prone to explain everything by them and neglect the more direct and primitive factors in organization.

For our own satisfaction we may take the liberty of restating and classifying Wertheimer's factors of organization. We have, then:

1. *Peripheral factors,* present in the given collection of stimuli. Here we have proximity, similarity, continuity, and common motion.

2. *Central factors,* originating in the organism and imposed on the stimuli: familiarity and set.

3. *Reinforcing factors,* analogous to the reinforcement of a conditioned response, or to the law of effect. Here we would place the factors of pregnance, good figure, and closure. If, while you are looking at a mass of dots or lines, some figure begins to emerge that is simple, symmetrical, like an object, or definite in any way, your natural reaction is to emphasize that figure and bring it out as fully as possible. This is a kind of "confirming reaction" (pages 73–74), a reinforcement of the emerging figure, and at the same time a manifestation of Wertheimer's law. If this suggestion should succeed in bridging the gap between two schools as divergent as the Gestalt and neo-associationist, it would be a very desirable closure.

THE DYNAMIC "FIELD" IN GESTALT THEORY

To understand the Gestalt theory of organization we must consider the field concept. Since the work of Faraday and Maxwell the field and its characteristics have been very important in the science of physics. The magnetic field and lines of force between and around the poles of a horseshoe magnet are shown in the familiar figure produced by the use of iron filings. The electric field is demonstrated by experiments on induced currents. When you lead a current of electricity through a circuit of copper wire, you may suppose as the older physicists did that you have confined the electricity to the wire, and you have so confined the actual current, but an electric field surrounds the wire and extends out some distance as shown by the fact that a current is induced in a neighboring circuit whenever the current in your wire starts or stops—the principle utilized in the induction coil and the transformer. The Gestalt psychologists attempt to apply this physical concept of a dynamic field not only figuratively but literally to the visual field, to the organism, and especially to the cerebral cortex.

The contrast between a dynamic field and a machine is brought out clearly by Köhler (1947, pages 100–35). In the action of a machine two factors are operative: the power supplied and the structure of the machine. The power or energy supplied would act in all directions if it were not restricted or "constrained" to produce motion in only the direction prescribed by the structure of the machine.

This structure is a system of constraints which determine what effect the energy shall produce. For a very simple example of a machine take a ball rolling along a groove. The energy may be supplied by gravitation if the groove slopes downward or by a thrust given the ball. The groove evidently supplies no energy but it constrains the movement of the ball, making it roll in a certain curve, for example. Or consider what happens in one cylinder of an automobile engine when a spark ignites the explosive mixture. The heated gas tends to expand in all directions, but the rigid wall of the cylinder restricts the motion and only the piston moves to any extent. The still surface of a pond is relatively free from constraints; if you apply energy at a certain point by dropping in a stone, the resulting wave moves in all directions.

The organism is constructed like a machine in some respects. The muscles are attached to the bones by tendons, and when kinetic energy is generated in a muscle its tendon pulls in one certain direction. The nerves, like insulated wires, constrain the nerve currents to go in certain prescribed directions, as from the retina to the interbrain and thence to the occipital lobe. But in the cortex or any mass of gray matter there would seem to be less constraint, more freedom, more chance for field effects. A nerve impulse coming in from the retina, like the stone dropped into the pond, would start a circle of waves in the cortex; these would be electric waves. A rapid series of nerve impulses, such as comes into the cortex from any stimulated point, would generate a rapid series of waves in the cortex and throw part of the cortex into a specific pattern of electric tensions, a pattern centered at the point which directly receives the nerve impulses from the retina. Just as two stones dropped simultaneously into the pond at different points produce a pattern of interacting waves, so two simultaneously stimulated points of the retina would give a definite pattern of electric tensions in the cortex. We may think of the pattern as analogous to two hills with a valley between, the valley and sloping hillsides being as much a part of the pattern as the hilltops. In seeing the two points, then, the observer gets not merely two points, but rather two points in relation. The relation consists physically in the cortical pattern of electric waves and tensions. If the two retinal stimuli are brought nearer together, the pattern becomes sharper (the slopes steeper). Any factor that flattens the pattern weakens the relation and makes the points look farther apart. Now there is a factor that flattens the pattern: continued stimulation of the same two retinal points, giving continued activation of the same cortical pattern of electric currents, produces increasing "polarization" in the cortex. In effect, resistance is built up to the currents.

The pattern flattens out, the two points become physically less closely related and so look farther apart than at first.

A study by Köhler and Wallach (1944) which demonstrated such visual distortion in "figural after-effects" attributed them to "satiation"—described as a temporary obstructing condition (electrotonus) in the cortical tissue affected by the fixation. This would presumably cause a deflection of nerve impulses coming to that area. J. J. Gibson had earlier observed a comparable distorting lag effect: prolonged inspection of a curved line makes a straight line viewed immediately afterward look as if it curved in the opposite direction (1933). He explained the phenomenon as the effect of kinesthetic adaptation. Köhler agrees that these "displacement" effects occur in kinesthesis, passive touch, and hearing, but insists that they can all be accounted for as instances of electrotonic satiation. "Even certain inhibitions which tend to impede learning may partly be caused by what we have called 'satiation' " (1958a, page 153).

Displacement phenomena have been verified by many later experimenters, and Köhler's daring "field theory" of cortical action has been scrutinized in a number of studies of electrical currents in the human cortex and in the exposed cortex of animals under various conditions of stimulation. (For detailed bibliography see Köhler, 1958.) Although an impressive array of data seems to support the electrotonic theory, competing explanations of figural after-effects have been offered. Osgood and Heyer (1952) propose one based on differential adaptation rate and recovery along a gradient of neural excitation determined by the "peak" and sharpness of a contour; Motokawa, *et al.* (1957) derive the effects from retinal rather than cortical processes; Fox (1951) is disposed to include the "adaptation" originally suggested by Gibson; and Story (1959) introduces the factor of the observer's expectation or "set." Besides the volume of research on the problem in the United States, much has been done in England, and even more in Japan (Sagara and Oyama, 1957). Many investigations have been reviewed by H. H. Spitz (1958) and by McEwen. The latter's conclusion is (1959): "The findings reported call for a more complex theory . . . than any so far put forward . . . they mean that perception is at least a two-stage process." (See also McEwen and Rodger, 1960.)

If the cerebral cortex is a free field for dynamic interaction, the old "machine theory" of the nervous system must be given up so far as the cortex is concerned, though it probably holds good of the nerves and of the vast system of nerve-fiber connections in the brain. The older psychologists had thought of each little item of stimulation coming in along the sensory nerves as remaining an independent unit in the cortex, so that the total sensation at any moment would be a mere collection or "mosaic" of sensory items. This mosaic seems to offer no chance for the relations and patterns which we have been speaking of and which are so real in actual sensory experience. Each sensory item would have to remain separate from all others, according to the machine theory as viewed by the Gestalt psychologists. But they do not do full justice to the possibilities of a machine theory. One pronounced anatomical characteristic of the cortex and other nerve centers is the *convergence* of nerve fibers (Hebb, 1949). Each cell has contact on the receiving side with several or many axons from different regions. So the various items of sensory stimulation, even if they do not interact, certainly *coact* or work together in producing the next phase of the total response. Within the framework of a machine theory, broadly conceived, a psychologist who regarded a pattern as a *response* to a combination of stimuli could perfectly well subscribe to Köhler's conclusion (1947, page 103):

> Our view will be that, instead of reacting to local stimuli by local and mutually independent events, the organism responds to the *pattern* of stimuli to which it is exposed; and that this answer is a unitary process, a functional whole, which gives, in experience, a sensory scene rather than a mosaic of local sensations.

Just because the Gestalt psychologists reject the machine theory we must not assume that they accept the vitalistic rather than the mechanistic view of the organism. They are strongly against vitalism, and that is indeed one reason for their emphasis on field dynamics. The field is a physical reality and at the same time corresponds to the psychological realities of behavior and experience. If we wish, as the Gestalt psychologists do wish, to fit the world of behavior and direct experience into the physiochemical world of natural processes, we must ask what physical patterns of brain processes can correspond with the known patterns of behavior and direct experience. Some correspondences are easily found. When we hear a sound grow softer and die away, the cortical process doubtless has the pattern of decreasing intensity. When we see a figure standing out as a unit from its background, the occipital cortex doubtless is active in such a way that a certain physical process is segregated from its surroundings.

In general, Gestalt theory postulates an *isomorphism* between patterns that we see or hear and the corresponding brain processes (Köhler, 1938, pages 185–232; 1947, pages 61–63, 301; Koffka, 1935, pages 53–68). The meaning of isomorphism may be understood by thinking of a map as compared with the country which it represents.

The map is very different from the country, just as our conscious experience is very different from any brain process. But certain shapes and relations in the map hold good of the country. What is higher up in the map is farther north in the country. What appears on the map as a wiggly line is present in the country as a river. If we could inspect a person's brain processes as well as we can see a map, and had learned the correspondences, we could read off his experiences as we read a map. So vague and unrealistic a prospect would have no appeal to the Gestalt psychologists, but as good experimentalists they try to derive from the postulate of isomorphism definite hypotheses which can be tested by psychological experiments, an excellent example being their work on figural after-effects, already mentioned. (See pages 224–25.)

SELF AND ENVIRONMENT IN DIRECT EXPERIENCE

The Gestalt psychologists object to behaviorism on several counts. They do not oppose objective methods and indeed agree that the final test of any hypothesis should be objective. But they insist on the psychological value of "direct experience." They approach the dynamics of behavior from the side of sensory experience, and with some success, as indicated in the preceding sections of this chapter. Pavlov regarded the conditioned reflex as a window for viewing the higher nervous activity, and motor behavior in general is such a window; but sensory experience is another window affording a view from another side, and perhaps a clearer and more direct view than can be got from the motor side. Apart from brain dynamics, sense perception has proved to be a very fertile field for experimental study even during these years of relative neglect by the behaviorists.

But the principal objection of Gestalt psychology to behaviorism has to do with the stimulus–response or S–R formula. The formula has meant different things to different psychologists, no doubt, but the behaviorists have meant by S the sum of stimuli acting on the sense organs at a given time, and by R the motor response. The dash or arrow between S and R has seemed to imply a direct connection between sensory stimulus and motor response, as if there were no intervening processes of any consequence. Stimulus and response are the objectively observable facts, and behaviorism as originally conceived was not to go beyond them. Watson's "implicit behavior" and the more recent "intervening variables" (page 137) do of course go beyond the objective data. And Watson really went beyond the objective data when he defined a stimulus as "any object in the general environment or any change in the tissues" (1925, page 6). The object out there is not the stimulus reaching our eyes or other sense organs. To identify the object with the stimulus is to assume in the organism the ability to perceive the object on receiving the stimulus. The behaviorist has tacitly assumed in the organism this process of perception intervening between stimulus and response. He has taken it for granted and refused to study it. As Köhler put the matter (1947, pages 164, 165, 200):

> The stimulus–response formula, which sounds at first so attractive, is actually quite misleading. In fact, it has so far appeared acceptable solely because Behaviorists use the term "stimulus" in such a loose fashion. . . . When the term is taken in its strict sense, it is not generally "a stimulus" which elicits a response. . . . A man's actions are commonly related to a well-structured field, most often to particular thing-units. The right psychological formula is therefore: *pattern of stimulation–organization–response to the products of organization.* . . . The stimulus–response formula . . . ignores the fact that between the stimuli and the response there occur the processes of organization, particularly the formation of group-units in which parts acquire new characteristics.

The Gestalt psychologists learned their "principles of organization" from the study of sensory experience, but they have gone on to apply these principles to behavior in a broader sense. Koffka (1935) made a valiant attempt to work out a comprehensive Gestalt theory covering learning, memory, emotion, voluntary and involuntary action, and personality. He tried to be as concrete as possible but could not help being sketchy and very abstract in spots, because some parts of the subject had not been directly studied by the Gestalt school.

Koffka's approach to behavior, however, is deserving of careful attention. We should regard behavior, he said, not as composed of separate responses to stimuli but as governed by a total field, the organismic field of interacting forces, a field that is self-organized into definite though changing patterns. This organismic field is of course physiological, but as operating in behavior and conscious experience it can be better called psychophysical. Its operations are physicochemical, cellular, or what have been called "molecular" (page 135), but they are at the same time "molar," occurring in patterns corresponding to significant units in experience and behavior. Some of these patterned operations are unconscious (the "unconscious" being part of the molar-physiological field), but some of them are conscious and make up the field of direct experience. There is no sharp, fixed boundary between conscious experience and the rest of the psychophysical field, and conscious experience is open to influences from the rest of the psychophysical field such as unconscious or only vaguely conscious desires.

The field of direct experience, as we all know it in adult life, has two poles, the ego and the environment. That is, we are aware of ourselves as surrounded by an environment. These two poles are like the poles of a magnet, with lines of force or stress between them. They are in constant and shifting interaction. Presumably the child does not at first make any distinction between the self and the not-self. But he discovers that his body is a unit distinct from anything else. Some things are in front of him, other things behind him, while he himself is in between. The great qualitative difference between the definite visual and auditory sensations and the background of bodily feelings may play a part in segregating the self from the environment. Tensions develop between himself and persons in the environment and thus the polarity of self and not-self is sharpened. The ego is not a mere pole; it is complex, structured into subsystems. Yet it maintains its identity in the flux of environmental happenings, without ever becoming static. It is never "completely balanced, completely at rest. . . . It is always going somewhere" (Koffka, 1935, page 332). The main point for the Gestalt theory is that there are always tensions within the ego as well as between the ego and the environment.

In a typical experience, I am doing something in the environment. The environment I respond to is of course the environment as it appears to me, and the appearance may not correspond perfectly to the reality. I behave in the apparent environment, which Koffka accordingly called the "behavioral environment." He introduced this concept with a striking example (1935, pages 27–28):

> On a winter evening amidst a driving snowstorm a man on horseback arrives at an inn, happy to have reached a shelter after hours of riding over the wind-swept plain on which the blanket of snow had covered all paths and landmarks. The landlord who came to the door viewed the stranger with surprise and asked him whence he came. The man pointed in the direction straight away from the inn, whereupon the landlord, in a tone of awe and wonder, said: "Do you know that you have ridden across the Lake of Constance?" At which the rider dropped stone dead at his feet.
>
> In what environment, then, did the behavior of the stranger take place? The Lake of Constance. Certainly, because it is a true proposition that he rode across it. And yet, this is not the whole truth, for the fact that there was a frozen lake and not ordinary solid ground did not affect his behavior in the slightest. . . . There is a second sense to the word environment according to which our horseman did not ride across the lake at all, but across an ordinary snow-swept plain. His behavior was a riding-over-a-plain, but not a riding-over-a-lake.

The geographical environment in this case was a lake, while the behavioral environment was a plain. Behavior which is well adjusted to the apparent or behavioral environment does not always fit the physical or geographical environment. The physical situation may be deceptive or at least difficult to grasp, our senses have their limits, and our desires may blind us to the real facts. Persons as well as things are not always what they seem. We may fail to discern their true attitudes and intentions, so that our behavioral social environment differs more or less from the real or geographical social environment. The behavioral environment is different for different individuals even when they are in the same geographical environment. It differs according to their several needs, interests, and abilities. One who is interested in gardening sees a nice garden plot in the spring beckoning him to spade it up and plant things, while to another person the same plot is merely bare ground with no appeal whatever. When a person is dreaming, his behavioral environment is a dream world very different from the room where he is sleeping. When anyone is asked to report what he sees, hears, tastes, smells, or touches, he reports things and other environmental facts, as a rule, and not the stimuli received which serve him as indicators. He is reporting his behavioral environment. When an animal's behavior is correctly adjusted to such environmental facts as the direction of a sound or the size and distance of a visible object, that animal is using stimuli as indicators in the same general way as a human being, and the psychologist, without assuming conscious experience in the animal, is still entitled to say that the animal's behavior is governed by a behavioral environment.

All this is familiar and acceptable enough to all psychologists except perhaps the most orthodox behaviorists. What, then, is the Gestalt psychologist's reason for insisting on it so strongly? There are two main reasons. First, the behavioral environment, as contrasted with an assemblage of stimuli, is *organized*, and behavior is governed by this organized field and not directly by the stimuli. This point has already been sufficiently emphasized. Second, the Gestalt principles of organization are held to explain why it is that the behavioral environment corresponds as well as it does with the geographical environment. A bunch of stimuli that are close together and similar gives rise to a segregated whole in the psychophysical brain field. Now such a bunch of stimuli very often comes from a definite object in the environment. Thus the principles of proximity and similarity make us see the environment as containing definite objects; and to this extent the behavioral environment corresponds to the geographical. The principles of continuity and closure operate to close accidental gaps in the stimuli received. The "central" factors of set and familiarity certainly are very important —more important than the Gestalt school is inclined to admit—in exploring the environment and building up an acquaintance with it, part by part. And a great deal could be said for the factors of pregnance and good figure, which we have regarded as factors of reinforcement (page 223). In spite of many discrepancies between the behavioral and the geographical environments, between appearance and reality, a good measure of agreement is guaranteed, according to the Gestalt theory, by the forces of the psychophysical field within the organism which receives the stimuli from the external world. Many "molar" characteristics of the physical world—patterns and relations—are reproduced in the psychophysical field and in the individual's direct experience and so made available as guides for his behavior in the environment. His motor behavior is determined in the same general way by the field forces; but this side of the theory has not been worked out into very definite form.

INSIGHT AND PRODUCTIVE THINKING

Two of the most interesting studies produced by the Gestalt school have to do with problem solving. These are Köhler's book on *The Mentality of Apes* (1917 in German, 1925 and 1927 in English) and Wertheimer's *Productive Thinking* (1945). Other Gestalt studies of problem solving which amply deserve more than this passing notice are those by Duncker (1935, 1945) and by Katona (1940).

Just before the First World War, in 1913, Köhler was made director of an anthropoid station at Teneriffe in the Canary Islands, maintained by the Prussian Academy of Sciences. Köhler proceeded to Teneriffe and began psychological studies of chimpanzees. Marooned there during the war, he had time for the thorough study shown in his book. The problem he undertook was whether the chimpanzee, representing probably the most intelligent group of subhuman animals, showed any genuine intelligence. By intelligence Köhler meant something more than trial and error in the solution of a novel problem. He meant insight, a seeing into the problem. Thorndike had been convinced by his experiments on cats, dogs, and monkeys that these animals attacked a problem by trial and error, i.e., by impulsively trying one thing after another until something succeeded, and that they learned by repetition and the Law of Effect, the successful reactions being stamped in and the unsuccessful ones stamped out. Though Thorndike's experiments had not extended to the anthropoid apes, the general impression left behind by his work was that trial and error represented the only animal line of attack on a problem. Köhler entertained serious doubts of this conclusion and believed that Thorndike's associationist background had led to ill-conceived experiments and false interpretation of results.

Thorndike had used mazes and puzzle boxes—blind situations, not lying open to the animal's inspection. He did this in order to give the animals something new to be mastered. If he had left a clear, unobstructed path to the goal, the animals would have gone straight to the goal without any problem to solve. Köhler agreed that there must always be some obstacle; the animal must be required to take a roundabout path, a *detour*, literally or figuratively, to reach the goal. But Köhler held that the animal should nevertheless be enabled to survey the whole situation, so that if he has the power of insight he will be able to solve the problem without blind trial and error. The pattern of the situation should be visible, and the question should be whether the animal can grasp the pattern and act accordingly.[1] In a complicated maze, an animal cannot see the entire path to the goal and is bound to show trial and error. Thus the maze does not give the experimenter a chance to see whether insight is possible for the animal; the same is true of Thorndike's puzzle boxes.

Köhler's chimpanzees solved with ease any problem which consisted literally in a roundabout path to a goal, if only the whole path were in clear view. Other kinds of "detours" gave them more trouble. While a chimpanzee is confined in a barred cage, a banana is placed on the ground outside at too great a distance to be reached by the hand, but with a string tied to it and laid along the ground to the cage. This single-string problem is easily solved, but if several strings are laid on the ground, all extending in the general direction of the banana but only one being attached to it, a chimpanzee often pulls the wrong string. Prompt insight is prevented by the complexity of the visual pattern and by the animal's haste.

The reaching-stick problem is simple when a suitable stick is laid on the ground between the cage and the banana, but becomes difficult if the stick is placed far away from the banana, especially if it lies at the back of the cage. A compact visual pattern is apparently a great help in gaining quick insight.

The chimpanzees learned rather quickly to use a box as a stool for reaching a suspended banana, but the use of two boxes, one to be piled on the other for reaching a still higher objective, was a dif-

---

[1] Köhler was anticipated in this criticism of Thorndike's work by the English scientist, L. T. Hobhouse (1901), who devised a variety of experiments similar to those later used by Köhler, tried them on several kinds of animals, and reached the conclusion that what he called "practical judgment," the ability to respond to patterns and relations, was within the power of animals such as the cat, dog, and monkey.

ficult problem though solved (with some assistance) by several of the animals. While they evidently appreciated the value of a high stool, they showed no insight in the matter of stability of construction, being content to pile the boxes carelessly and depend on their own agility to reach the objective before the pile collapsed.

The prize performance was the solution of the jointed-stick problem by "Sultan," the most intelligent of Köhler's chimpanzees. He was given two pieces of bamboo which could be fitted together into a long stick—long enough to reach a banana that could not be reached by either stick alone. After an hour spent in fruitless angling with the single sticks and other trial-and-error behavior, he gave up but continued idly playing with the two sticks. Happening to get them jointed together he immediately used the long stick for pulling in the banana and other things as well; and next day he showed almost perfect retention of what he had learned.

The behavioral evidences of insight in these cases are (1) the sudden transition from helplessness to mastery; (2) the good retention; and (3) what psychologists call "transfer." Insight gained in one situation can sometimes be carried over and utilized in another situation which has the same pattern though not the same details. If the trick of piling boxes to reach a banana has been grasped, it should be transferable to a situation where a trunk and a suitcase are available for reaching an apple. Insightful behavior does not consist in separate responses to separate stimuli but in an integrated response to the pattern of the whole situation. A problem amounts to a "gap" in the present situation, insight amounts to perceiving the gap, and insightful behavior closes the gap.

Insight ordinarily means a seeing below the surface of things, but this could not have been Köhler's meaning, since he insisted that the essential structure of the situation should be aboveboard and open to inspection. Insight may of course go much deeper, but it consists essentially in seeing the situation as an organized whole. A rudimentary form of perceptual insight is illustrated by a "transposition experiment." An animal is first trained to find food in a box marked by a certain shade of gray. Two boxes are always placed before him, A and B, box A being marked with a patch of light gray paper, box B with a medium gray. The two boxes vary in position, but the food is always in B, the darker of the two. When the animal has learned to choose B consistently, box A is removed and a new box C, darker than B, is substituted. Will the animal still choose B, responding to the same specific stimulus as before? As a rule he chooses C, the darker of the two visible boxes. What he has learned, therefore, is to choose the darker of two, not a particular shade of gray. He perceives the lighter–darker pattern or relation, and chooses the darker term of the relation.

This whole experiment fails to meet Köhler's requirement that the problem should be openly presented to the animal, for the food is not visible and there is nothing to indicate, at the outset, where the food will be, if anywhere. The animal has to try one box or another and run the chance of making an error. He usually makes many errors before settling down to a consistent choice. But what he learns is response to a relation between stimuli (or objects) and not response to an isolated stimulus. Insight in this rudimentary form consists in perceiving relations, perceiving them well enough to be governed by them in behavior.

In this experiment and many others the animal (or human being) learns by trial and error, or at least *after* some trial and error. Whether the trial-and-error behavior makes any contribution to the solution of a problem, or is simply so much waste motion, is a question for experimental study, and there have been many studies devoted to the question. We cannot pause to discuss this matter thoroughly, but will merely consider the relation of trial and error to Gestalt theory. The Gestalt psychologists speak very disparagingly of trial-and-error behavior and regard it as waste motion for the most part, though they admit that sometimes a blind action results in a better view of the whole situation (Köhler, 1927, page 193). It would seem, however, that the Gestalt disparagement of trial and error is illogical, and that trial-and-error behavior must *always* be needed whenever it occurs. For the Gestalt theory is not that we *ought* to organize the field but that we always *do* organize it. The field, including the ego and the behavioral environment, organizes itself, and behavior is governed by the resulting organization. Any false move was dictated by the organized field. The move was an error because the behavioral environment did not conform to the real or geographical environment. The false move made some change in the environment or in the individual's relation to the environment, resulting in a new organization and a new move. When the successful move occurs, it occurs because the just preceding false move has so altered the behavioral environment as to make it conform to the real environment. Therefore the last of the false moves is necessary for insight. And we could argue back in this vein, step by step, and reach the conclusion that the whole series of false moves was necessary, given the organism and environment as they were at the outset.

Thorndike's cat in the puzzle box, for example, sees the space between two particular bars as a way out, but on trying to squeeze through finds it not a way out after all. The cat's behavioral environment is changed to that extent, but several other false leads may have to be explored and eliminated before the door button stands out as something to be tried. Even this successful move does not usually clarify the situation completely for a cat, her perception of such a device as a door button being pretty vague. Köhler has recognized this fact when in his presidential address to the American Psychological Association in 1959 he confessed to past inconsistencies in his own early use of the term "insight." To say that the behavior of an ape reflects his awareness of an important relation between two features of a problem is not to say that the relation emerged through insight. When, as in Harlow's "oddity" problem (page 189, this book), the significant relational fact is set by the experimenter, a great many circumstances will enter into determining the animal's choices in the early trials "until he happens to attend, once or repeatedly, to the oddity relation just when he chooses (or does not choose) the right object. Gradually he will now attend to this particular relation in all trials; and he may do so even when entirely new objects are shown. Surely, such a process should not simply be called 'learning by insight'" (Köhler, 1959, page 730). When the solution does not depend entirely on the whim of the experimenter, insight, Köhler believes, may play a more important part, but is still not the only factor involved.

While the Gestalt psychologists have demonstrated the value of insight, then, they have not disproved the value of trial and error. By *trial and error* is meant exploratory or manipulatory behavior that is relatively "blind" in the sense of lacking foresight of the result of a move that is tried. Such blind exploration is inevitable when the situation itself is blind, as it often is in real life, animal or human; and even when the "geographical" situation is completely open to inspection, the "behavioral" situation may be different because of poor observation. By *insight* is meant good observation, perception of the situation as a whole, or perception of those parts of the situation that provide a route to the goal.

If it is true that problem solution depends on perceptual organization and on the field forces present at the moment—so that errors as well as genuine solutions are bound to occur—is there nothing that can be done to *improve* man's ways of attacking his problems, nothing to make his thinking more productive? A *teacher* can so present problems as to favor insight and can foster in his pupils a genuine problem-solving attitude; and the human individual can be his own teacher, once he grasps the principles of Gestalt psychology. Such was Wertheimer's message in his last book (1945). His case material ranged from the solution of simple geometrical problems by young children up to a personal study with Einstein of the thought processes that produced the theory of relativity. At all levels Wertheimer found examples of "genuine, fine, clean, direct, productive processes," though he also found "factors working against those processes as, e.g., blind habits, certain kinds of school drill, bias, or special interests" (1945, page 189).

Wertheimer's advice for one who would be a productive thinker is to let the whole dominate the parts and never to lose sight of the problem as a whole even while devoting the necessary attention to details. Avoid "piecemeal" thinking, which is sure to be blind. Concentrate on the "structure" of the situation, get that clearly in view and locate the gap in it which constitutes the problem. In scrutinizing details, be always "looking for structural rather than piecemeal truth," asking yourself what role each detail plays in the structure of the whole situation.

The science of logic, as Wertheimer and many others have pointed out, tests the validity of a conclusion but does not show the actual process of reasoning that leads a thinker to his conclusion. For example, the logical demonstration of a proposition as customarily given in a textbook on geometry enables you to meet the objections of any skeptic and prove to him that the proposition is valid; but if you work out the demonstration as an "original," your own thought process is very different from the formal demonstration given in the book. Other psychologists have emphasized the exploratory, zigzag, trial-and-error process that goes on in actual reasoning; such terms were very distasteful to Wertheimer, who emphasized instead the need for grouping and regrouping, organizing and reorganizing, centering and recentering the data. You may have to change your point of view, but you should always face toward the goal and take no step blindly. Proceed from above downward, from the whole to the parts. The piecemeal attack is sometimes very painstaking and conscientious, but it is blind, stupid, slavish, pedantic.

Wertheimer experimented in teaching children how to find the area of a rectangle by regarding it as divided into little squares—so many rows, each made up a certain number of squares, so that the area could be found by multiplying the number of squares in a row by the number of rows, i.e., by multiplying the base by the altitude. When he was sure that the child had a "structural" understanding of the area of a rectangle he presented an oblique parallelogram, usually a long, slender one, and asked the child how the area of the parallelogram could be found, suggesting that it be compared with a rectangle. Many older children, as well as adults, gave the "associationist" type of answer: "I haven't learned that yet," or, "I used to know that but I've forgotten." But some, even of the younger children, reached a "fine, genuine, original" solution. They saw that the middle portion of the parallelogram was like a rectangle and that only the oblique ends were troublesome; and then they saw that one end could be taken off by a vertical cut and fitted on at the other end so as to make a complete rectangle out of the parallelogram.

Wertheimer (and also Katona, 1940) experimented with a variety of mathematical and quasi-mathematical problems, seeking methods of leading children to see into the problems and not depend on blind following of rules. They concluded that school teachers tend to depend too much on repetitious drill in the application of authoritarian rules, and that in this way children are "educated" to depend on rules rather than on their own intelligence. They charged that the associationist and connectionist psychology, applied to education, supports the traditional emphasis on drill, and that only the Gestalt psychology offers any hope of improvement.

Some facts, to be sure, like the names of objects, are just facts and have to be learned by association strengthened by repetition. "Repetition is useful, but continuous use of mechanical repetition also has harmful effects. It is dangerous because it easily induces habits of sheer mechanized action, blindness, tendencies to perform slavishly instead of thinking, instead of facing a problem freely" (Wertheimer, 1945, page 112).

Trial and error, in Wertheimer's view, can play no part in productive thinking, except as an interference. He has described two examples of his own solution of mathematical problems in which, he felt, trial and error played no part, even though many hours or days were required to reach a solution. "There was no trial and error with regard to formulas, no trying of hypotheses. . . . Each step was a step in a consistent line of thinking; there were no arbitrary steps, no blind trial and error" (pages 155, 159). In spite of this strong assertion, there are instances in the reports of his trying a lead that he had to abandon because it was getting nowhere. In his interesting analysis of Einstein's progress toward the theory of relativity, again, there are clear instances of the same sort.

> For years Einstein tried to clarify the problem by studying and trying to change the Maxwell equations. He did not succeed. . . . In whatever way he tried to unify the question of mechanical movement with the electromagnetic phenomena, he got into difficulties. . . . But although these attempts did not lead to a solution, they were by no means blind. At that stage it was wholly reasonable to test such possibilities (pages 171, 188).

No one, certainly, would accuse Einstein of stupidity or of trying leads without some good reason. But he was "blind" in one important respect: he could not see his way through to his goal. Everyone is blind in this respect when confronted by a genuine problem, for if he could see through from the start to the finish there would be no problem. Even in mathematical problems such as Wertheimer used in his experiments, some exploration is necessary; and in concrete matters of fact everyone agrees that exploration is necessary. Even when you find nothing of positive value, you at least eliminate possibilities that looked promising at the start.

Wertheimer's advice to the would-be productive thinker is all to the good, even though he does not succeed in deriving from Gestalt principles any sure way of being productive all the time. The "field forces" will not always keep you out of blind alleys. On the contrary such factors as proximity and similarity are responsible for many misleading first impressions. The tendency to closure must sometimes be resisted for fear of adopting premature conclusions (pages 110, 195). "Good figure" is something to be found rather than something given in a problematic situation. "Set" is useful when it takes the form of an "attitude of looking for the objective structural requirements of a situation, . . . facing the issue freely, going ahead with confidence and courage" (page 64). But set is a dangerous handicap when it takes the form of excessive eagerness to reach the goal or the form of a blind reliance on habitual routine procedures (pages 113, 195). The recall of past experiments can be a great help in understanding a novel situation, but it is only too likely to lead to a piecemeal attack or to a superficial view based on the apparent familiarity of the present situation. In short the field forces operate to produce errors as well as genuine solutions.

Wertheimer's main contention, after all, is that human beings desire to think clearly and are able to do so. "To live in a fog . . . is for many people an unbearable state of affairs. There is a tendency to structural clearness, surveyability, to truth as against petty views" (page 199). And according to Gestalt theory, as opposed to the skeptical philosophy of Hume and the associationists, truth is attainable if we approach our problems "from above" and resolutely aim at structural understanding. To see evidences of clear thinking in children especially, or in his students, gave Wertheimer great joy. He was, as Köhler assures us (1944), a man of "extraordinary mind."

LEWIN'S FIELD THEORY

Kurt Lewin (1890–1947) may be counted either as an adherent of Gestalt psychology or as the founder of a closely related school. He began his career independently but was later closely associated with Köhler and Wertheimer at the University of Berlin, where he studied and taught before migrating to the United States in 1932. His psychological career can be divided into three periods:

1. At Berlin he developed a theory of motivation with relevant experiments mostly on adults but in part on young children.

2. At the State University of Iowa, 1935–1944, he was professor of child psychology, one of his outstanding achievements being the study of groups of children under democratic as compared with autocratic leadership. Research was necessary on methods of training democratic leaders as well as on the responses of the children and their groups.

3. In 1944 Lewin was called to the Massachusetts Institute of Technology to inaugurate a Research Center for Group Dynamics. There were many problems of industrial strife and of prejudice and hostility between groups, and Lewin from experience and originality was obviously the best man to get the necessary research started. So well did he do this in the few years of life left for him that his Research Center still remains active and scientifically productive in its new location at the University of Michigan. For an early report see Festinger (1950).

Lewin began his scientific career as an associationist, but with a particular interest in will and motivation. His early work (1917, 1922) convinced him that the associationist theory had to be radically revised. Associations, he said, were not sources of energy, but merely links or connections, like the couplings between the cars of a railroad train which do nothing except transmit the energy supplied by the locomotive. You have strong associations, for example, between common objects and their names, but these associations do not force you to name every object you see. If you have some motive for naming them, the associations enable you to do so easily; but without some motive the associations have no driving force. Even as passive couplings, associations are nevertheless of great importance, according to Lewin, and in this respect he diverged from the views of the major Gestalt psychologists who sought to get away from the notion of machine-like links or connections and to explain learning as well as perception in terms of organizational dynamics. Lewin said much later (1940, page 16):

Psychology cannot try to explain everything with a single construct, such as association, instinct, or gestalt. A variety of constructs has to be used. These should be interrelated, however, in a logically precise manner.

Throughout his three decades of psychological activity Lewin consistently devoted himself to what we may broadly call the motivation of human behavior. Associative machinery and instinctive machinery as well must be activated by driving forces, by needs and quasi-needs, the latter being temporary interests or intentions. This line of investigation differed considerably from the studies of perception and problem solving characteristic of the older Gestalt psychologists, who perhaps felt that the time was not ripe for such an extension, though we find Koffka using Lewin's results in his own attempt to write a comprehensive Gestalt psychology. Again, while Lewin had much to say of psychological forces, he did not attempt to relate them closely to physical forces, nor did he show much interest in the "isomorphism" of direct experience with brain dynamics (see Köhler, 1938, page 357; Koffka, 1935, pages 47–48). His interests led toward social rather than physiological psychology. The "field" of which Lewin had a great deal to say was not the brain field isomorphic with the individual's direct experience, but rather the environment containing one or more individuals.

Lewin did, however, regard the individual person as a field or system containing subsystems more or less separate but more or less capable of interacting and combining with each other. One subsystem might be friendship for a certain person; another might be love for a certain sport. When a person is engaged in a certain activity and intent on reaching a goal, one of his subsystems is in a state of tension. If he is interrupted, this subsystem remains tense for a while and causes him to resume the same activity as soon as the interruption ceases. If the same activity cannot be resumed, a similar activity may serve as a substitute and drain off the tension. A repetitious task will sooner or later drain off all the tension in its subsystem, leaving a state of satiation which tends with continued activity to spread to related subsystems ("cosatiation"). These and other inferences from Lewin's theory of motivation were put to experimental test and confirmed (Lewin, 1935).

By refusing to become involved in the problem of how motives originate, whether in instinct or in previous experience, and by experimenting instead on the present operation of motives, Lewin gave a new direction to the study of motivation and made real progress there.

His guiding field formula, as reported in his summary of his work on child behavior and development (1954), could be written,

$$B = f(P, E),$$

"Behavior depends on the interaction of the Person and the Environment." Application of the formula to a specific case becomes rather involved, since the psychological environment depends partly on the abilities and wishes of the person, and we are not perfectly sure of a person's present abilities and wishes until we see how he responds to the present environment. But we can proceed by successive approximation.

As a child develops, his personality system expands and becomes more fully organized into subsystems. His psychological environment expands in space and time and becomes "cognitively restructured," i.e., better understood, and he distinguishes better between the real world and the "irreal" world of his wishes and fears. He finds new social roles for himself and learns new social norms and codes.

Lewin clung to his "field theory" in spite of its difficulties. Late in his career (1940, pages 33, 36), he stated his creed as follows:

The possibilities of a "field theory" in the realm of action, emotion, personality are firmly established. The basic statements of a field theory are that (a) behavior has to be derived from a totality of coexisting facts, (b) these coexisting facts have the character of a "dynamic field" in so far as the state of any part of this field depends on every other part of the field. . . . According to field theory, behavior depends neither on the past nor on the future but on the present field. . . . This is in contrast both to the belief of teleology that the future is the cause of behavior, and that of associationism that the past is the cause of behavior.

Lewin's field is thus the "life space, containing the person and his psychological environment" (1938, page 2). The psychological (or behavioral) environment is of course the environment as perceived and understood by the person; but, more than that, it is the environment as related to his present needs and quasi-needs. Many objects which are perceived are of no present concern to him and so exist only in the background of his psychological environment. Other objects have positive or negative "valence"—positive if they promise to meet his present needs, negative if they threaten injury. Objects of positive valence attract him, while objects of negative valence repel him. The attraction is a force or "vector" directed toward the object, the repulsion a vector directed away from the object. A vector tends to produce "locomotion" in a certain direction. Often two or more vectors are acting on the person at the same time, and then the locomotion is some kind of a "resultant." The locomotion called for by the vectors is often impeded or completely blocked by a "barrier."

Some of these concepts call for a little further explanation. Locomotion includes any sort of approach or withdrawal, as for example turning the eyes toward a beautiful object or away from an ugly one, listening to agreeable music or attending to something else if the music is uninteresting. When you are absorbed in planning what to do tomorrow, your life space is not the room where you are now sitting but rather the place where you expect to be tomorrow, and your present locomotion in that anticipated environment consists in deciding on one course of action rather than another, according as the resultant of present vectors impels you toward one or the other.

Barriers are very important in the theory. A barrier is a "constraint" which has no valence at the outset and exerts no force until force is exerted on it, when it offers a certain amount of resistance. It may yield when force is applied to it or it may prove to resist your utmost efforts. How rigid it is you can discover only by trying it out, by exploration. A box stands in the way of getting something you want, but how heavy the box may be you have to discover by trying to move it. Some plan of yours may not entirely please your friend, but how much resistance he will put up you have still to discover. (Evidently some trial and error are necessary when an unexplored barrier stands in the way to any goal.) A barrier found to be impassable is likely to acquire a negative valence such as leads to an angry attack or execration.

An awakened need is a state of tension in the person, a readiness for action but so far without any very specific direction. A suitable object, when found, acquires a positive valence. So a vector is set up directing locomotion toward the object. Excessive tension (hunger, for example) may blur the individual's perception of the environment, prevent his finding an object of suitable valence, and so prevent the establishment of a definite vector. Again, frustration by a barrier, by increasing tension, may result in random or ill-directed activity (1938, page 160).

Lewin felt the need of some kind of mathematics to foster exact reasoning on problems of motivation and behavior. Statistics, so much used by psychologists, did not meet his requirements because he wished to deal adequately with the "single case" so as to predict an individual's behavior in a concrete situation (1935, page 68). He needed two things: some means of mapping the *life space* at a given moment so as to show all the possible goals and routes to the goals; and some means of taking account of *motives* so as to predict which one of the possibilities will be chosen by the individual. No existing form of mathematics was exactly suited to Lewin's requirements, but he found he could do fairly well with a combination of topology and vector analysis—topology for mapping the life space, vector analysis for taking care of the motives (1936, 1938, 1940; see also Leeper, 1943). He used only the rudiments of these two branches of mathematics but elaborated his own system both in the form of diagrams and in that of equations. One advantage of mathematical treatment is that the symbols used must be carefully defined. In order to apply mathematics to a concrete problem, we must define our symbols (1) conceptually, by relating one symbol to another, as for example by relating the concepts of need, valence, and vector to each other; and also (2) operationally, by indicating how the facts covered by our concepts are to be observed and measured. The operational definition enables us to secure our data, while the conceptual definition enables us to treat the data mathematically (1938, page 13). The diagrams and equations have some value at least in laying the situation distinctly before the investigator. They should also suggest hypotheses to be tested by experiment, and Lewin found his diagrams useful in this respect, as his pupils have also. One difficulty is that the resultant of two vectors cannot be found in the ordinary way by the parallelogram of forces. If a person sees one desirable goal to the north of him and another equally desirable one to the east, he does not advance eagerly to the northeast. He makes a choice. Probably he "restructures the field," sees it so that the two vectors are no longer equal in force. But about all that can psychologically be done with divergent vectors is to regard them as directly opposed to each other, so that only their relative strength needs to be considered. Even with this and other limitations, Lewin's mathematics has been regarded by many psychologists as a good start toward fertile experimentation in the study of motivation. (See Escalona, 1954; Deutsch, 1954; Hilgard, 1956.)

Whatever may be the fate of Lewin's mathematics, there can be no doubt of his success in devising incisive types of experimental research on motivation, on child psychology, and on social psychology. His latest and perhaps greatest achievement was his plan for "action research," designed for his Group Dynamics Center. He made contact with many organizations and individuals who wished to work for the improvement of group relations in industry and in the community. He saw that much research would be necessary.

The research needed for social practice can best be characterized as research for social management or social engineering. It is a type of action-research, a comparative research on the conditions and effects of various forms of social action, . . . leading to social action (Lewin, 1948, page 202).

Working teams will have to be organized and trained. By analogy with both military and medical strategy, action research calls for a repeated cycle of preliminary fact-finding, action, and subsequent fact-finding for appraisal of results.

Gardner Murphy's estimate of Lewin's work should be quoted: "Lewin's influence on social psychology is huge, on child psychology very large, on general theoretical psychology considerable. His vitality and originality demanded respect even when his formulations were rejected."

GESTALT PSYCHOLOGY IN THE 1950'S

The positive influence of Gestalt theory continues to be greatest in the field of sense perception. What has been called the "Gestalt revolution" (Hochberg, 1957) is the reaction against analysis of perceptual experience into elementary sensations supplemented by associations developed through past experience. Instead, the perceived "event" is taken as a whole and its conditions studied. Actually much of the old work on perception of depth and distance followed this procedure—work which properly belongs under the description of functional psychology (our page 17). An example is Stratton's famous experiment on the effects of long-continued wearing of lenses that inverted the field of view. After about a week of seeing the world under these unnatural circumstances, he found himself quite adapted to the new state of affairs, and no longer reached for objects above and to the right which were really below and to the left. Ivo Kohler (born 1915; professor in Innsbruck, Austria) has contributed some new data of the same sort from experiments even more daringly conceived. The glasses in one part of this study were half-prisms, distorting only half of the visual field in some particular respect. For instance, one half of the retina would receive a right-side-up image, the other an upside-down image; or one half would see things reversed as in a mirror, while the other would see them normally. In another experiment, colored goggles were used; the right half of each glass was yellow, the left half blue. After fifty days of the half-prisms, the wearer had adapted to the extent of seeing things only slightly distorted through them, but the rest of the field of vision by that time had become greatly distorted, and after removal of the experimental lenses forty more days were required before the subject again saw things normally.

This much of Kohler's data confirms the results Stratton earlier reported, and could be covered under the broad heading of adaptation effects. But the results produced by the bi-colored lenses are even more challenging. The wearer of these would see blue to the left and yellow to the right. After looking toward the left for a while, then turning his eyes toward the right he would see objects in that direction in an intensified yellow—a successive contrast effect. Still more interesting was the effect after several weeks of wearing the goggles: when he then removed them he noted for several days that eye movement to the left produced a blue sensation; eye movement to the right produced a yellow sensation. Would we be justified in describing it as a "conditioned sensation"? Kohler himself describes it as "conditioned adaptation," suggesting that it is of a more complex nature than common visual adaptation. He also concludes that the learning of an orderly sequence of stimulation would better account for his results than would the classical Gestalt doctrine of internal organization (1956, 1962).

The Gestalt point of view does not seem to hold the position in the psychology of perception that it once did. Floyd Allport, in his monumental critique (1955) of "theories of perception" (thirteen of them!) finds cause for complaint against the Gestalt theory: its treatment of whole and part is defective; organization does not proceed exclusively from whole to part, but depends also on the previously learned characteristics of the parts. Similar conclusions are reached by Weiner (1956) and by Vernon (1957). We have seen that the transactional theory of perception (page 52, this book) places much more emphasis on learning and on transfer from past experience. (For a Gestalt rebuttal of the transactional view see Zuckerman and Rock, 1957.) Protagonists of the Gestalt position continue to investigate the problems of perception, with more attention to the importance of the memory factor. Hans Wallach (born 1904; professor at Swarthmore) whose famous study, with Köhler, of figural after-effects we have already considered (page 225), has extended the Gestalt theory of spatial perception and demonstrated the importance of memory in such experience. (See Wallach and O'Connell, 1953; Wallach, O'Connell, and Neisser, 1953.)

GESTALT CONTRIBUTIONS IN OTHER AREAS. If the influence of Gestalt in the field of perception seems less dominant than it has been, part of the explanation may be that much of the wisdom of Gestalt may be said to be now in the "public domain." In learning and problem solving, on the other hand, the competing schools have not yielded much ground. In motivation theory we have already described the contributions of Kurt Lewin which have had a powerful influence upon psychological thought and research. Other significant American developments in Gestalt theory can be traced to the centers for Gestalt research and teaching which were established in the United States by Koffka in 1927 at Smith College, by Wertheimer in 1933 at the New School for Social Research in New York, and by Köhler in 1935 at Swarthmore College.

Fritz Heider (born 1896; long associated with Koffka at Smith, and now professor at the University of Kansas) has developed the Gestalt views along the line of social perception and interpersonal relations both normal and disturbed. In *The Psychology of Inter-*

personal Relations he undertakes the problem of the analysis of the individual within the "complicated causal network of the environment"—an environment that is made up of objects and people, of immediate and distal factors. "We try to make sense out of the manifold of proximal stimuli by ordering them in terms of the distal invariants and their relevant dispositional properties" (1958, page 296). "Why," you ask, "is X being so nice to me?" The proximal facts may not provide you with an adequate answer, so you work back, "layer after layer," to a more stable foundation in the form of an invariant disposition of X which will give you some assurance of control over this aspect of your environment.

A limitation of Lewin's topological approach was the difficulty of representing X's life space as a factor operating in A's life space. Heider's approach is in some respects like Lewin's but Heider's subjective environment includes the self and another person, and some new event for which, as in the example given above, some explanation is sought. A striking innovation in Heider's conceptual analysis of the social situation is his use of terms taken from the naive accounts of common sense psychology as it is expressed in everyday language. "Can," for instance, implies ability of the individual combined with an environment that offers no interference when that degree of ability exists; "try" involves both intention and exertion, corresponding to the direction and strength of motivation, etc. Heider's analytical vocabulary consists of these and several other mostly commonplace terms thoughtfully and thoroughly assayed to provide what he considers a "basic English" of social situations: Life Space, Perceiving, Causing, Can, Trying, Wanting, Suffering, Sentiments, Belonging, Ought (1938, pages 15–18). Although conceding some truth to Skinner's charge that "the vernacular is clumsy and obese" (Skinner, 1938, page 7), Heider argues that a young science does well to seek answers to its questions from any source available, and to work toward successive refinements of its methodology as the way becomes clearer. In turning to good effect through verbal analysis concepts implicit in popular language, he associates himself with philosophy of science principles formulated by Gilbert Ryle (1949) and by Rudolf Carnap (1953).

As Wertheimer's successors at the New School for Social Research we now find Mary Henle and Rudolf Arnheim. Mary Henle (born 1913) early in her professional career distinguished herself by doing a thoughtfully conceived systematic study of the predictive validity of Lewin's theory of task substitution. In this she tested the effectiveness of such factors as similarity, homogeneity, closure, interest, and success, as features of the substituted task, in satisfying the quasi-need induced by interruption of a task (1942). She has more recently concerned herself with the systems of psychology and problems of motivation and thinking (1957, 1962).

Rudolf Arnheim (born 1904), is a visiting professor at the New School, and also a member of the Sarah Lawrence College psychology faculty. He has been especially identified with the psychology of esthetics, an area which has received much attention from the gestaltists. In view of the emphasis which the school has placed upon perception and values this interest is understandable. In his *Art and Visual Perception* (1954) Arnheim ventures into the analysis and experimental investigation of little-understood problems of balance, form, color, meaning, etc., applying the theoretical and methodological assets of Gestalt psychology combined with his own rich, scholarly knowledge of art.

Solomon Asch (born 1907; now professor at Swarthmore College), has been a close disciple of Wertheimer. In his *Social Psychology* (1952) he has tackled from the Gestalt position some of the knotty problems of group behavior. What explains, for instance, the reckless disregard of law, decency, morality, and habitual personal standards that seems to take possession of a usually peaceable man when he becomes part of a mob? The concept of an independent group mind such as Durkheim proposed, or even McDougall's acceptance of some new synthesis growing out of the collective sentiments of the individual members of the crowd (1908) were not well received by tough-minded psychologists. To Floyd Allport (1924) a crowd is composed of egocentrically motivated individuals, and "the individual in the crowd behaves just as he would behave alone, only more so." To Asch, a generation later, the group mind problem offers another possible interpretation of human motivation. Man appears to be capable of transcending his own interests and of "representing to himself the situation that includes himself and others. . . . it would almost be right to say that there are group minds, but that they exist in individuals, and there are as many group minds as individuals in a group" (1959, pages 371 and 373). Asch concedes that the *mutual representations* that are associated with group feelings and group action often lead to aggression, but contrary instances may be cited in which the effect is in the cause of humanitarian goals and justice.

Mutual representation is not limited to mob or crowd behavior. Another perplexing problem is that of communication. How does one individual convey to another in a way that makes the experience real and vivid to the listener or observer the sense of what is necessarily locked up within the consciousness of the reporter? This can be quickly recognized as the issue which continues to divide phenomenologists from behaviorists in their views of what can be allowed as the proper content of scientific psychology, and what methods can be used to study it. But more than this, it is implicit in our everyday dealings with other human beings; it is essential for any appreciative understanding of literature, music, or art. The effect of another human being upon us is quite different from the effect of an inanimate object in our environment. To the former we respond as if there is purpose and meaning in his actions, and as if he expects to find these same characteristics in our reactions to him. To ignore this essential feature of human relationships, or reduce it to conditioned verbal responses without exploring its cognitive, affective, and motivational consequences, is to reduce social psychology to a study of "geometrical displacements" of objects. Yet, as Asch points out, even the most rigid behaviorist, once he steps out of his official role as a behaviorist and begins to write about social psychology, easily drops into off-guard admissions of the existence and significance of mutual representations in interpersonal behavior (1959, page 375).

Asch's research has been guided by his principle of abstracting from an experimental situation the full yield of a combined behavioral and phenomenological approach. He has undertaken a study of why certain words acquire a dual connotation, one physical, another psychological. Objects and people may be described as *warm* or *cold, hard* or *soft, bright* or *dull;* a road or a way of thinking may be *straight* or it may be *narrow,* etc. He has found that these extended meanings appear in other languages reflecting very different cultures, and that the resemblance between their metaphors and our own is substantial enough to suggest that it is not fortuitous. Of the possible explanations that such metaphors develop as a result of association by contiguity or association by similarity, Asch decides in favor of similarity on the grounds that the same terms which describe the properties and forces of nature are intuitively found suitable for describing fundamentally related characteristics in people (1958, page 93). In this conclusion he is apparently drawing upon the phenomena of synesthesia, a subject traditionally of interest to the Gestalt school (Hornbostel, 1927). Synesthesia is a tendency, more common in some people than others, to identify an experience they receive through one sense modality with an experience of a different sense. A rather usual form is "colored hearing," in which certain tones are immediately referred to certain color effects.

Asch has more recently carried his study of these "dual terms" further by investigating the appearance of metaphor in the language of children. Many other challenging studies which he has reported in his 1952 volume have attracted wide attention and stimulated a sizable volume of research by other psychologists.

In Germany, land of its birth, Gestalt psychology languished during the Hitlerian regime and the Second World War, but it showed new signs of vitality in the 1950's, participating in the general resurgence of psychology in West Germany. Gestalt psychology is well represented at the Free University in West Berlin and in the universities of Frankfurt, Münster, and Tübingen.[2]

Wolfgang Metzger (born 1899; professor at Münster) has written on various problems and applications of Gestalt psychology, including the laws of seeing, striving, and thinking. For a condensed general statement see his *Fundamental Concepts of Gestalt Psychology* (in German, 1954).

Edwin Rausch (born 1906; professor at Frankfurt) has experimented very extensively on visual configurations, detecting a general tendency to perceive them in such a way as to eliminate distortions (1952). He finds a similar tendency in auditory and tactile perception. The thought process is another of his fields of interest.

Kripal Singh Sodhi (born 1911 in India; professor at the Free University of Berlin) is a prolific investigator in the field of social psychology: comparison of trends in Europe and America; national prejudices and stereotypes; difficulties of communication and understanding between groups; social forces as factors in individual beliefs and judgments. See his survey of European social psychology (1954).

Wilhelm Witte (born 1915; professor at Tübingen) has applied the Gestalt approach to psychophysics and also to the projective techniques. He finds use for psychology in the diagnosis and treatment of physical (non-psychiatric) illnesses. With a co-editor, he has inaugurated a new research journal, *Psychologische Beiträge* (1953).

Besides the Berlin Gestalt school, there was, as noted earlier (page 219), an older Gestalt school in Austria. An outgrowth of this Austrian school was a Leipzig school, more commonly called the *"Ganzheit"* (Totality) school. It was founded by Felix Krueger when in 1917 he succeeded Wundt as head of the Leipzig psychology department. There was a tendency to maintain the traditional rivalry of the Leipzig and Berlin departments of psychology. The Leipzig group accused the Berlin gestaltists of limiting their scope to the cognitive processes and neglecting the all-embracing totality of the life of feeling; and of neglecting also the necessary study of how an organization develops.

[2] The author is indebted to Wolfgang Köhler for this information.

Friedrich Sander (born 1889; recently professor at Bonn) offered a comprehensive view of the totality psychology in the *Psychologies of 1930*. The school is still very much alive in Germany and is held to afford the most adequate scientific study of personality. (See Holzner, 1957–1958.) It seems not far removed from the personalistic psychologies which we have still to consider in our Chapter 11 (pages 356–62).

A. Wellek (born 1904; now professor at the University of Mainz) has written of the totality effect on musical knowledge which fuses mood and feeling with the perceptual experience (1958). His thinking is much akin to that of the Sander group (1955, 1957).

Many other well-known names might be added to our list of Gestalt psychologists, and it might be still further lengthened by names of those who warmly approve of some, if not all, of the principles identified with this school. In fact, some of the most distinguished defenders of such principles have been psychologists who have claimed only a qualified affiliation, as would be true of Katz and of Lewin. In assessing the movement, W. C. H. Prentice, formerly at Swarthmore, now the President of Wheaton College, has pointed out that despite the *Zusammenhang* of its theories, individual principles such as the antimosaic attitude, the concept of isomorphism, or the phenomenological method could well be "exported" into areas not yet covered by the gestaltists themselves (1959). There is no doubt that the eclectic psychologist can find much of value in the offerings of the Gestalt school.

9

Psychoanalysis
and Related Theories

The problems of perception, motivation, and learning which have kept experimental psychologists busy during the twentieth century have been investigated primarily with a view to reaching a better understanding of normal behavior. In the course of such research some light has also been thrown, incidentally, on abnormal responses and the conditions which produce them. We recall, for example, Pavlov's discovery of "experimental neurosis"; also the startling effects of sensory deprivation on the immediate behavior of human subjects and on the development of animals (pages 186–88). The search for answers to questions about normal brain functioning has also been pressed, we have seen, through various surgical techniques including electrical stimulation of finely localized nerve centers or the application of energizing, depressant, or toxic drugs which may have dramatic effects upon behavior.

But we come now to a school of psychology which did not originate in psychology itself, and which for many years after taking root showed very little interest in the academic psychology of the human or animal laboratory. We might add that the indifference was mutual. The original aim of the new movement was the better understanding of *abnormal* behavior and the discovery of successful methods of treatment. In the years since psychoanalysis arose within the fold of psychiatry, its orthodox spokesmen and those who have been sympathetic with some, but not all, of Freud's teaching have continued to work toward that end; but they have at the same time been building out of their experience with the emotional problems of human beings an elaborate structure of theory which has gradually spread closer and closer to the realms of interest of the academic psychologists. We have seen that the hard and fast lines separating the schools we have earlier considered are gradually fading. It is doubtful that the gap between these and the analytical schools will be as quick to close. But it is now evident that there are movements within both groups to discover and reconcile concepts which will lead to a better understanding of the individual and his responses to his environment.

SOME PRECURSORS OF PSYCHOANALYSIS. As a movement within psychiatry, psychoanalysis was a revolt against the dominant "somatic" tendency of the nineteenth century (page 11) and a springing into new life of the "psychic" tendency. Convinced at last that brain lesions could not be found in some mental disorders, psychiatrists were turning to the patient's emotional stress, weakness of will, suggestibility, and irrational habits. The history of this psychiatric development is a story by itself. It is partly the story of hypnotism. Brought to medical and scientific attention by Mesmer in 1780, hypnotism led a checkered career for a century, being associated with a great deal of charlatanism and almost universally rejected by the medical profession until the days of the famous rival schools of Paris and Nancy, along in the 'sixties, 'seventies, and 'eighties of the nineteenth century. The Paris school was dominated by Charcot (1825–1893), the leading neurologist of his day, a striking personality and a great teacher. Charcot made a special study of hysteria. He found that persons subject to hysterical symptoms could also be put into deep hypnosis, and he used this fact in treating hysteria as well as for interpreting hypnosis, which he inferred to be a peculiar pathological state of the organism. This view was vigorously opposed by the Nancy school which taught that a mild form of hypnosis could be induced in nearly all normal subjects and was merely a passive and receptive state produced by suggestion. They used it in the treatment of neurotic conditions. The strife between the two rival French schools was very keen.

Charcot had many pupils who became prominent in the study and treatment of the neuroses. Morton Prince of Boston (1854–1929) used hypnosis and suggestion in the treatment of "double personality." The report of a case of multiple personality by Thigpen and Cleckley (1954), later published under the title of *The Three Faces of Eve* (1957), was reminiscent of the interesting group of cases described by Prince (1913), the most famous of which was that of Miss Beauchamp. Like Eve White, Miss Beauchamp had several alternating personalities, some of which would appear spontaneously, others under hypnosis, each having her own integrated memories and attitudes. The two cases presented an additional interesting phenomenon for which Prince suggested the theory of "coconsciousness." Sally Beauchamp, and in the more recent case, Eve Black and "Jane," were also aware—as something quite alien to themselves—of what went on in the thinking and daily life of their *alter egos,* who did not share the same advantage. We have not heard much in recent clinical psychology of the problem of the coconscious, but, as William McDougall has pointed out (1926), it is a fact which will have to be covered in any adequate explanation of the integration of personality.

Pierre Janet (1859–1947) as a young professor of philosophy at the Lycée in Havre began his preparation for a medical degree by carrying on some interesting experiments in hypnotic somnambulism. Although he admitted some reservations about the significance of the results, they were striking enough to attract Charcot's attention, and several years later Janet became associated with Charcot in the Psychological Laboratory at Salpêtrière. There he continued his investigations of automatic writing and similar dissociated behavior (1889). In his medical thesis (1892) he presented the results of his work on these phenomena and of his continuing intensive study and treatment of the neuroses. Following up Charcot's work, he found that hysterical patients were able under hypnosis to recall experiences that seemed in the waking state to have been entirely forgotten. Emotional shocks were thus recalled, and particular symptoms such as the hysterical paralysis of one arm were traced back to their source. Moreover, if during hypnosis a suggestion were made by the physician that "That's all past and gone now," the hysterical symptoms connected with the emotional shock would disappear (although the patient was likely to develop other symptoms later that could be traced back to other shocks).

Whereas *les idées fixes* of the hysteric could usually be reached and treated by hypnosis and suggestion (1904, 1907), Janet found the case of the obsessive to be quite another matter. Scrupulous, overconscientious, stricken by a sense of worthlessness which Janet referred to as *"une honte de soi,"* obsessives appear to be unable to force themselves to make decisions (1903). Elton Mayo (1948) has summarized Janet's and his own characterization of them in these terms: "They are experts in an arduous rethinking of the obvious— they substitute an exaggerated precision in minor activities for that activity in major affairs of which they are or feel themselves to be, incapable." The loss of the ability to cope with social reality and the *lowering of psychological tension* which occurs when the obsessive is confronted with a task beyond his powers are the root of such symptoms.

The idea of "lowered tension" seems incompatible with the tenseness and agitation the obsessive shows in such a situation, but here tension has a meaning different from its common one. Janet conceived levels of mental tension as positively correlated with a hierarchy of mental functions ranging from simple reflexes to the most complex dealings with reality. The latter depend upon the integration of reflexes, habits, and skills of lower order, and wherever these are inadequate the higher processes will also fall short of requirements. In normal, effective attention these subordinate and contributory functions fall easily into place: they are *in equilibrium*. The greater the complexity of the act, the greater will be the mental tension required to maintain that equilibrium. The deficiency of the hysteric is at a relatively primitive level, usually affecting sensory awareness in one or another form; the deficiency of the *psychasthenic* —a term implying psychic weakness which Janet used to cover a syndrome of neurotic symptoms including phobias and obsessions— is at a higher level. In the case of the obsessive it appears to hinge essentially upon his ineptness in social adjustment. It is interesting to find in Janet's writings recognition of the same individual trends toward aggressive hostility, social withdrawal, or selfless docility in such cases as social analytic theorists later to be discussed have proposed:

. . . Previous indications of character, egocentricity, pride, susceptibility, authoritarian ideas—betray an inclination to objectify psychological troubles, to attribute to the machinations of other people the subject's own psychological insufficiencies. Moreover one finds in this group an increased tendency to systematization and less disposition to obsessive doubt. . . . Conversely, sweetness, humility, a tendency to perpetual subjective analysis are indications in a patient of the approach of indecision, doubt, and the typical overscrupulous attitude (Janet, 1903, as quoted in Mayo, 1948, page 93).

Particularly the latter type of obsessive does not use reflection in the way of a normal person to bring consistency and unity to his experience. Instead, he agonizes over a problem, freezing into inactivity and allowing it to absorb his attention with the effect of alienating himself further from his fellow-men. In such a case, Janet would seek out the source of this disequilibrium in a study of the subordinate functions, and then attempt to re-educate the patient. Janet's work, slightly antedating psychoanalysis, was beginning to exert considerable influence on both psychology and psychiatry when it was overtaken by the more dramatic conceptions of Freud and rather thrown into the shade. However, it seems not unlikely that his contributions may some day be reviewed and reappraised scientifically.

PSYCHOANALYSIS

Sigmund Freud (1856–1939), though a native of what is now Czechoslovakia, lived in Vienna from the age of four until the Nazi invasion in 1938. In the *gymnasium* he was a brilliant student, evidently suited to an intellectual career, but what line this should take was not clear to him. Civilization, human culture, and human relationships attracted him more than natural science; but Darwin's new and exciting theory of evolution opened up a scientific approach to the understanding of all life. After some hesitation Freud registered as a medical student at the University of Vienna, having no real desire to be a physician, but attracted by the biological and social sciences. He found physiology most to his liking, and worked for six years in the physiological laboratory. Of the clinical branches of medicine, only psychiatry had much appeal for him. Finding that he had no immediate chance of earning his livelihood in pure science, he decided to go into medical practice and in 1882 switched from the physiological laboratory to the hospital where he specialized as much as possible on the nervous system, its anatomy and organic diseases such as paralyses, aphasia, and the effects of brain injuries in children. The nervous diseases seemed to offer a good field not yet well developed in Vienna.

In 1885, attracted by the fame of Charcot, he went to Paris and studied with the master for a year. He was much impressed by Charcot's use of hypnosis in the treatment of hysteria. Charcot had got far away from the old view that this was essentially a woman's ailment (the name itself derived from the Greek *hystera* meaning womb), and he was able to demonstrate hysterical symptoms in some of his male patients. On his return to Vienna Freud reported to his medical colleagues Charcot's methods and results, including male hysteria, but was ridiculed by some of them for accepting such an absurdity. A few such rebuffs confirmed Freud's already formed conviction that his place was bound to be "in the opposition."

It was at this time, in 1886, when he was just about thirty, that Freud married and settled down to private practice in Vienna as a nerve specialist. Since the neuroses were a neglected field in Vienna he built up his practice in that direction. In hypnosis he had a method of treatment which produced remarkable cures in many hysteric patients. But he soon found difficulties with the method. First, the cures were apt to be temporary; and second, many neurotic patients could not be hypnotized. His indifferent success led him in 1889 to make another pilgrimage to France, this time to examine the work of the Nancy school which had claimed to hypnotize practically all subjects and to have great success in the use of curative suggestions given to hypnotized patients. He was disappointed to learn from the Nancy doctors that their success was not nearly so good with private patients as with the clinic patients. Apparently the private patients were too sophisticated to accept the suggestions wholeheartedly. Freud returned to Vienna and continued to treat his private patients by hypnosis, but still with only moderate success. Janet, as we have seen, was also beginning to use hypnosis at this time in therapy, but Freud did not know of Janet's work until later.

DEVELOPMENT OF THE PSYCHOANALYTIC METHOD. Freud owed a great deal to his friend, Joseph Breuer (1842–1925). Breuer was an eminent physiologist who had made important contributions to the study of respiration and of the semicircular canals, but who was devoting himself mostly to general medical practice. Quite incidentally he had undertaken to treat a severe case of hysteria, a gifted young woman who was incapacitated with a whole swarm of symptoms—paralyses, memory losses, and states of mental confusion. Breuer treated her by using hypnosis, and found as Janet did that under hypnosis a patient could remember emotional experiences that had given rise to specific symptoms. But Breuer's patient led him one step further: she reported that after remembering an emotional experience and talking it out with him while under hypnosis she found herself free from the particular symptom that dated from this experience. Breuer followed up this lead and succeeded after many such sessions in getting all her symptoms talked out and "abreacted." Abreaction was the term he used to describe the release of a blocked emotional charge through consciousness and movement, and in this case it seemed to account for the fact that the patient was able to resume her normal life. Freud took a keen interest in the information he received from Breuer and tried the method out successfully on other patients. They collaborated in publishing the results of a series of cases in 1893 and 1895. They applied the term *mental catharsis* to the new method because it worked by eliminating sources of disturbance related to past emotional experiences of the patient.

In spite of this promising beginning Breuer refused to make any further use of the cathartic method. It appears that his patient, after the long period of hypnotic sessions, and very close to complete cure, confessed she had fallen in love with him—an abreaction that led Breuer to decide that the new method presented problems for a doctor who wished to maintain a strictly professional attitude. Freud was soon faced with the same difficulty, but careful weighing of the possible explanations of this unexpected response led him to the conclusion that the love was transferred to him as a substitute for the real and original object toward whom it was directed. If he could continue to treat the patient while maintaining the professional attitude, he might even make use of this *transference* to hasten the cure. It was years before the theory of transference was fully worked out, but in time the techniques for managing and using it came to have a dominant place in psychoanalytic practice.

Freud believed that the use of hypnosis made the transference difficult to manage, which was one reason for his decision to give up hypnosis. Another reason was that he wished to reach neurotic patients who were not easily or deeply hypnotized. Hypnosis was a great aid in recovering the lost memories quickly, but he felt that even in the waking state it should be possible for the patient to revive them by trying hard enough. Following up this reasoning, Freud had his patients relax on a couch while he sat behind them watching without being watched. Then he urged them to search their memories, insisting that with effort they could remember the source of their present troubles. This was a strenuous procedure for both doctor and patient, and not always successful.

Freud was then led to take a most important step in the development of his method. Instead of urging his patients to search their memories, he instructed them to relax mentally and let ideas come up spontaneously. Borrowing a psychological term he called this the method of "free association." Although it was controlled to some extent by the whole doctor-patient relationship, it was free in the sense that Freud gave the patient the lead, making very few comments and interfering as little as possible with the course of the patient's thoughts. But the patient was supposed to accept the "fundamental rule of psychoanalysis" which was to give full expression to every idea as it came up, however embarrassing, unimportant, irrelevant, or even foolish it might appear to be.

Sometimes in the course of free association the patient reported a dream he had had, and Freud discovered that the dream made an excellent source of new associations (1900). The patient was instructed to let his mind play freely about each item of the dream. This led regularly to the patient's unearthing significant memories long forgotten which seemed to have a bearing on his problem. In studying the relationship between these buried memories and the dreams, Freud found that the "manifest content" which the patient could remember was a disguise for the real or "latent dream content," part of which might consist of current experiences or wishes, but a much more important part of which would be unfulfilled wishes dating from childhood. He made the surprising discovery, too, that some of the significant and shocking memories reported by his neurotic patients as a result of dream analysis had never really happened. A woman might "recall" having been sexually attacked by her father or some other male member of the family, but a subsequent check on the story would establish that it had no basis in fact. The frequency of this kind of distorted recall convinced Freud that in such cases a fantasy or daydream embodying a childish wish had become incorporated into the patient's memories as an objective event. That it had existed even as a fantastic wish made it significant in the patient's life history, for Freud felt it could lead to the core of the neurosis in childhood and ultimately to the patient's cure by helping her to recover the lost memories and to live over the wishes of that period.

Freud had already discovered that the revival of recent memories was not enough to effect a permanent cure, for it had often happened that patients dismissed as cured after superficial analysis returned later with slightly different complaints. But how to push the analysis back to early childhood—that was a problem! Only a few scraps of the rich experience of those first years were ever recovered. However, perhaps the entire *intellectual* recall of those early events was not as essential as the revival of the *emotional attitude*. Once this childish attitude, this unrealistic desire, was brought out into the open, the neurosis should be revealed in its true infantile character, and perhaps give way to better adjustment under the guidance of the analyst. Freud's reasoning took this general form.

When the patient thus revives his childish emotional attitudes without clear memory of the persons and events that accounted for them, the importance of transference becomes very clear. If the child's father was the object of love and also of defiance, the analyst as a father substitute becomes the object of the transferred emotional attitudes. Sometimes the patient is full of love and enthusiasm for the analyst; at other times he shows rebellion and even hate. Both the *positive* and the *negative* phases must be worked through with the help of the experienced and understanding father substitute, the analyst. As the analysis approaches its goal, positive transference is more evident, making it necessary for the analyst to wean the patient from this childish dependence on him and prepare him to assume his adult role in life.

Freud laid great stress on the necessity of helping the patient overcome his *resistances*. Often, "free association" does not operate freely; it seems to be blocked as if the patient were coming dangerously near to some memory or idea which is too painful or terrible or shameful to be faced—as if some emotional attitude were stirred which he is unwilling to recognize as his own—hatred, for example, toward someone near and dear to him, or unlimited selfishness. As a neurotic patient he admits he is in trouble, but he still has a very good opinion of himself and tends to repel any memory or any insight that would shame him. By degrees, under the guidance of the analyst, he begins to face the facts, though it is a painful process.

The forgotten experiences and unadmitted desires and attitudes that came to light in free association were so often of a sexual nature that Freud early came to emphasize the predominant if not exclusive importance of sexual difficulties and conflicts in the causation of any neurosis. Hostility motives and *ambivalence* (love and hate for the same person) also came to light but were regarded as arising from frustration of sex desires. From dream analysis he came to believe that certain types of objects in the manifest dream were regular symbols for sexual objects and processes. With his insight into the nature of these symbols the analyst could penetrate the disguises concealing the latent content of the patient's dream. Freud discovered that when, after reaching his diagnosis, he shared his conclusions with the patient, they were met with incredulity and resistance. Apparently a less authoritarian approach had to be devised. In a much later book (1920, pages 17–18) Freud has summarized the three stages of this approach:

> At first the endeavors of the analytic physician were confined to divining the unconscious of which his patient was unaware, effecting a synthesis of its components and communicating it at the right time. . . .
> Since the therapeutic task was not thereby accomplished, the next aim was to compel the patient to confirm the reconstruction through his own memory. In this endeavor the chief emphasis was on the resistances of the patient; the art now lay in unveiling these as soon as possible, in calling the patient's attention to them, and . . . teaching him to abandon the resistances.
> It became increasingly clear, however, that the aim in view, the bringing into consciousness of the unconscious, was not fully attainable by this method either. The patient cannot recall all of what lies repressed, perhaps not even the essential part of it. . . . He is obliged rather to *repeat* as a current experience what is repressed. . . . As a rule the physician cannot spare the patient this phase of the cure; he must let him live through a certain fragment of his forgotten life.

Freud's determination to effect a radical cure by penetrating to the core of every neurosis forced him to abandon any hope of expeditious treatment. Not less than five sessions a week for months or even years were required, he found. One analyst could handle only a few cases in the course of a year, and the number of analysts could not be rapidly increased since each one *must first be analyzed himself* and then work for two years under supervision before practicing on his own account. Countless neurotics must accordingly be deprived of the benefits of psychoanalysis as long as it remained under the discipline of Medicine. For this reason and also for the fact that medical schools of the period were disposed to stress physical rather than psychic causes for mental disease, Freud concluded that the practice of psychoanalysis should be an independent profession (1926b). Although there have been some well-known lay analysts, most of Freud's followers have been medically trained, and are inclined to reject this one opinion of the master no matter how orthodox they may be in other respects. As to the expanding group of consulting psychologists, many of them doubtless make some use of Freud's methods, but few are orthodox enough to seek for radical cures by the "classical analysis" such as Freud prescribed. They align themselves more nearly with those medical followers of Freud who seek to simplify the treatment so as to benefit a larger number of more or less neurotic individuals.

Even in the early days before 1913, some of Freud's followers attempted to simplify the psychoanalytic procedure by concentrating on the patient's present problems and maladjustments instead of working back to childhood. Freud vigorously opposed any such attempt, being convinced in his own mind "that the actual conflict of the neurotic becomes comprehensible and solvable only if it can be traced back into the patient's past history" (1914a, page 55). Since Freud's death, however, those who call themselves psychoanalysts and do all honor to Freud as the father of the movement have been showing considerable freedom in modifying his methods, and, as we shall later see, in modifying his theory as well. Franz Alexander, a leader of the Chicago group, points out (1953) two reasons why many analysts retained the classical procedures for so many years: the first being that they generally selected cases that could best be dealt with by those methods; the second, that these were best suited for research purposes. Alexander himself, however, was one of those who early recognized (Alexander and French, 1946) that the analyst could, with advantage to patient and to doctor, reduce the frequency of the sessions, in some cases spacing them widely. But such latitude in method will depend upon the seasoned analyst's understanding of the case and "appreciation of the momentary psychodynamic situation" (1953, page 284).

Countertransference, the character of the analyst's attitude toward the patient, has also become a more flexible device in the hands of the modern analyst. Alexander contrasts the Freudian concept of "the blank screen upon which the patient casts his emotional reactions" with the "two-way street" relationship of the later analyst and his patient. His own studies of the effects of various attitudes taken toward the patient by the analyst have led him to conclude that the circumstances of the case should be the determining factor:

> For example, if the patient in his self-assertiveness was originally intimidated by a tyrannical father, the most suitable analytic climate is an outspokenly permissive one. If, on the other hand, the patient's father was overindulgent and by his doting love evoked an oppressive type of guilt in his son, the analyst may advantageously behave in a more detached manner; at the same time he can be helpful without losing the basic nonevaluative attitude. In accordance with the patient's needs, the analyst can change the interpersonal climate from a more to a less detached one, or from a more to a less permissive one (1953, page 287).

There is much evidence that Freud was jealous in the defense of his own convictions, but this is understandable when we realize that both his method and his philosophy of mental development were to him the logical outgrowth of his clinical observations. It was this logic that he would not allow to be lightly challenged. When he changed his own theory, as he did from time to time, the revision reflected his critical reconsideration of the implications of his extensive clinical data. He did just what an experimental psychologist would be expected to do if the results turned up by his laboratory study did not support his hypothesis. The great difference between the two, of course, lies in the greater complexity of the data Freud dared to study.

Focusing sometimes on those theories that are hardest to believe, people sometimes tend to forget that before he engaged in this study he had been trained as a scientist and that he had, in fact, specialized in neurophysiology although he chose to cast his theory in psychological terms. In a remarkable piece written at the turn of the century, *Project for a Scientific Psychology* (unfinished and until recently unpublished, 1954), he worked out a series of postulates which amount to a neurological "model" to account for the facts of learning, memory, thinking, pain, stress, and pleasure. Reviewing these postulates Karl Pribram (1962), who has been currently engaged in neuropsychological research, points out a number of instances where Freud's theorizing had anticipated or approximated more recent thinking about the organization of the nervous system. Even those who disagree radically with his views rarely have doubted Freud's stature as a thinker.

FREUD'S EARLY THEORY

Freud always insisted that his theory did not pretend to cover all the topics usually included in a textbook of psychology, but aimed to explain what other psychologists were neglecting or leaving unsettled. It dealt almost wholly with motives and their conflicts, and with the effect of conflict not only in the neuroses but also in everyday behavior.

THE UNCONSCIOUS. The earliest of Freud's theories to take shape, according to his autobiography (1946), was his firm belief in unconscious mental or "psychic" processes. Experiments which he witnessed at Nancy in 1889 impressed him strongly. On awaking from a hypnotic trance the subject may be entirely unconscious of what has happened during the trance ("posthypnotic amnesia"), though he remembers it if put back under hypnosis. Breuer's patient and many patients treated by Freud could remember while under hypnosis past experiences which seemed entirely forgotten while the patients were awake. These memories, then, had not been really forgotten but had sunk into the unconscious from which they could not be summoned by the conscious self. Freud did not invent the concept of the unconscious. It had been used by a number of his predecessors and contemporaries, including Charcot and Janet, to account not only for pathological but also for normal behavior. The term *unconscious cerebration,* for instance, had been introduced by Carpenter in 1876 to explain the common experience of having an elusive memory or the solution to a stubborn problem suddenly pop into our heads after we have stopped thinking about it. (There are, of course, other ways of explaining such happenings.) "Unconscious cerebration" suggested a physiological activity; Freud chose the psychological term, *unconscious.* He believed that complex planning and deliberating could go on in the unconscious. He even came to believe that the whole psychic life was initially unconscious and for the most part remained so, with the quality of consciousness playing only a secondary role. Freud's study of dreams and his discovery that many of the "sexual episodes" reported to him had never occurred led him to reconsider his original "environmentalistic" hypothesis that the unconscious consisted merely of isolated experiences and emotions which had been repressed because of the moral and ethical pressures of society.

UNCONSCIOUS MOTIVES. His conception of the unconscious soon took on a special emphasis that was new and original. It appeared to him that the unconscious consisted essentially of motives. Those memories which his first patients got back while under hypnosis were, to be sure, memories of persons and events, but they were shot through with strong but unfulfilled wishes. A young woman's sense of duty to her sick father forced her to give up her love affair—that was the kind of memory that often came to light. Such a "forgotten" wish might still be very much alive in the unconscious, with queer effects on conscious behavior. The young woman in this case developed a hysterical paralysis which betrayed an unadmitted desire to be rid of the duty of nursing her father.

In one of his most interesting books, the *Psychopathology of Everyday Life* (1904), Freud assembled hundreds of examples of slips of the tongue and lapses of various kinds which by the method of free association in analysis were shown to be unconsciously motivated. Freud did not spare himself in these analyses. In one instance he had a lapse of memory which certainly appeared remarkable. In going over his account book at the end of one year he was mystified to find the name of a patient occurring repeatedly, though he had no notion who that patient could be—a patient in a sanitarium seen daily for several weeks during the previous summer. Finally he remembered—it was a young girl whom he had treated successfully for a hysterical condition and finally let go though she was still complaining of some abdominal pain. Two months later she was dead of cancer in the abdomen. He had made a regrettable error in diagnosis and his unfulfilled wish was that he had done a better professional job. From such examples, interpreted in his characteristic manner, Freud reached a new theory of forgetting: anything once well known was never forgotten though it might be banished to the unconscious. Without going quite so far as to assert that intentional forgetting accounted for all failures of memory, he did say there was good reason to suspect some motive in any pronounced case.

He said the same thing about any slip of the tongue or any "accident" such as losing or breaking anything. Every such act, he suspected, was intentional, though the intention might be unconscious. A bride loses her wedding ring—a sign that she has a smoldering wish to be free again or at least to be free of her present bridegroom. Freud offered evidence that wit, too, allowed the repressed content of the unconscious a chance to escape into the conscious. A pun, for example, or a *double entendre* joke may be enjoyed not so much for its apparent meaning as for the subtler meaning which would not be allowed expression in its frank form (1905b).

Besides free association and dream analysis there were other guiding principles that Freud found useful in turning up unconscious motives. One was that whatever is strongly forbidden must be strongly desired. If people did not want to do certain things prohibitions against such behavior would be unnecessary. On these grounds Freud argued that parricide and incest, being so abhorrent, must be strong, universal, unconscious desires. Another guiding principle was that whatever is strongly feared is really desired. This would apply particularly to irrational and excessive fears of the type known as phobias. Freud believed that such neurotic fears, and even the more normal worry and solicitude one individual may show for another's welfare really mask unconscious wishes for the very thing feared.

THE TOPOGRAPHICAL APPROACH. So far we have been focusing on an unconscious which is completely cut off from conscious awareness by an act of *repression*. Confronted with content from this part of his psyche a patient's unconscious *resistance* can cause him to disown it, quite innocently. But there are other kinds of unconscious experiences. Sometimes we voluntarily *suppress* a thought or a wish. We may be reminded of it many times in the course of a day, and each time it recurs we may push it out of our minds again. But this does not make it part of the unconscious; it still remains available in an area that Freud called the *preconscious* (also called the *foreconscious*). Actually the preconscious system is much broader than the conscious part of the psyche because it contains all the perceptual and motor experience we have at our command to summon into consciousness. For example, the thought you have in your mind at this instant may produce an association that was very remote when that thought first entered your mind, but it was part of the preconscious and so was accessible to consciousness. On the other hand the thought which preceded it has now passed into the preconscious. It can be seen that this is what happens in free association. That being so, the question arises as to how the *unconscious* idea that is causing the trouble can ever be reached through the association of ideas in an entirely separate stratum. Freud acknowledged the problem (1915b) and conceded that there was no simple explanation:

> On the border of the Pcs [preconscious] the censorship thrusts back the Ucs, but its derivatives can circumvent this censorship, achieve a high degree of organization, and in the Pcs reach a certain intensity of *cathexis* [that is, a concentrated channeling of psychic energy]; when, however, this is exceeded and they try to force themselves into consciousness, they are recognized as derivatives of the Ucs, and are repressed afresh at the new frontier by the censorship between the Cs and the Pcs. Thus the former censorship is exercised against the Ucs itself, and the latter against its preconscious derivatives. . . .
>
> In psycho-analytic treatment . . . we require the patient to produce freely derivatives of the Ucs, we pledge him to overcome the objections of the censorship against these preconscious formations becoming conscious, and, by overthrowing this censorship, we open up the way to abrogating the repression accomplished by the earlier one (page 125, italics and bracketed words added).

According to this early *topographical* scheme which interrelated conscious, preconscious, and unconscious, the *ego*, about which we shall soon have more to say, would obviously have to be conscious. Yet when it functions as a censor, it appears to be Janus-faced, for to do its job it must have some knowledge of the unconscious as well as of the preconscious and conscious. We have then the paradox of a conscious part of the psyche "unconsciously" repressing the forbidden wishes and emotions consigned to the unconscious, offering resistance to their revival, feeling anxiety when they press to be readmitted, yet providing these very exiles with disguises which allow them to slip through the barrier in the form of dreams, wit, symptoms, etc.! This inconsistency was one of the reasons why Freud later developed a different theory. But before we turn to that let us consider some of the features that remained common to both systems.

THE PRIMARY AND SECONDARY PROCESSES: PLEASURE AND REALITY PRINCIPLES. Like Janet, Freud believed that neurosis was a loss of *"la fonction du réel"* (page 253): the patient has turned away from reality, or at least from some aspect of it. The resemblance which he found between dreams and neurotic symptoms led him to conclude that both drew upon a mental process more primitive and less disciplined than that which operated in normal thought or perception. He called this the *primary process,* and identified it with the *pleasure principle,* since its function was to reduce tension arising from any excitation of the organism and so restore it to a state of tensionless equilibrium. The primary process, however, was at a serious disadvantage in this respect: having no contact with reality it could not tell the difference between real and hallucinated experiences. It might conjure up an epicurean meal that would have no more food value than one in a dream; in fact, the primary process was conceived to be the one which takes over in dreaming, or hallucinating, or in any confused mental condition. Lacking in any framework for the ordering of objects in time or space, it would have much of the nature of the earliest experience of the infant as Piaget (page 42) or Sullivan (page 330) describes his awareness. But the primary process is *not* conscious.

Its failure to provide any permanent satisfaction of needs, in spite of the variety of fantasy-satisfactions it can offer, leads to the development of the *secondary process.* As Freud put it (1911, page 14): "the mental apparatus had to decide to form a conception of the real circumstances in the outer world and to exert itself to alter them." The secondary process, then, is the *reality principle* to which is delegated the function of finding ways and means, using the same psychic energy that has formerly futilely dissipated itself in fantasy. To achieve its goal it must "bind" the energy which has been used freely by the primary process—unbound energy is described as *mobile*—and so delay immediate response to stimulation while the secondary process does some "reality testing." This requires the organization of memory-traces and the comparison of new objects with the memory of those which have or have not in the past brought satisfaction. Freud adds that one part of the thought process is forever cut off from reality testing: that part used in play, daydreaming, and any form of autistic imagination. It is clear, too, that reality testing is deficient in the neurotic whose phobia prevents him from living a normal life, in the obsessive whose overintellectualizing prevents him from coming to grips with his real problem, in the victim of melancholia who commits suicide because of his overpowering sense of worthlessness, and in the schizophrenic whose delusional systems isolate him in a world of his own making. They have all in varying degrees lost "the function of the real."

The concepts of the primary and secondary processes which Freud first introduced in *Die Traumdeutung* (1900) were of particular significance for several reasons: first, the primary process provided a link between the elaborate dream work—which conceals the latent meaning of a dream—and mechanisms which operate in other kinds of mental activity. For example, the mobile primary process could readily shift cathexis from one "object" to another, or from a part to the whole or the whole to the part. The terms *displacement, condensation, substitution,* and *symbolism* are all closely interrelated and all descriptive of this shifting of cathexis. In the dream an apparently innocuous element may arouse disproportionate emotion, or something which should be shocking leaves us strangely untouched. In such a case the *affect* is apparently displaced; and the object which produces it is probably a substitute or a symbol for some other object, or it may represent an economical condensation of a number of ideas. Freud wrote in 1910:

> . . . we have discovered from the analysis of dreams that the unconscious makes use of a sort of symbolism, especially in the presentation of sexual complexes. This symbolism in part varies with the individual, but in part is of a typical nature, and seems to be identical with the symbolism which we suppose to lie behind our myths and legends. It is not impossible that these latter creations of the people may find their explanation from the study of dreams (1910a, page 21).

In the course of time the term *displacement* has come to be used more freely than it was in its original usage to include substitutions which are devices of the secondary process or *ego* activity in its function of adapting to reality. A good example of this form of displacement is provided in play therapy when a child displaces upon a doll the hostility he has repressed toward one of his parents or a sibling. Although the experiments by N. E. Miller, described on page 151 of this book, seem to confirm the fact of displacement, the S–R explanation in terms of *stimulus generalization* is far removed from the Freudian concept of redirection of a certain quantity of psychic energy such as *libido*.

But what is libido? Freud's earliest formulation of his instinct theory was the second significant development related to his concepts of a primary and a secondary process. In this formulation he grouped together certain forms of behavior which his studies had led him to conclude provide sexual pleasure from infancy onward. *Libido* is the energy of the drives which produce such behavior and which will ultimately contribute to the mature reproductive behavior of the adult as it emerges after a series of *pregenital* phases of development. Since the sources of sexual pleasure in the first years of childhood are the erotogenic zones of the body itself there is no immediate problem in satisfying these infantile drives. The problems will come later when the child is old enough to have some understanding of the social "must-nots" attached to these pleasurable activities. On the other hand, the behavior which serves to nourish the body and protect it from harm also provides a form of pleasure, for according to Freud's hedonic principle, pleasure is a state of equilibrium undisturbed by any pain-producing or tension-producing excitations. Whenever such unpleasantness develops, it is the job of the primary process to get rid of the intruding excitation as fast as possible in whatever way possible, and restore the desired equilibrium. The *ego* motives are at a disadvantage in carrying out their part of the program, for, as we have already noted, they must take stock of the environment and substitute delaying tactics for the impulsive but ineffective or even dangerous "solutions" presented by the drive-directed primary process. Gradually, as we have seen, the secondary process comes to meet the need for more realistic solutions, and through it the ego eventually comes to establish a sort of custodianship even over the libido, and if it does not quite tame, it at least opposes the wayward, "peremptory" demands of this pleasure-ridden part of the psyche.

INFANTILE SEXUALITY. Freud's publication of his conclusions on the subject of infantile sexuality was received by his professional colleagues with shocked indignation. He was even for a time subjected to some ostracism. In his turn, he did not miss the chance of interpreting this reaction, according to the principles of his own theory, as the effect of repression and resistance on the part of his critics. When this first negative response wore off, the spectacular features of his new theory began to catch the *avant-garde* imagination with the consequent distortion which appears whenever a new "movement" becomes a fad. Freud then found himself in the position of having to defend his real theory against the radical "wild psychoanalysis" (1910b) that lightly offered diagnoses and prescribed treatment, disregarding the necessity for the painstaking and protracted study of the individual's life history which should be a prelude to such judgments. Again and again in his search for the original cause of a repression the trail led him back to the patient's earliest childhood. He said that his theory of infantile sexuality was a "theoretical extract from very numerous experiences"—experiences in obtaining free associations from his neurotic patients. Later, observation and analyses of young children confirmed his conclusions about the sexual life characteristic of that stage of development.

The sex drive of the infant has not nearly the intensity that it will have in adolescence when the sex glands and hormones have matured, and it does not yet have the definite aim of the sexually excited adult. It is diffuse rather than sharply focused, Freud said. It aims simply at bodily pleasure from any organ, from the mouth, from the anus, from the genitals. It is auto-erotic, not yet being directed toward any other person as a love object. It first gains satisfaction from the mouth in sucking. The sucking of a hungry baby, to be sure, is driven by hunger and not by the sex urge, but when a baby who is not hungry sucks his thumb or a pacifier with apparent pleasure, he cannot be motivated by hunger but must be driven by the pleasure-seeking motive, the rudimentary sex motive in Freud's conception. By the sixth month, biting begins to be a prominent feature of the infant's oral activities, a fact which will take on more theoretical significance when we come to Freud's later revision of his ego-libido polarity hypothesis (page 277). But for the present we might note the important practical implications of considering early oral behavior as the first phase of *psychosexual* development. It immediately opens up a great many questions as to the best methods of seeing the infant through this critical stage: What is the best kind of mothering care? What about feeding schedules? When and how should weaning be carried out? The literature of child psychology is rich with recommendations on these questions, some of them based on clinical studies, some on experimental data. Not all of it is Freudian, by any means, but a large part of it, including many cross-cultural studies of infant care procedures and their apparent effects on personality patterning (Erikson, 1950; Kardiner, *et al.,* 1945), has been sparked by Freud's theory that the normal forward movement of the libido in the successive phases of its development will depend first on how successfully the problems of the oral period have been met.

In the normal course of events, at the end of the first year the anal region becomes the predominant source of libidinal pleasure. Cathexis is not entirely withdrawn from the objects that gave pleasure in the oral stage; we must always eat; and some of us have enough interest left over for the objects of the oral phase to keep us chewing or smoking or talking or kissing a disproportionate amount of time throughout the rest of our lives! During the anal phase, however, the main cathexis is on the activities of the organs of elimination. The baby takes pleasure not only in the process of evacuation, but even, according to Freud, intensifies the pleasurable sensations by delaying that activity as long as possible. In this phase of development as well as in the oral phase there appears a pattern of hostility which, until his revised theory appeared, Freud explained as the result of the obstacles which prevent the free expression of the infant's libidinal impulses. In the third, the phallic, stage the genital region comes to be of absorbing interest, and here again his erotic activity encounters restriction and frustration from the social environment. Frequently he is subject to harsher discipline at this time than at the earlier periods not only because of the social taboos against masturbation, but also because by the fourth year a child begins to look to his patience-tried parents more like a fit subject for "higher education," particularly when he has been under foot all day. He may adjust himself adequately to the social demands, or he may react by first intensifying and then repressing the particular activity. When he represses, he "fixates" this particular urge in the unconscious where it persists unchanged, though it may obtain partial satisfaction through some form of "sublimation" which is socially tolerated or even approved.

Still other pleasurable activities of the child were regarded by Freud as belonging under the general head of sexuality: biting things and putting them in the mouth; rhythmical movements of the arms and legs in the baby, swinging and seesaw in the older child; tearing things apart and throwing things down; showing off and looking at things—especially, of course, exposing one's own naked body or looking at that of another person; and, in short, any activity which seems to afford the young child sensuous and natural pleasure. At a higher level Freud included under sex gratification all affectionate behavior and comradeship originating in the infant's attachment to the nursing mother. Love for art or music, too, he included under the sex impulse. Whatever we say in ordinary language that we love or love to do is classed by Freud as sexual. Well, you say, that is simply his use of terms; he chose to define sexuality as equivalent to love and pleasure-seeking in the broadest sense. But we must notice, on the other side, that Freud objected strenuously to anyone who attempted to "dilute" his theory by desexualizing it. He insisted that affection was truly sexual and that thumbsucking gave the baby genuine though rudimentary sexual pleasure. He insisted that his conception of sexuality was strict as well as broad (1905a, 1916).

THE OEDIPUS COMPLEX. Though the child's libido is at first autoerotic and does not cathect any external love-object, in the course of the early years it does begin to form some attachments. The first major attachment will be to the person who ministers to the child's needs, usually, of course, the mother. This is true whether the child is a boy or a girl. Rather early the girl shifts her affections to her father as a result of her discovery of an anatomical "deficiency" for which she holds her mother responsible. The boy, on the other hand, comes to have more and more an attitude of possessiveness toward his mother and a strong resentment toward his father as a rival for her love. If he gives overt expression to this by a public announcement that he intends "to marry his mother," or engages in play with her which reveals a sexual quality, he is likely to be sharply reprimanded. Some parents may even resort to threats of dire specific retaliation if his wickedness continues. Such threats take on a very realistic meaning to the boy when he discovers that a girl's body does not have a penis. Both children assume that the girl has been deprived of hers, and the boy is left with no doubt that the same fate will befall him if he does not give up the competition with his father for his mother's love. The fear of castration has the immediate effect of making him repress his incestuous love, and also the hostility that he has had for his father. In fact, normally at this time he comes to identify himself with his father—a solution that has other, more extended effects which we shall hear about when we come to consider the *superego* and *anxiety*.

The girl's reaction is somewhat different. She transfers her love to her father in the hope of compensating for what she lacks. Later in life, for the same reason, she takes special pleasure in having sons. Freud conceded that the oedipal situation is not limited to a single pattern (1923, pages 42–43):

> One gets the impression that the simple Oedipus complex is by no means its commonest form, but rather represents a simplification or schematization which, to be sure, is often enough adequate for practical purposes. . . . A

boy has not merely an ambivalent attitude towards his father and an affectionate object-relation towards his mother, but at the same time he also behaves like a girl and displays an affectionate feminine attitude to his father and a corresponding hostility and jealousy towards his mother. It is this complicating element introduced by bisexuality that makes it so difficult to obtain a clear view of the facts.

Whatever the individual variations, much of the force of the Oedipus complex is lost in the years of the latency period which stretch between the climax of the "family romance" and adolescence. However, according to Freud, its solution seems to come earlier for the boy than for the girl, hastened perhaps in the former case by the fear of castration.

What prompted Freud to seek in the Oedipus legend the underlying motives for the commonly observed preference of little boys for their mothers and little girls for their fathers? He had been impressed with the fact that modern audiences continue to be deeply affected by Sophocles' drama despite its seeming remoteness from reality. Why would this be so unless the theme touched buried, unacknowledged wishes which were common to all mankind? You will recall that Oedipus, the hero of the legend, was exposed to the elements with a spike through his feet by order of his father Laius, the king of Thebes, because an oracle had predicted that this child would slay his father and marry his mother. He was rescued by a shepherd and adopted by the king of a neighboring state, where he grew to early manhood in ignorance of his true parentage and of his predicted fate. On one occasion, however, when he visited the oracle, he was told that he would slay his father and wed his mother. To avoid such a calamity he remained away from his adopted home, but in his wanderings he encountered his true father, quarreled with him, and slew him. As he continued his wanderings he arrived at Thebes, where by solving the riddle of the Sphinx he freed this city from a long-standing pest and was consequently proclaimed king and given the widowed Queen Jocasta as his wife. Years later, when a plague was threatening to destroy Thebes the oracle warned that the city would be saved only when the murderer of Laius was driven out or destroyed. The truth about his own patricide and incest dawned upon Oedipus only when the charges of the seer Tiresias were confirmed in his mind by Jocasta's tale of the abandonment of an ill-fated baby, and by the knowledge of his own attempted flight from this very destiny. In despair he put out his eyes. Jocasta killed herself.

Freud's belief in the biological universality of the Oedipus pattern has been the target of attack from many directions. The anthropologist, Malinowski (1927), was probably the first to apply the cross-cultural test: What happens in a society that is structured differently from our own? In the Trobriand Islands, "mother-right" prevails, and the real head of the household is the maternal uncle. Malinowski found that in this situation there was no evidence of sexual rivalry between a son and his father, but there was considerable hostility directed against the uncle, who wielded the power. From this it might be reasonable to conclude that in some degree the boy's resentment of parental authority rather than his resentment of sexual competition accounts for his rejection of the father in the "oedipal" phase in our own society.

The psychoanalyst, Erich Fromm, takes a similar view of the matter, but has offered a more "psychoanalytic" support of his position. He challenges Freud's interpretation of the symbolism of the Oedipus legend (1951), pointing out that even in the first drama of Sophocles' trilogy, there is no evidence that Oedipus fell in love with Jocasta; she was merely part of the prize; she "went with the throne." Even more convincing is the evidence that the other plays of the trilogy, Oedipus at Colonus and Antigone, make no use of the incest theme, although father-son hostility and the defiance of authority are prominently featured. Fromm writes, supporting his conclusion with an interpretation of Greek mythology made by Bachofen in 1861 (see Bachofen, 1926):

> An analysis of the whole Oedipus trilogy will show that the struggle against paternal authority is its main theme and that the roots of this struggle go far back into the ancient fight between the patriarchal and matriarchal systems of society. Oedipus, as well as Haemon and Antigone, is representative of the matriarchal principle; they all attack a social and religious order based on the powers and privileges of the father, represented by Laius and Creon (1951, pages 204–5).

Abram Kardiner, also of the psychoanalytic group, commenting upon Cora Du Bois' study of the people of Alor (1945), points out that the mother's disproportionate burden of duties and the father's constant involvement in complicated financial huckstering throw the young child upon the tender mercies of older siblings or anybody else available to keep an eye out for him. Under these conditions he does not develop any strong positive or negative attitudes toward his parents or other people; but the frustrations he undergoes appear to add up to the later distrust and meanness which characterize his dealings with others.

Franz Alexander, on the other hand, concedes the influence of the society and of the period, but insists that Freud's biological foundation cannot be ignored (1942, pages 430–32). Emphasizing the long-extended dependency of the child for the satisfaction of his needs, Alexander finds it reasonable that hostility will be expressed against anybody who appears as a competitor for the attentions of the tending figure. Where long dependency is discouraged, as in the Marquesas, the child's attachment may be transferred to someone other than the mother who will have less frustrating standards. The oedipal relationship, in this sense, need not be based upon a libido drive, nor need it be a specific mother-son, father-daughter bond; but it is still closely associated with fundamental biological needs.

NARCISSISM. What does Freud have to say about the libido that encounters such rebuffs and frustrations? It is withdrawn from the original object, and if no suitable substitute can be found, it is drawn back, partially at least, into the self. This would be a form of regression, for it is only during the early months of life that the libido has no object-cathexis. At that period the infant is in that state of vague awareness, during the few hours that he is awake at all, which makes no distinction between experiences that arise in his own body and those that come from the outside. Even the pleasure he derives from feeding at the mother's breast is not identified as having an objective source. The breast is just as much a part of him—or we might also say as little a part of him—as his own fist which he may continue to suck when the breast is withdrawn. The pleasure he obtains is auto-erotic, and the libido development at this stage is described as *primary narcissism*.

When the child does begin to differentiate the environment—a secondary process function—and when he then begins to identify suitable "objects," his libido cathects them; but at least some libido is always retained by the ego. The balance between the two makes the difference between normal "self-regard," immoderate self-conceit, and the psychotic withdrawal of the schizophrenic. The schizophrenic has withdrawn his libido from the world and invested it entirely in himself.

THE LATENCY PERIOD. Freud believed that after the climax of the "family romance" the child's interest in sex becomes less active. Perhaps it would represent his position more accurately to say that the child during the period between six and twelve years seems to enjoy being with members of his own sex rather than with those of the opposite sex. On this account Freud has given the name "homosexual stage" to this phase of psychosexual development. It represents the next step in the normal sequence of libido movement toward maturity. However, many of Freud's followers in the psychoanalytic tradition as well as other critics regret his failure to explore more thoroughly this period of the child's adjustment to his peers and to a world of objects and standards and problems which he must learn to face independently. Hartmann, Erikson, Sullivan, and Piaget have had much to say of this period; but for Freud it seemed to hold little interest. R. W. White has written, "For once we can almost say that Freud underestimated the importance of sex" (1960).

PSYCHIC DETERMINISM. An event is "determined" if it has a cause. It is fully determined if it has a sufficient cause so that in every detail its character follows necessarily from the antecedent conditions, nothing being left to chance. Determinism is the belief or scientific postulate that all events in nature have their sufficient causes. As applied to the human organism determinism means that every act or thought or emotion has its sufficient causes, though these may be very complex and difficult to disentangle because of the complexity of the organism and of the environment. Freud believed heartily in determinism. He would not admit that any act "just happened" or that it was due to "free will." He pointed out that important actions and decisions are always ascribed to motives, and that it is only in unimportant matters that we are inclined to say that we could have acted this way or that but just decided arbitrarily to act in this way rather than that. Where there is no conscious motive there must be an unconscious one, he asserted. A slip of the tongue or any sort of "accident" must be motivated by some hidden desire. It is aimed at a certain goal, and though it may not fully reach its goal it interferes with the conscious purpose of the moment and produces unexpected results. A dream is not mere play of imagination but is governed by an unconscious wish and aimed at the fulfillment of that wish. For Freud motivation was practically the whole field of psychology.

In the realm of the abnormal, Freud did not accept Janet's view that neurosis could be explained as the result of low mental tension (page 254). He held that the neurotic wanted his phobia or obsession—unconsciously, if not consciously. Freud's followers, even those who parted from him on other questions have generally clung to psychic determinism. They believe that every symptom has a meaning in terms of unconscious motives and unconscious satisfactions. When we behave in a way that seems on the surface to be "reasonable" and can offer "good reasons" for our behavior the analyst may describe our explanation as "rationalization"—a form of pseudo-reasoning which our consciousness offers to account for what unconscious motives made us do or say. When we mislay something, forget or arrive late for an appointment, sprain an ankle skiing, he may attach little significance to the momentary distractions, external circumstances, imperfections of skill, or fatigue which *we* think of as the causes of such mischances. To him the essential explanation lies in the unconscious motive. However, he would admit that behavior may be *overdetermined*: that is, other causes are conceded to operate along with the motive (Rapaport, 1960). The manifest dream content, for example, is said to be partly the result of sensory stimulation affecting the sleeper as he dreams—as when a draft from an open window makes him dream that he is out of doors unclad; it is also partly the result of some current problem absorbing his attention; but along with these causes the ever-essential repressed motives contribute to the form the manifest dream takes.

With the increased emphasis since Freud's death on the ego functions (Hartmann, 1939; Rapaport, 1959, 1960), psychoanalysts are in a better theoretical position to grant that behavior may be at least partly determined by factors independent of, or at least relatively remote from, the instinctual motives. More about this development will be given on pages 285–91.

FREUD'S LATER THEORY

Freud was not quite satisfied with his theory as it stood in 1914. He had by that time, as we have seen, moved from his original idea of repressed wishes as motives to a theory of instincts in which there was polarity between the libido and the ego drives. But there were details which did not easily fall into place in this scheme. One was the concept of narcissism which Freud found very useful in accounting for certain neurotic and psychotic symptoms. But where did narcissism belong? Since it involves love, it should be part of the *libido* family; but in its practical effect it is just as closely related to the *ego*, because it tends to protect, support, and even inflate the self. Sadistic behavior presented another problem. Here the libido element is obvious; but how can the aggressive, hostile aspect of sadism be reconciled with the love motive? When the "mental casualties" of the First World War began to be studied still other questions on the validity of the older theory arose. The result was that between 1915 and 1926 Freud subjected it to a major overhauling.

He began first with a systematic re-ordering of his thinking on instincts and the "vicissitudes" or transformations which they undergo (1915a). Instinct he defined as an internal source of mental stimulation, but of a kind which "never operates as a force giving a *momentary* impact but always as a *constant* one." Only an adequate "object" will satisfy it. An instinct, therefore, has four aspects: a source, an aim, an object, and an impetus. The source is the bodily process itself that produces the excitation; the aim is satisfaction in some form or some degree; the object is that which is cathected because it can provide the satisfaction; and the impetus is the force behind the instinct. Freud also described the flexibility or variability in the way the instinct can manifest itself. We need not go into the complexities of Freud's reasoning about these defenses of the ego, since it was based upon a theory he was shortly to modify; but since the defenses remained as features of the new theory we may explain them with some simple examples. An instinct may be *sublimated*, as when sexually motivated curiosity is turned to good effect in biological research. The instinct may undergo *reversal into its opposite* as when the desire to inflict pain on another is replaced by the willing acceptance of the passive role of sufferer. In another form reversal takes the form of *reaction formation* in which love or pity unconsciously serves to mask hostility. Many illustrations of this could be offered. An older child may express the tenderest affection for a new baby that has replaced him as the center of his parents' attention. Without leaving the slightest conscious trace or even any obvious signs in his behavior, his hostility gives way to an acceptable "reaction." Love too may be turned into its opposite with the effect of making the relationship between one person and another *ambivalent*.

In *turning the instinct round upon the subject*, the object is changed. We have already had an example of this in the narcissism of the schizophrenic. But hostility as well as love may be turned upon the self, and may account for many symptoms, physical as well as mental. Freud considered the morbid depression of melancholia (1917) to be of this character, but even as trifling an incident as cutting oneself in shaving could also be explained as self-punishment according to the fundamental principle of psychic determinism.

The fourth defense, *repression*, is a concept of tremendous importance in Freudian theory, as all of these many pages we have devoted to it bear witness. In the first formulations of his thinking repression was a cornerstone; now it dropped into line with other forms of ego defense; but there were those who believed that it should still be considered basic to other defenses such as those just discussed. The disposition of the later analysts, however, has been to support Freud's decision to make it one of many mechanisms, rather than the primary mechanism; and to give greater prominence to the "ingenious" assortment of defenses the ego seems to have at its disposal.

LIFE AND DEATH INSTINCTS—EROS AND THANATOS.   In his two important publications of 1915 Freud was still struggling with the polarities of ego and libido, pleasure and pain, and the paradoxes which did not seem to fit neatly into that framework. Finally, in 1920, he took a drastic step in the direction of solving the problem. His reasoning took something of this line: The instincts of self-preservation and propagation of the species, though having different immediate goals, are ultimately alike in being aimed at growth and increase of life. Suppose we combine them into an inclusive *life instinct*. Then what would we have to oppose them? What, indeed, except a *death instinct!*

The assumption of a basic death instinct was not absurd as Freud saw the matter. He had observed the tendency for repetition to occur in behavior—repetition in many different forms and at all ages. A child seems to enjoy it in his play: he wants to hear the same story told over and over in the same words; he himself mutters and croons the same nonsense sounds for minutes on end; he repeats the same play theme day after day, and has the same daydreams. At a later age he may report the same nightdream or some feature of the dream repeating itself with disturbing frequency. Freud had found that his patients were even prone to repeat the same mistakes in their lives, chalking up failure after failure that showed the same pattern. Freud called this the *repetition compulsion*. In a sense Freud's basic doctrine was based on the idea of repetition, since the later ways of life were always traceable to the distribution of libido energy determined in the early stages. Any single life might be thought of as a "theme with variations."

Now, since life itself has presumably arisen from an inorganic state, Freud argued, why should there not be a disposition for it to return to, or repeat, that inorganic state? There must be a primal, unconscious drive toward death, and it must be present in every individual from the beginning to the end of his life. Here was polarity enough! Eros and Thanatos—Eros the principle of life and growth, Thanatos the principle of decay and death; Eros the loving and constructive, Thanatos the hateful and destructive.

If, however, there is a death instinct, it must somehow manifest itself in the feelings and behavior of human beings. Here Freud could reason as he did in the case of narcissism. Just as the libido is generated within the organism but attaches itself to external objects, so also with the death instinct. It manifests itself for the most part not as a desire to die but as a desire to kill. Turned outward it is the urge to destroy, injure, conquer. It is the hostility motive, the aggressive tendency, which certainly manifests itself abundantly.

Finding something outside to destroy, it does not need to destroy the self. But when frustrated in an external aggression it is likely to turn back upon the self as a suicidal tendency. Its scope, like that of libido, must be very wide. It is not limited to homicide and suicide but covers the milder forms of aggressiveness, whether directed toward the self or toward external objects. Self-punishment and self-condemnation are included, and so are jealousy among rivals and rebellion against authority.

INCREASING EMPHASIS ON HOSTILITY AND AGGRESSIVENESS. From the viewpoint of this later theory of motives, it seems strange that Freud did not accept the basic role of hostility much earlier. He had much to say of hostility even in his early writings. The unconscious wishes that were fulfilled in dreams were often spiteful wishes such as the childish desire for the death of a brother or sister. In the Oedipus complex the boy becomes hostile to his father as the one who is frustrating his love demands on his mother. But in the earlier theory Freud was satisfied to regard hostility as merely a self-evident corollary of frustrated libido. But with the death instinct accepted, Freud's view changed. "How can the sadistic drive which aims at injury to the loved one be derived from the life-sustaining Eros? Must it not stem from the death instinct?" (1920) And the love-hate ambivalence must be a fusion or alloy of the two basic drives rather than a mere distortion of libido alone. Any concrete motive is a fusion of love and hate, of constructiveness and destructiveness.

Man's constructive activities are at the same time destructive. To build a house he chops down trees. Any action on the environment destroys or at least disturbs the existing state of affairs. The muscles are primarily the agents of aggression, and in any dealing with the environment aggression leads the way, with Eros joining forces later. Such statements are found in Freud's later works.

In his earlier thinking on social psychology Freud had emphasized the conflict between the sexual demands of the individual and the restrictions made necessary by social life. In his later works he laid at least equal emphasis on the natural hostility of man to man as the great obstacle to civilization (1930). The individual's demand for justice and fair play arises from jealousy. Each child in a family wants to be the favorite but finally backs down to the extent of saying, "If I cannot be the favorite, neither shall you. We will all be equals" (1921). Eros tends to bind men together in families, clans, and ever larger groups, always with love and justice within the group but with hostility and aggression for outsiders. Civilization develops through the conflict and fusion of these two major drives.

The difference between Freud's earlier and later theories of moti-

SIGMUND FREUD

vation can be brought out by reference to family life. Since the family is based on the reproduction function and centers in the sex act, the earlier theory regarded family life as wholly motivated by the sex instinct. Freud ridiculed anyone who failed to see a woman's behavior in childbirth as a clear example of sex behavior driven by libido. Since the mammary glands are sex organs, nursing the baby is sex behavior, and by extension all care of the child is sex behavior. The child, being born into this sexually motivated milieu and participating in its activities, is necessarily sex-motivated when he nurses, when he is bathed, when he is loved and protected in any way. His demands on the family are sex demands, and even his jealousy and rebellion when his demands are not fully met are direct derivatives of the sex motive that dominates his entire life in the family circle. So far the earlier theory. But with the recognition of a primary destructive tendency the picture changes. Now the baby comes into the world with a primary tendency to fight his environment. This aggressive tendency accounts for his rebellion and jealousy. By itself it would make life impossible in the family group, but the erotic tendencies come to the rescue and by fusing with the destructive tendencies lead to behavior which is a workable balance between love and hate.

The death instinct was a bitter pill for many of Freud's loyal followers, nurtured as they had been on the libido theory. It gave a harsher picture of human life. To Freud it was more and more convincing in his old age (1932, pages 124–43; 1940), passed in a period of wars and persecutions. He became more conscious of an aggressive tendency in himself. He had always been a "good hater" according to the testimony of his most devoted disciples (Reik, 1940, page 6; Sachs, 1944, page 116); and some of his more polemical writings (1927, 1937) as well as the finality of his breaks with dissenting colleagues support this description, and suggest that his aggressive drive was not strongly repressed.

In Freud's earlier theory maladjustments were traced to the repression of libido, and a considerable change would be expected from any emphasis on the repression of the aggressive tendency. Without elaborating the effect, Freud hinted at it in such statements as these:

What we have recognized as true of the sexual instincts holds to the same extent, and perhaps to an even greater extent, for the other instincts, for those of aggression. . . . The limitation of aggression is the first and perhaps the hardest sacrifice which society demands from each individual (1932, page 143).

The holding back of aggression is unhealthy, creates illness (1940, page 14).

The great increase of literature on "psychosomatic" illness during the 1940's can certainly be attributed to Freudian theory. There was at that time, and to a less extent there still is (Ring, 1957), a suggestion that specific forms of disease are the result of the repression of one or another drive. For example, peptic ulcer was explained as the effect of repression or frustration of the need for love; asthma was another condition referred to the libido and more particularly to fear of separation from the mother. Essential hypertension and arthritis, on the other hand, were charged to repression of hostility. Alexander (1954) differentiates these by describing the hypertensive as more likely to have a history of a stormy childhood which may be followed in maturity by a rather abrupt change to patient forbearance and endurance at the cost of chronic and spiraling tension. The arthritic, in contrast, adapts to the social pressures by combining "self-control and a benevolent tyranny over others." The disease symptoms are precipitated when the object of the benevolent tyranny departs from the scene or revolts. More recently, Alexander has reported a collaborative experimental study (Alexander, et al., 1961) recording a variety of physiological changes, including alterations in thyroid function while and after a group of treated and untreated hyperthyroid patients viewed a hair-raising movie-drama of life-and-death adventure. Other data were obtained from the subjects through psychiatric interviews and tests. There is a clinical suspicion that thyrotoxicosis is related to death anxiety, and the study aimed at determining whether the existence of such anxiety or defense measures against it could be measured physiologically. Although there were few cases—fourteen thyroid patients and five controls—the differences in the three groups were sufficient to encourage the authors of the study to conclude that their methodology and instruments were effective in establishing the physiological-psychological correlation. On psychosomatic theory in general, Alexander takes the position that while many symptoms must be treated psychologically as well as physically if a permanent cure is to be achieved, the psychological component by itself does not, in cases of repressed drives, explain the chronic disease.

. . . The same emotional conflicts can be observed in persons who do not suffer from any organ symptoms. In order to explain the organic condition other predisposing factors—to which we may refer with the expression of specific organ vulnerability—must be postulated. This vulnerability may be either constitutional—transmitted by genes—or acquired early in life by childrearing practices or by previous diseases involving the organ system in question (1954, page 349).

THE STRUCTURAL APPROACH: EGO, ID, AND SUPEREGO AS PARTS OF THE PSYCHE. Another major alteration in Freud's theory, made at about the same time as his shift from the ego–libido polarity of motives to the life and death instincts, had to do with his doctrine of the unconscious. A belief in the reality and importance of unconscious mental processes was fundamental in Freud's thinking throughout his life. To review quickly his early position on the subject: at first he regarded the unconscious and the conscious as the two component parts of the mind (or psyche). There was also the preconscious, consisting of memories and wishes that could be easily summoned into full consciousness, but the conscious and preconscious belonged to one system as opposed to the unconscious material which lay beyond the reach of the conscious mind. The conscious self was in touch with the environment through the senses and acted on the environment by using the muscles. It was engaged in perceiving, thinking, remembering, and acting. The unconscious was constantly striving to emerge into consciousness, but was held down by the conscious self or *ego*. This had, along with other functions, the task of resisting the unconscious.

But this simple scheme ran into the difficulties already mentioned (page 265). Patients under analysis seemed not to be aware of their own resistances. Consciously they were trying to recall certain experiences or to engage in free association, but unconsciously they were resisting. Freud reasoned that the ego, as the resister, must be partly conscious and partly unconscious. In the revised theory (1923) he called that part of the mind "which behaves as though it were unconscious" the *id;* he thought of the ego as extending from the outer surface, where it is in touch with the environment, into the id where it is also in touch with the turbulent, unorganized, passionate motives of life and death, love and destruction driving toward expression. It comes to know the dangers of the environment and the necessity of restraining the id. Freud wrote (1923):

> Thus in its relation to the id it is like a man on horseback, who has to hold in check the superior strength of the horse; with this difference, that the rider seeks to do so with his own strength while the ego uses borrowed forces . . . .

The borrowed forces are the energies of the id which it must gradually "bind" and use in a way suitable to the exactions of reality. We still have here the old relationship between primary and secondary process.

As if the ego's task of controlling the id were not enough, a third part of the psyche emerges in early childhood to complicate the problem. Because the child is made to feel his weakness and inferiority in comparison with his parents and other adults, he takes these superior beings as models, "identifies" with them and builds up an ego-ideal, which is himself as he aspires to be. But these superior beings are not simply admired; they are feared. They punish him; they tell him he is naughty; they have rules of right and wrong which he must obey. Finally he adopts these external commands as his own internal laws of conduct and keeps watch over himself to make sure he does not disobey. Freud describes this identification as an incorporation or *introjection* of the "object" with whom the identification is made. In the course of life there may be many such identifications, but the earliest and usually the most significant will be that made with the parents. It is from them that the child first begins to learn, when he is five or six, what the rules are, and this knowledge forms a special core within the ego which is usually identified as the *superego*. This late outgrowth of the ego, then, seems to have two sides: the positive ego-ideal which sums up what the individual wants to be, and the superego which tells him what he ought to be. From this it would appear that the superego has at least some of the characteristics of conscience, at least in the sense of a compulsive conscience. The superego says "Thou shalt" and "Thou shalt not" without saying why. It cannot explain its commands because the source of its authority is buried in the unconscious. Freud believed that the rudiments of the superego were inherited from primitive mankind and that it took shape largely in each child's struggle with the Oedipus complex (page 270). Some neurotic patients are excessively conscientious. They are never satisfied with their own behavior but always accuse themselves of sins of omission and commission. They feel guilty for acts which they have not performed if they have merely thought of doing them, and they may go through elaborate rituals of self-punishment, making life miserable for themselves and their friends. They admit that their guilty feeling is irrational, but they cannot get away from it. Their superego is fierce and relentless. In general Freud held that the superego is motivated by the aggressive tendency turned inward against the ego. In other words, the superego appropriates some of the energy of the aggressive instinct for use against the ego.

FEAR AND ANXIETY. In this period Freud seemed to waiver between the idea of a weak ego hard beset by the many demands upon it, and a masterful ego with many assets and considerable power. The first position is taken in the following excerpt:

> The proverb tells us that one cannot serve two masters. The poor ego has a still harder time of it; it has to serve three harsh masters, and has to do its best to reconcile the demands and claims of all three. These demands are always divergent and often seem quite incompatible; no wonder that the ego so frequently gives way under its task. The three tyrants are the external

world, the superego, and the id. . . . The ego . . . feels itself hemmed in on three sides and threatened by three kinds of danger, towards which it reacts by developing anxiety when it is too hard pressed . . . (1932, page 103).

The problem of anxiety held an important position in Freud's theory from the beginning, and it had figured prominently in his thinking during the extensive revision which we have been discussing: in fact, one of the common translations of a monograph which he wrote in 1924, "*Hemmung, Symptom und Angst,*" is "The Problem of Anxiety" (1926a). Although this term is often used as a synonym of "fear," there are times when it carries a very different meaning. Fear is what Freud called "realistic anxiety," an emotion aroused by a truly threatening situation. There is good reason to fear wars, and exposed live wires, and earthquakes where earthquakes can be expected periodically to take lives and destroy property; but if a person were to become uneasy about living within the boundaries of civilization because of the fear of war, or refuses to turn on electric light switches for fear of being electrocuted, or expresses a terror of earthquakes where none has ever been reported, there seems to be some justification for believing that the real fear is of something quite different. These expressed fears would be symptoms of neurosis, and of course Freud was constantly confronted with such neurotic anxiety symptoms in his patients. Sometimes these groundless fears are fixed: these are phobias; sometimes they appear to be "free-floating": the patient gets over one worry, and it is promptly replaced by another. An aura of threat seems to hang over anything he undertakes.

Freud's first explanation of anxiety was that it represented in consciousness the effect of libido that was repressed, but not effectually repressed. The anxiety was a conversion of the "leak." By 1924, however, he had come to a different opinion about the cause of much—but not all—anxiety. His experiences in child analysis played an important part in his new formulation. In the Oedipus situation the child represses his libidinous wishes because of anxiety about the punishment they might bring down upon him: repression, then, was the effect of anxiety in such a case, not its cause. Thinking back to the earlier experiences of childhood where anxiety might appear, Freud noted the uneasiness of a small child when the mother disappears, or a little later when the child experiences her reproof for something she considers "naughty." Fear of abandonment, fear of loss of love, seemed to arouse the anxiety response. Finally he concluded that the primal source of anxiety was the birth process itself, at which time the infant is violently thrust into a new environment for which he is by no means fully prepared. Essentially the theory was that the psyche, as well as the nervous system, of the infant is at the time of birth overwhelmed with the flood of new stimuli; and he concluded that the resulting experience of helplessness was the prototype, and in a sense, the source of later anxiety aroused by situations too threatening for the ego to handle.[1] However, as the ego matured it learned to *anticipate* such situations, so that anxiety occurred before the threatening event occurred. Anxiety therefore became a device used by the ego to keep the id in line. It was really an adjunct of the reality principle.

All the instinctive motives (or emotions), except fear, belong primarily to the id. But fear, or anxiety, is a property of the ego, and, as such, contributes to its relative strength in the three-way struggle Freud describes above, for to the extent that the ego curbs the id it also may reduce the tyranny of the superego. The ego is strong, too, in the fact that it appropriates the energies of the libido and the destructive drive to use in *desexualized* and *sublimated* form. This fact and the occasional suggestions that appear in Freud's writings that the ego is not entirely without its own resources have become the basis for the recent developments of classical Freudian theory in the direction of "ego psychology," an extension along lines which, according to Heinz Hartmann, David Rapaport, and Anna Freud, would have received Freud's benediction, had he lived to know about it. We shall hear more of "ego psychology" shortly (pages 285–91).

But what of the merits of the system as Freud left it? He himself points out one difficulty in the tripartite division of the psyche just described: "I must add a warning. When you think of this dividing up of personality into ego, superego, and id, you must not imagine sharp dividing lines . . . we must allow what we have separated to merge again" (1932, page 103). This dividing of the individual into distinct entities which are always warring against one another gives an unreal picture of what actually goes on in thought, feeling, and behavior. For scientific purposes, to be sure, we require not so much a realistic picture as a working model, a conceptual framework in which we can think clearly and predict what behavior will occur under given circumstances. Did Freud himself in his later works find his system of scientific value? In some passages he indicates that it was of definite value, while in other passages he seems to be struggling with its complexities. The ego remains a somewhat am-

---

[1] Otto Rank, long one of Freud's close disciples, elaborated the "birth trauma" theme, but his additions were not well received by the master, and this contribution became the rock on which their association foundered. Rank later modified his own theory independently (1929).

biguous concept. In contrast with the id or superego it is the active, executive function. In contrast with the libido it is still the instinct of self-preservation. In contrast with the external world it is the entire individual, as it must be in narcissism, for the ego that is loved is not the executive function but the self as a whole. One must say, too, that if Freud overdid the libido in his early theory, he overdoes hostile aggression in the later theory. *Aggression* is an ambiguous word, sometimes implying anger and hostility, sometimes vigor and initiative. It must be a mistake, we feel, to regard all human activity as either erotic or destructive, in any reasonable sense, or as combining the two in some kind of fusion. There must be outgoing, constructive motives that are not erotic, and some energetic, enterprising motives that are not belligerent. In essence, Freud's theory seems to imply that something like this is the case: A sculptor and a mineralogist stand before a block of marble. The sculptor says: "I love that stone enough to embrace it. But I hate it too; I would like to smash it into powder. So I will compromise by carving it into the form of a beautiful girl." The mineralogist says: "I love it, I hate it, so I will compromise by cutting a thin section of it which I can examine through a microscope to bring out its inner structure." Must not other motives be present to govern the devoted attention which these two people will give to a block of stone? The contributions of the neo-classical Freudians offer an interesting answer to this question.

PSYCHOANALYTIC EGO PSYCHOLOGY

ANNA FREUD. In her book, *The Ego and the Mechanisms of Defense* (1946) Anna Freud clarified the status of the ego in current psychoanalytic theory, and at the same time sketched a plan for the direction further study of that concept might take. In the clarification, she pointed out that early psychoanalytic *theory* would have promptly rejected as apostasy any disposition to dethrone the id and to set up the ego as its independent partner. She attributed this dogmatism to the view that the term "psychoanalysis" should be limited to the "new discoveries relating to the unconscious psychic life." Psychoanalytic *therapy,* on the other hand, had from the beginning concerned itself with the unconscious only for the purpose of treating abnormalities and restoring "the ego to its integrity." The notion that psychoanalytic research should be restricted to depth psychology was exploded by Freud's own writings, *Beyond the Pleasure Principle* (1920) and *Group Psychology and the Analysis of the Ego* (1921). She might have added *Analysis Terminable and Interminable* (1938) in which her father had, perhaps most explicitly, expressed the conviction of an ego "endowed from the beginning with its own peculiar dispositions and tendencies"—a statement hard to reconcile with some of Freud's other views, but well chosen to justify what might otherwise have seemed a radical departure from orthodoxy in Heinz Hartmann's publication one year later of his epoch-making *Ego Psychology and the Problem of Adaptation* (1939). Hartmann's work could really be described as undertaking the task of exploring the ego's "contents, its boundaries and its functions and [tracing] the influences in the outside world, the id, and the superego by which it has been shaped"—the direction which psychoanalytic theory should take as Anna Freud later prescribed. The prestige of her endorsement has undoubtedly done much to lend strength not only to Hartmann's contributions but also to the work of Ernst Kris, David Rapaport, Erik Erikson, and others identified with the advancement of the concept of the autonomy of the ego.

Besides her recognition and study of ego devices which often play a predominant part in the defense mechanisms of neurotics, Anna Freud's own contributions to psychoanalytic ego theory have been incorporated into her active professional work with children at the Hampstead Child Clinic in England, her international lectures, and her regular articles in *The Psychoanalytic Study of the Child*, an annual publication presenting case reports, theories, and round-table discussions of psychoanalytic issues. Anna Freud has been a co-manager and co-editor since its establishment in 1945.

HEINZ HARTMANN.   The publication in 1939 of Heinz Hartmann's *Ich-Psychologie und Anspassungsproblem* (*Ego Psychology and the Problem of Adaptation*) may be thought of as a landmark not only in the development of psychoanalysis but also in the potential relationships of the schools. For psychoanalysis it might have meant only the rise of another rebel group. But Freud was no longer present to challenge the new movement; and Hartmann, with those who contributed to its launching (Hartmann, *et al.*, 1946; Kris, 1939, 1941, 1950), did not assume the rebel role. On the contrary, they sought in Freud's own somewhat ambiguous theorizing a justifying base for their radical proposals. Without surrendering the psychoanalytic concern with depth forces which "scientific" psychologists regarded with distrust, Hartmann proposed a revision of the concept of the ego which had the effect of freeing it at least partly from its dependence on the id, and so opened up the possibility of a new approach to questions of motivation, learning, thought, perception, and other activities in a form more akin to those which are the concern of the academic psychologist.

In the sense that Freud had identified the ego with the reality principle and the secondary process, it had long been associated with adaptation and survival value; but Hartmann was not satisfied with Freud's explanation of the derivation of the reality principle from the pleasure principle. How does the ego force the pleasure principle into adapting to reality? Taking his cue from a statement made by Freud in *Analysis Terminable and Interminable* (1938), Hartmann found a fresh solution to the problem. Freud had said, "We must not overlook the fact that the Id and Ego are originally one . . . ." Hartmann proposed that both arise as independent structures from an originally undifferentiated phase during which man's native endowments provide him with the means of adapting to an "average expectable environment":

> . . . There are no drives in man which would in and of themselves guarantee adaptation, yet on the average the whole ensemble of drives, ego-functions, ego-apparatuses, and the principles of regulation, as they meet the *average expectable environmental conditions*, do have survival value. Of these elements, the function of the *ego-apparatuses*—is "objectively" the most purposeful . . . (Hartmann, 1939, as translated by Rapaport, 1951, pages 382–83; italics added).

The physical and psychological "apparatuses" to which he refers include intelligence, perception, memory, and motility, which, as they mature, not only enable the child to cope with his environment but also provide intrinsic pleasure of a conflict-free nature. (This theme of "function pleasure," so-called by Karl Bühler, has much in common with features of the theories of J. Piaget, R. W. White, and R. S. Woodworth.) In time these pleasurable conflict-free activities, which have primary autonomy, may come to be used in the service of the id. Language, for instance, may be adapted to ego defense by the direction of sharp wit or ironic criticism against those who arouse hostility; what is seen or heard may be warped by id drives or the defenses against them; walking or dancing may be assimilated to the id system, etc. On the other hand, any habit once acquired as an ego defense may develop a *secondary autonomy* which insures its persistence even when the need for the defense no longer exists, as when meticulous orderliness long outlives the anxiety which originally accounted for its development. Here again, the possibility of the separation of a process developed in the service of a drive from that drive, and its subsequent functioning as an end in itself, had been earlier recognized by Freud in *Wit and Its Relation to the Unconscious* (1905b), so that Hartmann's argument that any particular response may be "triggered by the drive," may serve other needs, or may have become an end in itself is a less radical innovation than it at first glance appears to be.

As we survey the functions of the ego according to Hartmann's concept of its development, we realize its diversity and complexity: it tests reality; it controls and directs the discharge of motor energy; in response to danger signals it safeguards the organism through internalized trial responses and "detour activities" which result in "growing independence from the immediate impact of present stimuli"; through its defenses it inhibits instinctive drives. But in addition to these functions of adaptation and inhibition, Hartmann identifies also integrating and coordinating tendencies which he describes as the ego's *synthetic function* (1939) and which he suggests, further, seeks to maintain equilibrium with the adapting and inhibiting activities. The synthetic function seems to represent the person as something transcending the apparatuses and functions which comprise the ego.

We have seen that the same behavior, according to psychoanalytic ego theory, may be at various times (1) a simple adaptive response made to the environmental situation; (2) a conflict-free response made purely for the pleasure it gives to the performer; (3) an action which has become tied up more or less with the id; or which as an after-effect of this complication (4) now remains as a habit carried on with the neutralized energy of the aggressive or sexual drive it once served. With the first two points in mind we see, too, that thought activities once treated as "rationalizations" can now be accepted as reality-oriented means of dealing with the external environment. So, too, with memory or fantasy. The memory of past reality will contribute to the solution of immediate problems; the still freer imagination is not infrequently the source of brilliant invention and creativity.

ERNST KRIS. The concept of *neutralization* of drive energy allows for a gradation of effect between primary process and secondary process activities. The more remote from the primitive sexual or aggressive drive an idea or activity is, the more likely it is to be accepted and used by the ego; but regardless of the degree of neutralization, "the ego may use the primary process and not be overwhelmed by it. . . . the organizing function of the ego includes the control of regression . . ." (Kris, 1950).

This observation was made by Ernst Kris (1901–1957) whose contributions to the new psychoanalytic ego theory included a penetrating analysis of preconscious mental processes. Although Freud had probably not expressed himself finally on the subject of the preconscious, his later treatment of it as a mental quality characterizing those contents of the psyche which could readily become conscious failed to take into consideration the fact that not all ideas that can be recalled are recalled with equal ease or casualness. Some require considerable effort; some are attended by disturbing emotions. Kris was impressed, too, with the variety in the nature of the preconscious items, ranging from "purposeful reflection to fantasy and from logical formulation to dream-like imagery."

The fantasy, he concluded, used in the service of the id, will discharge non-neutralized libido and aggression, whereas reflective thought, serving the autonomous ego, will involve neutralized ego energy. Fantastic imagery may occur on the borderline between sleep and waking when the defenses of the ego are relaxed; on the other hand, it may represent the first, or inspirational, phase of what will develop into creative productivity. Controlled regression by the ego in its full strength, may draw from the primary process an inspirational cue which may then be the basis for elaboration into a scientific or artistic production. When the temporarily relaxed countercathexis [2] of the ego is renewed, the fantastic, idiosyncratic quality of the inspiration is worked over by the ego into a form that can be communicated to others. Without this translation the same experience might remain socially unintelligible, or even pathological nonsense. In this theory of the ego's regression "in order later to regain improved control," it is interesting to note a resemblance to Jung's understanding of the function of regression (page 308, this book). Kris applied his study of the preconscious to the interpretation of normal and pathological art (1952).

DAVID RAPAPORT. The untimely deaths of Ernst Kris and David Rapaport (1911–1961), two of the most distinguished proponents of the new psychoanalysis, have dealt a serious blow to the systematic development of ego theory. Rapaport, in his several major efforts to reconcile and integrate psychoanalytic principles with some of the academic mainline hypotheses and experimental findings (1951, 1959, 1960), showed the tremendous breadth and depth of his knowledge of the entire field bounded on the one hand by experimental psychology and on the other by psychiatry. He showed also his realistic grasp of the main areas of strength and weakness of psychoanalysis. In *The Organization and Pathology of Thought* (1951), he provided a richly annotated review of contributions to the psychology of thinking made by such theorists as Ach, Claparède, Bühler, Piaget, and Lewin, along with those made by others more immediately associated with the psychoanalytic movement. From

---

[2] Countercathexis describes the repressing force exerted against an idea which threatens to emerge from the unconscious.

these he formulated a tentative synthesis or first approximation of a psychoanalytic theory of thought which might provide a basis for experimental studies.

Similarly, his contribution to the 1960 Nebraska Symposium on Motivation presented the psychoanalytic position against a broad background of other motivation theory. His primary antagonist in this instance was R. W. White whose theory of *effectance motivation* and *competence* was presented on the same occasion. (See pages 293–95). Against White's emphasis on the motivational character of curiosity, exploration, activity, manipulation—all used by the child in gaining competence in dealing with his environment—Rapaport argued that all *causes* of behavior are not necessarily *motives*, and that the Freudian theory of *attention-cathexis* offers a non-motivational account of the environment-induced responses about which White focuses his proposal. For Rapaport's systematic explanation of attention-cathexis the reader must refer to the original paper (1960, pages 227–33). Here space limitations permit us to cite only some of the distinctions between motivation and attention-cathexis: the latter (1) involves energies which "do not strive for discharge"; (2) they "show no peremptoriness; they are commanded by excitations"; (3) they show "no appetitiveness" but rather a readiness for new excitation, being in that respect not unlike quasi-needs; (4) "unlike motives, [they] do not have goals or specific objects or selectiveness" and, other things being equal, any object may attract them.

Having thus set up an alternative proposal to White's theory, Rapaport conceded in the genuine spirit of the scientific inquirer that White's arguments represented a serious challenge which could be met fully only with further study of the whole question of motivation. In the same spirit Rapaport formulated the comprehensive structure of psychoanalytic theory for Sigmund Koch's series, *Psychology: A Study of a Science* (1959, Vol. III). From a theorist who contributed substantially to the *rapprochement* between psychoanalytic theory and the positions of the other schools, the following observations on theory-making should hold considerable interest:

The bane of the "single theory and single method" is in part synonymous with the plague called "schools of psychology." The investigator uses a method and becomes its captive. So do his students. He develops a theory which can only predict phenomena elicited by that method or a closely related one. What is not amenable to study by those methods ceases to influence the theory. In turn, all theories whose methods do not apply to the realm of phenomena in question are somehow considered "wrong," and if they are tested at all, it is by methods alien to them, and so they are obviously *found* wrong. Usually, however, they are ignored altogether. As a result, certain methods become "canonized," the study of a limited range of phenomena becomes the

only "proper study of man," and those who try to reunite the field of psychology, so fragmented by a few methods, are regarded as "philosophers" in the
pejorative sense of the word (1959, page 166).

Theoretical progress, he held, begins with facts and a knowledge of
the theories offered to explain them. It depends upon intuitive
hunches, some of which can, some of which cannot, be promptly
subjected to empirical testing. Although there are rules for codify-
ing science, there are no fixed rules for making discoveries or making
theories. Rapaport quotes (page 165) Dingle, the British historian
of science, who wrote: ". . . there is only one scientific method:
produce a genius and let him do what he likes . . . the best we can
do is to learn to spot natural genius . . . and protect it, by fiery
dragons if need be, from the god of planning" (*The Scientific Adventure*, Philosophical Library, 1953). For those who would approve
of such a dispensation, it might seem right to include under it both
Freud and the apologist who turned such brilliant efforts toward
integrating psychoanalytic theory into the fabric of scientific
psychology.

EGO IDENTITY AND "SOCIAL METABOLISM." Erik Erikson (born
1902; now Senior Consultant at the Austen Riggs Center), has remained in the Freudian camp while at the same time recognizing the
effect social factors will have upon the individual's development at
each of the psychogenetic stages. Although Erikson's thinking has
been influenced by field studies of the Sioux and Yurok Indians which
he carried on with the cooperation of the anthropologists, H. Scudder
Mekeel and Alfred Kroeber, he is not just concerned with the broad
cultural differences which come first to mind when we think of different ethnic groups, but also with the effect of "changing historical
reality" within an apparently continuous culture (1950). As gradual
as the evolution of automation in our own society may appear to have
been to those who have lived through it day to day, its effect on ego
development should not be underestimated. If Hartmann's view
that the infant is born with a readiness to adjust to an "average expectable environment" is correct, it follows that "only a perpetual
social metabolism and a constant (if ever so imperceptible) restructuring of tradition can safeguard for each new generation of infants
anything approaching an 'average expectability' of environment"
(1959, page 151). The ultimate basis for a healthy personality, according to Erikson, is security of personal identity; and the proto-
types—or models for identification—around which this may be built
are likely to be less available in a push-button society or in a society
with amorphous goals and ideologies, than in one with organized

values and social institutions. In the latter, an older generation must constantly "rejuvenate" and interpret these values and institutions for the young as they move through the crises of early child development toward maturity. Healthy mental adjustment will therefore depend upon a healthy mutuality between the child and the parent as the latter functions in the role of the agent of society.

Using his own terminology but the familiar psychosexual stages of Freud as his framework, Erikson describes the essential contributions of each phase to the gradual evolution of the individual's ego identity. Positive *psychosocial* effects at each stage will depend on how successful the parents are in handling the inevitable frustrations that represent the crises of each period. In the first "incorporative" phase a crisis arises as the infant finds himself abandoned at moments of discomfort with no way of knowing that relief is near at hand. Regular loving attention on these occasions will change *mistrust* to *trust*, which will express itself in the "infant's first social achievement . . . his willingness to let his mother out of his sight without undue anxiety or rage" (1950, page 219). From the later teething stage he develops his earliest "sense of badness," when the loved source of comfort is abruptly withdrawn as he bites hard to ease his own discomfort. With the transfer of interest to the anal zone, "holding on" and "letting go" become the focal *modes* on which the *social modalities* will depend. Parental firmness wisely used at this time will help the child to develop a generalized *autonomy* rather than leaving him subject to *shame* and *doubt*. At the phallic stage his behavior is characteristically "intrusive," not only in relation to the genital zone but in his handling of objects, walking about and getting underfoot, chattering and asking questions. This is the oedipal period; and how it will affect the individual's later personality will depend on how skillfully the parents manage to develop a sense of participation, responsibility, and *initiative* out of the child's propensities and interests, rather than impressing him with a sense of *guilt*. A cruel and rigid superego developed at this stage may have disastrous effects all through life.

By the latency period, the "organ modes" having been mastered, the child begins to develop the knowledge and skills which will from then forward make an important contribution to the confirmation of his identity. Not only in the family group but among his peers his status is largely dependent upon the number and kinds of things he can do. His activities become less random and more aimful. If he fails with the tools of his *industry*, his sense of *inferiority* may turn him back upon thoughts of his failure in the oedipal rivalry and leave him with a lasting belief in his own inadequacy.

At adolescence, the normal individual's ego will integrate the assortment of identifications, aptitudes, and role experiences which have accumulated through the earlier periods, and derive an identity which is distinctly his own, and which, he is confident, bears a reasonable resemblance to what others think of him. In contrast to this self-awareness and stability are the uncertainty and experimental quality of the transient identities tried out by the adolescent whose psychosocial odyssey has not been well guided, and who arrives at this stage of development with doubts about his place in society. "It is primarily the inability to settle on an occupational identity which disturbs young people," Erikson holds, although he notes also the effects of doubts about sexual identity as another possible factor contributing to *role diffusion*.

In the period of early maturity succeeding adolescence, the individual suffering from the uncertainty of role diffusion reveals the fact in his inability to lose himself in the intimacy of a friendship or a love relationship. A tentative "identity" cannot be subjected to the risk of the fusion of identities which intimacy involves. A series of superficial friendships, repeated failures in the attempt to establish a love relationship, or the selection of clearly unsuitable partners are symptomatic of such insecurity. "To fall in love then often means to fall into one's mirror image, hurting oneself and damaging the mirror" (1959, page 125). "Regression to bewilderment and rage," weak or overrepudiation of those in a group with which the individual does not identify, "diffusion of time perspective"—by which Erikson seems to mean a loss in faith that time can change a present state of affairs, along with the fear that it might, "surrender" to leadership, especially the negative leadership of antisocial groups, are some other symptoms of role diffusion.

In later maturity, according to Erikson, the "ability to lose oneself in the meeting of bodies and minds" expresses itself in solicitude for the next generation and its welfare. The alternative to this *generativity* is *stagnation*. And the final, culminating stage of life he describes as characterized by *ego integrity* or *despair*, the former an acceptant attitude toward the way one has ordered one's life, and a willingness to accept death.

AN ECLECTIC VIEWPOINT. Robert W. White (born 1904; now professor of clinical psychology at Harvard University), is a paradoxical addition to a section devoted to psychoanalytic ego theory. Although he was one of the group associated with Henry Murray in the projects of the Harvard Psychological Clinic (see page 362 of this book), and may well have been impressed by Murray's own positive disposition toward psychoanalysis, he has maintained in his own thinking a rugged independence of any single system while still recognizing their separate merits. He is introduced here because of his qualified general approval of Erikson's version of ego theory and his more specific approval of Erikson's emphasis on the importance of security in ego identity, and in autonomy, initiative, industry, and other outcomes of the "critical encounters" which the individual faces at successive stages of his development. White has proposed a theory of motivation which has a surface similarity to Erikson's position in stressing the importance of *competence* (White, 1959, 1960) as a requisite for healthy personality development; but White sees no reason to explain as libidinal satisfaction the delight an infant obviously finds in managing a spoon for the first time, or the pleasure he takes in the new world he discovers as he begins to creep or to walk, in climbing a tree, or in hitting a ball with a bat. Supporting his claim with references to a growing volume of physiological research and an increasing number of advocates for the idea that real alertness and interest in the environment begin when biological needs have been satisfied, White concludes:

> There is no longer any compelling reason to identify either pleasure or reinforcement with drive reduction, or to think of motivation as requiring a source of energy external to the nervous system. This opens the way for considering in their own right those aspects of animal and human behavior in which stimulation and contact with the environment seem to be sought and welcomed, in which raised tension and even mild excitement seem to be cherished, and in which novelty and variety seem to be enjoyed for their own sake. . . . It is proposed to designate this motivation by the term effectance, and to characterize the experience produced as a *feeling of efficacy* (1959, pages 328–29).

Effectance will be recognized for its resemblance to other theories which have recently stressed the stimulating power of the environment. Piaget's theme of assimilation and accommodation (page 42 in this book) has been one. Woodworth's behavior primacy theory (1958) is another. In this there is no pretense of ignoring the existence of organic needs, but their satisfaction is held to be secondary to the organism's primary interest in becoming acquainted with and dealing with the environment. Many a harassed mother will confirm the loss of minutes mounting into hours as she has impatiently waited for her two-year-old to finish his scheduled feeding while he busies himself with knocking the spoon on the tray and then trying to push it into her mouth, leaning over to pour a bit of his menu on the dog's head, reaching out for a toy he has just noticed on the window sill, and investigating its possibilities as a substitute for the spoon in which he has now lost interest. These do not seem to be the responses of an organism motivated by hunger; yet if the claims of S–R theory are to be accepted literally, a child fed regularly at a certain time should regularly develop a biological drive for food at that time. Apparently in this case the environment proves more interesting to him than the food. Nor can this be disposed of as a special case, nor as an example limited to the two-year-old level. The adolescent who rebels against the household routine of meals which interferes with his baseball or tennis, and the scholar who would rather miss a meal or much needed sleep than interrupt his ongoing research seem just as unconvincing witnesses for a theory of biological drives.

White's *effectance motive* is offered as a supplement rather than a substitute for Erikson's libido model and for Sullivan's interpersonal model, the value of which in their own places White is willing to concede. He applauds Erikson's derivation of the sense of industry from the latency period but he would reject any necessary tie-up of the interests of that period or any other with the neutralized drive energies proposed by Hartmann, Kris, and Loewenstein (1949).

White has expressed his interest in the effects of ordinary life events on the normal individual's personal development—a source of psychological information that has not been systematically explored. In *Lives in Progress* (1952) he has made a tentative approach to a problem which obviously presents great methodological difficulties, by collecting case histories of three young people and following up their stories several years later as they entered a more mature phase of their careers. Unfortunately, justice cannot be done here to the full range of his conclusions on "stabilizing ego identity," the limiting effect of unfavorable social relations on learning, the conditions for the deepening of interests, and the value of empathy in allowing the broader development of social understanding. White's conclusions on maturity and adjustment have much in common with those of Fromm, Piaget, and those who preach the doctrine of self-actualization (pages 351–56 in this book). The individual must find his role in society and stamp it with his own individuality. Conformity to existing social goals may be less healthy than a militant effort to formulate higher ones. The important thing for a parent to recognize is his child's own growth potential.

MELANIE KLEIN. A prominent leader of the Freudian school in England, Melanie Klein (1882–1960) established herself early in her professional career as a successful child analyst. For the traditional free-association method she substituted a play technique which made it possible for her to interpret even to a very young child the significance of his selections from an assortment of simple nonmechanical toys, how he treated them, and the evidences of his satisfaction or anxiety when they met an untimely fate at his hands. Her observations led her to graft upon orthodox Freudian theory changes which, among other effects, move down to the middle of the first year the earliest appearance of the superego and of the Oedipus complex. Klein and her followers have conceived of the child's mind as filled with bizarre fantasies of birth and intercourse, and these combined with his inability to distinguish between his own sensations and objective reality, or to recognize the unity of an external object, provide the background for the hostility and anxiety of the early months. When the mother's breast is satisfying it is "the good breast," and he would incorporate it within himself. When it is frustrating it is "the bad breast"; but this he cannot project or dismiss, as he would like. It becomes a persecuting agent within himself and the source of early anxiety. Klein described this earliest stage as the *paranoid-schizoid position,* taking account in the term not only of the persecutory delusion, but also of the splitting of the object into a good-bad dichotomy. When, a few months later, the child has come to realize that the "good" and the "bad" are really one, and that he cannot destroy the bad without destroying the good, he enters upon the *depressive position* in which the dominant anxiety is that the good object may be lost unless some reparation be made. If the pain, the hate, and the fear constantly overbalance the satisfaction and the love, the child may never fully attain the depressive position, or may regress to the paranoid, persecutory stage, even becoming schizophrenic.

Klein also placed the origin of the oedipal relationship in the second half of the first year at the stage of development in which all parts of the child's body crave satisfaction of both erotic and destructive desires. For the child of either sex the relationship involves both parents and takes a much more complicated form than that traditionally thought of as Freudian, one outstanding difference being that the child wishes not only to give but to have a baby. Jealousy of a sibling is therefore compounded by the child's realization that the baby belongs to the mother and not to him (Klein, et al., 1957).

10

Other Analytical Schools – Some Distinguished Dissenters

Having freshly in mind the many reconsiderations and alterations to which Freud subjected his own theory, the reader may find it hard to reconcile his image of this famous figure with the common characterization of him as inflexible, and intolerant of the contributions of others. Yet the story of his professional associations suggests that he was. When he was ready to revise, he revised. Until then he was inclined to be unreceptive or sharply critical of additions or modifications offered by even his closest associates. The story of the early development of psychoanalysis is a story of broken friendships; the first two theorists to be discussed in the pages following had been among the most trusted and most eminent of Freud's followers until they committed the outrage of publicly disagreeing with him.

ALFRED ADLER AND THE SCHOOL OF "INDIVIDUAL PSYCHOLOGY"

When Freud, in 1902, invited Alfred Adler (1870–1937) to join the Vienna psychoanalytic group, he certainly recognized the quick perceptive power of the young Viennese physician; but he would hardly have foreseen that within ten years the alertness and flexibility in the thinking of this new associate, who was soon to succeed him as president of the society, would lead to a permanent rift be-

tween them and the development of a new analytic theory. With
the wisdom of hindsight we see quite clearly today why the association between these two men could not survive long. One reason
lay in the opposing orientation of their thinking. Freud, as we have
seen, sought to account for all behavior in terms of the past; Adler's
theory, from its earliest formulation, faced toward the future. In
Freud's thinking the division of personality was essential: conscious
against unconscious, ego against id and superego; Adler's emphasis
from the beginning was on *unity*. At all stages in Adler's thinking
there has been implicit in one form or another—if it has not been
explicit—the idea that the organism or individual as a whole is pushing forward toward something better. At one period in his writing
Adler described this as a "striving for superiority," but the theme
appeared with variations as his theory developed.

As a physician Adler's concern focused at first, understandably, on
the body's effect upon the mind. In that early phase of his thought
he accounted for whatever the quality of an individual's adjustment
—whether apparently normal, neurotic, or superior—as the result of
organic inferiority. The organism meets the threat of the environment which results from the inferiority by *compensating*. Medical
illustrations promptly come to mind, but Adler included "compensation within the organ, compensation through a second organ, *compensation through the psychological superstructure*, and organic or
psychological overcompensation." (Quoted from Ansbacher and
Ansbacher, 1956, page 24; italics added.)

This brief listing of the possible forms compensation for physical
inferiority may take has some interesting implications. Notice first
how the unity of the organism is implied in the flexibility of compensation. A defect in vision may be compensated by an increase
in attention and interest for visual stimuli; overcompensation could
conceivably make a ranking artist or designer of an individual who
might otherwise have shown merely indifferent talent. Adler cites
the case of Schiller, called to his attention by Otto Rank: Schiller
suffered from eye defect throughout his life, yet his poetry is rich
with visual images, and perhaps more striking is his use, as a drama-
tist, of the *William Tell* theme which places a high premium on the
eye's control of the hand (Ansbacher and Ansbacher, 1956, pages
28–29). Here compensation is achieved through imagination rather
than through any building up of the function of the defective organ
itself. A third way of compensating for the same kind of defect
might be to become a better "listener," either in the sense of a physical sharpening of auditory acuity, or a greater willingness to lend a
sympathetic ear to others.

INFERIORITY FEELING. Adler's emphasis on organ inferiority lessened as he gave greater recognition to the effects of *social* forms of inferiority. Underprivileged socio-economic status, the dependency of childhood, the inequality of privileges granted to the eldest, middle, and youngest child in the family, or the disadvantages of being an only child or an unwanted child could cause feelings of inferiority and in their separate ways produce efforts to compensate or overcompensate. In his early writings in this vein there was an explicit connection between feelings of inferiority and hostility. In fact in 1908 Adler "invented" a superordinate *drive of aggression* which had the property of using up all the energy left over because of the thwarting of satisfaction for the primary drives. Even in the first months of life this would take the form of kicking, biting, screaming, tantrums, fighting; but it might also express itself later in the form of self-injury, or pathetic appeal. The last two do not appear obviously to be expressions of hostility against others, yet it is recognized that they may be used with that effect. Suicide may have a double edge: it releases the victim from his troubles, but it also implies to the world in general or to those who have been particularly close to him, "See what you have made me do!" The appeal to pity is the same device on a much smaller scale: the domineering mother who has been unsuccessful in persuading her son to remain *her* little boy by out-and-out domination may be much more effective if she takes on an air of patient suffering. Translated into verbal form the aggressive drive could be expressed as, "I do not want you to stop being *my object*." Its transformation takes the form: "See how you are hurting your poor mother." In this way the device can be recognized as one form of "reversal formation" as Freud described that mechanism—but according to the Ansbachers' carefully documented account of Adler's contributions to the analytic movement the latter's *transformation of a drive into its opposite* was formulated seven years before Freud's counterpart concept was described in *Instincts and their Vicissitudes* (Ansbacher and Ansbacher, 1956, pages 32–33).

Although the reactions to feelings of inferiority prompted by the drive for aggression were of a psychological character in contrast to the biological, homeostatic nature of the compensations for organ inferiority, they were alike in the variety of forms they could take. Among other effects, aggression could express itself in the choice of a career such as law, teaching, preaching, medicine, etc., which would provide an opportunity for dominating others in a socially useful way. This expression of the instinct would fall into the familiar category of "sublimation," or in Adler's terminology, the *displace-*

ment of the drive to another goal. Some of its forms of expression, unfortunately, were not useful: snobbishness, pomposity, overweaning conceit, flagrant disregard for the rights of others, criminal behavior—the list could be stretched out indefinitely. As Adler's theories became more and more widely circulated, somewhere along the line the terms "inferiority complex" and "superiority complex" came to be identified with them, although there seems to be no evidence that he ever had anything to do with them until he learned about their existence in America in the mid-1920's (Ansbacher and Ansbacher, 1956, pages 256–61). Adler's later references to them found a place for them within his theory but made it apparent that there was no technical significance in the term "complex." "Inferiority complex" might describe a normal feeling of inferiority for which the individual who experiences it finds a socially useful compensation. On the other hand, another individual might use his feeling of inferiority neurotically to excuse himself from making any social contribution at all. This would be a different kind of "inferiority complex." The difference between the inferiority and the superiority complex lies entirely in the individual's point of view—or perhaps in the observer's: Is the important thing to the person under consideration where he has been or where he is going? We probably think of people with ambitions, in both the good and bad sense of this term, as illustrating the "superiority complex"; but their striving is still away from inferiority even though the manifest result is their movement toward higher goals. Since the term "complex" adds nothing to Adler's fundamental concept, perhaps it would be a good application of the law of parsimony to allow these two terms to fade back into the void from which they seem to have sprung.

THE MASCULINE PROTEST. While still a member of the Freudian group, Adler introduced as a variation of his inferiority–superiority theme the idea that superiority could be equated with masculinity. One sought to be "a man." This calls to mind Freud's theory of the effect upon character formation of woman's "penis envy" and of man's "castration anxiety." But in these concepts Freud was talking about the shame or fear associated with *biological* castration, while Adler's term referred to the striving against *psychological* castration (1911). Strength and power were identified with masculinity, weakness and inferiority with the feminine role. He shortly narrowed the term further to apply to behavior, more or less neurotic, that clearly betrays a woman's rejection of her feminine role. The masculine protest could show itself in her choice of a profession, such as engineering, which is usually thought of as man's stronghold; or in her cultivation of man's interests in the world of business or sports;

it could be expressed in the adoption of clipped haircuts and what one disapproving dean of women has described as "bifurcated garments." It may appear also in physical symptoms such as dysmenorrhea and frigidity. However, in the broader sense of the term the masculine protest described any defensive reaction against the underdog role. Male or female, the individual reached toward the superiority implied in "being a man."

FICTIONAL GOALS. Adler had begun by repudiating Freud's theory of the primacy of the sex drive. His writings on the subject of the feelings of inferiority and the masculine protest made it clear that he was moving further away from the Freudian position by emphasizing socially determined attitudes rather than biological instincts as the causes of behavior, both normal and neurotic. There could be no place in the Freudian camp for a rebel who gave primacy to ego rather than libido, and who even replaced the concept of repression with *safeguarding tendencies* associated with the masculine protest. In 1911 Adler resigned the presidency of the Psychoanalytic Society under the fire of its founder and a number of its other members, and thereafter devoted himself to developing the theories of Individual Psychology. At about the same time he became deeply impressed with the philosophy of Hans Vaihinger who had just published a book called: *The Philosophy of "As If"* (English translation, 1925). It was Vaihinger's thesis that all life is built upon "fictions," shadowy structures that determine our thinking about things without manifesting themselves in any explicit way. In this sense, fictions were "unconscious" determinants of behavior. For example, one such fiction would be the concept of a "normal" man. "Superiority" and "inferiority" would themselves be fictional to the extent that the former is thought of as all good and the latter as all bad—a way of thinking particularly characteristic of the neurotic.

Adler adapted this philosophy to his own thinking on the development of the individual. He began to regard the goals of superiority toward which each person aimed as "guiding fictions." Even in the small child, for instance, his future goal is symbolized in the "strength" and the "wisdom" of his parents and teachers, in the "power" of the policeman or the "courage" of the soldier or the cowboy. His play, daydreams, and other interests will tell us a great deal about the character of his guiding fictions.

One advantage of this innovation in Adler's theory was to make scientifically defensible the idea of a future goal as a cause for present behavior. By reducing the goal to an ideal operating in the present, the objection against teleological causality was eliminated. Another advantage was that it freed Adler from a position of strict causal determinism, and made it possible for him to explain why essentially the same circumstances in the lives of two individuals could lead to widely different results. Neurosis is the effect, not of social or physical inferiority or traumatic experience, but of the use the individual makes of such circumstances in setting up his future goal. Leading the patient to an understanding of the fiction behind his life pattern became the task of the therapist. For Adler who stressed the unity of personality the "unconscious" was merely the "not-understood"; the fictional character of the individual's goal was in this sense his "unconscious" (1926, 1931).

SOCIAL INTEREST. Adler early recognized the need for some factor counteracting aggressiveness to account for the positive feelings that exist within and between groups (1908). In this connection he noted the child's needs "to touch, to look and to listen." He decided that these drives operating together constituted a "need for affection" which could be satisfied by those who cared for the child when they cuddled him, talked to him, and carried him about. The need for affection could also be used as a "lever" for socializing the infant by withholding the reward of affection until desirable behavior replaced aggressive behavior. When Adler abandoned his drive theory he had to revise his thinking on the balancing social factor. Consistent with the pulling force of fictional goals of superiority were *counter-fictions* (1912, 1926) which seemed to develop purely as a matter of expediency and which provided a calculated respect for the social amenities. One cannot get far along the road to superiority without taking one's fellow-man into consideration!

Happily, this cynical "fiction" of humanity was soon replaced by Adler's theory of social interest as an innate potentiality for cooperation, a central factor in determining the quality of man's adjustment (1929). Social interest and cooperation make the difference between the normal and the neurotic character, between striving for perfection and striving for superiority, between the "common" sense of reasoning and self-centered rationalization. There is much resemblance between what Adler had to say and what Sullivan had to say (our page 330) on the difference between the "private" and "social" use of intelligence. Translating Adler's thoughts into Sullivan's terminology we could describe the neurotic's use of his intelligence as *parataxic;* the reasoning of the individual with adequate social interest, on the other hand, will be in the *syntaxic mode* and the product is more likely to be *consensually validated* (1931).

STYLE OF LIFE: THE CREATIVE SELF. Adler held that as early as the fifth year each individual develops a style of life which gives consistency and unity to his thought and behavior. Adler at various times equated the style of life with the whole personality, individuality, or the self; and in his later writings he stressed the point that it is created by the individual, and, as the *self*, represents the creative function of the individual. In other words, according to Adler, man is not the passive product of infantile repressions nor even of the physical or social limitations which his life history may record. He "creates" himself by the attitudes he takes toward such accidents of his existence. Although many factors may contribute to the shaping of his style of life, the most significant is the amount of social interest he invests in it. Strangely enough, Adler found that the pampered and the neglected child may have similar life styles. He used the term *pampered life style* to apply to both. When they are similar it is only to the degree that neither has developed adequate social interest (1935). The pampered child expects always to command and let somebody else do the work. The bullied child takes the attitude of trying to escape to a safe distance. The oldest child in a family tends toward a conservative attitude, seeking to keep what he has and not be displaced by the second child, who tends to adopt the radical attitude of changing things in his favor. These attitudes or styles of life, formed in the first few years, are extremely persistent. Each individual adopts his style early in life and maintains it as he meets the problems of youth and adulthood. Thus Adler, no less than Freud but in a very different way, laid great stress on the family situation as formative of the individual's character.

While not questioning the importance of the sex impulse, Adler did not allow it the fundamental role assigned to sex in Freud's earlier theory. The first problems of life are not sexual, and by the time the urgent problems of sex are encountered the individual's style of life is already formed. Of the three typical problems of life —community living, occupation, sexual love—it is the social task that the child meets first, and his social adjustment sets the pattern for his approach to the other problems as they arise. If the child's social attitude is one of courage and cooperation, readiness to give and to receive, he can later take up the sex interest into this style of life and succeed in love and marriage. But if the child's social attitude is an anxious seeking to outdo his associates, sexuality will later be used as a means to this same end.

The neurotic, hampered by a style of life that is not realistic for community living, has to substitute pretense for genuine achievement. His unconscious aim is to score a fictitious superiority by

evading difficulties instead of conquering them. In Adler's words
(1930, pages 41, 46, 47):

> The problem of every neurosis is, for the patient, the difficult maintenance
> of a style of acting, thinking and perceiving which distorts and denies the
> demands of reality. . . . As the work of Individual Psychologists has abun-
> dantly proved, an individual goal of superiority is the determining factor in
> every neurosis, but the goal itself always originates in . . . the actual experi-
> ences of inferiority. . . . "If I were not so anxious, if I were not so ill, I
> should be able to do as well as the others. If my life were not full of ter-
> rible difficulties, I should be the first." By this attitude a person is able still
> to feel superior. . . . His chief occupation in life is to look for difficulties.
> . . . He does this more to impress himself than others, but naturally other
> people take his burdens into account and . . . he wins his way to a privi-
> leged life, judged by a more lenient standard than others. At the same time,
> he pays the cost of it with his neurosis.

Whatever is written about characteristic life styles must be read
with the reservation in mind that each life style is unique, created
by the individual and, in a sense, by its dispositions, continuing to
create or at least to maintain itself.

ADLERIAN THERAPY. In examining a patient the Adlerian psychologist seeks to discover the patient's peculiar goal of superiority
adopted in childhood and still pursued in some way or other. His
position in the family and the general family situation in childhood,
his earliest memory, his likes and dislikes, his "heroes" from history
or fiction, his occupational choices in childhood and later, all provide clues. His present manner of standing, walking, and sitting
may reveal his "style." His way of shaking hands may be revealing,
and even the posture he takes in sleeping.

> When we see a person sleeping upon the back, stretched out like a soldier
> at attention, it is a sign that he wishes to appear as great as possible. One
> who lies curled up like a hedgehog with the sheet drawn over his head is
> not likely to be a striving or courageous character. . . . A person who sleeps
> on his stomach betrays stubbornness and negativity (1930, page 215).

Dream analysis was accepted by Adler as one of Freud's major
contributions to psychotherapy. But the dream should not be regarded merely as a fulfillment of old wishes; rather, it can serve to
reveal the patient's emotional attitude toward his present problems.
It is a symbolic rehearsal of an act that the patient must soon perform in real life and indicates his personal attitude toward this act.
A man whose style of life was characterized by doubt and hesitation,
being on the point of getting married, dreamed that he was halted
at the boundary between two countries and threatened with im-
prisonment—a comparatively easy dream to interpret in Adler's way.
Adler interpreted the plot of an entire dream rather than the associ-

ations obtained from the separate items. He discarded the reclining couch of the Freudian technique, preferring a more direct, conversational approach, free of constraint and with a "good human relationship" of social feeling between patient and therapist, both cooperating in the task of understanding the patient. Tact must be employed by the therapist to avoid the appearance of preaching or moralizing. The patient cannot be forced; no demands must be made on him, but he can be led gently to the point of seeing how he has been trying to achieve superiority "on the useless side of life" while missing his opportunities "on the useful side." The whole treatment takes much less time than is required for the "classical" psychoanalysis.

Adler's theory has drawn harsh criticism from the psychoanalytic group, but has found warm loyalties in some other quarters. There is an unevenness in the quality of his concepts, a fact he himself must have recognized if we can judge by the haste with which he abandoned some of them. In general his theory has been held to be relatively superficial, probably because it does contain a large amount of common sense applicable to daily life. Just why that should be regarded as a defect in a theory is not quite clear, particularly if it has established its value in the treatment of maladjustment; and Adler's has been successful, particularly in the treatment of children. Certainly by stressing the "whither" rather than the "whence" as an explanation of man's behavior it offers a more optimistic outlook for the individual and for society. But in addition to that, a critical reader of what Adler has had to say in his many publications can find, along with the "common sense," many shrewd observations which would identify his thinking with some of the most valued contributions of Gestalt and field theory and with the more recent rising volume of protests against psychological engrossment with fragments of personality which give us no clue to the essentially human significance of meaning and purpose.

THE "ANALYTICAL PSYCHOLOGY" OF CARL GUSTAV JUNG

Outside of Vienna the early center of psychoanalysis was at Zurich in Switzerland, where Eugen Bleuler (1857–1939), the eminent psychiatrist who developed the concept of *schizophrenia*, became interested in Freud's work. His assistant, Carl Jung (1870–1961), had begun using Freud's methods along with a word association test which was proving useful in detecting "complexes," dissociated, emotionally toned systems of ideas which had been found to be a source of mental symptoms. Jung and Freud became acquainted, and together they founded an international psychoanalytic society of which Jung was the first president. But his independence of thought soon came under the bitter censure of Freud and brought the relationship to an end. In 1913 Jung established the schismatic school of *Analytical Psychology.*

Although he followed Freud in stressing the polarity of the conscious and the unconscious, his concepts of these areas of the psyche were radically different. As we shall see later, he assigned to the ego a role of much less consequence than that played by the Freudian ego, and he tenanted the deeper layers of the unconscious with shadowy symbolic forms which represented the collective wisdom of man's remote past, upon which the individual, he believed, could learn to draw with profit. What a person is not *consciously,* he is *unconsciously.* The capacities and potential interests left undeveloped remain latent but unorganized in the unconscious, preempting a disproportionate share of the total psychic energy. Jung granted that the circumstances of childhood might be predisposing factors in neurosis, but he looked for the effective cause in some current problem which the patient could not solve because consciousness did not have enough psychic energy at its disposal. (Here Jung was clearly showing the influence of Janet, whose lectures he had attended in Paris.)

JUNG'S CONCEPT OF LIBIDO. Perhaps his most unforgivable departure from Freud's creed was Jung's concept of libido. This he judged to be not exclusively sexual, but a generalized energy more in the nature of Bergson's *élan vital* or Schopenhauer's *will to live.* It finds its outlets in growth, reproduction, and all kinds of activity. During the first four or five years—the presexual phase—it serves the functions of nutrition and growth and is the source of the child's early pleasures. Jung scoffed at the idea of an early oedipal relationship of the kind described by Freud. The child's attachment to the mother is at first merely a dependency relationship with the understandable satisfactions and rivalries which would be associated with the nutrition function. However, with the appearance of the sexual tendency toward the sixth year new elements begin to enter into the "complex" with the effect of making it appear to be more like the Freudian concept. But in dealing with an oedipal attachment (or with the *Electra complex* in a woman), Jung would be as much concerned with having the patient understand the part it was playing in his present unsolved problem as with persuading him to recognize its origin as a means of freeing himself from it. By so considering the purposes served by the present neurotic symptom along with the contributing causes of the past, Jung sought to integrate the Adlerian and Freudian orientations. But Freud in the years before 1920 still maintained that the libido was genuinely sexual even in earliest childhood, and considered Jung's effort to "purify" it a betrayal of psychoanalysis. He approached Jung's concept somewhat, however, when he combined the sexual libido with the other life instincts as "Eros"; and the still later changes of Hartmann (1939) and other psychoanalysts who have emphasized the conflict-free sphere of the ego (our page 287) have brought the neoclassical Freudian position still closer to Jung's on this question.

The libido attaches itself to certain ideas and objects to the neglect of others. The *persona* of an individual, which is really the social role in which he casts himself, is made up of certain qualities of his total potential which have been developed into a sort of social mask. Behind this lies, untapped and unrecognized, a host of other qualities representing that which is disapproved, unconventional, evil. These latter remain in the unconscious, but are by no means inert; and under the right conditions they may be integrated with the qualities of the conscious personality to good advantage. As in any more or less "closed" energy system, Jung's model has a self-regulating feature. Whenever a value in one part of the system is reduced compensation occurs in some other part; and when there is an overabundance of energy in one part there tends to be a flow of that energy to an area of lower value. Jung did not consider this displacement of energy as something lying within the power of the person: "Psychic energy is a very fastidious thing which insists on fulfillment of its own conditions . . ." (1956, page 63). We may use one of Jung's cases to illustrate the method of energy interchange between the conscious and the unconscious. The patient was a young man in the grip of a depression which on the surface appeared to be related to fears about his health. No amount of reasoning, however, could drive out these fears because they had their source in the irrational unconscious. While he was in this state he reported a dream: he sees his fiancée running down the road toward the frozen river. As she runs out on the ice it cracks, and although he is afraid she will jump into the fissure he stands passively and helplessly by as she does just that.

Jung explained the dream as one of a series of fantasies springing from the rich accumulation of libido in the unconscious at a time when the patient's conscious world has become "cold, empty, and grey."

The unconscious has simply gained an unassailable ascendency; it wields an attractive force that can invalidate all conscious contents—in other words, it can withdraw libido from the conscious world and thereby produce a "depression," an *abaissement du niveau mental* (Janet). But as a result of this we must, according to the law of energy, expect an accumulation of value—i.e., libido—in the unconscious (1956, page 227).

Little by little the conscious mind can regain control over the displaced libido by "giving the unconscious a hearing"—heeding the content of the fantasies of the dreams which become more insistent in their significance, and observing the goal toward which they reveal the unconscious to be moving. But it is not enough for the patient to stand by helplessly as an observer. He must recognize the reality behind the dream fantasy. In the case just described the female figure represented not just the fiancée, but an important archetype of the male unconscious—his *anima*. This, clearly, is seen to be slipping away from the dreamer; but if instead of allowing that to happen in reality, the patient makes an effort to retrieve it, he can salvage some of the libido which will otherwise be lost to the unconscious.

> Conscious realization and experience of fantasies assimilate the unconscious inferior functions to the conscious mind—a process which is naturally not without far-reaching effects on the conscious attitude. . . . I have called this change, which is the aim of our analysis of the unconscious, the transcendent function (1956, page 232).

In this way blocking or frustration may produce a good effect by forcing a person to regress to fantasies of the unconscious from which he may draw the wisdom and energy to deal with his problem. The French phrase, *"reculer pour mieux sauter,"* would describe this useful function of regression as Jung conceives it.

THE PERSONAL AND THE COLLECTIVE UNCONSCIOUS. The unconscious, for Jung, consisted of layers varying in depth and accessibility. The most superficial, the *personal unconscious,* contains those personal experiences which an individual has repressed or of which he has never been fully conscious. Still deeper and more remote are the layers of the *collective unconscious* which carries the heritage of the ages impressed upon the structure of the more primitive part of the nervous system. Despite scientific rejection of the idea that acquired characteristics can become hereditary, Jung found the concept of inherited dispositions toward thinking no more objectionable than inherited dispositions toward behaving. The forms of archaic thought provided by the collective unconscious are *archetypes* which, when they manifest themselves in consciousness, as they do in dreams, fantasies, fairy tales, myths, or in the delusions of the psychotic, appear as symbols. These are variable but can be readily identified by the analyst or even by the patient who has made some progress through analysis. Jung conceived of the collective unconscious as comprising a great many of these vague thought forms which he has referred to as *a priori categories*, or *primordial images*. As we find them in dreams, in man's imaginative creations throughout the ages (1956, 1957–1958), and in the religions of the world, they are seemingly innumerable. An adequate understanding of them would require that we follow him through profound analyses of the symbols in primitive mythology and modern literature, primitive and world religions of the oriental and western cultures, as well as into the mysteries of psychotic thought. Even the practice of alchemy came under his scrutiny as a crude medieval concretization of the archetypal knowledge that something noble and good can come of the blending of superior and baser elements. Just such a blending occurs at the psychological level in the transcendent function referred to above.

Here we must limit ourselves to the archetypes which play an important part in everyday adjustments. Best known is the *anima* which figured in the dream just described. A man's anima represents the opposite-sex complement of his persona (page 307). Jung sometimes spoke of it as the "femininity of the soul," or sometimes even as the soul itself, although he made it clear that he used the term not in the religious sense. Common observations suggest that man's rejection of feminine characteristics is culturally determined: what becomes stereotyped as suitably masculine behavior in one age or in one part of the world may be widely different from what is prescribed at another time or place. It might seem then that the unwanted feminine qualities should be sought among the contents of the *personal* unconscious. But this is only part of the story, according to Jung's interpretation; for in the archaic *collective* unconscious there has been permanently impressed a "collective image of woman." The more a man, under social pressure, identifies himself with his persona, the more does he become the victim of the powerful compensating force of the unconscious. Unless he becomes aware of his anima it remains an autonomous personality dissociated from himself, making him do things he cannot explain rationally, interposing itself between him and the women he meets with the effect of distorting his judgment of them. In this last respect his failure to come to terms with the anima can have unfortunate consequences when he chooses a wife whose real traits turn out to be quite different from those which he has projected upon her.

The need for transcending her feminine persona applies equally to the woman, except that in her case the unconscious will be masculine—the *animus*, or *animi*. [Jung found that the dream symbols of the woman are more likely to take on the character of "an assem-

bly of fathers or dignitaries" who impose standards of judgment
upon her (1956, page 218). Since man is consciously concerned
with the general more than with the personal, his anima is singular;
woman, consciously more preoccupied with the personal, will find
her unconscious oriented more to the general.]

The *shadow* is another archetype with which man may become
acquainted through his dreams or through his projections. It represents the evil that is instinctive in man—not just those undesirable
traits which are repressed into the personal unconscious, but the
whole ugly burden of world evil which each one of us disclaims any
share in, yet projects upon his neighbor. In his last book Jung attributed much of the unhappy state of the world to the tendency of
men and of nations to project their shadows sanctimoniously upon
others.

> It is in the nature of political bodies always to see the evil in the opposite
> group, just as the individual has an ineradicable tendency to get rid of every-
> thing he does not know and does not want to know about himself by foist-
> ing it off on somebody else. Nothing has a more divisive and alienating effect
> upon society than this moral complacency and lack of responsibility, and noth-
> ing promotes understanding and *rapprochement* more than the mutual with-
> drawal of projections. . . . True, all sorts of attempts are being made to
> level out glaring social contrasts by appealing to people's idealism, enthu-
> siasm and ethical conscience; but characteristically, one forgets to apply the
> necessary self-criticism, to answer the question: *Who* is making the idealistic
> demand? Is it, perchance, someone who jumps over his own shadow to hurl
> himself avidly on an idealistic program that promises him a welcome alibi?
> (1957, 1958, pages 102, 103.)

Just what can be done about the problem in its social aspect Jung
has not made very clear. He did, of course, urge the importance
to each individual of achieving better acquaintance with the dynamic contents of the unconscious, and he suggested that those who
have achieved such insight could unintentionally influence others,
but he conceded that such catalysts could not be expected to produce quick results.

THE SELF.   In the sense that it must be created by an assimilation of the contents of the unconscious to the conscious mind, the
self is an archetype of a somewhat different sort from those we
have described. As this integration is gradually achieved, a new
center of equilibrium replaces the ego which has served as the center of gravity for the conscious personality. The persona is individual only in the fact that the combination of traits which compose
it is varied from one person to another; the traits themselves are
"collective" inasmuch as they belong with the stereotype of the
social role which the persona represents. Success in practical life

calls for specialization, and for the building up of such a stereotype. But in the second half of life, from about the age of forty, many people are oppressed by a sense of futility and emptiness, and the need for something deeper and more significant. Jung's theory and practice were largely directed toward such people. In his treatment he encouraged them to immerse themselves in mythology and to express themselves in some form of artistic activity. As we have seen, their dreams also, separately and in series, were analyzed for indications of disturbing features, and for evidence of constructive stirrings of the unconscious pointing toward a degree of self-actualization. The process of *individuation* by which self-realization is achieved is not to be construed as selfishness or rugged individuality. On the contrary,

> . . . individuation means precisely the better and more complete fulfillment of the collective qualities of the human being, since adequate consideration of the peculiarity of the individual is more conducive to better social achievement than when the peculiarity is neglected or suppressed. . . . Now in so far as the human individual . . . is composed of purely universal factors, he is wholly collective. . . . Hence the individualistic emphasis on one's own peculiarity is a contradiction of this basic fact. . . . But since the universal factors always appear only in individual form, a full consideration of them will also produce an individual effect, and one which cannot be surpassed by anything else, least of all by individualism (1956, page 183).

Although the self concepts of the two theories are widely different, there is in this passage a faint reminder of the Adlerian distinction between the striving for superiority and the life style characterized by social interest (page 302). Jung believed that the process of individuation was a slow one and that self-actualization was never completely achieved.

Many other archetypes, including the *mother-imago*, the *child archetype*, *birth* and *rebirth*, the *hero*, the *old wise man*, etc., have been described by Jung and identified in the arts, in literature especially (Jung, 1933; Bodkin, 1934; Fiedler, 1957). However, whether these are to be regarded as ageless sources of wisdom upon which modern man can draw, or merely as symbolized "fictions" of the sort eighteenth-century Jeremy Bentham found a serious threat to man's logic, must be carefully weighed. The well-known Freudian psychoanalyst, Edward Glover, who has little patience with Jung's mysticism, or indeed with any part of his theory, writes:

> . . . we may inquire why the whole content of the Collective Unconscious is so wise, wonderful and precious. . . . why is it so experienced? . . . the mind of that prehistoric man must have been immeasurably younger than the mind of modern man. . . . The racial unconscious is no more old than a baby is old. . . . So far from being particularly wise the archetypes are

of a predominantly superstitious and animistic nature. . . . there is some reason to think that the concept of the Collective Unconscious resuscitates that sentimental derivative of ancestor worship, the Myth of the Noble Savage (1957, pages 50-51).

Against Jung's elaborate theory of archetypes stand the strictures of modern science. Jung himself conceded that "the idea of a self is itself a transcendental postulate which, although justifiable psychologically, does not allow of scientific proof . . ." (1956, page 252). Yet a perplexing fact which has been used as an argument in favor of the collective unconscious is that there are easily recognizable resemblances among the primitive legends of peoples widely separated throughout the world, even though there have been no known means of intercommunication.

PSYCHOLOGICAL TYPES: ATTITUDINAL AND FUNCTIONAL. The last of Jung's contributions to be considered here has supplied a convenient pair of household terms for typing our acquaintances, although those we glibly describe as "introverts" or "extraverts" are not necessarily so in the Jungian sense of the terms. Observations of his patients had impressed him with the self-confident, unhesitating action of some, in contrast with the shrinking withdrawal of others confronted with a task or a problem. He concluded that the interest of the former, the extraverts, is directed primarily toward the physical and social environment, while the interest of the introverts is centered on what goes on within themselves; or to make the distinction in somewhat different terms, the libido has an outward thrust in extraversion, and an inward thrust in introversion. Jung speculated also on why it should be true that Freud consistently found past object-attachments to be the source of his patients' neuroses, while Adler just as consistently found the explanation for his patients' problems in their drive for superiority. He suggested the possible explanation that each of these famous practitioners might exercise an unconscious selectivity, corresponding to his own thrust of attitude, upon the sampling of patients he found he could treat successfully.

Jung did not claim originality or monopoly for this theory of polarity of attitudes: he pointed out its resemblance to William James's contrast between the "tender-minded" and the "tough-minded." Nor did he believe that any individual was exclusively introverted or exclusively extraverted. As in the case of other values, one would probably be consciously developed more than the other; and self-actualization would carry with it the more adequate development of the neglected value (1923, 1933).

Jung soon realized after publishing his theory of attitude-types that they did not take account of all the differences between people. There appeared to be different kinds of introverts and different kinds of extraverts. Further study led him to realize the importance of the dominant *functions* of each individual in addition to his specialized attitude disposition: ". . . our habitual reactions are normally characterized by the application of our most trustworthy and efficient functions. . . . An intelligent man will make his adaptation to the world through his intelligence . . . even though, now and then, in a fit of rage, he may make use of his fists" (1933, page 101). Jung distinguished two *rational* functions: *thinking* and *feeling*, which he conceived to be polar opposites; and two *irrational* functions: *sensation* and *intuition*, also polar opposites. A thinking individual will reach his conclusions entirely on the strength of hard, cold facts; whereas a feeling individual will allow emotion or sentiment to enter into his reasoning. At the irrational level, the sensation type will record facts strictly as his sense experience enables him to perceive them; the intuitive type, on the other hand, will supplement from inner subliminal sources the bare facts delivered to him through his senses. A person may be introvert or extravert, and at the same time show a marked disposition toward one of the rational and one of the irrational functions; but he cannot be both a thinking and a feeling individual, nor can he be at the same time a sensing and an intuitive individual. At each level one of the functional pairs must be less developed than the other; although, again, the goal of self-actualization is to make greater use of the lesser function. Jung's theory of types, through the variety of combinations made possible by the supplementing of the attitude types with the functional types, therefore becomes much less simple and stereotyped than the popularized version of it.

EXPERIMENTAL STUDIES OF INTROVERSION-EXTRAVERSION. Unlike the more mystical features of Jung's system, his type-hypothesis seems to invite experimental investigation. However, in the choice of test or rating-scale items on which to determine the distribution of responses in the population there is always the possibility that the experimenter's "construct" misses the essential meaning of the original idea. This may account for the inconclusiveness of some of the earliest studies. These ignored the functional variations of the attitude-types as Jung had described them, and concentrated entirely upon introversion and extraversion which they usually found to be normally distributed throughout the experimental populations sampled—a result which could scarcely be construed as supporting Jung's idea that people could be assorted as belonging to one or the other *type*. Only recently has a test been developed, the Myers-

Briggs Type-Indicator which explicitly takes into consideration the effects of the four functions (Mackinnon, 1962, pages 489–490).

In the intervening period a number of factorial studies have indicated that more than a single factor is involved in the introversion–extraversion dimension of personality. The elaborate study carried out by H. A. Murray, *et al.* (1938) revealed five different forms of introversion, to some extent intercorrelated, but identifiably different, not only statistically, but also in our casual appraisals of the people we meet. For example, there seems to be little in common between the shy, sensitive introvert who withdraws because he is unsure of social acceptance, and the smug, "reserved, inviolate" introvert who, with no conscious sense of inferiority, holds others at a distance; or between these and the imaginative introvert who must cut himself off from others as he gives himself up to creative work. J. P. Guilford (1940) has also found introversion–extraversion to have five different aspects: S, a measure of the shyness–sociability dimension; T, a measure of the preference for thought over action; D, a measure of depression, pessimism, guilt-feelings; C, a measure of cycloid tendencies—unpredictability of mood as against stability of emotions; and R, a measure of rhathymia—freedom from worry and a happy-go-lucky attitude toward life.

R. B. Cattell, whose early factor studies did not confirm a real trait of extraversion-introversion, now reports a second-order factor closely corresponding to Jung's concept (1957). H. J. Eysenck, too, has found it to be one of the three basic dimensions of personality which have emerged in the wide-scale statistical analysis of behavior-test results carried on over a period of years at the University of London Institute of Psychiatry under his direction (1947, 1952, 1960a). Neuroticism and psychoticism are the other dimensions. By identifying hysteria and psychopathic personality as extraverted neuroticism, and anxiety and obsessive states as introverted neuroticism, Eysenck has related Janet's and Jung's theories to his own, and brought them within the realm of empirically testable hypotheses. A question has been raised, however, as to whether hysteria does in fact fit statistically into this neat scheme (Sigal, Star, and Franks, 1958), and further studies are under way.

With his associates Eysenck has probably done more to stimulate scientific thinking about the introversion–extraversion dimension of personality and to develop a program of systematic exploration of correlated hypotheses than any other individual or group of investigators. Following Pavlov's idea that the relative strength of cortical excitation and cortical inhibition accounted for observable differences in temperament and in the speed and stability of conditioning in his dogs, Eysenck has theorized that excitation is strong in the introvert, inhibition strong in the extravert. From this beginning he draws a number of inferences for experimental verification, according to the hypothetico-deductive formula. For instance, the introvert, characterized by strong excitation and weak inhibition, should be subject to quick conditioning but slow extinction. The introvert's rigid moral standards and haunting anxieties might be accounted for in this way. The extravert, on the other hand, would condition slowly, and his response would easily be extinguished because of his greater cortical inhibition. The evidence from various studies seems generally to support these predictions. Reasoning from Hull's postulate on reactive inhibition (I_r)—the tendency for resistance to an activity to build up as the activity continues—Eysenck proposes that the extravert, in a long-continuing task, may be expected to show signs of wandering of attention or mental blocking sooner than the introvert, and that these "involuntary rest pauses" will last longer than the periods of reactive inhibition in the performance of the introvert. His prediction that after a substantial "programmed" rest pause the extravert will show a more marked upswing in his performance than the introvert—who has maintained a steadier pre-rest output—has received only rather weak support from a number of experimental studes, spurring Eysenck on to a still more exhaustive inquiry into just how introversion and extraversion do contribute to this "reminiscence" effect (1962).

The variant effects of stimulating and depressant drugs on members of the two constitutionally different types have also come under his attention. The introvert, strong on the excitation side, should become more extraverted through the effect of depressant drugs; the extravert should show more introverted behavior under the effect of stimulant drugs. Although scattered returns seem to confirm Eysenck's hypothesis, a great deal more research on this subject is needed before the results can be considered conclusive. Eysenck has also been interested in the effect of drugs upon the incidence and duration of figural after-effects. These illusions, which Köhler explains as the result of neural satiation (page 224), are in Eysenck's theory related to reactive inhibition. If such is the case, the extravert, being more disposed to reactive inhibition, should also be more susceptible to figural after-effect, and drugs increasing or decreasing satiation will have a corresponding effect upon the duration of the illusion. (For a summary of related findings, see Eysenck, 1960b.)

So, step by step, an adopted concept has led to a systematic program of research of which the features mentioned here represent but a small sample. Jung's theory has undergone transformation in moving from the consulting room to the psychological laboratory. Introversion and extraversion are no longer inward and outward "thrusts of libido," the one realized in the conscious, the other an unfulfilled potential in the unconscious of the individual. In the "tough-minded" terms of the behaviorist, they have been made over into hypothetical "constructs" which appeared to be statistically justified as they emerged from a great mass of test intercorrelations, and which are now constantly challenged by new test data that pile up as fast as experimenters can think of new questions relevant to the constructs. If the I–E dimension of personality justifies itself by providing satisfactory and consistent answers to such questions, the laurels must go to Eysenck's constructs rather than to Jung's theory; by the same token, failure would not necessarily disprove the latter.

Eysenck puts an even greater distance between himself and Jung on the subject of therapy. A patient should first be tested to place him accurately within the tridimensional schema of I–E, neuroticism, and psychoticism. Treatment appropriate to his constitutional disposition would then be determined, but this would include deconditioning or extinction of undesirable behavior patterns in the Pavlovian style. In this method of ridding the patient of his symptoms and working toward self-actualization the role of the collective unconscious is not conspicuous!

A GROUP OF SOCIAL ANALYTICAL THEORIES

Labels may be misleading. The group of theories we are now about to consider have at some time in the past been designated as "neo-Freudian." It is hard to understand why they should ever have been so described, and still harder to justify continuing the practice in view of the more recent and more moderate departures from Freudian tenets represented in the theories of Anna Freud, Hartmann, Rapaport, and others who have adopted the "conflict-free ego" concept with all its implications. It is true that some of the analysts classified as neo-Freudian were trained in Freudian analysis and even practiced it, but the same could be said of Jung and Adler to whom the term is not applied. When Jung and Adler strayed too far from the trail Freud was blazing they were cut off from the main artery and they accepted their excommunication. Jung continued to develop his own theory and called it "analytical psychology"; Adler further developed his as "individual psychology." Neither one deviated from Freudian orthodoxy any more than have Karen Horney, Erich Fromm, Harry Stack Sullivan, and several of the other analysts whose systems have been called neo-Freudian.

In fact, the question has recently been quite rightly raised as to why these theories would not better be described as neo-Adlerian (Ansbacher and Ansbacher, 1956, pages 16–17). Certainly they share with Adler's theory a primary emphasis upon the role of social environment rather than upon biological instincts as determinants of personality and its patterns of adjustment or maladjustment. Where the libido concept has not been explicitly abandoned as a means of accounting for such patterns, it has been pushed into the background in favor of one or another form of proposal of dynamic habit-systems which have been built up largely under the influence of early social experience. Horney's *neurotic trends,* Sullivan's *dynamisms,* Kardiner's *projective systems* are of this nature, and bear some resemblance to Adler's *style of life.* Some if not all of the theories in this group bring into sharp focus, as does Adler's theory, the dynamic effect upon the individual of conflicting representations of the self: a fictional or idealized image of the self as against, on the one hand, the kind of person one really is at the moment, or, on the other hand, the potential self that could be realized. Obviously, Freud did not overlook the self, but his ego, operating for the most part as an agent of the id on a borrowed allowance, bears only a shadowy resemblance to the self concepts of the theorists of the neo-Freudian group. Of the early Freudians, Paul Federn, a loyal supporter of the orthodox position, did recognize that there was an abiding awareness of the continuity of one's mental and physical experience which distinguished the normal from certain psychotic states (1952); and of the later Freudians, Hartmann's treatment of the synthetic function of the ego suggests some organization of parts into a unified whole. But in general the Freudians have not featured a structured impression of the "self" which an individual may examine objectively and, rightly or wrongly, identify as his own. Ruth Munroe (1903–1963), who was sympathetic with the Freudian tradition, noted this as a gap in the theory if not in the method (1955, pages 102–4), and predicted that it would eventually be corrected:

> Freud's concept of the ego-ideal should also be mentioned in so far as it differs from the superego. In his early writings Freud stressed the narcissistic elements of the ego-ideal—the love of the person for himself as object. Once he had fully developed the concept of the superego, this aspect of the problem of the self was neglected. Freud himself did not clarify the difference in his later writings. A few recent articles and conversation with some Freudians suggest a growing interest in the ego-ideal as distinct from the superego. Until the ego-ideal plays a more substantial part in Freudian thinking, I shall not elaborate upon it, although I may prophesy that this is a point in my account of Freudians that will require revision in a few years.
>
> At present neither the narcissistic components of the ego-ideal nor the

powerful Oedipal components of Freud's superego seem to take account adequately of the *psychosocial* determinants I would like to emphasize in the term *self image* (1955, page 609, footnote).

Munroe's own contribution was that the self image of an individual who strongly identifies with the parents regardless of their conformity with the existing culture pattern of the group will take on much of the character of the *superego*, whereas the self image in a situation where the parent-child relationship is less well-defined than the culture pattern will reflect the emphasis of the *social role*.

Turning now to the clinical methods of the neo-Freudians, a comparison with the standard procedures shows further deviations, some of which seem to imply a break with principles as well as with technique. (However, even among the avowedly loyal Freudians there may be considerable variability from one therapist to another.) The analyst's couch is often replaced by a face-to-face confronting of doctor and patient. Free association may be resorted to on occasions, but often the analyst takes a more active role in the session, not to the extent of blue-printing a better way of life for his patient, or intruding his opinions before the patient has gained his own insight, but by providing in the consulting room a social environment which can encourage the patient to discover in examining his current experiences, his dreams, his memories of childhood, etc., how and to what degree his perceptions and his attitudes have become slanted the wrong way. The meetings between doctor and patient may be less frequent, sometimes—depending upon the nature and progress of the case—with intervals of weeks or months to give the patient a chance to apply in real life situations the insights he has gained in the consulting room. It has been pointed out also that two or three, perhaps even one, meeting a week may be more favorable than a five-day schedule for germination of the ideas which have grown out of an interview.

It is significant that it is becoming more and more difficult to draw a firm line of demarcation between orthodox or "classical" Freudianism and the movements which may or may not be regarded as schismatic. It would appear that in this area as well as in current learning theory the rigid boundaries of the past have become more permeable, allowing a chance for greater diffusion of ideas that have proved of value. Any theory—unless it be perfect—must allow such assimilation to take place. Without alteration or repair, by virtue of its own internal consistency it may be able to stand by itself, but like great-grandmother's wedding gown, it will go more and more out of fashion and will no longer fit the figure of the modern age. Keeping this in mind we can see that neo-Freudians and "neo-classical Freudians," however they may disagree with Freud or with one another, are alike in representing the harvest of a great man's thought, and in assuring its preservation by adaptation rather than by embalming.

KAREN HORNEY. After fifteen years of practice as an orthodox psychoanalyst, part of that time in Germany, part of it in Chicago and in New York, Karen Horney renounced her strict allegiance to Freudian theory and methodology and moved toward the founding of a new system and an institute for the training of followers in her methods. The Association for the Advancement of Psychoanalysis and the American Institute of Psychoanalysis, with headquarters in New York, officially represented the new movement. The title of her first book, *The Neurotic Personality of Our Time* (1937) gives some clue to the general reason for her dissatisfaction with Freud's position. A half-century had produced enough cultural change in our society to throw doubt on some of his formulations which reflected the mores at the turn of the century. By 1937 not only attitudes about sex but also the "balance of power" between the sexes was changing rapidly; and it is possible that Horney's exposure to the American scene, where this transformation was perhaps even more evident than it had been in Europe, precipitated her withdrawal from the Freudian circle. High on her list of rejected features of Freud's thinking was his explanation of the female personality (page 270), but even more fundamental was her objection to his idea that a repressed wish or experience remains isolated and unchanged in the unconscious to crop up again and again in dreams, lapses, or neurotic disturbances:

Freud tends to regard later peculiarities as almost direct repetitions of infantile drives or reactions; hence he expects later disturbances to vanish if the underlying complexes are elucidated. . . . We recognize that the connection between later peculiarities and earlier experiences is more complicated than Freud assumed: there is no such thing as an isolated repetition of isolated experiences; but the entirety of infantile experiences combines to form a certain character structure, and it is this structure from which later difficulties emanate (1939, page 9).

Although Horney speaks here of the "entirety of infantile experiences" she emphasized the parents' role in determining the character structure of the child. Parental defaults of one kind or another —neglect, indifference, display of favoritism to another child, oversolicitude, spoiling—can produce *basic anxiety* which Horney defined in a vivid and often quoted fragment as "the feeling a child has of being isolated and helpless in a potentially hostile world" (1945, page 41). It may be hard to reconcile her definition of basic anxiety with parental oversolicitude and spoiling, but even the parent who squanders attention and love on a child may, because of his or her own neurotic character, lack the capacity for "genuine warmth and affection," and betray the fact in ways more apparent to the child than to a disinterested observer. The question can also be asked how Horney, who had repudiated libido theory and Freud's accounting for each new neurotic episode as merely another repetition of the infantile problem, now justified tracing neurotic symptoms back to an early parent-child relationship or the general social climate of early childhood.

The answer is that the desolating effect of anxiety once experienced can reappear as a dynamic force whenever the defenses that have been set up against it are threatened. "Desolating" sounds like a rather melodramatic adjective to use in connection with anxiety, but it does not overstate the case. Fear is conceded to be relatively easy to bear, because what we fear we can usually do something about: if we cannot avoid the cause of the fear altogether, we can usually find some way to mitigate it, since it at least has objective reality. Anxiety, on the other hand, is a vague, pervasive experience. It enshrouds its victims, moves along with them, makes escape virtually impossible.

The immediate effect of the feeling of isolation and helplessness in the young child is hostility, the response most likely to alienate others and lead to further rejection. The recognition of hostility in the behavior of the young infant has not been limited to Horney's theory: we have already found it featured in the theories of Freud and Adler, of Erikson, of Klein. In Horney's conception of the child's early experience, however, it plays a key role in shaping the characteristic pattern of social behavior which the individual will tend to use in life as a means of assuring security and coping with anxiety. The expression of "raw" hostility, the child discovers, just makes the situation worse. If he is to enjoy security, hostility must be repressed or disguised. He early begins to develop devices for lessening the discomfort of anxiety, and so begins to structure a personality designed to meet the specifications of his environment as he sees it, rather than to fulfill his real potentialities.

If through docility he finds favor with adults and his peer group, he may become submissive and compliant. He may discover in time to his own advantage that the meek may inherit the earth. If he finds, on the other hand, that he can fight down opposition to his will from parents, siblings, or playmates, aggressiveness may become his method of dealing with this "hostile" world. He may get his way by tempests or tantrums, or enjoy the satisfaction of beating down his opponents in high-pressure competition in school studies, games, or athletics. The "sore-loser" reaction would be symptomatic of this motivation. A third device to avoid the pain of anxiety takes the form of withdrawal or seclusiveness. The young child may find himself most secure in the moments of fantasy, reading, and solitary play which reduce the threat of rejection or criticism by others. In later years the same individual will probably maintain a strict reserve in his personal relations, his inability to form warm and sustained friendships being a "safety device." His detachment, on the other hand, puts him in a vulnerable position when trouble occurs because he can neither allow himself to depend upon others nor to fight back. Dependency and aggressiveness would both revive the dread anxiety, so he is left with no alternative but to run away from the problem.

Glancing back over these *neurotic trends*, we see why Horney has classified them in three directional categories: *movement toward, movement against*, and *movement away from* people (1945). In the normal course of life, circumstances occur which justify all of these forms of behavior, and in the secure person all of them will occur. In the neurotic, however, they become the source of *basic conflict*, because having once established his method of coping with anxiety he dare not risk any departure from the formula. The alternative attitudes are therefore repressed, and the effect of repression is to make matters worse. A person who is committed to undeviating amiability and long-suffering patience must in the course of human events build up a tremendous potential for hostility. But the hostility cannot be allowed expression. The same applies to the other two types. Even the meanest and most ruthless power-seeker, or the individual who has achieved almost complete detachment and insulation from his fellow-men will build up a need for a more balanced psychic structure through more normal social relationships. But any move in the direction of restoring equilibrium is defeated by the anxiety it stirs up anew, the hostility he sees, or fancies he sees in others, and the reinforcement of hostility within himself. Unity of personality is not within reach by the methods the neurotic uses when he tries to achieve it.

Among these methods, along with those we have already described, Horney featured especially in *Neurosis and Human Growth* (1950) the neurotic's *idealized self-image*. This is a concept which has much in common with Adler's guiding fiction even to the extent that it becomes a determining influence on the individual. But its primary use to the neurotic seems to provide him with the illusion that his personality has a unity which in fact it lacks. The idealized self-image also has some of the character of the *persona* in Jung's theory. Both serve as a mask-like front which on closer examination turns out to be an incomplete and misleading representation of the full potentialities of the personality. Further, as with the guiding fiction and with the persona, the idealized self-image stands in the way of the individual's coming to an understanding and acceptance of his "real" self. What the neurotic dares not recognize as his own qualities—what he has purged from his concept of himself as the price of freedom from anxiety and a sense of unity or consistency —he finds reason to condemn in the personalities of others. The qualities he scorns may be good or bad. If he has come to think of himself as a powerful leader, he will have no patience with sentiment or sensitivity, denied expression in himself because they once met, and might again meet, with rebuff. His gentle, loyal, acquiescent supporter, on the other hand, may cluck his tongue at an explosive expression of resentment from a third member of the group. The loyal supporter cannot afford to indulge in the luxury of "blowing his stack"; the very thought of it would overwhelm him with anxiety. His safety devices have made him quite unaware of the repressed hostility within himself.

Horney's idea of the mechanism of *externalization* is understandable when we realize the extent to which the neurotic's idealized image "alienates" him from his real self. He is not aware of the conflict set up between these two except in the form of the increasing unhappiness, dissatisfaction, and lack of fulfillment that must result when a substantial part of one's human heritage is ignored and left undeveloped. Not only does he project his own unconscious attitudes upon others, but he assigns to events, objects, and the behavior of people the cause of his own feelings, with no awareness of the contribution his own psychic conflict has made to the effect (1945).

Horney's listing of the possible causes of basic anxiety in childhood are inclusive enough to justify the question: How many children escape the experience? Her answer would be that the question is not whether one is or is not neurotic, but rather how neurotic one is! The defining of what is normal and what is sufficiently different from normal to warrant the label "neurotic" is not a simple matter. Horney pointed to the growing literature of cultural anthropology which shows how relative to the particular mores of a society the two concepts are. Even her criteria of neurosis—rigidity, and discrepancy between achievement and actual fulfillment—can be thought of as valid only within the framework of the society and age in which the individual develops. Within our own American culture we see the truth of this in the current variations in the norms of "permissiveness" which hold in different sections of the country, or in the attitudes toward conformity versus individualism (Riesman, 1950; Fromm, 1947).

Horney made a distinction, also, between *character neurosis* and *situational neurosis*. The former is the effect of a kind of splitting of the personality with consequent internal conflict. A situational neurosis may grow out of a present, well-defined, stressful problem such as the necessity of living in peace with a difficult mother-in-law, or keeping up standards in school with a full-time job on the side; or having to feed a family during a period of depression and unemployment. There is the comforting thought here that the victim of such circumstances will get over his neurosis when the problem ends. But there is a reservation. That hope will be fulfilled only when the neurosis is truly a *situation* neurosis. Unfortunately, people with character neuroses are prone to get themselves into "situations." When such cases are studied, the real source of the trouble is often found to lie not in the situation, but in the neurotic trends or in the idealized self-image of the individual caught in the situation.

ERICH FROMM. Like Horney, Erich Fromm (born 1900; now in practice in New York) was trained in psychoanalysis at the Berlin Psychoanalytic Institute, became associated with the Chicago Psychoanalytic Institute in the early 1930's, and eventually came to New York to practice and teach a socialized revision of Freudian theory. Fromm, who is at present associated with the William Alanson White Institute in New York, is one of the few analysts of Freudian derivation who does not have a medical degree; but you will recall that Freud recognized that this was not an essential requirement for the successful practice of psychoanalysis.

Fromm's first publication to receive wide popular attention was *Escape From Freedom* (1941) in which he declares his departure from Freud's biological position and describes his own social philosophy in these terms: "The most beautiful as well as the most ugly inclinations of man are not part of a fixed and biologically given human nature, but result from the social process which creates man . . . . Man's nature, his passions, and anxieties are a cultural product . . . "(1941, pages 12–13). Man's emergence from animal status has brought with it insecurity growing out of certain paradoxes or "existential dichotomies" (1947). He has become free, but he longs for continued dependency and belonging; he has a biological urge to live, but his human reason confronts him with the inescapability of death; unlike animals, he has the capacity to solve problems of his world by thought rather than by instinct, but his brief life span makes fulfillment of his potentialities improbable if not impossible.

Much of man's behavior suggests that he tends to run away from this qualified freedom—a "freedom from" rather than a "freedom to"—by resorting to devices such as masochistic submission to another individual or to a powerful group. In either case the effect is the destruction of "self" as a price for the security of relatedness and belonging. Sadism is merely the correlative of masochism: the relationship is "symbiotic," assuring for both individuals involved the avoidance of isolation. The same appeal can explain the mass surrender of people to a political philosophy they would otherwise reject, or to a class status thrust upon them by a social culture. Fromm has documented his theory with historical analyses of periods and movements which illustrate man's need for *rootedness*.

In what appears a more normal expression of this dependency, the escape from freedom takes the form of the "magic helper." Of the variety of personifications which the individual may force into that role, one is a parent. Fromm credits Freud with an important discovery in pointing out the central importance of the Oedipus complex, but considers the factor of sexual attraction of much less consequence than the dependency need:

> . . . when the parents, acting as the agents of society, start to suppress the child's spontaneity and independence, the growing child feels more and more unable to stand on its own feet; it therefore seeks for the magic helper and often makes the parents the personification of "him." Later on, the individual transfers these feelings to somebody else, for instance, to a teacher, a husband, or a psychoanalyst. Again, the need of being related to such a symbol of authority is not caused by the continuation of the original sexual attraction to one of the parents but by the thwarting of the child's expansiveness and spontaneity and by the consequent anxiety (1941, page 178).

Other forms of escape include withdrawal from the world, destructiveness of the sort which levels everything that points up the individual's awareness of his powerlessness, destructiveness which may take the form of a blocking of one's own capacities for enjoying life or for living sensitively and usefully, which may lead to suicide itself. Here Fromm is obviously covering much the same ground that Freud has covered with the death instinct, but he explicitly rejects Freud's biological basis and instead explains these hostile tendencies as the effect of "social conditions which make for the suppression of life" (1941, page 184). *Automaton conformity* is another defense about which he has much to say. In aptly chosen illustrations he presents his argument that "pseudo-thinking," "pseudo-feeling," and "pseudo-willing" too frequently substitute for the spontaneous and genuine responses suitable to certain circumstances. We find ourselves repeating as our own an opinion that can be traced to outside influences; wearing the social mask required by an occasion as long as the occasion lasts; even making the choices that in the judgment of those about us are expedient. In none of these cases are we daring to exercise the freedom to be ourselves.

In *Man For Himself* (1947) we find these several modes of meeting the need for relatedness classified as dynamic *orientations* of character, the "(relatively permanent) form in which human energy is canalized . . . ," making it possible for man to behave rather automatically and consistently in many different kinds of situation at different times. Fromm gives credit to Freud for focusing upon the core sources of individual responses, in this way accounting for such different forms of behavior as thumb-sucking, nail-biting, overeating, smoking, and talking too much as all related to oral libido. Fromm too emphasizes the central orientation, but, as you will guess, he explains it in terms of how the individual has learned to relate himself to things *(assimilation)* and how he has learned to relate himself to people *(socialization)* rather than on the basis of how his libido is distributed. The *receptive*, the *exploitative*, and the *hoarding* orientations are not only similar to phases of personality at the oral and anal stages, but also resemble Horney's three neurotic trends. The receptive orientation disposes an individual toward self-effacing submissiveness and dependency. Since his great need is to be loved, it is important that everybody be his friend. He *moves toward* people. Corresponding to the exploitative orientation —an aggressive form of adjustment—would be Horney's *moving against*. *Hoarding* and *moving away from* do not sound alike, but for Fromm the hoarding orientation covers a syndrome of traits in which distrust and rigidity toward people and ideas are mingled with frugality and meanness.

These three orientations run parallel to the Freudian pre-phallic stages of oral, anal-sadistic, and anal-retentive libido; but in the *marketing orientation* Fromm departs from the Freudian pattern. The marketing orientation imposes on the individual the automaton conformity described earlier. He plays a variety of socially applauded roles, more intent on selling himself at current market values than in fulfilling his real potential. When he seeks to discover his "own" self, like Peer Gynt "he finds that he is like an onion—one layer after the other can be peeled off and there is no core to be found" (1947, page 73). The fault is not limited to the development of his own personality; he carries it over into his evaluation of other people. Fromm considers this fourth orientation to be of modern vintage—the effect of the stiffer competition in our society for places at the top. Riesman (1950) and Whyte (1956) have found similar cause for complaint against the modern system.

Fromm conceived of the four orientations as a framework for an "ideal" typology—a typology in the sense that an individual's behavior may tend to gravitate predominantly toward one or another of the poles without being exclusively determined by that orientation. Further, although the traits associated with each are obviously not admirable, the same orientation under the transforming influence of the productive character yields praiseworthy qualities: the spineless submissiveness of the receptive type becomes patient devotion; the aggressiveness of the exploitative type becomes initiative; the stinginess of the hoarding type becomes economy; and the opportunism of the marketing type becomes purposefulness, etc. (1947, pages 114–16). The catalyst responsible for this change is the productive individual's recognition and development of his own unique potentials. To the extent that he allows himself that fulfillment, he can invest reality with something of his own powers: reality is not static, it can be adapted to the uses of man. He can recognize and respect the integrity of other men: he no longer sees them related to him merely as objects serving his own need for security. Always concerned with the ethical aspects of adjustment, Fromm in his more recent works (1955, 1956), takes on a still loftier tone of idealism. Pursuing the theme of the effect of society on man's adjustment and the quality of brotherly love, he describes a form of "Humanistic Communitarian Socialism" which may one day allow each individual an equal chance for self-realization (1955). Speculating on much the same issue but seeing it in perhaps even more distant perspective, Gardner Murphy (1958) envisages not one but an unpredictable number of dimensions of human nature emerging in the future:

> The point is that there is no meaning in the conception of fulfilling human personalities by rounding out a man and making him perfect, for he becomes qualitatively a new man as he grows; and there is no such thing as a society which will offer fulfillment to human nature, for human nature and society are evolving together, not only along a line indicating quantitative increase in this or that but into ever new qualities (page 311).

THE INTERPERSONAL THEORY OF HARRY STACK SULLIVAN. Although the *interpersonal theory* of Harry Stack Sullivan (1892–1949) was developed within the discipline of psychiatry, its heavy loading with content significant to the social psychologist, anthropologist, and political scientist has extended its influence upon modern thought, its impact growing even stronger since Sullivan's death through the writings and teachings of his disciples. Several years after receiving his medical degree and completing service in the First World War, he entered upon a psychiatric career in which he achieved great distinction. One of his early mentors was William Alanson White, a famous neuropsychiatrist at St. Elizabeth's Hospital in Washington, D.C. The William Alanson White Psychiatric Foundation, of which Sullivan was president for ten years (1933–1943) continues to carry on the Sullivan (and Fromm) tradition, and training in the principles and methods of these two contributors to analytic theory can be obtained at the William Alanson White Institute in New York. Adolf Meyer was a second dominating force in Sullivan's thinking. You will read later (on page 350) a quotation from Meyer in which he said: ". . . Mind . . . is a sufficiently organized living being in action; . . . ." As we discuss the interpersonal theory further, its kinship to this definition will become apparent.

Why Sullivan is thought of as in any sense Freudian is, as we have already pointed out, less clear from surface appearances. Libido theory does not enter into his system; sex is considered in its narrow sense, and then as significant only in the development of the individual from the stage of early adolescence onward; the Oedipus complex is reduced to the effects upon the child of the relatively peremptory handling he receives from the same-sex parent: the father feeling that he can "see through" his son, the mother having a similar assurance about her daughter, and both of them contributing to the building up of resentment in the child for that very reason. Even Sullivan's method of therapy was radically unlike the Freudian approach, growing naturally and logically, as we shall see, from his interpersonal theory. In thinking of him as a neo-Freudian, therefore, we may find it helpful to keep in mind Ruth Munroe's conclusion that, inasmuch as he was not a product of the Freudian tradition, "His position is not so much a rebellion as a qualified *rapprochement*" (Munroe, 1955, page 354). One reason why the *rapprochement* would necessarily be "qualified" was Sullivan's emphasis on the social aspects of development, although he by no means ignored the biological factors. His theory of how the self-system develops reflects the influence of George Mead; and he was much impressed also by the anthropological studies of Ruth Benedict and of Edward Sapir.

Sullivan was a dynamic and colorful person. Besides carrying on his own psychiatric practice and hospital work, he taught psychiatry, gave numerous lectures in this country and abroad, worked with UNESCO after World War II on the study of factors contributing to international tensions, and with other organizations concerned with the problem of international mental health, and edited *Psychiatry*, the journal of the William Alanson White Psychiatric Foundation. This full career left him little time for formal writing, but the interpretations of his lecture notes and of his lectures provided by his disciples and colleagues (Sullivan, 1953, 1954; Mullahy, 1948, 1952; Blitsten, 1953; Thompson, 1960) have supplemented and clarified the single volume in which he presented his theory as a whole (1947). Helen Swick Perry has provided an account of his work with schizophrenics at the Sheppard and Enoch Pratt Hospital between 1923 and 1930 in the introduction to her edition of a collection of his writings on schizophrenia (Sullivan, 1962).

Aside from a distinctive style and terminology which does not encourage popular or rapid reading, Sullivan's theory differs from those we have been considering in maintaining that the essential object of concern in the psychiatric study of neuroses and psychoses was not some psychic structure such as mind, personality, or self neatly enclosed within the skin of A . . B . . C . . etc., but rather the relatively enduring patterns of behavior derived through their interrelationships. The primary interpersonal relationship will be that between the infant and the "mothering one"; and very early out of this relationship come the infant's first significant responses to his social environment. Lying relaxed, well-fed, warm, undisturbed by irritating stimuli, he enjoys *euphoria*, a feeling of well-being that is periodically interrupted by unpleasant sensations such as hunger, wetness, cold, pain. These produce tension, but his euphoria is restored when his needs are adequately satisfied. So far we see something rather similar to the Freudian pleasure principle, the most desirable state being one free from excitation. However, in Sullivan's theory the behavior of the mother complicates the picture, for if she is tense in handling the baby as she takes care of his needs, her tension will be directly communicated to him through *empathy*. Empathy is a term with an interesting history in psychology. It was originally used by Lipps (1907) to account for our reactions to works of art or our understanding of the feelings of others on the basis of kinesthetic sensations which arise when we assume comparable postures, consciously or unconsciously. More commonly it has been used to cover any unexplained intuition about the feelings of another person, although in this sense it loses any claim to scientific justification.

Sullivan was less interested in the mechanics of empathy than he was in its effect. The first effect upon the infant, as we have just seen, is to make him tense, and so to deprive him of the satisfaction that would otherwise have come to him from being fed, changed, cuddled, etc. At first the source of the frustration is not recognized as a personal feature of his environment: the nipple of the tense nursing mother may come to be recognized as the "bad" nipple in contrast to the "good" nipple from which he receives satisfaction and relaxation. But gradually, through these tension-producing experiences, he learns something about the culture in which he is developing by learning about the attitudes of the significant persons in his environment. He discovers, too, that by delaying the satisfaction of his needs, he can lessen the tension communicated to him through these significant "others." In other words, *security*, a social need, comes to be valued enough to make him choose the more bearable tension of temporarily unsatisfied physical needs rather than enduring the *anxiety* of social insecurity. Here again we find an interesting parallel between Sullivan's theory and the Freudian compromise between the pleasure and the reality principle, between the id and the ego, between the primary and the secondary process, the essential difference between the two theories being that Freud conceived of the compromise as a matter of how the libido was used, whereas Sullivan explained it by the hypothesis of the *self dynamism*.

THE SELF DYNAMISM AND THE SELF. In the theories of Jung, Adler, and Horney we have already met self concepts. These were by no means alike, except in the fact that they were firmly contained within the boundaries of the organism. Without denying the possibility that such private structures may exist within an individual, Sullivan concentrated rather on the systems of habits which characterize the *interpersonal* responses of the individual. As tension-aroused anxiety teaches him to distinguish between approved and disapproved behavior, the child develops the patterns calculated to assure him the greatest security. The *self system*, or *self dynamism* —the terms are used interchangeably—is an "envelope" of such habits based upon the reflected approval or disapproval of others. When the child acts in conformity with social demands the "good-me" is in control; when he breaks the rules the "bad-me" subjects him to a flood of anxiety. A third *personification*, the "not-me" appears to consist of infantile experiences of terror or disgust which have been disassociated from the part of the self about which the individual can communicate without intolerable anxiety. Besides the self system the self comprises other patterns of behavior which have developed through learning, and interests that have no necessary connection with the avoidance of anxiety.

Modes of Experience.   The epistemological question of how we become aware of ourselves in relation to the surrounding environment has been a perplexing one to psychologists as well as to philosophers. We have already had before us Freud's answer in terms of the interplay between the primary and the secondary process. Sullivan's contribution was less an explanation than a description of what occurs. He identified three modes of experience which occur successively, but which once developed may continue to operate under certain circumstances at levels where a higher mode has typically supplanted them.

The most primitive mode, the *prototaxic*, characterizes the earliest confused and unorganized experience of the infant. He *is* his world. He has developed no framework of space or time, and so there can be no orderly succession of events, no orderly arrangement of objects. His experience consists of isolated, unrelated mental states in which there is neither "subject" nor "object" as these will later be distinguished. In its "oceanic" character this prototaxic mode has something in common with the Freudian primary process, and it suggests also Piaget's reconstruction of the infant's earliest experience (page 42).

Gradually the infant's world begins to take on some semblance of organization. He learns, for instance, that certain sounds—his mother's comforting call, or the sound of her steps—will soon be followed by that most delightful of all objects, his bottle; and that a different sound—a familiar bark—is a signal for the enthusiastic arrival on the scene of his good friend the dog. From such recurring sequences he begins to expect events and to explain them: "because B follows A, it is therefore the result of A"—a form of reasoning which is not only highly disapproved by logic professors but which is also quite unrealistic. Yet he comes to attach language symbols to certain objects and people in this way. He discovers that by making a certain strange sound he can prevail upon the "mothering one" to pick him up, and by making a different sound, he can persuade her to put him down. But he also learns that some of these signals cannot be depended upon to work at all times. His expectancies are not always realized in this *parataxic* mode, because they have "personal meaning" rather than the "consensually validated" meaning of the *syntaxic* mode. In the latter stage which he reaches when experience has begun to teach him something about the logical, or at least generally accepted, relationships, he finds that others share and confirm his views, and that communication with others is therefore easier and more reassuring (1953).

However, even after he has reached this stage of development and has long used consensually validated symbols, any individual may drop back without realizing it to the parataxic mode: a young wife may be convinced that her husband no longer loves her because he has remained rather silent at dinner; a disappointed week-ender is sure the weather has turned out to be bad because this was the particular week-end he chose to go to the beach. Neurotics, of course, are particularly prone to the parataxic mode; but even those who are judged to be solidly normal people mix the parataxic and syntaxic modes in their thinking. When this happens two people will find themselves completely at a loss in trying to understand each other, because they are in a sense talking different languages—one with subjective or *autistic* meaning, heavily weighted with the values he has incorporated into his "personifications" at an early age; the meanings of the other, perhaps, more closely tied in with reality. It is hardly necessary to add that daydreams and nightdreams are also in the parataxic mode. Sullivan believed, much in the manner of Freud, that dreams provide an outlet for the residue of the needs the self system only partly satisfies through *sublimation*.

STAGES OF DEVELOPMENT. In addition to the overall development represented by the modes of experience, Sullivan described what appeared to him the more specific stages of development. They are not genetic stages in the strictly Freudian sense, but they reflect genetic development as it is shaped by environmental experiences. *Infancy,* the earliest stage, lasts from birth until the child acquires some facility with language. A great many things happen during this short period, most of which we have already covered: he comes to recognize an objective world, and to focus special interest upon the reactions of people in that world on whose acceptance his security depends. He learns to tolerate minor tensions connected with bodily needs as he develops the security measures of the self system to reduce anxiety. In this period, too, begins the first crystallization of his values in such all-or-none personifications as "the good mother" and "the bad mother." These become the basis for many of his parataxic judgments of other people with whom he later comes into contact. His good "eidetic" people become a recurrent source of disillusionment for him, and his bad eidetic people become the unfortunate victims of his prejudices.

In the *Childhood* period, which extends to the time when he is ready to leave the constant supervision of his family for the company of other children, he is exposed to the hardships of the civilizing process. It is a period of developing new dynamisms and not infrequently reverting to old ones (regression). Anger is a common reaction to the frustrations of training, but Sullivan regards it also as a way of neutralizing anxiety at this time. If the training process is not tempered with some parental tenderness, any longing for tenderness comes to be connected in his mind with rejection and greater anxiety, and he undergoes what Sullivan has called "malevolent transformation," which makes him distrustful and hard in a world that he has found hostile. Some of the serious personality problems of later life can be traced to such inverted dynamisms. Language, of course, is one of the most prominent features in the acquisitions of this stage.

In the *Juvenile Era*, the child's age peers and his teachers begin to challenge the influence of the home. In this broader environment he gradually learns to see himself as others see him, and "reputation" comes to be a source of more anxiety for him. Cooperation begins to develop at this time, but it is motivated by the need for social acceptance, and if the social acceptance can be furthered more by competition or by independence and indifference, these patterns will be cultivated.

A significant change occurs in the period of *Preadolescence*, however. Sometime about the eighth year, the child normally picks up a special chum to whom he becomes dedicated, and who in turn is dedicated to him. Usually the chums are of the same sex; in fact similarities in various respects may be the basis for the development of the association. Sullivan considers this relationship to be the first genuine appearance of love in the child's life, love in the sense that the chum's security and satisfactions are at least as important as his own, and that he will make sacrifices to assure them. Up to this time he has portioned out his love selfishly in return for the satisfaction of his needs, or for security.

In *Adolescence*, the earlier idealistic "isophilic love" of the juvenile era gives way to the "lust dynamism." It is here that the contrast between Sullivan's position and Freud's becomes most striking. For Sullivan, the sex drive makes its appearance at this stage and interest begins to be directed to the opposite sex. It would seem reasonable to expect the unselfish love of the isophilic period to continue to express itself in heterosexual behavior, but this seems too rarely to be the case even at the later adolescent and adult stages. The cause for the trouble is not to be found in the biological sex drive and is certainly not traceable to early unsolved libido problems. Sullivan finds its source rather in the anxiety with which sex is associated from childhood onward because of the restrictive social attitudes of our culture. That anxiety stands in the way of the intimacy and tenderness which make satisfactory sexual adjustment possible. According to this standard of measurement many "adults" have not matured beyond the preadolescent level.

Sullivan's contribution to therapeutic technique has been important. Much of his work was done with schizophrenic patients, and in treating these he was outstandingly successful even at a time when medicine did not have available its present methods of increasing the accessibility of the schizophrenic to communication (1962). After a period of trial and error Sullivan capitalized on the idea of the interview as in itself an "interpersonal" situation. In that light the role of the interviewer as well as the behavior of the patient should be subject to critical study. The interviewer becomes the "participant observer" systematically noting what the patient does, what he says, and how he says it; but at the same time he must be alert to the possible intrusion of his own parataxic distortions or personifications which may trick him into "selective inattention"— that is, failure to notice what is incompatible with one's own attitudes. Empathy and reciprocal emotion are significant features in the Sullivan type of interview, setting it off in distinct contrast from the remote, objective role of the therapist as originally conceived by Freud.

11

Motivation and the Unity
of the Person

It has been difficult to choose an appropriate title for this chapter because its contents will be drawn from a variety of sources, some of them scarcely "contemporary" in the strictest sense of the term, some of them not easily differentiated from viewpoints considered in earlier chapters. What these theories will have in common, however, is their insistent recognition of man's experience and behavior as a reflection of his unity. They will be found not to be in agreement on the nature of the integrating or unifying principle, not in agreement on what might be the appropriate or best methods of studying this entity, not even in agreement on what it should be called—the "organism," "person," "personality," "self," "proprium." But what is very significant is that, despite their differences, these theorists pay more than lip-service to the fact that psychological understanding is contingent upon taking into consideration the *whole* individual. The fact of man's functional wholeness can hardly be disputed. Even Watson said that behavior, as contrasted with the action of muscles, glands, and other separate organs was the activity of the organism in relation to its environment; but in his enthusiasm for linking conditioned reflexes into chains of behavior, he seems to have lost sight of this organic relationship. In the theories about to be considered it remains paramount.

The problem of motivation takes on special significance when emphasis is laid upon the wholeness of the organism. In earlier chapters we have had the question of motivation before us in diverse forms: Thorndike's law of effect; Hull's drives and drive stimuli;

Tolman's latency learning, "need systems," and "belief-value matrices"; Spence's $r_G \sim s_G$ incentives—these are only a few reminders of the learning theorist's preoccupation with this subject. When we turn back to the pages dealing with clinical psychology, we could easily be persuaded that the question "Why?" in the sense of "What have been the patient's real motives?" makes up all but a small part of the theoretical concern of these schools.

It would be rash to say that the organism does not figure in the thinking of these two groups investigating in their different ways the important problems of behavior; but the thesis could be defended that by too highly spotlighting a particular aspect of an organism's behavior, they have seen in a distorted form what they had hoped to interpret. Modern ethologists complain that psychologists who confine their study of animal behavior to the controlled laboratory situation not only risk inducing deviant behavior in their subjects, but also tend to ignore all features of the animals' reactions other than those in which they are interested. Quantitative laboratory studies properly follow only after qualitative field observations (Hinde, 1959). The clinician's conclusions about the nature of human motivation are also drawn from dubious data. Unless we are prepared to agree that neurosis is universal and "normality" only relative—and the writer does not propose to take sides on this issue —we must concede the danger of overgeneralizing from the isolated symptoms of patients whose emotional problems arise from the particular circumstances of their lives or of the culture in which they have developed. In one instance a son's sedulous emulation of his father may be a reaction formation against an oedipal hatred; in another it may well be the result of the son's healthy value judgment of his father's social contribution and of his own ability to carry his father's work forward toward an envisioned goal. The motive is the product of the organism—not of just any organism, but of the organism concerned.

For the most part, the theories we shall be considering in the present chapter take as their point of departure the image—or fiction —of the healthy organism. They stress the unity of the organism. A quotation from William McDougall, whose hormic theory will be the first presented, might serve as a typical expression of the theme we shall find repeated again and again with variations in the theories to follow:

. . . all parts, all features and functions of the developed personality play their part in that integrated unity which is the person, make some contribution however slight towards determining the unique quality and flavour of that complex totality. . . . Personality should then be used to imply that totality: *not the sum of the distinguishable features and functions which by analysis we discover in it, but rather the synthetic unity of all features and functions in their intimate interplay* (1932, pages 368–69; italics added).

Finally, characteristic of these theories of the normal, unique totality which is variously described as *person, personality, self,* or *organism* in the pages to follow, is an emphasis on a "forward thrust," a tendency toward "self-actualization," toward "becoming" rather than "being." We find this a prominent feature of McDougall's teleological hormic psychology.

PURPOSIVENESS AND HORMIC PSYCHOLOGY

When psychologists turned to being scientific they found purpose a troublesome concept both introspectively and behaviorally. Titchener decided it came under the heading of meaning or value and therefore ruled it out of his existential-introspective structuralism. Watson classified it with sensation, perception, image, and desire—all outworn introspective fantasies which he threw overboard (1925). Z. Y. Kuo, an eminent Chinese behaviorist, characterized it as a "lazy substitute for . . . careful and detailed analysis" and predicted that the concept would disappear eventually with better understanding of the elements of behavior (1928).

But even if such analysis were ever to be successfully accomplished, the *fact* of purpose would be just as undeniable as the *fact* of water which seems to have successfully survived its chemical analysis into hydrogen and oxygen. Purpose is a molar fact (page 135), a distinctly psychological fact. Purposive behavior is the same as goal-seeking. In a full-fledged purposive act, as we know it ourselves, two factors are combined: desire and foresight. We foresee the goal and we desire to reach it. Foresight and desire do not always go together. The aviator in a certain predicament may clearly foresee that he is going to strike a tree—without desiring that result. The hungry infant desires a full stomach—without knowing what he desires. In the primitive kind of goal-seeking there is a striving without any clear foresight of the goal. Purposivism asserts the prime role of striving in all behavior; it emphasizes striving rather than foresight, though inclined to place much emphasis on foresight as well, even in animal behavior. It is because of its major emphasis on striving that McDougall adopted for his theory the name of hormic psychology.

WILLIAM MCDOUGALL. An Englishman by birth and education and for the larger part of his active career, William McDougall (1871–1938) was a distinguished student of biology and medicine and an active anthropological field worker before settling down in 1900 to the work of a psychologist, first at London and then at Oxford. During the First World War he was a medical officer in the British Army in charge of cases of war neurosis. After that war he became professor at Harvard and later at Duke University.

We have already noticed that McDougall was one of the first to define psychology as the science of behavior (pages 114–15). A mere science of consciousness seemed to him "sterile and narrow." The behavior of men and animals under all conditions of health and disease was the proper field for psychological study. McDougall himself was trained in physiological methods. He was fond of animals and from time to time used animal subjects in his psychological experiments. Accordingly he stressed the importance of objective methods, but he was by no means inclined to reject introspection. If we limit ourselves rigidly to objective observation, we are apt to get a mechanical view of an animal's behavior, and even a human being appears like a machine. But we know our own behavior from inside and know it to be purposive and not mechanical; and there is no point in forgetting what we know by introspection when we turn our attention to animal behavior. McDougall was not afraid of anthropomorphism.

What, then, is behavior? As we look around in the world we find some things that are inert and mechanical, moved by external forces, and other things that *behave*, that "seem to have an intrinsic power of self-determination, and to pursue actively . . . their own ends and purposes. . . . The striving to achieve an end is, then, the mark of behavior; and behavior is the characteristic of living things" (1912, page 20). McDougall cited several objective characteristics of goal-seeking behavior, as follows (1923, pages 43–46):

1. It *persists*. An activity may start in response to a stimulus but continue after the stimulus has ceased. A rabbit scurrying to its hole after a momentary noise is an example.
2. With all the persistence there is considerable *variation* of the activity. An obstacle is by-passed and the same goal is reached as if there had been no obstacle.
3. The activity *terminates* when the goal is reached, and some other activity takes its place. The cat makes a dash for a tree and up the trunk, but then sits down on a branch and calmly watches the dog.
4. The activity *improves* with repetition. Useless movements are eliminated, and the whole performance becomes smoother and quicker. In short the animal learns to reach the goal more efficiently.

These objective criteria of purposive behavior, first formulated by McDougall in 1912,[1] are about the same as those later adopted by Tolman and other behaviorists (page 135). Although most of McDougall's work was not well received by the behaviorists, we must credit him with considerable influence in this respect.

If behavior, both human and animal, is characterized by goal-seeking, a very important problem for psychology is to discover what goals are sought. The particular goals vary enormously, but they may fall into a few natural classes. The tree for the cat and the hole in the ground for the rabbit fall into the class of places of safety; they have the same fundamental appeal. What are the fundamental appeals or motives that lead to goal-seeking behavior? This is the question raised by McDougall in 1908 in his *Introduction to Social Psychology*, on the whole the most important of his many books. It was an effort to provide a psychological foundation for the social sciences. Up to that time the psychologists had made no serious attempt to provide such a foundation but had left each historian or economist or sociologist to improvise a psychology for his own use. The experimental psychologists had made good progress in the study of such intellectual processes as sensation, perception, learning, memory, and thinking, but what the social sciences seemed to need was knowledge of human motives, thus far almost neglected by the psychologists. Why do men live in groups, why do they follow leaders and submit to governmental regulation—through mutual fear, mutual helpfulness, or simply inertia and imitation? Is religion the result of a religious instinct, and political life the working of a political instinct? Is all conduct motivated by a desire to obtain pleasure and avoid pain? The social thinker who required an answer to these questions adopted the best answer that suggested itself to him, while psychology offered no solution.

McDougall's revolt against the existing state of affairs was twofold. He objected to the rough-and-ready psychology that he found in the social sciences, and he objected to the one-sided intellectualism of psychology. This intellectualizing tendency had led to the assumption that all human conduct was rational and dependent on foresight of consequences. But why should some consequences be chosen rather than others unless there were some basic needs and preferences? Or consider the doctrine of "psychological hedonism," that all desire is necessarily a desire for pleasure. This "axiom" puts the cart before the horse, at least in many cases. For when is eating pleasant? Only when you are hungry, i.e., have a desire for food. The pleasure depends on the desire, and the desire is more funda-

[1] In the fifth edition of his *Introduction to Social Psychology*, pages 354–55,

mental than the pleasure; and so it is with other appetites. To get down to fundamentals we must find the natural desires and goals of men, some of which like hunger and sex desire may be common to men and animals.

McDougall set to work in earnest in the hope of developing a systematic psychology of motives for the use of the social sciences. His general assumption was that there must be a number of fundamental motives which are natural and hereditary and that all other motives must be derived from these primaries in the course of the individual's experience. He chose to call the primaries by the old name of "instincts"—a choice which he later regretted. An instinct for him was not a mechanical affair like a reflex or chain of reflexes. It was, rather, a motive, a striving toward some type of goal. There was emotion in it—the emotion of fear, for example, in striving to escape from danger. And there was a cognitive element in it, a perception of danger in the case of fear. He regarded an instinct as a complete mental process at the primitive level, capable of analysis into three parts: (1) On the receptive side, it is a predisposition to notice significant stimuli—like food odors when one is hungry. (2) On the executive side, it is a predisposition to make certain movements or to approach a certain goal, or to find a safe place when afraid. (3) In between is the emotional impulse or striving, the core of the whole instinct. Sometimes a distinction can be made between the striving and the emotion, but on the whole McDougall later concluded that the two were scarcely distinguishable.

It was necessary for McDougall to work out a fairly adequate list of human instincts or *propensities,* as he later preferred to call them (1932). If any important ones were omitted, the motivation of human behavior would not be sufficiently explained. But he had to take care not to admit any secondary, learned motives into his list of primaries, and not to fall into the absurdity of "explaining" each human activity by assuming an instinct for it—a political instinct to explain politics, a religious instinct to account for religion, an instinct of workmanship to account for the high standards of the expert workman, etc. In 1908 McDougall listed twelve major human instincts. In a series of revisions he brought the list by 1932 to eighteen, most of them social in character, but the last a category of physical propensities relatively remote from the interests of a psychologist. It is instinctive, he believed (1932, pages 97–98):

1. To seek (and perhaps to store) food (food-seeking propensity).
2. To reject and avoid certain noxious substances (disgust propensity).
3. To court and mate (sex propensity).

4. To flee to cover in response to violent impressions that inflict or threaten pain or injury (fear propensity).
5. To explore strange places and things (curiosity propensity).
6. To feed, protect, and shelter the young (protective or parental propensity).
7. To remain in company with fellows and, if isolated, to seek that company (gregarious propensity).
8. To domineer, to lead, to assert oneself over, or display oneself before, one's fellows (self-assertive propensity).
9. To defer, to obey, to follow, to submit in the presence of others who display superior powers (submissive propensity).
10. To resent and forcibly to break down any thwarting or resistance offered to the free exercise of any other tendency (anger propensity).
11. To cry aloud for assistance when our efforts are utterly baffled (appeal propensity).
12. To construct shelters and implements (constructive propensity).
13. To acquire, possess, and defend whatever is found useful or otherwise attractive (acquisitive propensity).
14. To laugh at the defects and failures of our fellow creatures (laughter propensity).
15. To remove, or to remove oneself from, whatever produces discomfort, as by scratching or by change of position and location (comfort propensity).
16. To lie down, rest, and sleep when tired (rest or sleep propensity).
17. To wander to new scenes (migratory propensity).
18. A group of very simple propensities serving bodily needs, such as coughing, sneezing, breathing, evacuation.

This list, presented without McDougall's qualifications and explanations, does not do full justice to his theory. He observed, for instance, that the acquisitive propensity might perhaps more properly be broken down into a possessive propensity and a hoarding propensity; that the comfort propensity might include several distinct tendencies; that some individuals or races could have certain propensities in reduced degree, or even lack them altogether. The single-line description of the laughter propensity gives us an ugly shock until it is understood in the context of McDougall's theory of *primitive passive sympathy.* This is a capacity related to the gregarious propensity which enables animals or humans to share the emotional experiences of others. Without the countercheck of laughter man's sympathetic responsiveness to the distress of others would threaten him with constant pain and depression. Laughter brings with it not only wholesome physiological effects, but may "unlock" the laughter of the person whose minor woes have momentarily been exaggerated. "The great laugher is the person of delicately responsive sympathetic reactions; his laughter quickly gives place to pity and comforting support, if our misfortune waxes more severe. . . . Lord Byron wrote: 'And if I laugh at any mortal thing, 'tis that I may not weep' " (1923, pages 169–70).

Each of the instincts or propensities is to be regarded as a natural inclination or motive. The self-assertive and submissive propensities might be called the "pecking order" instincts, with reference to behavior observed in a henyard. The hens quickly establish a relatively permanent order of dominance, each one asserting her claim to any morsel of food as against certain other hens but yielding without resistance to certain others. Any particular pecking order is of course learned and not instinctive, what is instinctive being the tendencies to dominate as far as possible but submit as far as necessary. McDougall argued that submitting gracefully, following a leader happily, and being suggestible and imitative toward prestige persons were sufficient indications of a true native tendency to submit.

How seriously McDougall regarded his list of instincts or propensities can be seen from these words from the *Introduction to Social Psychology* (1908, page 44):

Directly or indirectly the instincts are the prime movers of all human activity . . . determine the ends of all activities and supply the driving power . . . and all the complex intellectual apparatus of the most highly developed mind is . . . but the instrument by which these impulses seek their satisfactions.

This quotation, however, tends to create a false impression of McDougall's system of motives, for he went on to show how the instincts become modified by learning and experience. The fighting instinct, for example, is modified in two principal ways. On the sensory side it becomes attached to new stimuli; it becomes conditioned, as Pavlov would say. The stimulus arousing angry behavior in an infant consists of physical restraint and interference with the infant's movements. Later, restraint or interference of a more subtle sort, exerted by an adult's verbal commands, will arouse the child's anger. On the motor or executive side, too, much modification occurs through learning. The infant's slashing and kicking give place to biting and scratching, to hair pulling and striking with the fist, to angry talk and various indirect ways of injuring the adversary. In spite of all these sensory and motor modifications the instinct remains the same at its core, the core being the angry impulse to fight. The infant who reacts to some one holding his elbows by movements of slashing and kicking, and the adult who reacts to an offensive letter by devising some scheme that will damage the offender's reputation, appear on the surface to be performing entirely different acts, and yet the angry impulse to hurt the enemy is there in both cases. When to fight and how to fight are learned, but the primary motive of fighting back against interference remains the same from infancy to old age.

With only so much modification of the instincts as already described, the infant would scarcely become a humanized adult. McDougall recognized another modification. The instinctive tendencies become combined into what he called *sentiments*. They become combined by being attached to the same object. A man's love for a certain woman includes sex desire and also some of the tender, protective tendency called the parental propensity. These two natural tendencies and probably others as well are attached to that one love object and make up the sentiment of love, which is a powerful adult motive. Patriotism is also a sentiment. There is no single instinct of patriotism, but a man's native land becomes the object of several instincts. His country in danger awakens fear in him; an attack on his country awakens his anger; his country in rivalry with another country awakens his self-assertive tendency; and as his home it stirs love and loyalty. The complexity of the sentiment, combining as it does a variety of instincts, gives some degree of organization to his thought and behavior, while, on the other hand, producing inconsistencies that may seem hard to explain. We find ourselves loving, hating, fearing, and pitying the same individual. It is proverbial that a parent may whip his own child for misbehavior, but still strongly resent any criticism of the same behavior from a neighbor. The combination of propensities that motivate the whipping is not the same as the one arousing resentment to the outsider when he intrudes his opinions, and the father's self-assertiveness seems to play a different role in the two situations.

Sometimes when we are guilty of inconsistencies of this sort we feel ashamed of ourselves. When this happens, according to McDougall's theory, it would be the effect of the *self-regarding sentiment* which is the central integrating force in personality at the highest level. It is the sentiment of self-regard that forces order and consistency on the lower levels of propensities and sentiments. When the father can say of his little son's behavior, "In all fairness, neighbor, I must admit he has been very naughty," his self-regarding sentiment has stepped in to make him judge the situation on its real merits. This superordinate integrating factor has some resemblance to the psychoanalyst's *ego ideal*, Adler's *creative self* (page 303), and

WILLIAM McDOUGALL

even to Horney's *idealized self-image.* All of these set up for the individual a motivating standard of conduct consistent with his idea of the kind of person he is or should be. We expect our "self" to be consistent. We may, as Horney believed (page 322), demand this consistency of ourselves so compulsively as to develop overpowering intrapsychic conflict. McDougall thought of the sentiment of self-regard rather as a *normal* integrating factor threading into unity motivational dispositions that would otherwise be a source of conflict.

McDougall, then, did not say, as he is sometimes supposed to have said, that adult human behavior is directly motivated by the instincts. What he said was that human behavior is motivated by sentiments derived from the instincts and still possessing the emotional striving of the instincts. Behavior, he said, is not driven by purely rational considerations, but by loves and hates, interests, zeals, rivalries, enthusiasms, all of which have an emotional and impulsive character derived ultimately from the native propensities of mankind. Social behavior, therefore, is not based on a single social instinct, but on loyalties and interests resulting from the instincts combined into sentiments. The gregarious propensity, by itself alone, would simply keep men together in groups; but group life gives a chance for all the instincts to become conditioned to social situations and combined into social sentiments.

EARLY AND LATER REACTIONS TO THE HORMIC PSYCHOLOGY. The psychology McDougall gave to the world in 1908 was received with enthusiasm by many psychologists, though not all of them, and quickly led to books and university courses on social psychology by psychologists. It created social psychology as a branch of psychology, where previously it had been treated almost exclusively by sociologists. By the social scientists, too, it was received with great interest and accepted for a few years as just what they needed. How social institutions are based on human instincts became the theme of a succession of books by sociologists and economists. Society, it was said, has to meet the instinctive demands of the individual. An industrialized society may get so far away from the primitive conditions of life to which the instincts were adapted that it can no longer satisfy the instinctive cravings of the individual. Mechanized industry may allow the workman too little play for his self-assertive impulse, and the delay of marriage tends to thwart the sex instinct. Frustrated instincts tend to produce restless, neurotic behavior. Society may have to be remodeled so as to afford scope for the instincts. Such was the line of thought of Graham Wallas, the English economist, in his *Human Nature and Politics* (1908) and *The Great Society* (1914).

McDougall's doctrine of instincts, though well received at first, ran counter to what may be called the professional bias of the sociologists. With their eyes fixed on the social group as the important object of study, they were less impressed with the natural demands of the individual than with another line of facts suggesting that the individual was molded by society. The individual derives his language, his manners and customs, and to a large extent his beliefs from the social environment. All that the anthropologists call the culture of the group appears to be imposed upon the individual and not demanded by him. While to the psychologist it may be self-evident that society is composed of individuals and must meet their demands, to the sociologist the main fact is that society is there before any given individual and imposes on him its demands and standards. We behave alike and "behave like human beings," not in the main because of our instincts, but because of the culture we all receive. Such is the characteristic approach of a sociologist or social anthropologist.

Among the sociologists, then, a long-smoldering discontent with the instinct doctrine broke into flame about 1920. The greatest single conflagration was a book by L. L. Bernard, in 1924, entitled *Instinct, A Study of Social Psychology*, which sought to show the absurdities of much of the current talk about instinct and to demonstrate the unimportance of instinct in society. One part of the author's task was easy enough. No two psychologists gave the same list of instincts. Some allowed over a hundred, while others by pruning and combining brought the number down to two or even one. Such disagreement argued against the validity of the whole conception.

Bernard's more serious criticism was that what were called instincts in common speech and even in the psychology books were far from being purely instinctive. They were complex activities, differing from culture to culture and acquired by the individual from the social environment. Mating behavior with its forms of courtship and marriage was an obvious example. The human mother's care of her baby is not instinctive mothering behavior but a complex activity acquired largely from older women or from the doctors. And so with self-assertion, acquisitiveness, and constructiveness—as we see them among men they cannot be hereditary units. McDougall's belief in an emotional "core" of an instinct, present as the driving force in all its varied activities, seemed to Bernard a touch of mysticism. No doubt there were many biological instincts, like breathing and sneezing, but they were small affairs of little social importance. They could not be allowed the important role that McDougall assigned to the instincts; they did not determine the goals and provide the motive force for man's social behavior.

What does determine the goals and provide the motive force, in Bernard's opinion, is the social environment. This supplies the formative factors in the development of intelligence and character. Man's environment is very different from the natural environment in which biological instincts would be appropriate. Mankind, in the course of many generations, has built up a highly artificial environment of houses, roads, and manifold material objects, and also of customs and institutions. No doubt society has to meet the individual's biological needs, but in the main the individual is plastic and is molded by environmental pressures. But you will find Bernard lapsing occasionally into a way of speaking that seems to give away his whole case. Notice what he says of "environmental dominance" (1926, pages 138–39):

> Civilization is itself in large part a system of sublimations and repressions. We do not give our pugnacious, sexual, gustatory, fear, and gregarious impulses free rein. . . . The best method of control . . . is by what we call sublimation. This involves the turning of the impulses into derivative and substitute channels. . . . Our formative institutions . . . should be able to devise a system which will bend the native impulses to the service of the best abstract ideals of a cultural civilization.

If this last quotation fairly represents Bernard's views, there is no fundamental difference between him and McDougall.

We have distorted the historical course of events by considering the sociological reaction against McDougall before the psychological. The psychologists had never accepted McDougall's treatment of the instincts with anything like unanimity. Both Thorndike and Watson soon criticized these broad instincts as poorly established and did not see much promise in the idea of native driving forces operating throughout life. But the main question for the psychologists was how far any complex behavior patterns were inherited rather than built up by the processes of learning. Doubts began to be raised whether complex actions were ever provided by heredity; it might be that only simple movements were so provided, while all complex behavior patterns, in man at least, had to be learned. At any rate, the native and the acquired elements in behavior were so interwoven as to make separation impossible (Dunlap, 1919). The first outcome of this discussion was to make psychologists more critical of instincts and more inclined to lay all their emphasis on learning. The pendulum has now swung back a little, and the reality of some unlearned complex behavior has been admitted, at least in animals.

This critical revision of the doctrine of instincts, however, has nothing to do with the essential doctrine of purposivism. Two different problems were mixed together in this debate on instinct. How far are behavior patterns native rather than learned? That is the question which has most interested the psychologists, and their answer has been the critical attitude of demanding proof before they will admit that a behavior pattern is native. The other problem has to do with native impulses or primary motives. It would not seriously damage McDougall's theory if he were forced to admit that almost all the behavior patterns of fear, anger, sex, curiosity, self-assertion, and the other instincts are acquired by learning. What his theory demands of the fighting instinct is not a skillful fighting performance but an innate tendency to combat any interference by an angry reaction. If that tendency exists in human nature, operating in different patterns at different levels of behavior, we are justified in accepting a primary pugnacious motive.

This distinction between motive and behavior pattern had been recognized by McDougall from the start. The emotional–impulsive "core" of the instinct, which was native and remained unchanged by experience and learning, was evidently the motive. The sensory and motor parts of the instinct, which were modified by learning, made up the behavior pattern. In speaking of instincts as being combined into sentiments he was evidently referring to their "cores" and not to their behavior patterns. Thus he used the word *instinct* in two senses: to refer to a native behavior pattern with its emotional–impulsive core, and to refer to the core alone. In his latest statement of the theory (1932, page 78) he recognized this source of confusion and needless controversy and dropped the use of *instinct* in referring to human motives and behavior. A typical instinct, such as the nest-building of a wasp, includes a native ability "geared to" a native propensity. The native ability is shown by the fact that the wasp builds the characteristic nest of her species without ever having a chance to learn the use or form of the nest. The native propensity is shown by the fact that when she has matured to the egg-laying stage she devotes all her energy to building and stocking the nest. The human being has many native abilities (or capacities) and quite a number of native propensities, but the abilities are not innately geared to the propensities. So the human being has no full-fledged instincts (except the "minor" ones like breathing and sneezing). If his self-assertive propensity is aroused, he draws upon any ability that is convenient ("See what I can do!"), not upon one particular preordained ability; or if it is the sex propensity that is aroused, he may utilize any ability that seems likely to "make a hit." The abilities (in McDougall's view) do not have any driving force in themselves, but must be driven by the propensities, either by the native propensities or by sentiments derived from the propensities. We may indeed acquire "tastes" for certain activities, like music or bridge, i.e., we learn to like to exercise certain abilities for their own sake, but such likes (and dislikes) have no strong motivating force. "Broadly speaking . . . we may say that, while our sentiments determine the major goals toward which we strive, our tastes determine our choice of means, the kinds of activities and instruments we use" (1932, page 239). Another late qualification of the theory was that an immediate goal has a strong pull, no matter what the ultimate motive may be. "If from any motive you set yourself to attain the goal"—the exit, for example, in a maze puzzle—"from that moment the exit becomes your goal, you foresee and desire the passing out through the exit. . . . It is the same whenever we solve a problem. . . . The solution is the goal towards which we look forward" (1932, page 348). In thus recognizing the motivating power of immediate goals, of which there is an indefinite number, and even of tastes, of which there are many, McDougall seems to some of us to have modified his theory quite radically (and desirably).

PRESENT STANDING OF THE HORMIC THEORY. Unfortunately, McDougall's theory is too little known and too little understood today for having been so thoroughly damned by its critics in the 1920's. It was "wrong" then because it was an "instinct" theory; yet in its application to man, insistence on the hereditary roots of behavior was really not necessary: the immediately effective motives (sentiments), as well as the objects to which they had become attached and the responses made, were all products of learning. As far as animal behavior is concerned, ethologists such as Tinbergen (1951, 1953) and Lorenz (1950) have done much, on the basis of their habitat studies, to restore interest and systematize thinking on the question of "instinct." The *fixed action pattern* (FAP) and the *innate releasing mechanism* (IRM) suggest that heredity plays a prominent if not the only role in the behavior so described. The former consists of a relatively stereotyped *consummatory* response, characteristic of the species, which occurs at or near the end of a searching, *appetitive* prologue. An innate releasing mechanism can be illustrated by the effect upon a territory-holding robin of a bunch of red breast feathers. These he will attack, although he may leave unmolested the figure of an adult-size immature robin that is speckle-breasted (Lack, 1939, 1943; Hinde, 1959, page 584). We cannot argue that the new data provided by ethologists have vindicated McDougall's instinct theory, but they do warrant taking it out of cold storage for reappraisal.

Again, McDougall was judged "wrong" because his theory was purposive and teleological. In 1930 he wrote (pages 3–4):

Fifteen years ago American psychologists displayed almost without exception a complete blindness to the most peculiar, characteristic, and important feature of human and animal activity, namely, its goal-seeking. All bodily actions and all phases of experience were mechanical reactions to stimuli. . . . Now, happily, all is changed; the animal psychologists . . . are busy with the study of "drives," "sets," and "incentives." . . . Much the same state of affairs prevails in current American writings on human psychology. . . . American psychology has become purposive . . . in the vague sense. . . . My task is the more difficult one of justifying the far more radical purposive psychology denoted by the adjective "hormic," a psychology . . . which asserts that active striving towards a goal . . . cannot be mechanistically explained or resolved into mechanistic sequences.

We know now that his optimism was premature. Not even Tolman at that time could sell purposivism to "tough-minded" American behaviorists. Some psychologists, indeed, after going to great pains to show how purposes could be natural behavior events, were still afraid to allow them any causal efficacy—which was rather absurd, for if purpose occurs as a natural effect, it can also be a natural cause for further effects.

Even by 1951, Lashley's analysis of the problem of the serial order in behavior as irrefutable evidence against a theory of simple mechanical causation (see page 175, this book) was received by many with polite interest, but not assimilated into their psychological thinking. But by 1960 "teleological causation" had acquired a new sponsor: the digital computer! McDougall's thesis had found at least partial support in a machine that could systematically go about the solution of problems by the use of Plans and Metaplans (see page 207, this book). Hebb, too, agreed that the time had come to push the investigation of the ordered thought process and the possible role of a "self [that] is neither mythical nor mystical" in intentional learning and in precontrolled sequences such as those Lashley had cited. He suggested that some "physiologizing" in line with Lashley's proposals or his own cell assembly and phase sequence theory might further clarify the interaction of Plan and Metaplan (1960, pages 743–44).

As Miller, Galanter, and Pribram tell the story, this is how the change in scientific climate toward teleology came about (1960, page 42):

Typical of the new freedom deriving from a deeper conception of what machines can be and do was the discovery that machines can behave purposively. In 1943 Rosenblueth, Wiener, and Bigelow shocked many psychologists by putting their very tough-minded reputations behind the assertion that machines with negative feedback were teleological mechanisms. At that time psychologists generally regarded "teleological" and "unscientific" as synonymous, and it was therefore surprising to realize that machines could strive toward goals, could collect information about the difference between their intentions and their performance and then work to reduce that difference. If entelechy was compatible with mechanism, then entelechy could be admitted as a respectable concept in psychology.

It is doubtful that McDougall would have been enthusiastic about this concept of teleology. The model he used in proposing his own teleological theory was not a hardware one, but Mowgli, "our natural man."

As he lies in his cave, imagining both the deer and the lions, impelled by hunger and restrained by fear, our natural man, Mowgli, may imagine himself taking refuge in a tree beside the pool, as he may have done when threatened by lions in the past. Then he imagines himself going in safety to the tree in daylight and remaining there till nightfall, and thence descending upon his game . . . when there is no sign of lions at hand. He would then, having imagined this line of behavior, which promises to satisfy his hunger without incurring great risk, proceed to work it out in action. He would have formed a plan. And, if he had imagined and successfully executed such plans several times, he would, when confronted with a new problem, probably set himself more or less deliberately to imagine a plan. In this way Mowgli would achieve real planning, the thinking out of a line of action before beginning to act. It is very doubtful whether any animal achieves this level of thinking. Animals, if they are confronted by a problem, solve it, if at all, *ambulando*, in the course of action; they do not sit down and think out a plan; still less do they sit down in order to think out a plan. Such planning, such purposive deliberation, would be the principal condition of the natural man's superiority to the animals. When confronted by difficulties, he would imagine alternative lines of action; and, when he had imagined a line of action which avoided or circumvented the difficulty or danger, he would proceed to action on that plan (1923, page 208).

Currently, perhaps the most vocal supporter of McDougall's thinking is Raymond B. Cattell (born 1905; now research professor at the Laboratory of Personality Assessment and Group Behavior at the University of Illinois), who has been partly guided in his multivariate factor analysis of personality by McDougall's concepts, and who has found his results generally favorable to them. In factoring out the innate motivational units (*ergs*), he has found adequate confirmation for six of McDougall's propensities, and partial confirmation for four others. For various reasons, five remain unconfirmed (Cattell, 1957). Propensities in McDougall's list for which Cattell has found full support are sex, gregariousness, parental protectiveness, exploration, escape, and self-assertion. Of the last he says: "It is interesting to note that, of the various descriptions of this self-assertive drive, McDougall's seems to have been the most unerring" (1957, page 518). Evidence appeared also for what seemed to be a relatively separate *self-sentiment* (page 525)—described by Cattell as an "environmental mold trait," in contrast to the "constitutional source trait" represented in the erg. His self-sentiment concept was based upon McDougall's self-regarding sentiment and Freud's ego and superego concepts. In the *dynamic lattice* by which he represents the integration of his factors, the self-sentiment appears to take the important role which McDougall had assigned it.

McDougall's influence has been probably greater than he thought, but it has been limited by his insistence that psychologists follow him beyond the boundaries of what they consider scientific into regions that are the province of philosophy.

ORGANISMIC PSYCHOLOGY

Let us notice first two main lines of attack against tradition that are suggested by the concept of the organism as a whole. The great enemy is sometimes the old mind–body dualism, and sometimes the still-prevalent tendency of psychologists to speak of separate functions and motives of the organism.

Adolf Meyer (born 1866; long professor at Johns Hopkins), who soon became the acknowledged leader of American psychiatry, rebelled as a young man against the mind–body distinction current in nineteenth-century psychiatry. The cleavage between the somatic and psychic theories (page 11) seemed to him wholly unrealistic and unprofitable. As he pointed out in 1897, the organism in its development from the one-celled egg begins and continues as a unit. "In this unit the development of the mind goes hand in hand with the anatomical and physiological development, not merely as a parallelism, but as a oneness with several aspects." And in 1908 he wrote: "It is unfortunate that science still adheres to an effete and impossible contrast between mental and physical. . . . Mind . . . is a sufficiently organized living being in action; and not a peculiar form of mind-stuff." He found this "psychobiological" concept a better working hypothesis for psychiatric work than the materialistic and mentalistic approaches that were customary. If somatic disorders are found, well and good—diagnose and treat the patient accordingly—but if none is demonstrable, it is futile to imagine some brain disorder underlying the symptoms; it is better to utilize the available facts of the patient's behavior and life history.

He should be seen as a person confronted with a situation that is too much for him, rather than merely as a "case" to be classified under some one of the recognized psychoses. His trouble can sometimes be traced in the Freudian manner to an unsolved problem of childhood, but often it has a more gradual development and amounts to a faulty habitual attitude toward social situations—a growing tendency, for example, to retreat from the real situation into the realm of fantasy. While not a prolific writer, Adolf Meyer was a great teacher and therapist and he built up in the Henry Phipps Psychiatric Clinic in Baltimore an outstanding and influential institution. His psychobiology has been found a very useful basis for psychiatric work. His point of view has found expression in psychosomatic medicine, which looks for mental or emotional factors operating in organic conditions and also for organic factors possibly present in cases of behavior disorder. (Compare pages 279–80, this book. For Meyer's teachings, see Rennie, 1943.)

Kurt Goldstein (born 1878; now in New York), one of the strongest defenders of the organismic point of view, believes that reflexes can offer only a misleading approach to any true understanding of the organism's behavior. The reflex is supposed to be a constant, uniform response to a constant stimulus, but such constancy of the single stimulus cannot be obtained except under constant conditions in the rest of the organism. A reflex is really an act of the whole organism and can be understood only as a particular manifestation of the whole organism. Even the knee jerk cannot be obtained in regular, uniform strength unless the leg is in a certain position and "isolated" from the rest of the organism by instructions to the subject to think of something else. How absurd, then, to expect to understand the organism's behavior as a combination of reflexes! We must begin, rather, with an impression of the organism's unitary action; then we can see the reflex playing its part in the whole and so make our view of the organism more detailed and diversified. We must proceed from the whole to the parts, not from the parts to the whole.

Isolation of pieces of the organism's behavior is characteristic not only of the physiologist's investigation of reflexes but also of the psychologist's study of habits, thoughts, motives, feelings, sensations, and perceptions. Every experiment demands constant conditions so as to isolate the particular phenomenon to be observed. Only by this isolating, analytic procedure can any scientific data be obtained. The organismic approach finds itself in a dilemma, since it wishes to see the organism in its behavioral wholeness and yet must resort to isolating observation in order to secure any dependable facts. It rejects the analytic-synthetic method of first examining the parts and then trying to piece them together. Instead it adopts the holistic-analytic method. First must come a holistic view of the behaving organism; then follows isolating observation which yields data for correcting and amplifying the first impression. The holistic or global impression plays the role of a working hypothesis which almost certainly can be improved in face of the particular facts as they are discovered. Or, the global view provides a framework for holding the facts, a framework that is not too rigid to accommodate itself to the growing mass of data. Or again, in Goldstein's words: "We do not try to construct the architecture of the organism by a mere addition of brick to brick; rather we try to discover the actual Gestalt . . . through which some phenomena may become intelligible. . . . We sketch a picture of the whole organism, which in turn, so long as we encounter discrepancies between this picture and factual experience, stimulates further questions and investigations" (1940, pages 23, 26).

The global picture or Gestalt shows an organism endowed with certain capacities and needs, continually challenged by the environment and seeking always to "come to terms with the environment" so as to achieve optimal performance. If the challenge is too severe, the organism is thrown into a "catastrophic" state of anxiety, a feeling of inability to perform its chosen tasks. Brain-injured men, closely studied by Goldstein in his medical capacity in Germany during and after the First World War, are especially subject to this feeling of "catastrophe," and their reaction is to get rid of the tensions so produced. But the normal tendency is not, as Freud and others have theorized, to get rid of tension, but rather to maintain an optimum of tension such as is necessary for accomplishment and progress. "Freud fails to do justice to the positive aspects of life. He fails to recognize that the basic phenomenon of life is an incessant process of coming to terms with the environment; he only sees escape and craving for release. He only knows the lust of release, not the *pleasure of tension*" (1939, page 333).

The behavior of neurotic and of brain-injured people manifests certain traits very strikingly, but we have to be on our guard here against the isolation error. A sick person's behavior is dominated by isolated needs, such as the need for self-preservation. Seen in isolation these needs appear unduly strong and rigid; in the normal person under normal conditions, such needs are not isolated from the general tendency to come to terms with the environment. The same error of isolation is likely to vitiate the experimental study of animal drives and even the much overvalued study of children, for the young child is still uncentered or unintegrated. Only the normal adult responding normally to a favorable environment gives the holistic picture, and he is animated by a single comprehensive motive, which Goldstein calls the urge toward self-actualization or self-realization, "the tendency to achieve the optimal performance of the total organism" (1947, page 228). Nevertheless, though the organism has this one holistic motive, it engages in various activities and seems to be seeking various goals. This is because it has various capacities and tends to actualize its potentialities.

The traditional view assumes various drives. . . . We assume only one drive, the drive of self-actualization, but are compelled to concede that under certain conditions the tendency to actualize one potentiality is so strong that the organism is governed by it. . . . The organism has definite potentialities, and because it has them it has the need to actualize or realize them. The fulfillment of these needs represents the self-actualization of the organism (1940, pages 144, 146).

Taken literally, these statements could apply only to an extremely self-conscious organism whose interests were wholly centered in the self and not in the environment.

We have spoken of "isolation" as a necessary though risky procedure of the scientific investigator, and we should also notice that isolation is an inevitable characteristic of the behavior of an organism, at least of a higher organism possessing various capacities. Though, in a sense, the organism always acts as a whole, it cannot actualize all its potentialities at the same time. Its behavior is governed by one need or capacity at a time. Here there are two extreme possibilities. The organism may yield itself passively to the configuration of the present environment, this being the "concrete attitude"; or, being self-conscious and aware of its own many capacities, the organism may analyze the situation and choose for itself which capacity to actualize, this being the "abstract attitude." The concrete attitude is rigid and cannot shift from one capacity to another so long as the concrete situation remains unchanged; but as soon as the situation changes, the response passively follows suit. The abstract attitude, on the contrary, can shift from one line of attack to another upon an unchanging situation, and it can maintain a persistent line of attack upon a changing situation. The normal human adult can adopt either attitude; in planning, choosing goals, and selecting ways and means, he takes the abstract attitude, while in carrying out a specific manipulation of the environment he necessarily acts concretely. Goldstein's study of brain-injury cases convinced him that their essential defect was the loss of the abstract attitude. They were unable "to break up a given whole into parts,

to isolate and to synthesize them . . . to abstract common properties reflectively . . . to plan ahead ideationally" (Goldstein and
Scheerer, 1941, page 4). With his several collaborators he has designed and adapted a number of tests for the abstract attitude and
has found that schizophrenics and the feeble-minded, as well as
young children, are more or less deficient in this ability. Here, then,
we find organismic psychology of a productive sort, though it is not
quite clear how the productive research depends upon the organismic viewpoint. Goldstein would claim, however, that his discovery
of the abstract and concrete attitudes was due to his firm determination to view the patient's symptoms and test results from the standpoint of the personality as a whole.

Is Goldstein to be counted as a member of the Gestalt school?
The leading Gestalt psychologists have claimed him, but he himself
is inclined to make a distinction. He thinks primarily as a biologist
rather than a psychologist. "Our basic view agrees in many respects
with Gestalt psychology. . . . Yet my guiding principle has been
a different one, inasmuch as the 'whole,' the 'Gestalt,' has always
meant to me the whole organism and not the phenomena in one field,
or merely the 'introspective experiences.' . . . Certain differences
arise between the views advanced by Gestalt psychologists and by
myself" (1939, page 369). For him a "good gestalt" is not merely
an organization of the perceptual field; rather, it is a performance
of the organism, a way of coming to terms with the environment as
well and economically as possible. Gestalt psychology has under-
valued the central factors, the "field forces" supplied by the organism itself and not by the stimulus configuration. And the existing
Gestalt theory does not allow sufficiently for the "abstract attitude."
Indeed, Goldstein's emphasis on the abstract attitude as a prime
necessity in science and in normal adult behavior seems exactly opposed to Wertheimer's abhorrence of any "piecemeal attitude."

Abraham Maslow (born 1908; now professor at Brandeis University) uses the term "self-actualization" in a more specific sense than
Goldstein's concept. He holds that certain basic needs may be considered generally, if not always, to have priority. The organism's
demands for food, sleep, warmth, comfort, etc., come first. When
these are satisfied the need for safety takes on greater importance.
If this is reasonably assured, the need for love and belongingness
becomes more pressing, and once this is adequately satisfied, the
individual will have more time to seek satisfaction of the need for
esteem. When all of these have been reasonably fulfilled he may
still be aware of a gnawing sense of incompleteness until he finds
some suitable way to express and develop his own special potentiali-

ties. This is the need for self-actualization—the fifth in the hierarchy of basic needs.

Maslow recognizes that in the course of satisfying these a person is bound to acquire certain knowledge and certain abilities. But he feels, as does an increasing number of psychologists, that too little attention has been given to the desire to know and to understand as an end in itself. That objects and activities are interesting for their own sakes as well as means to achieving goals has been a fact slow to be recognized in motivation theory. We have already discussed this lag in another connection (pages 191–93). Accordingly Maslow adds the need for knowledge, and the aesthetic need—which he considers to have been similarly neglected—to his need hierarchy. He makes it clear, however, that in practical operation the effects of the last two cannot be sharply separated from the activities motivated by the five basic needs.

We are reminded here of the interweaving effects of the primary and secondary autonomy of ego functions (page 287) as these have been conceived by Hartmann and others. But Maslow, of course, is not thinking in terms of libido, nor can he be in any way identified with the psychoanalytic school. He describes his own system as *holistic–dynamic* and essentially related to organismic and Gestalt theory. New experience, therefore, whether for better or worse, is not just added to the previously accumulated stock of the organism. It is assimilated to the organism as it exists at that moment, and changes it not in just one aspect but in its entirety. He adopts and adapts the medical term *syndrome* to describe the internal organization of personality. As he uses it, a syndrome would consist of the interacting and interchangeable, yet enduring and self-consistent modes of behavior an individual may use in "coping" with certain kinds of problem. Maslow makes the claim that the characteristic "flavor" of the syndrome's composition is distinctive enough to make it possible at times to identify its function by one single feature, as when we judge from the character of a person's laughter that he is insecure (1954).

The approach to personality from the direction of psychopathology has, in Maslow's judgment, overemphasized "coping" behavior to the neglect of relatively unmotivated forms which appear in normal people. Play, "loafing," artistic appreciation and expression, fun, daydreaming, even the patterning of perceptual experience may take a less motivated form in a healthy than in an unhealthy personality. The person who is insecure and needs to bolster his self-esteem must play competitively, and must maintain his interest in music because his social role demands certain status symbols. His daydreaming is directed toward means of consolidating his position; he dares not even see facts as they are but views a situation with the selective inattention or tendentious apperception which Sullivan and Adler noted to be characteristic of the neurotic.

Maslow's contribution to the study of normal personality consisted in a survey of the personality characteristics of 43 individuals, some living, some historical, some famous, some yet to receive recognition, but all judged to be, according to certain criteria, "self-actualizers." The details of their selection and the generalizations about their distinguishing personality characteristics are to be found in Maslow's *Motivation and Personality* (1954). We shall limit ourselves here to saying that they appeared to be generally more self-accepting; more likely to be interested in ends than in means to an end; more creative; less hostile in their humor; more selective in their deep friendships, although generally well-disposed toward humanity and its welfare; likely to be indifferent to convention but ready to accept it within reasonable limits; and more than the average person, inclined to cherish periods of privacy. If Maslow's observations are right these may be thought of as the by-products of self-actualization.

PERSONALISTIC PSYCHOLOGY

The reality of the self is as obvious to the introspectionist as the reality of the organism is to the behaviorist. We should have to go far back in the history of psychology to find the beginnings of the personalistic view. With the coming of empirical and experimental study of psychology the person tended to drop out of the picture because attention was focused on analytic data, separate sensations, images, and feelings. This way of approaching psychology was criticized by William James in his famous chapter on "The stream of thought" (1890, Vol. I, 224–25). On the contrary, he said:

> The first fact for us . . . as psychologists, is that thinking of some sort goes on. I use the word thinking . . . for every form of consciousness. . . . How does it go on? We notice immediately five important characters in the process . . . :
> 1) Every thought tends to be part of a personal consciousness.
> 2) Within each personal consciousness thought is always changing.
> 3) Within each personal consciousness thought is sensibly continuous.
> 4) It always appears to deal with objects independent of itself.
> 5) It is interested in some . . . objects to the exclusion of others.

Elaborating the third point, James wrote of the "warmth and intimacy" of our own thoughts remembered after a gap:

> . . . whatever past states appear with those qualities must be admitted to receive the greeting of the present mental state, to be owned by it, and ac-

cepted as belonging together with it in a common self. This community of self is what the time-gap cannot break in twain, and is why a present thought, although not ignorant of the time-gap, can still regard itself as continuous with certain chosen portions of the past.

Consciousness, then, does not appear to itself chopped up in bits. Such words as "chain" or "train" do not describe it fitly as it presents itself in the first instance. It is nothing jointed; it flows. A "river" or a "stream" are the metaphors by which it is most naturally described.

Mary Whiton Calkins (1863–1930), a pupil of James beginning in 1890, was for a decade the active head of the psychological laboratory at Wellesley, though she later switched mostly to philosophy. She invented the important "method of paired associates" for the study of memory. During the 1890's she became more and more dissatisfied with the Wundt–Titchener psychology and more and more impressed with the importance of the self as the integrating factor in conscious experience. In 1900 she came out strongly for "psychology as a science of selves," and in 1901 she embodied this view in her first book, An Introduction to Psychology. In this book she endeavored to do justice to both the atomistic and the personalistic views of psychology. She came to believe, however, that the atomistic data were significant only in relation to the self, and in 1909 her revised textbook, called A First Book in Psychology, made a radical innovation "by its abandonment of the duplex conception of psychology, as science alike of succeeding mental events and of the conscious self, in favor of a single-track self-psychology" (1930, page 40). She argued that the self, far from being merely a metaphysical concept, was an ever-present fact of immediate experience and fully worthy to be made the central fact in a system of scientific psychology.

The conscious self of each one of us . . . is immediately experienced as possessed of at least four fundamental characters. I immediately experience myself as (1) relatively persistent—in other words, I am in some sense the same as my childhood self; as (2) complex—I am a perceiving, remembering, feeling, willing self; as (3) a unique, an irreplaceable self—I am closely like father, brother, or friend, but I am, after all, only myself: there is only one of me. I experience myself (4) as related to (or conscious of) objects either personal or impersonal (1914, page 3).

The self is consciously related to its objects in various ways. It takes a receptive attitude toward an object in observing it, but a dominating attitude in managing it; it has the attitude of liking certain objects but of disliking others. To speak of pleasantness and unpleasantness as impersonal conscious states is as absurd as to speak of them as unrelated to objects, for the real datum is the self being pleased or displeased by an object. Among the "objects" of the self the most important are other selves. The self is consciously a social being. Only a self-psychology can provide the basis for a genuine social psychology. Behaviorism cannot make a start on social psychology without smuggling in assumptions contrary to its major principle of regarding individuals as not having conscious experience; for, no matter what the behaviorist may say, the individuals he is considering certainly treat each other as conscious beings. Aside from this fanatical negative doctrine of behaviorism, its positive research findings can be welcomed and assimilated by self-psychology.

Calkins was distinctly an introspectionist and approached the self from this point of view. In her textbook she constantly appealed to the student to introspect for himself and to see the personal significance of the different topics in psychology. But she was eager also to bring the schools together and hoped to accomplish this by securing general acceptance of the fundamental importance of the self or person in all the psychologies. Though she herself much preferred "the strictly psychological conception of the self-which-has-a-body" to that of the conscious organism, she became convinced that the "biological form of personalistic psychology provides a middle ground in which most schools of contemporary psychology may meet" (1930, page 50). She noted that the "psychosomatic personalists," such as Stern whom we shall soon consider, attributed to the "person" the same fundamental characteristics she attributed to the "self," and that "nothing forbids the self-psychologists from enriching their doctrine by distinctions stressed by these biological personalists." Nor does anything prevent the self-psychologists from utilizing the "atomistic" data of Titchener's existential school. "Only the great negation of existential psychology,[1] its outlawry of the self, its insistence on contents or ideas or experiences as the one concern of scientific psychology, is inconsistent with personalistic theory." She found herself in substantial agreement with Gestalt psychology except in its neglect of the "supreme illustration of the *Gestalt*"—that "integrated complex whole inclusive of parts" which is the self. And in psychoanalysis, which she regarded with a critical eye, she found the self appearing again and again in different guises—as the censor, for example, of Freud's earlier period and as the superego of his later theory (1930, pages 52–53). In fact it would be almost impossible to write psychology without lapsing, even against one's theoretical preconceptions, into the language of self-psychology.

---

[1] Not to be confused with current existentialism. (See pages 27–28, and pages 381–85.)

Why, then, should not all the schools unite in a personalistic psychology? Her plea seemed to fall on deaf ears, probably because
most psychologists felt there was little to be gained by continually
reiterating the truism of the reality and unity of the self or organism.
Yet, looking back over the past fifty years, one can see that psychology has been moving in the direction she desired.

William Stern (1871–1938) offered his personalistic psychology
to the world in 1906, just a few years after the self-psychology of
Calkins made its appearance. Stern was apparently unacquainted
with the work of Calkins; the Germans of 1900 or even of 1920 paid
little attention to the American output in psychology. The two
authors were alike in having a predominant interest in philosophy,
as well as in making substantial contributions to experimental psychology. Stern was an exceptionally enterprising and inventive
psychologist, a pioneer in the psychology of testimony and an active
contributor to applied, differential, child, and clinical psychology.
It was he who invented the IQ for use in connection with the Binet
tests. His most important position was at Hamburg (1916–1933)
where he was professor of psychology and director of the many-
sided Hamburg Psychological Institute, devoted largely to clinical
and guidance work in connection with the public schools.

Stern's great ambition throughout his career was to develop a
philosophy that should reconcile the atomistic tendency of science
with the human demand for real values in the world—that should
integrate mechanism and teleology; and, like Calkins again, he believed that the concept of *person* made this reconciliation and integration possible. The person has unity, value, and purpose. The
person is a whole of many parts, *unitas multiplex*. Taken part by
part he (the person) can and should be studied mechanistically,
i.e., in terms of cause and effect and the interaction of different factors; but taken as a whole he can be understood only in terms of
purposes, goals, and values. The typical person is an adult human
being; but a child is a person; an animal or any living organism is a
person under Stern's definition; and there are superindividual "persons," organized social groups having their own goals and composed
of individuals as the individual is composed of cells.

Each person has an environment selected by himself to some
extent, and it is characteristic of a person to be in active relations
with his environment. There are three levels of relations between
the individual and his environment: the biological level of nutrition,
etc.; the psychological level of conscious experience; and the valu-
ational level which Stern regarded as the province of philosophy.
Psychology is concerned with conscious experience. Its data are

the "phenomena" which the individual reports. But psychology goes behind the phenomena and recognizes "acts" of the person which are revealed by the phenomena, such as the acts of seeing, remembering, desiring. Psychology goes behind the momentary acts and recognizes enduring "dispositions" such as abilities and propensities, which are potentialities of the organism needing only to be awakened by stimulation from the environment. And finally psychology attempts to go behind the manifold dispositions and envisage the unitary person; but psychology cannot by itself reach this goal, because the unitary person is not purely mental but biological as well and also related to the world in a system of values which have to be approached from the philosophical angle (Stern, 1938, pages 70–84).

The true conception of the person dawned on Stern during his intensive studies of his own children in the home.

Here I became aware of the fundamental personalistic fact of *unitas multiplex;* the wealth of phenomena concomitantly or successively observable arrayed themselves in a unified life-line of the developing individual. . . . Here I discovered the fundamental form of personal causality: the convergence of the stirring character-traits in the developing child, with the totality of environmental influences (1930, pages 350–51).

This concept of *convergence* is important in Stern's system. The child's development is not due to heredity alone, nor to environment alone, nor to a mere sum of heredity and environment, but to the convergence (or synergy) of the two, convergence being possible because of the unity of the person. In the same way the person has a multiplicity of traits, but these converge in his unitary personality. He has a multiplicity of drives, but these converge in his unitary purposive behavior. Freud grossly underestimated the multiplicity of the individual's drives and motives, and he also failed to take due account of the unity of the person (1938, page 37).

Yet Freud's idea of a "depth psychology" is important, for there are depths in the person beneath the level of conscious experience. These depths are biological rather than psychological, but they have their influence on behavior. The unconscious cannot be rightly conceived in the categories of conscious activities such as ideas, memories, and definite desires. There is a gradation in depth extending from wholly unconscious biological activity of the organism, up through the various degrees of vaguely conscious feelings and activities, to the most sharply conscious and attentive perceptions and voluntary acts.

Whatever is sharply conscious was said by Stern to be *salient;* and whatever is salient is at the same time *embedded* in the deeper layers of the person. When you are closely observing a certain object, that observation is salient; but at the same time there is a background of feeling in which the specific observation is embedded; and the feeling itself is embedded in the unconscious life of the organism. "Everything that 'stands forth' from the whole nevertheless remains 'embedded' in it, despite its isolation, and receives from this relationship its sense and order" (1930, page 380). Stern suggested the analogy of the mountain range.

The peaks (cognition and acts of will) appear to stand out from the earth as sharply defined separate structures; but they are not separate from it, being held up by the mountainous mass (feeling) which, while visible itself, displays no shape of its own nor any sharp edge above and below; it is very near to the earth and is rooted, along with the peaks, in the invisible ground common to them all (sphere of the so-called "unconscious") (1938, page 531).

Feeling, regarded not in isolation but as personal background experience, is not limited to pleasantness and unpleasantness but has a great variety of shades and tones. It can be mapped in many dimensions, including excitement–tranquillity, activity–passivity, attraction–avoidance. It is "shapeless" but still has much influence on behavior.

Gestalt psychology, in its emphasis on shape or configuration, has neglected the important role of the non-Gestalt, the shapeless. It has said much of figure and ground but devoted all its attention to the figure and regarded the ground as a minor matter. But the ground is not simply the spatial background of a visual figure; it is, rather, the personal feeling in which the act of perceiving the figure is embedded. Visual figures, so much used by the Gestalt psychologists, are not suited to bring out the whole range of psychological dynamics. They are too much like the old isolated elements. A whiff of odor, a sunset, a breeze blowing on the skin, have a degree of salience though they are shapeless non-Gestalts rather than Gestalts. Such sensory experiences, along with the feelings, must have their place in our psychology. Salience and embedding are a more comprehensive and useful pair of concepts than figure and ground. Such was Stern's contention (1938, page 112).

Stern made practical application of his personalistic psychology in the clinical and guidance work of his Hamburg institute. The "total procedure" used there has been described by a colleague (Bogen, 1931). The mere accumulation of tests in the hope of sampling the individual on all sides is not entitled to be called a "total procedure," because limitations of time would not allow for a complete survey, and also because the totality principle would be neglected. The real requirement is to see the individual as a unity in his multiplicity. The focal question must be, "What goal is this person seeking—what situation is he trying to make real?" Each person was regarded as having two goals: (1) an intrinsic goal bound up with his individual nature, and (2) an adopted goal representing his adjustment to his social environment. The adopted goal is the resultant of the converging influences of the intrinsic goal and the environment. The psychologist's task was to discover the intrinsic as well as the adopted goal of the individual. Achievement and aptitude tests were given, also the Rorschach with some freedom of interpretation, and a typological questionnaire based partly on Kretschmer. But the main thing was to get the subject to tell the story of his life beginning as far back as he could remember. Freud's rule, to keep back nothing, was followed, but nothing like a full psychoanalysis was attempted, nor were the Freudian concepts used. The psychologist was on the watch for resistances, conflicts, and the subject's childhood feelings toward his environment. Special attention was given to what the subject could tell of his childhood play. Did he have his own favorite kinds of play, or did he follow the season and the crowd? Sometimes it seemed desirable to obtain from the subject an account of his relatives, especially of those whom he "took after" to his own knowledge. From all these indications an opinion and recommendation were offered and discussed with the subject before being regarded as final.

PERSONOLOGY. Henry A. Murray (born 1893; long Director of the Harvard Psychological Clinic; more recently professor of clinical psychology) has brought to the study of personality a rare combination of creativity and leadership, scientific and literary sophistication, and a penetrating interest in human beings. He has had little patience with the behaviorist's rejection of introspection and preoccupation with the reactions of lower animals in artificial laboratory situations. His medical training had demonstrated to him that man's reports of his own interior experiences could be valuable adjuncts to information obtained by other methods of observation, and so he has included such data among the "multiple methods of assessment" he has used in the study of personality. Some of these— notably the famous Thematic Apperception Test (TAT; Morgan and Murray, 1935; Murray, et al., 1938), and the ingenious situational tests contrived for selecting men for strategic services in World War II (Murray, et al., 1948)—represent important landmarks in the history of psychological testing.

From medicine, too, he had learned the importance of an adequate system of concepts for classifying data. Murray's elaborate terminology developed to serve this need presents something of a problem to those who confront it for the first time, but with familiarity it becomes less formidable, particularly as the kinship of his thinking with that of other theorists becomes more apparent. He acknowledges his debt to Freud, McDougall, and Lewin, as well as to Alfred North Whitehead, for the structure of his theory. Yet it was Jung who provided his earliest close contact with analytical thought, and there are many reflections of Jung's influence in his formulations. The Freudian influence—the result of a Freudian analysis and his later training by Franz Alexander and Hanns Sachs —is expressed in the unorthodox adaptation of the concepts of the id, ego, superego, and ego-ideal; and in his building upon the Freudian pregenital phases of development—the oral, anal, and phallic, to which he has added *claustral* and *urethral* sources of pleasure —an explanation of the development of later neurotic symptoms. Murray has been recognized as one of the first to attempt a large-scale reconciliation of psychoanalytic theory with the concepts of academic psychology.

The id, as he describes it, remains a primitive biological force, but one that is not wholly undesirable in its effects. On the contrary, it provides the basic energies, emotions, and needs which, used under the direction of the superego at the right *time,* in the right *place,* in the right *manner,* and toward the right *objects* (*t-p-m-o*), have a positive value. He still conceives of the superego as the social conscience of the individual, but its precepts are derived not only from parents and authority figures, but from the cultural heritage of literature, folk-tales, and even from the pressures of peer groups. The ego-ideal may or may not be congruent with the superego. It may be dominated by the id to the extent of making the individual completely asocial and criminal. If it is dominated by the superego, the effect is one of rigid conformity to social standards. If the individual can successfully balance these two possibilities, he is ego-dominated and "normal."

Murray's more characteristic terminology appears in the concepts which will be briefly treated next. [For a fuller account, Murray, *et al.* (1938), Murray and Kluckhohn (1953), and Murray (1959) should be consulted.] The influence of McDougall is clearly seen in Murray's definition of a *need,* the motivational unit he emphasized in his early theory:

A need is a construct . . . which stands for a force . . . in the brain region, a force which organizes perception, apperception, intellection, conation and action in such a way as to transform in a certain direction an existing, unsatisfying situation. . . . Each need is characteristically accompanied by a particular feeling or emotion and tends to use certain modes . . . to further its trend. . . . usually it persists and gives rise to a certain course of overt behavior (or fantasy), which . . . changes the initiating circumstances in such a way as to bring about an end situation which . . . (appeases or satisfies) the organism (1938, pages 123–24).

Not only in the function of the need, but also in the nature of some that he has specifically listed, can resemblances to McDougall's theory be found, as the following small sample will show:

Murray	McDougall
n Abasement, and n Defendance	Submissive propensity
n Affiliation	Gregarious propensity
n Aggression	Anger propensity
n Harmavoidance	Fear propensity
n Nurturance	Protective propensity
n Succorance	Appeal propensity

Other parallels and overlapping can be traced, although the lists are by no means identical, and Murray's is much the longer.

In his later thinking on the subject he found causes for dissatisfaction with the need categories, although they had been useful in classifying the overt behavior of the fifty subjects who had been intensively studied at the Harvard Psychological Clinic, and they had served also in the interpretation of the TAT stories. Listed as they are above in abstract detachment from the situations in which they would function or the actions to which they would lead, they appear to be, as Allport has pointed out (1937, 1961), standardized motivational categories presumably independent of one another, whereas in fact they would operate in an organized way, each need contributing to a situation jointly with others and modified to some degree by the others. The listed needs might provide a rough measure of the universal components of personality, but would fall short of providing an account of the unique motivation of an individual.

Murray, however, cannot be charged with leaving needs in a state of abstract isolation. He conceives of them as hierarchically organized, some taking precedence over others, or being prepotent, under certain circumstances. Sometimes two or more *fuse* to produce the same effect. A particular need may regularly find satisfaction in a certain kind of activity, and so become integrated with the ideas and behavior that have produced that satisfaction. This *need-integrate* concept has been cited by Allport as more closely approximating what he called in his earlier treatment of the subject (1937) an "individual trait," and what he has in his more recent account described as a "personal disposition" (1961). Murray has, in his own later writings, moved toward, if not beyond, Allport's position on motivation. He suggests, for example, that *thematic dispositions* would describe the properties of an individual personality better than needs. A *thema* relates a need to the circumstances, and although he does not subscribe to Sullivan's interpersonal conception of personality, he places great value on dyadic interaction as providing a relatively natural method of studying personality. (See Murray, 1963.) Of thematic dispositions he says: ". . . instead of saying that X possesses the trait of aggressivity . . . or need for aggression, one should, if possible, . . . say with more precision that two properties of his personality . . . are supersensitive dispositions to react with resentment and aggressive words (1) to apperceived insults to his self-respect and (2) to apperceived vainglorious boastings by an alter" (1959, page 34).

The "apperceived insults" and "apperceived boastings" fall into a category which Murray describes as *press*. Press would include the wide variety of environmental situations involving people and objects that can produce reactions: threats to security, the loss of prized possessions, the death or misfortunes of those dear to us, personal honors and opportunities, etc. Such situations can be appraised from two viewpoints—that of the reactor, and that of a relatively disinterested observer. A remark which seems innocuous or humorous to a by-stander *(alpha press)* may be loaded with malice and threat for the individual to whom it has been addressed, and it will be this significance *(beta press)* that will determine his reaction. *Beta* press corresponds to what Lewin called the "psychological environment" of the individual. By taking into consideration *alpha* press, which might be defined as the consensually validated "real" situation, Murray offers a criterion against which the individual's unique reaction may be matched, and so corrects a deficiency in Lewin's system: without some measure of *alpha* press "we shall never know how much of the external situation was rejected by the subject" (1959, page 27).

Murray insists that personality is more than "an inert aggregate of response patterns, which requires a stimulus to start it going"; it is, rather, a manifestation of *regnant*—that is, organized, integrative —neural processes in the brain, "a matrix of incessant functional processes" such as programs, goals, expectations, fears, etc., which may operate at an unconscious as well as at a conscious level, and which may initiate behavior as well as react to external press. *Process* activities or *modal* needs would be good illustrations of this. In these we meet again a principle of motivation recognized also by Karl Bühler (1924) under the concept "function pleasure"; by Piaget as the active searching to assimilate new "aliment" when new schemata have developed (page 42, this book); by White's theory of "competence" (page 294, this book); and by Heinz Hartmann and other psychoanalysts who have espoused the conflict-free theory of the ego (page 287, this book). The infant soon finds obvious pleasure in exercising some newly developed capacity such as releasing objects, watching them fall, and hearing the sound they make as they hit the floor; a few months later, in walking, climbing, and talking. Such playful activities may be intrinsically rewarding or may at times serve n Autonomy or n Achievement.

Satisfaction derived from performing with skill or elegance beyond practical requirements reflects the operation of a modal need. Notwithstanding his Freudian inclinations, Murray has not supported the traditional theories that assume motivation to be related to the organism's disposition to return to a tensionless state. He agrees that satisfaction may result from tension reduction, but it is in the process of reduction rather than in the tensionless state that the satisfaction is felt, and the greater the tension the greater the satisfaction. This is apparent when we set levels of aspiration for ourselves. When we are ambitious and confident, we raise our sights; when we have been made "realistic" by failure, we moderate our self-demands to avoid the unpleasantness of irreducible tension (Murray and Kluckhohn, 1953, p. 40).

Since his earliest formulations, Murray has never lost sight of the dimensionality and complexity of the problems involved in the study of human personality. In his later formulations on the dynamics of behavior he has focused more upon the cathected values of the individual and the positive or negative sentiments and dispositions expressed toward objects and people, rather than on the relatively unrealistic press–need concept (1959, 1963). Similarly, an isolated *proceeding,* a unit of behavior detached from the events which have preceded it and which will follow it, as well as those which accompany it but which may appear irrelevant to the experimenter, is an abstraction. It may be as brief and inconsequential as a nod to a passing acquaintance, or as weighted with significance as a final decision on the choice of a life partner or a career; but in assessing personality the psychologist may find that additional light is thrown on the subject if he takes into account the total ongoing activities of the individual at that instant. Murray describes such a cross-sectional sample of behavior as a *durance,* and in his multiple assessment techniques provides for the inclusion of such information by moving pictures, instrumental data of various kinds, and by later reports from the subject (1963). Sustained goal-directed behavior stretches into sequences of related proceedings which he calls *serials.* Over a period of hours, days, weeks, or years, serials will require thoughtful planning through *schedules* and *serial programs* to prevent conflicts and to promote the chances for attaining the goal. Much of Murray's treatment of this problem of *ordination* anticipates the more recent speculations of Miller, Galanter, and Pribram on the same topic (1960).

Murray's concept of the effects of the pregenital complexes, and the concept of a *Unity-Thema* give recognition to the threads of consistency in the individual's life pattern. "Every man is in certain respects (a) like all other men, (b) like some other men, (c) like no other man" (Kluckhohn and Murray, 1948, page 35). Viscerogenic needs would provide illustrations of the first category; the Icarus complex (1955), his name for a syndrome of characteristics related to the urethral complex—a history of enuresis, love of fire, overweening ambition which cannot survive the first prick of failure—would illustrate the second category; and the unique sentiments and values developed by the individual as the result of his particular life experiences would represent the third. These last may not always be clearly apparent in the complexities of the serials of an individual's life, but Murray believes that an original thema established early in life, or a reaction formation that has developed from it, may be found regularly in the later life record when it is scrutinized.

Although Murray has frankly conceded the difficulties of holistic studies of personality which at the same time conform with the rubrics of scientific method, he has proposed a plan (1963) to integrate the efforts of personologists and experimentalists toward such an objective. These would work together to build up a bank of comprehensive personality data on a criterion group of subjects. Once developed, this information could thereafter be used by later experimenters in interpreting new data, and in framing hypotheses to account for individual deviations from the general norms available.

Perhaps no item of Murray's multiple assessment program has attracted as much attention as the Thematic Apperception Test developed with Christiana Morgan in 1935. Since that time its method of administration and scoring, the interpretation of the responses made to the ambiguous social situations pictured, the number and assortment of the specific pictures used have been changed by the numerous investigators who have used it as an instrument of personality measurement or for the purpose of testing the validity of the assumption that the subject identifies with the hero (or some other character of the story told), projecting fantasies which grow out of his own unfulfilled needs.

Among those who have been particularly identified with the use of the test in a modified form have been David McClelland and his associates (1953) in their studies of n Achievement. Although McClelland would appear to be doubly identified with Murray through his *n Ach* and his use of the TAT, his motivation theory has little more than these features in common with Murray's theory. He defines motive in general as a cue-produced reinstatement of an affective change related to an earlier experience. The subject has learned to expect something to happen, and if what does happen is relatively close to what he has adapted himself to expect and take, the effect will be pleasant or at least tolerable. Great discrepancies between expectations and actuality will be unpleasant. (Compare Hebb, page 185.) With particular application to measuring *n Ach* by means of TAT, the theory raises the issue of whether the stories told will reveal the unfulfilled wishes for achievement, or elicit only the watered-down, anxiety-controlled aspirations of subjects who have come to protect themselves against failure and disappointment. Findings reported by McClelland and his associates (1953), and conflicting results with other needs (Holt, 1961; Lazarus, 1961; Wyatt and Veroff, 1956) leave some doubt about the validity of the TAT as its function was originally conceived, if not about its potential value as a measuring device if a better method of interpretation and scoring can be found. Magda Arnold's more recent use of the test by a prescribed method of assaying the import of each story in the sense of "what is implied . . . *from the point of view of the storyteller*" (1962, page 65) and, beyond that, of gleaning what further information is to be found in the sequence as a whole, offers promise of new uses and improved results from this controversial assessment device.

THE "UNDERSTANDING" PSYCHOLOGY—A PSYCHOLOGY THAT SEEKS TO UNDERSTAND RATHER THAN TO EXPLAIN. This is one of the oldest of still-contemporary schools. No sooner had the infant experimental psychology begun to show its hand than philosophers who were impressed with the richness of mental life and with the need for a broad, deep psychology as a basis for the social sciences began to utter wails of disappointment. Wilhelm Dilthey (1833–1911) if not the first was about the most outspoken and influential. In 1894 he urged that there should be developed a "descriptive and analytic psychology" very different from the "explanatory psychology" that was imitating the natural sciences and attempting to discover the elements of conscious experience and the laws of their combination. This explanatory psychology seemed doomed to depend on unverifiable hypotheses, while a direct appeal to consciousness would reveal a living unity calling for no such artificial constructions. The explanatory psychology had no means of approaching the motives of men or the achievements of great minds, and its natural-science techniques broke down altogether before the problems of social institutions and cultural history. The method of descriptive psychology, as applied to the individual, would start with the integrated totality of mental life and then examine parts of this totality in their intimate relation to the whole. "Understanding" cannot be purely intellectual but must be appreciative, sympathetic, feelingful. Values as well as facts are directly given in the inner life. The component parts discovered by true psychological analysis are seen in their relations to the whole. But the full scope of mental life cannot be gained from this introspective study; it is revealed in the achievements of great men and in human history and culture, envisaged as living processes. Dilthey's unremitting emphasis on the integrated whole *(Zusammenhang)* and on its articulated structure sounded a note that is common to many of his successors in Germany, such as Stern, Goldstein, and the Gestalt school. We should include here the *Ganzheit* ("wholeness") psychology of Felix Krueger, Wundt's successor at Leipzig. This school, well represented by Sander (1930), is sometimes called the Leipzig Gestalt School (see pages 249–50, this book). It sought to go beyond the Berlin School by recognizing the "emotive totality" of any experience and focusing on the development of personality. The *Ganzheit* school is still very much alive in Germany. What Dilthey had to offer was a project and not a descriptive psychology worked out to any extent, but he did offer the suggestion (1895–1896) that types of men, men with distinctive aims in life, would well repay psychological study.

This lead has been followed by Edouard Spranger (born 1882; professor of philosophy at Berlin). Spranger's interest in the problems and aspirations of young people, along with his interest in philosophy and the history of culture, led him to take up Dilthey's demand for an "understanding" psychology (1928). While the "explanatory" psychology was occupied with elements and physiological processes, understanding psychology must proceed at the higher level of meaningful acts and attitudes. A meaningful act has some goal, some value. What are the goals and values of really meaningful human activity? They are not limited to the biological goals of self-preservation and reproduction, for we find mankind seeking other values. Mankind finds value in knowledge, and one of its goals is the advancement of knowledge. Another is seen in the love for beauty and the age-long devotion to artistic production and enjoyment. By keeping in view both the living individual and the history of mankind we can develop a psychology of values and understand the individual's attitude toward life. After prolonged attention to the problem Spranger believed he could identify six typical human goals—six dimensions of human value, we might say —aside from the biological goals mentioned. Here is his list of goals, values, or attitudes:

The theoretical, knowledge-seeking
The aesthetic
The economic or practical
The religious
The social or sympathetic
The political or managerial

Spranger speaks of "types of men": the practical man, the religious man, and so on. He does not mean that people can be neatly grouped under these heads, for every individual will appreciate more than a single value. As a type, the "practical man" is idealized; and the same thing is true of the other types. Yet actual individuals differ in their interests, some inclining more toward the practical, others more toward the theoretical, others more toward the political. This is not only common observation, but it has also been demonstrated by the use of questionnaires based on Spranger's types, so that his system has found use in studies of personality. The well-known Allport-Vernon Study of Values (1931; third edition, 1960, with G. Lindzey) is one of these.

Gordon W. Allport (born 1897; now professor at Harvard University) took his undergraduate degree at Harvard in the social sciences and humanities, then spent a year teaching these subjects at Robert College, Istanbul. When he returned to study for his doctorate at Harvard, however, and during two years of post-doctoral study at the Universities of Berlin, Hamburg, and Cambridge, psychology was his major interest. So it was that during the period when behaviorism was becoming entrenched in America, with the white rat too rapidly assuming a star role, Allport was exposed to the more philosophically oriented psychologies of Europe which focused upon man as an individual. In his years as a member of the Harvard faculty, interrupted only by a four-year period at Dartmouth (1926–1930), Allport has been identified with the study of the person as an individual, and of the person in his relationships with other individuals.

His stress on the theme of the uniqueness of each personality has led him to the formulation of a theory of the integrative "structures" which account for the individuality, the direction, and the detectable consistencies of each person's thought and behavior. In this respect

his aim and thinking do not appear to be very different from Mc-
Dougall's (our pages 335–36), but Allport dismisses McDougall's
hormic theory or any theory which attempts to account for man's
present behavior entirely in terms of "unchanging energies" derived
from the past. Each person develops interests and habits which
become independent of their original motivating conditions. These
become *functionally autonomous* contemporary forces in the personality which not only assure its individuality but also keep it
moving toward new goals. These forces, for the normal person,
will not be scattered and disorganized, but will provide, through an
integrative system which Allport calls the *proprium*—corresponding
to the concept of the self—some degree of intentional control and
consistency in the selection and achievement of goals. But before
presenting Allport's thinking on the subjects of functional autonomy
and the proprium, let us take a look at some of the facts which influenced him to adopt his present position.

The publication of Allport's *Personality: A Psychological Interpretation* in 1937 brought into the academic arena a subject which
before that time had been associated in people's minds largely with
syndicated newspaper columns on how to win friends or how to
maintain mental serenity in the face of personal crises. There were,
of course, the analytical schools; but they were not yet thought of
as contributing substantially to the mainstream of scientific psychology, although occasionally a challenging concept, such as the introversion–extraversion typology, would filter through, usually to meet
with ignominious rejection at the hands of the increasingly "tough-
minded" experimental group. Much of this critical research was
incidental to the development of personality tests, which was the
first program of scientific psychology to include the problem of personality traits and types. The relative success of Woodworth's
Personal Data Sheet (1918a) in screening recruits during World
War I had set off a chain reaction of personality test construction.
Most of the post-war tests varied or elaborated the questionnaire
approach, some concentrating on a single dimension of personality;
others, like the Bernreuter, attempting to assess several factors.

COMMON TRAITS OR UNIQUE TRAITS? Among those which focused upon what appeared to be a single dimension was the A–S
Reaction Study (1928a, 1928b) jointly produced by Gordon Allport
and his brother Floyd. This enjoyed a good deal of popularity for
several years, subject to the qualification which applies to all questionnaire methods that depend upon *face validity*—viz., that many
of the questions invite the subject to check the socially acceptable
answer rather than the true one. It is interesting that Gordon All-

port later used the "ascendance–submission dimension" presumably measured by this test to illustrate the fictional character of the "common traits" discovered by statistical procedures (1937, pages 332–37). Certain test scores or groupings of test answers may suggest that they reflect real traits which are normally distributed in the population, whereas the truth may be that the "normal curve" is an artifact of the test constructor's choice of items and of the subject's choice of answers. The constructor eliminates questions that produce a distribution of answers incompatible with the normal curve, and the subjects tend to choose answers that conform with approved standards of behavior whether or not their behavior accords with such standards.

Common traits, according to Allport's mature judgment, are not real (*veridical*) traits, but are rather a reflection of social pressures that bring a semblance of conformity to the behavior of those who share a common culture. Relax the social standard, or change the conditions under which the trait is tested, and its ephemeral quality will become apparent. This can explain the results obtained in the elaborate Hartshorne, May, and Shuttleworth Character Education Inquiry (1930). In this there appeared clear evidence that children who would not steal money might cheat in the classroom; that those who would not cheat under supervision might when they were unsupervised; that those who would not cheat in arithmetic might have no scruples about misrepresenting their achievement on a physical task they had been left to perform in the gymnasium, etc. The investigators concluded that such inconsistencies argued in favor of specific habits rather than generalized traits of personality.

Allport construes the data differently. The surface inconsistencies in a person's behavior could still exist even though a single unifying principle—*radix*, to use Wertheimer's term for it—determined all his behavior. A book lover who cherishes every volume in his own library may return in bad shape a book he has borrowed from a friend. The question is, what is the veridical trait? It is certainly not love of books, but love of the extended self. What is his he values as he values himself; what belongs to others does not warrant such solicitous care. Allport's concept of personality, therefore, is constructed upon a theory of interwoven and integrating root traits—individual traits (1937), or, as he has more recently (1961) described them, *personal dispositions* ("p.d.'s").

Personality is the dynamic organization within the individual of those psychophysical systems that determine his characteristic behavior and thought (1961, page 28). . . . We view personality . . . as a network of organization, composed of systems within systems, some . . . somewhat peripheral to the central or propriate structure, other systems of wider scope at the core of the total edifice . . . some so culturally conforming that they can readily be viewed as "common"; others definitely idiosyncratic. But in the last analysis this network—employing billions and billions of nerve cells, fashioned by a one-time heredity and by environmental experiences never duplicated—is ultimately unique (1961, page 360).

In this account the "network of organization" results from the "forming of *patterns or hierarchies* of ideas and habits" (page 28; italics added). In one man specific habits of honesty, once developed in money situations, in school performances, in scrupulous reporting of facts rather than falsehood, may become organized into a higher order honesty of an abstract sort that becomes so rigid in its operation that he may be unable to relax it even to the extent of offering a graceful compliment or softening the blow of a crushing truth. In another person the precepts of honesty may become tied up with his attitudes toward society—general hostility to others, class prejudices, sentimentalities, resistance to conformity, etc.—which would determine just how, when, and toward whom his honesty would be called into play. The dishonesty of the tax-dodgers, the Robin Hoods, the slanderers, the demagogues and charlatans of our society is probably a reflection of the unique organization within each individual in these categories of a trait of honesty in the bad company of other traits which contaminate it and distort its expression. The infinite range of combinations guarantees the uniqueness of each individual. Roughly he may be fitted into a type or stereotype on the basis of some surface resemblance to others, but closer study of those who compose the "type" would reveal their differences.

THE PRINCIPLE OF FUNCTIONAL AUTONOMY. The word "dynamic" in Allport's definition is also significant. These uniquely organized structures within the person contribute in an important way to his motivations. Allport does not deny that visceral needs provide part of the answer to the Why of behavior. An infant will eat when and because he is hungry, but a child's hunger drive is not sufficient to account for an adult's eating behavior. The adult's taste for special foods, his regular hours for eating, the setting in which he customarily chooses to eat, and the equipment he uses all become part of the pattern, so that he may sometimes elect to stay hungry rather than compromise on the standards he has come to regard as "correct."

The Englishman in the jungle dining in formal attire could serve as a caricature of a principle of motivation proposed by Woodworth in 1918 as an alternative or supplement to McDougall's instinct theory: "Mechanisms may become drives" (1918b). The means to an end may become an end in itself. Illustrations can be offered from many commonplace activities of everyday life, and Allport has supplied some that have become famous in support of his principle of *functional autonomy*—the general law by which the proliferation of unique dynamic traits within an individual can be explained:

> An ex-sailor has a craving for the sea. . . . Now the sailor may have first acquired his love for the sea as an incident in his struggle to earn a living. The sea was "secondary reinforcement" for his hunger drive. But now the ex-sailor is perhaps a wealthy banker; the original motive is destroyed, and yet the hunger for the sea persists and even increases in intensity (1961, page 227).

By such a principle much of the compulsive behavior of old fogeys —and William James has pointed out that old-fogeyism begins to rear its head in the mid-twenties!—could be explained. On the more positive side so also could the commitment of a painstaking worker to turning out a high-quality product.

Allport has moderated his early position on functional autonomy, and in his 1961 version has come to grips with several criticisms leveled against his early presentation. To Neal Miller's argument (1951) that a strong acquired drive may be slow to extinguish if there is higher order reinforcement or if new reinforcing effects occur, Allport concedes that some apparently autonomous behavior may prove on investigation to be the effect of delayed reinforcement: ". . . if with the passage of time an acquired interest disappears (extinguishes) we are not dealing with functional autonomy; but many cases of 'delayed extinction' are apparently *permanently* delayed, and in these cases we conclude that functional autonomy is therefore involved" (1961, page 246). On challenges from other sources, including the psychoanalytic, he replies:

> . . . it is not always possible to determine whether a given motive is rooted in drives, in infantile fixation, in sublimations, or in wholly adult formulations of life. For that matter, a motive may reflect a combination of forces: infant and adult, instinctive and intentional, conscious and unconscious. . . . we cannot declare that a motive is always *either/or*. . . . motives may show many degrees of purity and impurity in respect to functional autonomy. . . .
>
> In principle, however, we can say that *to the extent that a present motive seeks new goals (i.e., manifests a different kind of tension from the motives from which it developed) it is functionally autonomous* (page 244).

THE PROPRIUM. Partly to avoid the ambiguities of the terms *self* and *ego*, partly to incorporate meanings associated with both, Allport has chosen the term *proprium* to designate those features of the personality that come to have a special "importance to the emotional life of the individual." It has been widely recognized that the newborn infant is selfless; that evidences of awareness of self in its several aspects appear gradually through adolescence and even into maturity (James, Piaget, Erikson, Sullivan, etc.), and that this development is closely related to the individual's social adjustment pattern. Allport has done much to bring order to the varieties of thinking on this subject of ego and self (1943, 1950, 1955) by summarizing and classifying under eight categories the formulations that have been offered. Among these will be recognized the contributions made by theorists we have discussed in earlier chapters. The aspects of the proprium are (1955, pages 41–54):

1. *Bodily sense:* the accumulation of sensory data from the body itself which eventually adds up to the individual's awareness of his own physical organism as an integrated object distinct from other objects, and different in the sense of being identified with him.
2. *Self-identity:* a growing sense of the continuity of one's existence, founded not only upon bodily sense, but to a great extent also on the building up of experiences in which one remembers having participated.
3. *Ego-enhancement:* the focusing of positive values upon the self—self-interest, self-esteem, self-love.
4. *Ego-extension:* the stretching of personal identity to include one's possessions, activities, thoughts, friends, groups, nation, etc.
5. *Ego as rational agent:* or in Allport's later phrasing, the self as *rational coper* either in the sense of providing defenses or in marshalling the resources of the organism to cope with the problems of the environment.
6. *Self-image:* that concept of oneself which, for better or for worse, plays an important part in steering and shaping one's personality development.
7. *Propriate striving:* the directive function, growing out of the higher order personal dispositions, which formulates aims and works toward goals far beyond the instant satisfaction of bodily needs and the release of tension emphasized in S–R theory. In Allport's view, as in Murray's, man is *proactive* as well as reactive. He can and does take initiative in reaching beyond the present moment to plan a future for himself—a future which may be costly in terms of his present and the intervening period, but for which he may even be willing to sacrifice his life.
8. *The self as knower:* Allport grapples here, as did William James, with the issue of whether there is a transcendent self ("the pure ego") beyond the self-aspects covered in the first seven categories. He concludes that scientific psychology must limit itself to the seven, lest the eighth aspect be contrived into an "homunculus"—

we might even call it an "intervening homunculus"—to take care of all unsolvable problems without the formality of scientific checks.

Allport has also distinguished *propriate functional autonomy* from *perseverative functional autonomy*. Some habits apparently perpetuate themselves without ever becoming geared into the central motivating systems. A limp may persist long after a fractured tibia has healed; the toss of a young head may outlast the wayward wisp of hair that originally required that gesture. Many of the routine activities of our lives would fit into the category of perseverative functional autonomy, for although we may develop favored ways of doing our daily chores, it would be hard to make a case for classifying these methods with the central motives that shape our lives. Unless they have some special significance for us, we are usually glad to have relief from the daily routines life imposes on us; and even the traditional busman who retraces his daily route when he drives the family to the beach over the weekend probably finds his pleasure in the differences that distinguish the holiday outing from the daily run, rather than in the resemblances. (Compare Hebb, page 185, this book.)

On the other hand, there are dedicated workers who cannot be persuaded to take a holiday. Propriate functional autonomy would account for some of these cases—those in which the workers have identified themselves with the task in which they are engaged. A research scientist does not regularly lock up his laboratory on Friday evening with the happy thought, "Well, I'm glad that's over!" When circumstances require that he separate himself from his project for a while, he "takes the project with him" or leaves a bit of himself behind for the interval. Propriate functional autonomy develops when a person has related a task, its purpose, or the manner of doing it with the central core of his personality. It has become an extended aspect of himself.

CONSISTENCIES OF PERSONALITY. Both common traits and p.d.'s contribute to the unity of personality, the latter perhaps more significantly than the former. The degree of unity will depend upon the number and the centrality of the motivational traits identifiable within any particular individual. Very rarely one hears of a person whose entire life or the major part of it can be understood on the basis of a single *cardinal trait*. Tolstoi has been described as such a person, his dominant disposition having been "simplification of life." We might venture to add some famous names from the history of the twentieth century whose cardinal trait has been power-lust; but in general the people we know are more likely to fit into the category of those who display several *central* dispositions of rather similar strength. The one-theme personality is likely to be found more often in fiction than in life. On the basis of some admittedly slender experimental evidence, Allport suggests that when adequate methods are established for determining the major p.d.'s on which a particular personality is structured, the answer will probably turn out to be between five and ten (1961, page 367). One of the difficulties in finding the answer to such a question is that earlier referred to in the study of honesty and in the example of the "inconsistent" book lover. The same surface behavior (phenotype) in different individuals may be an expression of quite dissimilar root motives (genotypes); or different phenotypes may arise from the same root motive. (Lewin and Allport have adapted to good effect this biological terminology in interpreting personality.) A high score in honesty on a classroom test may be the result in one case of strong ethical principles; in another, fear of getting caught; in a third, respect for the teacher; in a fourth, having complete assurance of knowing the answers to the questions! Deviations from honesty may be the result of anxiety, overcompetitiveness, underemphasis on the ethical breach when "only a school exam" is involved, or psychopathic personality. It is impossible to measure veridical traits on a scale designed to measure culture-determined behavior that will show a high degree of conformity as long as the cultural pressures are maintained.

Allport has also studied another kind of consistency which might be expected to reveal itself as the product of individual, integrated personal dispositions. This is a "congruence" which shows itself to some degree in expressive behavior such as handwriting, gait, voice quality, or—more generally stated—in "style." There has appeared much experimental evidence to support the hypothesis that *expressive* behavior, to the extent that it has been not too overlaid with conformity-producing learning, can be recognized and identified with some success if samples of behavior of the same subjects in different areas are matched by judges. *Coping behavior,* on the other hand, shows no such evidence of congruence across modalities. It is interesting that two samples of handwriting produced at different times will resemble each other more than two made on the same occasion when one is a deliberate copy of the other (1961, page 472). Ludwig Klages, the German characterologist and graphologist, has identified the influence of *Geist und Seele* upon behavior. These terms are usually translated literally as "mind" and "soul," but as he uses them they appear to have a sense closer to the superego and id (von Bracken, 1957, page 32. For a review of early work on the problem of expressive movement, see Allport and Vernon, 1933. For a summary of more recent studies, consult Bonner, 1961.)

THE BIOSOCIAL VERSUS THE BIOPHYSICAL APPROACH TO PERSONALITY. Although Allport has been one of our leading social psychologists and has made, alone and with others, memorable contributions to the experimental research and the literature of social psychology (1960), he has taken a biophysical rather than a biosocial position on the issue of personality. According to his view personality exists "within the skin" of each individual, notwithstanding the important influence of its transactions with the social and physical environments. In his 1961 revision he has given thoughtful consideration to the impact of culture and cultural roles and situations, but has maintained his original stand on the subject. His views therefore come into conflict with those of such theorists as Murphy, Nuttin, and Sullivan who believe that the person cannot be described realistically apart from the environmental context any more than he can be understood without taking into consideration his organic wholeness. It may be interesting, therefore, to contrast the account of the derivation of adult motives offered by two of these theorists with Allport's principle of functional autonomy, keeping in mind that they are all in agreement on the individuality of the person.

On the surface Murphy's principle of "canalization" seems to have a close resemblance to Allport's concept. In the satisfaction of his needs the individual adopts and uses consistently forms of behavior that he has found effective in the past. He turns again and again to the foods, the ways of thinking, speaking, writing, of "managing" people—even to the "fascinating" mistakes—that have proved in some way satisfying. In time he may progress to more effective canalizations, or he may regress to the earlier forms. But in Murphy's view (1947), the response is always made to reduce the same basic tissue tension, or—more correctly—to satisfy specific patterns of tissue tensions. Since it does not seek new goals or manifest a "different kind of tension from the motives from which it developed," it does not fit Allport's concept of functional autonomy. The two ideas are alike, however, in offering an account of the multiple motives which insure the uniqueness of each individual. (For more specific details, see Murphy, 1947, pages 178–80.)

Joseph Nuttin (professor of psychology at the University of Louvain, Belgium), applauds Allport's move to free adult motivation from any immediate connection with a limited number of organic needs or infantile drives; but he considers that the theory of functional autonomy "fails to provide personality with a dynamic system" (1957, page 185). Not all mechanisms become drives. In many cases the drive seems to grow out of the discrepancy between the results expected or hoped for and the achievement. When this gap is closed the activity may lose its attraction unless it can serve some other need in the ego–world relationship. A specific need is a "pattern of ego–world relations in a state of tension," and the tensions which arise at the adult level are not the same as those which arise in infancy, although there may be an identifiable similarity between the two. Nuttin's conclusion is that the abstract *fundamental need* will be represented at successive stages of development or in particular situations by a variety of concrete behavior patterns which in turn represent different degrees of generality. Gregarious behavior may be an expression of a relatively generalized need for contact with other human beings, or it may be an expression of a still more abstract need for self-actualization through better understanding and interaction with our social universe. The concrete need has an "I want" quality, and can be thought of as a task or project the individual undertakes to resolve his ego–world tensions. He may not understand the fundamental reason for the wanting, or may understand it only imperfectly; but failure in the task he has set for himself will have results beyond the temporary dissatisfaction that could be ascribed to an impersonalized tension that remains unreleased. "In a word, what hurts and disturbs is not the impersonal, unreleased energy, or the lack of need reduction, but the failure of the whole personality to accomplish the task or the project of satisfying the need" (1957, page 194).

Allport holds an impressive position in American psychology. He has found a way to balance and enrich it with the less rigid psychologies of Europe without losing sight of the values of the scientific approach. He has plotted a course for American psychology between the Scylla of tough-minded S–R theory and the Charybdis of "unruly" depth psychologies and existentialism. If the revised functional autonomy seems a less dependable marker than it appeared originally it at least serves to encourage other navigators to seek safe passage through that treacherous channel.

THE "PERSON" AS BEING AND BECOMING:
SOME CURRENT THEORY AND THERAPY

In the theory of the "person" which Carl Rogers (born 1902; now at the Western Behavioral Sciences Institute) has derived from observations and studies of the changes that take place in individuals in the course of *client-centered therapy* we meet many features that remind us of views set forth by the analytical theorists covered in the preceding chapters. We can identify in his formulations and in the protocols of his clients something analogous to the "idealized self-image" described by Horney. At times the impoverished "self" revealed by a patient seems to have the mask-like quality of Jung's "persona," lacking the real substance that is to be had just by reaching out and drawing upon the neglected wealth of the whole organism—a mine undiscovered or ignored because of defenses much like "selective inattention" or the "not-me" as these mechanisms have been conceived by Sullivan. In his stress upon the importance of understanding and of effective communication in the client–counselor relationship, Rogers is again close to Sullivan, closer, perhaps, than to therapists of the Freudian tradition. Yet though his views might have been considered in connection with any of these theories, they also fall naturally into place in a chapter devoted to theories which deal with personality as an organismic or holistic growth process. As basic to Rogers' position as to Goldstein's is the view that *self-actualization* is the single goal of the organism; and although at first sight his theory may seem to have little in common with the earlier theories of Calkins, Stern, and Dilthey, closer scrutiny reveals points of agreement that justify grouping his thought with theirs.

Rogers' first introduction to the problems, and the problem of personality, came through child guidance training at Teachers' College, Columbia University, New York. After a dozen or more years of applying that training, meanwhile building up his own convictions on the subject of effective techniques, he accepted a professorship at The Ohio State University in 1940. Shortly thereafter, through his publications (notably, *Counseling and Psychotherapy*, 1942) and his lecturing, he began to attract public attention to a new technique described as "non-directive," in which the role of the therapist appeared on the surface to be merely that of a permissive, understanding listener. However, in the full-blown development of the technique, it appears that a much deeper investment of himself is required of the therapist if the relationship is to be helpful to the client. For a vivid reconstruction of the empathic sharing of the patient's groping toward a healthy integration of his experiences, the reader is referred to Rogers' own accounts of the method (1961, Parts II and III).

His theory of the person has evolved in close relationship with this therapeutic method. Briefly, it presents a picture of the struggle between the self-actualizing *organism*, inherently ready to respond to everything in the *phenomenal field* (this being, much like Lewin's life space, the individual's interpretation of reality), and a *self* which selects some and rejects other features as a result of the values determined by experience and social norms. The self is really a part of the phenomenal field which has gradually come to be identified as "I" or "me," and which is therefore subject to the same subjective and objective evaluations as any other aspect of reality. Conflict may result from the discrepancies between his own evaluations and those introjected from parents and others who have a part in the development of the individual, with the consequence that he may distort or refuse to acknowledge aspects of himself or of his life experiences. When this unrealistic structure imposed upon the self leads to problems the individual can no longer cope with by himself, the therapist may help him to break through the rigid and distorted values by moving along understandingly, and with genuinely shared "affect," as the client gradually acknowledges and accepts the threatening feelings he had previously refused to recognize or had not dared to symbolize.

The effect upon the client is to replace the fixed self-image with a "process" of self-acceptance. According to the Rogerian view, the constant striving of the freely functioning organism does not allow for any final, completed fulfillment of the self. Consistency must be sought in the relationship between self and organism, rather than in the consistency of the self from day to day. In respect to this "process" concept of personality, Rogers is aligned with Adler, whose *creative self* implies the same continuing development, and with Gordon Allport who has emphasized "becoming" as an essential feature of the *proprium*. But in this feature of his theory and others, Rogers comes very close also to the existentialist position which has expressed itself prominently in the psychiatry and psychology of our era as well as in its philosophy, art, and literature. While he has maintained his independence of the existentialist influence, he has found merit in some of its principles and has also found methods of subjecting to research hypotheses derived from such principles (1961, Parts V and VI).

EXISTENTIAL PSYCHOLOGY. "To be that self which one truly is" epitomizes for Rogers the ideal relationship between the person and his organism. The words are a quotation from Sören Kierkegaard whose mid-nineteenth-century philosophy has had a strong influence on our contemporary existentialist thought. Kierkegaard objected to the prevailing philosophy of his day, Hegelian rationalism, which reduced man and truth to unrealistic abstractions by emphasizing "essence" rather than "existence." It is meaningless to speculate about man as a static object, for he is neither an "object," nor "static." He is, before and in spite of all speculation about him, a being, aware of his being and subject to anxiety at the threat of non-being. Kierkegaard has left a memorable treatise on anxiety— "the sickness unto death"—which has received greater recognition in the present existential movement than it commanded in its author's own lifetime (1954).

Truth, too, Kierkegaard held, must be recognized as something more than abstracted, objective reality. There is a subjective relational truth—that which the individual conceives to be true is true. Here what at first glimpse appears a shocking negation of reality can be recognized as another expression of the phenomenological view which has appeared several times before in these pages, implied in Lewin's *life space,* in Rogers' *phenomenal field,* in Murray's *beta press,* and in Allport's use of the concept of *proception* (Gordon Allport, 1961, pages 264–67) to describe the unique interpretation given by each individual to our common environment. Kierkegaard recognized, as do these others, that an observer with an "objective" attitude would remain far from the "truth" in any attempt to account for human behavior.

The "being" on which the existentialist bases his case is not easily described, and it can perhaps be best understood by citing instances in which the *sense of being* has been surrendered as the price of security. Fromm's "marketing personality" (1947) and Riesman's "other-directed" person (1950) would represent the repression of a sense of individuality or any acceptance of uniqueness. Rollo May, on the other hand, has referred to the emergence in a patient, during the course of therapy, of the *"I-am"* experience (May, *et al.,* 1958, page 43). In descriptions of existential theory, three terms appear together frequently: freedom, responsibility, courage. Man has the *freedom* to make choices, and the *responsibility* of fulfilling some purpose or giving some meaning to his life. Will he have the *courage to be?* (Paul Tillich has used these words as the title of his popular book, 1952.) In a somewhat different sense the courage to be is achieved through the ultimate self-affirmation of the Rogerian client who comes to acknowledge the feelings and emotions he had rigidly denied, or by the patient who at last comes to terms with the proscribed *not-me* (page 329, this book), or recognizes the falsity of an *idealized self-image* (page 321, this book).

The temptation is strong to trace the specific contributions to psychological thought which followed those of Kierkegaard in the philosophies of Friedrich Nietzsche, Edmund Husserl, Martin Heidegger, Karl Jaspers, Jean-Paul Sartre, Martin Buber, Gabriel Marcel, and others identified with the movement, but we must limit ourselves here to some generalizations on its significance. These might be classified under the following headings.

1. *The spotlighting of philosophical issues too often neglected in psychological literature and research.* The existentialist movement has drawn attention back to questions regularly pushed aside by those whose psychological horizons have been confined within the limits imposed by prevailing philosophies of science and principles of experimental design. The problem of man's freedom of choice, the problem of the self as "knower" and integrator as against the self as object, the problem of the differentiating effect upon human behavior of man's unique knowledge of the inevitability of death, are not matters on which psychologists have qualified themselves to give final answers; yet not infrequently the covert answer to one or another of these issues will be implicit in the experimental method used or the breadth of the generalization drawn. It is good to have such questions aired, even though the promise of reaching scientific agreement on them is slight.

2. *The development of new clinical concepts and techniques.* Existential therapists have not, as a group, identified themselves with a distinctive clinical procedure, although the movement has provided a growing pool of concepts and techniques which have been found effective in helping patients to recognize and fulfill their highest abilities. In this process *encounter* has been noted as playing an important part. This may be brief or enduring, may occur in or out of a therapeutic relationship; but the effect is a dramatic transformation of personality in which the significant social contact appears to operate as a catalytic influence rather than as a model with whom the patient identifies or on whom transference is established.

Viktor Frankl's *logotherapy* represents another variant of standard analytical procedure (1955). Existential analysis has the function of making the patient face his own responsibility for making decisions. Logotherapy, based on rational thinking about values rather than on the probing of emotional depths, is effective when the patient is struggling with situational problems for which he has no readily available philosophical solutions.

In distinguishing among the "biological, sociological, and psychological" factors involved in the shaping of human personality, Frankl is saying much the same thing as does Ludwig Binswanger who speaks of three "modes of world." Both these men, independently, have worked out systems of psychotherapy which depart radically from psychoanalytic philosophy. In contrast to Freud's emphasis on the pleasure motive, and to Adler's emphasis on the power motive, Frankl stresses the *will to meaning* as the primary dynamic force in man's life. Binswanger, once a member of the Zurich psychoanalytic group, transferred his affiliation to the Vienna Society when Jung defected from the Freudian camp. In the years following, with Eugene Minkowski, he was a leader in the development of a phenomenological psychiatry and a form of therapy designed around man as a "being-in-the-world," a concept of Heidegger's which imposes a biosocial significance on the term *personality* (see page 378, this book). Details of the rationale and development of the existential analytic movement, which has had a profound influence on European thought, can be found in *Existence* by Rollo May and others (1958).

Of the three modes of experience which play their part in man's life, according to Binswanger the *Umwelt* comprises the biological circumstances to which each person must adjust. The *Mitwelt* represents the world of the individual's social relationships (as distinguished from an objectively conceived world of people). The *Eigenwelt* involves the individual's relationship to himself. Of this last Rollo May says:

. . . What does it mean to say, "the self in relation to itself"? What goes on in the phenomena of consciousness, of self-awareness? What happens in "insight" when the inner gestalt of a person reforms itself? . . . Each of these phenomena goes on almost every instant with all of us . . . Yet, perhaps precisely because they are so near to us, no one knows what is happening in these events. This mode of the self in relation to itself was the aspect of experience which Freud never really saw, and it is doubtful whether any school has as yet achieved a basis for adequately dealing with it. *Eigenwelt* is certainly the hardest mode to grasp in the face of our Western technological preoccupations. It may well be that the mode of *Eigenwelt* will be the area in which most clarification will occur in the next decades (May, *et al.*, 1958, page 64).

The effect of disharmony among the modes and the disproportionate emphasis by the individual on one of them is illustrated in Binswanger's analysis of the case of Ellen West (May, *et al.*, 1958). Disproportionate emphasis on one or the other mode in any therapeutic method, Binswanger argues, will by the same token lead only to failure or partial results.

3. *The derivation from phenomenological philosophy and psychiatry of promising leads for experimental research.* The inconstancies of the experiences of space and time have invited speculation and study by many philosophers, including Husserl (1928) and

Heidegger (1949). Since these experiences seem to undergo systematic distortion in certain forms of mental disease they also receive careful attention from psychiatrists. Is the structure of space the same for a schizophrenic artist as it is for the normal man who views his creation with puzzlement? Time perception also presents problems. The relativity of the passage of time with age, with the degree of pleasure in the current activity; the estimate of time in the remote past or future, in contrast with the near past or future, are among the challenging questions considered by the phenomenologists and existentialists. The contributions of Minkowski (1933), Binswanger (1955), and Merleau-Ponty (1945) on such questions provide another tributary to the growing stream of interest in the psychology of perception. In the area of emotion, Jean-Paul Sartre's theory (1948) would be more difficult to reconcile with scientific standards, but even here careful distillation might provide something of value to psychology. (See Arnold's summary, 1960, Vol. 1, 158–61.)

The task of appraising the overall effect of existentialism upon American psychology is made difficult by the independent development in this country of somewhat parallel theories that have emphasized the uniqueness of the individual person, his forward drive toward self-actualization, and the character of the social interferences and the fears which may arrest progress on the way. Certainly there is much resemblance between what Goldstein, Maslow, Allport, and Rogers have to say and the thesis of the existentialists. But from the American group that has been most aware of the merits of the movement, including Rollo May who has been its able interpreter and commentator (1958, 1961) has come sharp criticism of its scientifically irresponsible features. Perhaps it would be correct to say that existentialism has reinforced the American revival of interest in conscious experience and has helped to counterbalance the extreme behaviorist's pull away from the "middle of the road."

12

The Middle of the Road

As we come now to the moment of taking stock, we are impressed with the significant changes that have taken place in the psychological scene since the half-way mark of the century. Shortly before that time we wrote, apropos of the different views and interests of psychologists:

> Their diverse lines of work do not usually result in the formation of "schools," . . . but to quite an extent the schools do represent different lines of work. The behaviorists are more interested in problems of learning, the Gestalt group more in problems of perception, the psychoanalysts more in motivation. The human individual, enmeshed in all the problems, is what holds the specializing groups of psychologists together, and we may hope that the interrelations of the problems will become increasingly evident with the general advance of the science. Already rapprochements are becoming visible (Woodworth, 1948, page 254).

In the years since, the *rapprochement* has been accelerated. If we pursue our traditional metaphor of the middle of the road, we might say that traffic has picked up in keeping with the times, for we find "cognitive" and "subjective" [1] behaviorists brushing shoulders with "experimental" psychoanalysts and self-theorists. We note, too, in the group, new impedimenta which have played a part in bringing the members of the procession closer together. In his day William James spoke with some concern about the threat of "brass instrument" psychology. What he had in mind was probably quite different from the digital computers and stereotaxic equipment [2] which have contributed so abundantly to psychological

[1] Miller, Galanter, and Pribram humorously describe themselves in this paradoxical way (1960, page 211).
[2] A device which makes possible precise localization of animal brain areas for purposes of experimental stimulation, cauterization, or implantation of electrodes.

theory on mental functioning; and he would probably welcome these as symbols of revived interest in the problems of the stream of thought, ideomotor action, and intention—matters which had given him cause for deep reflection.

Certainly one of the features of the present scene which distinguish it from that of the first half of the century has been the increased attention to long-neglected central factors in behavior. Perception is still a matter of interest to the Gestalt school. But it is no longer identified primarily with the Gestalt school, nor is it thought of now as a topic which can be disposed of neatly within its own narrow chapter of the textbook. It is now broadly recognized as an area of research that cannot be separated from motivation, learning, or personality. Perception is closely related to each of these, and they in turn have been found clearly to influence it (Bruner, 1951; Ittelson, 1960; Merleau-Ponty, 1945; Riesen, 1947; Witkin, *et al.*, 1954; Woodworth, 1947, 1958). Its functional role in the adaptation of the organism to the environment has been a prominent feature of many theories reviewed in these pages: Hebb's, Piaget's, Hartmann's, and Rapaport's, as well as Woodworth's, to mention only a few. Nominally behavioristic, functionalist, and psychoanalytic in their several points of departure, these have come to a measure of accord in the degree that they are all concerned with the "What?" "How?" and "Why?" of perception—the hallmark of the functionalist approach.

It would be a mistake to overstress the unanimity effect. Paradoxically, the same apparatus we have used as symbols of the *rapprochement* of the schools might serve also as symbols of division in their methods and their thinking. The renewed hope of discovering more exactly the physiological correlates of behavior revives the issue of "reductionism." The psychologist has much to gain by learning all he can about the functioning of the human organism; but his job does not end there. The molar aspects of human behavior—man's "plans," his "encounters" with the social environment, the uniqueness of his motivation, his normal sense of continuing self-identity—are among the countless problems that will not be thoroughly understood by pinpointing areas within the nervous system, however much such information may help in explaining some of their features. They represent an emergent dimension—a "different level of discourse."

Well apart from the middle-of-the-road group, we see, too, the mathematical theorists following in the paths cut by Bush and Mosteller, and by Estes. These have attracted much attention by the volume and the "elegance" of their research; yet, as we have seen, they have also drawn criticism for premature concern with method at the price of a narrowing range of interest in the kinds of psychological problems to be investigated. This charge has not been leveled only against the psychomathematicians, but against all the "tough-minded" caste bound by the orthodoxy of the philosophies of science that dominated the period between 1930 and 1950— the period of the rise of logical positivism, of the hypothetico-deductive method, of approved rigid formulas for developing psychological theory. Koch, who refers to it as the *Age of Theory* (1959, Vol. 3), has written a memorable passage summating the views of the scientific "code" of this period as they have been expressed by selected spokesmen for the various systems included in his volumes:

> No one is prepared to retreat one jot from the objectives and disciplines of scientific inquiry, but most are inclined to re-examine reigning stereotypes about the *character* of such objectives and disciplines. There is a longing, bred on perception of the limits of recent history and nourished by boredom, for psychology to embrace—by whatever means may prove feasible—problems over which it is possible to feel intellectual passion. The more adventurous ranges of our illimitable subject matter, so effectively repressed or bypassed during recent decades, are no longer proscribed.
>
> *For the first time in its history, psychology seems ready—or almost ready— to assess its goals and instrumentalities with primary reference to its own indigenous problems.* It seems ready to think contextually, freely, and creatively about its own refractory subject matter, and to work its way free from a dependence on simplistic theories of correct scientific conduct (page 783; italics as in the original).

Koch returns to this theme in a later paper (1961) in which he urges psychology to give up its slavish imitation of the "methods, forms, symbols of the established sciences," and develop its proper role as a social science—a "third force"—bridging the gap which separates the sciences from the humanities.

In another respect the psychological scene has been changing its complexion since World War II. Up to that time the pure science tradition which had been the heritage of psychology since the founding of the Leipzig laboratory of Wilhelm Wundt held undisputed sway, and the scientists bred in this tradition not infrequently assumed a Brahmin attitude toward their more practically oriented brothers in the clinical and industrial fields. With the rapid technological advances of the second half of the century, there has come a heavy demand upon the talents of psychologists by industry and by government. Within the same period the increased stresses of life, and a wider recognition of what the psychologist may be able to do to make them tolerable, have placed a heavier load upon those who concern themselves with the problems of mental health. The result has been a rather sharp rise in the number of psychologists engaged in "applying" psychology as against the number that dedicate themselves to academic research (Tryon, 1963). If the academic laboratory is conceived as the only or major source of the life stream of scientific psychology, this imbalance can obviously be a serious threat. But we have had evidence that scientific inquiry may be the more fruitful for having had its origin in the natural situations of real life. The modern ethologists make a special point of this desideratum. We have noted, too, the growing disposition of the clinician to turn to experiment, or to cast his theories in a form which makes experimentation by others possible (Rogers, 1961; Rapaport, 1960).

The rigorous empirical checks on the contributions of the "engineering psychologist" do not leave him long in doubt about the validity of his theorizing. One does not arrive at conclusions "intuitively" about the probable effects on man of traveling 17,500 miles an hour through outer space. Solutions for the more routine, prosaic problems of man's adjustment to his daily work environment demand no less realistic knowledge about the "human factors" involved. In our age of technology the "man–machine system" has been developed to minimize the margin of human error. The machine is designed to make optimal use of the operator's sensory and motor capacities; at the same time there is transferred to the machine any possible function which, left to the operator, might slow up reaction or in any way increase the risk of a faulty response. In this way a very technical task may be reduced to reading carefully designed dials ("displays"), and responding by manipulating ingeniously planned "controls." One might say that a new form of S–R chain goes into operation, since the response of one operator in a team provides the stimulus for the next in the system. But the jargon of the engineering psychologist is not that of the "schools." "Human behavior for this psychological *avant-garde* is a matter of inputs, outputs, storage, coding, transfer functions, and bandpass" (Taylor, 1957, 1960).

One more fact remains to be noted in our contrast of the current scene with that of the past. Much more prominent in the moving throng are distinguished representatives of other nations. We had become provincial for a generation or two in our attitude toward psychology, thinking of it mostly as a domestic product. American behaviorism was centered; and rather dimly we were aware, along the margins, of the contributions from abroad, mainly of our English-speaking colleagues and of those few other nations whose journals were most accessible to American readers. In this respect the situation has changed radically and happily. Our university libraries now provide the student of psychology with the increasingly rich output of many countries, and these journals, as well as our own, attest the active interchange of ideas that is taking place. We have mentioned earlier (page 8) the international conferences on current issues as another source of communication. During recent years a number of reports on international developments have appeared from time to time in the *American Psychologist*. It seems hardly necessary to add that with the lively inflow of concepts and methods from abroad, there is to be expected a gradual change of emphasis, interests, and even basic scientific philosophy.

What, then, of the schools? We have said little about them directly in these last few pages, yet they have had an implicit part in the selection of the items of our account. We have conceded that their outlines are now less firm than they were in the first two decades of the century, even less firm than they were in 1948 when our last accounting was made. The current practice is to speak or write about "theories" or "systems" of psychology, and this can be defended as perhaps a more appropriate description of the contemporary scene. But the "schools" are still with us. There are few psychologists even today who will shrug their shoulders indifferently at such questions as: "Are you a behaviorist?" "What do you think about psychoanalysis?" "Is there really any difference between organismic psychology and Gestalt?" British Associationism, the basis of much of our own behaviorism, is still an active movement. Even the teleological views of McDougall may receive another hearing in the light of cybernetic analogies. Perhaps we might describe the living, growing record of psychology as a palimpsest underneath which has been engraved the now somewhat obscured but ever enduring history of the schools.

Robert S. Woodworth:
A Bibliography

1897

Note on the rapidity of dreams. *Psychol. Rev.*, **4**, 524–26.

1898

(Asst. ed.) *Psychological Index.* New York: The Macmillan Co. Vol. V, 173 pp.

1899

The accuracy of voluntary movement. (Dissertation for the degree of Doctor of Philosophy, Columbia University.) *Psychol. Rev. Monogr.*, **3**, No. 13, 114 pp.

(Asst. ed.) *Psychological Index.* New York: The Macmillan Co. Vol. VI, 174 pp.

The best movement for handwriting. *Science*, **10**, 679–81.

(Review) *Les Origines de la psychologie contemporaine.* D. Mercier. Paris: Alcan, 1897, 486 pp. In *Psychol. Rev.*, **6**, 307–10.

(Review) *Zur Analyse der Unterschiedsempfindlichkeit.* L. J. Martin and G. E. Müller. Leipzig: S. A. Barth, 1898, 223 pp. In *Science*, **10**, 818–19.

1900

The exposition. The beautiful city of Paris, and other matters of interest from France. *Berlin [Connecticut] News*, September 27, 1900.

Fourth International Congress of Psychology. *Science*, **12**, 605–6.

With E. L. Thorndike. The influence of special training on general ability. *Psychol. Rev.*, **7**, 140–41.

Judgments of magnitude by comparison with a mental standard. *Psychol. Rev.*, **7**, 344–55.

Studies in the contraction of smooth muscles. *Amer. J. Physiol.*, **3**, 26–44.

1901

With E. L. Thorndike. The influence of special training on general ability. *Psychol. Rev.*, **8**, 164–65.

With E. L. Thorndike. The influence of improvement in one mental function upon the efficiency of the other functions. *Psychol. Rev.*, **8**, 247–61, 384–95, 558–64.

With E. A. Schäfer. Note on the results of circumsection of the motor cortex. *J. Physiol.*, **26** (Proceedings of January 26), xxiii–xxv.

On the fatigue of nerve centers. *N. Y. U. Bull. med. Sciences*, **1**, No. 3.

On the rate of fatigue of nerve centers. *Amer. J. Physiol.*, **5**, 4–5.

On the voluntary control of the force of movement. *Psychol. Rev.*, **8**, 350–59.

(Review) Beiträge zur Lehre von der Lage–und Bewegungsempfindungen. F. Kramer and G. Moskiewicz. *Z. Psychol.*, **25** (1901), 101–25. In *Psychol. Rev.*, **8**, 440–41.

(Review) *Bibliotics, or the study of documents*. P. Frazer. 1901, 266 pp. In *Science*, **14**, 291–92.

(Review) Creeping and walking. A. W. Trettien. *Amer. J. Psychol.*, **12** (1900), 1–57. In *Psychol. Rev.*, **8**, 439.

(Review) Experiments upon the control of the reflex wink. G. E. Partridge. *Amer. J. Psychol.*, **11** (1900), 244–50. In *Psychol. Rev.*, **8**, 316.

(Review) On the correlation of mental and motor ability in school children. W. C. Bagley. *Amer. J. Psychol.*, **12** (1901), 193–205. In *Psychol. Rev.*, **8**, 439–40.

(Review) Ueber den Einfluss einiger psychischer Zustände auf Kniephänomen und Muskeltonus. O. Vogt. *Z. Hypnotismus*, **10** (1900), 202–18. In *Psychol. Rev.*, **8**, 314–15.

(Review) Zur Kenntniss des Einflusses einiger psychischer Zustände auf die Atmung. D. Isenberg and O. Vogt. *Z. Hypnotismus*, **10** (1900), 131–58. In *Psychol. Rev.*, **8**, 314–15.

Section of Anthropology and Psychology of the New York Academy of Sciences. *Science*, **13**, 662–63, 864–65.

Section of Anthropology and Psychology of the New York Academy of Sciences. *Science*, **14**, 934–35, 971.

1902

Maximal contraction, "staircase" contraction, refractory period, and compensatory pause of the heart. *Amer. J. Physiol.*, **8**, 213–48.

(Review) *L'Audition*. P. Bonnier. Paris: Doin, 1901, 276 pp. In *Psychol. Rev.*, **4**, 323–24.

Section of Anthropology and Psychology of the New York Academy of Sciences. *Science*, **15**, 309–10, 547–627, 907–8.

1903

The electric conductivity of mammalian nerve. University of Liverpool. *Thompson Yates and Johnston Laboratories Report*, **5**, Part 1, 61–66.

Le Mouvement. Paris: Doin, 421 pp.

1904

With C. S. Sherrington. A pseudaffective reflex and its spinal path. *J. Physiol.*, **31**, 234–43.

Subcortical expressive reflexes and their spinal pathways. *Amer. Med.*, **7**, 4–5.

1905

Color sense in different races of mankind. *Proceedings Soc. Exper. Biol. Med.*, **3**, 24–26.

With H. D. Marsh. Motor correlations. *Psychol. Bull.*, **2**, 49.

(Review) W. H. Winch. Immediate memory in school children. *Brit. J. Psychol.*, **1** (1904), 127–34. In *J. Philos.*, **2**, 136–38.

(Review) Influence de l'intensité lumineuse sur certaines phases de l'excitation rétinienne. M. Bourdon. *Bull. Soc. scien. méd. de l'ouest.* Ier Trimestre, 1905. In *J. Philos.*, **2**, 585.

(Review) La Durée des sensations visuelles élémentaires. P. Janet. *Bull. Inst. Gén. Psychol.*, **4** (1904), 540–54. In *J. Philos.*, **2**, 584–85.

(Review) *Principles of physiological psychology*. W. Wundt. Trans. by E. B. Titchener. New York: The Macmillan Co., Vol. I, 1904, 347 pp. In *Science*, **22**, 789–90.

(Review) *Technique de psychologie expérimentale*. E. Toulouse. Paris: Doin, 1904, 335 pp. In *Science*, **22**, 523–24.

(Review) Über einige Grundfragen der Psychologie der Übungsphänomene im Bereiche des Gedächtnisses zugleich ein Beitrag sur Psychologie der formalen Geistesbildung. E. Ebert and E. Meumann. *Arch. gesammte Psychol.*, **4** (1904), 1–232. In *J. Philos.*, **2**, 136–38.

Section of Anthropology and Psychology of the New York Academy of Sciences. *Science*, **21**, 469–71, 860–61.

Section of Anthropology and Psychology of the New York Academy of Sciences. *Science*, **22**, 835–36.

With E. G. Brunner. Some sex differences. *Psychol. Bull.*, **2**, 48.

1906

The cause of a voluntary movement. In *Studies in philosophy and psychology by former students of Charles Edward Garman*. Boston: Houghton Mifflin Co., 411 pp. Chap. XII, pp. 351–92.

Discussion of papers at American Psychological Association. *Psychol. Bull.*, **3**, 61.

(Ed.) *Archives of psychology*. New York: Columbia University.

Imageless thought. *J. Philos.*, **3**, 701–7.

Psychiatry and experimental psychology. *Amer. J. Insanity*, **63**, 27–38.

(Review) *Das Farbenempfindungssystem der Hellenen*. W. Schultz. Leipzig: S. A. Barth, 1904, 227 pp. In *J. Philos.*, **3**, 21–25.

Section of Anthropology and Psychology of the New York Academy of Sciences. *J. Philos.*, **3**, 16–21, 267–71, 351–57.

Vision and localization during eye movements. *Psychol. Bull.*, **3**, 68–70.

1907

Non-sensory components of sense perception. *J. Philos.*, **4**, 169–76. (Abstract in *Psychol. Bull.*, **4**, 217–18.)

(Review) *La misura in psicologia sperimentale.* A. Aliotta. Firenze: Galetti and Cocci, 1905, 253 pp. In *J. Philos.*, **4**, 131–35.

Section of Anthropology and Psychology in the New York Academy of Sciences. *J. Philos.*, **4**, 76–79, 435–40.
El Movimiento. Spanish trans. by Domingo Vaca of *Le Mouvement*, 1903. Madrid: Daniel Jorro, 448 pp.

1908

The consciousness of relation. *Essays philosophical and psychological, in honor of William James, by his colleagues at Columbia University*. New York: Longmans, Green & Co., 1908, 610 pp. Part II, Chap. 11, pp. 483–507.
Function and feeling. *Psychol. Bull.*, **5**, 46–47.
Proceedings of the American Psychological Association. Chicago. *Psychol. Bull.*, **5**, 33–52.
Psychology. (A Lecture Delivered at Columbia University in the Series on "Science, Philosophy and Art," March 11, 1908). New York: Columbia University Press, 1908, 29 pp.
(Review) *Doctrine of primary and secondary sensory elements*. B. Sidis. *Psychol. Rev.*, **15**, 44–68, 106–21. In *J. Philos.*, **5**, 472–74.
(Review) *The integrative action of the nervous system*. C. S. Sherrington. New Haven: Yale University Press, 1906, 411 pp. In *Science*, **27**, 885–89.
Section of Anthropology and Psychology of the New York Academy of Sciences. *J. Philos.*, **5**, 41–44, 212–16, 412–15.
Section of Anthropology and Psychology of the New York Academy of Sciences. *Science*, **27**, 890–91.

1909

Hermann Ebbinghaus. *J. Philos.*, **6**, 253–56.
The physiology of the nervous system. *Psychotherapy*, No. II, 67–77; No. III, 81–92.
How the psychological mechanism works. *Psychotherapy*, No. IV, 68–84.
Present-day methods of teaching philosophy. Lake Erie College, Jubilee Commencement, 50th Anniversary. Cleveland, Ohio; pp. 121–30.
The problems and methods of psychology. Mimeographed.
(Review) *A text-book of psychology*. E. B. Titchener. New York: The Macmillan Co., 311 pp. In *J. Philos.*, **6**, 692–94.
Section of Anthropology and Psychology of the New York Academy of Sciences. *J. Philos.*, **6**, 208–14.
Section of Anthropology and Psychology of the New York Academy of Sciences. *Science*, **30**, 775–76.

1910

American education. *Science*, **32**, 760–61.
(Assoc. ed.) *Psychol. Bull.*, 1910 through 1925.
(Ed., Sections on Race and Individual Psychology) *Psychol. Bull.*, **7**, No. 10.
The puzzle of color vocabularies. *Psychol. Bull.*, **7**, 325–34.
Racial differences in mental traits. *Science*, **31**, 171–86.
(Review) Associative Massenversuche. G. Saling. *Z. Psychol.*, **49** (1908), 238–53. In *Psychol. Bull.*, **7**, 349–51.

(Review) Beiträge zur Associationslehre auf Grund von Massenversuchen. F. Reinhold. Z. Psychol., **54** (1909), 183–214. In Psychol. Bull., **7,** 349–51.

(Review) The distribution and functions of mental imagery. G. H. Betts. New York: Teachers College, Columbia University, 1909, 99 pp. In Psychol. Bull., **7,** 351–52.

(Review) Educational psychology. 2nd ed. E. L. Thorndike. New York: Teachers College, Columbia University, 1910, 248 pp. In Psychol. Bull., **7,** 342–46.

(Review) Lectures on the experimental psychology of the thought-processes. E. B. Titchener. New York: The Macmillan Co., 1909, 318 pp. In Science, **31,** 224–26.

(Review) Manual of mental and physical tests. G. M. Whipple. Baltimore: Warwick, 1910, 534 pp. In Psychol. Bull., **7,** 346–48.

(Review) An outline of individual study. G. E. Partridge. New York: Sturgis and Walton, 1910, 240 pp. In Psychol. Bull., **7,** 348.

(Review) A study of association in insanity. G. H. Kent and A. J. Rosanoff. Amer. J. Insanity, **67** (1910), 37–96. In Psychol. Bull., **7,** 349–51.

Section of Anthropology and Psychology of the New York Academy of Sciences. J. Philos., **7,** 216–18, 238–40.

1911

American educational defects. Science, **33,** 107.

With F. L. Wells. Association tests. Psychol. Rev. Monogr., **13,** No. 57, 85 pp.

Learning without insight in the chimpanzee. (Unpublished research done in the laboratory of G. S. Sherrington in 1902–3). A brief report in Physiol. Psychol. New York: Charles Scribner's Sons, 1911, 704 pp. Chap. VIII, pp. 552–53.

New York Branch of the American Psychological Association. J. Philos., **8,** 125–29, 460–67.

On factors contributing to a low scientific productivity in America. Science, **33,** 374–79.

With G. T. Ladd. Physiological psychology. Rev. ed. New York: Charles Scribner's Sons, 1911. 704 pp.

Psychology in the college course. Educ. Rev., **41,** No. 205, 499–506.

The psychology of light. Transactions of the Illuminating Eng. Soc., **6,** 437–71.

Reflex action. Psychol. Bull., **8,** 126–30.

Voluntary phenomena—experimental. Psychol. Bull., **8,** 375–78.

1912

(Address) German psychology—as observed during a visit in the summer semester of 1912. Bonn; 14 pp.

Combining the results of several tests: A study in statistical method. Psychol. Rev., **9,** 97–123.

Laboratory manual. Experiments in memory, etc. Mimeographed, 49 pp.

Mental efficiency. Mental Hygiene Congress, Report, 214–18.

National psychology. Psychol. Bull., **9,** 397–99.

(Review) *Geschichte der Psychologie.* O. Klemm. Leipzig: B. G. Teubner, 1911, 387 pp. In *J. Philos.*, 9, 218–20.

1913

Care of the body. New York: The Macmillan Co., 1913, 354 pp.

Cerebellum and brain-stem. *Psychol. Bull.*, 10, 138–42.

The preponderance of evidence. *Case and Comment*, 827–31.

The problems and methods of psychology. Part I. Rev. 1913, 132 pp. Mimeographed. (An edition antedating *Experimental psychology* by R. S. Woodworth and A. T. Poffenberger, 1920.)

(Review) *Nervous and Mental Disease Monograph Series.* Ed. by S. E. Jelliffe and W. A. White. 1907–1913. Vols. I-XV. In *Science*, 38, 927–31.

(Review) *The science of human behavior.* M. Parmelee. New York: The Macmillan Co., 1913, 443 pp. In *Science*, 37, 416–17.

1914

College curriculum. *Science*, 40, 315–16.

Conference on Individual Psychology. *Science*, 39, 731–32.

A contribution to the question of "Quick learning, quick forgetting." *Psychol. Bull.*, 11, 58–59.

(Ed., Sections on Race and Individual Psychology) *Psychol. Bull.*, 11, No. 10.

Experimental psychology. Part II. Rev. 1914, 115 pp. Mimeographed. (An edition antedating *Experimental psychology* by R. S. Woodworth and A. T. Poffenberger, 1920.)

Professor Cattell's psychophysical contributions. (The psychological researches of James McKeen Cattell: A review by some of his pupils.) *Arch. Psychol.*, No. 30, 60–74.

(Review) *Ancient Rome and Modern America: A comparative study of morals and manners.* G. Ferrero. New York: G. P. Putnam's Sons, 352 pp. In *Psychol. Bull.*, 11, 440–41.

(Review) *The elements of psychology.* D. B. Major. Columbus, Ohio: Adams, 1913, 413 pp. In *Science*, 40, 821.

(Review) *Mind and health, with an examination of some systems of divine healing.* E. E. Weaver. New York: The Macmillan Co., 1913, 500 pp. In *Science*, 39, 71.

Voluntary phenomena—experimental. *Psychol. Bull.*, 11, 402–4.

1915

The influence of retention of conditions favoring quickness of learning. *J. Philos.*, 12, 246.

(Review) *L'Année psychologique.* Nineteenth Year. 1913. Ed. by H. Piéron. Paris: Masson, 515 pp. In *J. Philos.*, 12, 329–32.

(Review) *The man of genius.* H. Türck. New York: The Macmillan Co., 1914, 483 pp. In *Psychol. Bull.*, 12, 421–22.

A revision of imageless thought. Address of the President before the American Psychological Association, at Philadelphia, December, 1914. *Psychol. Rev.*, 22, 1–27.

Voluntary phenomena. *Psychol. Bull.*, 12, 408–11.

1916

The better retention of longer memory lessons. *Psychol. Bull.*, **13**, 65.

Comparative psychology of races. *Psychol. Bull.*, **13**, 388–97.

(Ed., Sections on Race and Individual Psychology) *Psychol. Bull.*, **13**, No. 10.

Followers of Freud and Jung. *Nation*, **103**, 396.

Voluntary phenomena. *Psychol. Bull.*, **13**, 416–21.

1917

(Review) *Mental conflicts and misconduct.* W. Healy. Boston: Little, Brown and Co., 1917, 330 pp. In *Science*, **46**, 461–62.

Some criticisms of the Freudian psychology. *J. abn. soc. Psychol.*, **12**, 174–94.

1918

Dynamic psychology. New York: Columbia University Press, 210 pp.

1919

(Ed., Sections on Race and Individual Psychology) *Psychol. Bull.*, **16**, No. 11.

Examination of emotional fitness for warfare. *Psychol. Bull.*, **16**, 59–60.

Personal data sheet. Chicago: Stoelting, 1919, 4 pp.

1920

With B. T. Baldwin, Ed. of Child Education, Race and Individual Psychology. *Psychol. Bull.*, **17**, No. 11.

The teaching of psychology. In Klapper, P. (Ed.). *College teaching.* Yonkers, N. Y.: World Book Co., 1920, 583 pp. Chap. XVI, pp. 334–46.

With A. T. Poffenberger. Textbook of experimental psychology. Mimeographed in 1920, 285 pp.; remimeographed in 1932.

1921

Psychology: A study of mental life. New York: Henry Holt, 1921, 580 pp.

1922

Physiology and psychology. *Essays and studies in honor of Margaret Barclay Wilson.* New York: Columbia University Press, 1922, 151 pp. Chap. XV, pp. 136–48.

(Review) *The beloved ego, foundations of the new study of the psyche.* W. Stekel. London: Kegan Paul, 1921, 237 pp. In *New York Evening Post*, December 9, 1922.

(Review) *The depths of the soul.* W. Stekel. London: Kegan Paul, 1922, 216 pp. In *New York Evening Post*, December 9, 1922.

(Review) *Fundamental conceptions of psychoanalysis.* A. A. Brill. New York: Harcourt, Brace, 1921, 344 pp. In *New York Evening Post*, December 9, 1922.

(Review) *Mysticism, Freudianism and scientific psychology.* K. Dunlap. St. Louis: C. V. Mosby Co., 1920, 173 pp. In *J. Philos.*, **19**, 101–9.

(Review) *Psychoanalysis*. R. H. Hingley. London: Methuen & Co., Ltd., 1922, 190 pp. In *New York Evening Post*, December 9, 1922.

1924

Four varieties of behaviorism. *Psychol. Rev.*, **31**, 257–64.

Four varieties of behaviorism and the lack of inherent connection between them. *Psychol. Bull.*, **21**, 89.

1925

(Advisory ed.) *Psychol. Rev.*, 1925 through 1929.

Psychological experience with the interview. *J. Personnel Res.*, **4**, 162–65.

The relationship of man and animals. *Sci. Monthly*, **21**, 147–49.

(Review) *Social psychology*. F. H. Allport. Boston: Houghton Mifflin Co., 1924, 453 pp. In *J. abn. soc. Psychol.*, **20**, 92–106.

The Scopes case and "constitutional rights" of the teacher. *School and Society*, **22**, 274–75.

Similarities of structure show relationship of man and animals. *Science Service*, No. 222B, pp. 1–5.

Testing and training the memory. *Sci. Monthly*, **20**, 111–12.

1926

Contributions to animal psychology. (In honor of Edward Lee Thorndike on his twenty-fifth anniversary as Professor in Teachers College.) *Teachers College Record*, **27**, No. VI, 516–20.

Dynamic psychology. In Murchison, C. (Ed.). *Psychologies of 1925*. Worcester, Mass.: Clark University Press, 1926, 412 pp. Chap. V, pp. 111–25. Also in *Pedagog. Seminary*, **33**, 103–18.

Fact finding devices used in psychology. (A Memorandum Prepared for the Committee on Methods of Research in Industrial Relations, Personnel Research Federation.) 1926, 6 pp.

From the psychologist's point of view. *Amer. Child*, **8**, 4. Also *Elementary School J.*, **27**, 169–70.

Historical antecedents of the present child study movement. *Progressive Educ.*, **3**, 3–6.

Psychological data pertaining to errors of observation. *International Critical Tables*. New York: McGraw-Hill Book Co. Vol. I, 92–95.

[*Behavior psychology*]. Japanese trans. by N. Asahi of *Psychology*, 1921. Dairen, Manchuria, 446 pp.

1927

Gestalt psychology and the concept of reaction stages. (Washburn Commemorative Volume.) *Amer. J. Psychol.*, **39**, 62–69.

A justification of the concept of instinct. *J. abn. soc. Psychol.*, **22**, 3–7.

Motivation. Mimeographed. Lecture. 10 pp.

Table for finding the S. D. of the mental age distribution. New York: The Author, 4 pp.

1928

Computing the standard deviation and probable error of a Binet mental age. *Psychol. Bull.*, **25**, 167.

How emotions are identified and classified. In Reymert, M. L. (Ed.). *Feeling and Emotions; The Wittenberg Symposium*. Worcester, Mass.: Clark University Press, 454 pp. Chap. XVIII, pp. 222–27.
Woodworth's results. In Klineberg, O. An experimental study of speed and other factors in "racial" differences. *Arch. Psychol.*, No. 93, 111 pp. Chap. VI, pp. 87–90.

1929

Maturation and exercise. *Psychol. Bull.*, **26**, 14.
The nursery school and child development. *School and Society*, **29**, 497–504.
Psychology. In Gee, W. (Ed.). *Research in the Social Sciences*. New York: The Macmillan Co., 305 pp. Chap. V, pp. 151–77.
Psychology. Rev. ed. New York: Henry Holt, 590 pp.

1930

Christine Ladd-Franklin. *Science*, **71**, 307.
Dynamic psychology. In Murchison, C. (Ed.). *Psychologies of 1930*. Worcester, Mass.: Clark University Press, 497 pp. Chap. XVII, pp. 327–36.
How to discipline professors. *School and Society*, **31**, 398–99.
Ninth International Congress of Psychology. Report of the Treasurer. In *Psychol. Bull.*, **27**, 565–66.
(Review) *Colour and colour theories*. C. Ladd-Franklin. New York: Harcourt, Brace, 1929, 287 pp. In *Psychol. Bull.* **27**, 130–32.
(Review) *Foundations of experimental psychology*. Murchison, C. (Ed.). Worcester, Mass.: Clark University Press, 1929, 907 pp. In *J. gen. Psychol.*, **38**, 521–24.
(Review) *A history of experimental psychology*. E. G. Boring. New York: The Century Co., 1929, 699 pp. In *J. gen. Psychol.*, **38**, 521–24.

1931

(Amer. ed.) Contemporary Library of Psychology. 1931 onward.
Contemporary schools of psychology. New York: The Ronald Press Co., 232 pp.
Interrelation of statistical and case methods: Studies of young delinquents by John Slawson and Cyril Burt. In Rice, S. A. (Ed.). *Methods in social science*. Chicago: University of Chicago Press, 822 pp. Section VIII. Analysis 39, pp. 543–48.
Psychology. A quarter century of learning, 1904–1929. New York: Columbia University Press, 381 pp. Chap. VII, pp. 129–46.

1932

Old prejudices and new schools in psychology. (An address in the Psychology Series sponsored by the National Council on Radio in Education, on November 14, 1931. N. B. C.) In Bingham, W. V. (Ed.). *Psychology today*. Chicago: University of Chicago Press, pp. 38–46.
Robert S. Woodworth. In Murchison, C. (Ed.). *A history of psychology in autobiography*. Worcester, Mass.: Clark University Press, Vol. II, 359–80.

1933

Adjustment and mastery: Problems in psychology. Baltimore: The Williams
   & Wilkins Co., 137 pp.
Christine Ladd-Franklin. *Dictionary of American Biography,* 10, 528–30.

1934

(Address) Purposes of the Society for Research in Child Development.
   Washington, D. C., November 3, 1934.
Discussion on papers by Dr. Brickner and Dr. Fox and Dr. German. *Arch.
   Neurol. Psychiatry,* 31, 1120–21.
Edward Lee Thorndike: President of the American Association for the Ad-
   vancement of Science. *Sci. Monthly,* 38, 187–89.
Howard Crosby Warren. *Psychol. Rev.,* 41, 105–7.
Psychology. 3rd ed. New York: Henry Holt, 546 pp.
Shepherd Ivory Franz: 1874–1933. *Amer. J. Psychol.,* 46, 151–52.
(Special ed.) Psychology, Psychiatry, and so forth. *Webster's New Interna-
   tional Dictionary.* 2nd ed. Unabridged. Springfield, Mass.: G. and C.
   Merriam Co.

1935

With S. B. Sells. An atmosphere effect in formal syllogistic reasoning. *J.
   exper. Psychol.,* 18, 451–60.

1936

The psychophysical methods. Formulae, tables, and examples. New York:
   The Author, 19 pp.
Vi Og Umverda. Oslo: Det Norske Samlaget, 138 pp.

1937

The future of clinical psychology. *J. consulting Psychol.,* 1, 4–5.
Gamle Fordomar og ny Psykologi. *Norsk Pedagogisk. Tidskrift,* 21 Arg.,
   pp. 19–24.
Situation-and-goal set. Golden Jubilee Volume. *Amer. J. Psychol.,* 50,
   130–40.

1938

Experimental psychology. New York: Henry Holt, 889 pp.
Psykologia. Finnish trans. by U. Harva and E. S. Saarimaa of *Psychology,*
   3rd ed. Helsinki: Werner Söderström, Osakeyhtiö, 558 pp.

1939

Fundamental and applied research. *Mental Health.* Publication No. 9 of
   the American Association for the Advancement of Science, 59–61.
Individual and group behavior. *Amer. J. Sociol.,* 44, 823–28.
Psychological issues. New York: Columbia University Press, 421 pp.

1940

Charles August Strong: 1862–1940. *Amer. J. Psychol.,* 53, 302.

With M. G. Smith. *Class demonstrations in psychology.* New York: Henry Holt, 80 pp.
Livingston Farrand: 1867–1939. *Amer. J. Psychol.*, **53**, 302.
With M. G. Smith. *Notes for instructors, to accompany class demonstrations in psychology.* New York: Henry Holt, 12 pp.
Psychology. 4th ed. New York: Henry Holt, 639 pp.
Recent results on heredity and environment. *Transactions N. Y. Acad. Sci.*, **3**, 30–35.
(Review) *Human nature and the social order.* E L. Thorndike. *Science*, **92**, 36–38.
A revised standardized examination on Woodworth's psychology. 3rd ed. Forms A and B. New York: Henry Holt, 56 pp.

1941

Heredity and environment: A critical survey of recently published material on twins and foster children. *Soc. Sci. Res. Coun. Bull.*, No. 47, 1–96.
(Review) *General psychology.* J. McK. Cattell. *Science*, **94**, 116–17.
Successes and failures of experimental psychology. *Science*, **94**, 265–70.

1942

The Columbia University Psychological Laboratory: A fifty-year retrospect. New York: The Author, 23 pp.
Introduction, *Studies in personality: A contribution in honor of Lewis M. Terman.* McNemar, Q., and Merrill, M. A. (Eds.). 3–12.
Raymond Dodge: 1871–1942. *Psychol. Rev.*, **49**, 395–402.
(Review) *Sensation and Perception in the History of Experimental Psychology.* E. G. Boring. *Science*, **96**, 64–65.
(Review) *Unconsciousness.* N. E. Miller. *Science*, **96**, 114.

1943

The adolescence of American psychology. *Psychol. Rev.*, **50**, 10–32.
Bugünün Psikologi Cereyanlari. Turkish trans. by Mazafer Sherif [Başoglu] of *Contemporary schools of psychology*, 1931. Ankara: Ankara University, 210 pp.

1944

With M. R. Sheehan. *First course in psychology.* (Trade ed.: *Practical psychology of everyday life.*) New York: Henry Holt, 445 pp.
With others. James McKeen Cattell: In memoriam. *Science*, **99**, 151–65.
James McKeen Cattell: 1860–1944. *Psychol. Rev.*, **51**, 201–9.
[*Psychology.*] Arabic trans. by Abdul Hamid Kadhim of *Psychology*, 4th ed. Baghdad, Iraq, 788 pp.

1945

Edmund Burke Delabarre. *Science*, **102**, 369.

1946

Reinforcement of perception. *Amer. Psychologist*, **1**, 260–61 (abstract).

1947

Reinforcement of perception. *Amer. J. Psychol.*, **60**, 119–24.
With D. G. Marquis. *Psychology.* 5th ed. New York: Henry Holt, 677 pp.

1948

Contemporary schools of psychology. Rev. ed. New York: The Ronald
Press Co., 279 pp.
Margaret Floy Washburn: 1871–1939. *Nat. Acad. Sci. Biogr. Mem.*, **25**, 275–
95.

1949

Psychologie expérimentale. French trans. by André Ombredane and Irène
Lézine of *Experimental psychology*, 1938. Paris: Presses Universitaires
de France. 2 vols., 1183 pp.
[*Practical psychology of everyday life.*] Hebrew trans. by M. Kokhba of
First course in psychology, 1944. Tel-Aviv: Masadah, 262 pp.
(Review) *Theories of learning.* E. R. Hilgard. *J. abn. soc. Psychol.*, **44**, 124–
29.

1950

Edward Lee Thorndike: 1874–1949. *Science,* **111**, 250–51.

1951

Psychologie. Dutch trans. by P. P. J. Van Caspel of *Psychology*, 5th ed.
Antwerp: Standaard-Bockhandel; Utrecht: Spectrum, 693 pp.
With M. R. Sheehan. *First course in psychology.* Rev ed. New York:
Holt, Rinehart and Winston, Inc., 445 pp.

1952

Edward Lee Thorndike: 1874–1949. *Nat. Acad. Sci. Biogr. Mem.*, **27**, 209–
37.

1953

[*Psychology.*] Hebrew trans. by M. Elan-Rosenhach of *Psychology*, 4th ed.
Tel-Aviv: Masadah, 590 pp.
Psychkologi. Swedish trans. by Elsa Janson and Mils-Gustac Hildeman of
Psychology, 5th ed. Stockholm: Almqvist & Wiksell, 960 pp.

1954

With Harold Schlosberg. *Experimental psychology.* Rev. ed. New York:
Holt, Rinehart and Winston, Inc. 948 pp.
[*Contemporary schools of psychology.*] Hebrew trans. by B. Harel of *Con-
temporary schools of psychology*, rev. ed. Tel-Aviv: Hebrew Teachers
Union, 216.

1958

Psicologia. Portuguese trans. by Lavinia Costa Raymond of *Psychology*, 5th
ed. São Paulo: Campanhia Editors, National.
Dynamics of behavior. New York: Holt, Rinehart and Winston, Inc. 403 pp.

1959

John Broadus Watson: 1878–1958. *Amer. J. Psychol.*, **72**, 301–10.

Josiah Royce: 1855–1916. *Nat. Acad. Sci. Biogr. Mem.*, **33**, 381–96.

DAVIS, R. C. 1958. Physiological psychology: A view of fifty years. In Seward, G. S., and Seward, J. P. (Eds.). *Current psychological issues: Essays in honor of Robert S. Woodworth*, 249–77. New York: Holt, Rinehart and Winston, Inc.

References and
Author Index

The author wishes to express gratitude to the many publishers, organizations, and individuals who have extended permission for the use of numerous quotations that appear throughout this book.

Page numbers in italics refer to text pages on which specific publications are mentioned or discussed. When an author's general views have been cited frequently, such citations will be found listed immediately preceding his publications.

ACH, N. 1951. Determining tendencies; awareness. In Rapaport, D. (Ed.). *Organization and pathology of thought*, 16–38. New York: Columbia University Press. *289*

ADLER, A., *297–305; 312, 317, 320, 342, 381*
  1908. Der Aggressionstrieb im Leben und in der Neurose. In Adler, A., and Furtmüller, C. (Eds.). *Heilen und Bilden; ärtzlich-pädagogische Arbeiten des Vereins für Individualpsychologie*, 23–32. Munich: Reinhardt, 1914. *302*
  1911. "Verdrängung" und "männlicher Protest"; ihre Rolle und Bedeutung für die neurotische Dynamik. In Adler, A., and Furtmüller, C. (Eds.). *Heilen und Bilden; ärtzlich-pädagogische Arbeiten des Vereins für Individualpsychologie*, 103–14. Munich: Reinhardt, 1914. *300*
  1912. *Über den nervösen Charakter; Grundzüge einer vergleichenden Individual-Psychologie und Psychotherapie*. Wiesbaden: Bergmann. 4th ed., Munich: Bergmann, 1928. *302*
  1926. *The neurotic constitution*. New York: Dodd, Mead & Co. *302*
  1929. *The science of living*. New York: Greenberg, Publisher, Inc. *302*
  1930. *Problems of neurosis*. New York: Cosmopolitan Book Co. *304*
  1931. *What life should mean to you*. Boston: Little, Brown and Co. *302*
  1935. The structure of neurosis. *Internat. J. indiv. Psychol.*, **1**, No. 2, 3–12. *303, 304*

ALEXANDER, F., *363*
  1942. Educative influence of personality factors in the environment. In

The scope of psychoanalysis: Selected papers of Franz Alexander, 1921–1961, 424–39. New York: Basic Books, Inc., 1961. *272–73*

1953. Current views on psychotherapy. In *The scope of psychoanalysis: Selected papers of Franz Alexander, 1921–1961,* 276–89. New York: Basic Books, Inc., 1961. *260–61*

1954. The psychosomatic approach in medical therapy. In *The scope of psychoanalysis: Selected papers of Franz Alexander, 1921–1961,* 345–58. New York: Basic Books, Inc., 1961. *280*

1961. Experimental studies of emotional stress: I. Hyperthyroidism. (Written in collaboration with others.) In *The scope of psychoanalysis: Selected papers of Franz Alexander, 1921–1961,* 364–77. New York: Basic Books, Inc., 1961. *280*

ALEXANDER, F., and FRENCH, T. M. 1946. *Psychoanalytic therapy.* New York: The Ronald Press Co. *260*

ALLPORT, F. H. 1924. *Social psychology.* Boston: Houghton Mifflin Co. *247*

1955. *Theories of perception and the concept of structure.* New York: John Wiley & Sons, Inc.; London: Chapman & Hall, Ltd. *245*

ALLPORT, G. W., *370–79*

1937. *Personality: A psychological interpretation.* New York: Holt, Rinehart and Winston, Inc. *364, 371, 372*

1943. The ego in contemporary psychology. *Psychol. Rev.,* **50,** 451–78. *375*

1950. *The nature of personality: Selected papers.* Cambridge, Mass.: Addison-Wesley Publishing Co., Inc. *375*

1955. *Becoming: Basic considerations for a psychology of personality.* New Haven: Yale University Press. *374–76, 381*

1960. *Personality and social encounter: Selected essays.* Boston: Beacon Press. *378*

1961. *Pattern and growth in personality.* New York: Holt, Rinehart and Winston, Inc. *364, 372–73, 374, 377, 378, 382, 385*

ALLPORT, G. W., and ALLPORT, F. H. 1928a. *The A–S reaction study.* Boston: Houghton Mifflin Co. *371*

1928b. A test for ascendance–submission. *J. abn. soc. Psychol.,* **23,** 118–36. *371*

ALLPORT, G. W., and VERNON, P. E. 1933. *Studies in expressive movement.* New York: The Macmillan Co. *378*

ALLPORT, G. W., VERNON, P. E., and LINDZEY, G. 1960. *A study of values.* 3rd ed. Boston: Houghton Mifflin Co. *370*

ANANIEV, B. 1948. Achievements of Soviet psychologists. *J. genl. Psychol.,* **38,** 257–62. *94*

ANDREW, G., and HARLOW, H. F. 1948. Performance of macaque monkeys on a test of the concept of generalized triangularity. *Comp. psychol. Monogr.,* **19,** No. 3 (Serial No. 100). *190*

ANGELL, J. R. 1904. *Psychology: An introductory study of the structure and function of human consciousness.* New York: Holt, Rinehart and Winston, Inc. *30–31*

1907. The province of functional psychology. *Psychol. Rev.* **14,** 61–91 *31n*

1936. Autobiography. In Murchison, C. (Ed.). *A history of psychology in autobiography,* Vol. III, 1–38. Worcester, Mass.: Clark University Press. *31n*

ANOKHIN, P. K. 1961a. A new conception of the physiological architecture of conditioned reflex. In Delafresnaye, J. F. (Ed.). *Brain mechanisms and learning,* 188–229. Oxford: Blackwell Scientific Publications. *105–6, 110, 175, 208*

1961b. Electroencephalographic analysis of cortico-subcortical relations in positive and negative conditioned reactions. In Kline, N. S. (Ed.). *Pavlovian Conference on higher nervous activity. Annals N. Y. Acad. Sci.,* **92,** Art. 3, 899–938. (Editor in Chief, F. N. Furness.) *107, 177*

ANSBACHER, H., and ANSBACHER, R. 1956. *The Individual Psychology of Alfred Adler.* New York: Basic Books, Inc. *298, 299, 300, 317*

ARNHEIM, R. 1954. *Art and visual perception.* Berkeley and Los Angeles: University of California Press. *246–47*

ARNOLD, M. B. 1960. *Emotion and personality.* 2 vols. New York: Columbia University Press. *124, 152, 177, 385*

1962. *Story sequence analysis.* New York: Columbia University Press. *368*

ASCH, S. E. 1952. Social psychology. New York: Prentice-Hall, Inc., *125, 247–49*

1958. The metaphor: A psychological inquiry. In Tagiuri, R., and Petrullo, L. (Eds.). *Person perception and interpersonal behavior.* Stanford, Calif.: Stanford University Press; London: Oxford University Press. *198n, 248*

1959. A perspective on social psychology. In Koch, S. (Ed.). *Psychology: A study of a science.* Vol. III, 363–83. New York: McGraw-Hill Book Co. *247, 248*

ASRATYAN, E. A. 1961a. Some aspects of the elaboration of conditioned connections and formation of their properties. In Delafresnaye, J. F. (Ed.). *Brain mechanisms and learning,* 95–113. Oxford: Blackwell Scientific Publications. *79, 87, 107–8*

1961b. The initiation and localization of cortical inhibition in the conditioned reflex arc. In Kline, N. S. (Ed.). *Pavlovian Conference on higher nervous activity. Annals N. Y. Acad. Sci.,* **92,** Art. 3, 1141–59. (Editor in Chief, F. N. Furness.) *108*

ATKINSON, R. C. 1960. A theory of stimulus discrimination learning. In Arrow, K. J., Karlin, S., and Suppes, P. (Eds.). *Mathematical methods in the social sciences, 1959,* 221–41. Stanford, Calif.: Stanford University Press. *210*

BACHOFEN, J. J. 1926. In Schroeder, M. (Ed.). *Der Mythus von Orient und Okzident.* Munich: Ch. Becksche Buchhandlung. *272*

BAIN, A. 1855. *The senses and the intellect.* London: Edwin S. Parker, Ltd. *65–66*

1859. *The emotions and the will.* London: Parker & Son. *65–66*

1868. *Mental science: A compendium of psychology, and the history of philosophy.* New York: Appleton-Century-Crofts. *15*

BAUER, R. A. 1952. *The New Man in Soviet psychology.* Cambridge, Mass.: Harvard University Press. *94*

BEKHTEREV, V. M. 1913. *Objektive Psychologie; oder, Psychoreflexologie: die Lehre von den Assoziationsreflexen.* Leipzig: B. G. Teubner. First ed., 1907. *90, 92, 120*
1933. *General principles of reflexology.* Trans. from 4th (1928) Russian edition. London: Jarrolds. *92*

BENTLEY, M. 1926. The psychologies called "structural": Historical derivation; the work of the structuralists. In Murchison, C. (Ed.). *Psychologies of 1925*, 383–412. Worcester, Mass.: Clark University Press. *30*
1930. A psychology for psychologists. In Murchison, C. (Ed.). *Psychologies of 1930*, 95–114. Worcester, Mass.: Clark University Press. *30*

BERGMANN, G., and SPENCE, K. W. 1944. The logic of psychophysical measurement. *Psychol. Rev.*, **51**, 1–24. *21*

BERITOV, J. S., and BREGADZE, A. 1929. Physiology of animal behavior: Role of experimental setting in the production of reflex reaction of animals to complex sound stimuli. *Med. Biol. Zh.*, **5**, 83–101, 131–51. *82*

BERKELEY, G. 1709. *An essay toward a new theory of vision.* Dublin: N.P. *63*

BERLYNE, D. E. 1955. The arousal and satiation of perceptual curiosity in the rat. *J. comp. physiol. Psychol.*, **48**, 238–46. *185*

BERNARD, L. L. 1924. *Instinct: A study of social psychology.* New York: Holt, Rinehart and Winston, Inc. *344*
1926. *An introduction to social psychology.* New York: Holt, Rinehart and Winston, Inc. *345*

BETTELHEIM, B. 1943. Individual and mass behavior in extreme situations. *J. abn. soc. Psychol.*, **38**, 417–52. *56*

BEXTON, W. H., HERON, W., and SCOTT, T. H. 1954. Effects of decreased variation in the sensory environment. *Canad. J. Psychol.*, **8**, 70–76. *187*

BILLS, A. G. 1931. Blocking: A new principle of mental fatigue. *Amer. J. Psychol.*, **43**, 230–45. *33*
1935. Fatigue, oscillation, and blocks. *J. exp. Psychol.*, **18**, 562–73. *33*
1937. Blocking in mental fatigue and anoxia compared. *J. exp. Psychol.*, **20**, 437–52. *33*
1943. *Psychology of efficiency.* New York: Harper and Row, Publishers. *33*

BINET, A. 1903. *Étude expérimentale de l'intelligence.* Paris: Schleicher. *24*

BINSWANGER, L. 1955. *Ausgewählte Vorträge und Aufsätze.* Bern, Switzerland: A. Francke Verlag. *384–85*
1958. The case of Ellen West. In May, R., et al. (Eds.). *Existence: A new dimension in psychiatry and psychology*, 237–64. New York: Basic Books, Inc. *384*

BLEULER, E. 1911. *Dementia Praecox.* Leipzig and Vienna: Franz Deuticke. *40, 305*

BLITSTEN, D. 1953. *The social theories of Harry Stack Sullivan.* New York: The William-Frederick Press. *328*

BODKIN, M. 1934. *Archetypal patterns in poetry.* New York: Oxford University Press. *311*

BOGEN, H. 1931. Zur Methodik des "Totalverfahrens" in der berufseignungspsychologischen Begutachtung. *Z. angew. Psychol.,* Beihefte, **59,** 15–32. *361*

BONNER, H. 1961. *Psychology of personality.* New York: The Ronald Press Co. *378*

BORING, E. G. 1930. Psychology for eclectics. In Murchison, C. (Ed.). *Psychologies of 1930,* 115–27. Worcester, Mass.: Clark University Press. *30*
1942. *Sensation and perception in the history of experimental psychology.* New York: Appleton-Century-Crofts. *30*
1950. *A history of experimental psychology.* 2nd ed. New York: Appleton-Century-Crofts. *9n, 30, 219*
1953. A history of introspection. *Psychol. Bull.,* **50,** 169–89. *58*
1961. *Psychologist at large.* New York: Basic Books, Inc. *5, 188*

BORING, E. G., and STEVENS, S. S. 1936. The nature of tonal brightness. *Proc. Nat. Acad. Sci.,* **22,** 514–21. *30*

BOULDING, K. E. 1956. *The image.* Ann Arbor: University of Michigan Press. *206*

BOWER, G. H., and MILLER, N. E. 1958. Rewarding and punishing effects from stimulating the same place in the rat's brain. *J. comp. physiol. Psychol.,* **51,** 669–74. *154*

BOWLBY, J. 1951. Maternal care and mental health. Geneva: *World Health Organization Monogr.,* No. 2. *186*
1960. Grief and mourning in infancy and early childhood. *Psychoanal. Study of the Child,* **15,** 9–52. New York: International Universities Press, Inc., *186*

BRACKEN, H. VON. 1957. Personality theory in Germany. In David, H. P., and Bracken, H. von (Eds.). *Perspectives in personality theory,* 27–43. London: Tavistock Publications, Ltd. *378*

BRADY, J. V. 1962. Psychophysiology of emotional behavior. In Bachrach, A. J. (Ed.). *Experimental foundations of clinical psychology,* 343–85. New York: Basic Books, Inc. *177*

BRAINE, M. D. S. 1959. The ontogeny of certain logical operations: Piaget's formulation examined by non-verbal methods. *Psychol. Monogr.,* **73,** No. 5 (Whole No. 475), 1–43. *41*

BRAY, C. W. 1962. Toward a technology of human behavior for defense use. *Amer. Psychologist,* **17,** 527–41. *212*

BRELAND, K., and BRELAND, M. 1951. A field of applied animal psychology. *Amer. Psychologist,* **6,** 202–4. *163*
1961. The misbehavior of organisms. *Amer. Psychologist,* **16,** 681–84. *191–92*

BREUER, J., and FREUD, S. 1895. *Studien über Hysterie.* Leipzig and Vienna: Franz Deuticke. *256*
1936. *Studies in hysteria.* Trans. by A. A. Brill. New York: Nervous and Mental Disease Publishing Co. *256*

BROWN, J. S. 1953. Problems presented by the concept of acquired drives.

In *Current theory and research in motivation*, Vol. I, 1–21. Lincoln: University of Nebraska Press. *193*

Brown, R. W., and Lenneberg, E. H. 1954. A study of language and cognition. *J. abn. soc. Psychol.*, **49**, 454–62. *202*

Brown, T. 1820. *Lectures on the philosophy of the human mind*. Edinburgh: Tait, Longman. *64, 218*

Brožek, J. 1962. Current status of psychology in the U. S. S. R. In Farnsworth, P. R., *et al.* (Eds.). *Ann. Rev. Psychol.*, 515–66. *97, 98, 99*

Bruner, J. S. 1951. Personality dynamics and the process of perceiving. In Blake, R. R., and Ramsey, G. V. (Eds.). *Perception: An approach to personality*. New York: The Ronald Press Co. *387*
1960. Individual and collective problems in the study of thinking. In Furness, F. N. (Ed.). *Fundamentals of psychology: The psychology of thinking*. Annals N. Y. Acad. Sci., **91**, Art. 1, 22–37. *204*

Brunswik, E. 1934. *Wahrnehmung und Gegenstandswelt: Grundlegung einer Psychologie vom Gegenstand her*. Leipzig and Vienna: Franz Deuticke. *38, 51*
1939. Probability as a determiner of rat behavior. *J. exp. Psychol.*, **25**, 175–97. *38–39*
1952. The conceptual framework of psychology. *International Encyclopedia unified science*, Vol. I, No. 10. Chicago: University of Chicago Press. *38, 39, 53*
1956. *Perception and the representative design of psychological experiments*. Berkeley and Los Angeles: University of California Press. *39*

Bühler, K. 1924. *Die geistige Entwicklung des Kindes*. 4th ed. Jena: Gustav Fischer. *287, 289, 365*

Bush, R. R., and Estes, E. K. (Eds.). 1959. *Studies in mathematical learning theory*. Stanford, Calif.: Stanford University Press. *210*

Bush, R. R., and Mosteller, F. A. 1955. *Stochastic models for learning*. New York: John Wiley & Sons, Inc. *209, 210, 387*
1959. A comparison of eight models. In Bush, R. R., and Estes, E. K. (Eds.). *Studies in mathematical learning theory*, 293–307. Stanford, Calif.: Stanford University Press. *209, 210, 387*

Calkins, M. W. 1900. Psychology as a science of selves. *Philos. Rev.*, **9**, 490–501. *357*
1901. *An introduction to psychology*. New York: The Macmillan Co. *357*
1909. *A first book in psychology*. New York: The Macmillan Co. 4th ed., 1914. *357*
1926. Converging lines in contemporary psychology. *Brit. J. Psychol.*, *Gen. Sec.*, **16**, 171–79. *358–59, 380*
1930. Autobiography. In Murchison, C. (Ed.). *A history of psychology in autobiography*, Vol. I, 31–62. Worcester, Mass.: Clark University Press. *357–59*

Carmichael, L. (Ed.). 1946. *Manual of child psychology*. New York: John Wiley & Sons, Inc. *129*

Carnap, R. 1953. The two concepts of probability. In Feigl, H., and

Brodbeck, M. (Eds.). *Readings in the philosophy of science*. New York: Appleton-Century-Crofts. *246*

CARPENTER, W. B. 1876. *Principles of mental physiology*. 4th ed. New York: Appleton-Century-Crofts. *262*

CARR, H. 1930. Functionalism. In Murchison, C. (Ed.). *Psychologies of 1930*, 59–78. Worcester, Mass.: Clark University Press. *32–33, 111*
1936. Autobiography. In Murchison, C. (Ed.). *A history of psychology in autobiography*, Vol. III, 69–82. Worcester, Mass.: Clark University Press. *32*

CARROLL, J. B., and CASAGRANDE, J. B. 1958. The function of language classifications in behavior. In Maccoby, E. E., *et al.* (Eds.). *Readings in social psychology*, 18–31. New York: Holt, Rinehart and Winston, Inc. *202*

CATTELL, J. McK. 1904. The conceptions and methods of psychology. *Pop. Sci. Mo.*, **46**, 176–86. Included in *1860–1944 James McKeen Cattell–man of science*. Lancaster, Pa.: The Science Press, 1948. *114, 171*

CATTELL, R. B. 1956. Second order personality factors in the questionnaire realm. *J. consulting Psychol.*, **20**, 411–18. *314*
1957. *Personality and motivation structure and measurement*. New York: Harcourt, Brace & World, Inc. *349–50*

CHAPANIS, A. 1961. Men, machines and models. *Amer. Psychologist*, **16**, 113–31. *204*

CHARCOT, J. M. 1877. *Lectures on the diseases of the nervous system*. London: New Sydenham Society. *252, 255, 262*

CLAPARÈDE, E. 1930. Autobiography. In Murchison, C. (Ed.). *A history of psychology in autobiography*, Vol. I, 63–97. Worcester, Mass.: Clark University Press. *38, 39, 40*
1933. La genèse de l'hypothèse, étude expérimentale. *Arch. de Psychol.*, **24**, 1–154. *39, 289*

COFER, C. N. 1960. Experimental studies of the role of verbal processes in concept formation and problem solving. In Furness, F. N. (Ed.). *Fundamentals of psychology: The psychology of thinking. Annals N. Y. Acad. Sci.*, **91**, Art. 1, 94–107. *202*
1961. (Ed.). *Verbal learning and verbal behavior*. New York: McGraw-Hill Book Co. *36, 202*

CULLER, E., FINCH, G., GIRDEN, E., and BROGDEN, W. 1935. Measurements of acuity by the conditioned-response technique. *J. genl. Psychol.*, **12**, 223–27. *79*

DASHIELL, J. F. 1928. *Fundamentals of objective psychology*. Boston: Houghton Mifflin Co. *201*

DELAFRESNAYE, J. F. (Ed.). 1961. *Brain mechanisms and learning*. Oxford: Blackwell Scientific Publications. *97, 177*

DEMENT, W., and KLEITMAN, N. 1957. Cyclic variations in EEG during sleep and their relation to eye movements, bodily motility, and dreaming. *Electroenceph. clin. Neurophysiol.*, **9**, 673–90. *16*

DEUTSCH, M. 1954. Field theory in social psychology. In Lindzey, G.

(Ed.). *Handbook of social psychology*, Vol. I, 181–222. Cambridge, Mass.: Addison-Wesley Publishing Co., Inc. *243*

DEWEY, J. 1896. The reflex arc concept in psychology. *Psychol. Rev.*, 3, 357–70. *30–31, 39*

DILTHEY, W. 1894. Ideen über eine beschreibende und zergliedernde Psychologie. In his *Gesammelte Schriften*. Leipzig: B. G. Teubner, 1924, Vol. V, 139–240. *368, 380*

DINGLE, H. 1953. *The scientific adventure*. London: Pitman, 1952; New York: Philosophical Library, 1953. *291*

DOLLARD, J., and MILLER, N. E. 1950. *Personality and psychotherapy*. New York: McGraw-Hill Book Co. *149, 151*

DU BOIS, C. 1944. *The people of Alor*. Minneapolis: University of Minnesota Press. *272*

DULANEY, D. E. 1961. Hypotheses and habits in verbal "operant conditioning." *J. abn. soc. Psychol.*, 63, 251–63. *87, 203*

DUNCKER, K. 1935. *Zur Psychologie des produktiven denkens*. Berlin: Verlag Julius Springer. *231*
    1945. On problem-solving. Trans. by L. S. Lees. *Psychol. Monogr.*, 58, No. 270. *231*

DUNLAP, K. 1919. Are there any instincts? *J. abn. soc. Psychol.*, 14, 307–11. *345*

EBBINGHAUS, H. 1885. *Über das Gedächtnis*. Leipzig: Duncker & Humblot. *17–18, 23*
    1913. *Memory*. Trans. by H. A. Ruger and C. E. Bussenius. New York: Bureau of Publications, Teachers College, Columbia University. *17–18*

EDWARDS, J. 1754. *A careful and strict enquiry into the modern prevailing notions of that freedom of will which is supposed to be essential to moral agency, virtue and vice, reward and punishment, praise and blame*. Boston: Kneeland. *18*

EHRENFELS, C. VON. 1890. Über Gestaltqualitäten. *Vierteljahrschr. f. wiss. Philos.*, 14, 249–92. *218*
    1937. On Gestalt qualities. *Psychol. Rev.*, 44, 521–24. *219*

ELAM, C. B., TYLER, D. W., and BITTERMAN, M. E. 1954. A further study of secondary reinforcement and the discrimination hypothesis. *J. comp. physiol. Psychol.*, 47, 381–84. *86*

ELLIOTT, R. M. 1952. Autobiography. In Boring, E. G., *et al.* (Eds.). *A history of psychology in autobiography*, Vol. IV, 75–95. Worcester, Mass.: Clark University Press. *129*

ERIKSON, E. H., *291–93; 320, 375*
    1950. *Childhood and society*. New York: W. W. Norton & Co., Inc. *268, 291, 292, 295*
    1959. The problem of ego identity. In Klein, G. S. (Ed.). *Psychological issues: Selected papers by Erik H. Erikson*, 101–71. New York: International Universities Press, Inc. *291, 293*

ESCALONA, S. 1954. The influence of topological and vector psychology upon current research in child development: An addendum. In Carmichael, L. (Ed.). *Manual of child psychology*, 971–83. New York: John Wiley & Sons, Inc.; London: Chapman & Hall, Ltd. *243*

ESTES, W. K. 1950. Toward a statistical theory of learning. *Psychol. Rev.*, **57**, 94–107. *387*

——— 1959. The statistical approach to learning theory. In Koch, S. (Ed.). *Psychology: A study of a science*, Vol. II, 380–491. New York: McGraw-Hill Book Co. *210*

——— 1960. Learning theory and the new mental chemistry. *Psychol. Rev.*, **67**, 207–23. *210*

——— 1962. Learning theory. In Farnsworth, P. R., *et al.* (Eds.). *Ann. Rev. Psychol.*, **13**, 107–44. *209, 210*

ESTES, W. K., and BURKE, C. J. 1955. Application of a statistical model to simple discrimination learning in human subjects. *J. exp. Psychol.*, **50**, 81–88. *210*

EYSENCK, H. J. 1947. *Dimensions of personality*. London: Routledge and Kegan Paul. *314*

——— 1952. *The scientific study of personality*. London: Routledge and Kegan Paul. *314*

——— 1960a. *The structure of human personality*. 2nd ed. London: Routledge and Kegan Paul. *314*

——— 1960b. Drug postulates: Theoretical deductions and methodological considerations. In Uhr, L., and Miller, J. G. (Eds.). *Drugs and Behavior*, 352–59. New York: John Wiley & Sons, Inc. *315*

——— 1962. Reminiscence, drive and personality: Revision and extension of a theory. *Brit. J. soc. clin. Psychol.*, **1**, 127–40. *315*

FEDERN, P. 1952. *Ego psychology and the psychoses*. New York: Basic Books, Inc. *317*

FERSTER, C. B., and SKINNER, B. F. 1957. *Schedules of reinforcement*. New York: Appleton-Century-Crofts. *164, 165*

FESTINGER, L. 1950. Current developments in group dynamics. In *National Conference of Social Work, 77th Annual Meeting*, 253–65. *239*

FIEDLER, L. A. 1957. Archetype and signature. In Phillips, W. (Ed.). *Art and psychoanalysis*. New York: Criterion Books. *311*

FOX, B. H. 1951. Figural after-effects: "satiation" and adaptation. *J. exp. Psychol.*, **42**, 317–26. *225*

FRANKL, V. E. 1955. *The doctor and the soul: An introduction to logotherapy*. New York: Alfred A. Knopf, Inc. *56, 383*

——— 1963. *Man's search for meaning: An introduction to logotherapy*. New York: Washington Square Press. Original title: *From death-camp to Existentialism*. Boston: Beacon Press, 1959. *56, 383–84*

FRANZ, S. I. 1902. On the function of the cerebrum: the frontal lobes in relation to the production and retention of simple sensory motor habits. *Amer. J. Physiol.*, **8**, 1–22. *172*

——— 1907. On the functions of the cerebrum: the frontal lobes. *Arch. Psychol.*, No. 2. *172*

FRANZ, S. I., and LASHLEY, K. S. 1917. The effects of cerebral destruction upon habit-formation and retention in the albino rat. *Psychobiol.*, **1**, 71–139. *172*

FREIDES, D. 1957. Goal-box cues and pattern of reinforcement. *J. exp. Psychol.*, **53**, 361–71. *86*

FREUD, A. 1946. *The ego and the mechanisms of defence.* New York: International Universities Press, Inc. *285, 316*

FREUD, S., *255–85; 297, 298, 299, 300, 301, 303, 305, 306, 316, 323, 324, 325, 330, 331, 332, 333, 358, 360, 363*

    Gesammelte Werke. Chronologisch geordnet. Vols. I–XVII. London: Imago Publishing Co., 1940–1948. (*G.,* with a number following, in the Freud references indicates *Gesammelte* and the volume. References so marked are to the original editions, but quotations are from the respective translations.)

There is also now available, in twenty-four volumes, the Standard Edition of the *Complete Psychological Works of Sigmund Freud.* Trans. and edited by James Strachey. London: The Hogarth Press, Ltd., and the Institute of Psychoanalysis, 1953.

    Collected papers. First American Edition, 1959. Vols. I–V. New York: Basic Books, Inc. By arrangement with The Hogarth Press, Ltd. and The Institute of Psychoanalysis, London. References from these volumes are so indicated.

1900. *The interpretation of dreams.* New York: The Macmillan Co., 1913. 1st ed., German, 1900. (*G.,* II–III.) *22, 256, 262, 266*

1904. *Psychopathology of everyday life.* New York: The Macmillan Co., 1915. 1st ed., German, 1901. (*G.* IV.) *263*

1905a. Three contributions to the theory of sex. Trans. by A. A. Brill. *Nerv. ment. Dis. Monogr. Ser.,* 1910, No. 7. 1st ed., German, 1905. (*G.,* V.) *270*

1905b. Wit and its relation to the unconscious. In *The basic writings of Sigmund Freud.* New York: Modern Library, 1938, 631–803. *263, 287*

1910a. The origin and development of psychoanalysis. *Amer. J. Psychol.,* **21**, 181–218. (Quotation from p. 203.) Also in Rickman, J. (Ed.). *A general selection from the works of Sigmund Freud,* 1–36. Garden City, N. Y.: Doubleday and Co., Inc. (An Anchor Original), 1957. *266*

1910b. Observations on 'wild' psychoanalysis. In *Collected papers,* Vol. II, 297–304. New York: Basic Books, Inc. *268*

1911. Formulations regarding the two principles in mental functioning. In *Collected papers,* Vol. IV, 13–21. New York: Basic Books, Inc. *265*

1914a. *The history of the psychoanalytic movement.* New York: Nervous and Mental Disease Publishing Co., 1917. 1st ed., German, 1914. (*G.,* X.) *260*

1914b. On narcissism: an introduction In *Collected papers,* Vol. IV, 30–59. New York: Basic Books, Inc. 1st ed., German, 1914. (*G.,* X.) *273, 277*

1915a. Instincts and their vicissitudes. In *Collected papers,* Vol IV, 60–83. New York: Basic Books, Inc. *275, 277*

1915b. The unconscious. In *Collected papers,* Vol. IV, 98–136. New York: Basic Books, Inc. *264, 277*

1916. *A general introduction to psychoanalysis.* Trans. by J. Riviere. New York: Liveright Publishing Corp., 1920. 1st ed., German, 1916–1917. (*G.,* XI.) *270*

1917. Mourning and melancholia. In *Collected papers,* Vol. IV, 152–70. New York: Basic Books, Inc. *276*

1920. *Beyond the pleasure principle.* New York: Liveright Publishing

Corp., 1922. 1st ed., German, 1920. (*G.,* XIII.) *259, 268, 277, 278, 285*

1921. *Group psychology and the analysis of the ego.* London: International Psycho-analytic Press, 1922. 1st ed., German, 1921. (*G.,* XIII.) *278, 285*

1923. *The ego and the id.* London: The Hogarth Press, Ltd., 1927. 1st ed., German, 1923. (*G.,* XIII.) *270–71, 281*

1926a. *The problem of anxiety.* Trans. by H. A. Bunker. New York: W. W. Norton & Co., Inc., 1936. 1st ed., German, 1924. *Hemmung, Symptom und Angst.* (*G.,* XI.) *283*

1926b. *The problem of lay analyses.* New York: Brentano's, 1927. 1st ed., German, 1926. (*G.,* XIV.) *260*

1927. *The future of an illusion.* London: The Hogarth Press, Ltd., 1928. 1st ed., German, 1927. (*G.,* XIV.) *279*

1930. *Civilization and its discontents.* London: The Hogarth Press, Ltd. (*G.,* XIV.) *278*

1932. *New introductory lectures on psychoanalysis.* New York: W. W. Norton & Co., Inc. Copyright 1933 by S. Freud. Copyright 1961 by W. J. H. Sprott. 1st ed., German, 1932. (*G.,* XV.) *279, 282–83*

1937. *Moses and monotheism.* New York: Alfred A. Knopf, Inc., 1938. Translated from articles in *Imago,* 1937. *279*

1938. Analysis, terminable and interminable. *Internat. J. Psychoanal.,* **18,** 373–405. *285, 287*

1940. Abriss der Psychoanalyse. *Internat. Z. Psychoanal.,* **25,** 9–67. (*G.,* XVII.) *279*

1946. *Selbstdarstellung.* London: Imago Publishing Co. 1st ed., German, 1925. (*G.,* XIV.) *262*

1954. Project for a scientific psychology. Appendix in *The origins of psychoanalysis. Letters to William Fliess, drafts and notes, 1887–1902.* New York: Basic Books, Inc. *261*

FRICK, F. C. 1959. Information theory. In Koch, S. (Ed.). *Psychology: A study of a science,* Vol. II, 611–36. New York: McGraw-Hill Book Co. *212*

FROMM, E., *323–26; 295, 316*

1941. *Escape from freedom.* New York: Holt, Rinehart and Winston, Inc. *323, 324*

1947. *Man for himself: An inquiry into the psychology of ethics.* New York: Holt, Rinehart and Winston, Inc. *323, 325, 326, 382*

1951. *The forgotten language.* New York: Holt, Rinehart and Winston, Inc. *272*

1955. *The sane society.* New York: Holt, Rinehart and Winston, Inc. *326*

1956. *The art of loving.* New York: Harper and Row, Publishers. *326*

GALTON, F. 1880. Statistics of mental imagery. *Mind,* **5,** 301–18. *22*

GANTT, W. H. 1952. Russian physiology and pathology. In Zirkle, C., and Meyerhoff, H. A. *Soviet science,* 8–39. Washington, D. C.: A. A. A. S. *95*

GARNER, W. R. 1962. *Uncertainty and structure as psychological concepts.* New York: John Wiley & Sons, Inc. *212*

GIBSON, E. J. 1940. A systematic application of the concepts of generalization and differentiation to verbal learning. *Psychol. Rev.*, **47**, 196–229. *35–36*

1963. Perceptual learning. In Farnsworth, P. R., *et al.* (Eds.). *Ann. Rev. Psychol.*, 29–56. *55*

GIBSON, E. J., and WALK, R. D. 1960. The "visual cliff." *Sci. American*, **202**, 64–71. *55*

GIBSON, J. J. 1933. Adaptation, after-effect and contrast in the perception of curved lines. *J. exp. Psychol.*, **16**, 1–31. *225*

1959. Perception as a function of stimulation. In Koch, S. (Ed.). *Psychology: A study of a science*, Vol. I, 456–501. New York: McGraw-Hill Book Co. *52, 54, 55*

1960. The concept of the stimulus in psychology. *Amer. Psychologist*, **15**, 694–703. *55*

1963. The useful dimensions of sensitivity. *Amer. Psychologist*, **18**, 1–15. *55*

GIBSON, J. J., and GIBSON, E. J. 1955. Perceptual learning: Differentiation or enrichment? *Psychol. Rev.*, **62**, 32–41. *55*

GLOVER, E. 1950. *Freud or Jung?* New York: W. W. Norton & Co., Inc. (Pagination given refers to paperback edition, New York: Meridian Books, 1957.) *311–12*

GOLDSTEIN, K., *351–54; 380, 385*

1939. *The organism: A holistic approach to biology derived from pathological data in man.* New York: American Book Co. *352, 354*

1940. *Human nature in the light of psychopathology.* Cambridge, Mass.: Harvard University Press. *352, 353*

1947. Organismic approach to the problem of motivation. *Transactions N. Y. Acad. Sci.*, **9**, 218–30. *353*

GOLDSTEIN, K., and SCHEERER, M. 1941. Abstract and concrete behavior: An experimental study with special tests. *Psychol. Monogr.*, No. 239, 151. *354*

GOSS, A. E. 1961a. Early behaviorism and verbal mediating responses. *Amer. Psychologist*, **16**, 285–98. *202*

1961b. Verbal mediating responses and concept formation. *Psychol. Rev.*, **68**, 248–74. *202*

GOTTSCHALK, L. A. 1960. Introspection and free association as experimental approaches to assessing subjective and behavioral effects of psychoactive drugs. In Uhr, L., and Miller, J. G. (Eds.). *Drugs and behavior*, 587–90. New York: John Wiley & Sons, Inc. *56*

GRAHAM, C. H. 1958. Sensation and perception in an objective psychology. *Psychol. Rev.*, **65**, 65–76. *21*

GREENSPOON, J. 1962. Verbal conditioning and clinical psychology. In Bachrach, A. J. (Ed.). *Experimental foundations of clinical psychology*, 510–53. New York: Basic Books, Inc. *87, 204*

GUILFORD, J. P. 1940. *An inventory of factors STDCR.* Beverly Hills, Calif.: Sheridan Supply Co. *314*

GUTHRIE, E. R. 1938. *The psychology of human conflict.* New York: Harper and Row, Publishers. *161*

1952. *The psychology of learning.* Rev. ed. New York: Harper and Row, Publishers. *156, 160–62, 194, 210*

HARLOW, H. F., *188–94, 235*
1953a. Mice, monkeys, men, and motives. *Psychol. Rev.*, **60**, 23–32. *193*
1953b. Motivation as a factor in the acquisition of new responses. In *Current theory and research in motivation*, Vol. I, 24–49. Lincoln: University of Nebraska Press. *192–93*
1954. Motivational forces underlying learning. In *Learning theory, personality theory, and clinical research—The Kentucky Symposium*. New York: John Wiley & Sons, Inc. *193*
1958. The nature of love. *Amer. Psychologist*, **13**, 673–85. *193*
1959. Learning set and error factor theory. In Koch, S. (Ed.). *Psychology: A study of a science*, Vol. II, 492–537. New York: McGraw-Hill Book Co. *190–91, 192*
1962. The heterosexual affectional system in monkeys. *Amer. Psychologist*, **17**, 1–9. *186, 193*

HARTLEY, D. 1749. *Observations on man, his frame, his duty, and his expectations*. London: W. Eyres. *64*

HARTMANN, H. *286–88; 275, 307, 316, 317, 355, 365, 387*
1939. Ich-Psychologie und Anpassungsproblem. *Internl. Z. Psychoanal. Imago*, **24**, 62–135. *Ego psychology and the problem of adaptation*. New York: International Universities Press, Inc., 1958. *286, 287, 288*
1952. The mutual influences in the development of the ego and id: Introduction to the discussion. In Eissler, R., *et al.* (Eds.). *The psychoanalytic study of the child*, Vol. VII, 9–30. New York: International Universities Press, Inc. *288*

HARTMANN, H., KRIS, E., and LOEWENSTEIN, R. 1946. Comments on the formation of psychic structure. In *The psychoanalytic study of the child*, Vol. II, 11–38. New York: International Universities Press, Inc. *286*
1949. Notes on the theory of aggression. In *The psychoanalytic study of the child*, Vol. III–IV, 9–36. *295*

HARTSHORNE, H., MAY, M. A., with SHUTTLEWORTH, F. K. 1930. *Studies in the organization of character*. New York: The Macmillan Co. *372*

HEBB, D. O., *178–88; 104, 107, 226, 368, 376, 387*
1949. *The organization of behavior: A neuropsychological theory*. New York: John Wiley & Sons, Inc. *156, 179–85*
1955. Drives and the CNS (conceptual nervous system). *Psychol. Rev.*, **62**, 243–54. *179, 185*
1958. The motivating effects of exteroceptive stimulation. *Amer. Psychologist*, **13**, 109–13. *186*
1959. A neuropsychological theory. In Koch, S. (Ed.). *Psychology: A study of a science*, 622–43. New York: McGraw-Hill Book Co. *179*
1960. The American Revolution. *Amer. Psychologist*, **15**, 735–45. *178, 348*
1963. The semiautonomous process: Its nature and nurture. *Amer. Psychologist*, **18**, 16–27. *179, 180, 183*

HEBB, D. O., and MAHUT, H. 1955. Motivation et récherche du changement perceptif chez le rat et chez l'homme. *J. Psychol. normale et pathol.*, **52**, 209–21. *185*

HEBB, D. O., and THOMPSON, W. R. 1954. The social significance of animal studies. In Lindzey, G. (Ed.). *Handbook of social psychology*, Vol. I, 532–61. Cambridge, Mass.: Addison-Wesley Publishing Co., Inc. *186*

HEIDBREDER, E. 1933. *Seven psychologies.* New York: Appleton-Century-Crofts. *59n*

HEIDEGGER, M. 1949. *Existence and being.* Chicago: Henry Regnery Co. *28, 383, 385*

HEIDER, F. 1958. *Psychology of interpersonal relations.* New York: John Wiley & Sons, Inc. *124, 245–46*

HENLE, M. 1942. An experimental investigation of dynamic and structural determinants of substitution. *Contemp. psychol. Theor.,* **2,** No. 3. *246–47*
1957. Some problems of eclecticism. *Psychol. Rev.,* **64,** 296–305. *247*
1962. On the relation between logic and thinking. *Psychol. Rev.,* **69,** 366–78. *247*

HERBART, J. F. 1816. *Lehrbuch zur Psychologie.* Königsberg: Unzer. *66*
1824–1825. *Psychologie als Wissenschaft.* 2 vols. Königsberg: Unzer. *66*

HERON, W. 1961. Cognitive and physiological effects of perceptual isolation. In Solomon, P., *et al.* (Eds.). *Sensory deprivation,* 6–33. Cambridge, Mass.: Harvard University Press. *56*

HERON, W., DOANE, B. K., and SCOTT, T. H. 1956. Visual disturbances after prolonged perceptual isolation. *Canad. J. Psychol.,* **10,** 13–18. *187*

HILGARD, E. 1956. *Theories of learning.* 2nd ed. New York: Appleton-Century-Crofts. *32, 34, 58, 74, 126, 133, 149, 170, 209, 212, 243*

HINDE, R. A. 1959. Some recent trends in ethology. In Koch, S. (Ed.). *Psychology: A study of a science,* Vol. II, 561–610. New York: McGraw-Hill Book Co. *335, 348*

HOBBES, T. 1651. *Leviathan.* London: Printed for Andrew Crooke. *9, 60–62*

HOBHOUSE, L. T. 1901. *Mind in evolution.* New York: The Macmillan Co. *232n*

HOCHBERG, J. E. 1957. Effects of the Gestalt revolution: The Cornell symposium on perception. *Psychol. Rev..,* **64,** 73–84. *244*

HOLT, E. B. 1915. *The Freudian wish and its place in ethics.* New York: Holt, Rinehart and Winston, Inc. *129*
1931. *Animal drive and the learning process: An essay toward radical empiricism.* New York: Holt, Rinehart and Winston, Inc. *129–30*

HOLT, R. R. 1961. The nature of TAT stories as cognitive products: A psychoanalytic approach. In Kagan, J., and Lesser, G. S. (Eds.). *Contemporary issues in thematic apperceptive methods.* Springfield, Ill.: Charles C. Thomas, Publishers. *368*

HOLZNER, B. 1957. *Amerikanische und Deutsche Psychologie: Eine vergleichende Darstellung.* Würzburg: Holzner. *250*

HORNBOSTEL, E. M. VON. 1927. The unity of the senses. *Psyche,* **27,** 1–7. *248*

HORNEY, K., *319–23; 316, 317, 343, 380*
1937. *The neurotic personality of our time.* New York: W. W. Norton & Co., Inc. *319*
1939. *New ways in psychoanalysis.* New York: W. W. Norton & Co., Inc. *319*

1945. *Our inner conflicts.* New York: W. W. Norton & Co., Inc. *319, 321, 322*

1950. *Neurosis and human growth.* New York: W. W. Norton & Co., Inc. *321*

HOVLAND, C. I. 1952. A "communication analysis" of concept learning. *Psychol. Rev.,* **59,** 461–72. *209*

1953. A set of flower designs for concept learning experiments. *Amer. J. Psychol.,* **66,** 140–42. *209*

1960. Computer simulation of thinking. *Amer. Psychologist,* **15,** 687–93. *209*

HULL, C. L., *141–49; 109, 154, 157, 158, 159, 160, 178, 194, 200, 210, 214, 334*

1920. Quantitative aspects of the evolution of concepts. *Psychol. Monogr.,* **28,** No. 123. *141*

1925. An automatic correlation calculating machine. *J. Amer. Statist. Assn.,* **20,** 522–31. *142*

1928. *Aptitude testing.* New York: Harcourt, Brace & World, Inc. *142*

1930. Knowledge and purpose as habit mechanisms. *Psychol. Rev.,* **37,** 511–25. *142*

1931. Goal attraction and directing ideas conceived as habit phenomena. *Psychol. Rev.,* **38,** 487–506. *143*

1933. *Hypnosis and suggestibility.* New York: Appleton-Century-Crofts. *142*

1935. The conflicting psychologies of learning—a way out. *Psychol. Rev.,* **42,** 491–516. *142*

1937. Mind, mechanism, and adaptive behavior. *Psychol. Rev.,* **44,** 1–32. *147*

1943. *Principles of behavior: An introduction to behavior theory.* New York: Appleton-Century-Crofts. *86, 140, 142, 143, 147*

1950. Behavior postulates and corollaries—1949. *Psychol. Rev.,* **57,** 173–80. *140, 148, 153*

1951. *Essentials of behavior.* New Haven: Yale University Press. *148*

1952a. Autobiography. In Boring, E. G., *et al.* (Eds.). *A history of psychology in autobiography,* Vol. IV, 143–62. Worcester, Mass.: Clark University Press. *141, 148*

1952b. *A behavior system: An introduction to behavior theory concerning the individual organism.* New Haven: Yale University Press. *148, 200, 210*

HULL, C. L., and others. 1940. *Mathematico-deductive theory of rote learning: A study in scientific methodology.* New Haven: Yale University Press. *147*

HUME, D. 1739. *A treatise of human nature,* Vols. I, II. London: Noon. Vol. III. London: Thomas Longman. *63, 66, 215, 238*

1748. An enquiry concerning human understanding. In *Essays and treatises on several subjects.* London: Printed for A. Millar. *63, 66, 238*

HUMPHREYS, L. G. 1940. Extinction of conditioned psychogalvanic responses following two conditions of reinforcement. *J. exp. Psychol.,* **27,** 71–75. *86*

HUNT, J. McV. 1961. *Intelligence and experience.* New York: The Ronald Press Co. *40, 41, 47, 128*

HUNTER, W. S. 1926. Psychology and anthroponomy. In Murchison, C. (Ed.). *Psychologies of 1925*, 83–107. Worcester, Mass.: Clark University Press. *132*
1930. Anthroponomy and psychology. In Murchison, C. (Ed.). *Psychologies of 1930*. Worcester, Mass.: Clark University Press. *132*
1932. The psychological study of behavior. *Psychol. Rev.*, **39**, 1–24. *132*
1949. James Rowland Angell, 1869–1949. *Amer. J. Psychol.*, **62**, 439–50, *31n*
1952. Autobiography. In Boring, E. G., *et al.*, (Eds.). *A history of psychology in autobiography*, Vol. IV, 163–87. Worcester, Mass.: Clark University Press. *131*
HUSSERL, E. 1928. *Vorlesungen zur Phänomenologie des innern Zeitbewusstseins*. Halle a.d. Saale. *383, 384*

INHELDER, B., and PIAGET, J. 1958. The growth of logical thinking from childhood to adolescence. Trans. by A. Parsons and S. Milgram. New York: Basic Books, Inc. *41, 44, 46, 47–49*
ITTELSON, W. H. 1960. *Visual space perception*. New York: Springer Publishing Co. *53, 387*
ITTELSON, W. H., and KILPATRICK, F. P. 1952. Experiments in perception. *Sci. American*, **185**, 50–55. *52*

JACOBSON, E. 1932. Electrophysiology of mental activities. *Amer. J. Psychol.*, **44**, 677–94. *127*
JAMES, W. 1890. *Principles of psychology*. 2 vols. New York: Holt, Rinehart and Winston, Inc. *25–26, 30, 40, 59, 106, 111, 122, 220, 356–57, 374, 386*
1892. *Psychology: Briefer course*. New York: Holt, Rinehart and Winston, Inc. *25, 357*
JANET, P. *253–54; 256, 262, 265, 274, 307*
1889. *L'automatisme psychologique*. Paris: Alcan. *253*
1892. *L'état mental des hysteriques*. Paris: Ruell. *253*
1903. *Les obsessions et la psychasthénie*. Paris: Alcan. *253, 254*
1904. *Névroses et idées fixes*. 2nd ed. Paris: Alcan. *253*
1907. *The major symptoms of hysteria*. New York: The Macmillan Co. *253*
1930. Autobiography. In Murchison, C. (Ed.). *A history of psychology in autobiography*, Vol. I, 123–33. Worcester, Mass.: Clark University Press. *162*
JASPERS, K. 1954. *Psychologie der Weltanschauungen*. (*Psychology of world views*.) 4th ed. Berlin: Verlag Julius Springer. *28, 383*
JONES, M. C. 1958. A study of socialization patterns at the high school level. *J. genet. Psychol.*, **93**, 87–111. *57*
JONES, M. R. (Ed.). 1953–1963. *The Nebraska Symposium on Motivation*. Lincoln: University of Nebraska Press. *8*
Journal of the experimental analysis of behavior. No. 1, January, 1958. *163*
Journal of verbal learning and verbal behavior. No. 1, July, 1962. *202*

JUNG, C. G., *305–16; 329, 363, 380*
  1923. *Psychological types.* New York: Harcourt, Brace & World, Inc. *312*
  1933. *Modern man in search of a soul.* New York: Harcourt, Brace & World, Inc., *311, 312, 313*
  1953. *Collected works.* 18 vols. London: Routledge & Kegan Paul; New York: Pantheon Press (Bollingen Series No. XX; Copyright 1951 Bollingen Foundation, New York).
  1956. Two essays on analytical psychology. *Collected works*, Vol. VII. New York: Pantheon Press (Bollingen Series No. XX; Copyright 1951 Bollingen Foundation, New York.) (Pagination given refers to paperback edition, New York: Meridian Books, 1956.) *307–8, 309, 310, 311, 312*
  1957–1958. *The undiscovered self.* Boston: Little, Brown and Co. *309, 310*
  1958. *Psyche and symbol: A selection from the writings of C. G. Jung.* V. S. de Laszlo (Ed.). Garden City, N. Y.: Doubleday and Co., Inc. (An Anchor Original). *309*

KARDINER, A. 1939. *The individual and his society: The psychodynamics of primitive organization.* New York: Columbia University Press. *317*

KARDINER, A., LINTON, R., DU BOIS, C., and WEST, J. 1945. *The psychological frontiers of society.* New York: Columbia University Press. *268–69, 272*

KATONA, G. 1940. *Organizing and memorizing: Studies in the psychology of learning and teaching.* New York: Columbia University Press. *231, 237*

KATZ, D. 1911. Die Erscheinungsweisen der Farben und ihre Beeinflussung durch die individuelle Erfahrung. *Z. Psychol., Ergänzungsband*, **7**. *36*
  1925. Der Aufbau der Tastwelt. *Z. Psychol., Ergänzungsband*, **11**. *36*
  1930. *Der Aufbau der Farbwelt.* Leipzig: S. A. Barth. *36*
  1935. *The world of color.* Trans. by R. B. MacLeod and C. W. Fox. London: Stanley Paul & Co., Ltd. *36*
  1950. *Gestalt psychology: Its nature and significance.* Trans. by Robert Tyson. New York: The Ronald Press Co. *37, 55*
  1952. Autobiography. In Boring, E. G., *et al.* (Eds.). *A history of psychology in autobiography*, Vol. IV, 189–211. Worcester, Mass.: Clark University Press. *37*

KELLY, G. A. 1955. *The psychology of personal constructs.* 2 vols. New York: W. W. Norton & Co., Inc. *57*

KENDLER, H. H. 1959. Learning. In Farnsworth, P. R., *et al.* (Eds.). *Ann. Rev. Psychol.*, **10**, 43–88. *149*

KENDLER, T. S. 1960. Learning, development, and thinking. In Furness, F. N. (Ed.). *Fundamentals of psychology: The psychology of thinking. Annals N. Y. Acad. Sci.*, **91**, Art. 1, 52–65. *203*
  1961. Concept formation. In Farnsworth, P. R., *et al.* (Eds.). *Ann. Rev. Psychol.*, **12**, 447–72. *202, 203*

KEPPEL, G., and UNDERWOOD, B. J. 1962. Proactive inhibition in short-term retention of single items. *J. verb. learng. and verb. beh.*, No. 1, 153–61. *36*

KESSEN, W. 1960. Intellective development in children: A conference on Piaget's contributions in relation to other theories of children's thinking. *Items*, 14, 25–30. *41*

KESSEN, W., and KUHLMAN, C. (Eds.). 1962. Thought in the young child: Report of a conference on intellective development, with particular attention to the work of Jean Piaget. *Monogr. Soc. res. child. dev.*, 27, No. 2 (Serial No. 83). Lafayette, Ind.: Child Development Publications. *40, 46*

KIERKEGAARD, S. 1954. *The sickness unto death*. Trans. by W. Lourie. Garden City, N. Y.: Doubleday and Co., Inc. *28, 381–82*

KILPATRICK, F. P. (Ed.). 1952. *Human behavior from the transactional point of view*. Hanover, N. H.: Institute for Associated Research. *52*

KLAGES, L. 1949. *Handschrift und Charakter*. 23rd ed. Zurich: Hirzel. *377*

KLEIN, M. 1957. The psycho-analytic play technique: Its history and significance. In Klein, M., *et al.* (Eds.). *New directions in psycho-analysis*. New York: Basic Books, Inc. *295–96, 320*

KLINE, N. S. 1960. The organization of psychiatric care and psychiatric research in the Union of Soviet Socialist Republics. In *Annals N. Y. Acad. Sci.*, 84, Art. 4, 147–224. (Editor in Chief, O. v. St. Whitelock.) *97, 109*

1961. (Ed.). *Pavlovian Conference on higher nervous activity.* *Annals N. Y. Acad. Sci.*, 92, Art. 3. (Editor in Chief, F. N. Furness.) *97*

KLUCKHOHN, C., and MURRAY, H. A. 1948. Personality formation: The determinants. In Kluckhohn, C., and Murray, H. A. (Eds.). *Personality in nature, society, and culture*, 35–48. New York: Alfred A. Knopf, Inc. *367*

KOCH, S. 1954. Clark L. Hull. In W. K. Estes, *et al.* (Eds.). *Modern learning theory: A critical analysis of five examples*, 1–176. New York: Appleton-Century-Crofts. *147*

1959. (Ed.) *Psychology: A study of a science.* New York: McGraw-Hill Book Co. Study I. Conceptual and systematic. *8*
Vol. I. Sensory, perceptual, and physiological formulations.
Vol. II. General systematic formulations, learning, and special processes.
Vol. III. Formulations of the person and the social context. *388*

1962. Study II. Empirical substructure and relations with other sciences.
Vol. IV. Biologically oriented fields: Their place in psychology and in biological science. *8*

1961. Psychological science versus the science-humanism antinomy: intimations of a significant science of man. *Amer. Psychologist*, 16, 629–39. *388*

KOFFKA, K., *219–21; 228–30; 134, 141, 215, 216, 219, 245*
1922. Perception: An introduction to the *Gestalttheorie*. *Psychol. Bull.*, 19, 531–85. *134*

1925. *The growth of the mind*. New York: Harcourt, Brace & World, Inc. *221*

1935. *Principles of Gestalt psychology*. New York: Harcourt, Brace & World, Inc. *219–21, 226, 228–30, 240*

KOHLER, I. 1956. Die Methode des Brillenversuchs in der Wahrnehmungspsychologie mit Bemerkungen zur Lehre von der Adaptation. *Z. Exp. u. angew. Psychol.*, **3**, 381–417. *243–44*

1962. Experiments with goggles. *Sci. American*, **206**, 62–72. *243–44*

KÖHLER, W., *231–34; 178, 179, 180, 215, 216, 219, 245*

1925, 1927. *The mentality of apes.* New York: Harcourt, Brace & World, Inc. *231–34*

1929. *Gestalt psychology.* New York: Liveright Publishing Corp. *219*

1938. *The place of value in a world of facts.* New York: Liveright Publishing Corp. *221, 222, 226, 240*

1940. *Dynamics in psychology.* New York: Liveright Publishing Corp. *221*

1941. On the nature of associations. *Proc. Amer. phil. Soc.*, **84**, 489–502. *220*

1944. Max Wertheimer, 1880–1943. *Psychol. Rev.*, **51**, 143–46. *238*

1947, 1957. *Gestalt psychology: An introduction to new concepts in modern psychology.* New York: Liveright Publishing Corp. *180, 223–26, 228*

1951. Relational determination in perception. In L. A. Jeffress (Ed.). *Cerebral mechanisms in behavior: The Hixon Symposium,* 200–43. New York: John Wiley & Sons, Inc.; London: Chapman & Hall, Ltd. *179*

1958a. The present situation in brain physiology. *Amer. Psychologist,* **13**, 150–54. *179, 225*

1958b. Perceptual organization and learning. *Amer. J. Psychol.*, **71**, 311–15. *234, 235*

1959. Gestalt psychology today. *Amer. Psychologist,* **14**, 727–34. *235*

KÖHLER, W., and WALLACH, H. 1944. Figural after-effects: An investigation of visual processes. *Proc. Amer. philos. Soc.*, **88**, 269–357. *225, 245*

KORNILOV, K. N. 1930. Psychology in the light of dialectic materialism. In Murchison, C. (Ed.). *Psychologies of 1930,* 243–78. Worcester, Mass.: Clark University Press. *93*

KRAVKOV, S. V. 1934. Changes of visual acuity in one eye under the influence of the illumination of the other or of acoustic stimuli. *J. exp. Psychol.*, **17**, 805–12. *91*

KRETSCHMER, E. 1925. *Physique and character.* Trans. by W. J. H. Sprott. New York: Harcourt, Brace & World, Inc. *362*

KRIS, E. 1939. On inspiration. *Int. J. Psychoanal.*, **20**, 377–89. *286*

1941. Probleme der Asthetik. *Int. Z. Psychoanal. und Imago,* **26**, 142–78. *286*

1950. On preconscious mental processes. *Psychoanal. Quart.*, **19**, 540–60. *286, 288*

1952. *Psychoanalytic explorations in art.* New York: International Universities Press, Inc. *289*

KRUEGER, F. E. 1926. Über psychische Ganzheit. *Neue psychol. Stud.*, **1**, 1–123. *249*

KUO, Z. Y. 1928. The fundamental error of the concept of purpose and the trial and error fallacy. *Psychol. Rev.*, **35**, 414–33. *336*

KUPALOV, P. S. 1961. Some normal and pathological properties of nervous processes in the brain. In Kline, N. S. (Ed.). *Pavlovian Conference on*

higher nervous activity. Annals N. Y. Acad. Sci., **92**, Art. 3, 1046–53.
(Editor in Chief, F. N. Furness.) *86, 108–9, 110*

LACK, D. 1939. The behaviour of the robin. I & II. *Proc. Zool. Soc.
Lond.,* **A 109**, 169–78. *348*

1943. *The life of the robin.* London: H. F. and G. Witherby. *348*

LASHLEY, K. S. 1923. The behavioristic interpretation of consciousness.
Psychol. Rev., **30**, 237–72, 329–53. *171*

1929. *Brain mechanisms and intelligence.* Chicago: University of
Chicago Press. *172*

1931. Cerebral control versus reflexology: A reply to Professor Hunter.
J. genl. Psychol., **5**, 3–20, *173*

1934. Nervous mechanisms in learning. In Murchison, C. (Ed.). *A
handbook of general experimental psychology,* 456–96. Worcester, Mass.:
Clark University Press. *173*

1935. Studies of cerebral function in learning. XI. The behavior of the
rat in latch box situations. *Comp. psychol. Monogr.,* **11**, No. 22, 1–42.
174

1947. Structural variation in the nervous system in relation to behavior.
Psychol. Rev., **54**, 325–34. *173*

1950. In search of the engram. *Symposia of the Society for Experimental
Biology,* IV, 454–82. *174, 178*

1951. The problem of serial order in behavior. In Jeffress, L. A. (Ed.).
Cerebral mechanisms in behavior: the Hixon Symposium, 112–46. New
York: John Wiley & Sons, Inc.; London: Chapman & Hall, Ltd. *175,
348*

LAZARUS, R. S. 1961. A substitutive-defensive conception of apperceptive
fantasy. In Kagan, J., and Lesser, G. S. (Eds.). *Contemporary issues
in thematic apperceptive methods.* Springfield, Ill.: Charles C. Thomas,
Publishers. *368*

LEEPER, R. W. 1943. *Lewin's topological and vector psychology: A digest
and a critique.* Eugene: University of Oregon Press. *242*

LEWIN, K., *238–44; 245, 289, 363, 377, 380, 382*

1917. Die psychische Tätigkeit bei der Hemmung von Willensvorgängen
und das Grundgesetz der Assoziation. *Z. Psychol.,* **77**, 212–47. *239*

1921–1922. Das Problem der Willensmessung und das Grundgesetz der
Assoziation. *Psychol. Forsch.,* **1**, 191–302; **2**, 65–140. *239*

1935. *A dynamic theory of personality.* Trans. by D. K. Adams and K. E.
Zener. New York: McGraw-Hill Book Co. *240, 242*

1936. *Principles of topological psychology.* Trans. by F. Heider and G. M.
Heider. New York: McGraw Hill Book Co. *242, 246*

1938. The conceptual representation and the measurement of psychological
forces. *Contrib. to psychol. Theory,* **1**, No. 4. *241–43*

1940. Formalization and progress in psychology. *University of Iowa
Studies in Child Welfare,* **16**, No. 3, 9–42. *239, 241, 242*

1947. Frontiers in group dynamics. *Human Relations,* **1**, 5–41; 143–53.
243

1948. *Resolving social conflicts: Selected papers on group dynamics.* New
York: Harper and Row, Publishers. *243*

1954. Behavior and development as a function of the total situation. In
Carmichael, L. (Ed.). *Manual of child psychology,* 918–70. (See also
Escalona, S., 971–83.) New York: John Wiley & Sons, Inc.; London:
Chapman & Hall, Ltd. *240*

LIDDELL, H. S., JAMES, W. T., and ANDERSON, O. D. 1934. The comparative physiology of the conditioned motor reflex. *Comp. psychol. Monogr.*, 11, No. 51. *79*

LIPPS, T. 1907. Das Wissen von fremden Ichen. *Psychol. Untersuch.*, 1, 694–722. *328*

LOCKE, J. 1690. *An essay concerning human understanding.* London: T. Basset. *62, 66*

LONDON, I. D. 1949. A historical survey of psychology in the Soviet Union. *Psychol. Bull.*, 46, 241–77. *91, 92, 93, 94*
1952. Russian psychology and psychiatry. In Zirkle, C., and Meyerhoff, H. A. (Eds.). *Soviet science*, 40–47. Washington, D. C.: A. A. A. S. *94*
1954. Research on sensory interaction in the Soviet Union. *Psychol. Bull.*, 51, 531–68. *91*

LORENZ, K. 1950. The comparative method in studying innate behaviour patterns. *Symposia of the Society for Experimental Biology*, IV, 221–68. *347*

LUCE, R. D. 1959. *Individual choice behavior.* New York: John Wiley & Sons, Inc. *210*

MacCORQUODALE, K., and MEEHL, P. E. 1948. On a distinction between hypothetical constructs and intervening variables. *Psychol. Rev.*, 55, 95–107. *170*
1954. Edward C. Tolman. In Estes, W. K., *et al. Modern learning theory: A critical analysis of five examples*, 177–266. New York: Appleton-Century-Crofts. *140*

MACKINNON, D. W. 1962. The nature and nurture of creative talent. *Amer. Psychologist*, 17, 484–95. *314*

MALINOWSKI, B. 1927. *Sex and repression in savage society.* New York: Harcourt, Brace & World, Inc. *272*

MASLOW, A. H. 1954. *Motivation and personality.* New York: Harper and Row, Publishers. *354–56, 385*

MAX, L. W. 1937. Action-current responses in the deaf during awakening, kinesthetic imagery and abstract thinking. *J. comp. Psychol.*, 24, 301–44. *127*

MAY, R. (Ed.). 1961. *Existential psychology.* New York: Random House, Inc. *385*

MAY, R., ANGEL, E., and ELLENBERGER, H. F. (Eds.). 1958. *Existence.* New York: Basic Books, Inc. *382, 384, 385*

MAYO, E. 1948. *Some notes on the psychology of Pierre Janet.* Cambridge, Mass.: Harvard University Press. *253–54*

McCARTHY, D. 1954. Language development in children. In Carmichael, L. (Ed.). *Manual of child psychology*, 492–630. New York: John Wiley & Sons, Inc. *40, 46*

McCLELLAND, D., ATKINSON, J., CLARK, R., and LOWELL, E. 1953. *The achievement motive.* New York: Appleton-Century-Crofts. *368*

McDOUGALL, W., *335–50; 247, 363, 371, 390*
1905. *Physiological psychology.* London: J. M. Dent & Sons. *114*

1908. *Introduction to social psychology.* 5th ed., 1912. London: Methuen & Co. Ltd. *115, 338, 339, 341, 343*

1912. *Psychology: The study of behavior.* London: Williams and Norgate, Ltd.; New York: Holt, Rinehart and Winston, Inc. *337, 338*

1923. *Outline of psychology.* New York: Charles Scribner's Sons. *337–38, 341, 349*

1926. *Outline of abnormal psychology.* New York: Charles Scribner's Sons. *253*

1930. The hormic psychology. In Murchison, C. (Ed.). *Psychologies of 1930,* 3–36. Worcester, Mass.: Clark University Press. *348*

1932. *The energies of men: A study of the fundamentals of dynamic psychology.* London: Methuen & Co., Ltd. *335–36, 339–40, 346, 347*

McEwen, P. 1959. Figural after effects, retinal size and apparent size. *Brit. J. Psychol.,* **50,** 41–47. *225*

McEwen, P., and Rodger, R. S. 1960. Some individual differences in figural after-effects. *Brit. J. Psychol.,* **51,** 1–8. *225*

McGeoch, J. A. 1942. *The psychology of human learning.* New York: Longmans, Green & Co. *32, 35*

McGeoch, J. A., and Irion, A. L. 1952. *The psychology of human learning.* 2nd ed. Revised by A. L. Irion. New York: David McKay Co., Inc. *35*

McGeoch, J. A., and McDonald, W. T. 1931. Meaningful relation and retroactive inhibition. *Amer. J. Psychol.,* **43,** 579–88. *34*

McGeoch, J. A., and Underwood, B. J. 1943. Tests of the two-factor theory of retroactive inhibition. *J. exp. Psychol.,* **32,** 1–16. *35*

McGill, W. J. 1960. Mathematics: The other world. Review of Bush, R. R., and Estes, W. K. (Eds.). *Studies in mathematical learning theory. Contemp. Psychol.,* **5,** 284–85. *212*

McKellar, P. 1962. The method of introspection. In Scher, J. (Ed.). *Theories of the mind,* 619–44. New York: The Free Press of Glencoe. *22*

McNemar, Q. 1960. At random: Sense and nonsense. *Amer. Psychologist,* **15,** 295–97. *212*

Melton, A. W., and Irwin, J. McQ. 1940. The influence of degree of interpolated learning on retroactive inhibition and the overt transfer of specific responses. *Amer. J. Psychol.,* **53,** 173–203. *34*

Merleau-Ponty, M. 1945. Phénoménologie de la perception. Paris: Gallimard. *385, 387*

Mesmer, F. A. 1779. *Mémoire sur la découverte du magnétisme animal.* Trans. *Mesmerism.* London: MacDonald, 1948. *252*

Metzger, W. 1954. Grundbegriffe der Gestaltpsychologie. *Schweizerische Z. für Psychol. u. ihre Anwendungen,* **13,** 3–15. *249*

Meyer, A. 1897. A short sketch of the problems of psychiatry. *Amer. J. Insanity,* **53,** 538–49. *327, 350*

1908. The role of the mental factors in psychiatry. *Amer. J. Insanity,* **65,** 39–56. *350–51*

Meyer, M. F. 1911. *The fundamental laws of human behavior.* Boston: Richard G. Badger (The Gorham Press). *130*

1921. *The psychology of the other one.* Columbia: Missouri Book Co. *130, 201*

MICHOTTE, A., *24, 49–50, 55*
1946. La perception de la causalité. Louvain: Institut Supérieur de Philosophie. *51*
1952. Autobiography. In Boring, E. G., *et al.* (Eds.). *A history of psychology in autobiography,* Vol. IV, 213–36. Worcester, Mass.: Clark University Press. *49–50*
1963. The perception of causality. Trans. by T. R. and Elaine Miles. London: Methuen & Co.; New York: Basic Books, Inc. *51*

MILL, J. 1829. *Analysis of the phenomena of the human mind.* London: Baldwin. *65*

MILL, J. S. 1869. *Notes and annotations on J. Mill, Analysis of the phenomena of the human mind.* 2 vols. London: Longmans, Green & Co. *65, 67*

MILLER, G. A., GALANTER, E., and PRIBRAM, K. H. 1960. *Plans and the structure of behavior.* New York: Holt, Rinehart and Winston, Inc. *107, 175, 206–8, 348–49, 367, 386*

MILLER, N. E., *149–56*
1948a. Studies of fear as an acquirable drive: 1. Fear as motivation and fear-reduction as reinforcement in the learning of new responses. *J. exp. Psychol.,* **38**, 89–101. *85, 151*
1948b. Theory and experiment relating psychoanalytic displacement to stimulus–response generalization. *J. abn. soc. Psychol.,* **43**, 155–78. *151*
1951. Learnable drives and rewards. In Stevens, S. S. (Ed.). *Handbook of experimental psychology,* 435–72. New York: John Wiley & Sons, Inc. *151*
1954. Drive, drive reduction, and reward. *Fourteenth International Congress of Psychology,* Montreal. *193*
1957. Experiments on motivation: Studies combining psychological, physiological, and pharmacological techniques. *Science,* **126**, 1271–78. *153, 154*
1959. Liberalization of basic S–R concepts: Extensions to conflict behavior, motivation, and social learning. In Koch, S. (Ed.). *Psychology: A study of a science,* Vol. II, 196–292. New York: McGraw-Hill Book Co. *150, 153*
1961a. Some recent studies of conflict behavior and drugs. *Amer. Psychologist,* **16**, 12–24. *154, 374*
1961b. Analytical studies of drive and reward. *Amer. Psychologist,* **16**, 739–54. *154, 155*
1963. Some reflections on the law of effect produce a new alternative to drive reduction. In Jones, M. R. (Ed.). *The Nebraska Symposium on Motivation,* XI, 65–112. *107, 155, 156, 196*

MILLER, N. E., and DOLLARD, J. 1941. *Social learning and imitation.* New Haven: Yale University Press. *149, 153, 196*

MINKOWSKI, E. 1933. *Le temps vécu.* Paris: J. L. L. d'Artrey. *384, 385*

MINTZ, A. 1958. Recent developments in psychology in the U. S. S. R. In Farnsworth, P. R., *et al.* (Eds.). *Ann. Rev. Psychol.,* **9**, 453–504. *97, 98*
1959. Further developments in psychology in the U. S. S. R. In Farnsworth, P. R., *et al.* (Eds.). *Ann. Rev. Psychol.,* **10**, 455–87. *97, 98*

MORGAN, C. D., and MURRAY, H. A. 1935. A method for investigating fantasies. *Arch. neurol. psychiat.*, 34, 289–306. *362, 367*

MORGAN, C. L. 1894. *An introduction to comparative psychology.* London: Walter Scott. *69*

MORUZZI, G., and MAGOUN, H. W. 1949. Brain stem reticular formation and activation of the EEG. *Electroenceph. clin. Neurophysiol.*, 1, 455–73. *102, 176*

MOTOKAWA, K., NAKAGAWA, D., and KOHATA, T. 1957. Figural after-effects and retinal induction. *J. genl. Psychol.*, 57, 121–35. *225*

MOWRER, O. H., *194–98*
  1953. Neurosis, psychotherapy, and two-factor learning theory. In Mowrer, O. H. (Ed.). *Psychotherapy: Theory and research,* 140–49. New York: The Ronald Press Co. *194*
  1960a. *Learning theory and behavior.* New York: John Wiley & Sons, Inc. *156, 193, 194, 196*
  1960b. *Learning theory and the symbolic process.* New York: John Wiley & Sons, Inc. *156, 196, 197*

MULLAHY, P. 1948. *Oedipus—Myth and complex.* New York: Hermitage. *328*
  1952. (Ed.). *The contributions of Harry Stack Sullivan.* New York: Hermitage. *328*

MÜLLER, G. E. 1911, 1913, 1917. Zur Analyse der Gedächtnistätigkeit und der Vorstellungsverlaufes. *Z. Psychol., Erganzungsbd.*, 5, 8, 9. *23*

MÜLLER, G. E., and PILZECKER, A. 1900. Experimentelle Beiträge zur Lehre von Gedächtnis. *Z. Psychol., Erganzungsbd.*, 1. *34*

MÜLLER, G. E., and SCHUMANN, F. 1889. Über die psychologischen Grundlagen der Vergleichung gehobener Gewichte. *Arch. ges. Physiol.*, 45, 37–112. *23, 24*

MUNROE, R. L. 1955. *Schools of psychoanalytic thought.* New York: Holt, Rinehart and Winston, Inc. *317–18, 327*

MURPHY, G. 1947. *Personality: A biosocial approach to origins and structure.* New York: Harper and Row, Publishers. *378*
  1949. *Historical introduction to modern psychology.* Rev. ed. New York: Harcourt, Brace & World, Inc. *9n, 243–44*
  1958. *Human potentialities.* New York: Basic Books, Inc. *326*

MURRAY, H. A., *362–68; 293*
  1955. American Icarus. In Burton, A., and Harris, R. E. (Eds.). *Clinical studies in personality,* Vol. II, 615–41. New York: Harper and Row, Publishers. *367*
  1959. Preparations for the scaffold of a comprehensive system. In Koch, S. (Ed.). *Psychology: A study of a science,* Vol. III, 7–54. New York: McGraw-Hill Book Co. *363, 365*
  1963. Studies of stressful interpersonal disputations. *Amer. Psychologist,* 18, 28–36. *365, 366, 367*

MURRAY, H. A., et al. 1938. *Explorations in personality.* New York: Oxford University Press. *314, 362, 363, 382*

MURRAY, H. A., et al. (Office of Strategic Services Assessment Staff). 1948. *Assessment of men.* New York: Holt, Rinehart and Winston, Inc. *362*

MURRAY, H. A., and KLUCKHOHN, C. 1953. Outline of a conception of personality. In Kluckhohn, C., Murray, H. A., and Schneider, D. (Eds.). *Personality in nature, society, and culture*, 3–52. 2nd ed. New York: Alfred A. Knopf, Inc. *363, 366*

MUSSEN, P. H. (Ed.). 1960. *Handbook of research methods in child development*. New York: John Wiley & Sons, Inc. *40*

NEWELL, A., SHAW, J. C., and SIMON, H. 1958. Elements of a theory of human problem-solving. *Psychol. Rev.*, **65**, 151–66. *206*

NUTTIN, J. 1957. Personality dynamics. In David, H. P., and von Bracken, H. (Eds.). *Perspectives in personality theory*, 183–95. London: Tavistock Publications, Ltd. *378–79*

OLDS, J. 1958. Satiation effects in self-stimulation of the brain. *J. comp. physiol. Psychol.*, **51**, 675–78. *154*

OLDS, J., and MILNER, P. 1954. Positive reinforcement produced by electrical stimulation of septal area and other regions of rat brain. *J. comp. physiol. Psychol.*, **47**, 419–27. *177*

OSGOOD, C. E. 1953. *Method and theory in experimental psychology*. New York: Oxford University Press. *34, 199*

1962. Studies on the generality of affective meaning systems. *Amer. Psychologist*, **17**, 10–28. *199, 200*

OSGOOD, C. E., and HEYER, A. W., Jr. 1952. A new interpretation of figural after-effects. *Psychol. Rev.*, **59**, 98–118. *225*

OSGOOD, C. E., SUCI, G. J., and TANNENBAUM, P. H. 1957. *The measurement of meaning*. Urbana: University of Illinois Press. *197, 198, 199*

PAKOVICH, B. I. 1958. Concerning the minimal time of precedence of acoustic stimuli to a painful stimulus necessary for the formation of motor-defensive conditioned reflexes in dogs. *Papers of the U. S. S. R. Academy of Sciences*, **116**, 335. (In Russian.) *79*

PAVLOV, I. P., *74–78; 95–97; 35, 70, 143, 163, 178, 194, 227, 251*

1927. *Conditioned reflexes: an investigation of the physiological activity of the cerebral cortex*. Trans. by G. V. Anrep. New York: Oxford University Press. *78, 96, 141*

1928. *Lectures on conditioned reflexes*, Vol. I. Trans. by W. H. Gantt. New York: International Publishers Co. *78*

1932. The reply of a physiologist to psychologists. *Psychol. Rev.*, **39**, 91–127. *78*

1941. *Lectures on conditioned reflexes*, Vol. II. Trans. by W. H. Gantt. New York: International Publishers Co. *77*

1957. *Experimental psychology and other essays*. New York: Philosophical Library. *95, 96*

PENFIELD, W., and ROBERTS, L. 1959. *Speech and brain mechanisms*. Princeton, N. J.: Princeton University Press. *175–76*

PETERS, R. S. (Ed.). 1953. *Brett's history of psychology.* London: George Allen & Unwin, Ltd.; New York: The Macmillan Co. *9n*

PIAGET, J., *40–49; 203, 265, 287, 289, 295, 330, 365, 375, 387*
  1923. *The language and thought of the child.* Trans. by M. Worden. New York: Harcourt, Brace & World, Inc., 1926. *40, 41*
  1924. *Judgment and reasoning in the child.* Trans. by M. Worden. New York: Harcourt, Brace & World, Inc., 1928. *40, 41*
  1926. *The child's conception of the world.* Trans. by J. and A. Tomlinson. New York: Harcourt, Brace & World, Inc., 1929. *41, 45, 51*
  1927. *The child's conception of physical causality.* Trans. by M. Worden Gablan. New York: Harcourt, Brace & World, Inc., 1930. *40, 41*
  1932. *The moral judgment of the child.* Trans. by M. Worden Gablan. New York: Harcourt, Brace & World, Inc., 1932. *41*
  1936. *The origins of intelligence in children.* Trans. by M. Cook. New York: International Universities Press, Inc., 1952. *41*
  1937. *The construction of reality in the child.* Trans. by M. Cook. New York: Basic Books, Inc., 1954. *41, 44*
  1952. Autobiography. In Boring, E. G., *et al.* (Eds.). *A history of psychology in autobiography,* Vol. IV, 237–56. Worcester, Mass.: Clark University Press. *40*
  1953. *Logic and psychology.* Trans. by W. Mays and T. Whitehead. Manchester: Manchester University Press; New York: Basic Books, Inc. *47*

PILLSBURY, W. B. 1911. *Essentials of psychology.* New York: The Macmillan Co. *30, 115, 130*

POINCARÉ, H. 1913. Mathematical creation. In *The foundations of science.* Trans. by G. H. Halsted. Lancaster, Pa.: The Science Press. *209*

POSTMAN, L. 1962. Transfer of training as a function of experimental paradigm and degree of first-list learning. *J. verb. learng. and verb. beh.,* **1,** 109–17. *36*

POSTMAN, L., and ALPER, T. G. 1946. Retroactive inhibition as a function of the time of interpolation of the inhibitor between learning and recall. *Amer. J. Psychol.,* **59,** 439–49. *34*

POSTMAN, L., and STARK, K. 1962. Retroactive inhibition as a function of set during the interpolated task. *J. verb. learng. and verb. beh.,* **1,** 304–11. *36*

POSTMAN, L., and TOLMAN, E. C. 1959. Brunswik's probabilistic functionalism. In Koch, S. (Ed.). *Psychology: A study of a science,* Vol. I, 502–64. New York: McGraw-Hill Book Co. *39*

PRENTICE, W. C. H. 1959. The systematic psychology of Wolfgang Köhler. In Koch, S. (Ed.). *Psychology: A study of a science,* Vol. I, 427–55. New York: McGraw-Hill Book Co. *250*
  1961. Some cognitive aspects of motivation. *Amer. Psychologist,* **16,** 503–11. *178, 250*

PRIBRAM, K. H. 1962. The neuropsychology of Sigmund Freud. In Bachrach, A. J. (Ed.). *Experimental foundations of clinical behavior,* 442–68. New York: Basic Books, Inc. *261*

PRINCE, M. 1913. The dissociation of a personality. 2nd ed. New York: Longmans, Green & Co. *252*

PRITCHARD, R. M. 1961. Stabilized images on the retina. *Sci. American*, **204**, 72–78. *183*

PSHONIK, A. T. 1952. The cerebral cortex and the receptor functions of the organism. Moscow: *GIZ*, 240–95. *83*

RANK, O. 1929. *The trauma of birth*. New York: Harcourt, Brace & World, Inc. *284n*

RAPAPORT, D., *289–91; 316, 387*
1951. *Organization and pathology of thought*. New York: Columbia University Press. *287, 289*
1959. The structure of psychoanalytic theory: A systematizing attempt. In Koch, S. (Ed.). *Psychology: A study of a science*, Vol. III, 55–183. New York: McGraw-Hill Book Co. *275, 289, 290–91*
1960. On the psychoanalytic theory of motivation. In Jones, M. R. (Ed.). *The Nebraska Symposium on Motivation*, VIII, 173–240. Lincoln: University of Nebraska Press. *275, 289, 290, 389*

RAUSCH, E. 1952. *Struktur und Metrik figural-optischer Wahrnehmung*. Frankfurt-am-Main: Verlag Dr. Waldemar Kramer. *249*

RAZRAN, G. 1939. A quantitative study of meaning by a conditioned salivary technique (semantic conditioning). *Science*, **90**, 89–91. *100*
1949. Sentential and propositional generalizations of salivary conditioning to verbal stimuli. *Science*, **109**, 447–48. *100*
1952. Experimental semantics. *Transactions N. Y. Acad. Sci.*, **14**, 171–77. *100*
1957a. Recent Russian psychology: 1950–1956. *Contemp. Psychol.*, **2**, 93–101. *95*
1957b. Soviet psychology since 1950. *Science*, **126**, 1100–7. *90, 94, 95, 97*
1958a. Konstantin Nikolaevich Kornilov, 1879–1957. An obituary. *Science*, **128**, 74. *93*
1958b. Soviet psychology and psychophysiology. *Science*, **128**, 1187–94. *93*
1961a. The observable unconscious and the inferable conscious in current Soviet psychophysiology: Interoceptive conditioning, semantic conditioning, and the orienting reflex. *Psychol. Rev.*, **68**, 81–147. *97, 99, 100, 103, 104, 110*
1961b. Discussion: Part IV. In Kline, N. S. (Ed.). *Pavlovian Conference on higher nervous activity*. Annals N. Y. Acad. Sci., **92**, Art. 3, 1069–72. (Editor in Chief, F. N. Furness.) *109*

REIK, T. 1940. *From thirty years with Freud*. New York: Holt, Rinehart and Winston, Inc. *279*

RENNIE, T. A. C. 1943. Adolph Meyer and psychobiology; the man, his methodology and its relation to therapy. *Papers Amer. Congr. genl. Semant.*, **2**, 156–65. *351*

RESTLE, F. 1955. A theory of discrimination learning. *Psychol. Rev.*, **62**, 11–19. *210*
1957. Theory of selective learning with probable reinforcements. *Psychol. Rev.*, **64**, 182–91. *210*

RIBBLE, M. 1943. *The rights of infants: Early psychological needs and their satisfaction.* New York: Columbia University Press. *186*

RIESEN, A. H. 1947. The development of visual perception in man and chimpanzee. *Science,* **106,** 107–8. *180, 387*

RIESMAN, D. 1950. *The lonely crowd.* New Haven: Yale University Press. *323, 326, 382*

RING, F. O. 1957. Testing the validity of personality profiles in psychosomatic illness. *Amer. J. Psychiatry,* **113,** 1075–80. *280*

RIOPELLE, A. J. 1958. Progressive discrimination learning in platyrrhine monkeys. *J. comp. physiol. Psychol.,* **51,** 467–70. *189*

ROBACK, A. A. 1952. *History of American psychology.* New York: Library Publishers. *9n*

ROBINSON, E. S. 1932. *Association theory today: An essay in systematic psychology.* New York: Appleton-Century-Crofts. *33*
1934. Work of the integrated organism. In Murchison, C. (Ed.). *Handbook of general experimental psychology,* 571–650. Worcester, Mass.: Clark University Press. *33*
1935. *Law and the lawyers.* New York: The Macmillan Co. *32*

ROBINSON, E. S., and BILLS, A. G. 1926. Two factors in the work decrement. *J. exp. Psychol.,* **9,** 415–43. *33*

ROGERS, C. R., *379–81; 382, 385*
1942. *Counseling and psychotherapy.* Boston: Houghton Mifflin Co. *380*
1961. *On becoming a person: A therapist's view of psychotherapy.* Boston: Houghton Mifflin Co. *380, 381, 389*

RUBIN, E. 1915. *Synsoplevede Figurer.* Kobenhavn: Gyldendalske Boghandel. *37*
1921. *Visuell wahrgenommene Figuren: Studien in psychologischer Analyse.* Trans. from Danish. Kobenhavn: Gyldendalske Boghandel. *37*
1930. Psychology regarded as a positive science. *Ninth International Congress of Psychology,* 370–71. *38*

RUBINSTEIN (Rubinshtein), S. L. 1958. *O myshlenii i putyakh ego issledovaniya.* (*Thinking and methods of its study.*) Acad. Sci., Moscow, U. S. S. R. *99*
1960. *Protsess myshleniya i zakonomernosti analiza, sinteza i obobshcheniya: Eksperimental'nye issledovaniya.* (*The processes of thinking and laws of analysis, synthesis and generalization: Experimental studies.*) Acad. Sci., Moscow, U. S. S. R. *99*

RYLE, G. 1949. *The concept of mind.* London: Hutchinson & Co., Ltd. *246*

SACHS, H. 1944. *Freud, master and friend.* Cambridge, Mass.: Harvard University Press. *279, 363*

SAGARA, M., and OYAMA, T. 1957. Experimental studies on figural aftereffects in Japan. *Psychol. Bull.,* **54,** 327–38. *225*

SANDER, F. 1930. Structure, totality of experience, and gestalt. In Murchison, C. (Ed.). *Psychologies of 1930*, 188–204. Worcester, Mass.: Clark University Press. *250, 369*

SARTRE, J.-P. 1948. *The emotions: An outline of a theory.* Trans. by B. Frechtman. New York: Philosophical Library. *28, 383*

SCHNIERMANN, A. L. 1930. Bekhterev's reflexological school. In Murchison, C. (Ed.). *Psychologies of 1930*, 221–42. Worcester, Mass.: Clark University Press. *92*

SECHENOV, J. M. 1863. Reflexes of the brain. In Subkov, A. A. (Ed.). *Selected works* (Izbrannyyetrudy), 12. Institute for Experimental Medicine, Moscow, U. S. S. R., 1935. *90*

SENDEN, M. VON. 1932. *Raum- und Gestaltauffassung bei operierten Blindgeborenen vor und nach der Operation.* Leipzig: S. A. Barth. *180*

SHERMAN, M. 1927. The differentiation of emotional responses in infants. I. Judgments of emotional responses from motion-picture views and from actual observations. *J. comp. Psychol.*, **7**, 265–84. *123*

SIGAL, J. J., STAR, K., and FRANKS, C. M. 1958. Hysterics and dysthymics as criterion groups in the study of introversion-extraversion. *J. abn. soc. Psychol.*, **57**, 143–48. *314*

SIMON, B. 1957. *Psychology in the Soviet Union.* London: Butler and Tanner; Stanford, Calif.: Stanford University Press. *97*

SKINNER, B. F., *162–69*
1932. On the rate of formation of a conditioned reflex. *J. genl. Psychol.*, **7**, 274–86. *84*
1938. *The behavior of organisms: An experimental analysis.* New York: Appleton-Century-Crofts. *84, 86, 163, 176, 246*
1950. Are theories of learning necessary? *Psychol. Rev.*, **57**, 193–216. *163*
1953a. *Science and human behavior.* New York: The Macmillan Co. *163*
1953b. Some contributions of an experimental analysis of behavior to psychology as a whole. *Amer. Psychologist*, **8**, 69–78. *164*
1954. The science of learning and the art of teaching. *Harvard Educational Rev.*, **24**, 86–97. Also in *Psychology and the behavioral sciences.* Pittsburgh: University of Pittsburgh Press, 1955. Also in Skinner, B. F. *Cumulative Record*, 145–57 New York: Appleton-Century-Crofts, 1959. *166*
1956. A case history in scientific method. *Amer. Psychologist*, **11**, 221–33. Also in Skinner, B. F. *Cumulative Record*, 76–100. *86, 162, 163*
1957a. The experimental analysis of behavior. *Amer. Scientist*, **45**, 343–71. Also in Skinner, B. F. *Cumulative Record*, 100–31. New York: Appleton-Century-Crofts, 1959. *166*
1957b. *Verbal behavior.* New York: Appleton-Century-Crofts. *166–68*
1958a. Reinforcement theory today. *Amer. Psychologist*, **13**, 94–99. Also in Skinner, B. F. *Cumulative Record*, 131–41. New York: Appleton-Century-Crofts, 1959. *165*
1958b. Teaching machines. *Science*, **128**, 969–77. Also in Skinner, B. F. *Cumulative Record*, 158–82. New York: Appleton-Century-Crofts, 1959. *166*
1960. Pigeons in a pelican. *Amer. Psychologist*, **15**, 28–37. *166*

SMITH, S., and GUTHRIE, E. R. 1921. *General psychology in terms of behavior.* New York: Appleton-Century-Crofts. *125, 160*

SODHI, K. S. 1954. Mittel- und westeuropäische Sozialpsychologie. In Wellek, A. *Bericht über den 19 Kongress der Deutschen Gesellschaft für Psychologie,* 7–33. Göttingen: Verlag für Psychologie. *249*

SOKOLOV, E. N. 1960. Neuronal models and the orienting influence. In Brazier, M. A. B. (Ed.). *Central nervous system and behavior,* 187–239. New York: Josiah Macy, Jr. Foundation. *104*

SOLLEY, C., and MURPHY, G. 1960. *Development of the perceptual world.* New York: Basic Books, Inc. *53*

SOLOMON, P., KUBZANSKY, P. E., LEIDERMAN, P. H., MENDELSON, J. H., TRUMBULL, R., WEXLER, D. (Eds.). 1961. *Sensory deprivation.* Cambridge, Mass.: Harvard University Press. *187–88*

SOLOMON, R. L., and TURNER, L. H. 1962. Discriminative classical conditioning in dogs paralyzed by curare can later control discriminative avoidance responses in the normal state. *Psychol. Rev.,* **69,** 202–19. *80–81*

SPEARMAN, C. E. 1923. *The nature of 'intelligence' and the principles of cognition.* London: Macmillan & Co., Ltd. *88*

SPENCE, K. W., *157–60; 156, 335*
1936. The nature of discrimination learning in animals. *Psychol. Rev.,* **43,** 427–49. *157*
1937. The differential response in animals to stimuli varying within a single dimension. *Psychol. Rev.,* **44,** 430–44. *157*
1952a. Clark Leonard Hull: 1884–1952. *Amer. J. Psychol.,* **65,** 639–46. *149*
1952b. The nature of the response in discrimination learning. *Psychol. Rev.,* **59,** 89–93. *158*
1956. *Behavior theory and conditioning.* New Haven: Yale University Press. *157, 158, 159, 200*
1958. Behavior theory and selective learning. In Jones, M. R. (Ed.). *The Nebraska Symposium on Motivation,* VI, 73–107. *159, 160*

SPIELBERGER, C. D., and LEVIN, S. M. 1962. What is learned in verbal conditioning? *J. verb. learng. and verb. beh.,* **1,** 125–32. *87, 203–4*

SPITZ, H. H. 1958. The present status of the Köhler-Wallach theory of satiation. *Psychol. Bull.,* **55,** 1–28. *225*

SPITZ, R. A. 1946. Hospitalism: A follow-up report. *The psychoanalytic study of the child,* Vol. II, 113–17. New York: International Universities Press, Inc., *186*
1955. Childhood development phenomena: The influences of the mother-child relationship and its disturbances. In Soddy, K. (Ed.). *Mental health and infant development.* New York: Basic Books, Inc. *186*

SPRANGER, E. 1928. *Types of men: The psychology and ethics of personality.* Trans. of 5th German ed. by P. J. Pigors. Halle: Neimeyer. *369–70*

STERN, W. (sometimes L. W.), *359–62; 358*
1906, 1918, 1924. *Person und Sache: System der philosophischen Weltanschauung.* 3 vols. Leipzig: S. A. Barth. *359*
1930. Autobiography. In Murchison, C. (Ed.). *A history of psychology*

in autobiography, Vol. I, 335–88. Worcester, Mass.: Clark University Press. *360, 361*

1938. *General psychology from the personalistic standpoint.* Trans. by H. D. Spoerl from the German edition of 1935. New York: The Macmillan Co. *360, 361, 380*

STEVENS, S. S. 1939. Psychology and the science of science. *Psychol. Bull.,* **36,** 221–63. *4*

1956. The direct estimation of sensory magnitudes: loudness. *Amer. J. Psychol.,* **69,** 1–25. *56*

STORY, A. 1959. Figural after-effects as a function of the perceived characteristics of the inspection-figure. *Amer. J. Psychol.,* **72,** 46–56. *225*

STRATTON, G. M. 1897. Vision without inversion of the retinal image. *Psychol. Rev.,* **4,** 341–60; 463–81. *244*

STUMPF, C. 1883. *Tonpsychologie.* Leipzig: Hirzel. *130*

SULLIVAN, H. S., *326–33; 265, 316, 317 375, 378, 380*

1947. *Conceptions of modern psychiatry.* Washington, D. C.: William Alanson White Psychiatric Foundation. *328*

1953. *The interpersonal theory of psychiatry.* New York: W. W. Norton & Co., Inc. *295, 328, 330*

1954. *The psychiatric interview.* New York: W. W. Norton & Co., Inc. *328*

1962. *Schizophrenia as a human process.* In Perry, H. S. (Ed.). New York: W. W. Norton & Co., Inc. *328, 333*

SULLY, J. 1884. *Outlines of psychology.* New York: Appleton-Century-Crofts. *25*

SUPPES, P., and ATKINSON, R. C. 1960. *Markov learning models for multiperson interactions.* Stanford, Calif.: Stanford University Press. *210*

TAPPAN, H. P. 1841. *The doctrine of the will.* New York: Dodd, Mead & Co. *18*

TAYLOR, F. V. 1957. Psychology and the design of machines. *Amer. Psychologist,* **12,** 249–56. *211, 389*

1960. Four basic ideas in engineering psychology. *Amer. Psychologist,* **15,** 643–49. *389*

TAYLOR, J. A. 1953. A personality scale of manifest anxiety. *J. abn. soc. Psychol.,* **48,** 285–90. *160*

TEPLOV, B. M. (Ed.). 1956–1959. *Tipologicheskie osobennosti vysshei nervnoi deyatel'nosti cheloveka. (Typological characteristics of man's higher nervous activity.)* 2 vols. Acad. Pedagogical Sci., Moscow, U. S. S. R. *98*

THIGPEN, C. H., and CLECKLEY, H. A. 1954. A case of multiple personality. *J. abn. soc. Psychol.,* **49,** 135–51. *252*

1957. *The three faces of Eve.* New York: McGraw-Hill Book Co. *252*

THOMPSON, C. 1960. Theoretical framework of the William Alanson White Institute. In Hoch, P. H., and Zubin, J. (Eds.). *Current approaches to psychoanalysis,* 13–21. New York: Grune & Stratton, Inc. *328*

THORNDIKE, E. L., *69–74; 111, 125, 138, 139, 194, 195, 232, 334*

1898. Animal intelligence: An experimental study of the associative processes in animals. *Psychol. Rev. Monogr. Suppl.*, No. 8. Reprinted with other animal studies in the same author's *Animal intelligence*. New York: The Macmillan Co., 1911. *70, 86*

1905. *The elements of psychology*. New York: A. G. Seiler. *71*

1931. *Human learning*. New York: Appleton-Century-Crofts. *73*

1932. *The fundamentals of learning*. New York: Bureau of Publications, Teachers College, Columbia University. *73*

1933. *An experimental study of rewards*. New York: Bureau of Publications, Teachers College, Columbia University. *73*

1943. *Man and his works*. Cambridge, Mass.: Harvard University Press. *74*

TILLICH, P. 1952. *The courage to be*. New Haven: Yale University Press. *382*

TINBERGEN, N. 1951. *The study of instinct*. New York: Oxford University Press. *347*

1953. *Social behavior in animals*. London: Methuen & Co., Ltd.; New York: John Wiley & Sons, Inc. *347*

TITCHENER, E. B., *27–30; 131, 214, 357, 358*

1898. The postulates of a structural psychology. *Philos. Rev.*, **7**, 449–65. *27*

1899. Structural and functional psychology. *Philos. Rev.*, **8**, 290–99. *27*

1901, 1905. *Experimental psychology: A manual of laboratory practice*. 2 vols. New York: The Macmillan Co. *30, 39*

1909. *Lectures on the experimental psychology of the thought process*. New York: The Macmillan Co. *30*

1909–1910. *A textbook of psychology*. New York: The Macmillan Co. *28, 30*

1915. *A beginner's psychology*. New York: The Macmillan Co. *29*

1929. *Systematic psychology: Prolegomena*. New York: The Macmillan Co. *30*

TOLMAN, E. C., *133–41; 39, 147, 156, 160, 178, 194, 214, 335, 338, 348*

1920. Instinct and purpose. *Psychol. Rev.*, **27**, 217–33. *134*

1922. A new formula for behaviorism. *Psychol. Rev.*, **29**, 44–53. *134, 135*

1923. A behavioristic account of the emotions. *Psychol. Rev.*, **30**, 217–27. *134*

1932. *Purposive behavior in animals and men*. New York: Century Co.; Berkeley and Los Angeles: University of California Press, 1949. *134, 135, 136*

1935. Psychology versus immediate experience. *Philos. of Science*, **2**, 356–80. *136*

1938. The determiners of behavior at a choice point. *Psychol. Rev.*, **45**, 1–41. *136*

1942. *Drives toward war*. New York: Appleton-Century-Crofts. *136*

1948a. Kurt Lewin. *Psychol. Rev.*, **55**, 1–4. *136*

1948b. Cognitive maps in rats and men. *Psychol. Rev.*, **55**, 189–208. *136, 139*

1949a. There is more than one kind of learning. *Psychol. Rev.*, **56**, 144–55. *136*

1949b. The psychology of social learning. *J. soc. Issues*, Suppl. Series No. 3. *136*

1951. A psychological model. In Parsons, T., and Shils, E. A. (Eds.). *Toward a general theory of action*, 279–361. Cambridge, Mass.: Harvard University Press. *137, 138*

1952. Autobiography. In Boring, E. G. (Ed.). *A history of psychology in autobiography*, Vol. IV, 323–39. Worcester, Mass.: Clark University Press. *133, 139*

1955. Principles of performance. *Psychol. Rev.*, **62**, 315–26. *140*

1956. Egon Brunswik: 1903–1955. *Amer. J. Psychol.*, **69**, 315–24. *39*

1959a. Performance vectors: A theoretical and experimental attack upon emphasis, effect, and repression. *Amer. Psychologist*, **14**, 1–7. *140*

1959b. Principles of purposive behavior. In Koch, S. (Ed.). *Psychology: A study of a science*, Vol. II, 92–157. New York: McGraw-Hill Book Co. *140, 147*

TROLAND, L. T. 1928. *The fundamentals of human motivation*. New York: D. Van Nostrand Co., Inc. *88*

TRYON, R. C. 1963. Psychology in flux: The academic-professional bipolarity. *Amer. Psychologist*, **18**, 134–43. *389*

UNDERWOOD, B. J. 1945. The effect of successive interpolations on retroactive and proactive inhibition. *Psychol. Monogr.*, **59**, No. 3. *34*

1957. Interference and forgetting. *Psychol. Rev.*, **64**, 49–60. *36*

1961. Ten years of massed practice on distributed practice. *Psychol. Rev.*, **68**, 229–47. *36*

UNDERWOOD, B. J., and SCHULZ, R. W. 1960. *Meaningfulness and verbal learning*. Philadelphia: J. B. Lippincott Co. *36*

UNDERWOOD, B. J., and VITERNA, R. O. 1951. Studies of distributed practice. IV. The effect of similarity and rate of presentation in verbal discrimination learning. *J. exp. Psychol.*, **42**, 296–99. *36*

VAIHINGER, H. 1925. The philosophy of 'As if'; a system of the theoretical, practical and religious fictions of mankind. New York: Harcourt, Brace & World, Inc. *301*

VERNON, M. D. 1957. Cognitive inference in perceptual activity. *Brit. J. Psychol.*, **48**, 35–47. *245*

VERPLANCK, W. S. 1955. The control of the content of conversation: Reinforcement of statements of opinion. *J. abn. soc. Psychol.*, **51**, 668–76. *86, 204*

VORONIN, L. G., and NAPALKOV, A. V. 1959. Methodological techniques for the formation of complex systems of conditioned motor reflexes in animals. *Zh. vyssh. nervn. Deyatel.*, **9**, 788–91. *82*

WALK, R. D., and GIBSON, E. J. 1961. A comparative and analytical study of visual depth perception. *Psychol. Monogr.*, **75**, (15). *55*

WALLACH, H., and O'CONNELL, D. N. 1953. The kinetic depth effect. *J. exp. Psychol.*, **45**, 205–17. *245*

WALLACH, H., O'CONNELL, D. N., and NEISSER, U. 1953. The memory effect of visual perception of three-dimensional form. *J. exp. Psychol.*, **45**, 360–68. *245*

WALLAS, G. 1908. *Human nature in politics.* London: Constable & Co. Ltd. *343–44*

1914. *The great society.* New York: The Macmillan Co. *343–44*

WASHBURN, M. F. 1916. *Movement and mental imagery: Outlines of a motor theory of the complexer mental processes.* Boston: Houghton Mifflin Co. *30*

1930. A system of motor psychology. In Murchison, C. (Ed.). *Psychologies of 1930,* 81–94. Worcester, Mass.: Clark University Press. *30*

WATSON, J. B., *111–29; 92, 162, 173, 197, 198, 215, 334, 336*

1913. Psychology as a behaviorist views it. *Psychol. Rev.,* **20,** 158–77. *112, 201*

1914. *Behavior: An introduction to comparative psychology.* New York: Holt, Rinehart and Winston, Inc. *112, 122, 126, 129, 133*

1916. The place of the conditioned-reflex in psychology. *Psychol. Rev.,* **23,** 89–117. *120*

1919. *Psychology from the standpoint of a behaviorist.* Philadelphia: J. B. Lippincott Co. 3rd ed., 1929. *116, 117, 118, 119, 120–21, 122–23, 125, 134*

1920. Is thinking merely the action of language mechanisms? *Brit. J. Psychol.,* **11,** 87–104. *227*

1924. The place of kinaesthetic, visceral, and laryngeal organization in thinking. *Psychol. Rev.,* **31,** 339–48. *125, 126, 227*

1925. *Behaviorism.* New York: People's Institute Publishing Co. Rev. ed., New York: W. W. Norton & Co., Inc., 1930. *118, 123, 126, 127, 227*

1936. Autobiography. In Murchison, C. (Ed.). *A history of psychology in autobiography,* Vol. III, 271–81. Worcester, Mass.: Clark University Press. *116*

WEINER, M. 1956. Perceptual development in a distorted room: A phenomenological study. *Psychol. Monogr.,* No. 423, 1–38. *245*

WEISS, A. P. 1925. *A theoretical basis of human behavior.* 2nd ed., 1929. *130, 201*

1928. Feeling and emotion as forms of behavior. In Reymert, M. L. (Ed.). *Feelings and emotions: The Wittenberg Symposium,* 170–90. Worcester, Mass.: Clark University Press. *131*

1930. The biosocial standpoint in psychology. In Murchison, C. (Ed.). *Psychologies of 1930,* 301–6. Worcester, Mass.: Clark University Press. *131*

WELLEK, A. 1955. *Ganzheitspsychologie und Strukturtheorie.* Bern, Switzerland: A. Francke Verlag. *250*

1957. The phenomenological and experimental approaches to psychology and characterology. In David, H. P., and von Bracken, H. (Eds.). *Perspectives in personality theory,* 278–99. London: Tavistock Publications, Ltd. *250*

1958. Die Ganzheitspsychologischen Aspekte der Musikästhetik. *Bericht über den internationalen musikwissenschaftlichen Kongress Wien,* 677–88. *250*

WENDT, G. R., NOWLIS, H., and NOWLIS, V. 1956. The effects of drugs on social and emotional behavior. Unpublished progress report, University of Rochester, Project M–681(c). *56*

WERTHEIMER, M., *215–18; 235–38; 219, 245*
   1912. Experimentelle Studien über das Sehen von Bewegung. *Z. Psychol.,*
   61, 161–265. *50*
   1921, 1923. Untersuchungen zur Lehre von der Gestalt. *Psychol. Forsch.,*
   1, 47–58; **4**, 301–50. *221–23*
   1945. *Productive thinking.* New York: Harper and Row, Publishers.
   231, 235–38

WESLEY, F. 1961. Neither the soul nor the machine. Review of Rubinstein,
   S. L. *Grundlagen der allgemeinen Psychologie.* 2nd rev. ed. Trans.
   from Russian by H. Hartmann. Berlin, East Germany: Volkseigener
   Verlag, 1959. *Contemp. Psychol.,* **6**, 406–8. *94*

WHITE, R. W., *293–95; 45, 274, 287, 365*
   1952. *Lives in progress: A study of the natural growth of personality.*
   New York: Holt, Rinehart and Winston, Inc. *295*
   1959. Motivation reconsidered: The concept of competence. *Psychol.
   Rev.,* **66**, 297–333. *294*
   1960. Competence and the psychosexual stages of development. In
   Jones, M. R. (Ed.). *The Nebraska Symposium on Motivation,* VIII,
   97–144. Lincoln: University of Nebraska Press. *290, 294*

WHORF, B. L. 1956. *Language, thought, and reality: Selected writings of
   Benjamin Lee Whorf.* Edited by J. B. Carroll Cambridge, Mass.: The
   M.I.T. Press. *201–2*

WHYTE, W. H., Jr. 1956. *The organization man.* New York: Simon and
   Schuster, Inc. *326*

WIENER, N. 1948. *Cybernetics.* New York: John Wiley & Sons, Inc. *88,
   207*

WITKIN, H. A., LEWIS, H. B., HERTZMAN, M., MACHOVER, K., MEISSNER,
   P. B., and WAPNER, S. 1954. *Personality through perception.* New
   York: Harper and Row, Publishers. *387*

WOODWORTH, R. S. 1918a. *Personal data sheet.* Chicago: Stoelting. *371*
   1918b. *Dynamic psychology.* New York: Columbia University Press. *373–
   74*
   1938. *Experimental psychology.* New York: Holt, Rinehart and Winston,
   Inc. *180*
   1947. Reinforcement of perception. *Amer. J. Psychol.,* **60**, 119–24. *387*
   1948. *Contemporary schools of psychology.* 2nd ed. New York: The
   Ronald Press Co. *386*
   1958. *Dynamics of behavior.* New York: Holt, Rinehart and Winston,
   Inc. *45, 178, 287, 294, 387*

WOODWORTH, R. S., and SCHLOSBERG, H. 1954. *Experimental psychology.*
   Rev. ed. New York: Holt, Rinehart and Winston, Inc. *34*

WORTIS, J. 1950. *Soviet psychiatry.* Baltimore: The Williams & Wilkins
   Co. *93*

WUNDT, W., *10, 23, 24, 25, 26, 27, 69, 91, 131, 214, 215, 357, 388*
   1894. *Lectures on human and animal psychology.* Trans. from 2nd German edition (1892) by J. E. Creighton and E. B. Titchener. London:
   Sonnenschein. *69*
   1896. *Grundriss der Psychologie.* Leipzig: Engelmann. Trans. by C. H.
   Judd entitled *Outlines of psychology.* Leipzig: Engelmann. *25–26*

WYATT, F., and VEROFF, J. B. 1956. Thematic apperception and fantasy tests. *Prog. of Clin. Psychol.*, **2**, 3–57. *368*

ZENER, K. 1937. The significance of behavior accompanying conditioned salivary secretion for theories of the conditioned response. *Amer. J. Psychol.*, **50**, 384–403. *83–84*

ZENER, K., and GAFFRON, M. 1962. Perceptual experience: An analysis of its relations to the external world through internal processings. In Koch, S. (Ed.). *Psychology: A study of a science*, Vol. IV, 515–618. New York: McGraw-Hill Book Co. *17*

ZUCKERMAN, C. B., and ROCK, I. 1957. A reappraisal of the roles of past experience and innate organizing processes in visual perception. *Psychol. Bull.*, **54**, 269–96. *245*

Index

441